Animal Learning
and
Cognition

ALFRED A. KNOPF SERIES IN PSYCHOLOGY

SERIES ADVISORS:

GEOFFREY KEPPEL   •   STEPHEN E. GLICKMAN

BOTH OF THE UNIVERSITY OF CALIFORNIA AT BERKELEY

Animal Learning and Cognition

CHARLES F. FLAHERTY

RUTGERS UNIVERSITY

ALFRED A. KNOPF · NEW YORK

Library of Congress Cataloging in Publication Data

Flaherty, Charles F.
  Animal learning and cognition.

  Bibliography: p. 367
  Includes index.
  1. Learning in animals.   2. Cognition in animals.
I. Title.
QL785.F57   1985   591.5′1   84-23316
ISBN 0-394-33042-0

Manufactured in the United States of America

ACKNOWLEDGMENTS

Cover photographs courtesy of: Mary M. Thacher/Photo Researchers (top left), Ken Karp (top right), Ken Robert Buck/The Picture Cube (bottom left), Russ Kinne/Photo Researchers (bottom right).

Fig. 2–1 Copyright © 1981, The Society for Psychophysiological Research. Reprinted with permission of the author and the publisher from Becker, D. E., and Shapiro, D. Physiological response to clicks during Zen, Yoga, and TM meditation. Psychophysiology, 1981, 18, 694–699. Fig. 2–2 (top) Kandel, E. R. Cellular Insights into Behavior and Learning. The Harvey Lectures, Series 73. New York, Academic Press. Figs. 2–2 (bottom), 2–3, 2–4, 2–5, 2–8 Copyright 1970 Scientific American. All rights reserved. Kandel, E. R. Nerve Cells and Behavior. Scientific American, 1970, 223, 57–70. Fig. 2–6A Peeke, H. V. S. and Veno. Stimulus specificity of habituation aggression in three spined sticklebacks (Gasterosteas). Behavioral Biology, 1973, 8, 427–432. Fig. 2–6B Petroinovich & Peeke, H. V. S. Habituation to territorial song in the white crowned sparrow. Behavioral Biology, 1973, 8, 743–748. Fig. 2–6C Thompson, R. F., Groves, P. M., Teylar, T. J., and Roemer, R. A. A dual-process theory of habituation: Theory and behavior. In H. V. S. Peeke & M. J. Herz (Eds.), Habituation; Vol. I Behavioral Studies. New York, Academic Press, 1973. Fig. 2–7 Thompson, R. F., and Glanzman, D. L. Neural and behavioral mechanisms of habituation and sensitization. In T. J. Tighe & R. H. Leaton (Eds.), Habituation: Perspectives from Child Development to Animal Behavior and Neurophysiology, New York: Wiley, 1976. Table 3–1 Kimble, G. A. Hilgard and Marquis Conditioning and Learning. New York, Appleton-Century-Crofts, 1961. Table 3–2 Effects of partial reinforcement on conditioning, conditional probabilities, asymptomatic performance, and extinction of the rabbit's nictitating membrane response. Pavlovian Journal of Biological Sciences, 1975, 10, 13–22. Fig. 3–1 Berger, T. W., Clark, G. A., and Thompson, R. F. Learning-dependent neuronal response recorded from limbic system brain structures during classical conditioning. Physiological Psychology, 1980, 8, 155–167. Fig. 3–2 Fitzgerald, R. D., Martin, G. K., and O'Brien, J. H. Influence of vagal activity on classically conditioned heart rate in rats. Journal of Comparative and Physiological Psychology, 1973, 83, 485–491. Copyright 1973 by the American Psychological Association. Reprinted by permission of the publisher and author. Fig. 3–3 Liu, S. S. Journal of Comparative and Physiological Psychology, 1971, 77, 136–142. Copyright 1971 by the American Psychological Association. Adapted by permission of the publisher and author. Fig. 3–4 Neil Schneiderman, "Response System Divergencies in Aversive Classical Con-

Association. Reprinted by permission of the author. *Fig. 8–4* Seybert, J. A., Baer, L. P., Harvey, R. J., Ludwig, K., and Gerard, I. C. Resistance to extinction as a function of percentage of reward: A reinforcement-level interpretation. *Animal Learning and Behavior*, 1979, *7*, 233–238. *Figs. 8–5, 8–8, 8–9* Ferster, C. B., and Skinner, B. F. *Schedules of Reinforcement*. New York, Appleton-Century-Crofts, 1957. *Figs. 8–6, 8–11* Todd, G. E., and Coogan, D. C. Selected schedules of reinforcement in the black tailed prairie dog (Cynomys ludovicianus). *Animal Learning and Behavior*, 1978, *6*, 429–434. *Fig. 8–7* Reprinted with permission from *Physiology and Behavior*, *9*, Collier, G., Hirsch, E., and Hamlin, P. H., The ecological determinants of reinforcement in the rat. Copyright 1972, Pergamon Press, Ltd. *Fig. 8–10* Gentry, G. D., Weiss, B., and Laties, V. G. The microanalysis of fixed-interval responding. *Journal of the Experimental Analysis of Behavior*, 1983, *39*, 327–343. Copyright 1983 by the Society for the Experimental Analysis of Behavior, Inc. *Fig. 8–12* Mallot, R. W., and Cumming, W. W. Schedules of interresponse time reinforcement. *Psychological Record*, 1964, *14*, 211–252. Data redrawn. *Fig. 9–1* Fanselow, M. S., and Bolles, R. C. Naloxone and shock-elicited freezing in the rat. *Journal of Comparative and Physiological Psychology*, 1979, *93*, 736–744. Copyright 1979 by the American Psychological Association. Reprinted by permission of the author. *Fig. 9–4* Crawford, M., and Masterson, F. Components of the flight response can reinforce bar-press avoidance learning. *Journal of Experimental Psychology: Animal Behavior Processes*, 1978, *4*, 144–151. Copyright 1978 by the American Psychological Association. Reprinted by permission of the author. *Fig. 9–5* Azrin, N. H., Holz, W. C., and Hake, D. F. Fixed-ratio punishment. *Journal of the Experimental Analysis of Behavior*, 1963, *6*, 141–148. Copyright 1963 by the Society for the Experimental Analysis of Behavior, Inc. *Fig. 9–6* Anisman, H., de Catanzaro, D., and Remington, G. Escape performance following exposure to inescapable shock: Deficits in motor response maintenance. *Journal of Experimental Psychology: Animal Behavior Processes*, 1978, *4*, 197–218. Copyright 1978 by the American Psychological Association. Reprinted by permission of the author. *Figs. 9–7, 9–8* Rosellini, R., DeCola, J., and Shapiro, N. Cross-motivational effects of inescapable shock are associative in nature. *Journal of Experimental Psychology: Animal Behavior Processes*, 1982, *8*, 376–388. Copyright 1982 by the American Psychological Association. Reprinted by permission of the publisher and author. *Fig. 10–1* (bottom) Church, R. M., and Gibbon, J. Temporal generalization. *Journal of Experimental Psychology: Animal Behavior Processes*, 1982, *8*, 165–186. Copyright 1982 by the American Psychological Association. Reprinted by permission of the publisher and author. *Fig. 10–2* Harber, A., and Kalish, H. I. Prediction of discrimination from generalization after variation in schedule of reinforcement, *Science*, 1963, *142*, 412–413. Copyright 1963 by the American Association for the Advancement of Science. *Fig. 10–3* Blough, D. S. Steady state data and a quantitative model of operant generalization and discrimination. *Journal of Experimental Psychology: Animal Behavior Processes*, 1975, *1*, 3–21. Copyright 1975 by the American Psychological Association. Reprinted by permission of the author. *Fig. 10–4A* Halliday, M. S., and Boakes, R. A. Behavioral contrast and response independent reinforcement. *Journal of the Experimental Analysis of Behavior*, 1971, *16*, 429–434. Copyright 1971 by the Society for the Experimental Analysis of Behavior, Inc. *Fig. 10–4B* Mellgren, R. L., Mays, M. Z., and Haddad, N. F. Discrimination and generalization by rats of temporal stimuli lasting for minutes. *Learning and Motivation*, 1983, *14*, 75–91. *Fig. 10–4C* Flaherty, C. F., and Davenport, J. W. Three-level differential reward magnitude discrimination in rats. *Psychonomic Science*, 1969, *15*, 231–243. *Fig. 10–5* Hanson, H. M. Effects of discrimination training on stimulus generalization. *Journal of Experimental Psychology*, 1959, *58*, 321–334. Copyright 1959 by the American Psychological Association. Reprinted by permission of the publisher and author. *Fig. 10–7* Zentall, T., Collins, N., and Hearst, E. Generalization gradients around a formerly positive S−. *Psychon. Sci.*, 1971, *22*, 257–259. *Fig. 10–8* Halliday, M. S., and Boakes, R. A. Behavioral contrast and response independent reinforcement. *Journal of the Experimental Analysis of Behavior*, 1971, *16*, 429–434. Copyright 1971 by the Society for the Experimental Analysis of Behavior, Inc. *Fig. 10–9* Halliday, M. S., and Boakes, R. A. Behavioral contrast without response-rate reductions. *Journal of the Experimental Analysis of Behavior*, 1974, *22*, 453–462. Copyright 1974 by the Society for the Experimental Analysis of Behavior, Inc. *Fig. 10–10* Reynolds, G. S. Attention in the pigeon. *Journal of the Experimental Analysis of Behavior*, 1961, *4*, 203–208. Copyright 1961 by the Society for the Experimental Analysis of Behavior, Inc. *Table 11–1* McSweeney, F. K. Matching and contrast on several concurrent treadle-press schedules. *Journal of the Experimental Analysis of Behavior*, 1975, *23*, 193–198. Copyright 1975 by the Society for the Experimental Analysis of Behavior, Inc. *Fig. 11–1* Olton, D. S., and Samuelson, R. J. Remembrance of places passed: Spatial memory in rats. *Journal of Experimental Psychology: Animal Behavior Processes*, 1976, *2*, 97–116. Copyright 1976 by the American Psychological Association. Reprinted by permission of the author. *Fig. 11–2* McSweeney, F. K. Matching and contrast on several concurrent treadle-press schedules. *Journal of the Experimental Analysis of Behavior*, 1975, *23*, 193–198. Copyright 1975 by the Society for the Experimental Analysis of Behavior, Inc. *Fig. 11–4* Ito, M., and Asaki, K. Choice behavior of rats in a concurrent-chains schedule: Amount and delay of reinforcement. *Journal of the Experimental Analysis of Behavior*, 1982, *37*, 383–392. Copyright 1982 by the Society for the Experimental Analysis of Behavior, Inc. *Figs. 11–5, 11–6* Collier, G. H., and Rovee-Collier, C. K. A comparative analysis of optimal foraging behavior: Laboratory simulations. In A. C. Kamil and T. D. Sargent (Eds.), *Foraging Behavior: Ecological, Ethological, and Psychological Approaches*. New York: Garland STPM Press, 1981. Reproduced by permission of Garland STPM Press. *Fig. 11–7* Kaufman, L. W. Foraging strategies: Laboratory simulations. Unpublished doctoral dissertation, Rutgers University, 1979. *Fig. 11–8* Mellgren, R. L., Misasi, L., and Brown, S. W. Optimal foraging theory: Prey density and travel requirements in Rattus norvegicus. *Journal of Comparative Psychology*, 1984. Copyright 1984 by the American Psychological Association. Reprinted by permission of the publisher and author. *Fig. 12–2* Adams, C. D. *Quarterly Journal of Experimental Psychology*, 1982, *34B*, 77–98. Copyright 1982 by the Experimental Psychology Society. *Fig. 13–3* Capaldi, E. J., Nawrocki, T. M., and Verry, D. R. The nature of anticipation: An inter- and intravent process. *Animal Learning and Behavior*, 1983, *11*, 193–198.

For Mary, Brendan, and Jennifer

Preface to the Instructor

The investigation of animal learning is more interesting and relevant than it has ever been. The cluster of discoveries and theoretical developments that burst forth in the late 1960s and early 1970s reorganized the conceptual structure of animal learning research and stimulated an abundance of "normal science" investigations. I refer to such things as Kamin's work on blocking; Rescorla's contingency analysis of Pavlovian conditioning; Garcia's discoveries of the anomalous characteristics of conditioned food aversions; the Brown and Jenkins discovery of autoshaping; the Hearst and Jenkins work on sign directed behavior; the work of Maier, Overmier, and Seligman on learned helplessness; and the Wagner-Rescorla model of conditioning.

Activities following from these and other developments have merged with new trends which came to the fore in the late 1970s and continue to develop in the 1980s. These trends include an enhanced willingness to consider cognitive interpretations of animal behavior, rapid developments in understanding the neural basis of conditioning, the study of Pavlovian conditioning with drugs as unconditioned stimuli, the application of Pavlovian conditioning principles to the understanding of drug tolerance and addiction, and the beginning of the integration of laboratory and field studies of learning, particularly in the area of foraging.

In writing this text, I have attempted to integrate contemporary and traditional research and to include a brief historical introduction to each major topic. Although the majority of the material presented in the text is derived from laboratory research, I have tried to present this research in the context of evolution and to show how it is related to field studies of animal behavior. Thus, the first chapter is concerned principally with the relevance of evolution for learning and learning for evolution. This chapter also considers several ways in which the study of animal behavior has relevance for the understanding of human behavior. Chapter 2 explores sensitization and habituation using examples ranging from snails to humans and includes some of the simpler aspects of Kandel's cellular analysis of habituation in *Aplysia*.

Chapters 3, 4, 5, and 6 are concerned with Pavlovian conditioning, progressing from simple description and examples of human relevance through parameters of conditioning, the expansion of conditioning to include directed behaviors and conditioned food aversions, and some special topics such as inhibition, conditioning models of drug tolerance, and neural mechanisms of conditioning. This section ends with a consideration of theories of conditioning and a consideration of the relevance of conditioning research. Four chapters have been devoted to the subject because a great deal of contemporary research is organized around Pavlovian conditioning.

Chapter 7 introduces instrumental learning and considers ways of distinguishing it from Pavlovian directed behaviors. This chapter also presents the simpler information on reward variables. Chapters 8, 9, and 10 present further information on schedules of reinforcement, aversive conditioning, and stimulus control. Chapter 11 presents a somewhat detailed treatment of special topics. Choice behavior is examined in studies ranging from traditional and contemporary maze experiments to modern operant procedures. The matching law is also considered in this section.

Chapter 11 also examines foraging from the perspective of the complex choices that an animal must make in solving its daily survival problems. Foraging is considered in both field and laboratory studies, and some consideration is given to a cost/benefit analysis of this behavior. Chapter 12 presents an associative analysis of instrumental learning and considers how both Pavlovian and instrumental associations may be involved in typical learning tasks. Chapter 13 is concerned with a cognitive analysis of animal behavior. This analysis is applied to simple Pavlovian and instrumental tasks as well as to more complex situations such as those involving cognitive mapping, inference, concept formation, and possible self-awareness.

Finally, Chapter 14 considers the ways in which principles of learning discovered with one species of animal may or may not generalize to other species. This chapter includes examples of programmed learning, such as imprinting and bird-song acquisition, and considers why the law of effect may appear to "fail" in some situations. Also examined are some examples of selectivity in the formation of associations. The overall conclusion is that the principles of associative learning do seem to be quite similar across species, but the ways in which associations are expressed may depend upon the species' evolutionary history and the environmental niche to which the species has adapted.

The structure of the text is modular in the sense that some material may be omitted for lower level courses. For example, Chapters 1, 2, and 3 provide the basics of habituation, sensitization, and Pavlovian conditioning. Chapters 7, 8, 9, and 10 provide the basic information on instrumental learning. Thus, these seven chapters could be used for an elementary course. More detailed information on parametric relationships in Pavlovian conditioning could be included by adding Chapter 4. Chapters 5 and 11 present a series of selected topics in Pavlovian conditioning and instrumental learning, respectively. All of these chapters, or portions of them, could be added to enrich a lower level course. Chapter 13 extends the material to an analysis of animal cognition, and Chapter 14 addresses the question of the degree to which principles of animal learning are generalizable across species. Finally, Chapters 6 and 12, theoretical interpretations of Pavlovian conditioning and instrumental learning, respectively, may be added for a comprehensive course. If Chapter 6 is omitted, the concepts of contingency and blocking would have to be brought up in the lecture, since they are often referred to later in the text.

I believe that the study of animal learning will continue to expand. Neurobiologists such as Kandel are using the procedures and controls developed over many years of behavioral studies in their investigations of the cellular basis of Pavlovian conditioning. Kandel and other researchers not only see the relevance of the previous behavioral studies of animal learning for their own work but also have called for cooperative efforts between psychologists and neurobiologists in unravelling the mysteries of learning. The work of Richard Thompson on the neural basis of conditioning in higher organisms was built on years of behavioral research by Gormezano and his colleagues, and the two areas, behavioral and physiological, are now moving ahead in an integrated fashion. Similar progress is being made in other aspects of the study of learning.

The study of animal learning seems to be entering a new era: a time when behavioral studies will not be alienated from physiological and neurochemical investigations but will proceed in a coordinated and integrated fashion; a time when, instead of being isolated from each other, laboratory and field studies will supplement, support, and serve as correctives for each other; a time when laboratory animal research will not be interpreted as a sterile academic exercise but instead will be seen as contributing to applied fields such as behavioral medicine and the neural bases of learning and motivational disabilities as well as providing fundamental information on the learning process.

To the Student

Everything should be made as simple as
possible, but not simpler.
Albert Einstein

There is a lot of information in this text, but none of the material is
particularly abstract or complex. Proceeding through the book will be easier
and more rewarding if a few simple points and techniques of study are kept
in mind. First, the various aspects of animal learning considered in this text
are arranged from the simple to the complex and each may be summarized
concisely. Habituation, considered first, may be thought of as a process
whereby animals learn that a stimulus has no consequences for them—it is
unimportant. Sensitization, considered next, refers to an alerting process
through which an animal learns that environmental conditions may have
changed, that perhaps it should be wary and responsive to previously unimportant events. Pavlovian conditioning procedures are used to analyze how
animals learn that a particular stimulus is important, how they learn that it
signals something that will have an impact on them. These procedures are
used to study how animals learn about the relationship between environmental events that are beyond their control. Instrumental learning procedures are
used to study how animals learn that their own behavior may have an effect
on the environment, that they may be able to alter the environment in order
to bring about the occurrence of some preferred event or terminate or preclude the occurrence of some aversive event. Finally, several ways of studying complex learning in animals are considered. Among the questions asked
are: Are animals capable of learning rules and forming concepts? What are
some of the characteristics of animal memory? Can animals reason? Do they
have an awareness of self?

The learning and understanding of this material will proceed more
smoothly if a few simple study habits are adopted. First, I would suggest
glancing over the detailed outline presented at the beginning of each chapter
and the summary presented at the end of each chapter. This should help to

focus your attention on each chapter's structure and its major points. Then read the chapter through, perhaps underlining what seem to be the important issues and items of evidence. Finally, before an examination, review each chapter and take notes, using the outline at the beginning of the chapter as a guide. Ideally, a chapter should be read before the material is discussed in class and then outlined after such discussion has taken place. This allows for the integration of class and text material.

In reading a book such as this, there is more to notice than simply the content or facts presented. Among these more general lessons is the observation that animal behavior is orderly and may be studied systematically. Also notice that there is a positive and generative relationship between theory and data; theories suggest experiments, the results of which suggest modifications in theories, which suggest new experiments, etc. Something else to be aware of is that there are particular experimental methods for asking particular questions and that the answer to a question depends largely on the experimental procedures used. For example, there is some interest in whether animals are able to develop "cognitive maps" of the spatial relationships among items in the environment. A maze or similar apparatus is a more reasonable apparatus to use in asking such a question than is an operant chamber (Skinner box), so very often used in animal research. Finally, another lesson to be learned was perhaps best stated by Bertrand Russell: ". . . (what education) should produce is a belief that knowledge is attainable in a measure, though with difficulty; that much of what passes for knowledge at a given time is likely to be more or less mistaken, but that mistakes can be rectified by care and industry."

The completion of a textbook represents the cumulative effort and influence of many people. I would like to acknowledge my intellectual debt to my teachers, students, and colleagues. In particular, I would like to thank George Collier, Michael D'Amato, Leonard Hamilton and Seymour Rosenberg of Rutgers and Norman Spear of SUNY Binghamton for their continued support and intellectual stimulation over the years that we have had the opportunity to work together. I was also fortunate in having many people take the time to read and offer suggestions on all stages of the manuscript. Among these were Howard Becker, Philip Bersh, Regina Carelli, Alexis Collier, Mary Flaherty, William Gordon, Peter Holland, Ruth Maki, William S. Maki, Susan Mineka, Gary Olson, Herbert Roitblat, Robert Rosellini, Grace Rowan, David Thomas, and Jonathan Vaughan. The series advisors, Geoffrey Keppel and Stephen Glickman, offered encouragement and specific suggestions regarding text material.

Many people at Random House/Knopf contributed to the book. Among these were the senior psychology editor, Judy Rothman, and her assistant, Lucy Rosendahl, the manuscript editor, Niels Aaboe, and the copy editor, Harry Spector. I appreciate the dedication and thoroughness with which these people approached their work. I would also like to thank my secretary, Joan Olmizzi, for her patient and careful typing and retyping of the various drafts of this text. Finally, I would like to thank my wife, Mary, for her assistance in all aspects of completing this text.

Charles F. Flaherty
November 1984

Contents

1

The Study of Learning in Animals

*❝ The emergence of the capacity to learn is the triumph of evolu-
tion . . . learning frees the individual from the chains of its own
double helix.* ❞

Colin Blakemore, *Mechanics of the
Mind*, 1977

INTRODUCTION—LEARNING IN THE CONTEXT OF EVOLUTION

There are many factors that influence the place that each of us comes
to adopt in society. There are geographical and social circumstances of birth,
economic and cultural conditions present during our growth and later life,
talents and aptitudes that we may have inherited—all of these help shape the
careers and social roles in which we play out our lives. Whatever these various conditions may be, whatever the occupations we pursue, there is one
constant of which we can be quite confident—we will have to learn something.

There is learning involved in becoming an auto mechanic, a mailman, a
surgeon, a stockbroker, a housewife, or whatever. Even the non-occupational
positions that each of us holds as friend, family member, neighbor, etc., involve a certain amount of social learning. This fundamental role that learning
plays in human culture may resemble a role that learning had in evolution.
That is, learning helps each of us to adapt to a place in society, just as learning may have helped different organisms adapt to their environment during
the long history of evolution. Just as our society may select somewhat for
learning ability—those that do well in high school are more likely to be accepted by the colleges of their choice, and those that do well in college will
be recruited by the most desirable corporations, will get into the best law
schools, etc.—mechanisms of evolution may have operated to select for learning ability (or abilities) as well as other behavioral and structural modes of
adaptation to the environment. Let us briefly examine evolution and adaptation and see perhaps what relevance learning has for evolution and evolution
for learning.

Adaptation and Evolution

It is in the nature of things that living organisms reproduce themselves.
In order to accomplish this reproduction, certain needs must be met—the
organism must remain in environmental conditions friendly to its existence
(temperature, chemical composition, etc.), it must have nutrition sufficient to

keep it alive until reproduction takes place, if it reproduces sexually with a partner it must be able to locate and perform the species-typical mating behavior with the partner, the environment must be friendly for the survival and growth of the offspring, etc. All living species seem to have little trouble accomplishing these, in some cases, quite complicated feats. That is, living organisms seem to be well adapted to the environment in which they find themselves. How did this come about?

A fruitful way in which to interpret adaptation was provided by Darwin in his theory of evolution (1859, 1871). There are three aspects of Darwin's theory that are particularly relevant for the subject matter in this text: variation among individuals, differential reproduction, and natural selection. We shall consider each of these briefly.

Variation

Individual organisms within a species are not all identical—there is variability in physical structure and in behavior. What is the source of this variability? Although there was little known about genetics in Darwin's time, he was able to postulate that there must be some genetic material that is at the base of observed structural differences. Furthermore, he reasoned, when two individuals mate, their offspring will receive some combination of their parents' genetic material. The genetic material that the offspring receives would thus be similar to both parents, but different from either one. That is, the process of sexual reproduction allows for the creation of variability in the population—the creation of new combinations of genetic material. Sometimes the variation is obvious, as in the case of physical structure among humans; sometimes it is subtle, or perhaps apparent only under testing conditions such as pursuit by a predator, where one individual may be faster, more evasive, or more wily than another.

Differential Reproduction

Some individual differences may be irrelevant for meeting the challenges posed by the environment, but others, such as the anti-predator activity alluded to above, may be essential for survival. Individuals that happen to possess characteristics that are particularly useful for survival in their environment are more likely to have the opportunity to mate and produce offspring. That is, individual animals best suited to their environment will tend to have more offspring than animals less well suited to their environment.

Natural Selection

Those individuals that survive to reproduce will pass on the characteristics that led to their survival to some of their offspring. It is the difference in reproduction, based on adaptability to the environment, that Darwin referred to as natural selection. As a result of natural selection, successive generations of a lineage become more and more suited to the environment in which they exist, given that their genetic characteristics are such as to provide the basis for adapting to that environment.

A well known recent example of selection of this type is provided by the occurrence of industrial melanism among moths in England (Kettlewell, 1959). A certain species of moth *(Biston betularia)* occurs in two colorations: salt-and-pepper or black. These moths tend to rest on tree trunks that are covered with lichen. Against this background the salt-and-pepper moth is virtually invisible, but the black moth is highly visible. In the early nineteenth century, the black moth was relatively rare. However, after the onset of the industrial revolution in England the tree trunks in industrial regions tended to become covered with soot, which killed the lichen and turned the tree trunks black. Against this background, it was the salt-and-pepper moths that were highly visible and the black moths that were obscure. Over a period of a hundred years or so, the black moths came to outnumber the salt-and-pepper moths in the industrial areas, whereas the reverse continued to be true in the rural areas. The difference in the two populations was due to their differential likelihood of producing offspring, which, in turn, was due to their differential susceptibility to predation by birds. Thus, natural selection operated to produce two moth colorations, each adapted to a particular environment. It is not difficult to think of other structural adaptations brought on by natural selection, examples such as beak shape and size in birds, neck length in giraffes, body shape in fish and in mammals that have taken to the sea, etc. It is clear that structural change is a major mechanism by which many animal species have come to adapt to their environment—to survive and produce offspring.

Learning, Adaptation, and Natural Selection

It is also reasonable to suppose that behavior and psychological processes such as learning and memory play a role in adaptation and may also be selected for. One way to visualize the role that behavior may have played in evolution is to consider again some of the problems that an individual must solve in order to reproduce.

Consider, for example, the necessity of food. If food tends to be unevenly distributed in the environment, it would be to the animal's advantage to be able to learn and remember routes to the best food sources, cues that predict the availability of food, the route back to the nest site (if there is one), signs that predators might be in the vicinity of the food source and, if so, routes to alternative food sources. Also important would be the ability to learn and remember the distinguishing characteristics of toxic food substances. There is substantial evidence that learning is, in fact, important in food selection and foraging behavior, and we will consider this in some detail in several places in this text. For now it is important only to imagine that animals particularly efficient at these tasks would be more likely to produce offspring and hence pass on the ability to learn.

Is learning in regard to food-related behavior important in human culture? Just think of the substantial time allocated to such things as learning how to cook, recipe preparation, comparative food shopping, agriculture (requiring entire college curricula), the technology of fishing, and the dairy industry.

Anti-predator behavior is another problem faced by animals. Many animal species have evolved elaborate structural defenses such as camouflage colorations and morphology, and mimicry of toxic or dangerous animals. Some have developed evasive running behaviors; others have group defenses such as schooling (fish), herding (grazing animals), or mobbing (birds). (See Alcock, 1971; Gould, 1982 for a general discussion of these phenomena.) Learning also evolved to play a role in the safety of animals. For example, mobbing of a predator by birds not only serves to drive off the predator but also to acquaint the young with the nature of typical predators. For example, one species of monkey has different alarm calls for different types of predators, and these calls must be learned by the young (Seyfarth, Cheney & Marler, 1980).

It is interesting that the accumulated knowledge of human culture and technology is used for anti-predator behaviors in ways that mimic the structural and behavioral adaptations of other animals. For example, in warfare (humans are essentially the only predators that humans have to fear) protective coloration is used. Ski troops wear white, jungle troops wear green, desert troops wear khaki. There is even a "stealth" aircraft under development that is "invisible" to radar. Speed and evasive behaviors are used (in aircraft and ships, in particular). Repellent devices are used (weapons). All of these strategies employed by humans are based on learning in the sense of accumulated technology.

It is not necessary to elaborate any further on how learning may have evolved (been selected for) in other survival problems that all animals face, problems such as care of the young, habitat selection, social interactions with conspecifics, etc. The principal point is that survival problems can be solved in several ways: by structural changes that adapt the animal to its environment; by innate behaviors based on complex reflexes (e.g., Tinbergen, 1959); or by behavioral changes based on the ability to learn. There is an important difference among these modes of adaptation. Adaptation resulting from selection of the ability to learn and behave flexibly provides an enormous advantage in that it contains the basis of further adaptations in the lifespan of a single individual. An organism that has adapted solely on the basis of structural modification or innate behaviors faces difficulty if the environment changes; an organism that has adapted on the basis of learning may be able to learn new behaviors that will adapt it to the new environment. If this learning takes place, then such an individual will pass on its genes to future generations whereas the organism that has adapted solely on the basis of morphology or fixed behavioral mechanisms would be less likely to do so. Thus, the ability to learn would have been selected as an adaptive mechanism.

Perhaps the flexibility of learning can be emphasized by describing some examples of complex behavior that are surprisingly *inflexible*. A species of wasp provides food for its offspring by paralyzing its insect prey and depositing it in an underground nest for the larvae to feed upon. In doing this, the wasp goes through a regular sequence of behavior. When it first returns to the nest with its paralyzed quarry, it places the insect near the entrance and then goes down into the nest itself. The wasp soon returns, brings the insect down into the nest, and returns to the surface to close up the entrance. However, an interesting behavior occurs if, while the wasp is on its initial "inspection tour" of the nest, its prey is moved several inches away from where it was left at the edge of the nest. When the wasp now returns to the surface, it moves the prey back to the entrance and then goes down into the nest again—starting the sequence over. This apparently can go on ad infinitum as long as the prey is moved each time the wasp enters the nest. It is as if the wasp were caught in some program "loop" that must be completed before it can go to the next stage of its provisioning sequence. The wasp, in this instance, demonstrates remarkably inflexible behavior (Wooldridge, 1963).

Another example of inflexibility is the behavior of the wasp *Ammophila pubescens*. This wasp may maintain many burrows, with larvae at different stages of development in each. The wasp provides its young with food, giving each larva an amount appropriate for its size. Before setting off on the day's foraging the wasp visits all the burrows and then, eventually, returns with the proper amount of food for each burrow. If, however, the larvae are switched after it has made its first visit, the wasp does not adjust its behavior to the new occupants of the burrows. Instead, the amount of food placed in each burrow corresponds to the size of the offspring that had been there on its first visit—it does not correspond to the size of the current occupant. Again, the behavior of the wasp is complicated and is a performance that requires a considerable memory. But the behavior is also stereotyped and resistant to change based on changed conditions (Baerends, described in Gould, 1982).

In considering the evolution of learning, Pulliam and Dunford (1980) used the analogy of an investor and stockbroker. An investor could give his broker strict instructions to buy stock A, hold it for six months, then sell it and buy stock B, hold it for two years, and so on. This strategy might work if the stock market were perfectly predictable and the investor could see the future. However, if the stock market were unpredictable and other, more favorable opportunities for investment presented themselves, the broker would be helpless without further instructions from the investor. This situation is analogous to the set of genes that has constructed an organism to respond to environmental contingencies in certain, inflexible ways. If the environment remains the same as the one in which the organism evolved (was selected for), the programmed responses to contingencies should suffice to guarantee reproduction of the genetic material. But, if the environment changes, then the original program for survival (modes of adapting to the environment) might not be successful and, if so, the genes will be selected against and perhaps disappear from the population. In the example of wasp behavior given above, it could be said that the wasp's genetic programming was not prepared for the environmental changes brought about by the experimenters.

An investor could use a different strategy. He could give his money to a broker and instruct him to use his own experience and expertise with the stock market and invest the money as he saw fit, seeking the maximum return. If the broker were astute and knowledgeable, the investor would stand a better chance of doing well, in the face of an unpredictable market, using this strategy rather than the inflexible instructions described previously. This situation is analogous to a set of genes that has constructed an organism with a nervous system that has the ability to learn and vary its mode of adaptation to match changing environmental contingencies. If the nervous system learns well and applies its knowledge astutely, the chance of the genetic material being passed on to future generations is enhanced.

Throughout this text we will see how learning builds on a base of innate reflexes, and allows each animal to face the challenge of survival with the inherited predispositions handed down through the eons from generations of ancestors, plus the unique knowledge that it may have acquired in its own lifetime. We will see how animals learn to ignore stimuli that seem unimportant, how they learn to anticipate changes in their environment, to prepare for these changes and, where possible, to modify their environment and profit from the experience of being able to do so. However, before going on to a consideration of the simplest type of learning—habituation—we will first define learning more formally and specify some of the terms used in the experimental study of learning.

THE EXPERIMENTAL STUDY OF LEARNING

Definition of Learning

Learning may be defined as a ". . . more or less permanent change in behavior potentiality which occurs as a result of repeated practice" (Kimble, 1961). The phrase "more or less permanent change" is important to distinguish the process of learning from changes that are either very transient or very permanent. For example, transient changes in behavior result from processes such as receptor adaptation or muscle fatigue; e.g., the maximal running speed of the average individual is greatly reduced within a few hundred yards. This is clearly a change in behavior, but not of the type that we classify as learning, because the effect is only temporary and primarily involves the inability of the muscles to maintain a sustained level of forceful contraction.

At the opposite end of the range of changes are the permanent changes in behavior that are associated primarily with such processes as maturation. For example, the physical ability to lift a 20-pound weight does not develop for years following birth, but once developed, the ability remains throughout most of the lifespan of the individual.

The behavioral changes that reflect the process of learning are *relatively* permanent in that they fall between the two categories outlined above; that is, these changes in behavior typically remain in effect as long as they are appropriate to the environment but can change relatively quickly as the environmental requirements change. For example, a learned behavior may be "extinguished" if the environmental contingencies change.

The phrase *behavior potentiality* refers to the fact that the behavioral changes that result from learning need not necessarily be manifested by an immediate and overt response. For example, it is possible to learn a sequence of numbers without any overt response. The fact that learning has occurred can easily be demonstrated at a later time by dialing the sequence of numbers on the telephone. In Chapters 5 and 6, numerous examples of such "behaviorally silent" learning will be presented.

The phrase *repeated practice* refers to the observation that, under most conditions, repeated experience with the appropriate stimuli is necessary before learning can be demonstrated. However, we will provide examples in later chapters of cases in which learning occurs very gradually over many trials, and other cases in which learning takes place in a single trial.

Learning is a *process* that helps the organism adapt to the changing conditions of the environment. This process influences much of the observable behavior of mammals and other complex vertebrates.

Some Research Principles

A major goal of experimentation in any field of science is to determine the effects of one type of event upon another type of event. It has been determined, for example, that the amount of electric current that flows through a wire varies with the resistance of the wire. Events that influence other events in varying degrees are called variables.

In order to determine the relationship between one particular variable and a given event, all other variables that might influence the outcome must be held constant, that is, they must be controlled. For example, if you were interested in determining the injury likely to be suffered by drivers of different types of automobiles upon impact with a solid object, you would have to ensure that each different make of automobile impacted with the solid object at the same velocity. It would make no sense to compare a Toyota and a Cadillac if one is driven at five miles per hour and the other at 20 miles per hour. In other words, speed would have to be controlled for. Similarly, if seat belts were to be worn by the test mannequins, the experimenters would have to ensure that all seat belts were fastened to the same degree of tightness, etc.

Control must be used in the same way in research into learning. Consider an experiment in which you are interested in the effects of a certain drug on the ability of animals to learn a maze. You might have two groups— one injected with the drug and one not injected with the drug. What would have to be controlled in this type of experiment? Certainly, you would have to ensure that the two groups were as similar as possible before the start of the experiment. For example, it would make no sense if one of the groups had prior experience in learning mazes whereas the other group was naive; you would not be able to interpret any effect that the drug might have on learning. In this type of drug experiment, it might also be important to control for the effects of the injection itself. That is, the group not injected with the drug would ordinarily be injected with some inert substance such as physiological saline in order to ensure that the fact of receiving an injection itself would not produce differences between the groups.

Thus, in order to determine the effects of one variable on a particular event, all other variables that might influence that event must be accounted for—they must be controlled. A major part of the skill of an experimental scientist is in perceiving what factors should be controlled and in devising appropriate conditions or groups to accomplish that control. Without proper controls the results of an experiment may be misleading or uninterpretable.

Independent and Dependent Variables

The variable that is of interest in the experiment, the one that is manipulated by the experimenter, is termed the *independent variable*. The term *independent* is used because the experimenter decides whether or not to administer the variable and what levels of the variable to administer. In the two examples given previously, the different types of automobiles would be the independent variable in the collision-injury study, and the presence or absence of the drug would be the independent variable in the maze-learning study. The experimenter is interested in the effects of the independent variable on some other event. In order to determine these effects, the experimenter varies the independent variable while holding other variables constant.

In order to assess the effects of the independent variable, some measure of the event of interest must be taken. The variable used as a measure is termed the *dependent variable*. It is termed *dependent* because changes in this measure depend upon changes in the independent variable; it reflects the influence of the independent variable. In the examples above, some measure of damage to the mannequin might be the dependent variable in the automobile study, whereas the number of errors made in the maze might be the dependent variable in the drug study.

THE GENERALITY OF LEARNING

In the chapters that follow, we will be discussing particular areas of research in some detail. In each case, we will use experimental data to support the general conclusions that are reached. In most cases, the experimental subject cited will be the rat because of the widespread use of this animal as a subject. But is it reasonable to base general conclusions on the behavior of a specific organism? Would these same generalities apply to a sea slug, an insect, a chimpanzee, a fish, or a college sophomore? In many cases, the differences in behavior that would be observed by using another subject would be trivial. The purpose of this text is to develop an understanding of the basic principles of learning, and it is the contention of the author that most of these principles are applicable across species.

Although our major purpose is to develop general conclusions that apply to virtually all organisms, we will also examine a variety of situations in which the nature of the organism clearly interacts with the nature of the task. Some organisms, for example, easily acquire an active running response to avoid an aversive situation, but have difficulty learning to be passive and sit still; other organisms show the opposite patterns. Similarly, it will be seen that many birds tend to use the color of food as a cue in learning tasks in which rats respond to taste as a cue. Even considering only one kind of organism—pigeons, for example—we will see that the precise way in which a pigeon pecks at a signal for a reward differs depending upon whether the reward is water or grain.

Thus, although we will find many examples of generality in learning, we must also remember that each species evolved by adaptation to a particular niche in the environment and that both the structure and the brain of the organism must be somewhat specialized for the ecological niche to which it is adapted. For example, carnivores and herbivores have evolved quite different feeding behaviors. It would not be surprising to find that a cat (a carnivore) and a guinea pig (a herbivore) behave somewhat differently in learning tasks that use a food reward (see, for example, Collier & Rovee-Collier, 1981). However, although differing in detail, the general principles of learning remain similar in such divergent species. Similarly, cats tend to be solitary hunters or hunt in very small groups, whereas canids (dogs, wolves) tend to hunt in large groups. Again, it would be surprising if the long evolutionary history that adapted these animals to such different social behaviors did not also lead to differences in brain structure that would influence some types of laboratory learning tasks. When an animal is taken out of its niche and brought into the laboratory, the experimenter must be careful to temper any conclusions about learning ability or learning principles with a consideration of how the learning task might relate to the animal's behavior in its natural environment.

Later in the text we will consider in some detail how the evolutionary histories of various species may interact with the degree and type of learning that they exhibit in the laboratory.

WHY STUDY LEARNING IN ANIMALS?

Many undergraduates who enroll in learning courses are interested in human learning and they see little value in the study of animal learning. There are, however, several reasons to pursue such investigations. One such reason is that there may be similarities in principles and/or physiological processes underlying learning in humans and other animals. We will see many instances of this in subsequent chapters. For example, we well see how research on Pavlovian conditioning in animals has provided a way of understanding the learning of emotional responses in humans.

It is quite likely that there are substantial similarities if not identities in the physiology, neurochemistry, and learning principles governing emotional behavior across the animal spectrum. Knowledge of these similarities helps in the understanding and treatment of phobic behavior in humans, and it should soon help in the understanding of how emotional stress contributes to disease states such as hypertension and cancer. We shall also see how research in Pavlovian conditioning and food aversion learning in animals may have implications for the understanding of difficulties that cancer patients face when they undergo chemotherapy. Another example that may be cited in this regard is the widespread use and effectiveness of behavior modification techniques in treating various behavior problems. The basic understanding of these techniques was derived from animal research.

Many other examples of direct applications of animal learning to human behavior will become apparent throughout the text. One such example is the relevance of the study of punishment and aversive control in animals for the understanding of the relative effectiveness of reward and punishment in shaping the behavior of children. A second example is the relevance of the study of incentive relativity for the understanding of disappointment in humans.

Even the use of language —very likely unique to humans—as an instrument to produce a particular outcome may follow some of the same principles as instrumental learning in animals, where they learn that certain behaviors will produce particular changes in the environment. In other words, although the acquisition and many of the uses of language for cognitive processes may be unique to humans, the use of language as a tool in the service of motives and emotions may be similar to instrumental behavior in lower animals.

If these examples are relevant for the behavior of humans, why not study them directly in humans? In some cases that is possible after the relevance of the animal research is perceived. In other cases it is not possible because of the importance of the principle of control. We have seen how extraneous variables must be controlled if the effectiveness of a particular variable on behavior is to be understood. In many instances it is not possible to control factors that might influence learning in humans—not possible because of practical reasons and/or ethical reasons. For example, if the effectiveness of a particular treatment on learning is to be investigated, how is it possible to ensure that two groups of humans come into the experiment with the same past experience? It is not possible. Also, humans know when they are in an experiment and this knowledge itself may influence the outcome of an experiment. (There are somewhat related problems in animal research, but they are much easier to control.) Thus, research that may have direct relevance to human behavior is often best done with animals.

A second reason for investigating learning in animals is that it may help us to understand what is unique about human learning. Although there are many examples of similarities between human and animal learning, it is clear that there must also be many differences. Other animals, for example, do not have the language abilities that humans possess—even the apparent rudimentary language structure seemingly demonstrated in chimpanzees is under question (see Terrace, Petitto, Sanders & Bever, 1979). There are probably many differences in cognitive abilities between lower animals and humans, and the extent of these differences will become clearer the more we know about animal learning. That is, the knowledge we have of animal learning may serve as background against which the unique aspects of human learning may be perceived more clearly.

CHAPTER SUMMARY

Species of animals become adapted to their environment by means of differential reproduction and natural selection. The ability to learn may play a role in adaptation, and thus learning ability may have been selected for in the process of evolution. Adaptation by learning provides an advantage over adaptation by structural change in that the challenges of a change in the environment may be met by learning within the lifespan of an individual, rather than by structural changes that require many generations.

Independent and dependent variables are important concepts in the experimental study of learning. If, for example, one wished to study the effects of hunger on maze learning, two groups of animals could be tested in a maze:

one that was food deprived for 24 hours and another that was not food deprived. Hours of food deprivation (0 to 24) would be the independent variable—it is selected by the experimenter. The differences between two such groups could be determined by counting the number of errors made in learning the maze. Number of errors would be the dependent variable. All other factors, such as age of the animals, prior experience, etc., would be controlled by equating the two groups in these factors before the start of the experiment.

The study of learning in animals has yielded some general principles, conclusions that seem to be valid across a wide range of species and circumstances, as well as some conclusions that may be limited to certain species of animals and/or to certain types of learning situations.

Learning may be studied profitably in animals because, in many cases, the principles derived from animal research may be similar to principles of human learning—particularly in the case of learned emotional responses—and such a study may also help to highlight what is unique about human learning.

2

Habituation and Sensitization

" . . . to refrain from responding to insignificant stimuli is a necessary aspect of responding to significant stimuli. **"**

F. G. Worden, 1973

HABITUATION

Not long ago, in the older cities of the United States, elevated commuter railways wound through residential areas. Visiting someone who was unfortunate enough to live in a building bordering on the "el" was an interesting experience. The first train that roared by during the visit would be likely to elicit quite a startle response and perhaps an exclamation of "What's that?" To which the resident might respond, at the top of his voice as he braced glassware on the shaking table, "What's what?" Living in circumstances such as these would be impossible if one could not "get used" to regular disturbances. Indeed, the absence of a regularly scheduled train might evoke a sense of unease or alertness in a long-time resident.

Getting used to a loud noise that has no other important consequence is a form of *habituation*. In fact, we could define habituation as the waning of a response to constant or repeated stimulation, a waning that is not due to fatigue of the response process or to inactivation of the sensory mechanism. Habituation is a form of learning in that it represents a relatively permanent change in behavior that is the result of the experience of the individual and is not due to fatigue processes.

Habituation is a widespread form of learning, occurring in animals as simple as protozoa and the plant-like *Hydra*, and in animals as complex as humans (Wyers, Peeke, & Herz, 1973). The occurrence of habituation processes that are at least superficially similar across such a broad evolutionary spectrum suggests that habituation serves an important function in adaptation. And, indeed, it is not difficult to imagine that the ability to learn of the inconsequentiality of a particular environmental event could offer a selective advantage. Just imagine the behavioral paralysis and energy waste that might result if every change in the environment—every noise, etc.—always elicited a startle response of the same magnitude, always brought ongoing behavior to a halt. Little that might otherwise be important for survival could be accomplished.

Examples of Habituation

The Orienting Response

Habituation has been studied in complex responses of complex organisms, in simple responses of simple organisms, and in numerous intermediate situations. We will present only a few examples. One of the more complex response patterns occurs in the case of the *orienting response*. The presentation of a novel stimulus of moderate intensity will elicit a variety of behavioral and physiological changes. For example, the organism will tend to orient toward the stimulus, there may be a decrease in its heart rate, a decrease in skin resistance, a decrease in respiration, changes in the constriction of peripheral blood vessels, a change in muscle tone, and changes in the electrical activity of the cerebral cortex (Sokolov, 1963). If the stimulus is repeated a few times with no untoward consequences to the organism, then all of these responses will habituate, although perhaps at different rates.

Shown in Figure 2–1 is the habituation of one component of the orienting response—the change in skin conductance (Becker & Shapiro, 1981). The

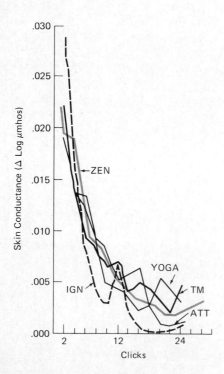

FIGURE 2–1 Habituation of one component of the orienting response, skin conductance, as a function of the number of clicks presented. Different groups of subjects practiced their usual meditational techniques, Zen, Yoga, or Transcendental Meditation (TM), or were instructed to ignore (IGN) or attend (ATT) to the loud clicks. The first few loud clicks produced a substantial increase from baseline (.000) in skin conductance (a measure of sympathetic nervous system activity) in all groups. Subsequent clicks produced less and less of an effect. The rate of habituation was not affected by the different states of consciousness. (Becker & Shapiro, 1981)

presentation of a loud clicking sound on the first two trials elicits a large degree of skin conductance caused by activity of the sweat glands, which, in turn, reflects the activity of the sympathetic nervous system. As the loud click is repeated, the degree of change in skin conductance diminishes until eventually there is little response to the noise. The subjects in this experiment were humans separated into five different groups. Three of the groups were composed of highly experienced meditators using different techniques [Zen, Yoga, and Transcendental Meditation (TM)]. These groups were instructed to engage in their standard meditating practice during presentation of the clicks. One of the other two groups was instructed to ignore the clicks (IGN) and the fifth group was instructed to attend to the clicks (ATT). As can be seen in the Figure, rate of habituation was approximately equal in all groups; apparently an inconsequential stimulus is an inconsequential stimulus in any of a variety of states of consciousness. Interestingly, Leaton and Jordan (1978) showed that habituation in rats to a loud noise, accomplished while they were awake, transferred to the sleep state. That is, rats that had been previously habituated were less likely to be aroused from sleep by the loud noise.

Gill Withdrawal Response

For another example of habituation, we turn from humans and rats to the lowly snail, in particular the sea snail *Aplysia californica*. This snail, illustrated in panel A of Figure 2–2, grows to an adult length of about 20 centimeters and has a number of characteristics that make it an interesting organism in which to study habituation. The first of these is that *Aplysia* has a readily elicitable response that habituates with repeated stimulation. This response is illustrated in the second and third panels of Figure 2–2. Tactile stimulation of the mantle shelf or siphon area of the snail causes it to retract its gill—a defensive reflex. However, if the stimulation is repeated and there are no adverse consequences to the snail, the degree of retraction becomes less and less, that is, the retraction response habituates.

A second feature that makes *Aplysia* an attractive organism to study is that its habituation shows many of the same functional relationships that have been found to apply to habituation in more complex organisms (Kandel, 1970, 1979a; Thompson & Spencer, 1966). A few of these relationships are shown in Figure 2–3. Panel C of the Figure shows that the response reappears after a rest period in which no stimulation is applied. This recovery is sometimes referred to as *sponataneous recovery*. Note that as the stimulation is repeated after the rest period, the response is rehabituated.

At first glance, this effect of a rest interval leading to the recovery of the response might indicate that the habituation is really due to a fatigue process and is not the result of learning. However, the next panel in Figure 2–3 illustrates the results of one of several procedures that may be used to

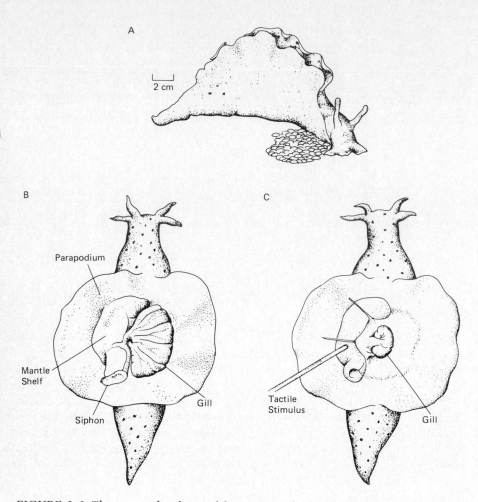

FIGURE 2–2 *The sea snail* Aplysia californica. *Tactile stimulation of the mantle shelf or siphon causes reflex retraction of the gill. This response habituates with repeated stimulation. (Kandel, 1979a—top; Kandel, 1970—bottom)*

show that habituation is not due to fatigue. This fourth panel (D) shows that habituation can be counteracted if the animal experiences another strong stimulus. For example, if *Aplysia* is touched somewhat roughly in the head and then the mantle shelf is stimulated, the previously habituated gill retraction response will reappear. This return of the response is referred to as *dishabituation*, and it indicates that the animal's muscle system is still capable of making the habituated response—it has not been lost because of fatigue.

The next panel of Figure 2–3 (E) shows that dishabituation itself may be habituated. That is, the dishabituating stimulus has less and less effect in

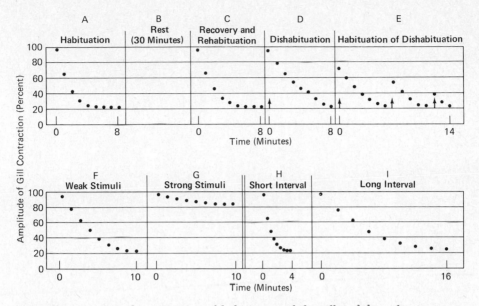

FIGURE 2–3 Some characteristics of habituation of the gill withdrawal response in Aplysia (Kandel, 1970). The various functions are explained in the text.

disrupting habituation as it is applied repeatedly. The final four panels (F–I) of the Figure illustrate two other relationships. They show that habituation is often more complete with less intense (weak) stimuli than with more intense (strong) stimuli, and that habituation may proceed faster if there is relatively little time between repeated presentations of the stimuli than if there is a long time interval between repeated presentations of the stimuli (Castellucci & Kandel, 1976; Kandel, 1970).

We have shown that Aplysia has a response that may be habituated and that many aspects of this habituation are similar to habituation in more complex organisms. The reason that these characteristics are interesting is that the nervous system of Aplysia is relatively simple, indicating the possibility of our coming to an understanding of the neural basis of habituation. Whereas the human brain may have a trillion (or 10^{12}) neurons, the nervous system of Aplysia has about 20,000 (or 2×10^4) neurons (Kandel, 1979a). Furthermore, these neurons are organized into nine separate groups (ganglia) each containing about 2,000 neurons. Many of these neurons are large and recognizable as particular cells occupying distinct locations and having distinct functions that are invariant in each individual (Kandel, 1979a). Some of this structure may be seen in the map of the abdominal ganglion of Aplysia presented in Figure 2–4. The motor neurons that control the gill withdrawal response are located in this abdominal ganglion (L7 is one of these motor neurons).

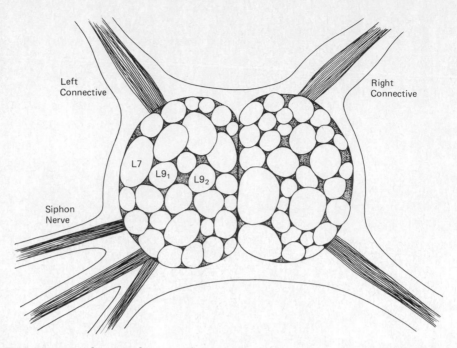

FIGURE 2–4 Schematic drawing of nerve cells in the abdominal ganglion of Aplysia. Many of the neurons are large and are identifiable in regard to location and function in different animals. The neurons labeled L7 and L9 (left 7, etc.) are involved in the gill withdrawal reflex. Also shown are nerve fibers connecting the abdominal ganglion to other parts of the nervous system. (Kandel, 1970)

The Neural Basis of Habituation in *Aplysia*

What happens at the neural level when a response becomes habituated? A long series of studies by Kandel and his colleagues (e.g., Castellucci et al., 1978; Kandel, 1979a, 1979b, 1983) has provided a substantial answer to this question in the case of the gill withdrawal response in *Aplysia*. A simplified version of their discoveries is presented in Figure 2–5. When the mantle shelf or siphon are touched, an impulse is initiated in sensory neurons. These sensory neurons influence (synapse with) the motor neurons controlling the gill withdrawal response. The first few times the sensory neuron is activated, there is substantial activation of the motor neuron and withdrawal of the gill. As the stimulus is repeated, there is less and less activation of the motor neuron. Does this mean that the motor neuron is becoming fatigued? No— because direct stimulation of the motor neuron shows that it is still capable of producing the complete gill withdrawal response. Is there less activity in the sensory neuron with repeated stimulation? No—Kandel's work has shown that the response in the sensory neuron is essentially undiminished by repeated stimulation.

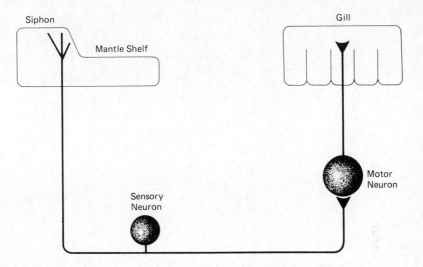

FIGURE 2–5 Simplified "wiring diagram" of the gill withdrawal response in Aplysia. The sensory neuron detects tactile stimulation of the siphon or mantle shelf area. The sensory neuron then releases a chemical transmitter (acetylcholine) from the axon terminal. The transmitter crosses the synapse and induces activity in the motor neuron (L7) which acts to retract the gill. With repeated stimulation, the amount of transmitter released becomes less and less. (Kandel, 1970)

It seems that the change that underlies habituation occurs in the region of the synapse between the two cells. Kandel has been able to show that this change involves the release of less and less transmitter substance by the sensory nerve as stimulation is repeated. With less transmitter substance released, there is less stimulation of the motor nerve and less of a gill withdrawal response. Is less transmitter substance being released because the supply is exhausted by repeated stimulation? No—the phenomenon of dishabituation indicates that this is not likely to be the case and, in addition, Kandel has shown that the release of less transmitter substance is an active process that results from other changes in the cellular chemistry of the sensory neuron (Kandel, 1979a).

Unfortunately, we will not be able to delve further into this cellular chemistry in this text. We will have to be satisfied with the knowledge that habituation of the gill withdrawal response in Aplysia has been traced to neurochemical processes taking place in individual cells. This knowledge will help greatly in the understanding of the neural bases of learning and memory in higher organisms.

Before leaving the topic of habituation, however, we should indicate that even this simple form of learning is not as simple as we have presented it thus far.

Some Complexities

Multiple Responses

One type of complexity may be seen in the field studies of habituation in sparrows by Petrinovich and Patterson (e.g., 1981, 1980, 1979). These investigators recorded the territorial song of a male white-crowned sparrow and played it back to a different sparrow pair through a speaker positioned within the territory of the pair. Various responses were recorded from the pair—for example, how often the male sang, how often it rose in flight, how closely it approached the speaker, how often it attacked the speaker, how often the female took to flight, etc. In addition, the songs were played back to sparrow pairs in different brooding conditions, that is, some were brooding eggs, some hatchlings, and some fledglings. The results of these studies indicated that habituation generally occurred, but the degree of habituation depended upon the brooding condition, the nature of the response, and the manner in which the song was presented. The point is that all responses may not habituate at equal rates and that the rate at which a given response habituates may depend on motivational states (here represented by brooding conditions) of the animal.

Different Processes

A second complexity is that all response changes that superficially appear to reflect the same process of habituation may not, in fact, reflect the operation of the same mechanism. For example, if rats are exposed to a loud click it will elicit a startle response that may be measured in terms of how much they jump. As the click is repeated, it produces less and less of a startle response. In other words, the startle response habituates. If a rat is exposed to a maze it has never experienced before, it will engage in a great deal of activity "patrolling" the maze. As the animal is given repeated exposure to the maze, its tendency to enter the various branches declines, that is, it seems to habituate. Although behaviorally there would seem to be the same process occurring in these two situations—decline of a response with repeated exposure to the stimulus—there is evidence that two different brain mechanisms may be responsible for the two declines. Leaton (1981) has found that damage to the hippocampus, a part of the brain implicated in memory processes in humans, prevents the decline in exploration seen with repeated exposure to the maze, but such damage has no effect on habituation of the startle response. That is, the startle response habituates in about the same way in brain-damaged rats and in normal rats, but the rate of decline in maze exploration is quite different in the two groups.

Thus, there may be a number of different brain mechanisms controlling different kinds of habituation. In fact, it has been argued that maze exploration involves the formation of cognitive maps—the remembering of spatial relations and the location of objects in space—and when the map is completed, exploration ceases (O'Keefe & Nadel, 1978; Tolman, 1948). O'Keefe and Nadel have also hypothesized that the hippocampus is necessary for the formation of these cognitive maps, and that without an intact hippocampus the animal cannot learn (or remember) spatial relations. Thus, exploration continues unabated. From this point of view, then, the apparently similar habituation curves of the startle response and maze activity would really represent two quite different processes—the learning of spatial relations in the case of the maze, and perhaps the learning that the loud click is unimportant in the case of startle.

Short- and Long-Term Habituation

As a final complexity, we shall mention the possibility that there are two basic types of habituation: short-term and long-term. One way of demonstrating the difference in them is to conduct a relatively brief series of trials and then check for recovery from habituation. Recovery usually occurs fairly quickly and completely, as shown in Figure 2–3. When, however, a longer series of trials is given, there is less recovery, and habituation is maintained over a longer time period (Kandel, 1979a).

Another way of demonstrating this is to present the stimulus to be habituated at two different interstimulus intervals (ISI) to two different groups of animals. For example, one group could be presented a stimulus every two seconds, whereas a second group could be presented a stimulus every 16 seconds. When this is done, the short ISI group shows more habituation than the long ISI group (Wagner, 1976). This type of relationship is also indicated in Figure 2–3. When, however, these same two groups are tested some time after the initial habituation session, then the long ISI group might be likely to show less recovery from habituation than the short ISI group (Wagner, 1976). It is possible that these two types of habituation may be related to differences in short-term and long-term memory in humans.

Given that there are two types of habituation, is it necessary to postulate that there are two different neural processes responsible for them? Some research by Kandel (1979a) indicates that the answer to this question is "yes and no." That is, in both short-term and long-term habituation, the sensory neuron of *Aplysia* becomes less effective in stimulating the motor neuron and the basis of this effect is that there is less transmitter substance released at the synapse (refer to Figure 2–5). Thus, the same basic mechanism seems to be involved in both types of habituation. However, there must also be a difference since synaptic activity is depressed for longer time periods in long-term than in short-term habituation. Kandel speculates that there may be some structural changes in the presynaptic terminal of the sensory neuron that result from the extended habituation training. These structural changes then contribute to the longer-lasting effects of habituation. However, the effects of these structural changes are reversible, as we shall see when we discuss our next topic: sensitization.

SENSITIZATION

Incremental Sensitization and Dishabituation

Sensitization refers to the augmentation of a pre-existing response by a strong, usually noxious, stimulus. There are two somewhat different ways in which the term *sensitization* is used. The first use is in referring to the enhancement of a response elicited by a stimulus with repeated presentations of that stimulus. We shall refer to this as *incremental sensitization*. It is clear from the definition that incremental sensitization describes a behavioral effect that is the opposite of habituation.

A period of sensitization often precedes habituation. That is, the behavioral effects of the second, third, or fourth presentation of a stimulus may be greater than the effects produced by the first presentation. Subsequent presentations may, however, lead to less and less of a behavioral effect. Habituation, therefore, may follow a period of incremental sensitization. Several examples of incremental sensitization are shown in Figure 2–6. The first panel shows an initial marked increase in the frequency with which a male three-spined stickleback fish *(Gasterosteus aculeatus)* bites another male introduced into its territory. After the fourth minute of intrusion, habituation of the attacks sets in. The second panel (Figure 2–6B) shows a similar process in the number of songs sung by a male white-crowned sparrow when the song of another male is played in its territory. In this case, the frequency of singing did not fall below the initial level during the course of the eight trials in which the "intruder's" song was played. The third panel (Figure 2–6C) shows changes in skin conductance in humans as a function of the intensity of sounds presented to them. Remember from our earlier discussion that skin conductance changes are one component of the orienting response (see Figure 2–1). Figure 2–6C shows clearly that the degree of sensitization depends upon the intensity of the stimulus presented. When loud sounds are presented, there is a period of incremental sensitization that precedes habituation.

A second way in which sensitization is often seen in behavior occurs when a stimulus, usually intense or noxious, is presented just prior to the presentation of an already habituated stimulus. In this use, the term *sensitization* is synonymous with dishabituation (Kandel, 1979a), as described in relation to Figure 2–3. It is as if the intense stimulus primes the animal (sensitizes it) to respond to any change in the environment. By thus priming the animal, the new stimulus undoes the effects of the previous habituation period. It is easy to imagine the potential adaptive value of the sensitization-as-dishabituation process. Once an animal has habituated to a stimulus, it is in

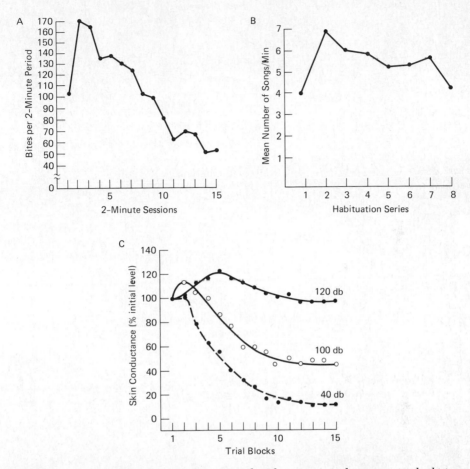

FIGURE 2–6 Examples of sensitization. Panel A shows an initial increase in the biting attacks of a three-spine stickleback fish toward a male conspecific introduced into its territory. This initial period of incremental sensitization is followed by habituation (Peeke & Veno, 1973). Panel B shows initial sensitization in the number of songs sung by a male white-crowned sparrow when the song of another male is played in its territory. This sensitization is followed by habituation back toward the original baseline (Petrinovich & Peeke, 1973). Panel C shows changes in human skin conductance as a function of the intensity of auditory stimuli. The least intense sound (40 db) produced only habituation; the more intense sounds produced more sensitization and less habituation (Raskin et al., 1969).

a vulnerable state should that stimulus suddenly become dangerous. The occurrence of dishabituation following the experience of another stimulus that is intense or noxious may serve to reduce this potential vulnerability. That is, the conditions under which habituation occurred may no longer be the same, and it may be safest for the animal if its nervous system is constructed so as to return to initial conditions (dishabituation) when the environment is changed.

Dual Process Theory

What accounts for functions such as those shown in Figure 2–6, where responsivity tends at first to increase before declining? Richard Thompson and his colleagues (e.g., Groves & Thompson, 1973; Thompson & Glanzman, 1976) have postulated that there exist two independent processes that are aroused by the presentation of a stimulus: habituation and sensitization. That is, each presentation of a stimulus has a tendency to sensitize an animal to future presentations of that stimulus so that such presentations will produce an enhanced response. At the same time, each presentation of a stimulus leads to an increment in habituation such that future presentations of the stimulus will tend to elicit a smaller response. The actual behavior that occurs represents the outcome of these opposed processes.

Some feeling for this theory may be gained from examining Figure 2–7. The two panels show hind limb flexor responses elicited by shock in cats. The cats in these experiments were prepared so that shock influenced only sensory neurons in the spinal cord, and the response of the cat's leg was controlled only by motor neurons in the spinal cord. The brain was not involved. In addition to the responses obtained in this experiment (represented by the solid lines), the Figure also shows the hypothesized course of the two proc-

FIGURE 2–7 *Habituation and sensitization of hind limb flexor response in cats. The data in panel A were obtained when a low intensity shock was used; the data in panel B were obtained with a high intensity shock. The solid lines in the two panels represent changes in the degree of flexor response. It is apparent that habituation predominated with low intensity shock, and sensitization with high intensity shock. The dashed lines in each panel represent theoretical processes of sensitization (S) and habituation (H) that underlay the obtained results. Sensitization is assumed to act always to offset habituation. The more intense the stimuli, the more pronounced the sensitization component. (Groves & Thompson, 1970)*

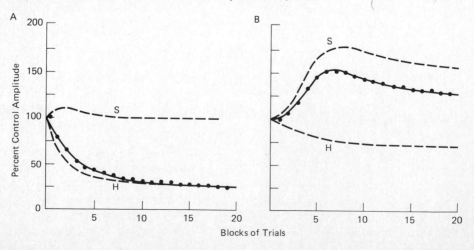

esses of habituation and sensitization (represented by the dashed lines). The behavioral data is assumed to reflect the interaction of these two processes.

The first panel of the Figure (2–7A) shows data and hypothetical processes when the intensity of the shock was low. In this case there was no evidence of incremental sensitization. The assumption is that at low intensities there is little sensitization and the habituation process predominates. The second panel (2–7B) shows the results and hypothetical processes when a more intense shock was used. In this case there was substantial incremental sensitization and little evidence of habituation. The inference drawn from these and similar data is that there is always some balance between habituation, which predominates when stimulus intensity is low, and sensitization, which predominates when stimulus intensity is high. One could imagine functions in between those presented in Figure 2–7, functions that might be obtained with intermediate levels of intensity (see Figure 2–6C).

Some evidence in support of this dual process interpretation of habituation and sensitization has been obtained at the physiological level. For example, Kandel and his colleagues (e.g., Kandel, 1979a) have studied sensitization in *Aplysia*. They found that a noxious stimulus applied to the head of *Aplysia* will greatly enhance a previously habituated gill withdrawal reflex. They have also found that this enhancement is brought about because of an increase in the amount of transmitter substance released by the sensory neuron (cf., Figure 2–5). Recall that in our earlier discussion of habituation in *Aplysia* we stated that habituation was due to a decline in transmitter release by the sensory neuron. Is sensitization a simple reversal of this process? Kandel's work indicates that there is more to it than that. When the head is stimulated by the noxious stimulus, a neural system different from the one shown in Figure 2–5 is activated. This neural system, represented in simplified form in Figure 2–8, makes contact with the presynaptic terminals of the sensory neuron that arises from the mantle shelf area. When the head area is stimulated, this additional neuron system causes the sensory neuron to release more transmitter substance, thereby enhancing the degree of gill withdrawal. Activity in the neural system arising from the head ganglion serves principally to modulate activity in the sensory neuron. That is, it affects the amount of transmitter substance released by the sensory neuron only when the mantle shelf is stimulated. Stimulation of the head without subsequent stimulation of the mantle shelf has relatively little effect on transmitter release and gill withdrawal activity.

Thus, the evidence adduced by Kandel and his colleagues agrees with the model proposed by Thompson and his colleagues—sensitization and habituation represent two separate and distinct processes. Other research supports this conclusion. For example, research by Kandel's group has indicated that the chemicals serving as transmitters are different in the two systems, at least in the case of *Aplysia*. Whereas acetylcholine is the transmitter released by the sensory neuron, serotonin is released by the neuron from the head

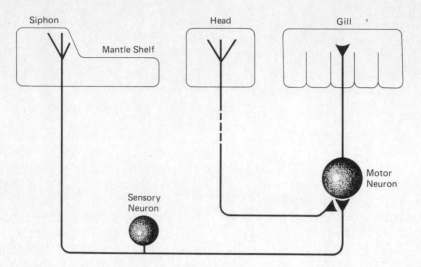

FIGURE 2–8 *Simplified diagram of dishabituation circuit in* Aplysia. *Tactile stimulation of the head area produces activity in a neuron that terminates on the presynaptic axonal area of the sensory neuron (see Figure 2–5). Release of a neurotransmitter (serotonin) from this head neuron enhances the release of transmitter (acetylcholine) from the sensory neuron when the mantle shelf area is stimulated. Thus, a second neural system mediates dishabituation.*

ganglion (Kandel, 1979a). Also, Thompson and his colleagues have found evidence that there are two types of neurons in the cat spinal cord: one type that shows only habituation and another type that shows sensitization (Thompson & Glanzman, 1976).

Thus, the evidence seems sufficient to conclude that the decrements in behavior that we see as habituation, and the increments in behavior that we see as sensitization, represent two distinct processes served by different neural systems. In general terms, we could think of habituation as representing a process of learning that a particular stimulus is not important—it has no consequences for the organism. However, if an aversive event occurs, then a motivation system is activated which enhances reactivity to environmental changes, even those that have been previously habituated.

Perhaps one more example will help to clarify habituation and sensitization. Imagine that you make it a regular practice to walk your dog at night in the dark, wooded back yard. There are a lot of sounds in the night—tree branches rubbing together, rabbits scurrying, etc. However, both you and your dog pay no attention to them—you have habituated to these noises. Then one dark night your dog suddenly starts barking and growling, but you see nothing. The next, previously inconsequential, sound that you hear is likely to elicit some attention and perhaps some behavior. In this example, the dog's barking served as a sensitizing stimulus, activating an arousing or alerting motivational system, which in turn dishabituated (sensitized) previously habituated behaviors.

CHAPTER SUMMARY

Habituation is said to occur when the response elicited by a stimulus declines with repeated presentation of that stimulus. Examples described included habituation of the orienting response in humans and habituation of the gill withdrawal reflex in *Aplysia*. Work with *Aplysia* has led to some understanding of the neural basis of habituation, at least in simple organisms.

Different responses may habituate at different rates, and the process of habituation may be influenced by motivational states. Finally, there may be both short-term and long-term habituation. Long-term habituation may occur after extended presentations of a stimulus and it may be related to structural changes in neurons.

Two forms of sensitization were described: incremental sensitization and dishabituation. Sensitization refers to the augmentation of a response which usually occurs after an intense and/or novel stimulus is presented. Sensitization seems to be a process independent of, and opposed to, habituation. Work with *Aplysia* and other animals has indicated that habituation and sensitization may represent two distinct and opposed processes, each with a different neural basis.

3

Pavlovian Conditioning I: Introduction and Basic Phenomena

INTRODUCTION AND HISTORICAL BACKGROUND

In the previous two chapters we have seen how learning may contribute to adaptation and how the ability to learn may have been favored by natural selection. We also considered some of the characteristics of habituation, a simple type of learning which involves the waning of responses to unimportant events. As we examine the topic of Pavlovian conditioning here and in the next three chapters, we will explore the circumstances in which animals learn that an environmental event is important. In particular, we will see how animals learn that one event may serve as a signal for another event. We will see how animals acquire knowledge of which stimuli are likely to be followed by motivationally important occurrences (e.g., food or an aversive stimulus) and which are unlikely to be so followed.

Empiricism and Nativism

There are two general traditions of intellectual inquiry concerning the origins of knowledge. One of these traditions, the *empiricist* view, is that all knowledge comes through the senses and is acquired during one's lifetime. According to this view there is no knowledge at birth, the mind (brain) is a blank slate *(tabula rasa)* to be written on by experience. This view has been argued by a number of philosophers, including Aristotle and some British political philosophers of the seventeenth, eighteenth, and nineteenth centuries. John Locke, for example wrote that ideas are the basic elements of the mind and these ideas derive from sensation, that is, from experience. The most fundamental ideas, those deriving directly from sensory experience, might be sensations such as hardness, redness, roundness, etc. Simple ideas (sensations) such as these, together with others, such as a particular taste, might be compounded into a more complex idea such as "apple," if they all occur together frequently. Thus, complex ideas were thought to result from the *association* of simple ideas.

Aristotle, Locke, and other philosophers such as David Hume and John Stuart Mill, elaborated lists of conditions that might lead to the formation of such associations among individual ideas. The condition mentioned most often was that of *contiguity*—closeness or proximity in space and/or time. Thus, the odor of smoke and the appearance of fire typically occur closely together in space and time and may become associated through experience, so that detection of the odor alone will bring to mind the image of fire. (A test of associations in humans is to present a word and ask the subject to state whatever comes to mind.) Another condition necessary for the formation of associations that was often mentioned by philosophers was repetition. Events are more likely to be associated if they occur together frequently than if their contiguous appearance is infrequent. We will see how contiguity, frequency, and other principles of association have experimental counterparts in the work of Pavlov.

A second philosophical position regarding knowledge is that of *nativism*, the view that some knowledge exists before experience; it is innate. According to this view, espoused in various forms by philosophers such as Plato, Descartes, and Kant, the mind is not entirely a blank slate to be written upon solely by experience. Rather, there are inborn components of knowledge or ways of interpreting experience.

The theoretical system developed by the Russian physiologist Ivan Pavlov combined nativism and empiricism in that it recognized two ways of responding to environmental events. One of these is innate, or, in Pavlov's terms, *unconditioned*. The second way of responding to environmental events is based on experience, and is learned during the life of the individual. This, in Pavlov's terms, is *conditioned* (Pavlov, 1927).

Reflexes

But what is it that is conditioned or unconditioned? Is it ideas, thoughts, or what? Pavlov's view of the nature of elementary knowledge was based on the concept of a *reflex*, a concept that developed in philosophy and was adopted by physiology. The origin of this concept may be traced back at least to René Descartes, the French philosopher and mathematician. Descartes believed that the body is a machine and that all of the behavior of animals and most of the behavior of humans can be explained in strictly physical terms, without the need for concepts such as mind or soul. According to Descartes, involuntary behavior (all animal behavior was thought to be involuntary) results from the passage of sensory information through the nerves to the brain, where it is *reflected* out (in the form of "animal spirits") through the "hollow tubes" that are the nerves, to the appropriate muscles, causing the organism to behave. This behavior was viewed as a "necessary reaction to some external stimulus" and the characteristics of the behavior were thought to be determined entirely by the nature of the stimulus and the internal "construction" of the organism.

This trend in thought was continued by I. M. Sechenov, a Russian physiologist, whose writings appear to have influenced Pavlov and anticipated in several details Pavlov's interpretations of conditioning phenomena. Sechenov went further than Descartes. He believed that the higher mental functions (as well as simple responses) can be explained in terms of reflexes. According to Sechenov, all forms of human behavior, including thought, are involuntary and reflexive in nature. This interpretation implied that higher mental functions could be subject to scientific investigation and analysis, and further, that the study of simple reflexes might have something to tell us about more complex forms of behavior. Scientific investigation of a form of learning apparently based on reflexes was initiated by Pavlov just at the turn of the century.

Pavlov had already made Nobel prizewinning contributions to the study of the digestive processes before he turned to the study of learning. In fact, observations that Pavlov made while studying digestion led directly to his investigation of the learning process. Pavlov noted that saliva and gastric secretions, which were initially elicited by the placement of food in a dog's mouth, eventually came to be elicited by a number of other stimuli that preceded the actual receipt of food by the dog. For example, salivation would eventually be elicited by the sight or smell of food, by the bowl that usually contained the food, or even by the sight of the person who usually brought in the food bowl.

The important observation here was that stimuli initially ineffective in eliciting a biologically important *reflex* (in this case secretion of digestive juices) began to elicit this reflex after the animal had some experience with the stimuli regularly preceding the food. If Pavlov had been trained differently, or lived at a different time, he might have been content to merely note these interesting observations (termed *psychic secretions*) and perhaps relate them to a principle of contiguity or repetition. However, for Pavlov, these observations were not the end but the beginning of the systematic study of the conditions that influence learning.

EXAMPLES OF PAVLOVIAN CONDITIONING

Before proceeding to a detailed analysis of Pavlovian conditioning, we shall present several examples of Pavlovian conditioned responses, some of which may be familiar, some not. Perhaps the most familiar example of Pavlovian conditioning comes from Pavlov's own research and concerns the conditioning of salivary secretions. When a hungry dog is presented with food, it will salivate. Salivation is a natural part of the digestive process. The salivary fluid, in addition to containing water that helps put food substances into solution, contains enzymes that begin the digestive process. Pavlov's initial observations indicated that environmental objects not biologically related to food (objects such as the room or bowl used to present the food) would also elicit

salivation after the animal had had some experience with the objects immediately preceding the presentation of food.

In order to investigate this apparent learning, Pavlov selected a stimulus
that did *not* normally elicit salivation—for example, the sound of a bell or the
beating of a metronome. By presenting these stimuli in conjunction with
food, Pavlov could determine how long it would be before these stimuli produced salivation. Of course, it was found that this procedure of pairing a bell's
sound with the presentation of food did indeed eventually lead to the sound
alone producing salivation.

In some ways, learning to salivate at the presentation of a stimulus regularly paired with the occurrence of food is an extrapolation of a normal biological process. The presence of food in the mouth normally initiates the secretion of digestive juices in the stomach sometime before the food actually
arrives there to be digested. As a result of the Pavlovian conditioning process,
salivation occurs in the mouth before food arrives there to be ingested and
digested.

For another example of Pavlovian conditioning let us turn again to a
process related to digestion. Insulin is a hormone secreted by the pancreas in
response to high levels of sugar (glucose) in the blood. Insulin causes the
removal of sugar from the blood and the storing of sugar in the liver. If a dose
of insulin is injected into an animal, it also removes sugar from blood, thereby
producing a temporary state of lowered blood sugar, or *hypoglycemia*. The
question of interest here is whether or not learning can take place within this
system. Can environmental events regularly correlated with the injection of
insulin produce an effect on blood sugar even if, on some occasion, no insulin
is actually injected? The answer is "yes." A number of studies have indicated
that animals given several insulin injections, say one every other day for a
few days, will show a drop in blood glucose levels when they are injected
with saline (Woods & Kulkosky, 1976). That is, the animals will respond as if
they have been injected with insulin when they have actually been injected
with a physiologically inert dose of salt solution. Animals previously injected
with saline solution only do not show a drop in blood glucose levels.

What this experiment shows is that the procedures and context related
to drug administration may themselves produce effects like the drug—even
when the drug is not administered.[1] Several examples of how Pavlovian conditioning processes may influence drug effects and how Pavlovian processes
may be involved in drug addiction will be considered in detail in Chapter 5.

Emotional responses too may be evoked by stimuli that were originally
neutral, through Pavlovian procedures. For example, a few administrations of
an electric shock, preceded by a mild clicking sound, will cause the clicking
sound to suppress behavior and release stress hormones (Mason, 1968; Mason

---

[1] It should also be noted that some investigators (e.g., Siegel, 1975) find conditioned hyperglycemia rather than hypoglycemia, and that under some conditions both may be obtained
(Flaherty et al., 1980). The reason for these differences has not yet been determined.

& Brady, 1956). The suppressed behavior and hormonal release are correlates of "fear" evoked by the clicking sound. We will consider many examples of Pavlovian fear conditioning in this text.

A final example of Pavlovian conditioning may be drawn from a medical setting. Some forms of cancer are treated by chemotherapy, a treatment which has many side effects including nausea and vomiting. Patients find this unpleasant but the great majority persist with the treatment because it may be a life or death situation. It has been found that Pavlovian conditioning processes may play a role in exacerbating the difficulty that patients experience with this treatment. Some patients find that, after a few treatments, they begin to feel nauseous when they enter the hospital, or when they prepare to leave home for the hospital, or even if a nurse calls them on the telephone to remind them of an appointment (Borysenko, 1982). Later we will consider evidence showing that conditioning involving agents that produce gastrointestinal disturbance is a very powerful form of Pavlovian conditioning in animals.

These four examples of Pavlovian conditioning have involved different species and quite different responses: salivation, change in blood glucose, stress hormones, and nausea; yet they share a similarity. The similarity is that stimuli which were originally neutral in regard to these responses lost their neutrality as a result of having been presented contiguously with other stimuli that elicited these responses. That is, neutral stimuli acquired new properties as a result of contiguous pairing with non-neutral stimuli.

We proceed now to some terminology and a more detailed analysis of Pavlovian conditioning.

ELEMENTS OF CONDITIONING

There are four basic elements in the conditioning paradigm: (1) the *Unconditioned Stimulus* (US); (2) the response that it reflexively elicits, the *Unconditioned Response* (UR); (3) an originally neutral stimulus, the *Conditioned Stimulus* (CS); and (4) the response that is eventually elicited, the *Conditioned Reponse* (CR).

The Unconditioned Stimulus and Unconditioned Response

We have already mentioned several USs and URs: the placement of food in the mouth (a US) reflexively elicits salivation (a UR), insulin (a US) elicits a decrease in blood sugar (a UR)[2], etc. Many other USs have been used

---

[2] The exact nature of the US and UR may not always be easy to specify when drugs are used in conditioning (Eikelboom & Stewart, 1982).

in the study of conditioning. For example, electric shock has been employed as a US for URs such as heart rate changes, vasomotor reactions, leg flexion reflexes, eyelid closure reflexes, and others. Morphine and poisons such as lithium chloride have been used to produce URs of nausea, vomiting, and general malaise. A number of USs and the URs they elicit are presented in Table 3–1.

The Conditioned Stimulus

Almost any stimulus can be utilized as a CS.[3] The two principal require-ments for the selection of a stimulus as a CS are (a) that it can be perceived or attended to by the subject, and (b) that it does not itself elicit the UR, that is, it should be initially neutral. Perception of a stimulus is often indicated by the behavior of the subject. For example, Pavlov noted that when a novel stimulus, such as the beat of a metronome, was first presented, the dog would turn in the direction of the sound. This response, called the investigatory reflex by Pavlov, but now more frequently termed the *orienting response*, provides behavioral evidence that the subject is attending to the stimulus (see Chapter 2).

The second requirement—that the CS be originally neutral with regard to the elicitation of the UR—is related to the definition and measurement of learning. If we want to measure the course of learning (the effects of experi-ence), then it is reasonable to start with a stimulus that does not initially elicit the response that will be used as the dependent variable to measure learning. For example, if the sound of a metronome always elicited salivation in dogs, then it would be a relatively poor choice for a CS if food is to be the US, because it would be difficult to measure any changes in behavior, any learn-ing, that occurred as a result of placing this sound in close contiguity with the food.

In practice, the selection of a neutral stimulus is sometimes a problem. Consider what happens when electric shock is used as a US. The application of the shock elicits a general activation of the sympathetic division of the autonomic nervous system. This general activation has many specific effects, the nature of which depends upon the organ system that the sympathetic branch innervates. For example, electric shock leads to an increase in heart rate, an increase in blood pressure, a constriction of peripheral blood vessels, and a decrease in skin resistance. This last measure, change in skin resis-tance, is termed *galvanic skin response* (GSR) and is a frequently used meas-ure in classical conditioning. The popularity of this measure probably relates

---

[3] There are some circumstances in which one type of stimulus is more likely than another type to enter into an association. For example, in mammals, taste-related stimuli are more likely to be associated with gastrointestinal distress than stimuli such as bells and lights. This matter will be discussed later in the text.

ADD ETHOLOGICAL LIST

TABLE 3–1 UNCONDITIONED RESPONSES AND THE STIMULI USED TO ELICIT THEM	
Response	**Stimulus**
Salivation	Dry food, acid
EEG Alpha Rhythm	Light
Change in skin resistance (GSR)	Electric shock
Pupillary reflex	Change in illumination, shock
Gastrointestinal secretions	Food
Vasomotor reactions	Shock, thermal stimuli
Nausea, vomiting, etc.	Morphine
Immunity reactions	Injection of toxin and antigen
Diuresis	Increased water intake
Flexion reflex	Electric shock
Knee jerk	Patellar blow
Eyelid reflex	Shock, sound, air puff
Eye movements	Bodily rotation
Change in respiration	Electric shock
Change in pitch of voice	Electric shock
Withdrawal movements	Electric shock
Mouth opening, swallowing	Food
Locomotion	Shock
Instructed responses	Various
Previously conditioned (higher order) responses	Various
Novel food aversion	X-irradiation, lithium chloride ingestion, apomophine injection, others
Change in blood sugar	Insulin injection
Catalepsy	Haloperidol
Body temperature changes	Morphine, alcohol
Immunosuppression	Cyclophosphamide
Changed epinephrine levels	Shock
Change in heart rate	Shock
Adrenocorticosteroid elevation	Cyclophosphamide

(Modified from Kimble, 1961)

to its relative ease of measurement and its covariation with the experience of emotion in humans. That is, events that produce emotions in humans also tend to produce GSR changes (a fact that the so-called lie detector takes advantage of; it is really an emotion detector).

However, the use of the GSR for conditioning presents difficulties for the selection of a neutral stimulus. This is so because GSR changes are also part of the orienting response (see Chapter 2, Figure 2–1); therefore, the presentation of any novel stimulus produces a decrease in skin resistance, which is the same response that the shock US produces. How then is one to study the acquisition of a conditioned GSR change with, say, light onset as the CS and shock as the US when both produce a GSR change from the beginning, without any training?

There are several procedures that may be used to alleviate this problem; we shall mention two. First of all, as you may have guessed, the GSR to shock is usually considerably greater than the GSR to something such as a light onset. Magnitude of the skin resistance change, then, could help discriminate between the two responses. The second solution to this problem deals with the fact that the organism eventually habituates to the novel stimulus so that the orienting response is no longer exhibited. Therefore, if the light is presented by itself a few times before the start of conditioning, it will eventually cease to elicit a GSR change. At this point, the conditioning trials can be initiated.

The basic facts to remember about selection of a CS, then, are (a) the stimulus should be within the sensory capacities of the subject; (b) the stimulus should not initially elicit the same response as the US; and (c) if the CS does elicit a component of the UR, certain procedures must be employed to circumvent this problem.

The Conditioned Response

The last of the four basic elements of conditioning we must discuss is the CR. It is the occurrence of the CR, upon the presentation of the CS, that tells us that learning has taken place. The CR is often quite similar in form to the UR, as we have seen already in the case of salivation and nausea. However, although grossly similar, the CR differs in detail from the UR. For example, the CR occurs before the UR and it may be of smaller magnitude than the UR. An example of this relationship is shown in Figure 3–1. Initially, the puff of air (the US) directed at the eye causes closure of the nictitating membrane. This closure is a reflex response to the air puff—it is the UR. The presentation of a tone before the air puff has no effect on the nictitating membrane. But, after the tone and air puff have been paired a number of times, the nictitating membrane begins to close during the CS period, before the US is presented. Eventually, after a number of pairings of the CS and US, the CR merges with the UR, resulting in a smooth and more gradual closure of the eyelid that *precedes* or anticipates the presentation of the US (see also Levey & Martin, 1968).

However, as the procedures used in Pavlovian conditioning experiments have become more varied, the specification of the nature of the CR has become more complex. For example, when electric shock is used as a US in heart rate conditioning, the UR is cardiac acceleration, but the CR may be

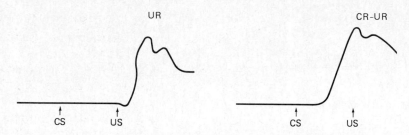

FIGURE 3–1 *Movements of the nictitating membrane (one of three "eyelids") at two stages of conditioning in the rabbit. The left panel shows that early in conditioning the US (an air puff directed to the eye) elicited closure of the nictitating membrane (the UR), but the CS (a tone which preceded the air puff by 250 milliseconds) did not cause movement of the nictitating membrane. The right panel shows that later in conditioning, the membrane closure occurred in response to the CS. This panel also shows how the CR (the movement elicited by the CS) blends with and becomes part of the UR. (Data from Berger, Clark, & Thompson, 1980.)*

either cardiac deceleration (e.g., Cunningham, Fitzgerald, & Francisco, 1977; Gallagher, Kapp, McNally, & Pascoe, 1981; Howard, Obrist, Gaebelein, & Galosy, 1974) or cardiac acceleration (e.g., Billman & Randall, 1980, 1981; Cohen, 1978). These differences in CR form may depend upon a number of factors including the species of animal used, how the animal is restrained, the experimental situation, etc.

A series of detailed studies by Holland (e.g., Holland, 1977, 1979, 1980a, 1980b) has provided information concerning some of the factors that influence CR form. Holland made a close observational analysis of the behavior of rats when various stimuli were used as the CS, when different time periods were tried between CS presentation and US presentation, and when different USs were used. Holland's data show that behaviors that occur early in the time period between CS presentation and US presentation are substantially influenced by the nature of the CS and, in fact, often resemble the orienting response initially elicited by these stimuli. For example, a light elicits rearing in the rat (standing on its hind legs) as an orienting response, and the frequency of this behavior is increased when the light regularly precedes food availability. In contrast, a tone elicits head turning behavior as an orienting response, and the frequency of this behavior increases when the tone precedes food availability. The tone elicits little rearing behavior either as an orienting response or as a CR.

Holland also found that behaviors that occur late in the CS–US interval, just before US presentation, are primarily influenced by the nature of the US, somewhat different behaviors occurring when sucrose solutions were used as the US than when solid food pellets were used. Thus, Holland's research indicates that the nature of the CR may be quite complex and may vary with a number of the conditions of the experiment.

To summarize, the CR is a response that develops to the presentation of the CS after it has been paired with a US one or more times. The CR usually precedes the occurrence of the US and may be similar to the UR. However, the exact nature of the CR is complex and there are situations in which it is quite different from the UR.

BASIC CONDITIONING PHENOMENA

Acquisition

Conditioning is measured by recording the presence or absence of the CR when the CS is presented. A function illustrating the progress of conditioning may be obtained if the presence or absence of a CR is examined on a trial by trial basis, a trial being defined by the presentation of the CS and US. In order to provide some concrete understanding of what takes place in a conditioning experiment, we will describe one such experiment in some detail.

An example of the acquisition of a CR is presented in Figure 3–2. The response conditioned in this experiment was heart rate in the rat.

FIGURE 3–2 Habituation, conditioning, and extinction of a decelerative heart rate response. See text for explanation. (From Fitzgerald, Martin, & O'Brien, 1973)

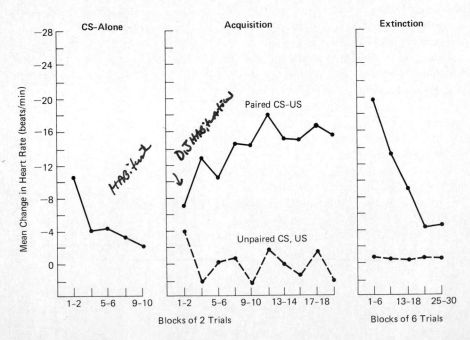

The CS in this experiment was a tone that was presented for 7 seconds. The US was an electric shock that was presented during the last second of the tone. Thus, the CS preceded the US by 6 seconds and overlapped it for 1 second. Heart rate was measured through electrocardiogram (EKG) elec- { SAY trodes attached to the rat. The time between trials was varied randomly be- } why tween 120 and 180 seconds.

Conditioning was measured by comparing the heart rate in the 6 second interval between CS onset and US onset with the heart rate during the 6 second period that immediately preceded CS onset.[4] These values are plotted on the ordinate of Figure 3–2. A minus number means that heart rate was slower during the CS period than in the 6 seconds immediately preceding the CS.

This experiment had three stages. The first stage was a habituation period in which the CS was presented alone. It is apparent in the first panel of the Figure that the initial presentations of the CS caused a slowing of heart rate. This slowing of heart rate is a component of the orienting response, as discussed in Chapter 2. It is also apparent in this first panel that the amount of heart rate deceleration that the tone produced diminished with repeated presentations of the tone so that by trials 9 and 10 there was little change in heart rate upon presentation of the tone. Thus, the change illustrated across the first panel of Figure 3–2 is habituation of heart-rate deceleration to the presentation of a tone.

Acquisition was begun in the second stage of this experiment. In this stage the animals that had been habituated in the first stage were randomly separated into two groups. Each of these groups was treated differently in acquisition. Half of the animals had the CS and US paired in the manner described above (i.e., CS preceding US by 6 seconds). This group is labeled as the Paired CS-US function in the Figure. The other group of animals also received the tone and the shock, but they were not paired (this group is labeled Unpaired CS, US in the Figure). For this group, the CS always followed the US by a time interval varying from 30 to 70 seconds; there was never any overlap between the US and the CS in this unpaired group. This unpaired group is termed a *control* group, and the presentation of the CS *after* the US is one of several different types of control procedure used in Pavlovian conditioning experiments.

The unpaired group controls for the importance of the temporal relationship between the CS and the US. Both paired and unpaired groups received exactly the same number of CS and US presentations, but they differed in the temporal arrangement of the two—the CS precedes the US and overlaps it in the paired group; the CS follows the US and does not overlap it in the unpaired group.

[4] Remember that the time between trials was varied randomly so, presumably, the rats could not predict when a trial would start.

It is apparent in the middle panel of Figure 3–2 that only the paired group showed the development of a CR. That is, as acquisition trials progressed, the paired group showed a progressively greater degree of heart rate deceleration upon presentation of the CS. The heart rate of the unpaired group showed no systematic changes during the acquisition period and, in fact, remained essentially unchanged from the end of the habituation period.

Suppose that Fitzgerald and his colleagues (1973) had neglected to include a control group. What would have been lost? For one thing, we would not know if the change demonstrated by the paired group was due to the pairing of the CS and US or whether it was due simply to the fact that the animals "occasionally" received shock as well as tone presentations. If the latter were the case, then the changes that occurred in the paired group may not have been due to a formation of an association between the CS and the US, but may simply have been due to sensitization (see Chapter 2). That is, the "occasional" occurrence of a shock may have sensitized the animals so that any change in the environment produced a slowing in heart rate. However, since the control group was included we know that such was not the case; the changes exhibited by the paired group must have been related to the temporal pairing of the CS and US.

Before leaving the acquisition phase of the Fitzgerald experiment, there are a few general comments regarding the measurement of conditioning that are appropriate at this point. In this experiment the CR was measured by recording changes that took place during the CS period before the presentation of the US. These responses are called *anticipatory* CRs in the sense that they occur prior in time to the US. The measurement of anticipatory CRs is one of the two principal ways of measuring the extent and course of conditioning. This procedure, however, may be used only when the time between CS presentation and US presentation is sufficiently long to allow for the occurrence of a response. If this time period is very short a *test trial* procedure must be employed. In this procedure, the US is occasionally omitted. If a response occurs to the CS on a test trial it must be a CR, not a UR, since there was no US. Test trials are generally presented infrequently, perhaps one out of every ten trials. A frequency score then may be obtained by recording the number of CRs that occur over a block of trials, and this score is used to plot an acquisition function.

There is one other general point to be made about acquisition measures. The data in Figure 3–2 represent average curves obtained across a number of subjects. Average curves such as these may mask wide differences among individual subjects in both rate and final level of conditioning. Therefore, it is not feasible to rely on averaged data to infer fundamental processes of conditioning. Averaged learning curves are much like average income figures for a community—they do not say that every individual is learning at the same rate (or making the same amount of money). Averaged curves are useful for a summary statement, but more detailed information may be gained from an inspection of the data from each individual subject.

Extinction and Related Phenomena

If, after acquisition training, the CS is presented over a number of trials without the US, the CR tends to diminish. This is apparent in the last panel of Figure 3–2. The term *extinction* is applied to both the procedure of presenting the CS without the US, and to the resultant phenomenon—the decrease in the magnitude and/or the probability of a CR occurring.

Extinction should be distinguished from forgetting. The change in the CR is due to the explicit operation of presenting the CS without the US. This is different from forgetting, which may take place over a time interval without a specific procedure such as presenting the CS alone.

Does the extinction of a CR mean that whatever had been learned originally in acquisition has been entirely erased by the process of extinction? Pavlov thought that this was not the case. Instead, he believed that extinction involved a process whereby the CR came to be inhibited from expression. A process of inhibition was thought to develop during extinction and this served to offset the excitation that developed during acquisition.

Two kinds of evidence will be mentioned which indicated to Pavlov that the association between the CS and US was not entirely erased in extinction. The first of these is *reacquisition*. If, after extinction, the US is again paired with the CS, the CR reappears and increases in strength (magnitude and/or probability of occurrence) across trials. Reacquisition is often faster than original acquisition, a fact that may indicate that the original association was not eliminated by extinction.

The second piece of evidence regarding Pavlov's view of extinction is the occurrence of *spontaneous recovery*. If a period of time is allowed to pass after a number of extinction trials have been administered, the strength of the CR appears to increase. For example, the data in Table 3–2 show that the probability of a CR increased over the 24-hour period from the last block of extinction trials on one day to the first block of extinction trials on the next day. Spontaneous recovery indicated to Pavlov that the association was not completely wiped out by the extinction process.[5] Applications of the extinction process to humans in the treatment of phobias and other undesirable behaviors will be considered later in this chapter.

Now that several of the basic phenomena related to extinction have been described, it is worthwhile to consider what an adaptive advantage the

---

[5] The processes of extinction and spontaneous recovery played a central role in the plot of *Gravity's Rainbow* (New York: Bantam Books, 1974), a somewhat bizarre novel by Thomas Pynchon.

TABLE 3–2 SPONTANEOUS RECOVERY

Two groups of rabbits, trained with different intertrial intervals (30 seconds or 60 seconds), showed CRs on approximately 100 percent of test trials at the end of acquisition. The remaining data show the percentage CRs in each group on the last block of 20 extinction trials on the first day of extinction and the first block of 20 extinction trials on the second extinction day. The percentage of CRs increased from the first to the second day of extinction— an example of spontaneous recovery. (From Gormezano & Coleman, 1975)

Intertrial Interval	Terminal Acquisition	Last Block of Extinction Trials— Day 1	First Block of Extinction Trials— Day 2
30 Sec	100%	40%	59%
60 Sec	100%	56%	75%

---

process of extinction must give to an organism, especially an extinction process that does not completely reverse the effects of prior learning. The extinction process permits the organism to modify its behavior when the environment changes; it permits a "tracking," as it were, of fluctuations in biologically important environmental events. That is, acquisition allows an animal to take advantage of a predictive relationship between a CS and a US and extinction allows the animal to disengage when the predictive relationship no longer holds. It is also interesting to note that, given the apparent importance and complexity of extinction related phenomena, a comparable process for eliminating unnecessary or no longer accurate associations was barely considered by those philosophers who speculated about learning without the availability of experimental data. This is perhaps just one of the many examples from the history of science where the availability of systematic, objective data has revealed interesting subtleties and interpretations that were not reached by methods of pure speculation.

Generalization

The tendency for stimuli other than the specific CS to elicit the CR was referred to by Pavlov as *generalization*. Research results from Pavlov's laboratory indicated, for example, that if the CS consisted of tactile stimulation of a restricted area on a dog's back, then stimulation of other areas of the dog's body would also tend to elicit the CR, but the farther away these areas were from the location of the original CS, the less likely they were to elicit the CR. Similarly, if the CS was a 1000 Hz tone, then tones of other frequencies, higher or lower, also tended to elicit the CR, but again, the farther away in frequency they were from the original CS, the less the probability (with some exceptions) that they would elicit the CR.

An example of generalization obtained in a Pavlovian conditioning experiment with rabbits is presented in Figure 3–3. In this experiment the rabbits were first conditioned with a 1200 Hz tone as the CS, and then were presented tones of other frequencies. It is apparent that the greatest proportion of responses were made to the original CS, but other stimuli also elicited the CR, even though they were never paired with a US.

The generalization process is quite possibly related to the development and treatment of some forms of abnormal behavior such as phobias. Phobias are not only characterized by an extreme and unrealistic fear of some object (e.g., a snake) or circumstance (e.g., confinement in a "small" space) but also by the spread of this fear to anything vaguely resembling the object or circumstance. For example, individuals who are abnormally afraid of snakes will fear not only snakes but will refuse to go near any object that resembles a snake or near any area such as a zoo, woods, or field that may contain a snake, and they may even find the word "snake" itself repulsive.

It is known that phobic-like behavior can be introduced by Pavlovian conditioning procedures. For example, in the famous (or infamous) Watson and Raynor "Little Albert" experiment (1920), a rat, which initially elicited

FIGURE 3–3 Relative generalization gradients. The number of responses made to each stimulus was divided by the total number of CRs elicited by all stimuli. The 1200 Hz stimulus was the CS. The data are expressed in terms of percentage of total responses made to all stimuli. (Redrawn from Liu, 1971)

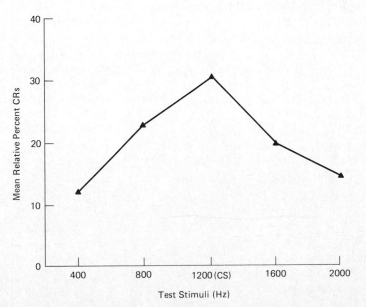

Mean Relative Percent CRs

Test Stimuli (Hz)

no fear responses in an 11-month-old child (Albert), was paired with a loud noise, an event which produced obvious startle and fear responses. It should be recognized that the rat was the CS and loud noise the US in this experiment. After a few pairings, the presentation of the rat alone began to elicit conditioned fear responses. As described in the protocol of Watson and Raynor: "Rat suddenly presented alone, Albert puckered [his] face, whimpered and withdrew body sharply to the left." And, on a later trial: "The instant the rat was shown the baby began to cry. Almost instantly he turned sharply to the left, fell over on left side, raised himself on all fours and began to crawl away so rapidly that he was caught with difficulty before reaching the edge of the table." These conditioned responses were not only elicited by the original CS, the rat, but also generalized to other stimuli such as a rabbit, a dog, a fur coat, a package of cotton, and a Santa Claus mask. These stimuli had been presented to Albert prior to conditioning and none had elicited fear responses at that time. The fear response did not generalize to wooden blocks.

The preceding discussion gives some indication of the importance of generalization as a basic phenomenon of conditioning. Pavlov gave an ecological interpretation to generalization, indicating, perhaps, why generalization should have evolved as an adaptive corollary of conditioning. In Pavlov's words:

> . . . natural stimuli are in most cases not rigidly constant but range around a particular strength and quality of stimulus in a common group. For example, the hostile sound of a beast of prey serves as a conditioned stimulus to a defense reflex in the animals which it hunts. The defense reflex is brought about independently of variations in pitch, strength and timbre of the sound produced by the animal according to its distance, the tension of its vocal cords and similar factors. (Pavlov, 1927, p. 113)

Application of Generalization and Extinction

We mentioned that the Watson and Raynor experiment indicated that phobic behavior in humans may be acquired by a process of Pavlovian conditioning. Some of the most successful methods of treating phobias in humans have developed as extensions of the extinction procedure. For example, one form of treatment for someone who is afraid of rats might be to have the individual listen to a tape recording that describes a scene in which rats are crawling all over a person, perhaps biting him. The idea behind this type of therapy, termed flooding or implosive therapy (Stampfl & Levis, 1967), is that the rat or the thought of the rat serves as a CS that elicits fear. If the rat (or the image) is presented a number of times without any aversive consequences to the individual, the fear should be extinguished. There is some evidence that this procedure works; however, some percentage of the patients find the treatment itself aversive and drop out of the therapy (Smith & Glass, 1977).

A different treatment makes use of the generalization gradient combined with extinction. For example, instead of presenting an individual who is afraid of rats with a rat, or the intense imagining of rats, the patient is shown or asked to imagine something that only remotely resembles a rat, such as a fur glove. If this elicits no fear, then an object that more closely resembles a rat is presented. If an object is encountered that elicits fear its presentation is continued until it no longer elicits fear. This procedure of working up a generalization gradient backward, as it were, is continued until the fear of the phobic object has been eliminated. Often this extinction procedure is combined with relaxation procedures, so that subjects are taught a specific relaxation exercise and then presented with the distant fear-eliciting objects while they are relaxed. The generalization hierarchy is then worked through, pairing each stimulus with the relaxation technique until fear has been eliminated. The process of pairing potential fear-eliciting objects with a contrary state of relaxation is termed *systematic desensitization*, a procedure that is very effective in eliminating phobias (Smith & Glass, 1977; Wolpe & Lazarus, 1966).

Discrimination

It is important that an organism generalize a conditioned response, but it is also sometimes important that an organism differentiate among stimuli that are followed by a biologically important event and those that are not. Pavlov initially believed that if one stimulus is followed often enough by a US then the organism would eventually respond to only that stimulus and no other. However, research in Pavlov's laboratory indicated otherwise. Complete differentiation between a stimulus consistently followed by a US, and other stimuli, was never obtained by this method, despite, in some cases, over a thousand presentations of the CS–US pair. If, however, two stimuli were repeatedly presented—one of which, the CS + was always followed by a US and the other, the CS – was never followed by a US—the subject quickly came to respond to the CS + only.

This procedure—presenting one stimulus that is consistently reinforced and another that is consistently unreinforced—is termed a *discrimination learning* paradigm. It is through such research paradigms that we can investigate how environmental stimuli come to acquire differential control over an organism's behavior. For example, in Pavlov's laboratory it was found that dogs could be conditioned to salivate only when a circle (the CS +) was presented and not when a square (the CS –) was presented. Pavlov and his colleagues investigated discrimination learning with many other stimuli, including tones of different frequencies, several different geometric shapes, tactile stimuli, and the sounds of metronomes and bubbling water.

An example of discrimination learning is presented in Figure 3–4. This experiment by Swadlow, Schneiderman, and Schneiderman (reported in Schneiderman, 1972) is interesting for several reasons. The differential stim-

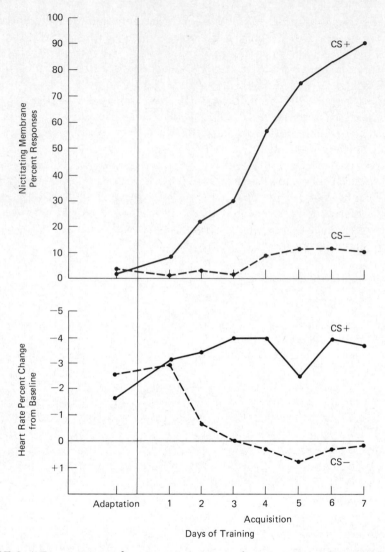

FIGURE 3–4 Discrimination learning. Acquisition of nictitating membrane and heart rate discriminative responses to an electric shock US applied near the rabbit's eyelid. See text for further explanation. (From Schneiderman, 1972)

uli (CS+ and CS−) were internal to the animal. Specifically, the CS+ was electrical stimulation (through implanted electrodes) of a visual relay nucleus (lateral geniculate body of the thalamus) on one side of a rabbit's brain, and the CS− was stimulation of the contralateral visual relay nucleus. The US was a brief electric shock applied near the rabbit's eyelid. Note that two responses were measured—closure of the nictitating membrane (one of the rabbit's three "eyelids") and heart rate—and that both showed differential conditioning to the same US and CS. Also note that during an adaptation phase both stimuli that were to serve as CSs elicited a decelerative heart rate response, but as conditioning was initiated and developed, only the CS + came to elicit the heart-rate deceleration.

This experiment, then, illustrates several general points. First is the phenomenon of discrimination learning itself; the CR comes to be elicited only by the reinforced stimulus (CS +). Second, it is possible for the CSs to be internal to the organism as well as external. Third, a number of responses may be conditioned simultaneously (e.g., Holland, 1980b). In this particular experiment two response measures were taken and both demonstrated differential conditioning. Although only a single response is measured in the majority of experiments, we should remember that the actual learning that is occurring may be quite complex, involving several responses and probably taking place in a number of different brain areas simultaneously.

CHAPTER SUMMARY

Philosophical speculation through two millennia focused attention on just a few principles that seemed critical for the formation of associations between stimuli and events. Most important among these principles were *contiguity* and *frequency*.

The experimental investigation of associative learning was begun by the Russian physiologist Ivan Pavlov just at the turn of the century. Pavlov found that if a stimulus (the US) which naturally elicited a reflex response (UR) was presented in close temporal contiguity with an originally neutral stimulus (the CS), then that originally neutral stimulus would eventually come to elicit a response (the CR) which has many of the characteristics of the original reflex response. Conditioning was found to proceed most efficiently if the CS preceded the US.

The presentation of the US was said to *reinforce* conditioning in the sense that as long as the US was presented the probability of a CR increased or remained high (*acquisition*), but when the US was not presented the probability of a CR decreased (*extinction*).

Conditioned responses tend to *generalize* to similar stimuli. However, if one stimulus is specifically reinforced (CS +) and another stimulus not reinforced (CS −), then an organism will eventually develop a discrimination between the stimuli so that the CR is more likely to be elicited by CS + than by CS −.

Experimental investigation of the associative processes has revealed a number of complexities that had not been considered in the earlier philosophical speculations on the subject. Some of these complexities are: that the CR may not resemble the UR; that there are alternative ways to measure the behavioral consequences of the new association (the CR); and that there is the likelihood that a number of different responses are learned at the same time, perhaps in different levels of the nervous system.

Pavlov believed that the phenomena of classical conditioning have important adaptive consequences for the organism because the acquisition of an association between a CS and a US provides the organism with a signal (the CS) indicating the impending occurrence of a biologically important event (the US). The study of classical conditioning investigates how these signaling functions are acquired.

4

PAVLOVIAN CONDITIONING II: EXPANSION OF THE PARADIGM AND PARAMETERS OF CONDITIONING

EXPANSION OF THE BASIC PAVLOVIAN PARADIGM

Directed Behaviors

Pavlov recognized that the behavior of his dogs in salivary conditioning experiments was not limited to salivation. Although their movements were restrained by harnesses, the dogs engaged in overt behaviors that developed during the course of conditioning and were clearly learned. Pavlov, however, chose to restrict his experimental observations to the secretory component of conditioning because the secretory response was easier to quantify than the diverse motor behaviors. He also believed that the secretory response would be less open to interpretation in anthropomorphic terms than the motor response (Pavlov, 1927, pp. 17–18). That is, Pavlov was wary of explaining behavior in terms of assumed "psychological" processes, such as postulating that the movements occurred because the dogs were "trying" to obtain the food, or because they may have "wanted" the food (see also Pavlov, 1932). It seems likely that the secretory component of conditioning fit more easily into the reflex model that was Pavlov's scientific guideline than does the more diffuse and variable motor behavior.

More recently, however, there has been substantial interest in the movements that occur in a Pavlovian conditioning experiment. An early and detailed analysis of the motor aspect of conditioning was provided by Zener in 1937. Zener observed and filmed dogs in a salivary conditioning experiment. The CS in this experiment was a bell and the US was a group of food pellets dropped into a pan fifteen seconds after the onset of the CS. Zener found somewhat different behaviors in different dogs, and found that the behaviors that occurred in any given dog were subject to change during the CS period and as the course of conditioning progressed. A typical pattern though, was a glance at the bell at CS onset and then a continued gaze at the food pan. There were occasional oscillations between the two, and some dogs held their heads at an angle between the locations of the bell and the food pan. There were also changes in bodily orientation toward the food pan. Some dogs initially approached the CS location and then, as the CS period progressed, moved back toward the US location. There were also other behaviors which Zener described as restless motions and which did not result in a change in position.

A more recent study examined dogs in a conditioning situation in which they had greater freedom to move than was the case in Zener's experiment. Jenkins and his colleagues (1978) placed dogs at one end of a small "room" and a food delivery device at the other end. In between, mounted on the side walls, were two lights to be used as CSs. In order for a trial to start, the dog had to be positioned at the end opposite to the food delivery location. The illumination of the light on one wall always signaled impending food delivery; thus, it was a CS+ (see Chapter 3). The illumination of the other light indicated the absence of food delivery; it was a CS−.

As in Zener's study, different dogs exhibited somewhat different behaviors during the course of conditioning. In general, though, the dogs did not make a direct approach to the US delivery site during a rewarded trial. Instead, they detoured in the direction of the CS. During the ten-second CS+ period one dog nosed the CS+. One dog variously pawed, nuzzled, licked, wagged its tail, and barked at the CS+. Another dog only deviated slightly toward the CS+ on its route to the US delivery site. Some of these behaviors are illustrated in Figure 4–1. In CS− trials, the dogs' behaviors were more desultory, with still a general tendency to approach the CS+ (which was not illuminated on CS− trials), and little tendency to contact the CS−.

This experiment, as well as Zener's, indicates that dogs will approach a stimulus that is a signal for impending reward but will not approach a signal that indicates the absence of reward. Other studies on pigeons and rats have demonstrated clear evidence of approach behaviors to stimuli signaling reward, and withdrawal behaviors away from stimuli signaling nonreward (e.g., Hearst & Franklin, 1977; Karpicke, 1978). The study by Jenkins and his colleagues demonstrated not only approach behaviors but also that dogs would engage in behaviors directed toward the CS+ that are typical of food soliciting behaviors for some members of their species.

Thus, it is clear that the behavior of animals in a Pavlovian conditioning situation is not confined to secretory responses and it is not passive. There are various terms currently used to describe these aspects of conditioning. As a general term, we shall use *directed behaviors* to refer to this approach–withdrawal component of the behaviors that occur in a Pavlovian situation. The behaviors directed toward the CS will be referred to as *sign-directed* behaviors and those directed toward the US will be referred to as *goal-directed* behaviors (see Boakes, 1977; Hearst & Jenkins, 1974).

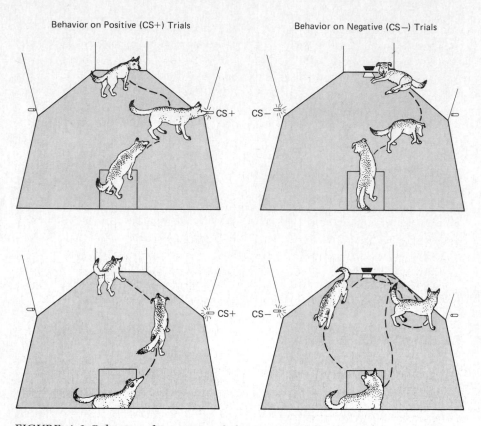

FIGURE 4–1 *Behavior of unrestrained dogs in Pavlovian conditioning. Left panel: behavior when CS + (light on right wall) predicts food at US site (far end). Right panel: behavior when CS − (light on left wall) predicts absence of food. (From Jenkins et al., 1978)*

Autoshaping

A particularly well-studied field of sign-directed behaviors is the phenomenon known as *autoshaping*. If the illumination of a small disc is made to regularly precede the presentation of grain to pigeons, an interesting pattern of behavior develops in the birds. First, there is a general increase in activity, such as pacing back and forth, particularly during a trial (i.e., while the disc is illuminated). As training continues, there is a progressive centering of movements around the area of the disc when it is illuminated. Finally, the pigeons begin to peck at the disc (Brown & Jenkins, 1968). The term *autoshaping* is used most often to refer to this behavior—where pigeons peck at a lighted stimulus correlated with the imminent delivery of reinforcement. Note that the pecks are not necessary to produce the reinforcement—it would occur whether or not the pecks were made.

This clearly seems to be an example of sign-directed behavior, quite similar to some of the behaviors described in dogs by Zener and by Jenkins and his colleagues. The discovery of the autoshaping behavior by Brown and Jenkins initiated a great deal of theoretical and research activity.

This research has shown, for example, that pigeons peck the disc differently when the illumination period is followed by grain from when it is followed by water. When grain is used the pecks are hard and straight at the disc, but when water is used the pecks may be characterized as shallow, scooping motions against the key (Jenkins & Moore, 1973). In other words, the pigeons behave toward the signal in a manner similar to their behavior towards the US (eating grain or drinking water).

A parallel result occurs when an illuminated disc signals the impending availability of a receptive female pigeon. In this case, the male pigeon eventually engages in aspects of courtship behavior directed towards the disc (Gilbertson, 1975). However, the response to the signal is not always similar to the response elicited by the US. For example, Wasserman (1973, 1981) placed baby chicks in a cool chamber and made the presentation of diffuse heat follow the illumination of a small disc. He found that some chicks eventually snuggled up to the disc, but most chicks pecked at it, a response quite different from their response to the heat, which included wing extension and napping.

In another study, Timberlake and Grant (1975) used the appearance of a rat as a signal for the imminent delivery of food to other rats. They found that the rats receiving the food showed a substantial increase in social behaviors directed toward the signal rat—they did not bite the rat as they did the food. Other groups of animals in this study were also exposed to the rat, but for them it did not predict food. These groups did not show levels of social behavior equal to the subjects for whom the rat was a signal for food.

In summary, the regular presentation of a signal before a US will, after a number of pairings of the signal and US, lead to the occurrence of a variety of complex behaviors directed toward the signal. These directed behaviors indicate that the establishment of a predictive relationship between a CS and US will activate complex approach or withdrawal behaviors centered on a signal, as well as less complex reflex behavior such as salivation. We turn now to a second major expansion of the Pavlovian paradigm, that of conditioned food aversions, probably the most active area of conditioning research in the last decade.

Conditioned Food Aversions

The palate reels like a wronged lover.
Was all that sweetness counterfeit?
Erica Jong

Plants as well as animals are subject to selective pressures that force adaptation or extinction. One of the environmental pressures impinging on plants arises from the fact that they are the fundamental food source of the animal kingdom. Various anti-consumer devices have evolved in the plant kingdom to fend off animals, as well as other plants. Among these defensive armaments is the production of compounds that are toxic to potential consumers. This development among plants in turn placed selective pressure on the animal kingdom to develop antitoxic mechanisms and, in fact, a variety of such mechanisms has evolved in different groups of animals. Among these mechanisms are digestive processes that detoxify the compounds, mechanisms for sequestering (segregating) the compounds (Whittikar & Feeny, 1971, cited in Domjan, 1980), and mechanisms that take advantage of the ability to learn. We will be concerned with the latter.

Rats will generally eat only a small amount of a novel food—a behavior pattern that has been termed *neophobia* or *bait shyness*. Barnett (1963) has suggested that bait shyness may be the result of natural selection based on the consumption of toxic substances. That is, if an animal consumed a large amount of a novel food and it happened to be toxic, the chances of that animal passing on offspring would be diminished. On the other hand, if an animal tended to consume only a small amount of a novel substance, and consumed no more if this ingestion led to harmful consequences (e.g., gastrointestinal distress, malaise) then this animal would be more likely to pass on offspring. Eventually, a genetic tendency to be neophobic would predominate in the population.

Notice that Barnett's suggestion implies an important role for learning. That is, in order for neophobia to serve efficiently, the animal should be able to learn which food substance resulted in sickness (and consume no more of that substance) and which food substance did not result in illness (and increase its consumption of that substance).

Indeed, early studies of rat poisoning indicated that rats that survived an initial poisoning tended not to consume the poisoned substance on reencounters with it. Some of the rats turned their heads away or pushed it aside with their forepaws if it was brought near them (Rzoska, 1953, cited in Garcia & Hankins, 1977; Richter, 1953).

Some of the early experimental work on learned food aversions was inspired by investigations into the effects of ionizing radiation. These early studies showed that animals allowed to consume a substance, such as a sucrose or saccharin solution, in conjunction with exposure to radiation, avoided consuming that substance when it was offered on future occasions (e.g., Garcia, Kimeldorf, & Koelling, 1955; Revusky, 1968; Smith & Roll, 1967). A surprising feature of these studies was that this apparent learning occurred even though the adverse consequences of radiation did not begin to affect the animal until several hours (in some cases) after the treatment. Such learning could also take place after a single trial.

Thus, these studies showed not only that animals could learn to avoid food that was correlated with sickness, but also that they could demonstrate such learning very quickly, and even with a relatively long time period between food consumption and the onset of sickness. This latter result begins to raise some question about the meaning of contiguity, a condition that for two thousand years has been thought to be essential for the formation of associations.

A third surprising finding in regard to food aversion learning was published in 1966 by Garcia and Koelling. In this experiment it was found that animals avoided consuming "tasty water" (a saccharin solution) if that solution was followed either by X-radiation or by sub-lethal doses of the poison lithium chloride. However, rats did not avoid consuming "bright-noisy water" (lights flashed and a clicking sound was made each time the rats licked) if it was followed by the radiation or poison. Apparently, the associative effects of the poison were limited to stimulation of the gustatory sense and were ineffective in producing learning when auditory and visual senses were involved.

In this study Garcia and Koelling also investigated the effectiveness of these two stimuli (taste and audiovisual) when electric shock was delivered two seconds after drinking was initiated. They found that the shock experience suppressed drinking of the "bright-noisy water" but did not effectively suppress drinking of the "tasty water." What the experiment seemed to indicate was that taste stimuli may be selectively associated with internal distress such as that brought on by poisons, whereas audiovisual stimuli may be selectively associated with external aversive events such as shock. Taste seemed not to be associable to the effects of shock, and audiovisual stimuli seemed not to be associable to the effects of internal malaise. Such data added a new dimension to Pavlovian conditioning research—the idea that some CSs and USs might be particularly easy to associate, and others particularly difficult (Seligman & Hager, 1972). Furthermore, these data indicated the potential importance of an evolutionary perspective for Pavlovian conditioning research. That is, the ability to rapidly associate a food with illness, even under unfavorable circumstances such as the occurrence of a long time period between food consumption and illness, should clearly have survival value.

Thus, early research concerned with learning, when the US was a substance that produced gastrointestinal distress, led to three interesting results: such learning could take place when long time periods (as much as 24 hours in some cases) elapsed between the CS and US; taste stimuli seemed to be selectively associated with such US events; and such learning occurred very rapidly. These early findings led to substantial research efforts (632 titles listed in a recent bibliography—Riley & Clark, 1977) concerned with the conditions under which such associations occur, and with the theoretical implications of this research. Conditioned food aversions, as well as directed behavior, will be referred to and considered again at several places in this text.

Applications

Before leaving the topic of conditioned aversions, several practical examples and implications will be considered. A conditioned food aversion was used to solve a problem that arose from efforts at reforestation following the logging of an area in northern California. Reforestation was failing because mice would eat the newly planted seeds. Killing the mice was ineffective because more mice simply moved into the depopulated territory. However, the addition of a nonlethal poison to the seeds proved to be effective because the mice learned to avoid them without vacating the territory for other mice (Tevis, 1956, cited in Domjan, 1980). Similarly, efforts have been made to control the predation of sheep by coyotes in western United States by mixing chunks of lamb ("lamburgers") with sub-lethal doses of lithium chloride. This treatment has shown some promise of being effective in reducing attacks on sheep by coyotes (e.g., Gustavson, 1977). Changing an animal's feeding habits by poisoning may be effective, however, only when there is an alternative food source available.

There is another way in which the research on conditioned aversions may have practical relevance. In Chapter 3 it was mentioned that chemotherapy treatments for cancer may have the side effect of conditioning nausea to various aspects of the treatment environment. Potential associative consequences of such treatments have also been demonstrated in a study which found that children undergoing drug treatment for cancer developed aversions for a novel ice cream flavor that they had during the treatment (Bernstein, 1978).

As well as being due to treatment effects, reduced appetite and weight loss are often accompaniments of tumor development itself. A recent study has indicated that at least part of this anorexia may be related to conditioned aversions developed to the usual diet because of its correlation with adverse consequences of tumor growth. When a novel diet was introduced to rats afflicted with tumors, there was a substantial increase in appetite (Bernstein & Sigmundi, 1980). The awareness that dietary aberrations may reflect the operation of associative processes brings a better understanding of the problem and may provide a means of correcting it through the application of another associative procedure, such as one of the variations of extinction described in the previous chapter.

The development of an aversion for a familiar diet and preference for a new diet may also be involved in some cases of natural nutritional wisdom. For example, if a rat's diet is made deficient in thiamine, the rat will gradually develop an aversion to this diet and will come to prefer a novel diet—a reversal of the rat's usual neophobia. If this new diet happens to contain thiamine, the rat will develop a preference for the flavor of the new diet (e.g., Rozin, 1967, 1969, 1977). Thus, rats seem to develop an association between the flavor of the new diet and the recovery from the internal consequences of the deficient diet. Although there are nonlearning mechanisms of food selection (see, for example, Richter, 1936; Zahorik & Houpt, 1977), the ability of animals to learn to avoid foods that have toxic or other undesirable side effects, and to learn a preference for foods that ameliorate nutritional deficiencies, clearly provides a flexible means for omnivores (such as rats and humans) to adapt to changing environmental contingencies (see Chapter 1 and the stockbroker metaphor).

PARAMETERS OF CONDITIONING

The study of the parameters or factors that influence conditioning is often viewed as tedious. For those who do not find such information inherently interesting (like baseball statistics), there is little that can be done to remove the tedium. Perhaps the task may be made more palatable if a brief overview is presented, and some comments on the potential usefulness of such knowledge are made.

The following pages will show that the temporal relationship between the CS and US often determines how much conditioning will occur, and the nature of the conditioning. In general, the best conditioning occurs when the CS precedes the US and there is some degree of overlap between the two. Also, in general, the more intense the CS and US, the better the conditioning. Duration of the CS and US does not have major effects on conditioning, except under certain limited circumstances, and preexposing animals to either the CS or the US before pairing the two, interferes with the development of conditioning. Intermittent pairing of the CS and US has somewhat complex effects. In general, such intermittent pairing may interfere with learning but prolong extinction. In addition, within some range, increasing the intertrial interval enhances conditioning.

Of what use is all this information? Basic research into the parameters of conditioning may be viewed as a set of recipes that describes the ingredients necessary for rapid conditioning, for slow conditioning, for persistent conditioning, etc. Such recipes may be used to facilitate other research. For example, if an investigator is interested in the effects of some drug or some type of brain damage on Pavlovian conditioning, the literature available on parametric data will be of help in setting up experimental conditions appropriate for the investigator's research interest.

The parametric data may also suggest questions, the answers to which will lead to an enhanced understanding of the basic nature of Pavlovian conditioning. For example, why is the temporal relationship between the CS and US so important? What is happening at the neural level that requires particular temporal relationships? Why do more intense CSs and USs promote better conditioning?

Finally, knowledge derived from parametric research may have practical applications. For example, the knowledge that novel tastes are more likely than familiar tastes to be associated with coincidentally produced nausea would suggest that novel foods should not be given to someone who is likely to experience nausea from illness or from some medical treatment such as radiation therapy. Or, the knowledge that such associations between novel foods and nausea will occur only if the novel food is consumed within a certain time period before the nausea is experienced would suggest a "safe" period when novel foods could be consumed without the danger of a conditioned food aversion developing.

For the most part, the organization of the following sections is such that the general results are given in the topical sentence of each paragraph, and the subsequent material provides experimental support and qualifications.

Temporal Factors

Conditioning is strongly influenced by the temporal arrangement of the CS and US. Some possible temporal arrangements between CSs and USs are illustrated in Figure 4–2. Early research from Pavlov's laboratory indicated that simultaneous conditioning—what would seem to be maximal contiguity—is not the most effective way to develop a CR. Instead, an overlapping CS and US, but with the presentation of CS onset slightly before US onset, was found to be more effective. This is delayed conditioning, where US onset is delayed for some time after CS onset.

The role of these temporal factors in conditioning will now be considered in some detail. Delayed conditioning will be described first, then trace conditioning (in which there is a gap between CS termination and US onset). Also considered will be simultaneous conditioning, in which CS and US onset coincide, and backward conditioning, where the US precedes the CS.

Delayed Conditioning

The essential characteristic of the *delayed conditioning* procedure is that CS onset precedes US onset and the CS continues at least up to the time of US onset. Separate terms are not given to the situations in which the CS terminates exactly at the time of US onset and situations in which the CS substantially overlaps the US or continues for some time beyond US offset. There are some data, however, which indicate that continuing the CS for some time after US termination does reduce the amount of conditioning obtained (Burkhardt & Ayres, 1978).

The proximity of two events has long been thought to be an important determiner of whether or not they will be associated. In the last chapter we described how the principle of contiguity, closeness together in space or time, has often been considered a condition fundamental for the formation of an association. The delayed conditioning procedure provides a way of quantitatively measuring the importance of contiguity. This question (how important is contiguity?) can be asked very simply by varying the time between CS

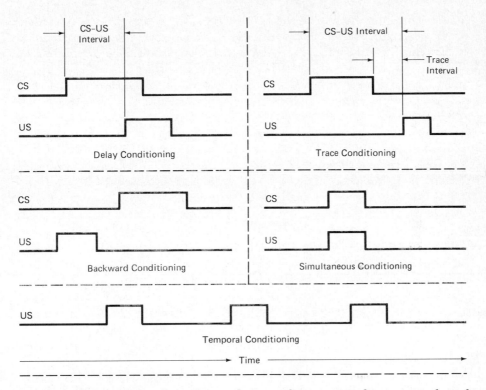

FIGURE 4–2 *Temporal relationships in basic conditioning paradigms. A number of different conditioning paradigms are labeled in accordance with the temporal relationships between CS onset and US onset.*

In delay conditioning, CS onset precedes US onset, and the offset of the CS either overlaps the US or coincides with US onset.

In trace conditioning, the CS terminates before US onset; thus there is a gap between CS termination and US onset. The length of this gap is referred to as the trace interval.

In both delay and trace conditioning, the time between CS onset and US onset is termed the CS–US interval.

In simultaneous conditioning, there is no CS–US interval; the CS and US coincide.

In backward conditioning, the US precedes the CS and may or may not overlap with it.

In temporal conditioning, the US is presented at regular temporal intervals; there is no explicit CS. Conditioning may be demonstrated in this paradigm by omitting the US occasionally and determining whether or not a response occurs.

onset and US onset. Such a variation provides a way of seeing if the proximity of stimulus onset of two events is an important determiner of associability. It seems a simple question, but it is important to note that the experimental method is required to answer it. No amount of reflection or speculation can tell us whether or not such a factor is important. In fact, just by thinking about it, it might seem that the time between CS onset and US onset would not be important. Why should it be, as long as the two events are coincident in the sense that CS termination is near to US onset? However, research has shown that this interval is a very important factor indeed.

The CS–US Interval. The time between the CS onset and US onset is referred to as the *CS–US interval*. The length of this interval affects the amount of conditioning that is obtained. However, the nature of the effect varies substantially in different conditioning preparations. There seem to be at least three "families" of CS–US interval functions. (1) When a simple reflex response, mediated by nerves controlling skeletal muscles (e.g. eyeblink) is conditioned, then there must be a very short period between the CS and US if conditioning is to be obtained. (2) When response systems mediated by the autonomic nervous system (e.g., heart rate, salivation) are conditioned, then a longer period may elapse between the two stimuli. (3) When the US produces gastric distress, as in conditioned food aversions, then conditioning may proceed with relatively long periods between the CS and US. Some data from each of these systems will be considered.

Simple Skeletal Reflexes. The results obtained in the conditioning of eyeblink reflexes in rabbits and humans have been consistent—an optimal interval for conditioning is usually found in the range of 0.5 seconds between CS onset and US onset (e.g., Frey & Ross, 1968a; McAllister, 1953). A detailed examination of the CS–US interval function is presented in Figure 4-3. The data presented in this figure were obtained from a study of the conditioned nictitating membrane response in rabbits (Smith, Colemen, & Gormezano, 1969). The top panel shows the gradual acquisition of the CR across 808 trials. The bottom panel shows the average percentage of CRs that occurred during the acquisition period for each CS–US interval. It is evident from the Figure that (a) no conditioning occurs with CS–US intervals of 50 milliseconds or less (the −50 millisecond point represents a backward conditioning paradigm); (b) there is apparently a sharp break in the conditionability of this system between CS–US intervals of 50 and 100 milliseconds; and (c) there is an optimal CS–US interval in the 200 to 400 millisecond range, with conditioning falling off on either side of that range.

A still further detailed examination of conditioning at several intervals in the range of 50 to 125 msec indicated no conditioning with intervals less than 67 msec (Salafia et al., 1980). However, if the CS is direct electrical stimulation of an area of the brain, rather than a CS applied externally to the the organism, then conditioning may be obtained at shorter CS–US intervals (Patterson, 1969, cited in Gormezano, 1972).

Autonomic Responses. Conditioning of functions mediated by the autonomic nervous system may routinely be obtained with CS–US intervals substantially longer than those found effective in eyeblink conditioning. For

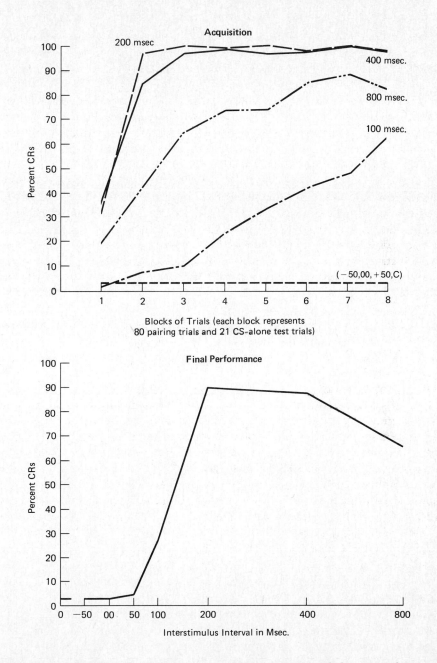

FIGURE 4–3 CS–US interval function in rabbit nictitating membrane conditioning. The top panel shows rate and level of learning obtained with the various CS–US intervals and the bottom panel presents the average number of CRs that occurred in acquisition for each CS–US interval. (Data from Smith, Coleman, & Gormezano, 1969.)

example, salivary conditioning may readily be obtained with a 25–30 second interval (Pavlov, 1927; Wagner, Siegel, Thomas, & Ellison, 1964), as can conditioned changes in heart rate (e.g., Billman & Randall, 1980, 1981). An optimal CS–US interval has not been mapped in detail in the case of these response systems, but effective conditioning has been obtained with intervals in the range of several seconds (e.g., Cunningham, Fitzgerald, & Francisco, 1977) as well as the longer intervals mentioned above. A clear upper interval for conditioning has not been obtained for these systems, but it probably does not extend very far into the minute range. For example, Manning, Schneiderman, and Lordahl (1969) found that a seven second CS–US interval produced better heart rate conditioning than a 21 second interval under the conditions of their experiment.

Conditioned Food Aversions. Conditioned food aversions may be obtained with very long time intervals between the CS and US. For example, presenting intense X-irradiation as much as 24 hours after rats are exposed to a novel saccharin solution will lead to some aversion of the saccharin (Smith & Roll, 1967); with less intense radiation, aversion to sucrose was produced with as much as a 6.5 hour CS–US interval (Revusky, 1968). Other US treatments will also produce aversions over long intervals; loading a rat's stomach with a 12.1-percent saline solution (normal salinity of body fluids is 0.9 percent) will produce an aversion to saccharin even if the stomach load is given 13.5 hours after the saccharin is consumed (Andrews & Braveman, 1975). Similarly, aversion to saccharin may be found if the nausea-producing drug apomorphine is injected over an hour after the saccharin is consumed (Garcia, Ervin, & Koelling, 1966). Also, aversion to saccharin may be found in rats if they are spun around at the rate of 70 revolutions per minute, 30 minutes after the saccharin is consumed (Haroutunian & Riccio, 1975). Some of these data are shown in Figure 4–4. The number of studies showing long delay conditioned flavor aversions, with a variety of US treatments, is voluminous (see, for example, Riley & Baril, 1976; Gamzu, 1977). These aversions to gustatory stimuli may be formed with very few pairings, often only a single pairing, of the CS and US.

Trace Conditioning

The trace conditioning procedure is like delayed conditioning in that CS onset occurs before US onset; it is different in that the CS terminates prior to US onset. Thus, there is a gap between CS termination and US onset, a gap referred to as the *trace interval*. In general, the trace procedure produces less conditioning than the delay procedure in animals and humans (Kamin, 1965; Little, cited in Rovee-Collier & Lipsitt, 1982; Manning et al., 1969; Schneiderman, 1966; Wasserman et al., 1977). Also, in general, the longer the trace interval, the less the conditioning (e.g., Kaplan & Hearst, 1982;

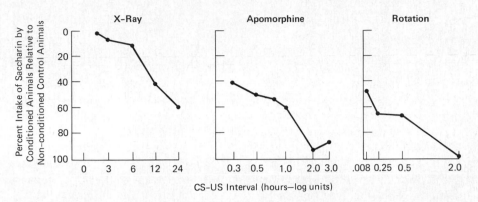

FIGURE 4–4 Aversions to saccharin solutions as a function of CS–US interval. Different USs and somewhat different procedures were used in the three studies. In all cases, however, percent intake of saccharin approaches control level (i.e., aversion decreases) as CS–US interval lengthens. (Data from Smith & Roll, 1967; Garcia, Ervin & Koelling, 1966; Haroutunian & Riccio, 1975)

Marlin, 1981; Wasserman et al., 1977). Data from the study by Wasserman and his colleagues, an experiment on autoshaping with baby chicks, are presented in Figure 4–5. It is clear that longer trace intervals led to less conditioning, and that the sharpest break occurred between the zero and five-second gap.

FIGURE 4–5 Autoshaping as a function of trace interval. The longer the trace interval the fewer the trials in which autoshaped responses (key pecks) occurred. (From Wasserman et al., 1977)

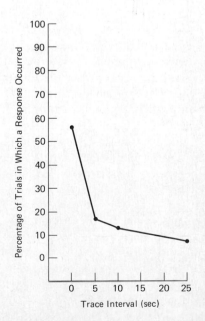

Note that the CS–US interval may also be varied in trace conditioning (see Figure 4–2). Variations in the CS–US interval have effects in trace conditioning that parallel the effects obtained in delayed conditioning (e.g., Manning et al., 1969).

An experiment that provides an insight into the learning that may take place during trace conditioning was published by Nancy Marlin (1981). Marlin's procedure was a variant of a conditioned fear experiment (see the Watson & Raynor and Mason experiments mentioned in Chapter 3). In this experiment water-deprived rats were given initial exposure to two kinds of apparatus. One was a two-compartment box, one side of which was black and the other white. The second apparatus was a clear plastic box that contained a water tube. In the conditioning part of the experiment the animals were assigned to eight groups. Six of these groups received fear conditioning, in which a tone (the CS) was paired with a foot shock (the US). Two of these six groups received a delayed conditioning procedure in which the CS terminated at US onset; that is, there was a 0-second trace interval. For two other groups there was a 10-second trace interval. The final two of these six groups received conditioning with a 30-second trace interval. The two remaining groups served as controls—they experienced the shocks but the shocks were not preceded by CSs. All eight groups received their shock experience in the black side of the two-compartment apparatus.

The effects of this conditioning experience were measured in two ways. For the first measure, one of each of the conditioning groups (0-, 10-, 30-second trace, and no-CS control) were placed in the apparatus containing the water and allowed to drink. However, after their fifth lick the CS that had been paired with shock was turned on and left on. The animals were not shocked during this test. The measure of the effectiveness of conditioning was how long it took the animals to reach their fortieth lick. It was assumed that if the animals had associated the CS with the shock, the onset of the CS should disrupt licking, thereby increasing the amount of time required for the rats to reach the fortieth lick. The results are presented in the top part of Figure 4–6. The licking of the 0-second trace group was interrupted the most by the CS, the 10-second group less, and the 30-second trace group even less. The no-CS group licked the water the fastest. Thus, these results indicate that the longer the trace interval, the less the conditioning.

For the second measure of conditioning the remaining four groups of animals were tested for their fear of the black side of the two-compartment apparatus, the compartment in which the conditioning experience was given. These data are presented in the bottom half of Figure 4–6 in terms of how much time, of a 300 second preference test, each group spent in the white compartment. These data show that the no-CS group spent the most time in the white compartment, and the amount of time spent by the conditioning groups was directly related to the length of the trace interval. Comparison of the top and bottom halves of Figure 4–6 reveals a clear relationship—the less

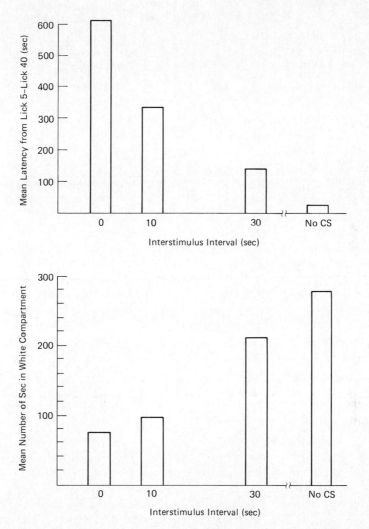

FIGURE 4–6 *Fear conditioning as a function of trace interval. Top Panel: The effect of CS paired with shock in producing suppression of licking declines with increasing trace intervals. Bottom Panel: Aversion to black compartment (where conditioning occurred) increases with increasing trace intervals. Data indicate that context conditioning occurs instead of CS–US conditioning with long trace intervals. (From Marlin, 1981).*

the conditioning to the CS, the greater the amount of time spent in the white compartment.

How should these data be interpreted? One possibility is the following. When there is close temporal contiguity between the CS and the shock, the animals learn to fear the CS and this fear disrupts licking for the water when the CS is presented. When there is not a close temporal contiguity between the CS and the shock, the animals associate the shock with the compartment in which it is given, rather than with the CS, and develop a fear of that compartment. This fear of the black compartment then produces a directed behavior away from the black and towards the white side of the apparatus. Thus, the animals in this experiment showed conditioning to the CS when there was close temporal contiguity, and conditioning to the general experimental context when there was little CS–US contiguity.

Other recent experiments show that the loss of conditioning to the CS that occurs when there is a trace interval may be overcome if an extra stimulus is made to occur during the CS–US gap. For example, trace conditioning may be made to occur with even a 60-second gap if an extra stimulus is inserted to bridge the gap (Kaplan & Hearst, 1982; Rescorla, 1982). A possible interpretation of this effect is the following. A Pavlovian conditioning session should be conceptualized as a repeating cycle of events: a CS, a gap (in trace conditioning), a US, a gap (the intertrial interval), etc. One of the problems that an animal may face in trace conditioning is discriminating between the intertrial interval gap and the trace interval gap. To the extent that this discrimination is facilitated by experimental procedures (e.g., increasing the intertrial interval relative to the trace interval, or inserting an extra stimulus in the trace interval), trace conditioning may be enhanced (Kaplan, 1984; Kaplan & Hearst, 1982; Lucas, Deich, & Wasserman, 1981; Martin, 1980, cited in Kaplan & Hearst, 1982; Mowrer & Lamoreaux, 1951). From this interpretation one would expect that insertion of the gap-filling stimulus would prevent the conditioning to context (background) stimuli observed in the Marlin (1981) experiment.

The conditioned food aversion paradigm is one situation in which trace conditioning apparently occurs with regularity. The gap between CS and US presentation may be a matter of many minutes or hours and robust conditioning is still obtained. The formation of associations over such long intervals makes the conditioned aversions data unusual. What serves to "bridge the gap" between the CS and US in this paradigm? Has natural selection led to specialization for food-toxin associations so that associations may be formed over long intervals even after only a single pairing (e.g., Garcia & Hankins, 1977; Seligman, 1970)? Are there perhaps some special characteristics of a gustatory stimulus as a CS which serve to lengthen its effective presentation period? That is, the metabolic and hormonal (e.g., insulin release) aspects of food ingestion may effectively prolong CS durations, thereby reducing the trace interval (Testa & Ternes, 1977). Conditioned food aversions will be considered in more detail in Chapter 14.

In summary, less conditioning occurs when a trace procedure is used than when a delay procedure is used. Inserting an extra stimulus in the trace interval may lead to conditioning occurring over longer than normal trace intervals. When there is no gap-filling stimulus and when trace intervals are relatively long, animals may associate US occurrence with the general experimental context rather than with the CS. Finally, conditioned food aversions may be learned over long trace intervals. Such learning may represent an adaptive specialization resulting from natural selection (evolution) but it may also reflect, in part, special characteristics of taste stimuli used as CSs.

Simultaneous Conditioning

Generally, little or no conditioning occurs with simultaneous CS and US onset (e.g., Pavlov, 1927; Smith, Coleman, & Gormezano, 1969). However, there is some evidence that simultaneous conditioning may occur when variations of the conditioned fear procedure are used. For example, a single simultaneous pairing of noise with shock may produce a conditioned fear response to the noise (Burkhardt & Ayres, 1978; Mahoney & Ayres, 1976). These studies also indicated that conditioning was greater if CS onset and offset coincided than if the CS continued past US termination. In fact, the longer the CS continued beyond US termination, the weaker the conditioning. Other studies of fear conditioning have also obtained evidence of conditioning with simultaneous CS–US presentation (e.g., Heth, 1976; Sherman, 1978) although the conditioning obtained with the simultaneous procedure is less than that obtained with delayed conditioning (Heth & Rescorla, 1973).

Backward Conditioning

Recent evidence indicates that conditioning may occur if the CS follows the US. In order to consider this evidence we must introduce the concepts of *excitatory* and *inhibitory conditioning*. In general, excitatory and inhibitory CSs have opposite effects on behavior—if an excitatory CS leads to an increase in behavior (e.g., salivation), then an inhibitory stimulus should produce a decrease in that behavior. If an excitatory CS leads to a decrement in behavior (as in the case of the heart rate CR in rats), then an inhibitory stimulus should lead to an increase in that behavior.

Both excitatory and inhibitory conditioning have been obtained when the CS is presented *after* the US (backward pairing). Inhibitory conditioning is a complex topic, one which will be considered in detail in Chapter 5. For the present, though, the description of inhibition as a process that opposes excitation, as given above, should be sufficient to understand the following data.

Excitatory Conditioning. Heth and Rescorla (1973) found evidence of fear conditioning when CS onset followed US onset by one or two seconds. The level of conditioning was less than that obtained in simultaneous and delay groups. Evidence of conditioned suppression of drinking (conditioned fear) has been obtained after only a single trial in which the onset of shock was followed four or eight seconds later by a CS. Furthermore, this conditioning following a single backward trial was retained over a 30-day retention interval (Shurtleff & Ayres, 1981). Evidence of excitatory backward conditioning has also been obtained in a number of other recent studies (e.g., Heth, 1976; Keith-Lucas & Gutman, 1975; Mahoney & Ayres, 1976; Wagner & Terry, 1975). A recent review of backward conditioning concluded that excitatory conditioning may be favored if a noxious US is used, if a small number of pairings are administered, and if the US occurrence is surprising to the animal (Spetch, Wilkie, & Pinel, 1981).

Inhibitory Conditioning. Plotkin and Oakley (1975) presented the CS either 0.2 or 0.5 seconds after US termination in a nictitating membrane conditioning study. One hundred and twenty five pairings were administered. They found no evidence of conditioning (see also Smith et al., 1969, and Figure 4–3 for lack of backward nictitating membrane conditioning). When, however, Plotkin and Oakley continued their experiment by presenting the animals with the same CS and US in a delayed conditioning paradigm with a 0.3-second CS–US interval (near optimal for conditioning—see Figure 4–3) they found that animals that had been exposed to the backward pairing were retarded in acquisition, relative to various control groups. This interference with acquisition may be considered to be an example of inhibition. That is, pairing a CS with a US at a 0.3-second CS–US interval should produce excitatory conditioning. However, the CS that had previously been used in a backward paradigm apparently acted to oppose the development of this excitatory conditioning. Therefore, it may be considered to be an inhibitory stimulus. Evidence for inhibitory effects of backward conditioning has also been obtained in other studies (e.g., Heth, 1976; Rescorla, 1966).

Both Excitation and Inhibition. Initial research in Pavlov's laboratory indicated that backward conditioning did not occur. Later, however, Pavlov found evidence that excitatory backward conditioning did occur when only a few trials were administered, but that excitatory conditioning could be transformed to no conditioning or to inhibitory conditioning when extensive training was administered. Research by Heth (1976) has supported Pavlov's conclusion. Heth, using a variant of the conditioned fear paradigm, found that excitatory conditioning occurred after 10 US–CS pairings. However, evidence of conditioning was diminished when 80 such pairings were administered, and 160 pairings led to evidence of inhibitory conditioning.

Thus, the conditioning process that occurs when the backward procedure is used is a dynamic one, changing in sign over trials. Animals may initially learn that there is a positive relationship between the CS and US if these are presented in close temporal proximity, even if the relationship is backward. After extended training, however, the animals may further learn that the CS does not predict the US, but instead predicts the absence of the

US (i.e., the intertrial interval). This latter learning may be the basis of the inhibitory effects of backward conditioning (see Rescorla, 1967).

Summary

Conditioning occurs most readily when CS onset precedes US onset and there is no gap between CS termination and US onset (delayed conditioning). The insertion of a gap between CS offset and US onset (trace conditioning) reduces the degree of conditioning, but this reduction may be ameliorated somewhat by the insertion of other stimuli as "gap fillers." In the absence of such gap fillers, the US may become conditioned to the general experimental context rather than to the CS. Conditioning may occur with the simultaneous presentation of CS and US, but this procedure is less effective than delayed conditioning and may occur more readily in fear conditioning than in other conditioning situations. A similar statement may be made about excitatory conditioning occurring with the backward paradigm. In addition, the sign of conditioning that occurs with backward pairings may change from excitatory to inhibitory as a function of number of training trials administered.

In the delay and trace paradigms, the degree of conditioning is strongly influenced by the length of the CS–US interval; conditioning diminishes as the interval increases. However, the absolute values over which conditioning will occur differ dramatically in different conditioning preparations; only short intervals are effective in eyelid conditioning, longer intervals in the conditioning of functions mediated by the autonomic nervous system, and quite long intervals in the conditioned food aversion paradigm.

Characteristics of the US

US Intensity

In general, the more intense the US, the greater the conditioning. For example, degree of eyelid conditioning increases with increases in US intensity (Hoehler & Leonard, 1981; Spence, 1956), as does degree of fear conditioning (e.g., Annau & Kamin, 1961; Randich & Rescorla, 1981; Sherman 1978). In the conditioned food aversion paradigm, conditioning is enhanced by increasing radiation dosage (e.g., Revusky, 1968), dosage of toxin administered (e.g., Nachman & Asche, 1973), or dosage of hypertonic saline ingested (Andrews & Braverman, 1975). Somewhat paradoxically, the tranquilizer chlordiazepoxide (Librium) will produce a conditioned food aversion if injected in large enough amounts; the larger the amount, the greater the food aversion (Gamzu, 1977).

If food or water is used as the US, then US intensity may be varied either by manipulating the degree of deprivation, or by varying the amount administered as the US. Degree of conditioning is directly related to the amount the animal is deprived of those substances (e.g., Pavlov, 1927; De-Bold, Miller, & Jensen, 1965). Similarly, dogs given greater amounts of food as the US show greater amounts of conditioned salivation (e.g., Gantt, 1938; Wagner, Siegel, Thomas, & Ellison, 1964).

US Duration

Variations in US duration usually have little effect on conditioning. Such results have been obtained in conditioned changes in skin resistance (GSR), a measure of emotion, with shock durations of 0.5, 3.0, and 15 seconds (Coppock & Chambers, 1959), in heart rate conditioning with shock durations of 0.1, 2.0, 6.0, and 15 seconds (Zeaman & Wegner, 1958), with eyelid conditioning with airpuff US durations of 0.05 and 1.0 seconds (Runquist & Spence, 1959), and in autoshaping with grain available for 4 or 60 seconds (Balsam & Payne, 1979).

Some effects of US duration have been obtained in one-trial simultaneous fear conditioning (Burkhardt & Ayres, 1978) and in eyelid and nictitating membrane conditioning (Frey & Butler, 1973; Tait et al., 1983). All in all, though, the effects of US duration appear to be small. The general lack of effect of US duration is somewhat puzzling since variations in duration would seem to be just another way of varying intensity. However, the large effects of US intensity, independent of duration, and the small effects of duration, indicate that it is the initial impact of the US that is most important in affecting degree of conditioning, rather than the cumulative effects that may arise from a long-lasting US.

US Preexposure

Conditioning is retarded if animals are preexposed to the US before it is paired with the CS. For example, Balsam and Schwartz (1981) found an orderly increase in the time taken by pigeons to autoshape if they were given 4, 8, or 64 feeder presentations prior to the pairing of such presentations with an illuminated disc (the CS in autoshaping). It has been argued that these retardation effects are due to the fact that the animal learns an association between the general apparatus stimuli and the feeder presentations. The formation of an association between the experimental context and the US in this case would be much like that described in the case of Marlin's trace conditioning experiment considered earlier. However, the present experiments go on to suggest that the formation of such a context–US association will interfere with the later development of a CS–US association (Tomie, 1976; Tomie, Murphy, & Fath, 1980). It is as if once an animal learns that the general experimental context predicts the US, it has difficulty learning that a discrete

CS presented within that context may be a more accurate predictor of the US.

Some experimental data that support the hypothesis that the retarding effects of US preexposure are due to context conditioning are presented in Figure 4–7. The left half of the Figure shows that the number of trials that are required for a pigeon to develop consistent autoshaped responding is increased when the birds have had 20 prior US exposures as compared to when they have had only 2 prior US exposures. The right half of the Figure shows that there is no retardation effect if the autoshaping training is administered in a context different from the one in which the US preexposures were given (see also Tomie, 1976).

Retardation from US preexposure has also been obtained in fear conditioning (e.g., Baker & Mackintosh, 1979; Baker, Mercier, Gabel, & Baker, 1981; Randich & LoLordo, 1979). Some of this research indicates that context conditioning may not account for the entire retardation effect obtained in the conditioned fear procedure. Rather, there may also be contributions made by adaptation to the aversiveness of the US and learning that the occurrence of the US cannot be predicted. Once the animals learn that the US in unpredictable, then it may take them longer to learn that it becomes predictable when it is regularly preceded by a CS. Retardation by US preexposure has

FIGURE 4–7 *Acquisition of autoshaping as a function of US preexposure and context change. The left half of the Figure shows that animals with 20 US preexposures required more trials to learn than animals with 2 US preexposures. However, when the learning context was different from the preexposure context, then there was no effect of US preexposure (right half of Figure). (From Balsam & Schwartz, 1981)*

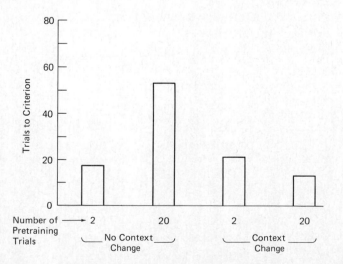

also been found to occur in the conditioned-food-aversion procedure (e.g., Best & Domjan, 1979; Cain & Baenninger, 1977; Domjan & Gemberling, 1980). Like other US preexposure effects, this one is also alleviated if the context is changed between preexposure and conditioning (e.g., Domjan & Best, 1980). However, as in the case of conditioned fear, the effect of US preexposure on conditioned food aversions may be mediated by more than one mechanism. One item of evidence supporting this view is the following. The retardation of conditioning that occurs with repeated US exposures is alleviated by context change prior to conditioning. However, retardation may also occur if a single US preexposure is administered close in time to the conditioning trial and this retardation is not alleviated by context change (Domjan & Best, 1980).

In summary, prior exposure to the US retards subsequent conditioning in a variety of situations. Conditioning of the US to the general apparatus context, which then interferes with conditioning to a CS introduced later, is probably a major part of this retardation effect. However, other mechanisms such as adaptation to the US or learned unpredictability may also be operating to contribute to the retardation effect. This topic is currently an area of active research.

Characteristics of the CS

CS Intensity

Generally, more intense CSs lead to better conditioning. For example, Gormezano (1972) reported a higher level of nictitating membrane conditioning in rabbits exposed to an 86 decibel (db) tone as a CS than in rabbits exposed to a 65 db tone. CS intensity effects have also been found in other situations such as heart rate conditioning (Hernandez, Buchanan, & Powell, 1981) and fear conditioning (e.g., Kamin, 1965; Imada, Yamazaki, & Morishita, 1981). In studies of human eyelid conditioning, CS intensity effects are more likely to occur if the same subjects experience both the high and low intensity stimuli than if different groups of subjects experience the two values of intensity (Grice & Hunter, 1964). Evidently, the more intense CS becomes particularly effective in humans only when they have an opportunity to compare stimuli of differing intensities. CS intensity effects have also been found, in some circumstances, to be greater in animals when they experience two different intensities (Frey, 1969).

Why do more intense CSs lead to better conditioning? One possibility is that more intense CSs produce greater or longer lasting neural activity, which serves to enhance the degree of association when the US is presented some time after the CS. Another possibility is that the absolute intensity of the CS is not critical, rather it is the degree of difference between the CS

and background stimuli that is important. The greater the degree of difference, the easier it is for the subject to discriminate the CS from the background (see Logan, 1954; Perkins, 1953). The data indicate that both the
absolute CS intensity and degree of difference from the background are important determiners of conditioning. For example, Kamin (1965) investigated
the effects of using as a CS either increases or decreases in the intensity of a
background noise. He found that the greater the degree of difference from
background levels, the greater the conditioning. However, he also found that
increases above background noise were more effective as CSs than decreases
of a comparable amount below background noise. Thus, CS intensity seems
to have two components: absolute intensity of the CS, and degree of difference from background stimuli.

Effects analogous to CS intensity variations have also been reported in
the acquisition of conditioned food aversions. In particular, more concentrated taste solutions lead to greater conditioning (e.g., Barker, 1976; Dragoin, 1971).

CS Duration

Duration of the CS normally has little effect per se on conditioning
(e.g., Kamin, 1965). Manipulations of CS duration, though, may influence
other parameters which do influence degree of conditioning. For example,
variations in the duration of the CS in which the US always coincides with
CS termination, would also represent variations in the CS–US interval, which
would influence conditioning. Burkhardt and Ayres (1978) have found that
increased CS duration that also increases the degree of overlap between the
CS and US enhances fear conditioning, but if the CS is maintained beyond
US termination, then conditioning is diminished.

One situation in which CS duration does seem to have effects is in the
conditioned food aversion paradigm. For example, Barker (1976) found that
increasing the duration of saccharin exposure in the range from approximately
one second to nine minutes led to increasing degrees of aversion when the
saccharin was followed by radiation. On the other hand, if the CS exposure is
too long, then the degree of aversion may be reduced (Deutsch, 1978; Rudy
& Cheatle, 1978).

Since the duration of CS exposure in the food aversion procedure is
confounded with amount consumed, these data indicate that there is a curvilinear relationship between consumption of the CS substance and degree of
aversion. Consuming either very little or a substantial amount of the substance before the US is presented may lead to less aversion than if an intermediate amount is consumed. There may be two explanations for this curvilinear effect. On the low end, it would seem reasonable that some minimal
amount of CS experience is necessary in order for the CS to become associ-

ated with the US. Indeed, Barker (1976) found that less exposure to saccharin was necessary for conditioning when the concentration of the substance was increased. Perhaps concentration (intensity) and duration of the CS may compensate for one another in promoting associability.

The decline in conditioned aversions with increased exposure may be due to another mechanism. Perhaps extended exposure leads to a decline in the novelty of the CS and novelty is an important factor in conditioned food aversion learning (Domjan, 1980; Rudy & Cheatle, 1978; Testa & Ternes, 1977).

CS Preexposure

Exposure to the CS prior to conditioning retards the development of conditioning. For example, Siegel (1972) found that giving rabbits extensive exposure to a tone CS prior to nictitating membrane conditioning more than doubled the number of trials required for the fifth CR to occur (the occurrence of the fifth CR was used as an index of conditioning). Retardation by prior CS exposure has also been obtained in a variety of other conditioning situations including heart rate conditioning (e.g., Hernandez et al., 1981), conditioned licking of water (Baker & Mackintosh, 1977, 1979), and conditioned food aversions (Elkins, 1973; Kalat, 1977; Kalat & Rozin, 1973).

Two different terms are used to describe these CS preexposure effects. In most conditioning situations the term *latent inhibition* is used (see Lubow, 1973). The idea behind this term is that the interference with conditioning brought about by CS preexposure is a form of inhibition—something that opposes excitation. It is latent because typically no measures of behavior are obtained during the preexposure period; the effects remain latent (unobserved) until conditioning trials commence. In the food aversion procedure the CS preexposure effect is often termed *learned safety*. The assumption here is that, with preexposure, animals learn that the CS substance does not make them ill and this learning then interferes with the learning of an aversion (Kalat, 1977). Whether there is any fundamental difference between latent inhibition and learned safety as processes is not clear at the present time.

Summary

Conditioning is facilitated by high intensity CSs and USs. Duration of the CS and US has relatively little impact on conditioning, except in a few special circumstances. Preexposure to either the CS or the US retards the course of conditioning. There are various theoretical interpretations of these latter effects.

Intermittent CS, US Pairings

Acquisition

What happens to acquisition if the US follows the CS on only some of the trials? Investigations of this question are termed studies of partial rein-forcement, and results obtained in one such study are presented in Figure 4–8. In this study of nictitating membrane conditioning in rabbits, one group received a US every time a CS was presented (the 100-percent group), but for the second group, only 50 percent of the CSs were followed by USs. It is clear in the Figure that the rate of acquisition of the 50 percent group was retarded compared to the 100-percent group, but that eventually both groups reached the same terminal level of responding (Gormezano & Coleman, 1975).

Another example of the acquisition effects of partial reinforcement is taken from autoshaping (Gibbon, Farrell, Locurto, Duncan, & Terrace, 1980). These data, presented in Figure 4–9, show the number of trials re-quired to reach a point where the animals responded on at least three out of

FIGURE 4–8 Acquisition of nictitating membrane response as a function of percent-age of reinforced trials (trials in which a CS is followed by a US). (Redrawn from Gormezano & Coleman, 1975)

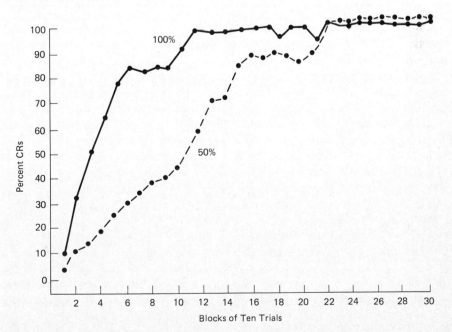

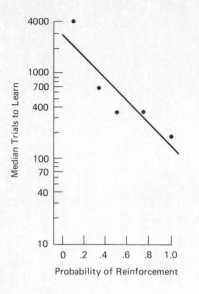

FIGURE 4–9 *Acquisition of autoshaped peck-ing response as a function of reinforcement schedule. A probability of 1.0 means all CSs were followed by USs, 0.8 means 80% of CSs were followed by USs, etc. The greater the probability of reinforcement, the fewer the trials required for learning. (Redrawn from Gibbon et al., 1980.)*

every four trials. It is clear that the lower the proportion of trials in which a US followed the CS, the more trials it required for the birds to develop the pecking response.

These data are representative of the effects of partial reinforcement on Pavlovian conditioning: acquisition is retarded. That is, if two groups are given the same number of trials (CS presentations), but one of these groups receives fewer US presentations than the other, the group with the fewer US presentations will show less rapid acquisition.

But note that there is another way to manipulate partial reinforcement. Suppose that one group is administered 100 trials on a 100-percent reinforce-ment schedule (CS always followed by US), and a second group is adminis-tered 200 trials on a 50-percent reinforcement schedule. These two groups will differ in percentage of reinforcement, but they will receive the same number of US presentations (100). The question arises as to whether there will be an effect of partial reinforcement on acquisition when number of USs are equated. Analysis of partial reinforcement in this manner is termed a *per reinforcement* analysis, as opposed to the *per trial* analysis described in the earlier part of this section.

It so happens that both the Gormezano and Coleman study and the Gibbon et al. study included groups of animals in which reinforcements were equated. Coleman and Gormezano reported evidence that acquisition was still retarded by a 50-percent schedule, even when reinforcements were equated. The data from the Gibbon et al. experiment, however, indicate only a slight retardation effect when reinforcements were equated, an effect so small as to be statistically insignificant. In their review of the partial reinforcement literature, Gibbon and his colleagues come to the conclusion that retardation effects of partial reinforcement on acquisition are less likely to be obtained when reinforcements are equated than when trials are equated.

Shift to Partial Reinforcement

What happens if animals are trained with a 100-percent schedule of reinforcement and then, after stable responding is obtained, they are shifted to a partial schedule? In a study of nictitating membrane conditioning it was found that CRs continue to occur at a high frequency with schedules of reinforcement as low as 15% (per trial), but a schedule of only 5 percent reinforcement produced a severe decrement in responding (Gibbs, Latham, & Gormezano, 1978). Thus, once stable responding is reached, nictitating membrane responding can apparently be maintained on very lean schedules of reinforcement.

Extinction

A number of studies have reported that partial reinforcement in acquisition enhances resistance to extinction. That is, animals reinforced on less than a 100-percent schedule take longer to extinguish than animals reinforced on a 100-percent schedule (e.g., Fitzgerald, 1963, salivary conditioning; Fitzgerald, Vardaris, & Teyler, 1966, heart rate conditioning; Poulos & Gormezano, 1974, conditioned jaw movements; Wagner, Siegel, Thomas, & Ellison, 1966, salivary conditioning). One example of the effect of partial reinforcement on extinction is shown in Figure 4–10. In this study the animals were first trained on a 100-percent reinforcement schedule before being shifted to various partial reinforcement schedules.

In Figure 4–10 it is apparent that there is a curvilinear relationship between schedule of reinforcement and resistance to extinction. That is, both very high and very low percentages of reinforcement accelerated extinction compared to intermediate reinforcement percentages.

In interpreting the effects of reinforcement schedule on resistance to extinction, there are two difficulties that the experimenter faces. First, animals given different percentages of reinforcement sometimes are responding at different levels at the end of the acquisition stage. For example, examine Figure 4–8 and imagine how the graph would look if acquisition were terminated after 100 trials. A difference in terminal acquisition levels complicates the interpretation of rate of extinction. Second, should resistance to extinction be interpreted on a *per trial* basis or on a *per reinforcement* basis?

Suppose there were two groups, one given 100-percent reinforcement for hundreds of trials, and one given 50-percent reinforcement for hundreds of trials. It could be that the proper comparison to make in extinction is response probability in every 200 trials for the 50-percent group compared to

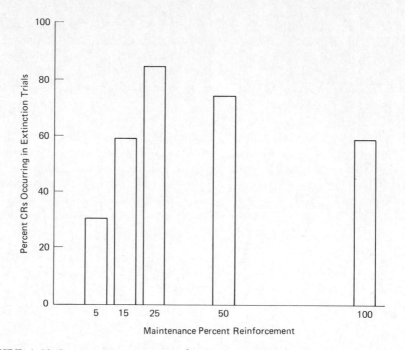

FIGURE 4–10 Percent CRs occurring during first 100 extinction trials as a function of percentage of reinforcement during the maintenance stage of the experiment. All groups were first reinforced on 100% of the trials, then shifted to the percentages indicated for 600 trials before the shift to extinction. (Redrawn from Gibbs et al., 1978.)

every 100 trials for the 100-percent group. This comparison makes particular sense if animals come to expect a particular *rate* of reinforcement (e.g., one every trial for the 100-percent group, and on the average of one every two trials for the 50-percent group, etc.). Thus, continuing with this example, if the 100-percent group were given 500 extinction trials, the 50-percent group would have to be given 1000 extinction trials in order to equate the groups in terms of number of US omissions experienced. Each 200 trial block of the 50-percent group would then be compared to each 100 trial block of the 100-percent group.

In their survey of the partial reinforcement literature, Gibbon et al. (1980) report that when extinction rates are examined proportionately to the animals' final level of acquisition performance (to equate for terminal acquisition differences), and also examined in terms of rate of extinction on a *per reinforcement* basis (instead of per trial), then there is little evidence that partial reinforcement increases resistance to extinction. In their own auto-shaping data, Gibbon et al. (1980) found that an examination of extinction over the first 250 extinction trials indicated a partial reinforcement extinction effect; the groups given the lower probability of reinforcement tended to make more responses over these 250 trials. However, the data were also analyzed over approximately 1200 extinction trials in terms of responses per omitted US (a 100-percent group would have 100 omitted USs in 100 extinction trials, but a 20-percent group would require 500 extinction trials before it experienced 100 omitted USs). When this per reinforcement analysis of extinction was used there were no differences in rate of extinction as a function of percentage of reinforcement.

Thus again, there seem to be two things to remember. Partial reinforcement tends to increase resistance to extinction, but this effect is reduced or eliminated if extinction is examined on the basis of number of USs omitted rather than on the basis of number of trials experienced (see Mowrer & Jones, 1945).

Intertrial Interval

Long intertrial intervals generally produce more rapid conditioning than short intertrial intervals (ITIs). Such an effect has been found, for example, in comparing 240-second versus 60-second, and 60-second versus 30-second ITIs in nictitating membrane conditioning (Frey & Ross, 1968b; Gormezano & Coleman, 1975); in comparing ITIs ranging from 15 seconds to 250 seconds in autoshaping (Gibbon et al., 1980); and in comparing ITIs ranging from 15 seconds to 135 seconds in human eyelid conditioning (Prokasy, Grant, & Myers, 1958).

There must be some limit to this facilitating effect, but the relevant parametric studies have apparently not been conducted. It is known that a 24-hour ITI (one trial per day) produces faster nictitating membrane conditioning than a 60-second ITI (Kehoe & Gormezano, 1974). This latter study showed another interesting effect of trial distribution: animals given 50 trials per day were slower to condition than animals given 5 or 10 trials per day; all had a 60-second ITI. Thus, within some limits, longer ITIs and fewer trials per day may promote better Pavlovian conditioning than the converse.

Long ITIs have also been found to produce faster acquisition of Pavlovian directed behaviors. Of particular importance seems to be the relationship between the length of a trial (CS and US presentation) and the length of the ITI. In general, the longer the ITI relative to the length of a trial, the more rapid the autoshaping (Gibbon et al., 1977), and the longer the ITI relative to the trace interval, the more likely an animal is to learn to approach the CS when a trace conditioning procedure is used (Kaplan, 1984).

CHAPTER SUMMARY

In this chapter we have seen that Pavlovian contingencies applied to relatively unrestrained animals will lead to approach or withdrawal behaviors contolled by CSs. In addition to simple approach response, animals will often direct toward the CS species-typical behaviors that are characteristically elicited by the US.

Conditioned food aversions, another expansion of the Pavlovian paradigm, were seen to be a particularly powerful type of conditioning, occurring after a single trial under parameters unfavorable for other types of conditioning.

Many factors influence the course of conditioning. Of particular importance is the temporal relationship between the CS and US. Trace conditioning is normally inferior to delay conditioning, and both diminish with long CS–US intervals. However, different families of CS–US interval functions were noted. With simple skeletal reflexes, such as eyeblink, effective conditioning demands only brief intervals between the CS and US. Autonomic functions such as heart rate and fear conditioning proceed with longer time periods between the CS and US. Conditioned food aversions form with quite long CS–US intervals. Some types of conditioning were found to occur with simultaneous presentations of the CS and US, and some with backward presentations. Backward presentations may lead to excitatory or inhibitory conditioning, depending upon other details of the experiment.

Conditioning is more pronounced with more intense CSs and USs, whereas CS and US duration have relatively little effect on conditioning, except in a few special situations. Preexposing the subjects to either the CS or the US before pairing trials has a deleterious effect on conditioning.

Intermittent reinforcement may have detrimental effects in acquisition and enhance resistance to extinction. But both of these effects may be reduced or eliminated if the data are considered on a per US rather than on a per trial basis.

Within limits, long intertrial intervals enhance acquisition. Recent evidence indicates that the *relative* length of the intertrial interval, compared to the length of the CS–US interval or trace interval, may be an important factor in determining the occurrence of conditioning.

5

Pavlovian Conditioning III: Selected Topics

I. Inhibition
  A. Definition and Examples of Inhibition
    1. Definition
    2. Examples of Inhibition
  B. Conditions that Do and Do Not Produce Inhibition
    1. Conditions that Do Not Produce Inhibition
      a. CS Preexposure
      b. Extinction
    2. Conditions that Produce Inhibition
      a. Explicitly Unpaired CS and US
      b. Random CS, US Presentations
      c. Trace Conditioning
      d. Long Delay Conditioning
      e. Discrimination Training
  C. Summary

II. Second Order Conditioning

III. Sensory Preconditioning

IV. Conditioned Drug Effects
  A. Conditioned Tolerance
    1. Morphine Analgesia
    2. Ethanol Hypothermia
  B. Other Conditioned Drug Effects
    1. Morphine Hyperthermia
    2. Cocaine Sensitization
    3. Methadone Withdrawal
    4. Hypoglycemia

V. Brain Mechanisms and Conditioning
  A. Cortical Mechanisms
  B. The Limbic System
  C. The Midbrain and Brain Stem
  D. Other Research

VI. Chapter Summary

> " *Inherited reflexes contain a static description of the events of high probability in the past experience of the species, but learning allows each animal to add a stock of personal secrets to its description of the probabilities of the world.* "
>
> Colin Blakemore, *Mechanics of the Mind*, 1977

INHIBITION

Pavlov's M.D. thesis was concerned with aspects of the dual innervation of the heart. Heart rate is controlled by both the sympathetic and parasympathetic branches of the autonomic nervous system. Increases in the activity of the sympathetic nerves to the heart increase heart rate, whereas increases in the activity of the parasympathetic innervation of the heart decrease heart rate. This dual control may be thought of as excitation and inhibition of the heart. Perhaps because of the influence of this early work, Pavlov's interpretations of his conditioning research relied heavily on the dual processes of excitation and inhibition.

Pavlov recognized two basic types of inhibition. One of these, external inhibition, was thought of as based on a reflex response to a distracting event that occurred in the environment. For example, if a sudden loud noise occurred during the acquisition phase of conditioning there would probably be a decrease in the magnitude of the CR on the trial following the disruption. This decrement in conditioning Pavlov referred to as *external inhibition* and he attributed it to the operation of the orienting response (see Chapters 2 and 3), which interfered with the conditioning process.

The second category of inhibition Pavlov termed *internal inhibition*. This type of inhibition, Pavlov believed, was learned under certain conditions of CS and US presentation. It is this learned inhibition that will be of concern in this text. The study of learned inhibition is a complex topic and one with some inconsistency in the terms used to describe various types of learned inhibition. We will consider only some of the simpler demonstrations of inhibition, and the experimental conditions that lead to such inhibition.

Definition and Examples of Inhibition

Definition

Excitatory conditioning may be defined as the learning that the occurrence of two events (e.g., CS and US) is positively correlated—they tend to occur together (Rescorla, 1975). If a CS derives its excitatory properties (tendency to elicit a CR) because of its predictive relationship with the US (i.e., it always precedes it in time), what arrangement of the CS and US should lead to the CS acquiring inhibitory properties? The answer would seem to be any arrangement that leads to a negative correlation between the CS and US (Hearst, 1972; Rescorla, 1975). By negative correlation is meant a situation in which the CS predicts the *absence* of the US. Note how this way of defining excitation and inhibition in terms of procedures used to produce them (positive and negative CS,US correlations) parallels the definition given in Chapter 4 in terms of the effects of excitation and inhibition. That is, the procedures used to produce excitatory and inhibitory CSs are opposite, and the effects of excitatory and inhibitory CSs on behavior are opposite. If one enhances behavior, the other will reduce it, and vice versa. Thus, an inhibitory CS is defined in relation to an excitatory CS—it opposes the tendency of the excitatory CS to elicit a CR.

There are two particular tests that a CS must pass in order to be considered inhibitory. These are the retardation test and the summation test, and they will be discussed in detail over the next several pages. But now we will describe two examples of inhibition; then we will go on to consider the experimental conditions that lead to a stimulus having inhibitory effects.

Examples of Inhibition

An experiment that examined a variety of possible inhibitory conditions was conducted by Siegel and Domjan (1971). This was a study of eyelid conditioning in the rabbit, in which there were five groups of animals. One of the groups received a *backward* pairing of the CS and US. That is, the US was immediately followed by the CS. Since there was an average one-minute intertrial interval between each US and CS presentation, the CS always preceded a period of US absence. Thus, the sequence of events experienced by this group was US, then CS, then a relatively long "empty" period. Five hundred and fifty such presentations were given. Four other groups in the experiment received either CS-only presentations, US-only presentations, a random presentation of both the CS and US, or were simply placed in the apparatus during this time and received exposure to neither the CS nor US.

In the next stage of the experiment all the groups were given identical acquisition training, with the CS preceding the US by a 0.5 second CS–US interval. The results of this acquisition stage are presented in Figure 5–1. It is apparent that all of the groups given pretreatment were retarded in acquisition. The group given the backward pairing was more hindered than the random group, which was more hindered than either the CS-alone or US-alone groups. These last two did not differ.

This test for inhibition is termed the *retardation test* and it is clear that the group for whom the CS explicitly predicted the absence of the US (the "backward" group) showed the greatest retardation of acquisition. The results

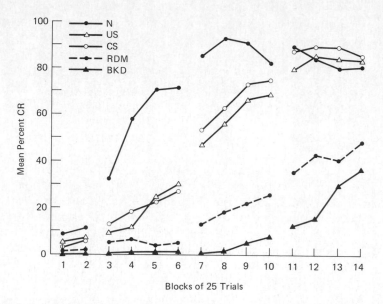

FIGURE 5–1 Acquisition of a nictitating membrane CR as a function of prior conditioning treatment. N = no prior conditioning, US = prior US-alone exposure, CS = prior CS-alone exposure, RDM = prior exposure to random CS and US presentation, BKD = prior exposure to a backward CS–US pairing. (Data from Siegel & Domjan, 1971)

are consistent with those reported in the backward conditioning section of Chapter 4.

In this experiment, inhibition was manifest as a decrement in behavior. However, the concept of an inhibitory CS is one that counteracts an excitatory CS. Inhibition does not necessarily mean a behavioral decrement. There are situations in which inhibition will lead to enhanced behavior. Consider, for example, conditioned fear. In the conditioned fear experiment a CS precedes the delivery of foot shock to a rat. The effects of such conditioning are determined by assessing the degree to which a behavior such as bar pressing for food is suppressed by the CS.[1] Thus, in this situation the excitatory CS (predictor of shock) acts to produce a decrement in behavior (bar pressing). If an inhibitory stimulus were to counteract the excitatory CS it should, in effect, enhance behavior.

Siegel and Domjan (1971) investigated this possibility with the same five treatment conditions as in the above experiment. The results of this experiment are presented in Figure 5–2. The group with no prior CS or US experience showed the greatest suppression of behavior, and the group with the

---

[1] It may take some experience with the US–CS pairing before the CS becomes inhibitory with the backward pairing. See Chapter 4, the section on Backward Conditioning.

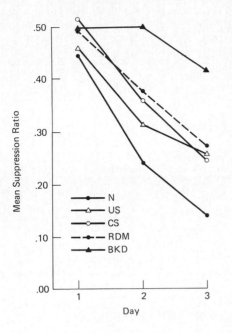

FIGURE 5–2 Acquisition of a conditioned fear response as a function of prior conditioning treatment. The group identifications are the same as in Figure 5–1. The suppression ratio is a measure of how much an animal's bar-pressing for food is suppressed by a CS that signals impending shock. The fewer the bar presses that the animal makes when the CS is on, the smaller the suppression ratio. Small ratios indicate greater fear and thus more learning of the CS–US relationship. In this graph the N group shows the most suppression or the best learning, and the BKD group the least. (Data from Siegel & Domjan, 1971)

prior backward experience showed the least suppression of behavior. Thus, the prior experience with the backward pairing of the CS and US (which, in this case, made the CS correlated with a period of shock absence) endowed the CS with inhibitory properties—properties that interfered with learning that the CS signaled the impending occurrence of shock. In this experiment the CS-alone, US-alone, and random groups showed an intermediate level of interference with acquisition.

Thus, experiments by Siegel and Domjan show that an inhibitory stimulus interferes with both behavioral enhancement and behavioral suppression caused by excitatory CSs. Similar effects have been obtained in other experiments (e.g., Baker & Mackintosh, 1977).

The opposing natures of excitation and inhibition may be seen in at least two other ways. Hoffman and Fitzgerald (1982) compared conditioned heart rate responses under two conditions: when the CS correlated with shock onset, and when the CS correlated with the absence of the shock US. They found that the CR elicited by the excitatory CS (correlated with shock onset) was a decelerative change in heart rate. The CS correlated with the absence of shock was not neutral—it provoked an accelerative change in heart rate. Thus, the excitatory CS produced a decrease below baseline in heart rate; the inhibitory stimulus produced the opposite response, an increase above baseline.

A final example of these opposed processes may be drawn from directed behavior experiments. In autoshaping and related studies, a CS correlated with the availability of food produces approach responses to the CS, whereas a CS correlated with the absence of food produces withdrawal responses away from the CS, sometimes to the opposite side of the cage (e.g., Green & Rachlin, 1977; Hearst & Franklin, 1977; Karpicke, Christoph, Peterson, & Hearst, 1977; Wasserman, Franklin, & Hearst, 1974).

Conditions that Do and Do Not Produce Inhibition

We will now consider two experimental procedures that do not produce an inhibitory stimulus and several procedures that do produce inhibition. Those procedures that do not produce inhibition are CS preexposure and extinction. The conditions that do produce inhibition are explicitly unpaired CS and US (such as backward conditioning), random presentation of the CS and US (under some circumstances), trace conditioning, long delay conditioning, and discrimination training.

Conditions that Do Not Produce Inhibition

CS Preexposure. We have seen in Chapter 4 and, to some extent in the Siegel and Domjan experiment just described, that CS preexposure retards acquisition. However, the retardation of acquisition is not sufficient evidence to conclude that the CS is an inhibitory stimulus. Such retardation could be due to some other factor. For example, perhaps CS preexposure simply leads to habituation (see Chapter 2) so the CS becomes less salient (less noticeable, less attention-getting). In this way, habituation, rather than inhibition, could account for retarded acquisition.

There is a test that is used to help distinguish inhibition from processes such as habituation. This test is termed the *summation test* (Rescorla, 1969). The logic and procedure of the summation test are as follows. If a stimulus is inhibitory, it should reduce the tendency of an excitatory CS to elicit a CR. Therefore a stimulus that is thought to have inhibitory properties is presented in compound (i.e., at the same time) with another stimulus that is known to have excitatory properties. If conditioned responding is less in the presence of the compound than in the presence of the excitatory stimulus alone, the added stimulus is said to have inhibitory properties. However, in order to be certain about this conclusion, a control condition is necessary. The degree of decrement in responding produced by the suspected inhibitory stimulus must be greater than the degree of decrement produced by a novel stimulus placed in compound with the excitatory stimulus. This controls for the possibility that the decrement might be produced by the novelty per se of the compound.

A study by Solomon, Brennan, and Moore (1974) examined the effects of CS preexposure on the summation test. In this study, rabbits were first given acquisition training (500 trials) with a light as the CS. This established the light as an excitatory stimulus. Then half of the animals were given an additional 450 presentations of a tone alone. The remaining half of the animals spent an equivalent amount of time in the apparatus, but did not experience the tone during this stage of the experiment. In the final stage of the experiment all animals received some trials in which the light (an excitatory CS, because of its previous conditioning) was presented alone, and some trials in which the light and the tone were presented as a compound. No USs were presented during any of these test trials. The results of this experiment are shown in Figure 5–3.

It is apparent that presentation of the compound reduced the number of CRs as compared to presentation of just the excitatory light CS. However, animals that had experienced 450 presentations of the tone alone showed less of an effect (a smaller decrement in CR percentage) than the animals for

FIGURE 5–3 *The summation test for inhibition. In the left pair of bars a conditioned excitor (light) is presented alone (L) and in compound (LT) with a tone that is novel to the animal. The tone produced a decrement in responding. In the right pair of bars a light-conditioned excitor is presented alone and in compound with a tone that the animals had experienced 450 times without a US. The tone produced less of a decrement in this group than in the novel group. If the tone were inhibitory the decrement would have been greater than that occurring to a novel stimulus. Thus, a preexposed tone is not inhibitory by this test. (Data from Solomon, Brenman, & Moore, 1974)*

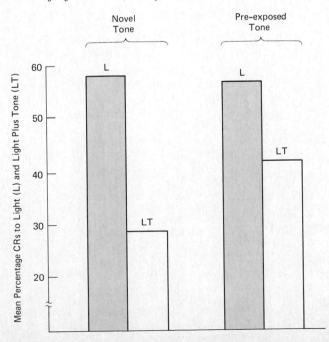

whom the tone was novel. These results indicate that the initial presentations of the tone alone did not cause the tone to become an inhibitory stimulus. Evidence of inhibition would be provided only if presentation of the preexposed stimulus led to a greater decrement than presentation of the novel stimulus.

Other experiments have also found that exposure to a CS-alone retards subsequent acquisition, but does not show evidence of inhibition on other tests such as the summation test (e.g., Reiss & Wagner, 1972; Rescorla, 1971). Thus, we may conclude that CS-alone presentations do not produce inhibition. The retarding effects that such experience has on acquisition may be due to some other process such as habituation and lack of attention to the CS.

Extinction. There is no substantial evidence either from summation tests or from retardation tests that extinguished CSs have inhibitory properties (Rescorla, 1969). Autoshaping studies have shown that reacquisition is faster after standard extinction (i.e., US omitted) than after extinction produced by explicitly unpaired or random presentations of the CS and US (Tomie, Hayden, & Biehl, 1980; Tomie, Rohr-Stafford, & Schwam, 1981). In fact, rather than being retarded, reacquisition is usually faster than original acquisition (Pavlov, 1927). An example of this faster reacquisition is shown in Figure 5–4. Thus, extinguished CSs are not inhibitors.

Conditions that Produce Inhibition

The failure of extinction and CS-alone treatments to produce inhibition is consistent with Rescorla's procedural definition of inhibition given at the beginning of this section. That is, the CS must predict the absence of the US. Perhaps the US must be sometimes present and sometimes absent in order for animals to learn that a CS predicts the absence of the US. In the CS-alone treatment and in extinction the US is never present. We will now consider several situations in which the US is sometimes present and sometimes absent, in all of which a CS that predicts US absence will acquire inhibitory properties.

Explicitly Unpaired CS and US. The term *explicitly unpaired* refers to the presentation of a CS and US in a manner not favorable for excitatory conditioning. Usually this means that the CS is presented after the US (backward conditioning) or is very remote from US occurrence. An example of remote presentations of CS and US is a study by Baker (1977) who presented CSs and USs on alternate days in a conditioned fear experiment. On some days the subjects experienced two CSs during a 30-minute session, but no USs; on alternate days they experienced four USs, but no CSs. Baker found that this procedure substantially retarded acquisition when the CS was later

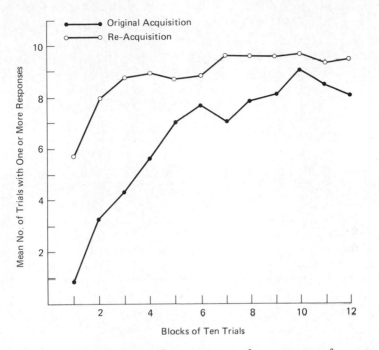

FIGURE 5–4 *Original acquisition and reacquisition after extinction of an autoshaped response. Reacquisition was faster. (Unpublished data from Tomie & Rhor-Stafford, 1983)*

paired with a US. In a second experiment he found also that the explicitly unpaired CS detracted from an excitatory stimulus in fear conditioning when the two were presented together in compound. Thus, Baker's procedure led to evidence of inhibition on both retardation and summation tests.

Earlier in this chapter we presented evidence that stimuli correlated with the absence of a US in heart rate conditioning led to a response (cardiac acceleration) that was opposite to the CR. There was evidence too that animals would withdraw from a stimulus signaling the absence of food but would approach a stimulus signaling the presence of food. Thus, stimuli paired with the absence of a US produce responses opposite to the CR, interfere with acquisition (the retardation test), and counteract the effects of an excitatory CS (the summation test). Explicitly unpaired CSs clearly become inhibitory.

Random CS,US Presentation. Random presentation of the CS and US retards acquisition to a degree greater than CS-alone preexposure, but to a considerably lesser degree than an explicitly unpaired CS. Furthermore, the random procedure often does not give evidence of inhibition when the summation test is used (e.g., Baker, 1977; Hinson & Siegel, 1980; Siegel &

Domjan, 1971). Neither does it lead to heart-rate changes that are opposite in direction to the CR (Cunningham, Fitzgerald, & Francisco, 1977).

Is it possible that the retardation of acquisition that occurs following the random presentation of the CS and US is due simply to the combined effects of CS and US preexposure? No; Baker and Mackintosh (1977, 1979) found that random presentation of the CS and US led to retardation effects greater than those of either CS or US preexposure. They also presented evidence that the retardation produced by the random condition might not be reducible to the combined CS and US preexposure effects. Something other than simple preexposure seems to be involved when the animals experience both the CS and US.

One possibility is that the animals learn that there is no relationship between the two (Baker & Mackintosh, 1979). This learning would be different from habituation to the CS and different from learning that the CS is correlated with the absence of the US. The learning of no relationship could interfere with acquisition (it may be hard then to learn that there is a relationship). But it could not interfere with the summation test, because the animals have already learned that the CS has no relationship to a US and therefore the CS does not add to or subtract from the effects of the excitatory CS. This interpretation is still in the realm of speculation. What is clear is that the random treatment has effects that are different from the CS preexposure treatment and from the explicitly unpaired treatment.[2]

Trace Conditioning. Evidence was presented in Chapter 4 which showed that trace conditioning was difficult to obtain, and that with long trace intervals, conditioning to the context may occur. In this section evidence will be presented to show that the trace conditioning procedure may produce an inhibitory CS.

Normally, no conditioning of a nictitating membrane response will occur if there is even a brief gap between the CS and US (Meredith & Schneiderman, 1967). In a more recent study Hinson and Siegel (1980) found no evidence of nictitating membrane conditioning in rabbits with a 10-second trace

---

[2] Another factor that must be considered in regard to the effects of the random treatment is the exact nature of the CS and US events. That is, the random presentation of the two may lead to some excitatory pairings (e.g., CS immediately precedes US, and/or some inhibitory pairings; (e.g., CS correlated with absence of US). For example, Benedict and Ayres (1972) found that excitatory conditioning could occur with random presentations of the CS and US if a few CS–US pairings occurred at the beginning of training. If non-pairings preceded any CS–US pairings, then no excitatory conditioning was obtained. In another study Witcher and Ayres (1980) found that a group that experienced both CSs and USs would show evidence of both retardation and inhibition in the summation test if only 10 percent of the CS presentations were paired with a US, but a group that had 20 percent of such pairings showed reduced retardation and no evidence of inhibition on the summation test. Thus, the effects obtained with the random treatment clearly depend on the nature of the CS and US events that the animal actually experiences when the "random" schedule is presented. If there are few CS–US pairings and thus the CS predicts the absence of the US, then the CS from a random treatment may be inhibitory. If, however, there are several CS–US pairings, then the CS will not become inhibitory.

interval. However, when the CS from this trace conditioning phase was used as a CS in a delayed conditioning situation with a 0.5 second CS–US interval (optimal for conditioning nictitating membrane responses), it was found that the trace conditioning experience retarded acquisition. In a second experiment Hinson and Siegel found that a trace conditioned CS also produced a decrement in conditioning when compounded with an excitatory stimulus in the summation test. Thus, by both the retardation and summation tests, a trace conditioning procedure that showed no signs of excitatory conditioning (no CRs developed) was found to endow the CS with inhibitory properties.

Long Delay Conditioning. Pavlov (1927) noted an apparent inhibitory effect in delayed conditioning when the CS duration was particularly long (e.g., three minutes). That is, during the early part of acquisition the CR tended to occur just after the CS was presented. But, as training progressed, the locus of the CR occurrence moved away from CS onset and toward the point of US onset. Thus the CR occurred later and later in the CS–US interval. This effect, which Pavlov termed inhibition of delay, has been noted by other investigators in other conditioning paradigms (e.g., Kimmel & Burns, 1975, in GSR conditioning). Pavlov's evidence that this delayed CR is a form of inhibition was derived from the presentation of a novel stimulus, a procedure that resulted in the reappearance of the CR at a point early in the CS–US interval. Pavlov's interpretation of this result was that the novel stimulus had disinhibited the CR.

Rescorla (1967a) found that the CS from a long delay conditioning experiment has inhibitory properties when superimposed on an excitatory baseline. Thus, long delay conditioning, like trace conditioning, may allow the CS to develop inhibitory properties. It is interesting to note that these procedures share a similarity with the explicitly unpaired treatment. That is, the CS in both the trace and long delay procedures is correlated with a regular period of US absence. Pavlov reported that some of his dogs fell asleep during long CS–US intervals, and sleep, Pavlov thought, was an extreme form of inhibition.

Discrimination Training. In discrimination training one stimulus (CS +) is correlated with the presentation of the US and a second stimulus (CS −) is correlated with the absence of the US (see Chapter 3). Evidence indicates that the CS − acquires inhibitory properties. For example, Hammon (1967, 1968) obtained evidence from both retardation tests and summation tests that a CS − in a conditioned fear experiment functioned as an inhibitor. Similarly, Grossen and Bolles (1968) found that a CS − from a conditioned fear experiment would reduce excitation in a fear-evoking situation.

Another quite different experimental procedure also yielded evidence of the inhibitory effect of CS −. In this study the US was direct electrical stimulation of the motor cortex of a dog. The UR was a leg-lifting response in the dog; that is, the low levels of electric current applied directly to the motor area of the brain caused the dog's leg to lift (Wagner, Thomas, & Norton, 1967). If the application of the US was preceded by a CS −, it was found that the amount of current necessary to raise the dog's leg was increased, indicating that the leg-lifting was being inhibited by the CS −. Evidence of inhibitory effects of a CS − has also been obtained in autoshaping studies (e.g., Tomie & Kruse, 1980) and in heart rate conditioning (Hoffman & Fitzgerald, 1982). Thus, the evidence indicates that standard discrimination training endows the CS − with inhibitory properties (see also Hearst, 1972).

Pavlov developed the procedures for another type of discrimination training, one that provided evidence of particularly powerful inhibition. In this second procedure, which Pavlov termed *conditioned inhibition*, one stimulus, the CS + is presented in some intermixed fashion, across trials, with a compound stimulus that is nonreinforced. This compound stimulus is composed of the same stimulus that serves as the CS + and a second stimulus. For example, an animal trained in such a paradigm might receive a tone as a CS + and a tone–light compound as a CS −. This procedure will eventually lead to differential responding—the tone will elicit a CR whereas the compound will tend not to elicit a CR.

Inhibition may be demonstrated by taking the added element in the compound (the light in our example) and using it in one of the standard tests of inhibition. Both retardation tests and summation tests have shown that the added element acquires substantial inhibitory effects (see, for example, Rescorla & Holland, 1977; Rescorla & Wagner, 1972; Wagner & Rescorla, 1972). A retardation test conducted in a heart rate conditioning study has indicated that inhibition using this "conditioned inhibition" procedure may be greater than that obtained with standard discrimination training (Hoffman & Fitzgerald, 1982).[3] Thus, evidence derived from both standard discrimination training and the form of discrimination training using a compound CS − indicates that a CS − develops inhibitory potential.

Summary

If excitatory conditioning is viewed as a learned relationship between the occurrence of the CS and US, then inhibitory conditioning may be considered a learned relationship between the occurrence of the CS and the

[3] There is a terminological problem in this area in that Pavlov used the term "conditioned inhibition" to refer to the compound stimulus procedure. More recently conditioned inhibition has been used to refer to all types of inhibition based on learning (e.g., Rescorla, 1969). Pavlov himself recognized that his conditioned inhibition procedure could be subsumed as a special case of discrimination training (Pavlov, 1927, p. 125). Therefore, we will follow Rescorla and use the term "conditioned inhibition" to be synonymous with learned inhibition, meaning all forms of learned inhibition.

absence of the US. The inhibitory properties of a CS may be measured in a variety of ways, including (1) the ability of the CS to retard acquisition, (2) the ability of the CS to subtract from excitation in a summation test, and (3) tendencies of an animal to withdraw from the CS.

Tests of inhibition have indicated that the following procedures endow a CS with inhibitory properties: any degree of negative correlation between the CS and US, including backward conditioning and other explicitly unpaired CSs and USs; discriminative conditioning; trace conditioning; and long delay conditioning. The evidence that random presentation of the CS and US leads to an inhibitory CS is equivocal. The effects of such random presentations are greater than the effects of CS-alone plus US-alone preexposure, but the inhibitory nature of such a CS may depend upon the exact sequence of CSs and USs that the animal experiences.

Two conditions that seem not to lead to the CS acquiring inhibitory properties are CS preexposure and extinction. CS preexposure does retard acquisition, but such effects may represent a form of habituation rather than inhibition.

SECOND ORDER CONDITIONING

After conditioning has been established, the CS elicits a response that is in some way related to the response elicited by the US. In a manner of speaking, the CS has become something like the US. Does this mean that the CS can function like a US and support conditioning to a new stimulus? The procedure for investigating this question is illustrated below. The first phase of such an experiment is a standard conditioning procedure in which a CS (termed CS_1) is paired with a US. After conditioning has been established with CS_1, it is then paired with a second CS (termed CS_2). If, as a result of this pairing, CS_2 comes to elicit a CR, then *second order conditioning* is said to have taken place. The occurrence of second order conditioning shows that CS_1 will serve to reinforce new learning, much like a US does.

Original Conditioning	*Second Order Conditioning*
CS_1	CS_2
US	CS_1

An experiment by Rashotte, Griffen, and Sisk (1977) will be examined as an example of second order conditioning and of the controls needed to adequately demonstrate such conditioning. The experiment was a study of autoshaping with pigeons. In the first phase of the experiment an illuminated disc was paired with the presentation of grain. The disc was illuminated with white light six seconds before the availability of grain. Thus, the white illuminated disc was the CS (CS_1) and the grain was the US. The animals received 20 daily sessions in which there were 30 pairings of CS_1 and the US in this first order conditioning stage. During the second order conditioning phase the disc was illuminated with blue light (CS_2) six seconds before it was illuminated with white light (CS_1). No US was presented on these second order conditioning trials. However, during this phase of the experiment alternate days were given over to first order conditioning. That is, Day 1 was all second order trials, Day 2 was first order trials, etc. This procedure was used because second order conditioning is also extinction for the first order CS (no US is presented). Thus, the alternate day procedure was employed to maintain CS_1 as an effective reinforcer.

The results obtained over second order sessions are presented in Figure 5–5. The curved labelled P-P shows that the birds learned to peck at CS_2 when it was regularly followed by CS_1. Thus, CS_1 acted like a US in its ability to promote new learning.

This experiment also included two control groups whose purpose was to ensure that the responses elicited by CS_2 were due to pairing in both stage 1 and stage 2. That is, one control group had CS_1 paired with the US in stage 1, but in stage 2 the CS_1 and CS_2 were presented randomly in relation to one another. This paired random (P-R) group controlled for the possibility that pairing in stage 1 alone would be sufficient to produce responses to CS_2 in the second stage of training. The occurrence of this result might be attributed to sensitization processes rather than to associative learning. Figure 5–5 shows that no CS_2 responding occurred in this group.

The second control group received a random presentation (R-P) of CS_1 and the US in the first stage of the experiment, but a paired presentation of the CS_1 and CS_2 in the second stage of the experiment. This group assessed

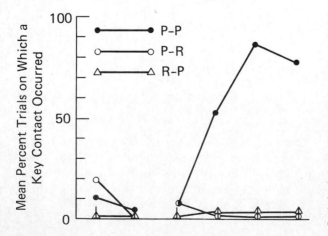

FIGURE 5–5 Acquisition of a second order autoshaped pecking response. Solid line represents responses to CS_2 when it is paired with CS_1. Two other groups that received either random CS_1, US presentations or random CS_1–CS_2 presentations showed no responses to CS_2. Thus, pairing of both CS_1 with US and CS_2 with CS_1 is necessary for second order conditioning. (Data from Rashotte et al., 1977)

the necessity of CS_1–US pairing for the second order conditioning. Figure 5–5 shows that no CS_2 responding occurred in this group. Thus, this experiment shows that pairing in both stages of the experiment (P-P) was necessary for second order conditioning to develop.

Second order conditioning has been investigated in other paradigms and is, for example, obtained in nictitating membrane conditioning (Kehoe, Feyer, & Moses 1981) and readily obtained in fear conditioning (e.g., Rescorla, 1980). Second order conditioning also seems to follow many of the parametric relations obtained in first order conditioning. For example, a CS_1 paired with a more intense US is more effective in second order conditioning than a CS_1 paired with a less intense US (O'Connell & Rashotte, 1982); CS_1–CS_2 interval functions may parallel CS_1–US interval functions (Kehoe et al., 1981); intermittent reinforcement may produce an acquisition decrement when measured on a per-trial basis (Rashotte, Marshall, & O'Connell, 1981); and trace conditioning is less effective than delay conditioning (Popik, Stern, & Frey, 1979).

Second order conditioning may also be used as an analytic device to answer practical and theoretical questions about Pavlovian conditioning. One such use of the second order paradigm is to reveal the presence of otherwise behaviorally silent associations. For example, if a tone is used to signal the impending availability of grain for pigeons, no pecking behavior develops to this diffuse auditory stimulus (note that this is like the autoshaping paradigm, but there is no localized CS). However, if this tone is used as CS_1 and paired with an illuminated disc as CS_2, then pecking will eventually develop to the disc. Since the tone serves to reinforce CS_2, the animals must have formed an association between it and the US, but this association was not observable in pecking behavior (Nairne & Rescorla, 1981). More detailed presentaton of second order conditioning research may be found in Rashotte (1981) and Rescorla (1980).

SENSORY PRECONDITIONING

We have seen ample evidence that an association is formed when a CS and a US are presented in specified temporal relationships. The presence of the association is indicated in behavior by the development of a CR. Sometimes an association is behaviorally silent but we have seen that special techniques (e.g., second order conditioning or tests for inhibition) may be used to examine for the presence of a behaviorally silent association. Now, what happens if two "neutral" stimuli are presented together under conditions that would normally lead to the formation of an association if one of the stimuli were a US? Is an association formed? For example, what if a bell and a light are paired? Will an animal learn the signaling relationship between the two even though neither has any particular biological importance?

The procedure used to study the possible development of associations between neutral stimuli is termed sensory preconditioning, a procedure apparently developed independently by Pavlov in the early 1930's (Kimmel, 1977) and by Brogden (1939). The basic procedure in these experiments is outlined in the table below.

Phase 1	Phase 2	Phase 3
S_1	S_2	S_1
S_2	US	

An experiment by Pfautz, Donegan, and Wagner (1978) illustrates the procedure as well as a control condition that helps to assess the degree of sensory preconditioning. In the first phase of the experiment subjects received a tone (S_1) paired with a light (S_2). The tone was 30 seconds in duration and terminated at the onset of the light, which was ten seconds in duration. Sixteen of these pairings were given. In the second phase, S_2 (the light) was paired with shock in a conditioned fear procedure. The light was presented for 10 seconds and terminated with the onset of a 0.5 second shock. Eight such trials were administered. In the third phase of the study, S_1 (the tone) was presented. The tone had never been paired with shock. The question of interest was whether the tone would suppress food related behavior. The degree of suppression in behavior produced by various conditions in this experiment is shown in Figure 5–6.

The left bar shows how much behavior was suppressed by S_2, the stimulus directly paired with shock. Presentation of S_2 led to an approximate 88-percent reduction in behavior. The right bar shows how much the preconditioned stimulus S_1, which had been paired with S_2, reduced behavior. There was an approximate 42-percent reduction when this stimulus was presented. Thus, even though S_1 was never paired with shock, it became an effective suppressor of behavior.

A sensory preconditioning interpretation of these data is that the animals had learned, in stage 1, that the tone (S_1) and the light (S_2) were associated, and in stage 2 that the light (S_2) and the shock were associated. The presentation of the tone in stage 3 then elicited the chain of associations tone–light–shock and the animals did what they do in the presence of a stimulus correlated with the occurrence of shock—they decreased their responding for food. Note, however, that the suppression to S_1 was not as great as it was to S_2, the stimulus directly paired with the shock US.

Several different control conditions may be used to assess the degree of sensory preconditioning. For example, a group of animals could be exposed to stage 2 conditions only, then presented with S_1 as a novel stimulus in stage

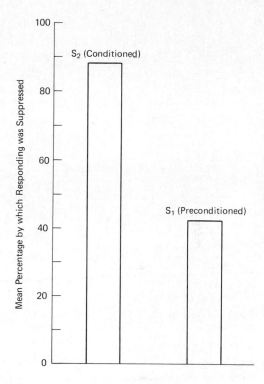

FIGURE 5–6 Sensory Preconditioning. Percentage by which behavior was suppressed by presentation of different stimuli: S_2 was
directly paired with shock; S_1
was a preconditioned stimulus; it
was paired with S_2 prior to the
pairing of S_2 with shock. (Redrawn
from Pfautz et al., 1978)

3. The S_1 from a paired group should show better evidence of conditioning
than S_1 from the control group if sensory preconditioning occurred.[4]

Other recent studies of sensory preconditioning using paired flavors in
the conditioned aversion paradigm may be found in Rescorla (1980) and in
Gillette and Bellingham (1982). The importance of the sensory preconditioning research is that it shows that animals may learn associations between relatively neutral stimuli and that the associations may not be apparent in the
animals' behavior, but they can be exposed if appropriate test conditions are
devised.

[4] Pfautz et al. (1978) used a more complex control condition. The same animals that had S_1
and S_2 paired in stage 1 had two other stimuli, S_3 and S_4, also paired. Trials on which S_1 and S_2
were presented together alternated trials on which S_3 and S_4 were presented together. During
stage 2, however, only S_2 was paired with the shock US; S_4 was not presented. In stage 3, the
test for sensory preconditioning, S_3 was presented on some trials and S_1 on other trials—S_3 resulted in about an 18-percent reduction in bar-pressing behavior. Thus the sensory preconditioning treatment led to greater suppression (42 percent) than the control condition, but it is also
clear from the control condition that some suppression would be expected even without the US
pairings in stage 2. Thus, the overall suppression due to sensory preconditioning may be rather
small.

Students often confuse the second order conditioning procedure and the sensory preconditioning procedure. The difference is principally one of sequence. In the sensory preconditioning procedure two "neutral" stimuli are first paired, then one of them is paired with a US, and then the other is tested. In the second order conditioning procedure the pairing with the US comes in the first stage; in the second stage the two CSs are presented. In sensory preconditioning two events are associated before either one of them is "important" and then one of them is made important. In second order conditioning one event is first made important (by pairing it with a US) and then its importance is transferred to another neutral event.

CONDITIONED DRUG EFFECTS

Conditioned Tolerance

The repeated administration of pharmacological agents often leads to the development of tolerance. That is, with repeated exposure, more and more of the drug is needed to produce the original effect. This lessening of the effectiveness of a drug with repeated administration may be due to a number of metabolic changes that occur as a result of experience with the drug. Recently, a body of research has developed which indicates that there may also be a learned component to drug tolerance (e.g., Krasnegor, 1978). Many of these studies indicate a role for Pavlovian conditioning processes in tolerance development. The essence of this evidence is that tolerance may be situation specific. [That is, animals may show tolerance to a drug only in the environment in which they have experienced the drug.] In a different environment they are not tolerant to the drug. If tolerance had a simple metabolic basis it would be expected that tolerance would be the same in all circumstances.

Morphine Analgesia

The analgesic (pain-reducing) properties of morphine make it a drug that is frequently used in medicine. However, when morphine is administered repeatedly, tolerance develops to its analgesic effects. The development of tolerance may be seen in several ways. For example, when tolerance develops, higher doses of the drug are required to produce the same degree of pain reduction. Alternatively, if the same dose of the drug is administered it has less and less pain-killing effect with repeated administration.

There are several physiological mechanisms that may account for tolerance (e.g., more rapid metabolism of the drug). Of particular interest, though, is recent evidence that some aspects of tolerance may involve Pavlovian conditioning. The evidence that supports such a conclusion is that tolerance to morphine, at low and intermediate doses, has been shown to be situation specific. That is, animals that are repeatedly injected with morphine and develop tolerance will demonstrate that tolerance only in the environment in which the drug has been injected. If rats are repeatedly injected with morphine and then tested for tolerance in an environment different from that in which they had received their injections, they show little evidence of tolerance (Siegel, 1976, 1978; Siegel, Hinson, & Krank, 1978; Tiffany & Baker, 1981).

An example of this effect is shown in Figure 5–7. In this experiment pain sensitivity was measured by putting pressure on the paw of a rat. The pressure at which the rat withdrew its paw was used as an indication of pain sensitivity—the lower the withdrawal pressure, the more sensitive the rat was to pain. The Figure illustrates the results obtained with two groups of animals that had a number of morphine injections. The group labeled "same" was given a morphine injection and then a pain sensitivity test in the same environment in which it had always received the morphine injections. The group labeled "different" was given a morphine injection and tested in an environment different from that in which it had received its past morphine injections. The Figure shows that the animals in the "same" group withdrew their paws at a lower pressure than the animals in the "different" group. Since both groups received the same morphine injections, these data show that the pain-killing properties of morphine were reduced in the environment where animals had a history of receiving the morphine (the "same" environment). That is, the animals showed more tolerance to morphine in the "same" environment than in the "different" environment. It is this situation-specificity of tolerance that indicates a role for conditioning—the situation (environment) is acting as a CS and the morphine is the US.

What is the basis of this apparently learned tolerance? Siegel's interpretation is that the predictive relationship between a CS and a drug allows for

FIGURE 5–7 Test for conditioning of morphine tolerance. The Figure shows the amount of pressure (grams-gm) that it was necessary to apply before rats would move their paws. Both groups were injected with morphine, the "same" group in an environment where they had a history of morphine injections, the "different" group in an environment different from where they had received previous morphine injections. The "same" group was more sensitive to pain (more tolerant to the analgesic effects of morphine). This "same" group withdrew their paws after 100 grams of pressure was applied, whereas 300 grams was necessary in the "different" group. (Data from Siegel, 1978)

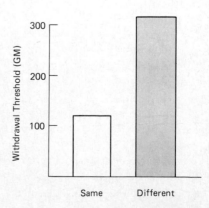

the development of a CR that functions to offset the effects of the drug. It is this opposing or "compensatory" CR that is at the basis of tolerance—it is why more and more of the drug is needed to produce the same effect. Krank, Hinson, and Siegel (1981) reported some behavioral evidence for such a CR that opposes the effects of morphine. In this study, rats were injected with a placebo (saline) in the environment in which they had a history of morphine injections. This procedure is analogous to a test trial for conditioning in the usual Pavlovian experiment. That is, the CS is presented (the environment plus the injection procedure) but the US (morphine) is not presented. The results showed that animals presented with the CS-only were hyperalgesic— they were more sensitive to pain than normal. This greater sensitivity to pain is consistent with the idea that the CR opposes the effects of morphine (which reduces sensitivity to pain). The physiological basis of such a hyperalgesic CR is not yet known.

In summary, Siegel's model of morphine tolerance is that the environment in which a drug is administered functions as a CS, the drug functions as a US, the normal effect of the drug (analgesia in this case) is the UR, and a CR develops, over trials, that opposes the effects of the US—thus diminishing the effectiveness of the drug. Changing the environment is equivalent to changing the CS and should therefore lead to a reduced CR (see Figure 3–3 for the effects of changing the CS in a more typical Pavlovian experiment).

An important prediction of this conditioning interpretation of morphine tolerance is that extinction should take place. That is, once tolerance develops it should be extinguishable. This is not a prediction that would be made by a pure physiological interpretation of tolerance. Some evidence in support of the extinction of tolerance has been reported (Siegel, Sherman, & Mitchell, 1980). In this study rats were first made tolerant to the analgesic effects of morphine by repeated injections in a particular environment. Then one group of rats was extinguished, that is, they were repeatedly exposed to the conditioning environment but injected with a placebo. This amounted to presentation of the CS without the US. A second group was just rested for an equivalent period of time. In a test for tolerance it was found that the extinguished group had lost its tolerance to morphine but the group that was just allowed to rest had not lost its tolerance. This is a particularly interesting result since previous data had indicated that morphine tolerance dissipates very little with the passage of time (Siegel, 1978). The conditioning interpretation indicates that tolerance may be removed fairly quickly by the application of the extinction procedure.

Other data that support a conditioning interpretation of tolerance include the findings that partially reinforced animals take longer to acquire tolerance than continuously reinforced animals (see Chapter 4), and that preexposing animals to the CS retards the development of tolerance (Siegel, 1978). One caution that should be mentioned is that the evidence available thus far supporting the conditioning interpretation of morphine tolerance has been derived principally with relatively low doses of morphine.

Ethanol Hypothermia

The injection of alcohol produces a drop in body temperature (hypothermia). With repeated injections the degree of hypothermia decreases gradually, that is, tolerance develops to the hypothermic effects of ethanol administration. It has been shown that this tolerance development is importantly influenced by signalling stimuli. On a test day, animals injected in the presence of cues that have always been paired with ethanol injection show more tolerance than animals injected in a stimulus context different from that in which they usually received the alcohol injection (Crowell, Hinson, & Siegel, 1981; Lè, Poulos, & Cappel, 1979). Thus, the presence of a cue that predicts the injection seems to be important for the full appearance of tolerance.

Is an opposing, compensatory, response the basis for this tolerance? Lè and his colleagues (1979) tested for this by giving animals a placebo injection (saline) in a stimulus context where they had usually received ethanol. They found that the placebo injection led to a rise in body temperature if it was given in the presence of cues that usually predicted alcohol, but the placebo injection did not result in an increase in body temperature if it was given in the presence of stimuli that had not been paired with alcohol. Similar results were noted by Crowell and his colleagues (1981). The rise in body temperature seen when the placebo injection is given is a CR—it is a CR that opposes the hypothermic UR produced by ethanol. Thus, these data support Siegel's hypothesis that conditioned drug tolerance is due to the development of a CR that acts to oppose the effects of the drug.[5]

A number of other studies have also obtained data that support the idea that at least a component of drug tolerance is due to Pavlovian conditioning (e.g., Bardo, Wellman, & Hughes, 1981; Mansfield & Cunningham, 1980; Siegel, 1977; Tiffany & Baker, 1981). This theory has important practical implications. Consider human addiction. If tolerance in humans is situation specific, then addicts to a drug such as heroin (where addiction involves tolerance) may run the risk of a drug overdose if the drug is administered under atypical environmental conditions. That is, if the effects of the drug are not signaled by the usual stimuli, then the compensatory CR may not develop and, as a result, the usual drug dose will have effects much greater than usual. Although specification of signaling stimuli in humans is much more

---

[5] Eikelboom and Stewart (1982) have proposed that apparent compensatory CRs may be due to the conditioning of homeostatic mechanisms activated by the disequilibrating effects of a drug. CRs that mimic the UR, on the other hand, may be due to the conditioning of the direct effects of the drug on the central nervous system.

complex than in animals (because for example ideas may be signaling stimuli) there is some evidence that conditioning factors may play a role in death from drug overdose (Siegel et al., 1982).

Other Conditioned Drug Effects

Morphine Hyperthermia

Drug effects other than tolerance may be conditioned. For example, morphine, in addition to its analgesic effect, has a hyperthermic effect. It acts to raise body temperature. Sherman (1979) and others have shown that this hyperthermic effect of morphine may be conditioned, so that after a number of pairings of a CS with morphine, the CS will act to raise body temperature independent of a morphine injection.

Cocaine Sensitization

When cocaine is used there seems to be a sensitizing effect rather than the development of tolerance; thus the behavioral effects of cocaine are augmented with repeated use of the same dose (e.g., Post et al., 1980). There is now some evidence that this sensitizing effect may also be context specific. Hinson and Poulos (1981) found that the sensitization effect is more likely to occur if the cocaine is administered in the presence of cues normally paired with the drug than if the cocaine is administered in the presence of different cues. Furthermore, these investigators found that the sensitization effects are extinguishable if a placebo is administered in the presence of the usual drug-correlated stimuli.

Methadone Withdrawal

Another study of drug conditioning to be considered is one of conditioned narcotic withdrawal symptoms. In this study former heroin addicts (humans) were maintained on daily doses of methadone, a synthetic narcotic. During conditioning, different subjects were injected with either naloxone, a narcotic antagonist, or saline. The administration of naloxone caused mild withdrawal symptoms, which included decreased skin temperature, running nose, tearing, and increased heart rate and respiratory rate. The injections of the drug were paired with a compound CS consisting of odor plus a tone. On test trials for conditioning, all subjects were administered saline injections in the presence of the CS. The results of the experiment showed that the CS had acquired the ability to elicit withdrawal symptoms (O'Brien et al., 1977). That is, under the influence of the CS the subjects behaved as if they had been injected with naloxone, which blocks the effects of methadone, rather than with saline, which has no physiological consequences.

Hypoglycemia

Insulin is a hormone normally released by the pancreas to aid in the metabolism of food. One of the principal functions of insulin is to aid in the removal of sugar (glucose) from the blood and to promote its use by body tissue and its storage in the liver. If insulin is injected it too will act to remove glucose from the blood. Some diabetics need insulin injections because their own production of insulin is deficient and, as a result, their blood sugar levels are too high. Thus, the injection of insulin in diabetics helps to restore blood glucose to normal levels.

The injection of insulin when blood sugar is already at a normal level will produce a condition of low blood sugar—hypoglycemia. There is substantial evidence that hypoglycemia produced by insulin injection is conditionable. That is, if rats are given several insulin injections in a particular stimulus context, and then are injected with a placebo (saline) in that context, their blood glucose levels will show a drop. The effects are not as great as when insulin itself is injected, but the decline is statistically reliable (e.g., Flaherty et al., 1980; Woods, 1972; Woods & Kulkosky, 1976). Animals given only saline injections do not show a drop in blood sugar.

There is also some evidence that the natural release of insulin may be conditionable. Animals fed only once per day and always at the same time show higher levels of insulin at that time of day than at other times (Woods et al., 1977).

It is not known at the present time whether or not the occurrence of hypoglycemic conditioning has any practical relevance. One interesting observation, though, is that a hypoglycemic condition may be correlated with increased irritableness and aggression (Davis et al., 1978). Thus, the possibility that blood sugar levels may be influenced by psychological factors (expectancies brought about by conditioning) may have potential practical importance.[6]

The mechanisms of drug conditioning are not yet understood, nor are the factors that determine what type of CR will be conditioned (i.e., one that opposes the effects of the drug, or one that mimics the effects of the drug). (This latter issue is reviewed in Eikelboom and Stewart, 1982.) However, it is clear that drug conditioning is a very important area of research. All medication as well as "recreational" drugs are consumed in some stimulus context. An understanding of what effects to expect from a medication or other drug

---

[6] In some circumstances a conditioned rise in blood glucose (hyperglycemia) may be obtained (Flaherty et al., 1980; Siegel, 1972, 1975). The factors that determine whether conditioned hypoglycemia or conditioned hyperglycemia will be obtained are not yet known.

may depend, in part, upon the conditionability of the physiological effects of the drug and on the directionality of that conditioning.

BRAIN MECHANISMS AND CONDITIONING

This is not a textbook about physiological psychology. However, there is now increased interest and progress in understanding the neural substrate of conditioning, and it would seem reasonable to present some of the relevant evidence in a textbook about learning. The presentation will not be detailed and will be confined, for the most part, to brain structures that are usually described in an introductory psychology course.

Cortical Mechanisms

Pavlov's principal interest in conditioning was in using the technique to develop an understanding of the functioning of the brain, particularly the cerebral hemispheres. Ironically, there is now substantial evidence which indicates that the cortex is probably not necessary for the formation of at least some types of Pavlovian associations. For example, a series of studies by Oakley and Russell (e.g., 1976, 1977) has shown that removal of the cortex in rabbits does not seriously interfere with the development of a conditioned nictitating membrane response, nor does it hinder an already learned response if the cortex is removed after the learning has taken place. In fact, rabbits without a neocortex actually perform better in a discrimination task than do normal rabbits. Recent evidence also indicates that the areas of the cortex underlying taste sensitivity are not essential for the development of conditioned food aversions (Braun et al., 1982). These results do not rule out the possibility that the cortex may be necessary for Pavlovian conditioning involving other procedures, such as trace conditioning (Thompson et al., 1983).

The Limbic System

The limbic system is a subcortical group of structures that borders on the cortex ("limbic" means border). Many of the structures in this system are known to be involved in emotions and motivation. There is also recent evidence that some of them are involved in some way with nictitating membrane conditioning. In particular, the hippocampus seems to function as a monitor of some sort during the conditioning process. For example, the data presented in Figure 5–8 show nictitating membrane responses and levels of neural activity in the hippocampus at two stages of conditioning. The left part of the Figure portrays events early in conditioning. At this stage, presentation of the US (air puff) causes closure of the nictitating membrane and a correlated increase in activity in the hippocampus. There is no response to the CS.

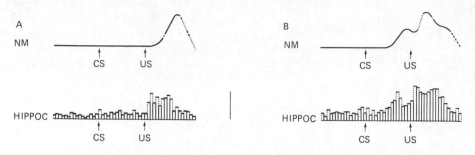

FIGURE 5–8 Conditioning of hippocampal neural activity. Left side: nictitating membrane response and hippocampal activity to CS and US early in conditioning. Only a UR occurs. Right side: nictitating membrane response and hippocampal activity later in conditioning. A CR occurs in both nictitating membrane and hippocampal activity. (Data from Berger, Clark, & Thompson, 1980)

The right portion of the Figure portrays events later in conditioning. Now there is a CR elicited by the CS. The CR is clearly visible in the nictitating membrane activity as an anticipatory closure—anticipatory to the presentation of the US. There is also activity in the hippocampus correlated with the occurrence of the behavioral CR. The hippocampal activity in both UR and CR precedes the nictitating membrane response (Berger, Clark, & Thompson, 1980).

These data and several other studies show that there is a strong correlation between neural activity in the hippocampus and the development of nictitating CRs. In fact, the hippocampal activity precedes the occurrence of the behavioral response, and the level of a particular type of neural activity in the hippocampus may be used to predict accurately which animals will develop CRs (Berger & Thompson, 1977; Berry & Thompson, 1978; Thompson et al., 1980).

There is a puzzle in these data, however. Lesions of the hippocampus or its closely related structure, the septum, do not prevent the occurrence of conditioning, and, in some cases, hardly affect it at all (Berry & Thompson, 1979; Moore, 1979; Schmaltz & Theios, 1972; Solomon, 1977; Solomon et al., 1983). Destruction of the hippocampus does eliminate the retarded acquisition that normally follows CS preexposure, and some other forms of habituation (Leaton, 1981), but conditioning itself is not greatly affected. What then is the function of the hippocampus in conditioning?

Some indication that an intact hippocampus does influence conditioning was provided by a recent study which showed that altering the normal neural activity of the hippocampus by administering a drug (scopolamine) seriously retarded nictitating membrane conditioning (Solomon et al., 1983). What this may mean is that the hippocampus is involved in some parallel conditioning circuits. Removal of the hippocampus would allow conditioning to proceed normally in the alternative circuits. However, disrupting the activity of an intact hippocampus may adversely influence operations in the parallel circuits. Evidence of parallel pathways in conditioning has been obtained in research with pigeons by Cohen (e.g., Cohen & Goff, 1978).

The role of the hippocampus may become more important when conditioning procedures that place greater demands on the animal are used. For example, some evidence indicates that the presence of the hippocampus is essential for trace conditioning, but not for delayed conditioning (Weisz, Solomon, & Thompson, 1980). Thus, the evidence indicates that the hippocampus must play some role in the conditioning process. That role may vary with the type of conditioning but an understanding of the role awaits further research.

The Midbrain and Brain Stem

There is evidence from lesioning and electrical stimulation studies that the locus of nictitating membrane conditioning may be in the phylogenetically primitive brain stem. Conditioning may involve the reticular formation, a part of the brain known to be important for arousal and consciousness, and the abducens nucleus (VI cranial nerve), the nerve group that controls the nictitating membrane response (Mis, 1977; Mis, Gormezano, & Harvey, 1979; Moore, 1979; Powell, Berthier, & Moore, 1979). However, the strongest evidence supporting the involvement of lower brain structures in conditioning concerns the cerebellum, a structure usually thought of in terms of its function in motor coordination. It has been shown that the electrical activity of one part of the cerebellum, the dentate nucleus, models the behavioral conditioning process (Thompson et al., 1983). That is, the development of a conditioned nictitating membrane response is paralleled by the development of neural activity in the dentate nucleus that corresponds to the conditioned response. These electrical changes in the cerebellum precede the behavioral response on each trial by a substantial period of time (.05 seconds). Furthermore, lesions of this area of the brain eliminate the conditioned response but do not influence the unconditioned response. This latter finding is important because it shows that the animals are still capable of the nictitating membrane response after the lesion. Thus, the lesion is not eliminating conditioning simply because it is interfering with the motor system. Thompson and his colleagues believe that these data imply that an important part of the memory trace controlling the conditioned nictitating membrane response is localized in the cerebellum.

Other Research

David Cohen and his colleagues have carried out an extensive series of studies investigating the neural basis of heart rate conditioning in the pigeon. The heart rate CR in the pigeon, when a shock is used as the US, is acceleration. Cohen and his colleagues have determined that the sympathetic branch of the autonomic nervous system is the principal contributor to the acceleratory CR. This research has also indicated a likely output path of the CR, which involves the brain stem, the hypothalamus, and a part of the pigeon brain that corresponds to the amygdala in mammals. (The amygdala is another part of the limbic system in the mammalian brain.) Lesions of the avian amygdala or the hypothalamus prevent the development of the heart rate CR.

In the input side, Cohen has traced the possible pathways of the visual CS used in his research. There are three pathways through which visual information could reach the higher brain areas from the pigeon's retina. If all three are lesioned, conditioning cannot take place. But, if any one of the three is left functioning conditioning may still occur. This result indicates parallel and substitutable routes for the CS involvement in associations.

Cohen has also recorded neural activity from various structures in the visual system and found a number of neurons whose activity changes as a function of conditioning. An interesting aspect of these data is that the neurons that show conditioned changes respond to both the CS and the US before conditioning. Their response rate to the CS is augmented as a result of the paired presentation of the CS and US (Cohen & Goff, 1978, 1980; Gibbs, Cohen, Broyles, & Solina, 1981; Wall et al., 1980).

CHAPTER SUMMARY

In this chapter we have reviewed several topics in Pavlovian conditioning. A CS may be made to function as an inhibitory stimulus if it is correlated with the absence of the US. Evidence relevant to five ways of producing this negative correlation was considered. The five ways are: explicitly unpaired CS and US, randomly presented CS and US, trace conditioning, long delay conditioning, and discrimination training.

An inhibitory CS retards acquisition, interferes with the effects of an excitatory stimulus in a summation test, and often elicits withdrawal behavior. Extinguished CSs and preexposed CSs were not inhibitory by these criteria.

In the second order conditioning procedure a CS that has been paired with a US will come to function like a US itself in that it will support new learning to a different CS. The sensory preconditioning procedure is used to show that an association may be formed between two neutral stimuli.

There are a variety of conditioned effects that may develop when drugs are administered. In some cases drug tolerance may be influenced by conditioning processes, as seems to be the case with morphine analgesia and ethanol hypothermia. In other cases a CS paired with a drug will come to have effects like the drug itself. Several examples of this effect were reviewed.

Pavlovian conditioning, at least of the nictitating membrane response and conditioned food aversions, seems not to require the cerebral cortex.

Pavlovian
Theoreti
Practi

Neural activity in limbi[c]
tures, is highly correlate[d]
occurrence. However, t[he]
ing. There is some evid[ence]
old parts of the brain—t[he]
conditioning in pigeons
tioning and the possibil[ity]
respond to both the CS

By conditioning selectively to good predictors of reinforcement . . . animals succeed in attributing events of consequence to their most probable causes.

N. J. Mackintosh, 1978

The preceding chapters in Pavlovian conditioning have presented many examples of how a stimulus comes to possess new properties after it has been presented in conjunction with some biologically important event. A simple light may be turned into a stimulus that causes an animal to blink its eyes, to salivate, to experience a change in heart rate, to release various hormones of stress. It may be converted into a stimulus that an animal approaches or one from which an animal withdraws. A preferred flavor such as saccharin may be converted into one which apparently nauseates an animal (or human). A potential pet such as a fuzzy animal may be converted into an object that elicits fear. What is the essential characteristic of these different examples of learning? What do these various examples of Pavlovian conditioning have in common? Why does Pavlovian conditioning occur?

CONTIGUITY AND CONTINGENCY

One way to approach a theoretical understanding of Pavlovian conditioning is to examine what is necessary for its occurrence. A factor that has been implicated from the time of earliest speculation about associative learning is contiguity (see Chapter 3). In Chapter 4 substantial data were presented showing that, indeed, the temporal relationship between CS and US presentation is important for the development of a CR. However, these data also indicated that the effects of such temporal relationships are not simple. How close in time a CS and US must occur apparently depends on what is being conditioned, an eyeblink or nausea, for example.

In the next section evidence will be considered which indicates that temporal contiguity between the CS and US may not, in itself, be sufficient to produce learning.

Blocking

A series of experiments published in 1969 by Kamin found that CS–US contiguity did not lead to conditioning when the following procedure was used: Animals were first trained with a noise as a CS paired with shock as a

US. In the second stage of this experiment the same noise-CS was presented simultaneously with a light, and both were paired with a shock US. In the final stage of the experiment the light *or* noise was presented alone—without the US. The results showed that the noise elicited a CR, but the light did not. The important aspect of these experiments was the failure of the light to develop an association with the shock, despite the fact that the two were presented contiguously in the second stage of the experiment. These experiments have had an important influence on theories of conditioning so they will be considered in some detail.

The general method involved training rats to press a lever for a food reward that was delivered only intermittently. This procedure led to steady rates of responding in the rats over a two hour test session. After the animals had had extensive experience in this situation, four CS–US pairings were introduced during each daily session. The CS and US were scheduled to occur independently of the animals' bar-pressing behavior. That is, pressing the lever had no effect on the occurrence or nonoccurrence of the CS and US, and similarly, the CS and US did not affect the availability of food for lever pressing. The CS was typically 3 minutes long and was followed immediately by a 1 mA electric shock for 0.5 second as the US. The dependent variable was an index of how much the rat suppressed its bar pressing during the CS. The CS itself was either a white noise (N), a light (L), or a compound stimulus made up of both the light and the noise (LN).

Kamin's experimental approach was to determine whether prior experience with one element of a compound CS would prevent the second element from acquiring control over behavior when it was subsequently presented in compound with the first element. A typical experimental design and results are illustrated in Table 6–1. There were three groups. Group 1 was first given 16 noise–shock pairings, then 8 pairings of the noise–light compound with the shock, and finally they were given a test trial with the light alone. As is apparent from the data presented in Table 6–1, the light did not function as an effective CS for this group—it did not suppress behavior. However, in Group 2, which received only the 8 light–noise compound trials, the presentation of the light alone in the test phase led to virtually complete suppression of responding. Thus, the comparison of Group 1 and Group 2 shows that prior experience with one element of the compound CS *blocked* the other element from acquiring control over the animals' behavior.

The extent of this blocking is evident in the comparison of Groups 1 and 3. Group 1, which had 8 trials with the light in compound, paired with shock was equivalent in SR to Group 3, which never experienced the light. Neither showed suppression to the light. Thus, despite the fact that both Groups 1 and 2 received 8 contiguous pairings of the light (in compound with the noise) and shock, they differed radically in the degree to which the light led to behavioral suppression. Group 2 showed nearly complete suppression; Group 1 showed essentially no suppression.

	TABLE 6–1			

Suppression ratios (SR) obtained in three groups of rats trained in a conditioned fear experiment. The CS was either a light (L), a noise (N), or a compound stimulus composed of the light and noise presented simultaneously (LN). The US was a shock. The US was paired with the CS in Phases I and II. As a test for conditioning the light was presented alone following Phase II. The suppression ratios refer to this test. A suppression ratio close to 0.50 indicates no suppression (equal responding both before and during the CS); suppression ratios close to 0.0 indicate a lack of responding during the CS. The lower the suppression ratio, the more the conditioning that occurred to the light. (Modified from Kamin, 1969)

	Phase I	Phase II	Test	SR
Group 1	N (16)	LN (8)	L	.45
Group 2	—	LN (8)	L	.05
Group 3	—	N (24)	L	.44

In other experiments Kamin demonstrated that the blocking effect is a function of pretraining with one of the stimuli, and it doesn't make much difference whether the light or the noise is used as the pretraining stimulus, because one blocks the acquisition of conditioning by the other stimulus. If only the compound training is given, and then each stimulis is presented separately, each is found to have acquired some degree of conditioning. Thus, in Kamin's experiments, it is clearly the pretraining that produces the blocking.

To what is this blocking due? One possibility entertained by Kamin was that the animal does not notice or perceive the second stimulus in the compound because its "attention is focused" on the first element. A second possibility is that the animal does notice the second element, but does not condition to it because it is redundant. Evidence against the first possibility was obtained when Kamin examined the animals' behavior on the *first trial* in which the compound stimulus was presented. He found that the group that had the light added to the noise CS showed less suppression of behavior than animals that continued with noise alone. It is important to note that the behavioral measure was taken during the three-minute CS–US interval, before the US was presented. Therefore, the animals' behavior had changed because of the addition of the light to the noise, not because of any effects of the US event, which had not yet occurred. Thus, the animals must have perceived the light.

Because of this observation, Kamin favored the second interpretation; that is, if nothing new is predicted by the added stimulus, then it will not acquire any associative strength. In Kamin's experiments the noise already predicted the occurrence of the shock; the added light was thus redundant as a predictor of this US. Kamin argued that the US must be surprising to the animal in order for learning to take place. If the US is already predicted by the noise CS, it is not surprising and the added light CS does not become conditioned.

Many experiments have been conducted to test this idea of surprise or predictability. A common procedure is to change the US at the same time that the extra CS is added. If the US is different it should not be adequately predicted by the original CS, and therefore the added CS should become conditioned. This is the case. Blocking is reduced—if the US is increased in intensity when the compound trials are introduced (Kamin, 1969); if a second brief shock is presented a short time after the first (e.g., Dickinson, Hall, & Mackintosh, 1976; Dickinson & Mackintosh, 1979); if an additional CS is presented shortly after the end of the compound trial (Gray & Appignanesi, 1973); if an expected US is omitted on compound trials (e.g., Dickinson et al., 1976; Kremer, 1980; Mackintosh, Dickinson, & Cotton, 1980) or if an expected second US is delayed briefly from its usual time of occurrence (Dickinson et al., 1976). Thus, changes in the US event lead to conditioning of the added stimulus (a reduction in blocking). This result supports Kamin's hypothesis that conditioning occurs when the US is not completely predicted by the CS.

But note that this also means that contiguity alone is not sufficient for conditioning. The blocking data indicate that a CS must not only be contiguous with a US, it must also be informative—it must predict something not already predicted by other stimuli present.

Contingency

The idea that predictability is important in Pavlovian conditioning was also suggested by Rescorla (1966, 1967b, 1968). The idea of a predictive relationship between the CS and US has been formulated in terms of *contingency*. Contingency means a dependence or a correlation. There is a contingent relationship between the occurrence of rain and certain other weather conditions, particularly the presence of clouds. Thus, the presence of clouds, to some degree, predicts the occurrence of rain. There is a contingent relationship between conception and sexual intercourse (except in special cases of artificial insemination). Note that a contingency may be probabilistic—it does not rain every time that there are clouds, nor (fortunately) does conception result from every instance of sexual intercourse. Yet, even though the relationship is only probable—not certain—there is the contingency. It does not rain without clouds and there is no conception without intercourse.

Rescorla expressed the importance of CS–US contingency in Pavlovian conditioning in terms of a pair of conditional probabilities: the probability that the US would occur given that a CS had occurred—written as p(US | CS)—and the probability that a US would occur given that no CS had occurred—written as p(US | $\overline{CS}$). The best way to conceptualize these probabilities is to imagine a training session as being divided into a series of time periods. The example given in Table 6–2 shows a 16-minute training session divided into a stream of two-minute time periods. During each two-minute block a CS could occur, a CS and US could occur, a US could occur, or neither could occur. The top line of the Table shows that CSs were presented during four of these time periods and every time a CS was presented it was accompanied by a US. Thus, the probability of a US occurring, given that a CS had occurred—p(US | CS)—was 1.0, as indicated in the appropriate column in the right-hand part of the Table. On the other hand, in the same training session a US never occurred in any of the two-minute blocks in which *no* CS occurred, therefore p(US | $\overline{CS}$) = 0. This first line of the Table would represent the typical case in conditioning experiments in which the animals were on

---

TABLE 6–2

Manipulation of CS, US contingency. Experimental session is divided into eight two-minute time periods. A CS, a US, both a CS and US, or neither may occur during these periods. The two right-hand columns show probability of a US occurring, given that a CS has occurred, and the probability of a US occurring, given that no CS has occurred.

	Two-minute Time Periods								p(US | CS)	p(US | $\overline{CS}$)
	1	2	3	4	5	6	7	8		

	p(US | CS)	p(US | $\overline{CS}$)
CS / US	1.00	0.0
CS / US	0.50	0.0
CS / US	0.50	0.25
CS / US	0.50	0.50
CS / US	0.0	0.50
CS / US	0.0	1.00

a 100-per cent reinforcement schedule (see Chapter 3). In our weather analogy, this would be the case if it rained every time there were clouds—
p(rain | clouds) = 1.00—and if it never rained in the absence of clouds—
p(rain | $\overline{\text{clouds}}$) = 0.

In the second and third sections in the Table it can be seen that a US
occurred on only two of the four periods in which a CS occurred, thus, p(US |
CS) = 0.50. This would be the case in the usual partial reinforcement experiment in which the animals were on a 50-per cent reinforcement schedule.
However, there is a difference between sections 2 and 3. In section 3 a US
was presented in one of the four two-minute periods in which there was *no*
CS. In other words, there was a 0.25 likelihood that the US would occur in
the absence of the CS. This is not the case in the usual partial reinforcement
experiment. Going back to the weather analogy again, section 3 in the Table
would be interpreted to mean that it rained half the time in which clouds
were present, but it also rained one quarter of the time in which no clouds
were present. The comparison of sections 1–3 gives an appreciation of how
these conditional probabilities are related to predictability. Under the conditions of section 1 there is perfect predictability—every time there is a CS
there is a US (every time there are clouds it rains). In section 2 there is less
predictability since a US occurs only half the time when there is a CS (it rains
only half the time when there are clouds, yet it never rains without clouds).
Thus, although an animal in this situation can't be sure that there will be a
US when a CS is presented, it can be sure that there will be no USs in the
absence of a CS. In section 3, however, predictability is substantially weak-
ened. The US occurs half the time when a CS occurs, and it also occurs one
quarter of the time when there is no CS (as if it could rain with and without
clouds, but it is more likely to rain when there are clouds). The reader can
continue this reasoning down through the Table. For example, in section 4 it
is easy to see that there is no predictability at all afforded by the CS, whereas
in sections 5 and 6 the CS predicts the *absence* of the US.

In general, when p(US | CS) exceeds p(US | $\overline{\text{CS}}$), then the US is to some
degree predictable by the CS. Under these conditions excitatory conditioning
should take place (the CS should come to elicit a CR). When the two probabilities are equal (as in section 4 of Table 6–2), then no learning should take
place. When p(US | CS) is less than p(US | $\overline{\text{CS}}$), then the CS predicts the
absence of the US. Under these conditions inhibitory learning should take
place (the CS should act to suppress the occurrence of a CR; see Chapter 5).
The weather analogy for this latter condition would be that the presence of
clouds indicated a reduced likelihood of rain.

We will now examine two experiments in which these conditional probabilities were manipulated. Keep in mind the relevance of this topic to contiguity—from a contiguity analysis the presentation of the US in the absence
of a CS seems to make no sense. With what is the US contiguous? How could
it influence conditioning?

Examples of Contingency Manipulation

Autoshaping—Gamzu and Williams. Gamzu and Williams (1973) varied conditional probabilities in an autoshaping experiment. Recall that in autoshaping with pigeons a small disc is illuminated shortly before grain becomes available. Under these conditions pigeons will peck at the disc even though such responses are unrelated to the availability of food (see Chapter 4). In the Gamzu and Williams experiment one group of birds was exposed to the conditions labelled "Differential" in Figure 6–1. For these animals the probability of grain being available when the disc was illuminated was only 0.03, but grain was never available when the disc was not illuminated. For a second group the probability of grain being available was 0.03 both when the disc was illuminated and when it was not illuminiated. As the Figure shows, the differential group, for whom $p(US \mid CS) > p(US \mid \overline{CS})$, showed substantially more autoshaped responding (pecks at the disc) than the nondifferential group, for whom $p(US \mid CS) = p(US \mid \overline{CS})$. Thus, animals for whom the CS (disc illumination) was a differential predictor of food acquired the pecking response; animals that had just as many contiguous pairings of the CS with the food, but for whom the CS was not a differential predictor, did not acquire the pecking response.

FIGURE 6–1 Acquisition of autoshaped key-peck response as a function of CS–US contingency. For the differential group the probability of a US (access to grain) occurring given that a CS occurred was 0.03. The probability of a US occurring in the absence of a CS was 0.0 for this group. In the nondifferential group both conditional probabilities equaled 0.03—grain was equally likely to be available in the presence and absence of the CS. (Data from Gamzu & Williams, 1973)

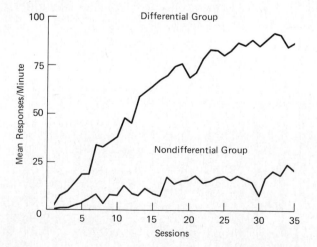

Conditioned Suppression—Rescorla. Our second example of the operation of contingency is derived from a fear conditioning experiment with rats. The experimental procedure employed by Rescorla (1968) was similar to that used in Kamin's experiments. Rats were first trained to press a lever for food under conditions that led to steady rates of responding. Then a CS and a US (shock) were presented in the bar-pressing context. As in Kamin's experiments, the degree of conditioning was indexed by how much the rats suppressed their bar-pressing behavior when the CS was presented.

There were four groups of rats in the portion of Rescorla's experiment that we will examine here. For all of these groups the probability of a US occurring, given that a CS had occurred, was 0.40. This means that only four out of every ten CSs were followed by a US. The four groups differed, however, in how likely they were to experience a US in the absence of a CS. These different $p(US \mid \overline{CS})$ values are indicated in Figure 6–2. Thus, all four groups received an equal number of contiguous CS–US pairings, but they differed in the number of USs presented in the absence of a CS. The results of the experiment presented in Figure 6–2 show that these different likelihoods of "unannounced" US presentations controlled the degree of conditioning. That is, animals for whom $p(US \mid CS) = p(US \mid \overline{CS})$ showed no conditioning (suppression ratio $= 0.5$). The greater the extent that $p(US \mid CS)$ exceeded $p(US \mid \overline{CS})$ the greater was the conditioning (the lower the suppression ratio). In other words, the more predictive the CS was for the occurrence of shock, the more suppression the animals showed in the presence of the CS. This experiment, like the Gamzu and Williams experiment, shows that CS–US contiguity alone is not sufficient to produce conditioning. What seems to be important is the relative likelihood of the US occurring in the presence or absence of the CS. If there is equal likelihood of US occurrence in the presence or in the absence of the CS, then animals do not condition to the CS, no matter how many contiguous pairings of the CS and US they experience. Reverting to the weather analogy—if it is equally likely to rain in the presence or in the absence of clouds, then we might assume that clouds have nothing to do with the occurrence of rain.

The Contingency Space

Figure 6–3 illustrates a way of representing all possible combinations of the two conditional probabilities relevant for the contingency analysis of conditioning. The diagonal line represents points of equality, where $p(US \mid CS) = p(US \mid \overline{CS})$ and where no conditioning is expected to occur. The space above and to the left of the diagonal represents the area in which $p(US \mid CS)$ is greater than $p(US \mid \overline{CS})$ and where excitatory conditioning is expected to occur. The filled circles in the figure represent the values used in the Rescorla (1968) experiment just discussed. Notice that the greater the distance the

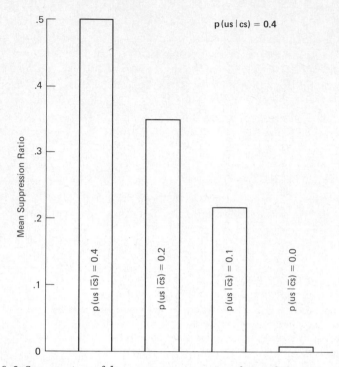

FIGURE 6–2 Suppression of lever pressing in a conditioned fear experiment as a function of CS–US contingencies. For all groups the probability of a shock occurring, given that a CS had occurred, was equal to 0.40 (40% of CS presentations were followed by a shock). The four groups differed in the probability of a shock occurring in the absence of a CS. For Group 0.0 shocks never occurred in the absence of a CS. For the other three groups the probability of a shock occuring in CS absence was 0.1, 0.2, or 0.4. The greater the difference between p(US) | CS) and p(US | CS), the greater the conditioning. When the two were equal, there was no conditioning. (Data from Rescorla, 1968)

circles are above the diagonal the greater the difference between the two conditional probabilities and the greater the degree of excitatory conditioning there was (see Figure 6–2). The value from Rescorla's experiment that is shown on the diagonal represented no conditioning. The space below the diagonal represents conditions in which p(US | CS) is less than p(US | CS), a situation in which inhibitory conditioning is expected to take place.

The contingency space is useful because it captures concisely the essence of the contingency analysis and because it indicates the way to further systematic experiments. The Figure contains clear predictions about the relative degrees of conditioning that should be obtained from selecting different values of the two conditional probabilities.

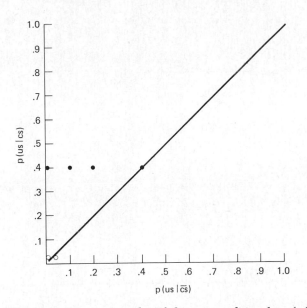

FIGURE 6–3 *The contingency space. Plot of the two conditional probabilities. When they are equal, no conditioning should occur. Excitatory conditioning should occur with values above the diagonal, inhibitory conditioning with values below the diagonal. The filled circles represent data from the Rescorla experiment, the open circles indicate data from the Gamzu and Williams experiment.*

The contingency analysis also has implications regarding the proper control procedures for a Pavlovian conditioning experiment. If the nature of Pavlovian conditioning is that animals learn the predictive relationship between the CS and US, then the proper baseline against which to measure this learning would seem to be a condition where no relationship exists. A condition that satisfies this would be the one represented by the diagonal in Figure 6–3, namely where $p(US \mid CS) = p(US \mid \overline{CS})$. One approach to this baseline condition is to present the CS and US randomly and independently of one another (Rescorla, 1967). Indeed, several experiments have indicated that such a control represents a condition in which no learning takes place, a condition which may be used to evaluate learned contingencies (e.g., Rescorla, 1966).

However, one may wonder if a lack of behavioral change following exposure to random CS–US presentations always indicates a lack of learning (Sheldon, 1973). It could be, for example, that animals exposed to random CS–US presentations learn *something*; they may learn that the CS and US are unrelated to each other and therefore that the CS has no implications regarding the possible occurrence of the US. There are some data that are consistent with the hypothesis that animals exposed to the random presentation of the CS and US may learn that there is no correlation between the two. For example, exposing animals to such random presentations will interfere with subsequent learning that the CS predicts the presence of the US, or subsequent learning that the CS predicts the absence of the US. That is, an experience with uncorrelated presentation of the CS and US interferes with both excitatory and inhibitory conditioning (Baker & Mackintosh, 1977).

This result is consistent with the idea that animals exposed to the random control condition have learned that there is no predictive relationship between the CS and US. Similarly, Baker and Mackintosh (1979) have shown that exposing animals to the random presentation of the CS and US has interfering effects with subsequent learning that are greater than those obtained if the animals are exposed to the CS or US alone. This indicates that the interfering effect on learning produced by the uncorrelated condition is not due simply to the sum of CS-alone preexposure (latent inhibition) and US-alone preexposure (context blocking; see Chapter 4, p. 73) effects. Thus, it may be that animals are able to learn about all three types of correlations: learning that CS predicts the US, learning that the CS predicts the absence of the US, and learning that the CS has no predictive value for the occurrence of the US.

Investigation of the random control condition itself has produced some interesting data. Any random procedure gains its randomness from the way it is produced, and the randomness may be apparent in the long run but not in the short run. For example, if a long table of randomly generated numbers is examined, a short sequence such as 1, 2, 3, 4, 5 may appear at some point in the table—a sequence that does not look random. Similarly, if CS and US presentations are scheduled randomly, it is possible for some "pairings" of the CS and US to occur by chance.

Do such pairings in a random group have any tendency to produce conditioning? They may or may not, depending on when the animal experiences them. Current evidence indicates that the occurrence of chance CS–US pairings early in an experiment tends to produce conditioning, which may then weaken with extended exposure to the random schedule. Furthermore, the occurrence of unpaired USs prior to the occurrence of chance pairings tends to prevent the chance pairings from producing conditioning, and the occurrence of unpaired USs after chance pairings tends to weaken any conditioning produced by the chance pairings.

Although both unpaired CSs and USs may have an effect of opposing conditioning, unpaired USs have a more potent "anti-associative" effect than unpaired CSs. In addition, the occurrence of both unpaired CSs and USs has a greater effect than the occurrence of either alone (Benedict & Ayres, 1972; Keller, Ayres, & Mahoney, 1977; Wasserman et al., 1977). All of these effects of unpaired presentations of the CS and US are consistent with the contingency analysis, that is, unpaired presentations of either stimulus event weaken the contingency (predictive relationship) between the two events.

Summary and Conclusions

Both the blocking and the contingency related experiments show clearly that CS–US contiguity in and of itself is not sufficient to produce conditioning. The various types of unblocking experiments all indicate that conditioning will occur if the added CS predicts something different, that is, if the occurrence of a new event is correlated with the occurrence of the added CS. The contingency experiments also indicate that the CS must differentially predict the occurrence of the US if a CR is to develop.

Random presentations of the CS and US will tend to preclude conditioning. Chance pairings of a CS and US in a random schedule will tend to produce a CR if the chance pairings come early in the animals' experience, but continued exposure to the random schedule will tend to eliminate the effects of early chance pairings. It is possible that animals exposed to an uncorrelated presentation of the CS and US, rather than learning nothing, do learn that the CS and US are, in fact, uncorrelated. However, this contention is difficult to show conclusively.

COGNITIVE INTERPRETATIONS OF PAVLOVIAN CONDITIONING

Introduction

Pavlov's research represented an extension of the concept of a reflex, a concept credited to Descartes (see Chapter 3). Pavlov extended the concept in that he explained conditioning in terms of two reflexes: one innate, the elicitation of the UR by the US; and one based on experience, the elicitation of the CR by the CS. The development of the learned reflex is dependent upon a particular contiguous (or, as we have just seen, contingent) relationship between the CS and US.

Over the years there has been uncertainty as to how best to conceptualize the nature of the associative process in Pavlovian conditioning, and how narrowly to define Pavlovian conditioning. As far as the association is concerned, early American behaviorists (e.g., Watson, 1913; Hull, 1943) tended to consider that an association was formed between the CS and UR, an association apparent in the elicitation of the CR by the CS. The CR was assumed to be, and often is, similar to the UR. However, Pavlov himself wrote as if an association was formed between the CS and US. After such an association was formed, the CS would then substitute somewhat for the US and activate the brain mechanisms controlling the UR. Both the CS–CR reflex interpretation and Pavlov's CS–US stimulus substitution interpretation imply that the CR and UR should be somewhat similar. Current theorists who wish to narrowly define Pavlovian conditioning in the reflex tradition also argue that the CR and UR must be closely related if the behavior in question is to be considered a form of Pavlovian conditioning (Gormezano & Kehoe, 1975).

There is, however, another interpretation possible, one that assumes that Pavlovian conditioning represents just a special case of associative learning (see, for example, Dickinson, 1980; Estes, 1975; Hulse, Fowler, & Honig, 1978). According to this more cognitive view, Pavlovian conditioning is special simply because one of the stimuli entering into a stimulus–stimulus association (the US) happens to reliably elicit a response. This fact allows the course of associative learning (CS–US association) to be traced by following the development of the response to the CS. The cognitive view differs from the narrower reflex view in that any behavior that changes reliably as a result of the pairing of the CS and US will be accepted as reflecting the development of an association (Rescorla, 1975; 1978). It is not necessary that the CR and UR resemble each other.

The difference between cognitive and reflex interpretations of Pavlovian conditioning may, perhaps, be exemplified by returning to an issue introduced at the beginning of Chapter 4, namely, the expansion of the basic Pavlovian paradigm. In that section we indicated that Pavlov had noted a difference between "secretory" behaviors and "motor" behaviors that developed during conditioning. When food was paired with a CS, the CS eventually came to elicit not only salivation, but also a variety of general motor behaviors, which were studied in greater detail by Zener (1937) and Jenkins et al. (1978). These more complex behaviors we termed directed behaviors in that earlier discussion. A reflex interpretation of Pavlovian conditioning would seek to restrict the definition of Pavlovian conditioning to the secretory response, a response that resembles the UR, and develop some other term to refer to the more complex directed behaviors, which do not resemble the UR (Gormezano & Kehoe, 1975). However, a cognitive view would include both directed and reflex behaviors as reflecting the development of a CS–US association.

Thus, from a cognitive view, behavior reflects the development of some underlying association. The association may be reflected behaviorally in a variety of ways, or, sometimes the association may be behaviorally silent, that is, not observed in behavior except under special circumstances. In this regard, cognitive interpretations of conditioning tend to make a distinction between learning and performance; the absence of behavior may not necessarily mean the absence of an association. Let us go on now to further characterize the cognitive view of conditioning.

Responding is Not Necessary for Conditioning

Various kinds of evidence have been adduced to show that the performance of a peripheral response is not necessary for the formation of a Pavlovian association. For example, in the Pavlovian procedure in which a brief shock, paired with a CS, is delivered to a dog's paw, the dog will eventually develop a CR of lifting its leg when the CS is presented (note that this response does not influence the presentation of the US—the animal is still shocked following CS presentation). Is the performance of this response during training necessary for conditioning to take place? Studies in which the spinal motor nerves have been crushed before conditioning, thus preventing the leg-lifting response, have shown that the answer is "no." When the nerves have regenerated, the dogs show a leg-lifting response to the CS even though it was not possible for them to perform this response during the conditioning trials (Light & Gantt, 1936). Similarly, substantially suppressing the degree of cardiac deceleration by using a drug during conditioning does not prevent the formation of a conditioned cardiac deceleratory response—a response that becomes manifest when the drug is no longer administered (Fitzgerald, Martin, & O'Brien, 1973). Nor does the paralysis of an animal with the drug curare prevent the formation of Pavlovian associations which later influence behavior when the drug is no longer acting (Leaf, 1964; Solomon & Turner, 1962).

Further evidence in this regard obtained from autoshaping experiments has been summarized by Hearst (1978). These experiments showed that pigeons exposed to a positive correlation between disc illumination and feeder presentation (i.e., the feeder always followed disc illumination) developed an autoshaped response faster than birds exposed to a negative correlation (i.e., the feeder presentation never followed the disc illumination closely). These results were obtained even though access to the feeder was blocked during the exposure period and even if approach movements in the direction of the feeder did not occur during the exposure period (Browne, 1976). A study found similar results when access to both the disc and feeder was prevented by a transparent barrier during the observation part of the experiment (Parisi & Matthews, 1975).

Another study exposed satiated birds to the positive or negative correlations between the disc and feeder illumination. While they were satiated, birds exposed to the disc and feeder contingencies made very few approaches to either the disc or the feeder, and groups exposed to positive and negative correlations did not differ in their frequency of responding. However, when the birds were food deprived, those subjects that had experienced the positive disc–feeder pairings while they were satiated learned the autoshaping response faster than subjects that had been exposed to the negative correlations (Deeds & Frieman, reported in Hearst, 1978). Also, a study by Boakes and Ismail exposed birds to either correlated or random presentations of the disc illumination and an *empty* food hopper. When food was placed in the food hopper on later trials the subjects that had been exposed to the positive correlation between disc illumination and hopper presentation learned the autoshaping response sooner than subjects that had been exposed to the random presentation of the two events (reported in Hearst, 1978).

In summary, these studies indicate that actual performance of the response is not necessary for the subjects to learn the predictive relationship between the CS and US. These studies favor the hypothesis that a CS–US association is learned in Pavlovian conditioning rather than just a CS–CR association.

Behaviorally Silent Conditioning

In addition to experiments designed to determine the necessity of peripheral responding for conditioning, other studies have also demonstrated that an association may be formed in the absence of any overt behavioral change. The many examples of inhibition considered in Chapter 5 typically represent learning that is not manifest in behavior unless special tests such as the retardation procedure or the summation procedure are used to assay for the presence of learning. This may be so because an inhibitory stimulus has little effect on behavior on its own, but serves principally to modify the effectiveness of excitatory stimuli in producing behavior (Konorski, 1948, as discussed in Rescorla, 1979). That is, an animal may learn that a CS predicts the absence of a US, but such learning may not be manifest in behavior unless there is an opportunity for the inhibitory CS to modify the effectiveness of an excitatory CS. The brakes on a car will serve to stop the car, but this can't be observed unless the car is in motion (has been "excited" by application of the accelerator).

Still another example of a behaviorally silent association was presented in the discussion of second order conditioning in Chapter 5. Nairne and Rescorla (1981) paired a tone with delivery of grain for pigeons. There was no behavioral evidence that the animals had acquired an association between the tone and the delivery of grain. However, it was found that the tone would serve as a reinforcer in a second order paradigm (see Chapter 5), thus indicating that the animals had learned a relationship between the CS and US even though this was not behaviorally observable in the first part of the experiment.

The data on sensory preconditioning also considered in Chapter 5 represent still another example of the formation of associations between events that themselves have little impact on behavior (see the Boakes & Ismail study described previously).

The existence of a learned association may be manifest with some response measures but not with others. For example, VanDercar and Schneiderman (1967) found evidence of conditioning of heart rate changes but little evidence of conditioning of nictitating membrane responses in the same animals when the CS and US were separated by a 6.75-second interval (see Chapter 4). Thus, measurement of the nictitating membrane CR alone would have produced little evidence of the formation of an association, but simultaneous measurement of heart rate showed that the animals had formed as association between the CS and US. The association was behaviorally visible as a heart rate CR but not as a nictitating membrane CR.

Further information regarding behaviorally silent associations may be found in Dickinson (1980), Rescorla (1978), and Weisman and Dodd (1979).

Performance Factors

The preceding sections illustrate that associative learning is not always manifest in performance. This section will consider some of the factors that influence the type of CR exhibited when an association is formed. Pavlov (1927), Konorski (1967), and others who have adopted the position that an association is formed between the CS and US in Pavlovian conditioning, have also stated that, as a result of this association, the CS becomes a substitute for the US. However, such a position would seem to demand that the characteristics of the CR should be determined primarily by the US and that in general the CR should resemble the US (see Mackintosh, 1974, pp. 100 ff.). However, there are many instances in which the CR does not resemble the UR (see Hearst, 1978, 1979). Of particular concern here will be studies which show that the characteristics of the CR may be strongly influenced by the nature of the CS.

Holland (1977) paired a tone or a light with the delivery of food. He found that general activity increased, across days, to the presentation of the tone (i.e., an activity CR developed) but there was no general activity increase in animals for whom the light was paired with the food US. Detailed examination of the animals' behavior showed that the tone as a CS tended to elicit sharp head-jerking responses as a CR, a behavior that registered as an activity increase in Holland's apparatus, whereas the light tended to elicit a rearing response as a CR, a response that did not register as an increase in activity. Thus, the CR that developed in this experiment varied with the nature of the CS. Did the fact that different responses occurred to the two CSs mean that the nature of the association was different? Apparently not, since the two CSs functioned equivalently as reinforcers in a second order conditioning paradigm. In addition, combining both light and tone CSs led to a summation of their reinforcing effects in a second order paradigm despite the fact that the two CSs elicited different, and incompatible, responses.

In other studies Holland found that the nature of the CR was influenced by the localizability and vertical distance of a light CS from the rat. Holland also noted that the nature of the CR that develops to a CS is related to the orienting response (Chapter 2) that the CS initially elicits, and that the character of the CR may vary during the CS–US interval; it is related to the CS early in the interval and to the US late in the interval (Holland, 1979, 1980a, 1980b).

Thus, Holland's research clearly shows that characteristics of the CS influence the nature of the CR. Other factors that may influence the CR are discussed in Hearst (1979), Rescorla (1978), and, in the case where drugs are used as the US (see Chapter 5) by Eikelboom and Stewart (1982).

CS and US Representation

We have stated that a cognitive interpretation of conditioning assumes that associations are formed between the CS and US. Of course, the associations must be formed between some internal representations of these external stimuli. Thus, an additional aspect of cognitive interpretations of conditioning is that the CS and US have an internal representation (e.g., Rescorla, 1978; Wagner, 1981). These representations may be thought to be the result of perceptual processing of external stimuli, much in the manner described in terms of Sokolov's model of habituation considered in Chapter 2. That is, when a stimulus is experienced, a "model" (Sokolov, 1963) or "gnostic" (knowing) unit (Konorski, 1967) is formed in the central nervous system. This unit or model constitutes the perceptual representation of the external stimulus. If two such stimuli are presented in a contingent relationship, then an association is formed between the representations.

Once an association is formed, arousal of the CS representation will call forth the representation of the US. Some investigators speak of the CS producing an image (e.g., King, 1979) or an hallucination (Konorski, 1967) of the US. Some simply refer to the more abstract concept of a representation (Rescorla, 1978), whereas others consider that the CS calls forth the representation of the US from a long term memory storage system into short term memory, where it is said to be in an active state and subject to modification (see Chapter 13 and Wagner, 1981).

An advantage of these cognitive views is that the idea of a separate representation for each stimulus element raises the possibility that the behavioral effects of an association may be modified simply by changing the representation, without altering the association. Thus, if behavior is somehow produced by the CS representation activating the US representation, then changing the US representation after the association has been formed should change the behavior the next time that the CS is presented. There is some evidence that this is the case.

Several studies, for example, have found that presenting a US of increased intensity after conditioning has been established will lead to an enhanced CR the next time that the CS is presented, a result termed a US inflation effect (e.g., Rescorla, 1974; Randich & Rescorla, 1981). It is important to note that the inflated US is presented without being paired with the CS in this procedure. Sherman (1978) showed that the US inflation effect is obtained only when there has already been a strong CS–US association previously formed. This representational model also predicts that weakening the US representation after conditioning should result in a diminished CR. There is some evidence to support this prediction (Holland, 1981b; Holland & Straub, 1979; Rescorla, 1973, 1978). In another experiment Holland and Rescorla (1975) first paired a CS with the presentation of food. The CR measured was an increase in activity when the CS was presented. They then paired the food with rapid rotation of the animals, which produces a conditioned food aversion (see Figure 4–4). There was a substantial reduction in the activity elicited by the CS on its next presentation. The Holland and Rescorla interpretation of this result was that the US representation had been devalued by having been paired with the rotation.

The idea of representational processes may also be used to conceptualize some of the inhibitory processes considered in Chapter 5. For example, Pearce and Hall (1980) assume that a conditioned inhibitor activates a representation of US absence—a no-US representation—and that this no-US representation then acts to diminish (inhibit) the US representation. And we have just mentioned evidence indicating that a diminished US representation will result in a diminished CR.

An earlier study by Wagner, Thomas, and Norton (1967) presented some data that is consistent with this account. This study was concerned with conditioning a leg-lifting response in dogs. The US was direct electrical stimulation of the brain region involved in controlling such a response so that current applied through an implanted electrode caused the dog's leg to lift. These investigators found that the threshold (minimal amount) of current needed to cause the dog's leg to lift was increased when the current application was preceded by an inhibitory stimulus. This result is consistent with the hypothesis that activity in a US area is diminished by presentation of an inhibitory CS. Rescorla and Holland (1977) have also obtained evidence that is consistent with the idea that an inhibitor has its effects by inhibiting activation of a US representation.

Response Generation

The occurrence of the CR is somewhat of a problem for cognitive theory. From a reflex view a CR represents a transference of a reflex from US to CS. But, as we have seen, any response that changes reliably as a function of exposure to a CS–US contingency may be an index of the formation of an association—it is not necessary that the response be like the UR or reflex in nature. Also, as we have seen, a cognitive interpretation accepts the possibility that associations may be formed without the occurrence of a behavioral change. Where does the CR come from, what form should it take, and when should it occur?

One possibility is the following. A tendency of an animal to approach or withdraw from a stimulus may be a fundamental dimension of behavior. Pointing to such a possibility is a great deal of evidence drawn from the comparative analysis of animal behavior (Maier & Schnierela, 1964), from an investigation of the neurophysiological basis of reward (Glickman & Schiff, 1967; Stellar, Brooks, & Mills, 1979), and from analysis of Pavlovian conditioning (Hearst & Jenkins, 1974; Karpicke, Christoph, Peterson, & Hearst, 1977; Wasserman, 1981). Our earlier discussion of directed behaviors provided examples of such approach responses. Further evidence has indicated that the motor mechanisms underlying approach behaviors may be innate—animals do not have to learn the responses involved in approaching a positively valued object or withdrawing from a negatively valued object. Such responses may be a characteristic of the primitive nervous system (e.g., Glickman & Schiff, 1967; Tinbergen, 1951) and only await activation. The activation may be provided by the CS–US representational system. Thus, arousal of a US representation may also activate the motor program for an approach response. As we have just seen, a US representation may be activated by the US itself, or, after an association is formed, by the CS representation. Therefore presentation of a CS to a conditioned animal may, by activating the US representation, also activate innate approach (or withdrawal) motor programs (see Bolles, 1978). The activation of the motor program may be observed, however, only if the animal is relatively unrestrained, as in the Jenkins et al. (1978) experiments discussed earlier, or in an autoshaping type experiment.

There may also be innate motor programs for specific consummatory behaviors such as feeding, drinking, mating, defensive behaviors, and curiosity behaviors (Glockman & Schiff, 1967). These behaviors, which are more specific than general approach or withdrawal, may be initiated also by the activation of CS or US representations. Examples of some of these behaviors were described in the discussion of autoshaping in Chapter 4.

A question for cognitive theory to resolve is just when specific consummatory behaviors, general approach-withdrawal behaviors, and no behavior at all will be activated by CS and US representations.[1] A possible solution to this problem has already been indicated in the preceding discussion. For example, general approach behaviors cannot be observed unless the animal is relatively unrestrained. Specific consummatory behavior activation may depend upon the nature of the US, the species of animal (see the discussion on autoshaping in Chapter 4; also Bolles, 1978), and nature of the CS (see Wasserman, 1981). This issue is considered in more detail in Chapter 14.

Holland's research discussed above has shown how important the nature of the CS is in determining the nature of the CR, and how the CR itself seems to shift from CS influence to US influence as the CS–US interval elapses. If a stimulus has no major motivational significance for an animal, as in the usual case of sensory preconditioning, then activation of the "US" representation would not be expected to activate any of the innate, motivationally related motor programs. Thus, in this case, an association may be formed in the absence of behavior.

---

[1]Konorski (1967) distinguished between preparatory responses (which are somewhat like the directed behaviors described in this text) and consummatory responses (which are like the reflex or consummatory responses discussed here). Konorski's distinction is discussed by Hearst (1979) and Mackintosh (1974).

Summary

Cognitive interpretations of Pavlovian conditioning assume that animals learn a relationship between events. This learning is in the form of associations established between internal representations of external stimulus events. Once an association has been formed, activation of the CS representation will, because of the association, activate the US representation. This activation may be thought of as moving a memory of the US from long term memory, where it is inactive, into short term or "working" memory, where it is active.

A cognitive interpretation of conditioning, unlike a reflex interpretation, does not assume that a particular response is necessarily learned—conditioning may be behaviorally silent. The nature of the CR that develops may be related to the UR, the orienting response originally elicited by the CS, or to both. The cognitive view assumes that any behaviors that change as a result of the formation of an association are meaningful measures of that association (Rescorla, 1978). These behaviors may be general approach-withdrawal behaviors, or more specific, reflex-like, consummatory behaviors. Either type of behavior may be initiated by activation of innate motor programs by a CS–US representational system.

PREPARATORY RESPONSE INTERPRETATION OF CONDITIONING

Data presented previously in this chapter have indicated that animals learn the contingent relationship between the CS and US in a Pavlovian conditioning paradigm. Is the learning of this relationship of any value to the animal? Pavlov and many others have commented on the likely adaptive value of the ability to associate an initially neutral stimulus (CS) with the impending occurrence of a biologically important event (US). That is, if the learning of a contingent relationship between the CS and US allows the animal to predict the occurrence of the US, this predictability should be of some functional value to the animal. One approach toward understanding this potential adaptive value is to examine behavioral changes that seem to prepare the animal for the effects of the impending US. Components of the CR may modify the impact of the US, and this modification may be one way in which the learning of a contingent CS–US relationship has adaptive value for an animal (see, for example, Perkins, 1968). Some of the evidence in regard to the learning of preparatory responses will now be examined.

On a motor level, the occurrence of directed behaviors may be regarded as preparatory. That is, an approach response will bring an animal nearer to a positively valued US, and a withdrawal response will remove an animal from the vicinity of an aversive US. These behaviors will thus modify the effects of the US on the animal.

More discrete reflex-like consummatory responses may also serve to modify the impact of the US on the animal. For example, there is a tendency in many Pavlovian conditioning preparations for the CR to occur at about the time that the US is normally presented. Such results have been obtained in salivary conditioning (Ellison, 1964), rabbit nictitating membrane conditioning (Sears, Baker, & Frey, 1979), human eyelid conditioning (Levey & Martin, 1968), human galvanic skin response conditioning (Kimmel & Burns, 1975), and rabbit heart rate conditioning (VanDercar & Schneiderman, 1967).

When two CS–US intervals are presented there is a tendency for two CR peaks to occur, one at each of the two times a US might be presented (Millenson, Kehoe, & Gormezano, 1977). The data presented in Figure 6–4 show the times of peak CR occurrence in groups that experienced either 200 milliseconds, 700 milliseconds, or both values, as CS–US intervals in a nictitating membrane conditioning study. Note the occurrence of peak CR magnitudes at about the times that the US would be delivered.

It is possible that the occurrence of the CR at about the time that the US occurs has an ameliorative effect on the impact of the US on the animal.

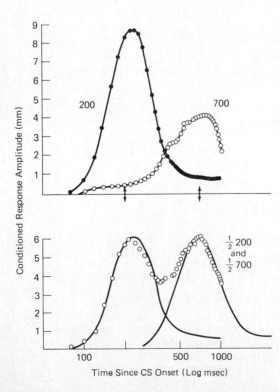

FIGURE 6–4 Amplitude (degree of closure) of the nictitating membrane as a function of time since CS onset and as a function of CS–US interval. The top panel presents data from groups with either a 200- or a 700-msec CS–US interval. Notice that the peak amplitude coincided with time that the US was due. The bottom panel shows data from a group in which the US was equally likely to occur 200 or 700 msec after CS onset. Notice that this group showed two amplitude peaks— one corresponding to each CS–US interval. (Data from Millenson, Kehoe, & Gormezano, 1977)

For example, in human eyelid conditioning it seems reasonable to assume that eyelid closure would reduce the impact of a puff of air used as the US (see, for example, Levey & Martin, 1968); in human galvanic skin response conditioning it is possible that a change in skin resistance at the time shock is delivered reduces the intensity of the shock (Kimmel & Burns, 1975); and so on.

It should be noted that there are two ways of interpreting the apparent adaptiveness of having the CR occur at about the same time as the US. In one interpretation, the occurrence of the CR modifies the US in a way that is advantageous to each individual animal. As a result, over the course of conditioning, the CR becomes "shaped" to occur at a point where it maximally influences the US (Levey & Martin, 1968). An alternative interpretation is that the nervous systems of animals may have been molded by evolutionary pressures because of the general adaptiveness of CR–US co-occurrence, so that the CR tends to occur at the time the US is presented, regardless of the benefit to the particular animal in question (Sears et al., 1979). This latter interpretation is more consistent with some data which indicate that there are situations in which co-occurrence of the CR and US would not seem to have any particular value for the animal—but they co-occur anyway (Coleman, 1975; Gormezano & Coleman, 1973).

Other data, possibly indicating a way in which a predictive CS–US association may allow an animal to prepare for and modify the effects of a US, may be found in some drug conditioning studies. For example, we reported in Chapter 5 that injection of ethanol reduces body temperature, but this effect (the UR) diminishes when the injections are repeatedly given in the same stimulus context (Lè et al., 1979). The CR that develops when ethanol is injected as the US is an increase in body temperature (Crowell, Hinson, & Siegel, 1981; Lè et al., 1979). Thus, the CR serves to offset (compensate for) the effects of the US.

Similar compensatory responses have been reported in other drug injection procedures (Siegel, 1978; Siegel, Sherman, & Mitchell, 1980). Siegel and his colleagues (1982) have argued that such compensatory responses may be important in drug addiction and, possibly, in death from drug overdose. For example, if a drug is administered regularly in a particular environment, and if a compensatory response (CR) develops which acts to offset the effects of the drug, then more and more of the drug will have to be administered to have the same psychological effect. If the usual dose of the drug is administered, but in an environment different from the one in which the drug is normally administered, the compensatory CR may be missing or diminished (because the context—the CS—is different) and, therefore, the drug may have an unexpectedly strong effect.

Other examples of the possible preparatory role of Pavlovian CRs may be found in Perkins (1968), Wagner et al. (1967), and Thomas (1971). This matter is discussed also by Miller and Balaz (1981), who indicate that the preparatory role of Pavlovian associations cannot be fully appreciated unless considered in the context of an unrestrained animal.

FORMAL MODELS OF CONDITIONING

Formal models of conditioning specify assumptions regarding the conditioning process fairly precisely, usually in terms of mathematical relationships, so that specific predictions may be derived and the model tested by experiment. The predictions are typically of a qualitative rather than a quantative nature. There are a number of formal models of conditioning; two will be considered here. One, the Wagner-Rescorla model, will be considered in some detail; the other, the Pearce-Hall model, will be covered more briefly, and principally as a counterpoint to the Wagner-Rescorla model. Both models are multifaceted, but our discussion will focus on how the two models account for blocking (described at the beginning of this chapter).

The Wagner-Rescorla Model

A principal assumption of the Wagner-Rescorla model is that each US has the ability to support a limited amount of conditioning. Once this limit has been reached no more conditioning will occur, no matter how many times the CS and US are paired. The model is not concerned with behavior directly, but with a hypothetical "associative strength" which is assumed to result from CS–US pairings, and, in turn, influences behavior. Wagner and Rescorla assume that associative strength, the strength of the connection between the CS and US, increases with repeated CS–US pairings, with most learning occurring within the earlier CS–US pairings, and less and less learning occuring on subsequent trials. Thus, the model assumes a learning function much like that shown in Figure 4–7.

Since the model was developed in part to account for blocking, the formal equations of the model are concerned with the associative strengths acquired by each element of a compound CS. In simple terms, the model assumes that when the reinforcing properties of a US are exhausted by one CS, then another CS paired with that same US will not be able to acquire any associative strength and, therefore, no CRs will develop in the presence of this added CS. Thus, the essence of the model is that blocking may occur if one CS "monopolizes" all of the associative strength that it is possible to obtain with a particular US. Let us now see how the model accomplishes this in formal terms.

There are two basic equations. The first shows how associative strength (symbolized by V) changes on each trial for one element of a compound stimulus (symbolized by A). The second equation shows how associative strength changes on each trial for the second element of a compound stimulus (symbolized by X). These equations are as follows:

$$\Delta V_A = \alpha_A \beta \, (\lambda - V_{AX})$$

$$\Delta V_X = \alpha_X \beta \, (\lambda - V_{AX})$$

The two equations describe the change in associative strength (V) that will take place in *each* component of a compound stimulus (AX) when that compound is followed by a US. This model has two learning rate parameters, one for the CS (α, or alpha), and one for the US (β, or beta). Learning rate parameters determine how rapidly learning occurs, and this rate may vary as a function of characteristics of the CS and US. The greater the learning rate, the greater the amount that will be learned on each trial. Thus, more intense CSs and USs may have higher learning rate parameters (i.e., promote faster learning) than less intense CSs and USs (see Chapter 4).

The model also assumes that there is a maximum level of associative strength that will be supported by the US. This maximum is symbolized by lamda (λ). With a given US, only so much learning can occur, and, in general, the more intense the US, the greater λ is (the more learning that can occur). An important additional assumption made by the model is that the associative strength of a compound stimulus (V_{AX}) is a simple additive function of the associative strengths of the component stimuli:

$$V_{AX} = V_A + V_X.$$

In summary, the model assumes that there is a limit to the associative strength supported by the US (symbolized by λ) and that the rate at which learning occurs on each trial is influenced by characteristics of the CS (symbolized by α) and characteristics of the US (symbolized by β). Remaining to be explained is the parenthetical part of the equation ($\lambda - V_{AX}$). This term of the equation gives the amount of associative strength that is available for conditioning on each trial. The amount available for conditioning is determined by the maximum amount that can be conditioned with that US (λ) minus what has already been conditioned to both CSs (symbolized by V_{AX}). Thus, the more the associative strength that has already been conditioned to each CS, the less will be available for conditioning on each subsequent trial. It is this characteristic of the model that allows it to generate curves of the shape of the curve in Figure 4–7, which shows less and less new learning occurs with each trial.

How does this model account for blocking? Pretraining with one element of the compound (as in Kamin's experiments) should increase the total associative strength of the compound (V_{AX}) close to asymptote (maximum) because of the assumption that $V_{AX} = V_A + V_X$. If V_{AX} is close to maximum (λ), the quantity $(\lambda - V_{AX})$ will be small—there will be little remaining associative strength that can be supported by the US. Thus, when the second CS element is added to the compound it should acquire little associative strength.

An example of how the model explains this type of blocking is illustrated in Table 6–3 and Figure 6–5. In this example a single CS (A) was paired with the US for eight trials. After this, the compound of AX was paired with the

---

TABLE 6–3 WAGNER-RESCORLA MODEL OF BLOCKING

Trial by trial changes in associative strength of stimulus A over first eight trials, when A is presented alone, and both A and X on subsequent trials, when both are presented as a compound. The left-hand columns give the associative strengths of Stimulus A, Stimulus X, and A+X, at the start of the indicated trial. The parameters were set to $\alpha_A = 0.4$, $\alpha_X = 0.4$, $\beta = 0.5$, $\lambda = 100$.

$$\Delta V_A = \alpha_A \beta(\lambda - V_{AX})$$

$$\Delta V_X = \alpha_X \beta(\lambda - V_{AX})$$

V_A	V_X	V_{AX}	Trial	A-Only Trials
0	0	0	1	$\Delta V_A = (.4)\ (.5)\ (100 - 0) = 20$
20	0	20	2	$\Delta V_A = (.2)\ (100 - 20)\ \ \ \ \ = 16$
36	0	36	3	$\Delta V_A = (.2)\ (100 - 36)\ \ \ \ \ = 12.8$
48.8	0	48.8	4	$\Delta V_A = (.2)\ (100 - 48.8)\ \ = 10.24$
59.04	0	59.04	5	$\Delta V_A = (.2)\ (100 - 59.04) = 8.19$
67.23	0	67.23	6	$\Delta V_A = (.2)\ (100 - 67.23) = 6.55$
73.78	0	73.78	7	$\Delta V_A = (.2)\ (100 - 73.78) = 5.24$
79.02	0	79.02	8	$\Delta V_A = (.2)\ (100 - 79.02) = 4.20$

Compound Trials

V_A	V_X	V_{AX}	Trial	Compound Trials
83.22	0	83.22	9	$\Delta V_A = (.2)\ (100 - 83.22) = 3.36$
			9	$\Delta V_X = (.2)\ (100 - 83.22) = 3.36$
86.58	3.36	89.94	10	$\Delta V_A = (.2)\ (100 - 89.94) = 2.01$
			10	$\Delta V_X = (.2)\ (100 - 89.94) = 2.01$
88.59	5.37	93.96	11	$\Delta V_A = (.2)\ (100 - 93.96) = 1.21$
			11	$\Delta V_X = (.2)\ (100 - 93.96) = 1.21$
89.80	6.58	96.38	12	$\Delta V_A = (.2)\ (100 - 96.38) = 0.72$
			12	$\Delta V_X = (.2)\ (100 - 96.38) = 0.72$
90.52	7.3	97.82	13	$\Delta V_A = (.2)\ (100 - 97.82) = 0.44$
			13	$\Delta V_X = (.2)\ (100 - 97.82) = 0.44$
90.96	7.74	98.70	14	$\Delta V_A = (.2)\ (100 - 98.70) = 0.26$
			14	$\Delta V_X = (.2)\ (100 - 98.70) = 0.26$
91.22	8.00	99.22		

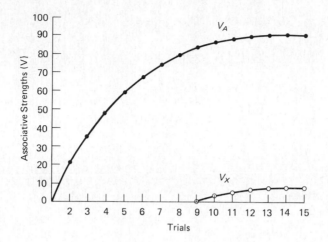

FIGURE 6–5 Trial by trial accumulation of associative strength to elements A and X
of an AX compound. A is presented alone for eight trials, then in compound with X.
(Data from Table 6–3)

US on each trial. Table 6–3 shows how the associative strengths of each element change on a trial by trial basis and it also shows the total associative
strengths of each element and of the compound at the end of each trial.

The Table is read as follows. At the beginning of trial one (first line)
neither CS (A or X) has any associative strength. The change in associative
strength (ΔV_A) that takes place in stimulus A when it is presented with the US
on that trial is found by multiplying together the learning rate parameter
associated with A (0.4), the learning rate parameter associated with the US
(0.5), and the associative strength available for conditioning on that trial. The
associative strength available for conditioning is the maximum supported by
the US (100) minus that already conditioned (0 on the first trial). The result
of this multiplication is 20, a value that represents the amount of associative
strength gained by stimulus A on the first trial. This value of 20 also represents the *total* associative strength of the compound AX (because of the assumption that $V_{AX} = V_A + V_X$) and is thus subtracted from λ on trial two,
etc.

Starting on trial 9, both stimulus A and stimulus X are paired with the
US on each trial, and thus both gain associative strength from that trial on-
ward. But, because V_A has already "used up" most of the conditioning that
the US can support, V_X shows only small changes on subsequent trials.

Figure 6–5 plots the associative strengths of A and X as a function of
trials. It is clear that A not only has vastly more associative strength than X,
but, because of the assumptions of the model, it has blocked X from ever
gaining much associative strength. Notice that after seven compound trials X

has not gained as much associative strength as A did on the very first trial, and X has essentially reached the limits of its associative strength.

Thus, the Wagner-Rescorla model can explain blocking by some simple mathematical assumptions. The model also makes clear that extra training with the compound would not alleviate blocking (see Figure 6–5), a result found by Kamin (1969). Reducing the amount of pretraining should reduce blocking—also a result found by Kamin (1969). The model also accounts for the reduction in blocking obtained when the US intensity is increased or a second US is given at the start of compound trials. According to the model, those manipulations increase the asymptote to which associative strength may go. Thus, there is more "room" for the added element to acquire associative strength. This may be seen by increasing the λ value in Table 6–3 and recalculating the data points.

Thus, the model is quite successful in interpreting a number of blocking manipulations. The model has also been successful in accommodating a variety of other blocking data (Rescorla & Wagner, 1972), and some of the inhibitory phenomena described in Chapter 5 (Wagner & Rescorla, 1972), as well as in generating some unusual predictions that have been confirmed (Kamin & Gaioni, 1974).

In summary, the Wagner-Rescorla model is successful in explaining blocking through the assumption that a given US can support only a limited amount of conditioning no matter how many stimuli may be paired with it. If the associative strength of one stimulus that paired with this US is near the maximum that can be supported by that US, then added stimuli will not develop an association with that US—they will not be conditioned.[2] Expressed in Kamin's terms, once a US becomes adequately predicted, it will not support any more conditioning; the US loses its associability when it is predictable. Only "surprising" (unpredicted) USs will support the formation of an association between a CS and a US.

The Pearce-Hall Model

Blocking: Further Evidence

Studies reviewed previously showed that an increase in shock intensity or the addition of a second shock reduced blocking that normally would occur to an added CS. These results are understandable in the context of Wagner-

---

[2]The model may be applied to explain the lack of conditioning that occurs in some of the contingency manipulations, where the US is presented in the absence of the CS. The explanation of these data assumes that presentation of the US in the absence of the CS leads to the conditioning of the context (apparatus) to the US. Thus, the context, and the explicit CS, may be thought of as a compound stimulus. In some contingency manipulations the unpaired presentations of the US may lead to the context acquiring enough associative strength to block the occurrence of conditioning to the CS.

Rescorla theory because both of these manipulations should increase λ, thereby allowing the added stimulus to gain associative strength. However, one impetus for the Pearce-Hall (1980) model was a number of blocking studies the results of which could not be readily explained by the Wagner-Rescorla model. These studies have shown that the postponement of an expected second shock or the omission of an expected second shock will also reduce blocking (Dickinson, Hall, & Mackintosh, 1976; Mackintosh, Dickinson, & Cotton, 1980). These results are inconsistent with the Wagner-Rescorla model. If there is no US, how can unblocking be explained in terms of increased λ? It seems that surprise itself—any change in the US event, even its absence—can produce unblocking (conditioning to the added element).

A second difficulty with the Wagner-Rescorla model is related to *when* blocking is supposed to take place. According to the Wagner-Rescorla explanation, blocking should occur on the first compound trial, or the first time the new CS is introduced. This prediction derives from the nature of the model's explanation of blocking—all the associative capacity of the US is "exhausted" because of the intial trials with the single stimulus. Thus, no learning can take place to the new stimulus when it is added to the first stimulus. However, a number of recent studies have indicated that learning takes place normally to the added CS when only a single compound trial is administered (Mackintosh, 1978; Mackintosh, Bygrave & Picton, 1977; Mackintosh et al., 1980). These experiments show that the occurrence of blocking may require multiple compound trials, something not predicted by the Wagner-Rescorla explanation.

What seems to happen when multiple trials are given—the usual Kamin procedure—is the following. Conditioning occurs normally to the added stimulus on the first trial in which it is added. If the US event at the end of that trial is not different from what the animal had experienced all along, no more conditioning occurs to the added stimulus on subsequent trials. If, however, the US event at the end of the first compound trial is novel (such as extra US, missing US, etc.), then the animal continues to show conditioning to the added CS element on subsequent trials. It is as if the animal attends to the new CS when it is first added and, because of this, learns of the contingency between this added CS and the US. However, if that US is not surprising, then the animal no longer attends to the added CS and thus learns nothing more about the contingency between it and the US. In fact, Mackintosh (1978) has data which indicate that the presentation of a surprising US for the first time at the end of the second compound trial has no effect on conditioning. It does not reduce blocking on subsequent trials. This result is consistent with the idea that the animal stops attending to the added CS after the first compound trial if it predicts nothing new.

The Pearce-Hall model takes these data into account by assuming that the locus of blocking in the Kamin paradigm is in the CS, not the US, as Wagner-Rescorla assume. That is, the Pearce-Hall model assumes that the tendency of a CS to enter into associations (its associability) is gradually lost as it comes to predict the US better and better. When a CS eventually becomes a good predictor of a US, it can no longer enter into associations with that US. The associability of a CS is enhanced, however, if it does not accurately predict its consequences (the US). Thus, any novel event that follows a CS should act to maintain its associability.

The Model

The formal properties of the Pearce-Hall model will only be sketched. Basically, the associative strength (V) that a stimulus acquires on a learning trial is a function of three factors: the intensity of the CS, the intensity of the US, and the associability of the CS. This latter factor, the associability of the CS, is a function of how well the CS predicts the US. The more the US is adequately predicted by the CS, the less associable the CS is. When the US is perfectly predicted, the CS cannot gain any more associative strength—it has lost its associability. The operation of these factors on a trial may be understood by examining Figure 6–6.

The central aspect of this figure is a processor unit that contains representations of the CS and US on trial n of a conditioning experiment. Presentation of a CS (CS input) does two things. It activates a memory of the US, the strength of which is a function of the strength of the association (V) between the CS and US. The CS input is also shunted, if it is intense enough

FIGURE 6–6 Hypothetical processes in the Pearce-Hall model of conditioning. See text for explanation. (Figure from Pearce & Hall, 1982)

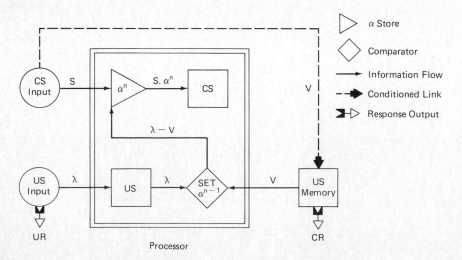

(S), to the processor where it must first pass through a system termed the associability (α) store. The associability store screens out stimuli whose associability had been set to zero on the previous trial, and it sets the associability of admitted stimuli for the next trial.

US input gains access to the processor as a function of US intensity (λ). The US does not have to enter a storage system; it always gains access to the processor if it is intense enough. Gaining access to the processor is equivalent to eliciting a representation. The US also, independent of gaining access to the processor, elicits a UR.

Inside the processor the following events take place. The US representation activated by US input is compared to the US memory activated by the CS. This comparison takes place in a comparator system (marked "set" in Figure 6–6). The output of this comparator is a value ($\lambda - V$) that represents how well the US is predicted by the CS. This value is used to set the associability of the CS in the store. When the CS accurately predicts the US, there is no discrepancy between the US memory and the US representation. As a result, the output of the comparator ($\lambda - V$) is zero and the associability of the CS (α) becomes zero. When its associability is zero a CS cannot gain access to the processor unit. It can, however, still elicit a CR by the associative memory link.

The formation of an association in this model is a function of the strengths of the CS and US representations active concurrently in the processor unit. Thus, once a CS becomes an adequate predictor of a US it will be denied access to the processor and it will acquire no more associative strength. It will, however, continue to elicit a CR via the conditioning-US memory link.

The model explains blocking in the following way. When more than one stimulus is present the degree of associative strength (V) is assumed to represent the associative strength of all stimuli present. Thus, in the typical Kamin procedure, when the second CS is added to the first, the V of the compound is taken as the sum of the Vs of the two CSs. On the first compound trial the added CS will enter the processor unit to a degree which is a function of its intensity. The α store will have no α value for it since it hadn't been experienced before. By entering the processor unit it will produce a CS representation, and conditioning will occur when the US representation is activated by US presentation. Thus, this model predicts that the added CS will gain associative strength on the first compound trial. However, if the US event is the same one that had always followed the first CS, then ($\lambda - V$) = 0 and the associability of the added CS would be set to zero for the next trial. That is, if the US event is already adequately predicted by CS_A, then CS_B would not have any associability after the first compound trial. Therefore, with repeated presentations of CS_A + CS_B no more conditioning to CS_B would occur—blocking would take place. Neither CS_A nor CS_B would have access to the processor. This analysis conforms to the experimental results we reported: blocking does not occur on the first compound trial, only on subsequent trials.

The model also deals in the following manner with the various ways of producing unblocking. The basic mechanism that determines the associability of the CS, and hence how much learning will occur on a subsequent trial, is how well it predicts the US. Any change in US characteristics, changes such as a postponement or omission of an expected US, will produce a mismatch between the US representation and the memory of the US elicited by the CS. Such a mismatch will lead to a non-zero value of $(\lambda - V)$ output from the comparator. Thus, the associability of the CS will be set to some value greater than zero and learning will take place on the next trial. Therefore, any change in the US should produce learning on the second compound trial, a prediction that is in accord with the data we have presented.

The model was also designed to explain the CS preexposure effect ("latent inhibition") and the various inhibitory phenomena described in Chapter 5. However, that discussion will not be included in this text (see Hall & Pearce, 1982; Kaye & Pearce, 1984).

In summary, both the Wagner-Rescorla model and the Pearce-Hall model were developed to provide explanations for a series of experiments, particularly blocking experiments, that challenge some of the assumptions regarding the fundamental role of CS–US contiguity in conditioning. The Wagner-Rescorla model was able to accommodate much of the blocking data with a formal model that emphasized the loss of the reinforcing properties of the US when it became fully predicted by a CS. The Pearce-Hall model was designed to accommodate a number of recent experiments that could not be explained by the Wagner-Rescorla model. It does this by using a different formal structure with different assumptions, assumptions that emphasize the conditions in which a CS is able to enter into an association. The Pearce-Hall model emphasizes the predictive importance of the CS. When the CS does *not* adequately predict its consequences it is available to form associations. When it does adequately predict its consequences it loses its ability to enter into associations.

The Pearce-Hall model is more comfortable with the cognitive interpretation of conditioning described earlier in this chapter than is the Wagner-Rescorla model. In addition, the Pearce-Hall model is somewhat similar to theories that emphasize the role of attentional processes in learning (Mackintosh, 1975). In fact, the model could be stated in attentional terms: when the consequences of a CS are uncertain, the CS is attended to; when the consequences of a CS are well known, the CS is not attended to. Only when a CS is attended to will it be capable of entering into an association.

These models do not, of course, represent the final word on formal interpretations of conditioning. In fact, Wagner (1981) has another model emphasizing memory processes in conditioning that is somewhat different from the treatment of memory in the Pearce-Hall model. Also, a study by Balaz, Kasprow, and Miller (1982) questions the finding that blocking does not occur on the first compound trial, a finding important for the Pearce-Hall model. And Grossberg (1982) has a considerably more complex model of conditioning that emphasizes both formal properties and the presumed neurophysiological substrate of these properties. Rather than being considered as final products, each of these models should be thought of as intermediate species in the evolution of an understanding of the data and mechanisms of conditioning.

RELEVANCE OF PAVLOVIAN CONDITIONING RESEARCH

There are two ways of considering the relevance of research into the principles of Pavlovian conditioning. In the first place, such research provides information regarding the conditions under which animals learn the predictive relationships among environmental events, and information about the behavioral and physiological consequences of such learning. As such, the research helps us to understand the role played by the learning of inter-event relationships in animal behavior and provides basic information regarding the learning process—information important for the eventual understanding of the neural basis of learning.

On a more practical level, Pavlovian research may have consequences for the understanding of human behavior. For example, the Pavlovian conditioning paradigm has long been thought of as a model for understanding the association of emotions with environmental events, and the physiological concommitants of such associations. In fact, as was discussed in Chapter 3, Pavlovian concepts are often used in attempts to understand the acquisition of phobias and in the development of treatments for phobias or other, more rational, fears.

We also discussed in Chapter 3 how chemotherapy treatment for cancer is often complicated because some patients show anticipatory nausea responses, and directed behaviors away from the events and places associated with the treatment. For example, they get sick at the thought of going to the hospital for their treatment, and some tend to resist undergoing the treatment. Such fears and behavior may be treated by systematic desensitization therapies that are related to Pavlovian constructs, as discussed in Chapter 3. Recent research has also indicated that the formation and extinction of conditioned food aversions in humans from excessive alcohol intake and from binge eating (bulimia) follows the same principles as the conditioned aversions described in Chapter 4 (Logue, Logue, & Strauss, 1983). This knowledge may help understand the development and treatment of these problems in humans.

More mundane fears, such as fear of going to the dentist, may also be treated with the systematic desensitization process (Gatchel, 1980), a process that could be thought of as restructuring the CS–US representation network. Such a treatment diminishes the fear and anxiety associated with the dentist and various dental utensils and treatments.

More recent research has expanded the potential importance of Pavlovian or Pavlovian-like processes to the fields of immunology, infectious disease, and cancer. It has been shown that stress responses suppress the activity of the immune system. Such suppression provides an opening for a variety of infectious diseases, including certain forms of cancer. It is known also that the suppression of the immune system may be brought under the control of neutral stimuli by Pavlovian processes (Ader, 1982). Thus, a contingent relationship between a particular environment and a stress response that suppresses the immune system may mean that exposure to that environment (the CS) will act to suppress the activity of the immune system. Thus, a consequence of this CR would be an enhanced susceptibility to infectious disease when exposed to that CS. The potential role of stress, particularly psychological stress, in modifying the course of cancer, will be mentioned later in this text.

We have also seen earlier in this chapter, and in Chapter 5, how Pavlovian processes may be of fundamental importance in drug effects and drug addiction. Conditioned responses may contribute to the reduced effect that many drugs have with repeated administration, and because of the conditioning, this reduced effect would occur only if the drug is administered under the usual environmental (CS) conditions (e.g., Siegel et al., 1982). If the same drug is administered in a different context it may have exaggerated effects because of the absence of conditioned compensatory responses. It is also possible that the pharmacological effects of some drugs may be elicited by the stimulus context in which they have always been administered; the environmental cues themselves may come to produce drug-like effects in the absence of the drug (see Eikelboom & Stewart, 1982; Flaherty et al., 1980; Woods & Kulkoski, 1976).

The conditions in which compensatory responses (which oppose drug effects) and responses that copy drug effects are obtained are not yet understood. However, it is clear that research into Pavlovian processes and drug effects is of fundamental importance since all medication is taken in some context and the data obtained thus far imply that conditioned responses developed to a context may modify the effects of the medication. This research on drug effects is also clearly related to the placebo effect, the fact that some people, administered an inert substance, will respond as they would to certain drugs if they are told that such drugs have been administered. In fact, approximately one third of the population will show an analgesic effect if they are given a placebo but are told that they have been administered a pain killer (Gatchel & Baum, 1983; Levine, Gordon, & Fields, 1978).

It is clear that such placebo effects could well be related to the drug effects we have described and to the general topic of expectations produced by prior experience, that is, to learned inter-event associations. It should be added that placebo effects are not "mystical." They have a physiological basis. In fact, the study by Levine and his colleagues (1978) provided evidence that the analgesic effects produced in the placebo subjects were probably due to the release of endorphins, which are normal hormone-like substances involved in pain suppression.

Finally, on a more speculative level, research into Pavlovian processes may help to bring about an understanding of the need for, and attempts at, prediction in human behavior. A litttle thought makes one realize how pervasive are attempts at prediction in our culture. The myriad of tests, particularly standardized tests, that a typical student is exposed to, all have, as one of their purposes, the possibility that they may be used to predict performance, and thus they may be employed for selection. Aptitude tests and intelligence tests are also used, in part, for the same purpose—to predict future performance. Personality tests, perhaps on an even more general level, also have as one of their goals the prediction of behavior. Indeed some personality tests are used to select individuals for certain occupations.

Beyond the individual level we have meteorologists and economists attempting to predict (with only marginal success) short and long term trends in the weather and economy; pollsters attempting to predict the outcome of elections; market researchers trying to predict who will buy product X at price Y; sportscasters and bookies trying to predict who will win, and by how much, in various sporting events; and so on and on. It is doubtful that Pavlovian research will provide us with specific information regarding all these activities. But such research may help us to sharpen our concepts and theories and may provide us with new analytical tools with which to understand the importance of prediction in human behavior.

CHAPTER SUMMARY

Research using the blocking procedure has shown that CS–US contiguity itself is not sufficient to produce conditioning. It seems that a CS must also be informative, be predictive, if it is to enter into an association with a US. The results of the CS blocking experiments, in conjunction with other data, support a cognitive view of conditioning.

According to this cognitive view, animals form associations between events based on their contingent (predictive) relationship, and these associations have behavioral consequences more complex than eliciting simple reflexes. The evidence favoring such a cognitive interpretation includes the importance of contingency, the fact that conditioning may be behaviorally silent, the fact that the occurrence of a behavioral response is not necessary for conditioning, the evidence favoring the representational view of CS and US events, and the complex nature of many CRs. The nature of the response that follows such inter-event associative learning may depend on the motivational value of the US, the orienting response originally elicited by the CS, the localizability of the CS and US, the opportunities available for the animal to engage in directed behaviors, and the species of the animal. In some cases the occurrence of the CR may alter the impact of the US on the animal.

Formal models of conditioning have had some degree of success in capturing the essence of a broad spectrum of data, particularly that of research related to contingency and blocking. The Wagner-Rescorla model can account for much of the blocking data in terms of a diminished ability of the US to support conditioning when it is predictable. The Pearce-Hall model, which accounts for blocking data not adequately explained by the Wagner-Rescorla model, emphasizes the loss of CS associability when a CS comes to predict its consequences.

Research in Pavlovian conditioning has potentially wide areas of applicability for a basic understanding of learning processes and for practical use in human behavior. Examples of the latter include the acquisition and elimination of emotional responses, learned food aversions, conditioned influences on the immune system and subsequent susceptibility to infectious disease, drug addiction, and the effects of drugs and medication in general. Pavlovian conditioning research may help in the understanding of the importance of predictability in behavior.

7

Instrumental Learning I: Introduction and Effects of Deprivation, Reward Magnitude, and Reward Delay

INTRODUCTION

The study of instrumental learning is the study of how the consequences of an animal's behavior affect its subsequent behavior. The term *instrumental* is used in the sense that the animal's responses serve as an instrument, a tool, to attain some end. Instrumental and Pavlovian experiments are usually distinguished by the procedures involved in each. In the Pavlovian situation the experimenter arranges a correlation between a CS and a US. These two events occur regardless of the subjects' behavior. And, as we saw in the last chapter, the current interpretation is that animals learn this contingent relationship between events that are beyond their control. They develop an expectancy that if the CS occurs, then the US will or will not occur, depending on the contingency.

In an instrumental learning experiment the experimenter arranges a situation in which some event will occur, but only if the animal makes a certain response. For example, the animal will receive a bit of food, but only if it finds its way through a maze, or presses on a lever, or pecks at a lighted disc, etc. In other words, a contingency is established between a certain response and an outcome. The specific response must be made in order for the outcome to occur. Thus, instrumental and Pavlovian conditioning experiments differ procedurally in terms of whether a response is necessary for the occurrence of an event such as the presentation of food.

Examples of Instrumental Learning

Before proceeding further in the definition of instrumental learning, and the distinction between it and Pavlovian conditioning, let's first examine some simple examples of instrumental behavior. Some of the traditional apparatuses used to study instrumental learning, and results obtained in them, are shown in Figure 7–1. The performance of rats in complex mazes was first studied by Small in 1901 (Munn, 1950). Subsequent research used a variety of mazes, one example of which, an elevated multiple-T maze, is shown in Panel A of Figure 7–1. The maze was constructed of narrow (1⅝ inch) boards set up 23 inches above the ground. The animal, in running through the maze, faced a series of choice points where it could go either right or left. At the end of the maze there was a small food reward. The graph to the right of the maze (Panel B) shows learning in the maze (reduction in number of errors as a function of number of runs through the maze) in two groups of animals. Animals trained under normal conditions learned the maze quite rapidly, but animals for whom the visual stimuli in the room (location of lights, tables, etc.) were constantly changed made considerably more errors. This last fact shows that rats used visual cues from the environment to help them learn their way through the maze (Honzik, 1936).

The straight runway illustrated in Panel C of Figure 7–1 represents a maze simplified to the extreme. All the animal must do to obtain the reward is to run from one end to the other. Learning in this apparatus is measured in terms of an increase in the speed with which an animal traverses the runway. Several graphs showing running speed in such an apparatus will be presented later in the text (e.g., Figures 7–4, 7–7, 7–8).

The next illustration (Panel D) is of one of the puzzle boxes used by Thorndike in his pioneering research on animal learning (Thorndike, 1898, 1911). Thorndike would place an animal (e.g., a cat) in this box with food visible on the outside. The box could be arranged so that any one of a number of responses would open the door and allow the animal access to the food. For example, the cat may have to step on the treadle on the floor, or put its paw in a loop and pull down, etc. The progress of learning was measured by the time required for the animal to make the "correct" response. With repeated practice this response came faster and faster.

Illustrated in Panel E is one of the modern successors to the puzzle box—the operant chamber or "Skinner box." In this apparatus the rat is required to press a lever in order to obtain a small amount of food or water. The lever may be in place permanently so that the animal is free to respond at any time, or the lever may be retractable so that it is inserted automatically when a trial is to be presented. The graph (Panel F) shows a learning curve for rats that were presented with a lever-pressing task. In this example the lever was inserted for each trial and learning was measured in terms of time elapsed before the rats responded on the lever after it was inserted. In this particular example the rats were given no prior experience with the apparatus and no pretraining. The data reflect learning in totally naive rats. A modification of the operant chamber for a pigeon is shown in Panel G. The lever is replaced with a small disk on which the pigeon is required to peck.

All of these examples of instrumental learning have one thing in common—the animals must make some response before they receive the sub-

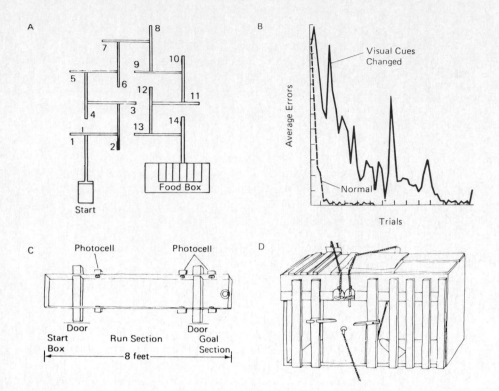

FIGURE 7–1 *Various types of apparatus used to study instrumental learning: Panel A, an elevated multiple-T maze (see text) used by Honzik (1936); Panel B, decline in errors in multiple T-maze across trials for animals with visual cues constant or varied on each trial (see text); Panel C, a straight runway; Panel D, a puzzle box used by Thorndike (1898), see text; Panel E, an operant chamber or "Skinner box" and a*

stance used as a reward. That is, the delivery of the reward is response contingent, and this is the defining characteristic of instrumental learning.[1]

The Law of Effect

Thorndike summarized the outcome of his research in terms of a principle—the law of effect. This "law" reads, in part, as follows: "Of several responses made to the same situation, those which are accompanied or closely

[1]The term *operant* is sometimes used in the way we are using *instrumental*. Operant comes from the writings of B. F. Skinner (e.g., 1938) and it means that the animals operate on the environment—they change the environment. We will use operant and instrumental synonymously.

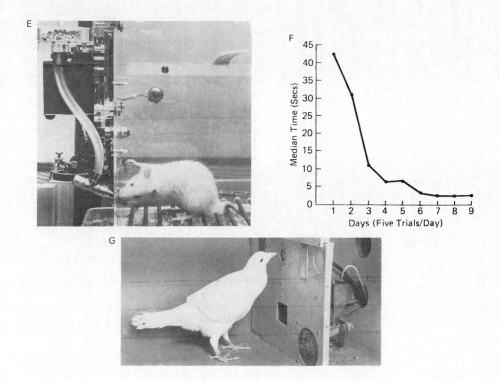

graph (Panel F) showing learning in terms of decreasing latencies to press a lever for a food reward when the lever was inserted in the chamber (see text—unpublished data, Flaherty and Kaplan). Panel G is an operant chamber for pigeons. The pigeons peck on the lighted disc or "key." Panel E photo: courtesy Chas. Pfizer and Co., Panel G photo: Ken Karp.

followed by satisfaction to the animal will, other things being equal, be more firmly connected to the situation, so that, when it recurs, they will be more likely to recur. . . ." Paraphrased, this law says that responses which produce rewards will tend to increase in frequency. Thus, instrumental learning may be viewed as a process of response selection—a particular response is selected by rewarding its occurrence. Common examples of the application of the law of effect, of the importance of response consequences, would be such things as training a dog to give you its paw or to roll over. When the "correct" response occurs the dog is rewarded with a choice bit of food or a pat and some friendly words. More generally, parents frequently attempt to use consequences in order to increase the frequency of some response; for example, "You may watch television *if* you do your homework." "You may have dessert *if* you eat your dinner." In some sense a capitalist society is oriented around a law of effect principle. People are paid for the work they do; they are paid *if* they work. (The contingency between pay and work, though, is sometimes lost!)

After we have explored instrumental behavior more thoroughly and become familiar with some of the parametric data, we will consider modern interpretations of the law of effect.

Shaping

In order for a behavior to be increased in frequency by the presentation of a reward, the behavior must first occur. What if it doesn't? There are several approaches that may be taken. One is to simply wait until it does and then reward the response. The data presented in Panel F of Figure 7–1 were obtained in exactly this way. It required a long wait until the first bar press was made.

An approach frequently used when there is not unlimited time is to "shape" the response by rewarding behavior that more and more closely approximates the desired behavior. For example, a rat may be rewarded at first if it is on the same side of the operant chamber as the lever, then only if it moves close to the lever, then only if it touches the lever, then only if it presses the lever. By successive approximations the exact response is drawn out of the animal. Similarly, if parents wish to establish a contingency between an hour a day of reading and television watching by their children, they may start by requiring a five minute reading period before access to the television. This time period may then be gradually increased.

In some situations it is possible to passively produce the response in an animal and then reward it for this response. Eventually, the response may become active. For example, if a dog's paw is lifted by a trainer and the dog is given a bit of food at the same time, the dog should eventually come to lift its paw by itself, at which time the behavior may also be rewarded (Kornorski, 1948; Kornorski & Miller, 1937).

Pavlovian Directed Behaviors and Instrumental Learning

Some of the instrumental behaviors that we have been describing may look suspiciously like some of the Pavlovian directed behaviors described in Chapters 4 to 6. The establishment of a Pavlovian CS–US contingency is sufficient to cause animals to approach the CS and even perform specific behaviors such as the autoshaped pecking responses described in Chapter 4. Are these behaviors different from instrumental behaviors? Take for example the runway behaviors described in regard to Figure 7–1. As illustrated in the Figure, food is presented at one end of the runway. The animal's task is to run down the runway and get it. Thus, there is a response contingency—if the animal does not run down the runway it does not get the food. However, the stimuli in the goal region of the runway may legitimately be considered to be CSs and the food a US. So there is also a contingency between the spatial location of the goal box and the presentation of a US. On the basis of the directed behavior data discussed previously, the animal would be expected to approach a CS that signals food. Therefore the animal should approach the goal region because of the *CS–US contingency*. What then is controlling the animal's behavior? Is it the contingency between a stimulus and a reward, the contingency between the response and the reward, or both?

The Omission Procedure

An experiment by Lajoie and Bindra (1978) sought to answer this question by comparing response rates of rats exposed to each contingency and then examining the effects of an omission contingency on these response rates. An omission contingency means that an animal must *refrain* from making a response in order to obtain a reward. A common example might be rewarding someone each day that he/she does *not* smoke.

The experimental situation employed by Lajoie and Bindra was much like the usual autoshaping procedure used with pigeons. There was a square panel located in one wall of a chamber. Illumination of this square served as the signal for impending availability of reward. The reward was a small amount of water that became available just above the panel. One group of animals was required to press the panel during the eight seconds that it was illuminated on each trial. This group had a response–reward contingency; they had to make a specific response in order to be rewarded. A second group of animals was exposed to only a stimulus–reward contingency; they received a reward at the end of the eight-second panel illumination period without the requirement that they make a response. This is the usual autoshaping procedure.

The responses generated in the two groups by these contingencies are shown in Figure 7–2. Two sets of data are presented; the response rate (responses per each two-second period) and the trials on which at least one response occurred. In both cases it is apparent that the response contingent group made more responses than the stimulus contingent group. However, it is interesting to note that the stimulus–reward contingency was sufficient to generate responding and, in terms of number of trials on which at least one response occurred, there was not too much of a difference between the two groups. In other words, the response contingency seemed to have its greatest effect on response rate, as compared to whether a response would occur or not.

The omission contingency was put into effect in the second half of this experiment. During this period a reward was not given if the rats pressed the panel. This omission contingency applied to both groups. It is clear from the

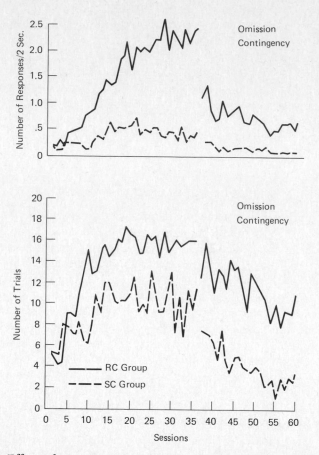

FIGURE 7–2 Effect of response–reward and stimulus–reward contingencies on a panel-pressing response. The response contingent group (RC) had to press the panel when it was illuminated in order to obtain a reward; the stimulus contingent group (SC) received a reward at the end of the illumination period whether or not it had pressed the panel. Left portion of the figure presents acquisition data for two response measures; right portion illustrates the effect of an omission contingency. (Data from Lajoie & Bindra, 1978)

right half of Figure 7–2 that imposition of the omission contingency led to a decline in responses in both groups. However, the animals with a prior history of a response–reward contingency maintained a response level somewhat above the animals with a prior history of a stimulus–reward contingency. The outcome of this experiment indicates that both stimulus–reward contingencies and response–reward contingencies may generate simple approach responses. The response–reward contingency has a more powerful effect, particularly in terms of generating higher rates of responding.

There have been many studies whose purpose was to evaluate the relative importance of stimulus–reward and response–reward contingencies in the autoshaping paradigm. Other than stating that the general outcome of these studies is that both contingencies do play a role in maintaining behavior and that the stimulus–reward contingency in itself is sufficient to maintain some level of responding, we will not delve into this research (see Locurto, Terrace, & Gibbon, 1978; Locurto, Tierny, & Fitzgerald, 1981; Peden, Browne & Hearst, 1977; Williams & Williams, 1969).

Negatively Correlated Reward

A second way of demonstrating the importance of the response–reward contingency in instrumental learning is to make the availability of reward negatively correlated with a particular behavior (Logan, 1960). In the usual instrumental runway task animals receive reward as soon as they reach the goal box (see Figure 7–1). In a sense, the faster the animal runs, the sooner it receives reward. Speed of running and reward receipt are positively correlated. It is possible to set a contingency such that the animal must take *longer* than a certain time period to reach the goal box. If the animal arrives at the goal before the criterion time has elapsed, it receives no reward. This procedure produces a degree of negative correlation between running speed and the receipt of food. The animal must run slowly, or at least take a long time, to reach the goal area.[2] A number of studies reported in Logan (1960) show that animals can learn to take a certain length of time (e.g., five seconds) to traverse the runway if there is a contingency between this time requirement and the availability of a food reward.

Another study has shown that animals will show appropriate running behavior in a situation in which reward is available as soon as they reach the goal box in a runway of one brightness, but in a runway of a different brightness the reward is available only if they take longer than five seconds to reach the goal area (Rashotte & Amsel, 1968). Thus, the animals' behavior adjusted to the response–reward contingencies in the two alleys. Similar effects may be noticed in a situation where a rat must press a lever to obtain food. A schedule may be arranged so that a rat must wait a certain time between lever presses if the presses are to be rewarded. Rats and pigeons will adjust their behavior to the response–reward contingencies in such a schedule (e.g., Gage, Evans, & Olton, 1979; Hemmes, Eckerman, & Rubinsky, 1979).

Thus, both the omission procedure data and the negatively correlated reward data show that the response–reward contingency has a strong influence over behavior in a situation in which there is also the potential for a

[2]This procedure is referred to as discontinuous negative correlation. It is discontinuous because there is a criterion of cut-off time that must elapse rather than a complete negative correlation between running speed and reward receipt (Logan, 1960).

stimulus–reward directed approach response. It is this response–reward behavior, namely behavior controlled by its consequences, which will be of primary interest in these chapters on instrumental learning. Later in the text we will return to the question of the relationship between Pavlovian and instrumental behavior.

Extinction

If a reward is no longer presented following the completion of an instrumental response, the animals eventually cease performing the response. There are many interpretations as to why this extinction takes place (see, for example, Mackintosh, 1974). In the remainder of this chapter, in the next chapter, and in several other sections of this text there will be occasion to describe the effects of a number of variables on the course of extinction. At this juncture let us just reiterate something that was mentioned earlier in regard to Pavlovian conditioning. That is, the occurrence of extinction would seem to be adaptive. If the environment changes so that an outcome that was rewarding no longer occurs when a particular response is performed, then it would seem in the best interests of the animal to cease making that response—to change its investments, in the analogy of the stockbroker described in Chapter 1. The processes of acquisition and extinction allow an animal to track the opportunities in its environment. They provide for flexibilities in behavior rather than rigidities.

REWARD VARIABLES

This section will be concerned with how the conditions of reward presentation influence performance in simple instrumental learning tasks. Most of the data presented in this section were derived from experiments using straight runways of the type shown in Figure 7–1. However, most of the conclusions derived apply also to more complex behaviors such as maze performance and behavior in operant chambers. This will be indicated at the appropriate places. Later, behavior that occurs in these more complex situations will be examined in more detail.

Deprivation State

Activating Effects

When a rat is deprived of food, many aspects of its behavior appear to become more energetic. For example, rats given the opportunity to run in a wheel will show great increases in activity when they are deprived of food and water (Collier, 1969). An example of this effect is shown in Figure 7–3.

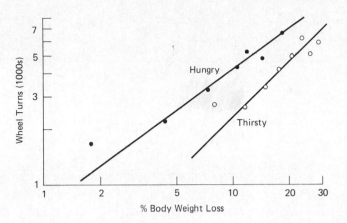

FIGURE 7–3 *Number of wheel turns as a function of percentage body weight loss in hungry and thirsty rats. Both axes are calibrated in log units. (From Collier, 1969)*

Note that the wheel-running in this experiment was not an instrumental response—it did not obtain food for the animals. This increase in activity may have adaptive functions if, in the natural environment, such increases in activity are likely to carry the animal to a different location, perhaps one where it is more likely to encounter the substance needed to satisfy the deprivation condition (see Craig, 1918; Eibl-Eibesfeldt, 1970). However, under laboratory conditions, deprivation does not always increase activity; it seems most likely to do so when there is opportunity for extensive physical movement and/or where there are changing environmental stimuli (Bolles, 1975; Campbell & Sheffield, 1953).

Acquisition Effects

Instrumental behavior also increases in vigor as a function of deprivation. The data presented in Figure 7–4 illustrate the effects of food deprivation on running speed for a food reward (Weiss, 1960). The experiment was conducted in a straight runway and the data are presented in terms of running speed for various periods of food deprivation. It can be seen that running speed increased as food deprivation was increased from 2 through 48 hours, and that the greatest speeds occurred in the middle section of the runway.

One interpretation of the effects of deprivation on runway behavior is that the rats do not really run *faster* as deprivation increases; they take less time to get from the start box to the goal box because responses such as sniffing and grooming, which would normally compete with running forward, are eliminated to an increasing degree as deprivation increases (Estes, 1958). This interpretation implies that behavior does not become more vigorous or

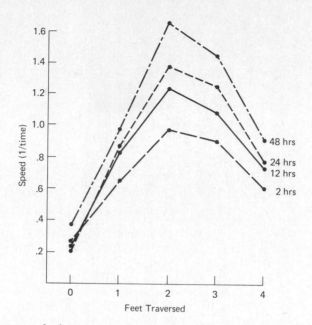

FIGURE 7–4 Speed of running in runway as a function of hours of deprivation and distance traveled in the runway. (From Weiss, 1960)

energetic as a function of deprivation, it simply becomes more direct. However, this interpretation has not received complete support from the data. For example, Porter, Madison, and Senkowski (1968) carefully observed rats' behavior in the runway and recorded the trials and runway sections in which competing responses occurred. As can be seen in Figure 7–5, there was a decrease in competing responses as deprivation increased and, furthermore, competing responses were at a minimum in the middle sections of the runway. These data nicely parallel the speed data presented in Figure 7–4. However, the investigators went one step further and analyzed their data after removing the effects due to competing responses. They did this by examining the effects of deprivation on trials where no detectable competing responses at all occurred and/or by subtracting the time consumed by the competing responses. When this was done, a relationship between deprivation and running speed was still found. The greater the deprivation the faster the rats ran.

So it appears that competing responses are eliminated as deprivation increases but, in addition, it also appears that rats run faster as deprivation increases. In other words, it is meaningful to think of an organism's behavior as becoming more energetic or vigorous as deprivation increases, as well as more direct (fewer competing responses).

These energizing effects of deprivation have been found in a variety of other situations such as operant bar-pressing tasks (e.g., Carlton, 1961), with

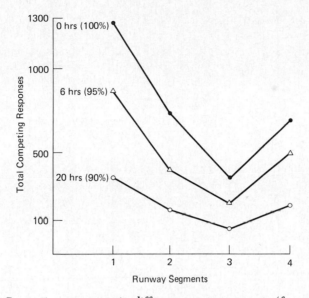

FIGURE 7–5 *Competing responses in different runway segments (from start to goal) as a function of deprivation. Each curve is labeled by the hours of food deprivation (0, 6 and 20) and the correlated percentage of free-feeding weight (100 percent, 95 percent and 90 percent). (From Porter et al., 1968)*

other rewards such as sucrose solutions (e.g., Collier, 1962) and saccharin (e.g., Snyder, 1962), a nonnutritive sweet-tasting substance.

Extinction Effects

When an animal is no longer rewarded for performing an instrumental task, its performance deteriorates. The effect of the removal of a reward appears to be directly analogous to the extinction effects that occur in Pavlovian conditioning when the CS is no longer followed by the US. The deprivation state of the animal has an effect on the rapidity with which the extinction occurs. Animals under more extreme conditions of deprivation during extinction take longer to extinguish (e.g., Barry, 1958; Capaldi, 1972; Pavlik & Reynolds, 1963).

It is also possible to shift the deprivation state between acquisition and extinction. The question of interest in such shifts is whether or not there is a carry-over effect from acquisition to extinction. In other words, does the rate of extinction depend only on the level of deprivation during extinction or is it also influenced by the deprivation levels that prevailed during acquisition but are no longer in effect? The answer to this question has not been easy to come by and it appears that the degree of carry-over between acquisition and

extinction may depend on the apparatus used (Bolles, 1975) and the deprivation parameters. But, to the extent that generalizations can be made, it appears that high deprivation during either the acquisition or extinction phase
retards extinction, but this effect is more pronounced when deprivation is
manipulated during the extinction phase (Barry, 1958, 1967; Capaldi, 1972).

Reward Magnitude

Acquisition Effects

In general, the larger the reward, the better the performance in simple
instrumental tasks. Animals tend to run faster in runways and mazes and
press levers at a higher rate when reward is large as compared to when it is
small (e.g., Crespi, 1942; Mellgren, 1972; Osborne, 1978; Pubols, 1960). In
addition to increasing the vigor of many types of instrumental behavior, there
is some evidence that large rewards serve a general activating function, like
deprivation, and increase the level of behaviors not directly related to a response–reward contingency (Killeen, 1975; Osborne, 1978). An animal's level
of activity while it is waiting for a reward to become available tends to be
higher the larger the reward that will eventually become available (Osborne,
1978).

Qualitative differences in rewards influence instrumental performance
in a fashion similar to quantitative differences in reward. For example, rats
will press levers faster or run faster in runways for more highly concentrated
sugar solutions (e.g., Flaherty & Caprio, 1976; Guttman, 1954). There is also
some evidence that there may be a perceptual and/or consummatory aspect
of reward magnitude effects. Wolff and Kaplon (1941) found that chickens
rewarded with a piece of popcorn cut into four sections ran faster in a runway
than chickens rewarded with a single whole piece of popcorn. Similar effects
have been found in studies with rats (Campbell, Batsche, & Batsche, 1972).

Despite the general simplicity of the effects of reward magnitude, there
are a few exceptions to be noted. In some circumstances the effects of reward
magnitude will disappear if the rats are trained in an instrumental task for a
long period of time. After extended training, there may be no difference between animals receiving large and those receiving small magnitudes of reward
(McCain, Ward, & Lobb, 1976). Other exceptions to the general rule will be
considered when we discuss schedules of reward later in the text.

Reward Relativity

A factor that importantly influences the effects of amount of reward on
behavior is whether the animals experience one, or more than one, level of
reward. If animals experience more than one level of reward, then the effects
of amount of reward on behavior may be exaggerated. This effect is illustrated

in Figure 7–6, which shows differences in the lick rate for 32-percent and 4-percent sucrose solutions under two conditions. The bars labeled "32" and "4" present data for animals that received only one sugar solution, either 32 percent or 4 percent. As indicated, the animals receiving the higher concentration licked more. The bars labeled "32(4)" and "4(32)" present data for animals receiving both the 32-percent and 4-percent solutions. The solutions were presented to these animals in alternation (i.e., 4-percent then 32-percent, then 4-percent again, etc). The animals also drank more for the higher concentration under these conditions, but the difference between the amounts they drank of the two solutions was exaggerated; more 32-percent was consumed and less 4-percent was consumed as compared to the rats that received only a single solution.

These results show that reward has relative as well as absolute effects. The absolute effects are demonstrated by a "between-subjects" comparison,

FIGURE 7–6 Incentive contrast. Lick rates for sucrose solutions as a function of sucrose concentration (32 percent or 4 percent) and method of presentation. The two interior bars represent data obtained from rats that received either 32 percent or 4 percent sucrose only. The difference between these two bars measures the difference in absolute rewarding properties of the two solutions. The exterior bars show that rats that had an opportunity to taste both 32 percent and 4 percent consume more 32 percent and less 4 percent sucrose than the control groups. Thus, experience with both solutions exaggerates the difference in lick rate. This exaggeration of differences illustrates incentive relativity or contrast. (Data from Flaherty & Largen, 1975)

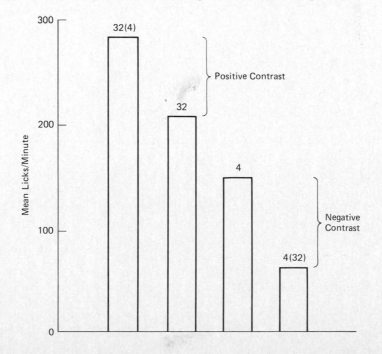

where each group received only one reward. Under these conditions each reward produces a certain level of responding. The relative effects are illustrated by comparing the "within-subjects," where the same animals receive the two solutions, and the between-subjects data. This comparison shows that the effects of a particular reward are influenced by other rewards that the subjects have experienced. Thus, the apparent value of the 4-percent solution is decreased (the animals drink less of it) if the animals have experience with a "better" (sweeter) solution, and conversely, the apparent value of the 32-percent solution is raised (they drink more of it) if the animals have had experience with a less sweet substance.

These reward relativity effects correspond to what is referred to as "psychological" in everyday language. To an outside observer, both groups of animals receiving the 4-percent solution are receiving exactly the same thing. Yet one group finds the solution less rewarding than the other, not because there is anything different about the solution each group receives but because there is something different about the experience that the groups of rats have had. It may be that this effect is analogous to something like disappointment or the spoiled child effect in humans—once a rat discovers that something better than 4-percent sucrose exists in the world, the 4-percent becomes less attractive.

Examples of reward relativity effects may be found in all types of simple instrumental learning tasks, including running in straight runways (Crespi, 1942; Mellgren, 1972), maze behavior (Elliott, 1928; Shanab & Ferrel, 1970), lever pressing by rats (Guttman, Sutterer, & Brush, 1975), and pecking behavior of pigeons (McSweeney, 1982; Williams, 1983). In this literature the two aspects of reward relativity are conventionally referred to by different terms. These terms may be illustrated by referring again to Figure 7–5. The enhanced responding for the 32-percent solution shown by the animals that receive both 32-percent and 4-percent is referred to as a *positive contrast effect*. The decrement in responding for the 4-percent solution shown by the within-subjects group is referred to as a *negative contrast effect*. Thus, positive and negative contrast effects are defined in terms of the difference in response rate between animals that receive only one reward level and animals that receive two or more reward levels.

The reward relativity literature has recently been reviewed and a substantial amount is known about the conditions that influence these contrast effects (Flaherty, 1982; Williams, 1983). Some of these conditions are as follows. Generally speaking, the greater the discrepancy in reward magnitude, the greater the contrast. There is also some evidence that increasing deprivation will enhance contrast, at least negative contrast (Cleland, Williams, & DeLollo, 1969; Ehrenfreund, 1971). When animals are rewarded on only some trials, or when the amount of reward that they receive is varied from trial to trial, then degree of contrast seems to be related to the average amount of reward that they receive (McHose, 1970; Peters & McHose, 1974). Contrast also occurs when the percentage of trials in which animals receive a reward is changed either upward or downward (e.g., McCain, Lobb, & New-berry, 1976; McHose & Peters, 1975; Seybert, 1979; Shanab & Cavallaro, 1975).

What causes contrast effects? The answer to this question is not entirely clear, but there are some suggestions. First, the animal must establish some expected level of reward based on its past experience (Capaldi, 1974) and there must also be some comparison process in which new rewards are com-pared to this expected level. The animal must also be able to detect a differ-ence between the expected level and the new reward, a process that must involve memory (Gonzalez, Fernhoff, & David, 1973; Spear, 1967) and, pos-sibly, perceptual processes. If the detection and comparison processes reveal that the reward is different from what was expected, an emotional response may be generated that may facilitate behavior in cases of better than expected reward, or interfere with the instrumental behavior in cases of lower than expected reward (Crespi, 1944). There is substantial evidence that emotional processes may be involved in negative contrast (Flaherty, 1982). For exam-ple, the shift to a smaller than expected reward may release stress hormones (Becker, Flaherty, & Pohorecky, 1984; Goldman, Coover, & Levine, 1973). Also, the behavioral effects of such a shift may be ameliorated by drugs that reduce anxiety in humans; drugs such as the tranquilizer Librium (Becker & Flaherty, 1983), alcohol (Becker & Flaherty, 1982), and barbiturates (Flaherty & Driscoll, 1980; Ridgers & Gray, 1973). Whether an emotional response such as elation somehow energizes or focuses behavior in a positive contrast situation has not yet been determined.

There are probably many examples of everyday life in which contrast-like processes are important. We constantly develop expectations and goals, some of which are met, some are not. The emotional consequences of these various outcomes may be major or minor, depending on the importance of the goals. Contrast-like processes are probably a factor in labor relations, par-ticularly in influencing salary demands. Realistic or unrealistic expectations may be important in job satisfaction. On a larger social level, some political scientists see a possible connection between social violence and unmet expec-tations (e.g., Feierabend, Feierabend & Nesvold, 1969).

Extinction Effects

The extinction procedure is formally similar to a negative contrast ex-periment in that the subjects are downshifted in amount of reward. The dif-ference, of course, is that in extinction the new reward is always zero. The question we are asking here is whether or not there is any relationship be-tween amount of reward received in acquisition, and resistance to extinction (R to E).

A number of studies have indicated that there is an inverse relationship between amount of reward in acquisition and resistance to extinction. That is, large rewards in acquisition apparently lead to faster extinction than do small rewards in acquisition (e.g., Armus, 1959; Burdette, Brake, Chen, & Amsel, 1976; Ison & Cook, 1964; Wagner, 1961). An example of this relationship is shown in Figure 7–7.

There are a number of plausible explanations for this outcome. One is that large rewards in acquisition lead to an emotional response, such as frustration, in extinction (Amsel, 1967). Frustration may, in turn, lead to behaviors that interfere with the performance of the instrumental response. This apparent similarity between extinction and negative contrast is supported by some data. For example, both negative contrast and extinction shifts lead to behaviors that could be classified as irritable. Both types of shift also lead to increases in stress hormones (Dantzer, Arnone, & Mormede, 1980; Goldman et al., 1973). Both negative contrast and R to E are influenced in a similar fashion by pharmacological agents (Flaherty, 1982; Gray, 1982). And both negative contrast and the effects of magnitude of reward on R to E are influenced in a similar fashion by comparable retention intervals (Gonzalez et al., 1973). However, there is not enough evidence yet to justify the conclusion that frustration completely accounts for the effects of acquisition reward on R to E. At the present time, the frustration interpretation can be regarded as a hypothesis deserving of further investigation.

A complicating factor is that some studies have not shown the inverse relationship between amount of reward and R to E. They find instead a direct relationship—the greater the reward the greater the R to E (e.g., Hill & Spear, 1962). A possible explanation for these conflicting data is that the effects of amount of reward on R to E may be related to the number of acquisition trials. The inverse relationship might be found only after extended ac-

FIGURE 7–7 Effect of magnitude of reward on extinction. Animals given large rewards in acquisition (300 mg pellet) extinguished faster than animals given small rewards (45 mg pellet) in acquisition. (Data from Burdette et al., 1976)

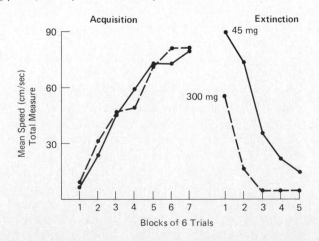

quisition training, whereas after minimal training there may be a direct relationship, or possibly no effects, due to amount of reward during acquisition. There is some evidence in the literature that supports this line of reasoning (e.g., D'Amato, 1970; Ison & Cook, 1964; Senkowski, 1978; Traupman, 1972; Wilton & Strongman, 1967).

Thus, the present state of knowledge might be summarized as follows. Large reward in acquisition often leads to faster extinction than small reward in acquisition. However, this effect may be apparent only if a relatively large number of acquisition trials are given. One possible explanation for the magnitude of reward effect is that extinction (shift to zero reward) elicits an emotional response such as frustration and this response interferes with the learned behaviors. The larger the reward that is expected, based on the acquisition experience, the more frustration there should be in extinction (Amsel, 1967; Capaldi, 1974) and, thus, the faster the extinction. One difference between negative contrast and extinction that should be borne in mind is that in the contrast experiment the animals are still rewarded, although at a lower level; in extinction no rewards are presented.

Delay of Reward

Acquisition Effects

It is well established that delaying the presentation of a reward until some time after the completion of an instrumental response results in a decrement in behavior. For example, animals run slower in a runway for a delayed reward than for an immediate reward, and, in general, the longer the delay the slower they run (e.g., Capaldi, 1978; Davenport, 1962; Logan, 1960; Mackintosh & Lord, 1973). This relationship is shown in Figure 7–8. Similarly, if animals are rewarded for choosing one arm of a T-maze, the learning that this arm is the correct (rewarded) arm proceeds much more slowly if the reward is delayed (Renner, 1964).

Some of the conditions that enable an animal to learn even when reward is delayed were investigated in early experiments by Perkins (1947) and Grice (1948). Grice trained his rats in the two-choice apparatus illustrated in Figure 7–9. In this experiment reward was correlated with a particular brightness. For example, black may have been designated as the correct stimulus for a particular rat. In order to obtain a reward the animal would have to choose the black section of the apparatus. After the animal made its choice it passed through the black area into the delay compartment, which was of a neutral brightness. The animal was confined in the delay compartment for the duration of the delay interval, after which it was allowed to enter the goal box. If the animal had made the correct choice (black) there would be a reward waiting in the goal compartment. Under the conditions of his experiment, Grice

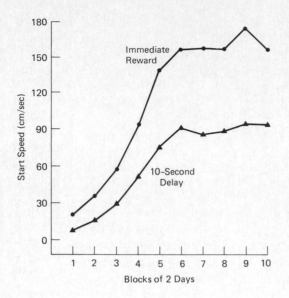

FIGURE 7–8 Effect of delay of reward on running speed. Rats for whom reward was delayed for 10 seconds after they reached the goal box ran slower than rats that received immediate reward (Capaldi, 1978).

found that a delay in reward of as little as two seconds virtually eliminated learning.

Comparison of Grice's results with earlier studies, which had shown that animals could learn with longer delays (e.g., Watson, 1917), indicated the importance of waiting out the delay period in the presence of cues correlated with the delivery of reward. If animals are allowed to wait in the presence of such predictive stimuli (e.g., the black compartment in Grice's study) they may be able to learn with relatively long delays. However, if there are no

FIGURE 7–9 Apparatus used by Grice to investigate influence of reward delay on learning to approach one brightness in a runway. The rats had to choose between entering a black or white runway, only one of which was rewarded. Before it could enter the goal area it was held in the delay chamber, where there were no discriminative cues. Thus, the delay was interposed between the rat's experience with the choice stimuli and the receipt of reward if correct and nonreward if incorrect (Grice, 1948).

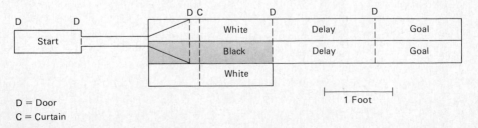

cues present during the delay interval, then learning may be substantially disrupted by even brief delays.

A more recent series of experiments, using an apparatus similar to Grice's, indicated another way in which animals may bridge a time gap and learn a choice response with a delay of reward as long as a minute or two. These studies showed that the presentation of an unusual or particularly salient stimulus just after the animal had made its choice (correct or incorrect) would help it to learn even though reward was delayed for some time and even though the animal was confined to a delay chamber without the presence of cues predictive of reward. The stimuli used in these experiments were events such as handling the animals just after they made the choice response, or presentation of a brief loud sound or bright light just after they made their response. The investigators in these experiments speculated that these stimuli served to "mark" the criterion response (the choice) in the memory of the rats. Then when the reward was received after the delay period the animals would be more likely to recall the response that they had made a minute or two earlier and associate that response with the presentation of the reward (Lieberman, McIntosh, & Thomas, 1979).

Another recent series of studies by D'Amato and his colleagues has indicated conditions in which animals may learn with substantial delays, even when there is only a single acquisition trial. These experiments involved training rats (and monkeys) to choose one arm of a T-maze. The experiments differed from traditional studies in several ways. First, the animals were given extensive preexposure to both arms of the maze (the arms were of differential brightness and complexity, e.g., striped). On a training trial the animal was confined to its nonpreferred arm of the maze (the one it had spent the least time in during preexposure) for a long period of time (say 20 minutes). Following this, the animal was removed to a waiting area in a cage outside of the experimental apparatus, where it remained for the delay interval (there were no cues predictive of reward in this situation, like Grice's experiment). After the delay period had expired (it was as long as 120 minutes in some experiments) the animals were moved to a different location (e.g., a wastebasket) and given a large reward such as 15 minutes access to a sugar solution. Finally, two days later the animals were tested for learning by placing them in the start box of the apparatus and allowing them to make a choice again of the two arms. Learning was measured in two ways: by determining the choice that the animal made, and by allowing the animal to move freely between the two arms after it had made its choice and then measuring where it spent most of its time (a measure of preference).

These experiments showed that animals learned which area was rewarded even with a 30-minute delay of reward and after only a single trial— if the learning was measured by the preference data (how long the animals remained in each arm). The initial choice response did not indicate any learning, but the preference measure clearly showed that the animals had learned something about the arm in which they were confined before reward. Thus, the conclusion drawn from these experiments is importantly influenced by the dependent variable chosen to assess learning.

Other results obtained in other experiments showed that animals could learn to avoid a maze arm in which they had been poisoned (by sub-lethal doses of lithium chloride), even with a delay in the poisoning, and that increasing the duration of exposure to the CS increased the delay over which learning could take place (D'Amato, Buckiewicz, & Puopolo, 1981; D'Amato & Safarjan, 1981; D'Amato, Safarjan, & Salmon, 1981).

Performance Effects

Performance of an already well-learned response deteriorates when a delay of reward is introduced. This was shown in an experiment by Shanab & Biller (1972). In this experiment, it was found that when rats were shifted from a 0-second to a 15-second delay of reward in a runway task, there was a decrease in running speed to a level approximately one quarter of that which prevailed before the shift. Interestingly, it was also found that if the reward was shifted up from 1 pellet to 12 pellets at the same time the delay of reward was added, there was considerably less of a decrement in performance.

Similar decremental effects of delay of reward on well-learned behavior have been found in other rat experiments (e.g., Mackintosh & Lord, 1973; Shanab, Sanders, & Premack, 1969) and in some experiments conducted with monkeys. In these latter studies, D'Amato and Cox (1976) have found that the introduction of a delay of reward as short as only 8 seconds can lead to the decline from virtually 100-percent correct responding to chance responding (50-percent correct) in a simple two-stimulus discrimination problem. The point here is that the monkeys apparently "knew" what the correct stimulus was—they had been performing at a very high level for hundreds of trials—and yet they began selecting the incorrect stimulus as often as the correct stimulus when the 8-second delay was introduced.

A motivational rather than a learning interpretation would seem to be appropriate for these effects of delayed reward on well-learned tasks. Such an interpretation has been advocated in the past (e.g., Spence, 1956; Tolman, 1932) and the general idea is that delays reduce the reward value of the goal event. Tolman wrote that reward delays would serve to reduce that animal's "demand" for the goal object; "demand" referring to the incentive value of the reward. We shall now review some studies that are consistent with this motivational interpretation of reward delay.

Interaction of Delay with Other Variables

In a series of experiments, Davenport (1962) and Logan (1965) studied the behavior of rats given a choice between responding for a small reward presented after a short delay or a larger reward that was available only after a longer delay. For example (in Davenport's experiment), rats were given a choice of going to one side of a Y-shaped chamber for a 2-pellet reward delivered after a 1-second delay, or going to the other side for an 8-pellet reward delivered after a 10-second delay. There were actually many such combinations and Davenport found that the rats would eventually develop consistent choices for one side or the other and that, in general, larger rewards could offset longer delays, at least to some degree. The percentage choice of the large reward side of the maze under various delay and reward conditions is presented in Table 7–1. It is clear that the effects of delay depend on the size of the reward.

A more extensive investigation of this "decision making" by rats was undertaken by Logan (1965). Logan's data were remarkably consistent with Davenport's in those cases where similar delay and reward values were employed. Taken together, these experiments as well as those mentioned above in which delay was introduced late in training, indicate quite strongly that

---

TABLE 7–1 RELATIONSHIP BETWEEN DELAY AND MAGNITUDE OF REWARD

Percent choice of large reward as a function of reward and delay differences. The row labels indicate the reward differences associated with each choice, the column labels indicate the delay differences. The longer delays were always associated with the larger rewards. The percentages listed in the cells represent final level of choice of the *large reward* side. Separate groups of rats were tested under each condition. The upper left cell shows that the animals always chose the 16 pellet reward (as opposed to a 2 pellet reward) when both were delayed by 1 second. The upper right hand cell shows that there was no preference between 16 and 2 pellets when the 16 pellet reward was delayed 30 seconds, but the 2 pellet reward was delayed only 1 second, etc. (After Davenport, 1962)

Amount of Reward (number of pellets)	Delay of Reward (seconds)					
	1 vs. 1	4 vs. 1	7 vs. 1	10 vs. 1	15 vs. 1	30 vs. 1
16 vs. 2	100%	100%	100%	100%	60%	50%
8 vs. 2	100%	100%	100%	60%	85%	25%
4 vs. 2	100%	100%	50%	25%	0%	0%

the effects of delay may be interpreted in motivational terms; i.e., delay of reward detracts from the reward value of the goal event but this detraction may be offset somewhat by increasing the amount of reward. The finding of Shanab and Biller (1972), also mentioned above, that the detrimental effects of the introduction of a 15-second delay may be offset by a simultaneous increase in reward from 1 pellet to 12 pellets, is also consistent with this interpretation. Other studies (e.g., Renner, 1963) have shown that the detrimental effects of delay of reward are offset also by higher levels of deprivation. The more food-deprived an animal is, the less effect a reward delay has on instrumental performance. Clearly, all of these variables (delay, reward magnitude, deprivation) may be interpreted as influencing the same thing, the incentive value of the goal event.

Extinction Effects

If reward is delayed on some, but not all, acquisition trials, there is an increased resistance to extinction (Shanab & Birnbaum, 1974). Presenting animals with varying durations of delayed reward during acquisition (e.g., reward is sometimes not delayed, sometimes delayed 30 seconds, etc.) also seems to increase resistance to extinction (Logan, 1960).

Summary—Reward Delay

Delaying reward reduces approach speed in a simple instrumental task. Delaying reward also interferes with the acquisition of a two-choice learning task; the effects of reward delay are greater when rats are required to learn a brightness discrimination than when they are required to learn a spatial discrimination (Grice, 1948; Perkins, 1947). The elimination of cues correlated with reward availability severely restricts the delay over which animals may learn traditional discrimination learning tasks. Rats may be able to learn a choice task with quite long delays of reward if special procedures are used. These procedures include extensive exposure to the correct stimulus prior to the delay interval, relatively novel stimuli, large rewards, and measures of preference rather than just simply choice.

Delay of reward in acquisition may, in some circumstances, enhance resistance to extinction.

CHAPTER SUMMARY

Instrumental behavior differs from Pavlovian conditioning operationally in terms of the degree of control the subject's response has over the reinforcing event. In Pavlovian conditioning the CR may or may not modify the US, but in instrumental learning the subject's response is *necessary* for the presentation of the reinforcer. The effect that the subject's response has on the environment determines whether the probability of that response occurring again will increase or decrease. The importance of the instrumental contingency on behavior may be studied by using the omission procedure or by using negatively correlated rewards.

Degree of deprivation increases general activity, in most situations, and increases both the vigor and directedness of instrumental behavior.

The vigor of instrumental behavior also tends to vary directly with both amount and quality of the reinforcement. Reinforcements have relative as well as absolute value. That is, shifting from a more preferred to a less preferred reinforcement will have deleterious effects on performance, and shifting from a less preferred to a more preferred reinforcement will tend to enhance performance. There are several possible theoretical explanations for these contrast effects.

The relationship between amount of reward in acquisition and resistance to extinction is a complex one but it seems that, at least in some situations, a larger reward in acquisition leads to faster extinction.

Delay of reward impedes instrumental behavior. Many of the deleterious effects of delay can be attributed to motivational factors in that they may be offset, to some extent, by increasing the amount of reward. Also consistent with a motivational interpretation is the fact that the effects of delay become manifest even when delay is introduced in a highly trained task. It is likely that delay of reward in acquisition also interferes with the formation of associations between the performance of the instrumental response and the availability of reinforcement.

8

Instrumental Learning II: Schedules of Reinforcement

We need to go beyond mere observation to a study of functional relationships. We need to establish laws by virtue of which we may predict behavior, and we may do this only by finding variables of which behavior is a function.

B. F. Skinner, *Behavior of Organisms*,
1938

INTRODUCTION

In the everyday world of humans and lower animals it is rare that each instance of a goal directed response is met with success or reward. It is more often the case that repeated attempts must be made before a given outcome is attained. For example, it has been reported that lions are successful in only about 8 percent to 30 percent of their attempted captures (Schaller, 1972). In this regard it is noteworthy that intermittently rewarded behavior is more resistant to extinction than is continuously rewarded behavior. In addition, the characteristics of the responding that occurs in acquisition vary systematically depending on the exact way in which intermittent rewards are scheduled to occur.

Two research procedures have been used to investigate the effects of reward schedule on behavior. One, termed *discrete trials procedure*, typically involves the use of a straight runway and exposes the animals to relatively few trials. These runway studies are termed *discrete trial* because the animal is placed in the apparatus and removed from the apparatus by the experimenter, usually for one trial at a time. The animal is able to respond only when the experimenter places the animal in the apparatus. Experiments using this procedure typically provide information regarding behavior changes that take place during the initial stages of learning and during the transition from acquisition to extinction.

The second procedure typically uses an operant chamber in which the subject is placed for an hour or two each day for weeks, months, or years. The subject is usually free to respond at any time that it is in the chamber, and the rate of this responding is measured. These "free operant" studies are particularly adapted to measuring the effects of schedules of reward on *steady state behavior,* that is, behavior characteristic of long exposure to the schedule.

The consideration of schedules of reward will begin with the discrete trials procedure.

DISCRETE TRIALS EXPERIMENTS

The typical effects found in runway studies may be stated concisely: Partial reward in acquisition tends to have no detrimental effects on runway behavior and may, in some cases, enhance running speed. Also, a history of partial reward in acquisition tends to increase resistance to extinction.

A study clearly showing the acquisition effects was conducted by Goodrich (1959). He found that rats rewarded on a random 50 percent of their trials ran faster in the start and run sections of a runway than did rats rewarded on 100 percent of their trials. In the goal section of the runway the 100-percent rewarded group ran faster than the 50-percent group. A more recent study by Capaldi (1978) showed that these partial reinforcement acquisition effects may be exaggerated if the animals are also given a constant 10-second delay of reward. There is as yet no completely adequate account as to why partially rewarded animals run faster than continuously rewarded animals in the early sections of the runway but slower in the later sections.

The increased resistance to extinction produced by partial reward has been shown by a large number of studies, and indeed is one of the more robust findings of the animal learning literature. For example, Weinstock (1954) found an inverse relationship between percentage of reward in acquisition and resistance to extinction in different groups of rats rewarded on 30 percent, 50 percent, 80 percent, or 100 percent of their acquisition trials. A more recent example of this partial reinforcement extinction effect (PREE) is shown in Figure 8–1. This experiment shows that 100-percent rewarded animals extinguish faster than 67-percent rewarded animals, and it shows that

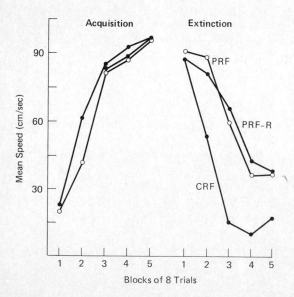

FIGURE 8–1 The partial reinforcement extinction effect (PREE). Animals rewarded on every trial (continuous reinforcement, or CRF) extinguish faster than animals rewarded on 67% of their acquisition trials (partial reinforcement, or PRF). There were two partially reinforced groups, one that received the same number of trials as the CRF group, and one that received the same number of reinforced trials (Group PRF-R) and thus more total trials. (From Burdette et al., 1976)

the greater persistence in the intermittently rewarded rats occurred in both trials equated and reward equated groups (see Chapter 4).

These extinction effects of partial reward may seem paradoxical from a common sense view. Why should animals that are rewarded only some of the time be more persistent than animals that are rewarded all of the time? The search for an answer to that question has generated many theories and a very large number of experiments. We will be able to give only the briefest exposure to this literature.

Frustration Theory

Amsel (1958; 1967; Amsel & Stanton, 1980) has argued that the partial reinforcement extinction effect occurs because animals trained with a partial reward schedule learn to persist under conditions of frustration. Amsel's model assumes that the following processes occur in animals exposed to a random schedule of partial reward. During the initial trials in the apparatus the animals develop an expectancy of receiving a reward in the goal box. The development of this expectancy is assumed to be mediated by Pavlovian conditioning processes, as described in Chapter 6. Once the animals develop the reward expectancy, the occurrence of nonreward elicits an emotional response of frustration. This frustration is assumed to be an aversive event.

It is important to note that nonreward is not assumed to be frustrating unless a reward is expected. Once the animals experience frustration they should come to expect frustration as well as reward when they reach the goal box. The acquisition of anticipatory frustration is assumed to be a Pavlovian process much like the acquisition of the expectancy of reward. Since the partial reward schedule is random, the animals cannot predict which trials will be rewarded and which trials will be nonrewarded. Thus, the animals should be in a state of conflict at the start of each trial. The conflict is generated by the opposing tendencies to approach the goal because of the expectancy of reward and to withdraw from the goal because of the expectancy of frustration.

The final stage in the acquisition process envisioned by Amsel is one of counterconditioning or conflict resolution. This stage comes about because animals continue to approach the goal with the mixed expectancies of reward and nonreward. Since the approach response is rewarded on some trials, and since the expectancy of both reward and frustration are assumed to be present on these trials, both of these expectancies should become associated with making the approach response. That is, the internal states associated with the expectancy of either reward or frustration should act as a stimulus that signals the animals to make the approach response in order to obtain reward. This process is termed *counterconditioning* because the original tendency of anticipatory frustration to promote withdrawal becomes reversed as this internal cue becomes associated with making the approach response. (We have previously considered the concept of counterconditioning in regard to phobias, in which case relaxation may be associated with a stimulus that originally elicited fear (see Chapter 3, p. 47).

The theory then explains the PREE in the following way. All trials are nonrewarded in extinction and these trials should be frustrating since the animals would have developed an expectancy of reward during acquisition. Eventually, in extinction the animals should come to expect frustration when exposed to the start box stimuli. This anticipatory frustration should elicit a tendency in the animals to withdraw from the goal box, or at least not to approach it. Thus, frustration should aid in the extinction of the running response. However, animals with a history of partial reward enter into extinction with an association that controls an approach response when frustration is anticipated. Thus, animals with a history of partial reward should approach longer in extinction than animals with a history of 100 percent reward. The latter group has not had the opportunity to learn persistence—to have anticipatory frustration associated with approaching the goal.

This is a fairly complicated model to explain the seemingly simple behavior of animals running in a runway. The model has, however, aided in understanding animal behavior because it has generated a greal deal of research. We shall briefly consider some of the evidence relevant to this frustration theory of the PREE.

Is Nonreward Aversive?

There are several items of evidence that support the idea that the absence of an expected reward is an aversive event. First, we have mentioned studies earlier in this text which showed that animals will withdraw from the locus of nonreward (e.g., Green & Rachlin, 1977; Hearst & Franklin, 1977; Karpicke et al., 1977). We have also mentioned earlier that extinction causes the release of stress hormones in animals and increases the likelihood that animals will fight (e.g., Dantzer et al., 1980).

There is also evidence that rats will learn a new response in order to escape from the presence of a stimulus which had previously been associated with nonreward (Brooks, 1980; Daly, 1974). Daly, for example, first gave rats a series of rewarded trials and then shifted them to extinction. Concurrent with the introduction of nonreward was the presentation of a new stimulus (e.g., a light onset) in the goal region. In the final phase of this experiment, the rats were placed in the start box of a hurdle-jumping apparatus and the stimulus that had previously been paired with nonreward was introduced. The rats could terminate this stimulus by jumping over a hurdle into a neutral goal box. The rats that had the stimulus paired with nonreward learned rapidly to jump over the hurdle to escape the stimulus. In comparison, rats that also had the same stimulus paired with nonreward, but that had never been rewarded in the apparatus (and therefore the nonreward should not have been frustrating) showed little tendency to jump the hurdle.

These results support the hypothesis that the occurrence of nonreward after a history of reward is aversive and that this aversiveness may be transferred to an initially neutral stimulus. Brooks (1980) showed that as few as five rewarded trials were enough to make subsequent nonreward aversive, as measured by the hurdle-jumping escape response.

There is substantial evidence also that animals exposed to nonreward after a history of reward leave odor trails that other rats find aversive and withdraw from (e.g., Collerain & Ludvigson, 1977; Ludvigson, McNeese, & Collerain, 1979). These aversive odors develop when extinction follows as few as four previously rewarded trials (Collerain, 1978).

In addition there is evidence regarding the influence of certain drugs on the PREE. If the PREE is related to the experience of frustration during the acquisition period, then drugs that ameliorate the effects of aversive events might be expected to reduce or eliminate the PREE. The data in this regard are suggestive but not conclusive. For example, one study (Willner & Crowe, 1977) found that the tranquilizer chlordiazepoxide (Librium) eliminated the PREE when it was administered to animals during acquisition only (the animals were not drugged during extinction). This finding is clearly consistent with the idea that the animals must experience the aversiveness of frustration in acquisition in order to show increased resistance to extinction. Another study (Demarest & MacKinnon, 1978) failed to replicate this result. It found no effects of Librium on the PREE, but the dose of the drug used was lower than in the Willner and Crowe study.

Another drug that reduces anxiety in humans, a barbiturate, has also produced conflicting results. Some studies found that it reduces the PREE (Gray, 1969, 1979, 1982) but other studies failed to support this conclusion (Ison & Pennes, 1969). What may be needed here are more parametric studies, varying drug dose and the conditions of partial reward.

Collectively, the evidence regarding withdrawal, hormonal release, aggression, odor trails, and conditioned aversiveness clearly supports Amsel's contention that nonreward when reward is expected is an aversive event for animals. This finding from animal research is also consonant with introspective reports and a variety of experimental evidence from humans showing that incentive loss is an aversive and frustrating experience (e.g., Klinger, 1977). An advantage in having an animal model of such frustration is that it permits research into the experimental, physiological, and genetic bases of the behavior. This is research that could not be conducted with humans.

Is There Conflict?

There has been little research bearing directly on this aspect of Amsel's theory. However, there is one study that seems to provide some support for a role of conflict and conflict resolution in the PREE. Henke (1974) found an increase in the trial to trial variability of rats' running speeds about halfway through an acquisition series of 48 partially rewarded trials. This increased variability eventually subsided before the start of extinction. There was no such pattern of variability increase and decrease in animals continuously rewarded—it occurred only in partially rewarded animals. Henke also found that the partially rewarded animals were more resistant to extinction than the continuously rewarded animals.

Further support for the observation that this change in variability of approach behavior might be related to the PREE was found in another aspect of Henke's experiment. In addition to normal animals, Henke also used animals with a specific part of their brains damaged. The damage was in the septum, a part of the limbic system (see Chapter 5, p. 106) that has been implicated in emotions, memory, and sensory processing. Henke found that these brain-damaged animals trained on a partial reward schedule did not show a PREE, and they also did not show the pattern of increased and then decreased variability. However, when another set of brain-damaged animals was tested with twice the number of acquisition trials they did show the changes in variability and they also showed a PREE. Thus, these experiments indicate that changes in the variability of approach behavior during acquisition may be related to the PREE. They do not, of course, give unqualified support for the idea that Amsel's hypothesized conflict mechanism is at the basis of the variability.

It seems quite reasonable to assume that animals in a state of conflict in regard to approaching or withdrawing from the goal should show more variable behavior than animals that are not in a state of conflict, but other interpretations are possible (e.g., D'Amato, 1962). However, the results are at least consistent with the idea that conflict and conflict resolution may be important factors leading to the PREE.

Other Data

An appealing aspect of frustration theory is its apparent ability to integrate a variety of data. For example, it was mentioned earlier that extinction following 100% reward tends to be more rapid after large reward in acquisition than after small reward. This result may be interpreted in frustration terms by assuming that a history of large reward in acquisition leads to greater frustration in extinction than a history of small reward. The greater frustration, in turn, leads to a greater tendency to avoid the goal area and hence to more rapid extinction of the running response. Earlier in this text the concept of frustration was also seen to apply to negative contrast effects, and their amelioration by tranquilizers.

Another example of the integrative application of frustration theory may be seen in the joint effects of amount of reward and schedule of reward on resistance to extinction. As we have just mentioned, animals that are rewarded on every trial in acquisition show faster extinction after large reward than after small reward—a result that may be interpreted in frustration terms.

However, when animals are given partial reward in acquisition, the effects of reward magnitude on extinction are reversed. That is, animals given large reward on an intermittent schedule take longer to extinguish than animals given small reward on an intermittent schedule (see, for example, Hulse, 1958; Wagner, 1961).

This reversal of results, however, can also be interpreted in terms of frustration theory. The reasoning is as follows. The nonrewarded trials of a partial schedule are assumed to be frustrating during acquisition. It is also reasonable to assume that animals given large rewards in acquisition will be more frustrated on the nonrewarded trials than animals that receive small reward in acquisition. But according to Amsel's theory, this frustration and resulting conflict is eventually resolved in that the cues from anticipatory frustration become a signal for the approach response. It is possible, then, that animals given large reward intermittently learn to approach the goal under greater levels of frustration than animals given small reward intermittently. This learning to tolerate greater frustration may then carry over into extinction and mediate the prolonged persistence of animals with a history of partial large reward. In a sense, this explanation says that the greater the frustration in acquisition, the more resistant to extinction the animals will be.

It is apparent that frustration theory has substantial experimental support and potentially wide applicability (see Amsel & Stanton, 1980; Daly and Daly, 1982; Rashotte, 1979). It should be recognized, however, that Amsel's frustration theory is not a complete account of extinction, nor even of the effects of partial reward on extinction. For example, extinction still eventually occurs even in partially rewarded animals. It has also been shown that the sequence of rewarded and nonrewarded trials has an effect on resistance to extinction, a result not taken into account by Amsel's theory. (Some of these data will be reviewed below.) There are also issues regarding the concept of frustration itself. Some scientifically conservative psychologists resist the attribution of human emotions to animals. (In some cases, even to humans!) There are potential difficulties in the use of such terms, not the least of which is a tendency to assume understanding of the animal data because of our own introspective ideas regarding frustration and related emotions, and the tendency to very readily generalize from the animal to the human and vice versa, when such terms are used. However, if these dangers are recognized, then a model like Amsel's seems amply justified in terms of the research it has generated and because of its potential integrative functions.

Sequential Theory

In order to obtain a schedule of reward that is less than 100 percent, some intermixture of rewarded and nonrewarded trials must be arranged. For example, consider an experiment in which four trials a day will be given and only two of these trials will be rewarded (i.e., a 50-percent schedule). It is obvious that several sequences of reward (R) and nonreward (N) are possible, namely RNNR, RRNN, RNRN, NRRN, NRNR, and NNRR. All of these are 50-percent schedules of reward but they differ in the actual sequence of rewarded and nonrewarded trials. In the usual partial reinforcement experiment, the sequence is determined randomly. However, Capaldi (1966) has found that the sequences themselves may have differential effects on behavior. For example, note that the sequence NRNR contains two transitions between nonrewarded and rewarded trials (NR transitions); the sequence RNRN contains only one NR transition; and the sequence RRNN contains no NR transitions. All three sequences are 50-percent reward schedules. Thus, the number of NR transitions is a variable that can be manipulated independently of percentage of reinforcement.

It has been shown that the number of NR transitions may have an important influence on behavior. For example, Spivey (1967) found that after only ten acquisition trials, a group that had experienced three NR transitions in acquisition was more resistant to extinction than a group that had received one NR transition. This latter group was, in turn, more resistant to extinction than a 100-percent reward group. These effects of NR transitions were found independent of differences in resistance to extinction produced by differing percentages of rewarded trials.

A second example of the influence of reward sequence may be seen in an experiment by Seybert, Mellgren, and Jobe (1973). In this experiment three groups were given a total of 16 acquisition trials each (one trial per day). In two of these groups 10 of the 16 trials were rewarded (a 62-percent schedule), but the groups differed in the sequence of rewarded and nonrewarded trials. The actual sequence each group experienced is presented in Table 8–1. The groups differed in number of NR transitions. One group experienced six NR transitions whereas the second group experienced only two NR transitions. The results of this experiment (presented in Figure 8–2) show that 6 NR transitions led to more resistance to extinction than 2 NR transi-

---

TABLE 8–1

Rewarded (R) and Nonrewarded (N) trial sequences received by the 3 groups in Experiment 1 by Seybert, Mellgren, and Jobe (1973). There were 16 acquisition trials.

Group	Trial Sequence
6NR	R R N R R N R N R R N R N R N R
2NR	R R R N N N R R R N N N R R R R
100%	All Rewarded

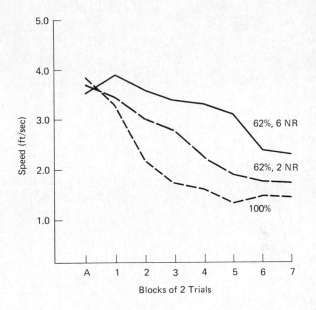

FIGURE 8–2 Effects of reward sequence on extinction. Mean running speeds for the last day of acquisition (A) and 14 days of extinction. The three groups received the trial sequences indicated in Table 8–1. Only 16 acquisition trials were given each group. (From Seybert, Mellgren, & Jobe, 1973)

tions, and that both partially rewarded groups were more resistant to extinction than the 100-percent rewarded group.

Two other sequential variables that influence resistance to extinction are N-length and the number of different N-lengths that an animal experiences during acquisition. The variable called N-length refers to the longest run of consecutive nonrewarded trials that an animal experiences in acquisition. In general, animals are more resistant to extinction when they experience long N-lengths in acquisition (e.g., Capaldi, 1966; Seybert et al., 1979). It seems to be the case too that experience with a variety of different N-lengths during acquisition enhances resistance to extinction (e.g., Campbell, Knouse, & Wroten, 1970; Capaldi, 1967).

Of the three sequential variables considered here (number of NR transitions, N-length, and number of different N-lengths), the NR transition factor seems to be most potent in determining resistance to extinction when there is a small number of acquisition trials. The other two factors become important determinants of resistance to extinction when the acquisition period is long (e.g., Capaldi, 1966; Seybert et al., 1973).

What is the mechanism by which these sequential variables exert their influence on resistance to extinction? One possibility is that animals form an association between the memory of nonreward and the eventual occurrence of reward. Thus, the sequence NR would promote resistance to extinction because during acquisition animals would learn to approach the goal area when they remember that they were *not* rewarded on the last trial, and during extinction this memory would promote performance, since all trials are nonrewarded. A similar explanation could be applied to the other sequential variables: N-length and number of different N-lengths experienced.

Support for some role for memory in sequential effects is derived from an experiment by Mackintosh (1970). It has been shown that increasing the intertrial interval reduces the size of the PREE. Mackintosh showed that long intertrial intervals were particularly effective in reducing the PREE when they were inserted between N and R trials. This result is consistent with a memory hypothesis on the assumption that a long intertrial interval will reduce the likelihood of an animal forming an association between the memory of nonreward and the eventual occurrence of reward.

A question arises as to whether all the effects of partial reward on resistance to extinction are due to sequential factors. The answer seems to be "no." Several studies by Seybert et al. (1979) have shown that percentage of reward influences resistance to extinction under conditions in which sequential variables are held constant. The results of one of these studies are presented in Figure 8–3. These data show that increasing N-length and decreasing percentage of reward have independent effects in prolonging extinction. Thus, intermittent reward may have effects that are not accounted for by the exact ordering of N and R trials. Given the extent of the evidence supporting both frustration theory and the sequential theory it seems likely that both have captured at least some of the reasons that intermittently rewarded animals are more persistent than continuously rewarded animals.

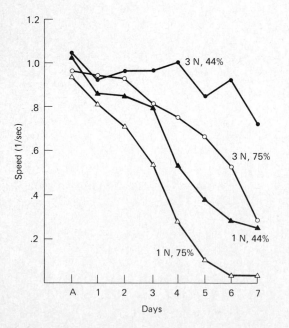

FIGURE 8–3 Effects of reward percentage and reward sequence on extinction. Mean speeds for the last day of acquisition (A) and seven days of extinction. Different groups received N-lengths of either 3 (3N) or 1 (1N) and reward percentages of either 44% or 75% in acquisition. Both percentage and N-length affected resistance to extinction. (From Seybert et al., 1979)

Before concluding the discussion of sequential variables, it should be indicated that reward sequence effects may also occur in acquisition. In particular, if a sequence is presented repetitively, rats may learn the sequence and this learning may affect their behavior. For example, if animals are given a regularly alternating sequence of rewarded and nonrewarded trials (for example, RNRNRN), they will eventually run faster on the rewarded trials than on the nonrewarded trials (e.g., Burns, 1976; Tyler, Wortz, & Bitterman, 1953). This differential behavior apparently develops because the animals learn to use the sequence or the reward outcome on the previous trial as a predictor of what will happen on the next trial—it is not the result of some artifact such as the odor of food, or odor trails left behind by the animal that immediately preceded them in the apparatus (e.g., Flaherty & Davenport, 1972).

Reinforcement Level

This explanation of why partial reward increases resistance to extinction focuses on the difference between the amount of reward expected as a result of the acquisition experience and the total absence of reward experienced in extinction. It is reasonable to assume that reward expectancy varies directly with percentage of reward. The greater the percentage of reward the greater the reward expected. Proponents of the reinforcement level explanation of the PREE also assume that resistance to extinction varies inversely with reward expectancy. The greater the reward expectancy, the faster the extinction (Capaldi, 1974; Seybert et al., 1979). Extinction itself is thought to be due to the development of some inhibitory process that opposes the approach response. The greater the reward expectancy the greater the inhibition.

These assumptions clearly account for the main PREE—animals given partial reward are more resistant to extinction than animals given 100-percent reward. The assumptions also account for the often-found result that higher percentages of reward in acquisition, even if they are less than 100 percent, lead to faster extinction than lower percentages of reward (e.g., Seybert et al., 1979; Weinstock, 1954). Some tests of other predictions derived from reinforcement level theory, tests that cannot be considered in detail in this text, have not been entirely supportive of the theory (Dyck, Dresel, & Suthons, 1978; Mellgren, Seybert, & Dyck, 1978).

It may be possible to relate the basic concepts of reinforcement level theory to frustration, but in a way somewhat different than Amsel's theory, which we have described. For example, one could assume that the higher the percentage of reward in acquisition (and the greater the reward expectancy), the more frustrating extinction is. The more the frustration in extinction, the greater the avoidance of the goal area, and therefore the faster the extinction. This use of the frustration concept is sometimes referred to as *primary frustration* to distinguish it from Amsel's interpretation of the PREE. Recall that

Amsel's interpretation relies on animals learning to approach the goal area under conditions of frustration experienced during acquisition. It is an explanation based on learned persistence that results from repeated experiences with frustration and conflict. The primary frustration concept emphasizes relative differences in withdrawal from the goal region based on initial encounters with frustration. The primary frustration interpretation of the PREE is somewhat similar to the way frustration was used as an explanation of negative contrast effects described earlier in this chapter—the greater the discrepancy between preshift and postshift reward, the greater the frustration and the greater the contrast effect. Some recent experiments have provided evidence in support of a primary frustration account of the PREE, particularly when small numbers of acquisition trials are administered (e.g., Brooks, 1980; Collerain, 1978; Ludvigson, McNeese, & Collerain, 1979).

There seems to be no basic incompatibility between the Amsel frustration account, Capaldi's sequential account, the reinforcement level account, and the primary frustration interpretation of reinforcement level. What may be needed are further integrative efforts that attempt to determine the relative contributions of these different factors in producing increased resistance to extinction. There are many other explanations of the PREE that space does not permit considering in this text. Other views may be found in Flaherty et al. (1977); Humphries (1939); Mackintosh (1974); Robbins (1971); Tyler et al. (1953).

What has not been fully explored in any of these accounts is the possible evolutionary adaptiveness of the PREE. An effect that is so robust in the laboratory must have some significance for the animal in the wild. Observation of animals in natural settings indicates that all attempts at attaining a goal are not met with success—there is some intermixture of success and failure (see, for example, Schaller, 1972). What would seem to be needed under these circumstances is some balance between giving up too soon and persisting too long. Whatever the mechanism that lies behind the PREE, as seen in laboratory studies, it may have evolved to solve this problem of optimal persistence in the face of natural food procurement situations.

STEADY STATE BEHAVIOR

The effect of intermittent reinforcement on well practiced behavior has been investigated almost exclusively with the free operant research paradigm. In free operant research, subjects (usually rats or pigeons) are placed in an operant chamber for long time periods (an hour is typical) and during this time the response object (a lever for rats or a lighted disc for pigeons) is continually available. Thus, the subject is free to make the instrumental response at any time (hence the term free operant), a characteristic of many real life situations.

This section is titled *steady state behavior* because the free operant experiments that we will consider here examine the effects of reinforcement schedules applied to subjects over numerous test sessions and many hours of experience. This is in contrast to the discrete trials experiments, in which even a relatively long experiment involving about 60 acquisition trials may take only a half hour of actual subject time. Long testing sessions are made possible through the use of automated equipment that minimizes the time demand on the experimenter and tends to maximize control over variables in the environment that are extraneous to the experiment.

Another difference between the discrete trial studies and the free operant paradigm is in the dependent variables typically employed. Whereas time measures such as latency or speed are typically used to measure runway performance, rate of responding is the usual dependent variable in free operant experiments. Response rate, recorded in cumulative form, as illustrated in Figure 8–4, provides a continuous record of behavior over the long test sessions that the subject spends in the operant chamber.

FIGURE 8–4 *Operant behavior is often studied with the help of cumulative response records. This Figure illustrates how differences in rate of responding appear on a cumulative record. This illustration was obtained with paper moving from right to left while each response served to deflect a pen slightly upward. The faster the rate of responding, the steeper the slope of the cumulative record. Pauses in responding produce horizontal lines due to no pen deflections and continued paper movement. At the top of the recording paper the pen resets to the bottom, ready to continue recording. Different schedules of reinforcement produce characteristic response patterns in a cumulative record.*

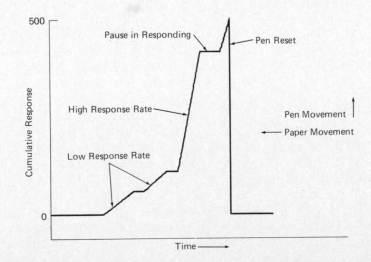

In the remainder of this chapter we will consider the basic "simple" schedules of reinforcement used in free operant experiments. More complex schedules will be considered in later chapters.

Continuous Reinforcement (CRF)

Animals may be rewarded for every response that they make, a situation directly analogous to a 100-percent reinforcement schedule in a runway task. This schedule of continuous reinforcement will produce a high and steady rate of responding but it is not used often in free operant studies because animals will quickly satiate on such a schedule and cease responding.

Fixed Ratio (FR)

On a fixed ratio schedule, the ratio of responses to reinforcements is fixed and regular so that every nth response that the subject makes produces reinforcement. For example, if every fifth bar press was rewarded with a food pellet, the schedule would be characterized as an FR-5. This schedule is analogous to piece work pay rates in industry where, for example, an employee may be paid a certain amount or given a certain bonus for every fifth electronic device assembled. Fixed ratio schedules of reinforcement produce a high rate of responding with, if the ratio is large enough, a pause after the delivery of the reinforcement.

A cumulative record showing fixed ratio performance when every 200th response is reinforced (FR-200) is presented in Figure 8–5. This is a record obtained from a pigeon that had extensive experience on fixed ratio schedules (over 4,000 reinforcements; Ferster & Skinner, 1957). The postreinforcement pauses, which varied from a few seconds to more than a minute, are clearly visible.

A second example of FR responding, this one obtained from prairie dogs, is shown in Figure 8–6. The Figure shows that postreinforcement pauses increase in length as the ratio requirement increases and that responding becomes erratic and tends to cease at higher ratios. This effect, high ratio requirements leading to a cessation in behavior, is termed *ratio strain*. Whether or not ratio strain is obtained may depend on a number of characteristics of the experiment, characteristics such as the degree of abruptness with which the schedule is introduced (gradually increasing the ratio reduces the likelihood of ratio strain), the deprivation conditions, the species of animal, the nature of the response, etc.

The development of characteristic fixed ratio behavior in a rat across successively more stringent ratios is shown in Figure 8–7 (Collier, Hirsch, & Hamlin, 1972). In this experiment the animals lived in the experimental apparatus twenty-four hours a day. Every time they completed the ratio requirement, they had access to food. This access was terminated if ten minutes

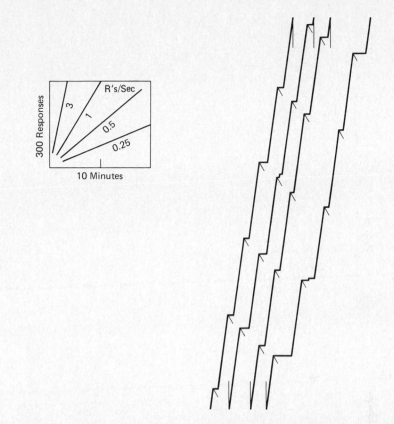

FIGURE 8–5 Cumulative record obtained from a highly trained pigeon on a FR-200 schedule. The short diagonal slashes indicate the points of reinforcement delivery. The inset provides an index of response rate. (From Ferster & Skinner, 1957)

elapsed in which the animals did not eat. Other studies using this procedure have shown that animals reduce the frequency of eating, but increase the duration of a "meal" as the ratio requirement increases. Using this procedure, it has been shown that rats and guinea pigs will respond on FR schedules up to FR 5120, but they will eat only once per day when so much "work" is necessary to produce access to food (Hirsch & Collier, 1974). Cats (Kanarek, 1974) respond on an FR schedule as high as 10,240 under these conditions. Even at these extreme ratios the characteristics of fixed ratio behavior are maintained: There is a postreinforcement pause that lasts many hours and then sustained responding at a high rate until food is obtained. The high rate of responding obtained in fixed ratio schedules is probably related to the direct response–reinforcer contingency: the faster the subject responds, the sooner reinforcement is obtained.

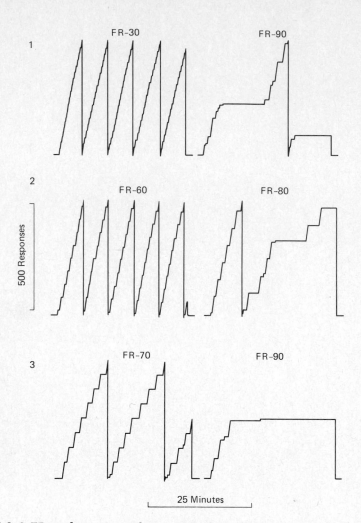

FIGURE 8–6 FR performance in three prairie dogs. The long pauses at the high ratios indicate "ratio strain" (see text). (From Todd & Cogan, 1978)

Variable Ratio (VR)

In a variable ratio schedule there is a relationship between the number of responses the subject makes and the delivery of reinforcement, but the relationship is varied rather than fixed. For example, the first reinforcement may be delivered after 10 responses, the next after 20 responses, the third after 15 responses, etc. The VR schedule is characterized by the average number of responses required to produce a reinforcement. For example, if the three ratio values just given (10, 20, 15) were the only ones used, and they were presented in an irregular order, then the schedule could be char-

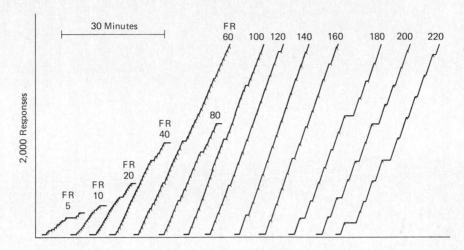

FIGURE 8–7 Performance with increasing ratio requirements in a single rat. (From Collier, Hirsch, & Hamlin, 1972)

acterized as a VR-15, since, on the average, it would take 15 responses to produce a reinforcement. A more complete description of a VR schedule would include a specification of the actual ratios reinforced and the sequence of their presentation.

The behavior associated with VR schedules is similar to the behavior produced by FR schedules in that there is generally a high rate of sustained responding interrupted by occasional pauses. However, on VR schedules these pauses are less frequent and are not correlated with the delivery of a reinforcement. An example of high rates of responding (approximately one per second) for relatively infrequent reinforcement on a VR-360 schedule is presented in Figure 8–8.

Fixed Interval (FI)

In a fixed interval schedule the delivery of a reinforcement depends upon both the passage of a time interval and the occurrence of a response. For example, in a fixed interval one-minute schedule (FI-1′) the first response after the passage of one minute produces a reinforcement. Note that in FI schedules the subject may ideally obtain reinforcement by making only one response each interval; responses that occur before the interval has passed have no bearing on the availability of reinforcement. Although the behavior produced by FI schedules does not match this theoretical ideal, it is influenced in a systematic fashion by the passage of the time period. Generally, there is a pause after the delivery of the reinforcement and then a gradual increase in the rate of responding as the availability of a reinforcement

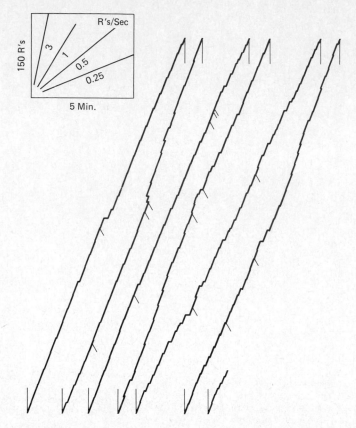

FIGURE 8–8 *Performance of a pigeon on a VR-360 schedule. Short diagonal slashes indicate reinforcement delivery. (From Ferster & Skinner, 1957)*

draws near. This behavior produces a pattern termed a *scallop* on a cumulative record (see Figure 8–9).

In comparison with FR schedules, FI schedules produce lower overall rates of responding, and the transition from the pause after reinforcement to responding tends to be less abrupt on FI than on FR schedules. An example of this scalloping may be seen in Figure 8–10, which presents data averaged across a large number of sessions. The gradual increase in response rate as the time period elapses is clear in both FI-5' and FI-15' schedules.

The rate of responding on FI schedules is related to the length of the interval: the longer the interval the lower the overall rate of responding (Wilson, 1954). This lower overall rate of responding on long FI schedules is quite likely related to the length of the pause after reinforcement, which tends to increase directly with the length of the fixed interval (Sherman, 1959). In speculating about the processes controlling this typical FI behavior it seems

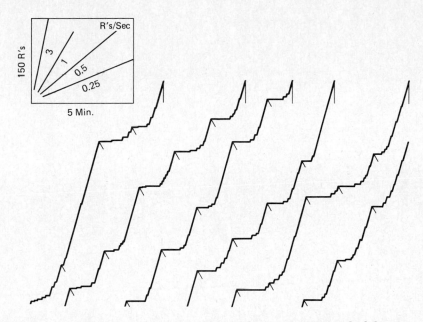

FIGURE 8–9 *Performance of a pigeon after 66 hours on a FI-4' schedule. Diagonal deflections indicate reinforcement delivery. (From Ferster & Skinner, 1957)*

FIGURE 8–10 *Average scallop on two FI schedules. The curves show the average number of responses, across 21 sessions, made at each tenth of the interval (i.e., after each thirty seconds in the FI-5' group and after each ninety seconds in the FI-15' group). The progressively increasing response rate as time of reinforcement availability approaches is clear. (From Gentry, Weiss, & Laties, 1983)*

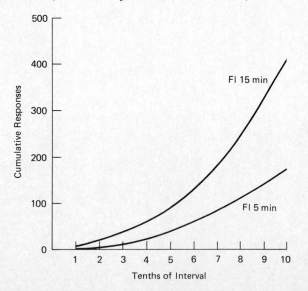

quite likely that subjects form a temporal discrimination, with the delivery of a reinforcement serving as a cue that another reinforcement will not be forthcoming for some time. Evidence in support of this contention comes from studies in which an animal is first exposed to a fixed time (FT) schedule for an extended period and then shifted to a FI schedule with the same time value. On a FT schedule the reinforcement is delivered after the passage of a particular time interval, *without the necessity of a response on the animal's part*. Thus, a FT schedule is really a Pavlovian procedure—no response is required of the animal.

The point to be made here is that exposure of animals to a FT schedule prior to shifting them to a FI schedule with the same time value leads to rapid development of scalloping (Trapold, Carlson, & Myers, 1965). The interpretation of this result is that scalloping on FI schedules is due, at least partly, to the formation of a temporal discrimination on the part of the animal. They learn approximately how long it is between the availability of successive rewards and they initiate responding near the time of reward availability (Schneider, 1969).

Before leaving the FI schedule we should note that a scalloping pattern of behavior occurs in many situations in which there is a fixed deadline for some important event such as an examination, or the completion of a paper or a book.

Variable Interval (VI)

A variable interval schedule is similar to a FI schedule except that the length of time between the availability of successive reinforcements is varied rather than fixed. For example, the first reinforcement may be produced by the first response following a one-minute interval, the second reinforcement by the first response following a three-minute interval, the third by the first response following a two-minute interval, etc. Such a schedule with different time intervals occurring in a random order may be designated by the length of the average interval. In the example given, if only one-, two-, and three-minute intervals were used and if they were presented in a random order and used equally often, then the schedule could be designated as VI-2'. Thus a VI schedule compares to a FI schedule in the same way that a VR schedule compares to a FR schedule.

In the VI, as in the VR schedule, the irregular changes in the availability and/or delivery of reinforcement deprive the subject of any cue that it can reliably use to predict the occurrence of the next reinforcement. And, in the VI as in the VR schedule, the subjects' behavior is less regular; there is no consistent pattern like scalloping associated with VI schedules. Instead, the typical steady state behavior produced by VI schedules is characterized by generally consistent rates of responding, as shown in Figure 8–11.

These four basic schedules of intermittent reinforcement include con-

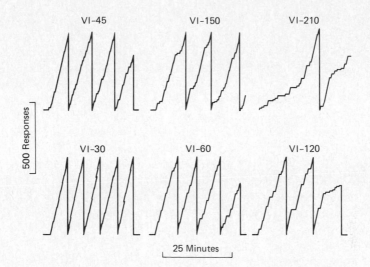

FIGURE 8–11 *Performance of two prairie dogs on three different VI schedules.* *(From Todd & Cogan, 1978)*

ditions in which the delivery of reinforcement is either directly related to the number of responses (ratio schedules) or depends on the passage of time as well as on a response (interval schedules). Either of these schedules may be regular (fixed) or irregular (varied). In general, ratio schedules produce higher rates of responding than interval schedules, and fixed schedules produce more patterned behavior than varied schedules. The exact relationship between schedules depends on the parameters of the schedules.

We have presented only the briefest consideration of these simple reinforcement schedules. More detailed treatments may be found in many sources, ranging from the seminal work by Skinner (1938) to a catalogue of schedule effects in pigeons (Ferster & Skinner, 1957), as well as more recent theoretical analyses (e.g., Gentry et al., 1983; Schoenfeld, 1970). However, even in this brief treatment it should be obvious that these simple schedules have, in general, regular and predictable effects on the behavior of organisms and therefore they may be used as important tools in the experimental analysis of behavior. One more schedule of particular interest remains to be described in this chapter. More complex schedules will be considered where appropriate in later chapters.

Differential Reinforcement for Rate

In ratio schedules there is a contingency between rate of responding and reinforcement such that the higher the rate the sooner the subject receives the reinforcement. In interval schedules there is less of a contingency between response rate and the delivery of a reinforcement but, nevertheless, there is some contingency between rate and reinforcement in the sense that subjects responding at a higher rate are more likely to be responding at the end of the criterion interval and are thus more likely to receive reinforcement sooner.

It is possible to reinforce rate of responding directly by establishing a contingency that reinforces either specific high rates or low rates of responding. This is called *differential reinforcement for rate*. The key to setting up such a contingency is the concept of *interresponse time (IRT)*: the time between successive responses. In a differential reinforcement schedule for high rates of responding (DRH), the subject will obtain a reinforcement only if it emits a specified number of responses *prior* to the completion of a time interval. For example, the subject may be required to emit 10 responses in a 5-second period in order to obtain reinforcement. Each time that this requirement is met a reinforcement is delivered.

Of more interest is the schedule that differentially reinforces low rates of responding (DRL). On this schedule the subject must refrain from responding for a specified period of time. Responses prior to the completion of that time period reset a clock so that the time period starts all over again. The first response after this time period has elapsed produces a reinforcement. For example, on a DRL 10-second schedule the subject must allow an IRT of 10 seconds to elapse in order to obtain reinforcement. The first response after 10 seconds have elapsed will deliver a reinforcement. Responses before that time will reset the clock so that 10 seconds will have to pass again before a reinforcement is available.

Performance on a DRL schedule may be assessed by determining the percentage of possible reinforcements that the subject obtains and/or by examining the distribution of IRTs. A typical distribution of IRTs obtained on a DRL 20-second schedule is shown in Figure 8–12. It is apparent that well practiced subjects are most likely to respond just after the criterion interval has timed out and thus obtain reinforcement. Errors tend to be concentrated in the time intervals just before the criterion interval is timed out and just after the delivery of a reinforcement.

Current interpretations of DRL performance favor the hypothesis that there are two underlying processes mediating the behavior in a DRL situation: the formation of a temporal discrimination, and the active inhibition of responding (e.g., Ellen & Aitken, 1971; Gage, Evans, & Olton, 1979; Hemmes & Rubinsky, 1982). There are also data which indicate that animals engage in ancillary or collateral behaviors that interfere with the criterion operant response (e.g., key-pecking); these collateral behaviors (pecking places other than the key, etc.) help to "pass the time" until the criterion interval has elapsed (e.g., Hemmes, Eckerman, & Rubinsky, 1979; Wilson & Keller, 1953).

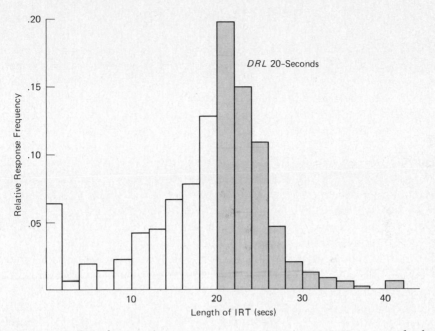

FIGURE 8–12 *Distribution of interresponse times (IRTs) on a DRL 20-second schedule. Responses in 2-second intervals are plotted as a ratio of total responses. The shaded area indicates reinforced IRTs. In well practiced subjects the greatest proportion of responses occurs just after the criterion interval has passed. (From Mallot & Cumming, 1964)*

These interpretations are particularly interesting in that they indicate that the DRL schedule may be used as a technique for investigating an organism's time estimating skills and/or an organism's ability to inhibit responding for a specified time. For example, the DRL schedule has been used in studies concerned with the neuroanatomical and neurochemical basis of inhibition and timing (e.g., Ellen, Aitken, Sims, & Stahl, 1975; Johnson, Olton, Gage, & Jenko, 1977).

Some variables that have facilitating effects on other schedules interfere with performance on DRL schedules. For example, larger amounts of reward generally facilitate responding where there is a direct relationship between responding and the receipt of the reward. For example, running speeds in a runway are generally faster the greater the reward, and in simple operant schedules, where there is a direct relationship between rate and the receipt of reinforcement, there is also a general facilitating effect of amount of reward (e.g., Keesey & Kling, 1961; Meltzer & Brahlek, 1968). In DRL schedules, however, large rewards interfere with DRL performance (Beer & Trumble, 1965). It is as if the subjects have a more difficult time inhibiting responses with large rewards.

CHAPTER SUMMARY

This chapter has been concerned with the effects of intermittent reward on instrumental behavior. The principal message of these data is persistence—animals trained on intermittent schedules are more resistant to extinction and they persist in acquisition even when rewards occur only infrequently.

The first section of the chapter was concerned with discrete trials studies of intermittent reinforcement. These studies are typically conducted in runways, they involve a brief sample of the animal's behavior, and have been mostly concerned with a theoretical analysis of the partial reinforcement extinction effect (PREE). Three theoretical positions were presented in some detail: Amsel's frustration theory, Capaldi's sequential theory, and the reinforcement level theory. The frustration theory focuses on the aversiveness of nonreward and assumes that the PREE is due to a learned persistence in the face of frustrating events. Sequential theory has highlighted the effects resulting from actual reward–nonreward sequences in a partial reward experiment. Reinforcement level theory is concerned with differential reward expectancies developed by partial and consistently reinforced animals. Each theory has a degree of support and, in general, they are not incompatible with one another. However, there is, as yet, no all-encompassing account of the PREE obtained in discrete trials experiments.

The steady state experiments provide data concerning the long term effects of exposing animals to various schedules of intermittent reinforcement. Each of the basic schedules reviewed (continuous reinforcement, fixed interval, fixed ratio, variable interval, variable ratio, differential reinforcement for low rate) leads to a particular pattern of responding. The characteristic behaviors associated with these schedules probably reflect a variety of psychological processes, including timing behaviors and inhibitory processes. The schedule-associated behaviors will be useful for the eventual understanding of these processes.

The robustness of the effects produced by intermittent reinforcement in laboratory experiments implies that performance under conditions of intermittent reinforcement may be an important factor in an animal's adaptation to its environment. Since an animal's attempts at food procurement are unlikely to meet with success in every instance, it may be that some balance between quitting too soon and persisting too long is necessary for optimal adaptation. In this regard, an analysis of the PREE in terms of animals that have different food procurement strategies and success might be useful.

9

Instrumental Learning III: Aversive Conditioning

> " . . . *the literature has become so voluminous that it must be almost a physical impossibility for any person burdened with the normal obligations of life to become conversant with the data, let alone reduce it to some systematic order.* "
>
> James A. Dinsmoor, Commentary in
> *Behavior and Brain Sciences,* 1982

INTRODUCTION

Hoofed animals on the plains of the Serengeti in Kenya are prey to a variety of predators, such as the lion, cheetah, leopard, hyena, and wild dog. The various predators have somewhat different hunting styles, and the various types of prey, in turn, employ different antipredator behaviors. These include such behaviors as having a "flight distance" that varies with different predators. When a predator approaches within the flight distance the prey animal flees, escaping from the vicinity of the predator. Other defensive patterns include running speed, zigzag running, herding (a lion has much less success attacking a herd than attacking a single animal), the tendency to avoid dense cover, drinking in the daytime rather than at night, etc. (Schaller, 1972).

It is probable that a defensive response of an animal represents a combination of innate and learned behavior patterns. The learned patterns could be based on individual experience (since capture attempts are only fractionally successful, an animal may learn some defensive behavior if it is attacked and escapes) or culturally transmitted from the actions of other animals in the herd (Schaller, 1972). Thus, the survival of an animal in the wild depends on its ability to escape or avoid its "natural enemies" and to strike some kind of balance between defensive behaviors and its need for sustenance. An animal cannot spend all of its time running and hiding.

A second situation in which aversive events may importantly influence an animal's behavior is in the adjustment to its own society. For example, many animal species are territorial and the boundaries of a given territory may be learned partly on the basis of combat between conspecifics, with an aversive outcome. The result of this combat may determine which animal avoids what territory. Also, many animal societies are organized around dominance hierarchies, structures that may be established by agonistic behavior, sometimes with physical and perhaps with psychologically damaging consequences to the losers (e.g., Eibl-Eibesfeldt, 1970; Lore, Nikoletseas, & Takahashi, 1984). It is likely that the avoidance of further aversive consequences helps maintain the dominance hierarchy once it is established.

A third case in which aversive consequences may be important in controlling natural behaviors is in the process of development. Young animals may be "taught" species-correct behaviors and independence by punishments administered by the mother, playmates, or other conspecifics (e.g., Jeffers & Lore, 1979). A substantial degree of control in human society is exerted, at least in theory, by the potentially aversive consequences of behaviors that society (including parents) has judged to be undesirable.

In this chapter we will be concerned with laboratory studies of the ways that aversive events influence learning and performance. These investigations have been concerned with elaborating situations in which aversive consequences of behavior may be studied, with establishing parametric details of aversive control, and with developing a theoretical understanding of how aversive consequences control behavior. Only within the past decade has there been any substantial interest in relating the laboratory situation to behaviors that might be appropriate for the animal under natural conditions. In this chapter we will consider a sampling of research and theory developed in several different experimental procedures.

CONDITIONED SUPPRESSION

We have encountered the conditioned suppression procedure earlier. It is not an instrumental learning paradigm per se, but one in which Pavlovian conditioning is measured by its effects on instrumental behavior. We bring it up again here because some of the data obtained with this procedure are important in theoretical interpretations of other procedures to be considered below.

In the usual conditioned suppression procedure an animal is first trained in an instrumental task, such as lever pressing, under conditions that will produce steady, persistent responding over long periods of time. The variable interval (VI) schedule described in the preceding chapter is often used for this purpose. After the animals reach a point of stable responding, a Pavlovian manipulation is superimposed on this instrumental baseline. For example, several times during a daily two-hour session a CS may be presented (e.g., a tone for three minutes) and, at the termination of the CS, an aversive event such as a shock will be presented. The presentation of the shock is independent of the animals' bar-press behavior—it is not response contingent. It is correlated only with CS presentation. After several such pairings the presentation of the CS leads to a suppression in instrumental responding. The degree of suppression in instrumental responding is taken as an index of the effectiveness of the Pavlovian conditioning. The amount of suppression is usually measured by comparing responding in the period immediately preceding CS presentation with that occurring during the CS. A number of examples of conditioned suppression were considered in Chapters 4 to 6 and data from such experiments were presented in Figures 5–2 and 6–2. These Figures show how degree of suppression was influenced by the Pavlovian manipulations investigated in those experiments.

Conditioned suppression is influenced in a straightforward fashion by a number of variables. For example, the greater the shock intensity, the greater the suppression (Annau & Kamin, 1961); a delayed conditioning paradigm produces more suppression than trace conditioning (Kamin, 1965); good conditioning is obtained with relatively long CS–US intervals (Kamin, 1965); the greater the stimulus change associated with CS onset, the greater the suppression (Kamin, 1965). Suppression of instrumental behavior will occur even if the shock itself is never experienced in the instrumental situation. That is, if the CS–US pairings are administered in a different context and the CS is then introduced into the instrumental context (Kamin, Brimer, & Black, 1963), it will produce suppression. A more detailed discussion of the variables influencing conditioned suppression may be found in McAllister and McAllister, 1971.

Why does the suppression occur? There are several possibilities. One is that the CS elicits an emotional response such as fear or anxiety and the presence of this emotional state is incompatible with ongoing instrumental behavior for a food reward. In this regard, the conditioned suppression procedure is often referred to as *fear conditioning*, or a *conditioned emotional response procedure* (see Brush, 1964; Estes & Skinner, 1941; McAllister & McAllister, 1971). The possibility of an emotional response is certainly plausible, and there are substantial data consistent with this idea, but it must be remembered that the existence of the emotional state is an inference—it is not directly measured in behavior.

There are behavioral events that may be directly measured in the conditioned suppression paradigm. One of these is a decline in activity on the part of the animal (Bolles & Collier, 1976; Bouton & Bolles, 1980). The percentage of time the animals spend immobile following the presentation of the CS increases with the intensity of the shock predicted by the CS (Fanselow & Bolles, 1979; Sigmundi, Bouton, & Bolles, 1980). These data are presented in Figure 9–1. Recall that suppression of instrumental behavior also increases with increasing shock intensity.

It seems likely that this immobility or "freezing" response may be part of the rats' innate defensive behaviors in dangerous situations. Bolles (1970, 1978) refers to freezing as a species specific defense reaction (SSDR), a response that is innate and may be elicited by danger signals in situations where other behavior, such as fleeing, is not possible. In this regard it is interesting that rats show similar "crouching" responses to both an arbitrary stimulus that has come to predict shock and to a natural predator—the cat (Blanchard

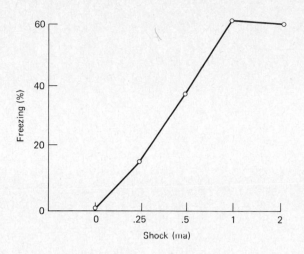

FIGURE 9–1 *Percentage of observations in which "freezing" occurred during an 8-minute period following CS presentation. More freezing occurred with increased shock intensity. (Data from Fanselow & Bolles, 1979)*

& Blanchard, 1969). It is clear that these freezing or crouching responses are incompatible with a response such as lever pressing and thus could be said to cause the suppression of instrumental behavior observed in this paradigm. Whether the freezing is, in turn, caused by fear is another question.

Freezing is not the only behavior that may be incompatible with instrumental behavior in the conditioned suppression experiment. A second possibility is that the animals may withdraw from the vicinity of the place where the response must be made. Indeed, there is evidence that animals will move away from a localized stimulus that signals shock, and if that stimulus is located near the lever more suppression will be obtained than if the stimulus is located on the opposite side of the chamber from the lever (e.g., Karpicke et al., 1977; Sigmundi et al., 1980). It is also the case that less freezing and more activity will occur in a longish rectangular box than in a square box in both of which shock has been administered (Bolles & Collier, 1976). This result may indicate that the longer box is more consistent with the fleeing SSDR whereas the square box is more consistent with a freezing SSDR (Bolles, 1978).

Thus, it seems that a signal, which the animal has learned predicts shock (a Pavlovian or S–S association), will elicit SSDRs such as freezing or fleeing, depending on such things as the location and localizability of the signal and the configuration of the apparatus; and these behaviors will, in turn, lead to a suppression of ongoing instrumental behavior. It is often assumed that this suppression reflects a state of fear in the animal. In fact, in the sections to follow several experiments will be presented that use the conditioned suppression procedure as an assay for level of fear in the context of other aversive learning situations (see Kamin, Brimer, & Black, 1963; Starr & Mineka, 1977).

ESCAPE BEHAVIOR

Experimental situations may be readily arranged in which the animal has an opportunity to escape from the presence of an aversive event such as shock, or from a signal for an aversive event. Escape behavior may be studied in a runway, in which the start and middle sections have a grid floor that may be electrified, and a goal area that is free from shock; or in a two-compartment box, where the animal may escape from shock or from a stimulus that had been paired with shock, by crossing from one compartment to the other; or in any of the typical instrumental tasks described in Chapter 7.

Performance in escape situations has been shown to be influenced in a systematic manner by a number of variables. For example, the larger the amount of reinforcement, as defined by degree of shock reduction, the better the escape performance (e.g., Bower, Fowler, & Trapold, 1959; Nation, Wrather, & Mellgren, 1974; Trapold & Fowler, 1960). Also, as is the case with positive reinforcement, delaying reinforcement (e.g., delaying shock termination) results in a decrement in escape performance (Fowler & Trapold, 1962).

Partial reinforcement has different effects on escape behavior than it has on runway behavior for positive reinforcement. Recall that rats rewarded with food on a partial schedule usually do not show a decrement in instrumental behavior and sometimes show an enhancement (Chapter 8). However, partial reinforcement in escape learning produces substantial decrements in behavior (Bower, 1960). This result may possibly be interpreted in terms of conflicting innate response tendencies elicited by the escape situation. That is, escape behavior may normally result from the animal fleeing from the vicinity of an aversive event or from the vicinity of a stimulus that it has learned predicts an aversive event. However, in a partial reinforcement experiment some of the fleeing responses are not reinforced—they do not remove the animal from the aversive situation. This failure may tend to elicit freezing, a response that would never be successful in escaping from the aversive event in these laboratory experiments. Thus, the decrement in escape behavior produced by partial reinforcement may be related to these conflicting responses of fleeing or freezing. This is an interpretation that is in the realm of speculation at the present time.

There are other data that indicate some of the factors that are important for successful escape behavior. For example, prior familiarity with the escape apparatus, a highly discriminable difference between the shock and "safe" areas, and the opportunity to spend a relatively long period in the safe area, all promote better escape learning (Franchina, Kash, Reeder, & Sheets, 1978;

McAllister et al., 1972; McAllister & McAllister, 1967). All of these data are consistent with the idea that the animal must clearly recognize a safe area if it is to flee a dangerous situation successfully.

One interesting sidelight to this research is the finding that the rats' performance in escape learning tasks is hampered if they are removed from the safe area by being picked up by the tail instead of the body. A possible interpretation of this result is that the rats find being carried by the tail an aversive experience. Thus, they are escaping from one noxious situation to another, and their performance suffers as a result (McAllister et al., 1980).

AVOIDANCE LEARNING

In the avoidance learning paradigm an aversive event is *not* presented if the animal makes some criterion response within a specified time period. For example, an animal may have to cross from one compartment of a two-compartment chamber to the other, or press a lever, or run in a running wheel within *x* seconds after the presentation of a warning signal. If the animal makes the correct response no aversive event is presented and, in effect, the animal has avoided the presentation of the aversive stimulus.

The quotation from Dinsmoor at the beginning of the chapter applies particularly well to the literature on avoidance learning. There is an abundance of both data and theory but as yet no certain understanding of the mechanism of avoidance learning. The great interest in this research topic probably arises from the number of paradoxes and puzzles presented by avoidance learning. Among these are the following. How does an animal avoid what is going to happen in the future—can animals see into the future? What is the reinforcement in avoidance learning, since, if the avoidance response is successful, no aversive event occurs, so how can the absence of something be a reinforcer? Avoidance learning is often found to be very resistant to extinction—why is this so? What is the role of fear in avoidance learning? Must an animal be afraid in order to perform successfully in an avoidance task? Does an animal actually avoid at all, or is the avoidance response taking place only from the experimenter's perspective, and not from the animal's?

One of the difficulties in dealing with the topic of avoidance learning is that avoidance has been studied in a large number of different experimental situations and in many cases the nature of the results obtained is very much influenced by the apparatus used or by other aspects of the experimental procedure. Our approach in reviewing this topic will be to describe the typical results obtained in several of the most frequently used avoidance procedures and concurrently to describe how these results are influenced by a number of independent variables. After the basic procedures and data have been described we will briefly examine some theoretical interpretations of avoidance behavior and relate them to the paradoxes we have mentioned and to the data presented.

Avoidance Tasks and Results

One-Way and Jump-Up Avoidance

Animals will learn an avoidance response within several trials if a *one-way* or *jump-up* avoidance task is employed. In these experiments the animal is simply required to cross from one compartment in which a shock is delivered to another (one-way) in which shock is never administered, or to leap (jump up) from one compartment up to another (see Figure 9–2). In some experiments just the placement of the animal in the apparatus is used as the cue that shock will be presented. In other studies a warning signal (e.g., light or tone) is presented for some time period before the shock is administered.

Although animals learn quite quickly to go to the safe compartment before shock is administered, there are some experimental parameters that influence the rate of this learning. For example, the more intense the shock, the more rapidly the animals learn (e.g., Deiter, 1976; Moyer & Korn, 1966). Some other variables that influence the rapidity of this learning include the distinguishability of the two compartments. The more distinctly different they are, the faster the learning (Knapp, 1965). The greater the amount of time the animals are allowed to spend in the nonshock chamber the faster is the learning (e.g., Denny, 1971).

Two-Way Avoidance

Two-way avoidance studies may be conducted in an apparatus like the shuttle box shown in Figure 9–2. The apparatus is modified so that shock may be presented in either chamber. The impending occurrence of shock is then signaled by the onset of a cue, usually a light, in whichever chamber the rat is occupying. If the rat crosses over to the other chamber before the shock is presented, the signal (hereafter called a *warning signal*, WS) is terminated and the shock is not presented. If the animal does not cross over before the passage of the WS–shock interval (usually a 5- to 10-second period), then shock is presented in the chamber occupied by the animal. The animal may then escape the shock by crossing over to the other compartment. Thus, the animal may either avoid or escape shock, depending on whether or not it responds during the WS–shock interval.

The principal difference between the one-way and two-way paradigm is that shock may be presented in either compartment of the two-way apparatus, so no compartment is always safe—each is safe only for a time. This added complexity greatly increases the difficulty of learning for the rat (e.g., Bolles & Grossen, 1969).

FIGURE 9–2 Top panel: jump-up apparatus used in the study of avoidance (from Denny, 1971). Bottom panel: shuttle box that may be used in the study of one-way or two-way avoidance.

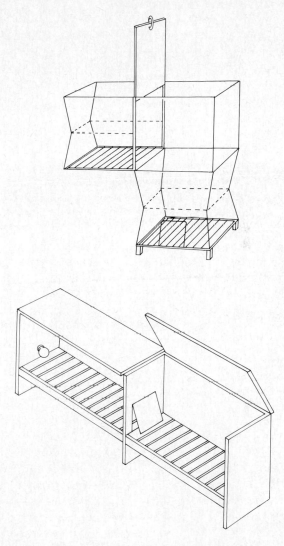

The effects of variations in shock intensity are more complex in two-way avoidance than in one-way avoidance. Generally speaking, the more intense the shock, the *poorer* the avoidance responding in the two-way task (McAllister, McAllister, & Deiter, 1976; Moyer & Korn, 1964). A possible explanation for this paradoxical finding will be considered below when the presumed role of fear in avoidance behavior is discussed.

Two-way avoidance learning is also hindered if the two compartments are distinctly different (e.g., black and white) as compared to when they are homogeneous (e.g., both black). Again, this result is opposite to that obtained in one-way avoidance. One possible explanation for this result is that the animals must learn that neither compartment is absolutely safe, and each is safe from shock only for a time—when the WS is not on. Distinctly different compartments may interfere with learning that it is the warning signal that is the best predictor of shock, not the compartments per se (Denny, 1971; Denny, Zerbolio, & Weisman, 1969).

Termination of the warning signal when the animal makes a crossing response is important. Avoidance learning is hindered if the offset of the WS is delayed for some time after the animals make the crossing response (Bower et al., 1965; Kamin, 1957). However, this interference effect may be largely eliminated if an extra stimulus (sometimes termed a "feedback" stimulus) is presented in the safe compartment when the animals make the crossing response (e.g., Bolles & Grossen, 1969; Bower et al., 1965). Several possible explanations for these effects will be considered below when theories of avoidance behavior are described.

Two-way avoidance learning may be considerably facilitated if the grid floor in the safe compartment is covered with a platform when the animal crosses in response to the WS onset (e.g., Modaresi, 1978). The platform may function somewhat like the feedback stimulus described above, but it seems to have a more potent effect than a feedback stimulus in facilitating avoidance behavior (Modaresi, Coe, & Glendenning, 1975).

A final factor that will be considered here is the occurrence of an "anticipatory" response. An anticipatory response is a crossing response that occurs during the interval between WS onset and the presentation of the shock. There is no possibility for the animals to detect that an avoidance contingency is available unless they respond during this period. In the absence of such responses the avoidance paradigm is essentially a Pavlovian conditioning experiment—the WS is repeatedly paired with a shock (in fact, the WS is often referred to as a CS). The Pavlovian contingency itself is sufficient to maintain only a very low level of responding (Kamin, 1956; see Figure 9–3) and Pavlovian processes alone are insufficient to account for avoidance performance (see Mackintosh, 1974, pp. 302–303). It is responses during the WS–shock interval that allow the animal to detect the possibility that its behavior will prevent the occurrence of shock (D'Amato, 1970). The available data indicate that any experimental condition that increases the likelihood of such anticipatory responses also facilitates two-way avoidance learning (e.g., Collins & D'Amato, 1968; D'Amato & Fazzaro, 1966; D'Amato, Keller, & Biederman, 1965; Hamilton, 1969).

Signaled Bar-Press Avoidance

Rats may learn a standard lever-press response as an avoidance response, but the learning is apparently difficult, usually requiring large numbers of trials, and the terminal performance is often at a low level (see Bolles,

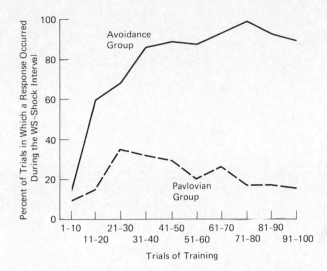

FIGURE 9–3 *Response occurring during WS–shock interval as a function of response contingency. In the avoidance group a response during the WS–shock interval terminated the WS and prevented shock presentation. In the Pavlovian group responses during the WS–shock interval had no effect. (Data from Kamin, 1956)*

1970, 1978; D'Amato, Fazzaro, & Etkin, 1968). Thus, bar-press avoidance is as difficult as, or more difficult than, two-way avoidance learning. This outcome may relate to the fact that the avoidance response (lever press) does not change the environment much—it does not move the animal to a different place. In fact, it has been shown that bar-press avoidance may be substantially improved if the lever-press response allows the animals to move to a different place, and it doesn't make much difference whether the animals themselves run or they are carried by the experimenter (Crawford & Masterson, 1978). These effects are shown in Figure 9–4.

Some other factors that influence bar-press avoidance will be briefly reviewed. In bar-press avoidance, as in two-way avoidance, high levels of shock intensity interfere with avoidance learning (e.g., Bolles & Warren, 1965; D'Amato & Fazzaro, 1966; D'Amato et al., 1968). Avoidance responding is enhanced if the shock is made discontinuous rather than continuous (e.g., D'Amato et al., 1968). In the discontinuous procedure the shock is on for a brief time period (e.g., 0.2 seconds) then off for some time (e.g., 2.0 seconds) then on again, etc. One possible explanation for the facilitating effect of discontinuous shock on bar-press avoidance is that rats may be less likely to freeze in this procedure. It is known that escape responses are more likely to occur during the off periods than during the on periods when discontinuous shock is employed (D'Amato, Keller, & Biederman, 1965).

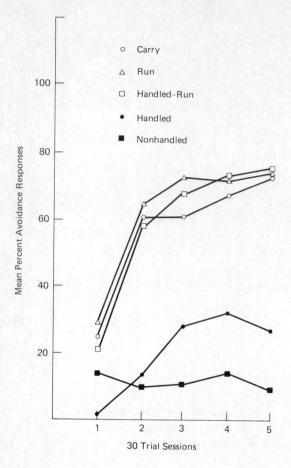

FIGURE   9–4 Bar-press avoidance as a function of opportunity to leave operant chamber. All groups could avoid shock by an appropriate bar press. The "carry" group was carried out of the chamber after an appropriate bar-press response. The "run" group was allowed to run out of the chamber. The "handled-run" group was handled and then allowed to run out of the chamber. The two remaining groups could not leave the chamber after an avoidance response. (Data from Crawford & Masterson, 1978)

If an avoidance response is well learned under favorable shock conditions (e.g., low intensity discontinuous shock) and then the intensity of shock is varied, a different effect is found. The more intense the shock, the better the performance (D'Amato, Fazzaro, & Etkin, 1967). Thus, there are two effects of shock intensity in bar-press avoidance. During the learning process high shock intensity interferes with avoidance behavior. But once the avoidance response has been well learned, then high shock intensity has a facilitative effect on the maintenance of that avoidance behavior.

It should also be noted that the detrimental effects of failure of WS termination mentioned in regard to two-way avoidance apply also to bar-press avoidance. In addition, these detrimental effects of the failure of WS termination may be offset to some extent by providing the animals with a feedback stimulus coincident with the occurrence of the avoidance response (D'Amato et al., 1968).

Unsignaled Avoidance

Perhaps the most difficult avoidance task for an animal is the *unsignaled avoidance* procedure, employed both in the two-way shuttle box and in the operant chamber. In the unsignaled procedure the only cue that an animal has as to when shock will occur is the passage of time. For example, a typical experimental arrangement may be that an animal is shocked every 20 seconds unless it responds (crosses to the other chamber or presses a lever). Once it responds it then has 20 seconds again in which no shock will be delivered. Thus, an efficient strategy for a rat in this situation might be to make a response every 19 seconds (see Anger, 1963; Church, 1978; Gibbon, 1972; Sidman, 1966, for reviews of animal timing behavior). By doing so the rat would always avoid shock and it would not have to respond too often. The poor performance of rats in this situation (a substantial number can never learn the avoidance response) is probably related to the fact that this procedure has all of the problems of the signaled two-way avoidance (the animals get shocked in both compartments) and the bar-press avoidance (they never leave the aversive situation), plus the fact that there are no cues other than those from an internal clock to tell the animal when shock will occur.

Increased shock intensity in unsignaled avoidance increases rate of responding, but decreases efficiency of responding. That is, with higher intensities of shock the rats are likely to respond when they are a short way into a response–shock interval instead of allowing a relatively long time interval to pass before responding (Myers, 1977). At low shock intensities the addition of a WS to an unsignaled avoidance task greatly increases the efficiency of the rats—they tend to wait for the WS before responding (Keehn, 1959; Myers, 1977). This advantage is largely lost, however, at high shock intensities—the rats become inefficient again (Myers, 1977).

Theoretical Interpretations of Avoidance Behavior

The recognition of apparent avoidance learning in the 1930's (e.g., Brogden, Lipman, & Culler, 1938) posed a problem for the strict behaviorist interpretation of animal learning. If animals cannot anticipate the consequences of their behavior, as Thorndike had argued, how could they learn an avoidance response? Even the term "avoidance" implies anticipation, the prevention of something that *would* happen if a particular response is not made.

One solution to this problem was developed by Mowrer (e.g., Mowrer & Lamoreaux, 1946). He hypothesized that there was no avoidance learning, at least from the animal's point of view, there was only escape behavior. This explanation involved the presumed operation of two factors. One of these factors was the Pavlovian conditioning of fear to the WS presented in the avoidance apparatus. Thus, in the presence of the WS the rat is shocked (the US) a number of times. The pairing of the shock with the WS leads to the conditioning of fear to the WS (see the Watson & Raynor "Little Albert" experiment described in Chapter 3). This learned emotional response is the first factor in Mowrer's theory.

The second factor involves escape from the WS. In the shuttle box task the animals may escape from the WS by moving to the "safe" compartment. This escape response should reduce fear since the animals have drawn away from a danger signal. The fear reduction should, in turn, serve to reinforce (increase the likelihood of) such an escape response with future occurrences of the WS. But note—if the animal escapes from the WS by crossing to the other compartment (and terminating the WS, as is the usual practice in avoidance experiments) it also has avoided the presentation of the shock. Thus, Mowrer's theory was an inspired application of known principles to explain apparent avoidance behavior without having to assume that the animals were actually avoiding a future event. They were simply escaping an aversive stimulus, an escape response that appeared to be an avoidance response because of the way in which the psychologists had designed the apparatus and conceptualized the experiment.

The research relevant to Mowrer's theory over the past 45 years has been truly voluminous. Only the briefest mention of this evidence may be made here. The principal evidence concerns the role of fear. First of all, there is no question that pairing a CS with shock leads to the development of an aversion to the CS. This has been demonstrated in many ways. For example, such a stimulus will cause the release of stress hormones (e.g., Mason, 1968); it will cause changes in heart rate (e.g., Cohen, 1980; Fitzgerald et al., 1973); rats will escape from the vicinity of such a stimulus, given the opportunity (e.g., Karpicke et al., 1977; McAllister et al., 1983); such a CS will suppress ongoing behavior controlled by a food reward (Karpicke et al., 1978); such a CS will increase the rate of avoidance behavior if it is superimposed on either unsignaled avoidance (e.g., Rescorla, 1966) or signaled avoidance situations (e.g., Rescorla & Solomon, 1967; Solomon & Turner, 1962). It has been shown also that rats will bury metal prods from which they have received a shock (e.g., Pinel & Triet, 1978) and they will also bury a light that is used to signal a shock (Anderson et al., 1983; Davis et al., 1983). It is reasonable to assume that all these behaviors could reflect an emotional state that physiologically and psychologically resembles fear in humans.

There is less certainty regarding the second aspect of Mowrer's theory, that escape from a fear-eliciting stimulus is the basis of avoidance learning. This lack of certainty arises from several problems presented by the data and from alternative theoretical interpretations. Some of these problems and alternative interpretations will be described briefly.

The Role of Shock Intensity

Mention was made above that there is a direct relationship between shock intensity and avoidance performance in one-way avoidance tasks, but an inverse relationship in two-way and bar-press avoidance. The poor performance with high shock levels seems inconsistent with an explanation of avoidance in terms of escape from fear. More intense shock should produce more fear, which should, in turn, result in superior avoidance learning.

A possible resolution of this paradox in terms that would still support a role for fear in avoidance learning has been suggested by the McAllisters. This explanation rests on a distinction between fear of the WS and fear of the situational cues (stimuli arising from other aspects of the apparatus), and on some assumptions regarding the reinforcing properties of fear reduction.

The argument runs as follows (McAllister et al., 1979, 1983). Since both the apparatus stimuli and the WS elicit fear (both are paired with shock in a two-way apparatus), the fear reduction that occurs when animals make a crossing response following WS onset should be incomplete. That is, the animals escape from a combination of WS plus apparatus cues in one compartment to just apparatus cues in the alternative compartment. Thus, the animals are going from a situation of greater fear to one of lesser fear—a degree of fear reduction that is apparently sufficient to reinforce learning.

The paradoxical effects of shock intensity are assumed to result from the following further considerations. The more intense the shock, the greater the fear conditioned to both the WS and the situational stimuli. With intense fear produced by intense shock the fear reduction brought about by the avoidance response is small and, thus, avoidance learning is poor. This argument follows the proportionality effects known to occur in perception. For example, going from a room illuminated with a 100-watt bulb to one illuminated with a 25-watt bulb would result in a clearly noticeable change in brightness. However, going from a room illuminated with a 1000-watt bulb to one illuminated with a 925-watt bulb would not result in a very noticeable change, even though the change in wattage is the same in both cases (75 watts). Effects of this type have been found with variations in shock intensity in the escape learning paradigm. For example, a change from a 300-volt to a 200-volt shock produces better escape learning than a change from a 400-volt shock to a 300-volt shock (e.g., Campbell, 1956; Campbell & Kraeling, 1953). What the McAllisters have done is to move this type of argument to the assumed psychological dimension of fear—a given amount of fear reduction is more reinforcing when overall fear is at a relatively low level than when it is at a high level.

Some evidence supporting the role of situational cues in this argument was obtained in a study by the McAllisters (McAllister et al., 1979). In this study they preexposed the rats to the apparatus for several days before the start of shock administration. There was no WS present during these preexposures, only the general situational cues. The rationale for this experiment was the following. Preexposing animals should have led to the development of latent inhibition (see Chapter 5). That is, the animals should habituate to the apparatus cues (one explanation of latent inhibition) so that when the shock is introduced later, they would be less likely to form an association between the apparatus cues and shock. Instead, the WS should become a singular predictor of shock. If the apparatus cues do not become associated with shock, then they should not elicit fear. If this is the case, then only the WS will elicit fear and the more intense the shock the more intense the fear. And, since the apparatus cues do not elicit fear, the greater should be the fear reduction when the animals make the crossing response. Thus, the prediction in the McAllister experiment was that preexposing the animals to the apparatus should lead to the finding that more intense shocks produce better avoidance learning—a reversal of the usual paradoxical finding. The results of their experiment supported this prediction. A similar argument should apply to the effect of shock intensity on bar-press avoidance, although the appropriate experiments have apparently not yet been conducted.

Thus, the complex effects of a seemingly simple variable, shock intensity, may be explained, but with the help of several assumptions and a somewhat complex interpretation. This explanation resolves the apparently paradoxical effects of shock intensity so the data may now be seen to support the fear hypothesis.

The Measurement of Fear During Avoidance Learning

A more difficult problem regarding the role of fear and fear reduction in avoidance learning is raised by studies which have attempted to measure the amount of fear elicited by the WS at several stages in the acquisition of an avoidance response.

These measurements were carried out by taking rats from an avoidance experiment after different numbers of acquisition trials and presenting the WS from the avoidance task in the context of a conditioned suppression procedure. The assumption behind these studies was that the greater the fear elicited by the WS, the greater the suppression of behavior there would be in the conditioned suppression paradigm. The results showed that rats given a relatively large number of trials in an avoidance task show less fear to the WS than rats given a small number of trials (Kamin et al., 1963; Starr & Mineka, 1977). Thus, a paradox—avoidance performance improves with increased numbers of trials (see Figure 9–3), but fear of the WS apparently declines. This result is not consistent with Mowrer's theory since, according to the theory, avoidance is really escape from the WS reinforced by fear reduction. If the WS becomes less fearful with repeated trials it would seem that avoidance should deteriorate, not improve.

Why does fear decline? Starr and Mineka (1977) have shown that the decline in fear is not due simply to a decrease in the number of shocks that occur as the animals learn an avoidance response. They showed this by having a group of subjects yoked to an avoidance learning group.[1] The yoked group experienced the same WS shock conditions as the avoidance group did, but the behavior of the yoked animals could have no influence on the occurrence or nonoccurrence of shock. If the avoidance group made a successful avoidance, then the yoked group also did not receive a shock, etc. Using the conditioned suppression test to measure amount of fear at different stages of learning, Starr and Mineka found that the avoidance group showed less fear to the WS with increasing numbers of successful avoidances in the avoidance task. However, the fear demonstrated by the yoked group did not decline over the same number of trials. Both groups received exactly the same numbers of shocks. Thus, this experiment indicates that it is something about the behavior of the avoidance learning animals that leads to a decline in fear of the WS. That is, the response contingency itself, the ability to terminate the WS and prevent the occurrence of shock, may be responsible for the decline in fear to the WS—it is not just the fact that shocks occur less frequently with experience in the situation.

In another experiment Starr and Mineka (1977) provided further evidence concerning what aspect of the response contingency leads to a decline in fear. In this experiment one group of animals received a feedback stimulus every time they made an avoidance response (see earlier discussion on page 206 regarding feedback stimuli in avoidance learning). A second group of animals was yoked to this avoidance group. They could not avoid the shock themselves, but they received all shocks and/or feedback stimuli that the avoidance group received. A third group was also yoked to the avoidance group in terms of number of shocks received, but this third group did not receive a feedback signal. The results of this experiment showed that both groups which received a feedback signal showed a reduction in fear to the WS; the third group, which received no feedback signal, did not show a reduction in fear to the WS. Thus, this experiment shows that the occurrence of a signal that indicates the absence of shock will lead to a reduction in fear to the WS.

One interpretation of this result is that animals in an avoidance situation learn that there is a stimulus condition which signals the absence of shock (safety), and once they learn this (and how to produce it), their fear diminishes. However, it may never completely disappear (see Mineka, 1979, p. 993). This position of safety may, in a sense, be similar to the flight distance of grazing animals in the Serengeti. That is, a lion or a jackal is not a danger signal sufficient to elicit flight (fear?) as long as the predator stays

---

[1] A control group yoked to ("tied to") an experimental group in an instrumental learning experiment typically experiences all the same stimulus and reward events as the experimental group, but the rewards are not response-contingent in the yoked group—instead they are produced by the behavior of the experimental group.

beyond the outer limits of the flight zone. Distance acts as a safety signal. In the avoidance task this safety may normally arise when the subjects learn that there is a contingency between their behavior and stimuli correlated with the absence of shock. Once the subjects learn how to produce these stimuli with the appropriate instrumental response (crossing to the other compartment, pressing a lever, etc.), then fear to the WS diminishes.

Some Conclusions Regarding Avoidance Learning

In this section we will synthesize some of the preceding material into a simplified model of avoidance learning and relate certain aspects of this model to other theories.

What an animal learns first in an avoidance task is that there is "danger" (an aversive event) and that there is a predictor of this danger (the WS). This learning is essentially a Pavlovian S–S association. Then it may learn that there is safety if it can produce the correct stimulus condition (WS termination, safety signal, different compartment, etc.). Once it learns this, its fear of the WS diminishes because, in a sense, the animal now has a coping response—it has a way of getting out of danger should that become necessary. This latter learning may be instrumental (R–S learning); the animal learns that its behavior has a rewarding outcome. The rewarding outcome is the absence of shock (and accompanying cognitive or emotional states such as safety or relaxation—Denny, 1971). Learning about the absence of shock has meaning only after the animal learns that shock may be present. This idea is essentially the same as that of frustration produced by the absence of reward. The absence of a reward has no meaning and cannot be frustrating unless reward is expected. This account differs somewhat from Mowrer's in terms of this second stage learning; it emphasizes the learning of an R–S contingency that leads to the absence of shock or predictors of shock.

This is perhaps an oversimplified account of avoidance behavior, but it will have to do in a textbook such as this. Many investigators have developed theories of avoidance learning, some of which emphasize different aspects of the problem that the animal faces in an avoidance task. For example, Denny (1971) has argued that the reinforcement for avoidance learning is "relief" and the opportunity for "relaxation" that is presented to the animal when it makes a successful avoidance response. This relaxation may be an emotional accompaniment to learned safety.

D'Amato (1970) has argued that the animal needs an opportunity to detect that an avoidance contingency exists (e.g., by performing anticipatory responses during the WS–shock interval). It also needs some stimulus support (e.g., response contingent stimulus change—feedback stimulus, etc.) to inform it that it has made a response that has had some consequence on the environment. The relative ease of detecting the avoidance contingency may influence the rapidity with which the second stage learning (R–S) takes place in the model presented above.

Bolles (1970, 1978) has argued for the importance of Pavlovian processes in avoidance learning (S–S associations) and for the role of species specific defense responses (SSDRs). By SSDRs Bolles means, in particular, freezing and fleeing. Freezing does not prevent the aversive stimulus in the tasks that we have described—the rat must flee. The order of difficulty with which the different avoidance tasks are learned (as described above) corresponds, Bolles believes, to their relationship to the rats' SSDR of fleeing. The one-way task is learned most easily because the animal may actually flee to a place different from where shock is administered. In the two-way task and in the bar-press task the rat cannot totally leave the danger situation, therefore avoidance performance is relatively poor.[2]

Bolles' emphasis on SSDRs may be consistent with the model presented above. That is, the situations that are most difficult to learn also involve difficult-to-detect safety stimuli for the rat, thus increasing the difficulty of the R–S stage of learning. Whether this is necessarily related to SSDRs remains to be seen.

A recent theory by Masterson and Crawford (1982) hypothesizes that a danger situation activates an emotional-motivational state in an animal. This state, in turn, brings to the fore certain stimulus situations that will satisfy the motivational state. For example, food deprivation activates a motivational state that may be satisfied by the stimuli associated with food. Danger activates a motivational state that may be satisfied by safety. Any response that produces safety will be reinforced and learned. One difference between this theory and the model presented above is that Masterson and Crawford emphasize an innate component of the avoidance behavior—danger innately primes the animal to seek stimuli correlated with safety. The cues that provide safety may differ somewhat with different species of animals, but they may also be based on learning, as our model emphasizes.

Masterson and Crawford also make a distinction between a danger signal that causes alarm and one that causes wariness. This idea would seemingly relate to the flight distance concept that we have described. Predators outside the flight distance may make an animal wary, predators inside the flight distance may alarm the animal. In the standard avoidance situation, it may be that the WS initially alarms the animal, but later, after the avoidance response is learned, the WS only makes the animal wary, a fact that would be

---

[2] Actually, this ordering is consistent with all the theoretical positions presented thus far. The stimulus support (or ease of detecting the difference between the dangerous stimulus conditions and the safe stimulus conditions) may decrease in moving from a one-way to a two-way to bar-press avoidance, and is least of all in the unsignaled avoidance procedure (the animal cannot leave and has only its sense of time to tell safety from danger).

consistent with the reduction in fear elicited by the WS at late stages of avoidance learning (see Keehn, 1959).

All of these theories may be seen as somewhat similar (especially in the simplified form presented here) and consistent with the abstracted model that we have presented.

In summary, an animal's task in a laboratory avoidance situation is to learn (1) what predicts danger (shock), (2) what predicts safety (the absence of shock), and (3) how to change stimulus situation 1 to stimulus situation 2. The different experimental variables reviewed at the beginning of this section may be seen to relate to these tasks (e.g., delaying CS termination may make stages 2 and 3 particularly difficult). The various theories briefly reviewed emphasize somewhat different aspects of the problem faced by the rat and suggest somewhat different mechanisms of solution. Our view is that stage 1 learning involves the formation of a Pavlovian association based on the contingent relationship between an originally neutral stimulus and an aversive event; stage 2 learning is also a Pavlovian association based upon the pairing of a stimulus (safety signal, different compartment, etc.) with the *absence* of an *expected event* (the absence of shock); stage 3 is seen as instrumental learning—the animals learn that there is a contingency between a particular response and the occurrence of the safety stimuli.[3]

Extinction of Avoidance Responding

Extinction of avoidance behavior has presented several puzzles. The first is concerned with Mowrer's original theory. The theory seems to predict that the acquisition process should really be a series of acquisition and extinction cycles. That is, once the animal learns to fear the WS and starts avoiding, fear of the WS should extinguish (since it is no longer paired with shocks) and, hence, avoidance responding should also cease (there being no more fear to motivate such behavior). But, once the avoidance responding ceases the animals would again receive shocks, which should start the process all over. As described in the previous section, this sequence of events does not occur. Instead, avoidance responding in acquisition tends to be stable (see Figure 9–3). This failure of cyclical extinction to occur is evidence against Mowrer's theory as a satisfactory account of avoidance learning.

A second puzzle is that extinction often does not readily occur in avoidance learning when the shock is no longer presented (e.g., Seligman & Campbell, 1965; Solomon & Wynn, 1954; Wahlsten & Cole, 1972). However, this persistence of avoidance responding in the absence of the shock may not really be a puzzle. That is, if the animals have learned that a partic-

---

[3] Other views of avoidance learning may be found summarized in the Masterson and Crawford paper, and in peer commentary following the paper; in Herrnstein and Hineline (1966); and in Flaherty et al. (1977, Chapter 6).

ular response leads to the absence of shock, then they may have little opportunity to discover the extinction contingency. As long as they keep responding they will not experience the fact that shock will no longer occur even if
they don't respond (see Mackintosh, 1974, pp. 331–340; Seligman & Johnston, 1973).

Extinction of avoidance responses may be made to occur quite rapidly
if procedures other than just eliminating the presentation of shock are used.
For example, if the avoidance response fails to terminate the WS, then extinction proceeds more rapidly than it normally does (e.g., Davenport & Ol-
sen, 1968; Reynierse & Rizley, 1970). Also, if shocks are presented independently of the animal's behavior (thereby removing the R–S contingency that
the animal had learned), then extinction proceeds quite rapidly (e.g., Bolles,
Moot, & Grossen, 1971; Reynierse & Rizley, 1970). Another effective way of
extinguishing avoidance responding is termed "flooding." In the flooding procedure the subject is prevented from making the avoidance response, often
by being confined in the situation in which shocks were administered. This
procedure leads to rapid extinction of the avoidance behavior (e.g., Baum,
1970; Mineka & Gino, 1979). However, if the avoidance response itself is
extinguished by the flooding procedure, there may still be some residual fear
present (e.g., Coulter, Riccio, & Page, 1969; Riccio & Silvestri, 1973). This
latter result (showing the presence of fear after the avoidance response itself
has extinguished) supports the hypothesis that there are at least two aspects
to avoidance learning: learning what is aversive (what to fear) and learning a
response that is effective in eliminating the aversive situation.

Two versions of the flooding procedure are sometimes used as therapy
for phobias. In one procedure, termed *implosive* therapy, the patients are
asked to imagine close contact with whatever it is that they fear (rats, snakes,
cockroaches, etc.). The imagining process is aided by various techniques employed by the therapist. In the *flooding* procedure the patient is actually
brought abruptly into contact with the feared object. That is, the patient may
be given a snake to handle. This procedure may be exemplified by a somewhat unusual case in which a woman was extremely afraid of meat, particularly pork. Her father had died recently of cancer and she came to fear many
things that might have been connected with his death, eventually focusing on
pork as a potential disease carrier. This fear was so great that in her efforts to
avoid meat or anything that reminded her of meat she could not lead a normal
life. The therapist's approach was to bring her into a room that contained a
tableful of raw pork covered with a cloth. The therapist asked the patient to
remove the cloth and touch the meat. He then asked her to make meatballs
out of some minced pork that was on the table. The patient and therapist
played catch with the meatballs until some broke and splattered all over the
patient (Baum & Poser, 1971). By using this procedure of abrupt and direct
contact with the feared object, the therapist hoped to eliminate the avoidance
response. Flooding often works as therapy, but there are some patients who

cannot tolerate this approach and there is also some question as to whether fear is ever completely eliminated by this procedure (recall that the animal studies of flooding indicate residual fear).

PUNISHMENT

Punishment is the response-contingent application of an aversive stimulus (D'Amato, 1970). This definition stresses the idea that the aversive event is applied in relation to a specific response. Defined in this way, the term *punishment* is not synonymous with the term *aversive stimulus*. An aversive stimulus may be used as a punishment (i.e., its application may be made response contingent), or it may be used in some other way such as to promote escape or avoidance learning, or it may be applied independently of the subjects' behavior.

When punishment is applied, it is usually done to suppress or eliminate undesired behavior. Is punishment effective in doing this? For some time it was thought that punishment would lead to only a temporary and perhaps slight suppression of behavior (Estes, 1944; Skinner, 1953; Thorndike, 1932). However, now that a great deal more research has been completed, the evidence is quite strong that punishment can, under some conditions, produce nearly complete suppression of behavior, and that in general, punishment is an effective way of controlling behavior (see Solomon, 1964). However, the effectiveness of punishment depends upon the conditions under which it is applied. Some of the conditions that are known to influence the effectiveness of punishment will be reviewed below. (For more complete reviews, see Campbell & Church, 1969; Dunham, 1971; Fowler, 1971; Walters & Grusec, 1977).

Variables that Influence the Effectiveness of Punishment

Intensity of Punishment

The more intense the punishment, the greater the suppression of behavior. This relationship has been demonstrated a number times (e.g., Azrin & Holz, 1961; Church, Raymond, & Beauchamp, 1967; Pearce, 1978). In the Church, Raymond, and Beauchamp study, virtually total suppression of a bar-press response that was reinforced with food on a VI 1-minute schedule was found when the subjects (rats) were given a 2.0-milliampere shock for responding. In contrast, a 0.1-milliampere shock produced very little suppression and even this small amount of suppression seemed to disappear as the animals had extensive experience with the shock.

Duration of Punishment

Duration of punishment has effects much like intensity. In general, the longer the duration of a punishment of a given intensity, the greater the suppression (Church et al., 1967). In Church's study it was found that a 0.16-milliampere shock applied for 3.0 seconds led to virtually complete suppression of a bar-press response rewarded with food on a VI 1-minute schedule. Shocks of less duration (i.e., 1.0, 0.50, 0.30, and 0.15 seconds) produced less suppression, and with the shorter duration punishments there was a tendency for suppression to recover as a function of experience with the shock.

Degree of Deprivation

In laboratory investigations punishment is typically administered contingent upon responses that have been learned on the basis of food reward. In the examples we have given, the punished subjects were responding on VI schedules for food. Of interest here is the degree to which food deprivation influences the effectiveness of punishment. In an investigation of this problem Azrin, Holz, and Hake (1963) trained pigeons on a VI 3-minute schedule of reinforcement with a food reward. The suppressive effects of an intense electric shock applied after every 100th response were examined, with the pigeons at a number of different body weights (body weight loss is a method of varying food motivation; see Figure 7–3). It was found that the punishment was intense enough to produce complete suppression when the pigeons were tested at 85 percent of their free-feeding weight. However, when the pigeons were made hungrier by reducing them to lower body weights (e.g., 75 percent, 65 percent, 60 percent) the shock had less suppressive effects and, in fact, when the pigeons were at 60 percent of their free-feeding weight they maintained a very high rate of responding despite the shock (see Figure 9–5).

These data indicate that the motivational level of the subject must be taken into account in assessing the suppressive effects of punishment. It appears that the more motivated the subject is, the less suppression will be obtained by a given aversive event. It would be expected that amount of reward would have effects similar to those of deprivation, but perhaps not to as great a degree.

Strength of Punished Response

Many drugs, such as alcohol or tranquilizers, that normally disrupt a learned task have much less of an effect if the task has been highly practiced. There is some evidence that punishment works in a similar fashion. For example, Miller (1960) found that an electric shock was more effective in disrupting running behavior in the runway if rats had relatively few training

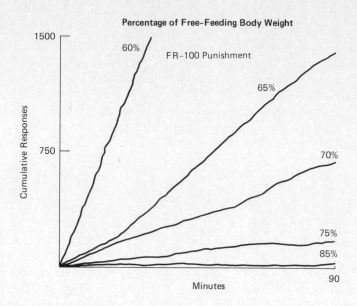

FIGURE 9–5 *Effect of food deprivation (percent free-feeding body weight) on punished responding. The data are from a single pigeon responding on VI 3-minute schedule of food reinforcement and punished by a 160-volt shock on an FR-100 schedule. (From Azrin, Holz, & Hake, 1963)*

trials than it was after rats had more extensive training. However, considerably more research will be needed before any complete understanding of this relationship will be available (see Born, 1967).

Schedules of Punishment

Azrin et al. (1963) examined the effects of a number of fixed ratio (FR) schedules of punishment on key-pecking behavior in pigeons. The results indicated that the more frequently punishment was administered (e.g., FR-1, FR-100, as opposed to FR-500, FR-1000) the greater the suppression. Thus, increasing the frequency of punishment has effects much like increasing the intensity or duration of punishment.

Gradual Introduction of Punishment

Miller (1960) demonstrated that the suppressive effects of electric shock are attenuated if the shock is very gradually increased in stages across a large number of trials. After approximately 750 trials in a runway, a group which had experienced no shock was abruptly shifted to a 335-volt shock. A second group was also receiving a 335-volt shock at this time, but the shock had been gradually increased over most of the previous 750 trials. The suppression of running behavior was much greater in the group that had experienced the abrupt introduction to shock (also see Terris & Wechkin, 1967).

Delay of Punishment

Shock has much greater suppressive effects if applied immediately than if delayed (e.g., Camp, Raymond, & Church, 1967; Kamin, 1959). In this regard, the effect of delay on punishment is much the same as the effect of delay on reward (see Chapter 7). For example, Camp et al. (1967) found that the suppression of a lever-press response was approximately only half as great if punishment was delayed 30 seconds as it was when punishment was administered immediately. Delayed punishment may be less effective because the delay removes the aversive event from immediate contact with the behavior to be suppressed. This removal allows other behavior to intervene between the target response and the actual delivery of the shock. Thus, from the subject's point of view, there may be a difficult problem of determining exactly what response is being punished. For example, if an electric shock is delivered 30 seconds after the rat presses a lever, at the time of the shock the rat may be nowhere near the lever and it may be engaged in some other unrelated behavior such as eating or grooming. These behaviors may be partly suppressed by the shock. The point is that punishment seems to suppress the behavior with which it is most contiguous.

Effect of Punishment on Alternative Responses

Most laboratory studies have measured the effects of punishment only on the response being punished. What happens to other behaviors in the subject's response repertoire? Some studies have begun to provide an answer. For example, Dunham (1971) allowed gerbils free access to a drinking tube, food, and paper for shredding. Each of these behaviors was punished in separate groups of animals and the duration of time spent in each of the behaviors, punished and unpunished, was measured. Dunham found that each class of behavior was effectively suppressed when punished, and in each case the behavior next most likely to occur under nonpunished conditions (as measured by duration) increased in preference. For example, the punishment of eating suppressed eating but increased paper shredding; punishment of paper shredding decreased that behavior but increased eating. In another study Dunham allowed gerbils the opportunity to run in a wheel, paper shred, eat, or scratch in dirt. When eating was punished there was an increase in the time spent running in the running wheel (Dunham, 1978). These studies indicate that the subject's behavior stream has dynamic and flexible properties such that punishment may have important effects on nonpunished behaviors.

Early studies in this area showed that the effects of punishment in suppressing behavior may be particularly large if the subject has some alternative response to perform that will also obtain it reward (Whiting & Mowrer, 1943). In this case, the subject's behavior simply shifts in the direction of the non-punished alternative, a fact that would seem to be of considerable importance for the practical effectiveness of punishment.

Cue Value of Punishment

If shock is not too intense, it may be used as a cue to signal the availability of a positive reward. Under these conditions subjects may be trained to approach an electric shock. For example, electric shock given for the correct response (in addition to food) may facilitate learning of a discrimination, and an electric shock may increase resistance to extinction (e.g., Fowler et al., 1973; Meunzinger, Bernstone, & Richards, 1938. Also Fowler, 1971, for review of this literature).

Increased Persistence from Intermittent Punishment

If rats are punished on only some of the trials on which they also receive a food reward, their resistance to continuous punishment is enhanced. For example, in an experiment by Banks, rats were first trained to run in a straight runway for a food reward. Following this, the animals were divided into two groups and one of these groups received a shock on a randomly selected 3 of the 10 daily trials. The second group of rats never received shock during this stage of the experiment. After 80 trials of such training, all rats were shifted to continuous shock. The continuous shock had a much greater disruptive effect on the rats that had no prior experience with intermittent shock (Banks, 1966a, 1966b). Similar effects of intermittent punishment have been found in other studies, and in some cases the increased persistence has been found to generalize to aversive stimuli other than the ones used in original training (e.g., Banks & Torney, 1969; Terris & Barnes, 1969).

These effects of intermittent punishment on later experience with continuous punishment are similar to the effects that experience with intermittent reward has on later experience with extinction (see Chapter 8). Both will increase persistence. Furthermore, enhanced resistance to extinction may be produced by mixing intermittent punishment with 100% reward prior to extinction (e.g., Fallon, 1968, 1969; Linden, 1974; Logan, 1960). The converse is also true—intermittent reward produces increased resistance to both extinction and to punishment (Brown & Wagner, 1964; Linden & Hallgren, 1973). This similarity in the effects of intermittent punishment and intermittent reward indicates that the two may have something in common. One possible mechanism for explaining the similarity between punishment and nonreward is the assumption that both conditions lead to similar emotional responses—frustration in the case of nonreward, and fear or pain in the case of punishment.

Thus, it may be that Amsel's account of the partial reinforcement extinction effect described in Chapter 8 could be extended to a more general theory of persistence. That is, if animals learn to persist under somewhat unfavorable circumstances (such as frustration due to intermittent reward, or fear due to intermittent punishment), they will be less affected if circumstances take a turn for the worse, such as extinction or continuous punishment (see Amsel & Stanton, 1980; Martin, 1963; Wagner, 1969).

Summary

Punishment may be very effective or ineffective in suppressing the behavior of lower animals. The degree to which it is either, depends upon a number of factors. In general, punishment is most effective if it is intense, long lasting, consistently applied from the beginning, and administered in close temporal proximity to the behavior that is to be suppressed. Punishment may be more effective in suppressing one behavior if an alternative behavior can be rewarded contemporaneously with the administration of punishment. Punishment is also likely to have effects on unpunished behaviors, thus altering their likelihood of occurrence. Finally, the more motivated the subject is, the less effective is punishment, other variables being equal.

LEARNED HELPLESSNESS

Earlier in this chapter we presented data showing that rats will readily learn a response that allows them to escape from an aversive stimulus. In this section we shall consider evidence showing that an initial experience with unavoidable and inescapable shock interferes with the later acquisition of an escape response. Although the data showing this interference effect are substantial, there is some disagreement over the mechanism by which inescapable shock interferes with later acquisition of an escape response. Current evidence indicates that such experience with inescapable shock may have several effects on the animal, effects such as reduced motor activity, depletion of certain neurotransmitters, a degree of analgesia to shock, and the production of an associative deficit. We will consider some of the basic data, the interpretations of the *helplessness* effect, and some possible relevance to the human condition.

The Interference Effect

The decrement in escape learning following experience with inescapable shock was first described by Overmier and Seligman (1967). In the basic procedure dogs were given a series of intense and long duration (e.g., 5 seconds) shocks that they could neither escape nor avoid. The next day the dogs were placed in a typical two-compartment shuttle box and given shocks that were escapable and avoidable. The performance of dogs given the prior treatment with inescapable shock was poor compared to animals that did not have such prior experience. For example, in one experiment it was found that the average escape latency of dogs pretreated with long inescapable shock was 54 seconds, and 5 out of 8 dogs never learned to escape at all. The comparable figures for dogs not exposed to inescapable shock were 22 seconds to escape and 1 out of 8 dogs never learned. The average across a series of such experiments indicates that approximately 63 percent of dogs given experience with uncontrollable shocks generally fail to escape when they have the opportunity, whereas only about 6 percent of untreated dogs fail to escape (Seligman, Maier, & Solomon, 1971).

This decrement in escape learning following experience with uncontrollable shock has been found in a number of other animals, including rats (e.g., Seligman, Rosellini, & Kozek, 1975), mice (e.g., Anisman, deCatanzaro, & Remington, 1978), and guinea pigs (Fenton, Calof, & Katzev, 1979). Some possible analogs to this deficit have been obtained in humans (see Garber & Seligman, 1980; Seligman, 1975).

An example of the interference effect obtained with mice is presented in Figure 9–6. In this experiment there were three groups of mice. In preliminary training one group was allowed to escape from shock. A second group was yoked to this group so that they received the same number and duration

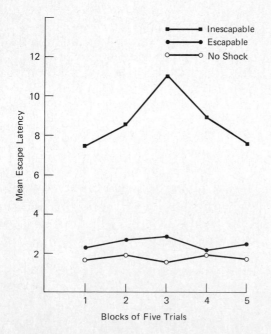

FIGURE 9–6 Mean escape latencies in three groups. Mice given prior exposure to inescapable shock had slower escape latencies than animals given prior exposure to the same number of escapable shocks and slower latencies than animals given no prior shock. (Data from Anisman et al., 1978)

of shocks, but their behavior had no effect on the shock, therefore this was an inescapable shock group. The third group was simply placed in the apparatus and experienced no shocks. Twenty-four hours later all groups were placed in a shuttle box and allowed the opportunity to escape from shock. It is apparent that the inescapable shock group had much longer escape latencies than the other groups. This experiment, and many like it (see Maier & Seligman, 1976) showed that the interference effect is a result of experience with uncontrollable shock, not simply with shock per se. Remember that in this experiment the escape group and inescapable group received exactly the same number and pattern of shocks during the pretraining phase. The only difference between the two groups was in the controllability of the shock.

Other studies have shown that the interference effect of uncontrollable shock may be eliminated if the subjects are first given experience with escapable shock. The sequence in such an experiment would be: first escapable shock, then inescapable shock, and finally the opportunity to escape again. This prior experience with control over shock is sometimes said to "immunize" the rats to the usual deleterious effects of experience with inescapable shock (Seligman et al., 1975). The interference effect may also be reduced after the fact by forcibly exposing animals to experience the escape contingency. For example, if dogs that do not escape are dragged back and forth across a shuttle box, they may eventually learn the escape response. This effect is sometimes referred to as "therapy" for learned helplessness (e.g., Seligman, 1975, pp. 56 ff.).

Interference from uncontrollable shocks is most likely to be obtained in rats if the task is somewhat difficult, such as requiring rats to cross both ways in a shuttle box before the shock is terminated (called an FR-2 response) or requiring them to press a lever three times to escape shock (called an FR-3 lever-press response). Simpler tasks are often not interfered with by prior experience with uncontrollable shock (e.g., Maier, Albin, & Testa, 1973; Seligman & Beagley, 1975).

Interpretations of the Interference Effect

Activity Deficit

Experience with uncontrollable shock leads to a decline in activity that is still likely to be present 24 hours after the experience with inescapable shock (e.g., Anisman et al., 1978; Drugan & Maier, 1982, 1983; Maier & Jackson, 1979; Weiss, 1981). This decline in activity follows uncontrollable shock but not controllable shock (e.g., Drugan & Maier, 1982). There seems to be little doubt that in some circumstances, particularly the shuttle box, this activity deficit may be a major determinant of the interference with escape learning produced by inescapable shock (e.g., Maier & Jackson, 1979). It is easy to see why this might be the case, particularly since rats are most likely to show an escape deficit in the shuttle box or bar-pressing tasks when they are required to cross in both directions (FR-2) or press a lever three times (FR-3).

This behavioral activity deficit may be related to neurochemical changes produced by experience with inescapable shock. For example, Anisman (e.g., Anisman, Pizzino, & Sklar, 1980; Anisman & Sklar, 1979) and Weiss (e.g., Weiss et al., 1975; Weiss et al., 1981) have shown that there is a substantial degree of covariation between depleted levels of the neurotransmitter norepinephrine and a decline in activity following inescapable shock. It is important to note that the lowered norepinephrine levels, as well as the lowered activity, are brought about only by uncontrollable shock, not by shock per se. Thus, we might think of this decline in a brain chemical as being a psychological effect—a result due to the psychological dimension of uncontrollability.

Analgesia

A second change brought about by experience with inescapable shock is the production of analgesia. Several studies have shown that experience with inescapable shock reduces sensitivity to pain (i.e., produces analgesia). The analgesia requires a large number of inescapable shocks (60 to 80), and it normally diminishes within a few hours, but may be reinstated again 24 hours later by brief exposure to shock.

The analgesia seems to be produced by the activation of an endogenous opiate system (e.g., endorphin) and it may be blocked by the administration of an opiate blocker such as naloxone. It is important to note once again that this type of analgesia is produced only by inescapable shock, not by escapable shock (Drugan & Maier, 1983; Hyson, Ashcroft, Drugan, Grau, & Maier, 1982; Jackson, Maier, & Coon, 1979; Maier, Drugan, & Grau, 1982; Maier, Sherman, Lewis, Terman, & Liebeskind, 1983).

This analgesic effect of uncontrollable shock may be blocked by first giving animals experience with escapable shock (Moye et al., 1981). Thus, the same experience that "immunizes" an animal from the activity deficit produced by inescapable shock also prevents the occurrence of analgesia.

Is the activity decline and escape deficit seen after experience with inescapable shock due simply to the fact that the rats are analgesic? That is, do they fail to escape because they do not feel the shock? The evidence in this regard is not entirely clear at the present time. Some data do, in fact, show that blocking an opioid neurotransmitter system blocks both the analgesic effect and the activity deficit produced by inescapable shock (Drugan & Maier, 1983). This result would indicate that the two are closely, perhaps causally, related. However, other recent data indicate that the activity deficit and analgesia may be two independent effects produced by inescapable shock and that analgesia does not cause the activity deficit (see MacLennan et al., 1982a, 1982b).

So, at the present time, it is perhaps best to remember that inescapable shock produces an activity deficit, analgesia, and interference with escape behavior. The activity deficit is clearly related to interference with escape, as evidence mentioned above indicates. Whether the activity deficit is related in any simple manner to analgesia is not clear at the present time.

Associative Deficit

A decline in activity and analgesia are not the only consequences of experience with inescapable shock. It also seems that experience with uncontrollable events increases the difficulty of *learning* that events can sometimes be controlled. That is, it increases the difficulty of learning that outcomes may be controlled by one's own behavior. For example, inescapable shock interferes with later choice learning, such as learning whether a left turn or a right turn in a Y-maze will avoid shock (Jackson & Maier, 1979). Rosellini and his colleagues also found that experience with inescapable shock interfered with the subsequent learning of a choice response in which the correct response was rewarded with food (Rosellini, DeCola, & Shapiro, 1982). In this experiment the rats had to learn to poke their noses through a hole in order to get food. There were two holes, only one of which was rewarded.

The mean correct responses for different groups in one of these experiments is shown in Figure 9–7. It is apparent that animals that had experienced inescapable shocks required more trials to learn this food-based choice response than animals that had experienced an equal number of escapable shocks.

Rosellini and his colleagues also found that the rats that had experienced inescapable shock were less active in the food reward situation and were

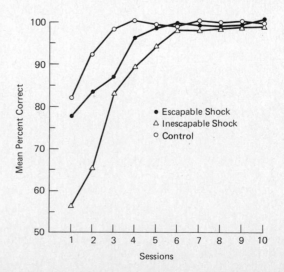

FIGURE 9–7 Mean percent correct responses in a position discrimination. Rats had to learn whether poking their noses in holes located on the left or right would lead to a food reward. Different groups had prior experience with inescapable shock, escapable shock, or no shock. The group with prior inescapable shock experience was the slowest to learn. (Data from Rosellini et al., 1982)

slower to respond when a trial started. An example of the activity deficit is shown in Figure 9–8. Is the activity deficit the cause of the poorer choice performance? Rosellini and his colleagues argued that it is not. There were two reasons for this position. In the first place, an examination of Figures 9–7 and 9–8 shows that there was still a pronounced difference in activity between inescapably shocked animals and control animals long after there was no difference in their performance on the choice task. Second, Rosellini et al. (1982) conducted another study in which the correct and incorrect responses were reversed after the animals had learned the choice response. Thus, if the left hole had been correct, the right hole was correct in the reversal phase of the experiment. The results of this study showed that experience with inescapable shock interfered with the animals' ability to reverse their choices even though there were no differences in the activity of the animals in this stage of the experiment. Based on this evidence, Rosellini et al. concluded that there was a deficit in the animals' ability to learn associa-

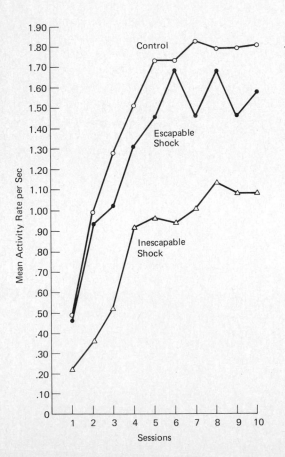

FIGURE 9–8 Mean activity level for the same groups that are shown in Figure 9–7. (Data from Rosellini et al., 1982)

tions between their behavior and environmental outcomes that was independent of the deficit in activity produced by inescapable shock.

Other evidence which supports the hypothesis that inescapable shock interferes with an animal's ability to form instrumental (R–S) associations includes the following. The deficit in choice behavior produced by inescapable shock lasts for at least a week after the shock experience (Jackson, Alexander, & Maier, 1980), a period which is considerably longer than the activity deficit usually lasts (see Weiss, 1981). In fact, studies with guinea pigs and rats have indicated that exposing these animals to inescapable shock soon after birth interferes with learning when the animals are adults (Fenton, Calof, & Katzev, 1979; Hannum, Rosellini, & Seligman, 1976). Also, inescapable shock has been shown to produce deficits on tasks in which little activity is required (Rosellini & DeCola, 1981; Samuels, DeCola, & Rosellini, 1981). This indicates that activity is not the only cause of the deficit.

Animals that are exposed to shock which they cannot escape, but shock whose intensity they can control, do not show a deficit in subsequent learning. This study implies that immunization against learned helplessness may be provided by control of any salient characteristic of shock, not only escape (Alloy & Bersh, 1979). In other words, once animals learn that there is a contingency between some aspect of their behavior and some aspect of the shock, they do not have trouble learning another association between their behavior and a different aspect of the shock.

Other studies show that the interfering effect of exposure to inescapable shock generalizes to situations in which food is used as a reward and to situations in which a quite different response is required of the animal. These studies may be taken as support for a generalized deficit in a readiness to form response–outcome associations (e.g., Goodkin, 1976; Rosellini, 1978; Rosellini et al., 1982).

It is this deficit in associative learning to which the label *learned helplessness* applies. Learned helplessness means that animals have a deficiency in learning that their behavior may influence the environment, they have a deficiency in learning R–S associations (e.g., Seligman, 1975).

This deficiency is conceptually similar to what may happen in Pavlovian conditioning when animals are exposed to a random sequence of CS and US presentations. In such a situation animals may learn that the CS and US are unrelated. This is a type of learning which may then interfere with the animals' learning at some later time that there is a relationship, when one does exist (e.g., Baker & Mackintosh, 1979; Baker, Mercier, Gabel, & Baker, 1981; Mackintosh, 1974).

In summary, experience with inescapable shock seems to have several effects on an animal. It produces an activity deficit, a deficit closely correlated with a decline in the neurotransmitter norepinephrine; it produces analgesia, possibly mediated by the activation of an endogenous opiate system; and it diminishes an animal's ability to form associations between its own behavior and subsequent changes in the environment.

Possible Human Relevance

Seligman has extended the learned helplessness research to human behavior. There are two principal aspects to this extension. One of these is that experience with uncontrollable events may produce a deficit in cognitive processes so that future learning is more difficult. A second aspect is that experience with uncontrollable events may lead to an emotional deficit, possibly even depression. Adequate coverage of the evidence relevant to Seligman's hypothesis in regard to the human aspects of learned helplessness is beyond the scope of this text. However, a brief description of these ideas will be presented here.

Cognitive Deficit

Evidence regarding a deficit in an ability to learn, paralleling the associative deficit obtained in animals, has come primarily from studies involving such tasks as the control of noise or the solution to puzzles such an anagrams. In the typical experiment there are three groups of subjects. One group is given experience with uncontrollable noise, say; one with controllable noise; and one is not exposed to noise. Then all subjects are exposed to a situation where noise may be controlled. Those exposed to the initial uncontrollable noise are less likely to discover that the noise may be controlled by them, or less likely to believe that they can really control the noise even after they do exert some control over it.

Similar results are obtained when puzzle solution is employed rather than control over noise (see Abramson, Garber, & Seligman, 1980; Alloy & Abramson, 1980; Miller, Rosellini, & Seligman, 1977; and Seligman, 1975, for reviews of this literature). Other parallels exist between these experiments with humans and those with animals. For example, prior experiments with solvable puzzles or controllable noise "immunizes" the subjects from the interfering effects of experience with unsolvable puzzles. However, the extent to which these experiments completely match the data obtained with animals is still a matter of active research and ongoing debate (see Alloy & Abramson, 1980).

Motivation Deficit—Depression

Animals exposed to inescapable shock are slower to initiate responses (e.g., Rosellini et al., 1982) and are less active overall. Could this pattern of behavior provide a model for investigating depression in humans? Seligman and others (e.g. Seligman, 1975; Miller, Rosellini, & Seligman, 1977) have advanced such a hypothesis. There are many aspects of human depression that are similar to the helplessness syndrome in animals. For example, depressives are inactive, unlikely to initiate behavior, and tend to view themselves as having little control over what happens to them. They may even interpret actions of theirs that do change the environment as being due only to chance (Miller et al., 1977). Of particular interest is the fact that norepinephrine depletion is often cited as being related to depression, and as we saw earlier, there is substantial evidence that norepinephrine depletion is a concomitant of learned helplessness. Also, many of the drugs used as antidepressants in humans act to increase the amount of functional norepinephrine in the brain.

What happens if these human antidepressants are administered to rats made helpless by exposure to inescapable shock? Recent research indicates that the antidepressants ameliorate the effects of helplessness in rats (e.g., Sherman, Sacquitine, & Petty, 1982; Weiss, Glazer, & Pohorecky, 1976). Furthermore, Sherman et al. (1982) tested a wide variety of drugs and found that the antidepressants were particularly effective in alleviating learned helplessness in rats, whereas other compounds such an antianxiety drugs or antipsychotic drugs, stimulants, and depressants were not. Sherman and colleagues also found that electroconvulsive shock, an effective treatment for some cases of depression in humans, also alleviated learned helplessness in rats.

Human depression is a complex state and there is almost certainly more than one type of depression. It is unlikely that the helplessness procedure will mimic all of the symptoms of all types of depression. Nevertheless, the model seems to be a reasonable animal approximation to the human condition, one certainly deserving of continued research.

Immuno-Suppression

Recent evidence has indicated that there is a third way in which the psychological effects of uncontrollability may have important consequences. That is, experience with uncontrollable shock appears to be a stressor which enhances susceptibility to cancer (Sklar & Anisman, 1979) and increases the rate of tumor growth (Visintainer, Volicelli, & Seligman, 1982). These effects of uncontrollable shock are probably mediated by decreases in the activity of the immune system (Laudenslager, Ryan, Drugan, Hyson, & Maier, 1983).

These data imply that the psychological dimension of uncontrollability may have important consequences for physical health. It is likely that this topic will be an active research area in behavioral medicine (Gatchel & Baum, 1983).

CHAPTER SUMMARY

The aversive consequences of behavior, or the anticipation of aversive consequences of behavior, may be important in predator-prey relationships, in the formation of intraspecific group structure, and in the "routine" operation of societies—human and lower animal.

In this chapter we have reviewed several laboratory procedures used to investigate the effects of aversive events on instrumental behavior.

A stimulus paired with an aversive event will suppress ongoing instrumental activity rewarded by food. This is influenced by a number of parameters such as shock intensity, method of pairing the CS with the aversive event, etc. Examination of the animals' behavior in these tasks shows that the CS may lead to freezing or withdrawal of the animals away from a localized CS. Both freezing and withdrawal are incompatible with the usual instrumental response, and thus may be a "cause" of the suppression of instrumental behavior. Many investigators assume that the conditioned suppression paradigm provides a measure of degree of fear elicited by a CS.

If the situation is so structured that animals may *escape* from an aversive event, or a stimulus predictive of an aversive event, they will readily learn to do so. A number of parameters that influence the rapidity of escape learning were reviewed.

Animals will also learn to perform an instrumental response that will prevent the onset of an aversive event. Such *avoidance learning* has been subject to a variety of theoretical interpretations and has been investigated using a number of instrumental procedures. Ease of avoidance learning is correlated with the nature of the instrumental response required of the animal and with a variety of parameters, such as shock intensity, whether or not the warning signal terminates concurrently with the instrumental response, etc. Important roles in avoidance learning are apparently played by: the degree to which the experimental situation facilitates anticipatory responses (responses during the WS–shock interval); the amount of stimulus change correlated with the occurrence of the avoidance response; the opportunity for safety or relaxation after the avoidance response is made; and the degree to which the experimental situation is compatible with natural defensive tendencies of the animal. Our summary interpretation was that the animal must learn what stimuli predict the aversive event (danger), what stimuli predict the absence of the aversive event (safety), and what instrumental response is required to go from danger to safety.

An aversive event made contingent upon the occurrence of a particular response is termed *punishment*. The degree to which punishment suppresses behavior is a function of a number of parameters. In general, punishment that is intense, long lasting, consistent, and applied immediately after the criterion response is effective in suppressing behavior. Gradually introducing punishment decreases its effectiveness in suppressing behavior. The more motivated the subject is the less effective a given level of punishment will be. Punishment that is applied intermittently will produce behavior that is resistant to the effects of continuous punishment applied later. Punishment of one response may have effects on other, unpunished behaviors.

If animals are exposed to a series of uncontrollable shocks they are later deficient in learning to escape or avoid shocks that they may have control over. Exposing animals to such inescapable shocks has a number of effects. It produces a decline in activity, a depletion of the neurotransmitter norepinephrine, analgesia, and an associative deficit. This complex of behaviors is often referred to as *learned helplessness*. To the extent that learned helplessness means a deficit in learning that one's own responses can influence the environment (an instrumental or R–S contingency), the term should perhaps be restricted to the associative deficit.

There are procedures that will "immunize" an animal from the effects of exposure to inescapable shock, and other procedures that will "cure" the animal from the effects of earlier experiences with inescapable shock. It has been suggested that deficits in human cognitive behavior and in human motivation may be modeled by the helplessness syndrome in animals. It is thought, in particular, that much may be learned about the cognitive and motivational components of human depression by studying the effects of exposure to uncontrollable shock in animals.

10

Instrumental Learning IV: Generalization, Discrimination, and Attention

GENERALIZATION

It seems inevitable that each deer hunting season a few cows are shot, apparently mistaken for deer. Other mistakes based on apparent similarity sometimes lead to tragedy, as when a police officer shoots a suspect thought to be holding a dangerous weapon—a weapon that turns out to be a toy or a piece of pipe. On a more mundane level we all encounter someone who sounds or looks like another acquaintance. It is possible to investigate what things are apparently perceptually similar to animals by using procedures termed *generalization tests*. These tests provide data on how animals behave in the presence of some criterion stimulus, usually one that was used as a rewarded stimulus in some task, and how they behave in the presence of other stimuli to which they were not specifically trained but which may bear some physical similarity to the trained stimulus.

In Chapter 3 we briefly considered generalization of Pavlovian CRs (see Figure 3–3). This section will be concerned with generalization obtained in instrumental behavior. Several examples of generalization are presented in Figure 10–1. The data in the top panel were obtained from pigeons trained to peck at illuminated discs on an intermittent schedule of reinforcement (Guttman & Kalish, 1956). For different groups, the discs were illuminated with different colors. The wavelengths of the impinging light for the various groups were 530, 550, 580, and 600 nanometers (nm). For humans, these wavelengths range from yellowish green to red.

Generalization testing was begun after the key-pecking response was well learned. The procedure consisted of illuminating the response key with wavelengths other than that used during training. For example, the pigeons trained with a 580 nm stimulus were presented with the response disc illuminated at wavelengths of 520, 540, 550, 560, 570, 580, 590, 600, 610, 620, and 640 nm. These stimuli were presented in a random order. The data shown in the top panel of Figure 10–1 are a plot of the number of responses the pigeons made in a given time period to each of these test stimuli. As is apparent in the Figure, most responses were made to the stimulus associated with reinforcement during training. However, responses were made also to

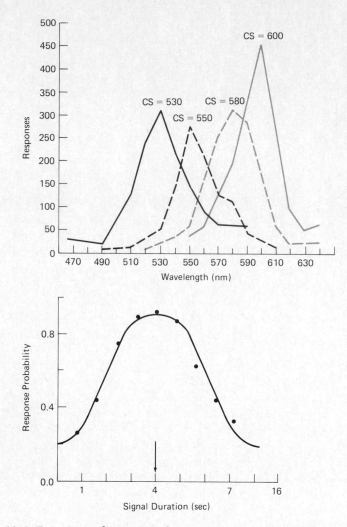

FIGURE 10–1 Top: Generalization gradients. Four curves were obtained with four different groups of pigeons, each trained with a different discriminative stimulus (530, 550, 580, or 600 nm), and then tested with other stimuli in extinction. (From Guttman & Kalish, 1956)

Bottom: Generalization gradient obtained with rats trained to respond after a four-second signal duration and then tested with signals of differing durations. (From Church & Gibbon, 1982)

other stimuli and the greater the physical difference (in nm) between these stimuli and the training stimulus, the fewer the responses made in their presence. The function shown in the Figure is termed a *generalization gradient*. It can be seen that the general symmetrical shape of the generalization gradient was similar in the four groups given different wavelengths as the trained stimulus. This graph shows that pigeons will respond to stimuli other than those rewarded during training, but the less like the rewarded stimulus they are, on the physical dimension of wavelength, the less likely the pigeons are to respond.

Generalization testing in this experiment was carried out in extinction. In investigating generalization, we are asking how likely it is that an animal will respond in a stimulus context different from the one in which it was trained. This question is most clearly answerable when the animal is not also reinforced for responding in the new stimulus context. One of the advantages of the Guttman and Kalish procedure of training the animals initially on an intermittent schedule of reinforcement is that extensive generalization testing may be conducted because of the greater resistance to extinction produced by such intermittent reinforcement schedules (see Chapter 8).

A second example of generalization is presented in the bottom panel of Figure 10–1. In this experiment (Church & Gibbon, 1982) rats were rewarded if they pressed a lever after the houselight (light that illuminated the interior of an operant chamber) had been turned off for a period of four seconds. After they had learned this response, generalization was tested for time periods of different durations. The Figure shows that the rats were most likely to respond after the four-second interval, and increasingly less likely to respond the greater the difference between the trained time interval and the test time interval. The training and testing procedures used in this experiment were somewhat different from those used by Guttman and Kalish. The difference is not of concern in this text. What is important to remember about this experiment is that it shows that orderly generalization gradients may be obtained in the estimation of time intervals by rats. Church and Gibbon (1982) have developed a mathematical model characterizing this time estimation ability of rats.

The shape of the generalization gradient is influenced by the schedule of reinforcement used in acquisition. In an experiment by Haber and Kalish (1963) generalization was examined following training on VI 15-second, VI 1-minute, and VI 4-minute schedules of reinforcement. Training was conducted with a 550-nm light, and generalization was examined by presenting a number of different wavelengths toward the short end of the spectrum. Two ways of looking at the degree of generalization obtained are presented in Figure 10–2. The absolute number of responses made to each stimulus is presented in the left-hand panel. This method of presentation indicates that there were only minor differences in the degree of generalization as a function of schedule of reinforcement. However, when the data are plotted in terms of the ratio of responses made to the test stimulus as a function of the response made to the training stimulus, a different picture emerges. These data, plotted in the right-hand portion of Figure 10–2, show that more generalization occurred following training on the VI 4-minute schedule than occurred following training on the other two schedules. But when we use the term generalization in this way, it must be clear that it is a *relative* measure of generalization: *the amount of responding made to the test stimulus in com-*

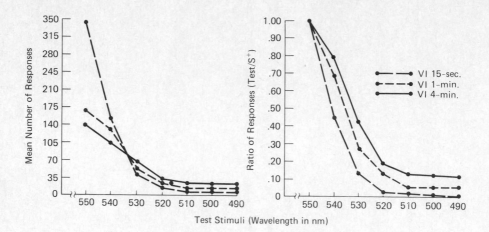

FIGURE 10–2 Generalization gradient as a function of schedule of reinforcement. Presented in the left panel are the absolute number of responses made to each test stimulus following training with a 550-nm light. Presented in the right panel is the ratio of responses made to the test stimuli as a function of responses made to the training stimuli. (Modified from Haber & Kalish, 1963)

parison to the amount of responding made to the training stimulus. The relative measure of generalization takes into account different rates of responding that occurred to the training stimulus among the three groups.

Other studies have also indicated that schedules which provide infrequent reinforcement or schedules that require that animals refrain from responding for certain time periods (see Chapter 8), produce broader generalization gradients than schedules that provide frequent reinforcement or schedules that do not require that animals learn to refrain from responding (Gray, 1976; Hearst, Koresko, & Popper, 1964).

A change in generalization within a schedule is shown in Figure 10–3. In this experiment pigeons were trained on an FI 20-second schedule and rewarded in the presence of a 597 nm illumination of the pecking disc (Blough, 1975). In the generalization test, wavelengths above and below this training value were presented. Blough examined response rates at different quarters of the FI 20-second schedule and it is clear that the nature of the generalization gradient changed during the course of the 20-second period. Over the initial 5 seconds response rates were low and there was a fairly sharp gradient. As time of reinforcement availability approached, response rates increased and the generalization gradient broadened. Thus, at the time when reinforcement was due, the pigeons were likely to peck at any color illumination, but when reinforcement was remote, the pigeons were quite selective in making their responses.

Another case in which a high response rate was correlated with greater generalization was reported by Thomas and Switalski (1966). They compared

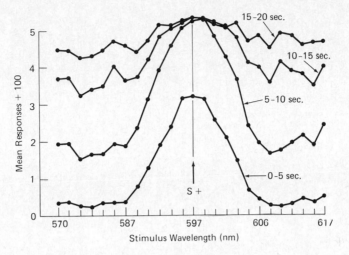

FIGURE 10–3 Generalization gradients obtained in four successive 5-second periods of a fixed interval 20-second schedule. As time of reinforcement approaches, response rate increases and the generalization gradient broadens. (From D. Blough, 1975)

generalization following training on comparable VI and VR schedules and found a broader generalization gradient following VR training, the schedule that produced the higher response rates.

Thus, various aspects of reinforcement schedules may influence the shape of the generalization gradient, but there seems to be no consistent relationship between the rate of response controlled by the schedule and degree of generalization. For example, both DRL, which leads to a low response rate, and VR schedules produce broad generalization. Some as yet undetected characteristics of the schedules must influence the breadth of generalization.

Aspects of generalization that we have not covered may be found in reviews by Bitterman (1979b) and by Honig and Urcuioli (1981).

GENERALIZATION AND DISCRIMINATION

Degree of generalization is importantly influenced by discrimination training. In discrimination training animals are specifically reinforced for responding in the presence of one stimulus and not reinforced for responding in the presence of a different stimulus. For example, in an operant chamber a pigeon may be rewarded for pecking on a green key and not rewarded for pecking when the key is red. Or a rat may be rewarded when a light is on, but not when it is off (rats have no color vision). Many other situations in which discrimination learning is studied will be mentioned in the course of this chapter and the next. As a result of discrimination training an animal will be more likely to respond when the stimulus signaling reward (termed S+) is present than when the stimulus signaling the absence of reward (termed S−) is present.

The term *stimulus control* is often used in conjunction with discrimination learning. It is used to describe the relationship between external stimuli and behavior. A behavior that is more likely to occur in one stimulus context than in another is said to be under stimulus control. A film on operant conditioning distributed by a publishing company several years ago contained an interesting example of stimulus control. The film showed a pigeon in an operant chamber. When the response disc was illuminated with "peck" the bird would run over to the disc and peck at a rapid rate. While the pigeon was pecking, the signal on the disc would switch to "stop" and the pigeon would abruptly stop and walk away from the disc. This behavior was brought under stimulus control by discrimination training in which the bird had a long history of responding for reward when "peck" appeared and of not being rewarded when "stop" appeared.

There are many analogies to the process of stimulus control in human behavior, brought about though by (possibly) more complex mechanisms. For example, libraries are places to whisper very loudly and, on college campuses, to socialize. College dormitories are places to play radios loudly. Child rearing provides many instances of learned stimulus control. Parents' efforts to stop an unwanted behavior such as cursing or smoking establishes them as an S−; the behavior occurs in their absence but not in their presence.

Examples of Discrimination Learning

Three examples of discrimination learning are presented in Figure 10–4. Panel A shows data from three pigeons trained to peck in an operant chamber. The birds were trained on what is termed a *multiple schedule*. On a multiple schedule there are usually two cues, each associated with a different schedule of reinforcement. The cues are made available one at a time, according to some alternation plan. In the Halliday and Boakes (1971) experiment illustrated in Figure 10–4 the response discs were either blank (white) or contained an angled line. During the initial stages of the experiment the reinforcement schedule was the same in the presence of both stimuli (a VI 1-minute schedule). During the second phase of the experiment the schedule was maintained at VI 1-minute in the presence of one of the stimuli but shifted to extinction in the presence of the other stimulus. As the Figure shows, the animals' behavior came under stimulus control. Their response rates were much higher in the presence of the rewarded stimulus than in the presence of the nonrewarded stimulus.

A second example of discrimination learning is presented in panel B (Mellgren, Mays, & Haddad, 1983). This experiment was conducted in a runway with rats. The discriminative stimuli in this experiment were different time periods. A trial was rewarded if a one-minute period had elapsed be-

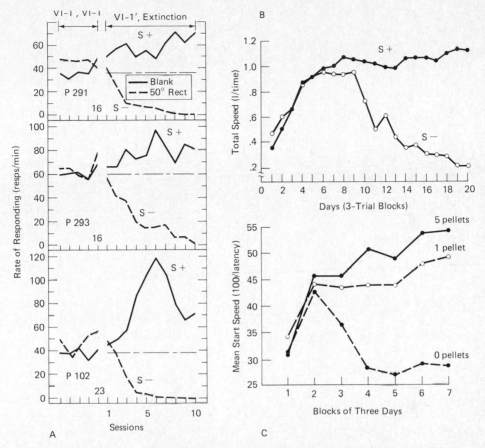

FIGURE 10–4 Panel A: Response rates of three pigeons during five sessions of non-differential training (both stimuli reinforced on a VI 1-minute schedule) and during ten sessions of discrimination training (blank key reinforced on VI 1-minute schedule, no reinforcement in presence of 50° rectangle). The dashed line indicates extrapolated baseline (nondifferential) response rates. (From Halliday & Boakes, 1971)
Panel B: Running speed following reinforced (S+) and nonreinforced (S−) intertrial intervals. Discriminative responding was based on time difference between trials (see text). (From Mellgren et al., 1983)
Panel C: Mean speed of initial lever press to stimuli signalling three levels of reward. (From Flaherty & Davenport, 1969)

tween the end of one trial and the start of the next trial, but running in the runway was not rewarded if a 10-minute period elapsed between trials. Thus, the rat had to learn the difference between 1- and 10-minute intertrial intervals, learn that this difference predicted the presence or absence of reward, and remember which intertrial interval had occurred most recently. The data in Figure 10–4 indicate that the rats developed this discrimination and ran considerably faster following 1-minute intertrial intervals than following 10-minute intertrial intervals. Control groups in this experiment (not shown in the Figure) indicated that differences in the intertrial interval themselves did not lead to differences in running speed. The intertrial interval differences had to be correlated with differential reward in order for differential responding to occur.

A third example of discrimination learning is presented in Panel C of Figure 10–4. This experiment was conducted in an operant chamber with retractable levers. At the start of a trial the lever was inserted into the chamber and a cue was presented. The dependent variable used in this experiment was the speed at which the rat first pressed the lever after the start of a trial. There were three cues: flashing light, tone, and clicking sound. Each cue was correlated with a different level of reward: five, one, or zero food pellets. It is clear in the Figure that rats readily learned to discriminate among the three cues and that response speeds corresponded to the size of the reward available to the animal. Control conditions insured that the differences in speed were due to the reward differences and not to other stimuli.

These three experiments give some indication of the variety of situations and stimuli that may be employed to study discrimination learning and they may provide a feeling for what is meant by stimulus control. The animals responded differently in the presence of different stimuli—their behavior was influenced or "controlled" by these stimuli—and this influence was related to the animals' experience with what the stimuli predicted.

Influence of Discrimination Training on Generalization

The remainder of this section will be concerned with the influence of discrimination training on generalization. Discrimination training usually has several effects on generalization. Some of these effects are illustrated in Figure 10–5. The Figure shows a portion of the data obtained in an experiment by Hanson (1959). One group, represented by the curve labeled "Generalization Gradient," was given training with a response key illuminated with a 550-nm light and then was given standard generalization tests in extinction. The group represented by the "Postdiscrimination Gradient" was reinforced for responding when the response key was illuminated with the 550-nm light (the S+) and not reinforced for responding when the key was illuminated with a 560-nm light (the S−). Following discrimination training, this group was also given a generalization test over the same range of stimuli as the control group.

Differences between the two groups in the results of this generalization testing are apparent in the Figure. These differences consist of three aspects: (a) The peak level of responding in the discrimination group is shifted to a stimulus other than the S+ (i.e., more responses were made to stimuli of

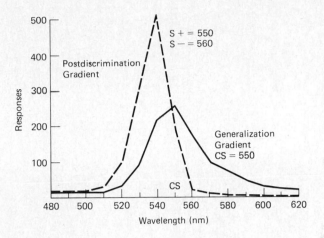

FIGURE 10–5 *Generalization gradients obtained following discrimination training with an* S+ *at 550 nm and an* S− *at 560 nm, and following nondiscriminative training with the 550-nm stimulus. (Modified from Hanson, 1959)*

shorter wavelength than S+ even though these stimuli were never experienced in training; (b) maximum level of responding is considerably higher in the postdiscrimination gradient than in the generalization gradient; and (c) the postdiscrimination gradient is steeper than the generalization gradient.

These three differences between postdiscrimination gradients were also found with other stimuli as S+ in the Hanson study and in numerous experiments since Hanson (see Honig & Urcuioli, 1981; Purtle, 1973; and Weiss and Dacanay, 1982, for reviews). What is it about discrimination training that moves the maximal point of responding from S+ to another stimulus in a direction away from the S− (referred to as *peak shift*), raises the overall level of responding, and sharpens the gradient of generalization? Some theory and data that relate to these characteristics of the postdiscrimination gradients will now be considered.

Peak Shift

One explanation of the shift in the peak of responding to a stimulus other than S+ may be derived from a theory of discrimination learning offered by Spence (1937). This explanation is based on the idea that a tendency to refrain from responding will develop in the presence of S− and that this tendency to not respond will generalize to similar stimuli. This generalized tendency to not respond will then detract from the tendency to respond in the presence of S+. We will consider this theory in more detail to see exactly how it predicts peak shift and we shall also consider the evidence relevant to several aspects of the theory.

Gradients of Excitation and Inhibition. Spence assumed that discriminative responding reflected the combined influence of excitatory tendencies acquired by S+ as a result of having been paired with reinforcement, and inhibitory tendencies acquired by the S− as a result of having been paired with nonreinforcement. That is, S− comes to control a tendency to *not* respond during the course of discrimination learning (see Chapter 5). Spence further assumed that this inhibitory tendency, like the excitatory tendency, would generalize to similar stimuli.

Hypothetical gradients of excitation and inhibition are shown in Panel A of Figure 10–6. The stimulus dimension illustrated in the Figure is one of stimulus size (area) and the gradients presented are those hypothesized to exist following discrimination training with a 256-cm² figure as S+ and a 160-cm² figure as S−. A further assumption by Spence was that these gradients of excitation and inhibition combined algebraically. Response tendencies that should exist at each stimulus value following such algebraic combination are indicated within the gradients. The numbers presented under the curve were derived by subtracting levels of inhibition from levels of excitation. The *absolute* value of these numbers is not important for our purposes. What is important is the *relative* value, that is, the resultant excitatory value at each stimulus size compared to the values at other stimulus sizes. It is these relative values that predict how the animals should respond at each stimulus size.

Examination of these relative values shows that Spence's model accounts quite readily for the peak shift obtained in a postdiscrimination gradient. The prediction of peak shift may be seen in the relative excitatory tendencies resulting from the subtraction of the inhibitory gradient from the excitatory gradient. These relative values are plotted as the postdiscrimination gradient in Panel B of Figure 10–6. Note that the maximal tendency to respond ("6.68") exists at a stimulus value of 655 cm², not at the original S+

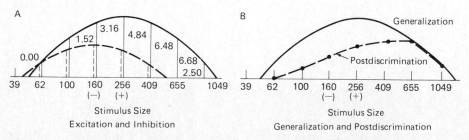

FIGURE 10–6 *Left panel: Hypothetical gradients of excitation (solid line) and inhibition (dashed line) obtained following discrimination training with a 256-cm² figure as S+ and a 160-cm² figure as S−. Differences between S+ and S− in "excitatory potential" are shown within the Figure. (From Spence, 1937)*
Right panel: Hypothetical generalization and postdiscrimination gradients drawn from the data presented in the left panel. Note the peak shift.

of 256 cm² (where the tendency to respond is equal to "4.84"). Thus, the greatest tendency to respond is found at a stimulus value shifted away from the S— value. This is the result obtained by Hanson (Figure 10–5) and many others (see Honig & Urcuioli, 1981).

Spence's explanation of the peak shift assumes the existence of gradients of inhibition and excitation. Evidence for a gradient of excitation exists in the form of the standard generalization curve. That is, the typical generalization gradient may be thought of as representing gradients of excitation—tendencies to respond to the presented stimulus. Figures 10–1, 10–2, and 10–3 all show that animals will respond to stimuli other than the originally rewarded stimulus.

There is also evidence supporting the existence of gradients of inhibition. An example of such a gradient is presented in Figure 10–7. In this experiment, pigeons learned a discrimination in which pecking on a blank disc was reinforced whereas pecking on a disc with a vertical line superim-

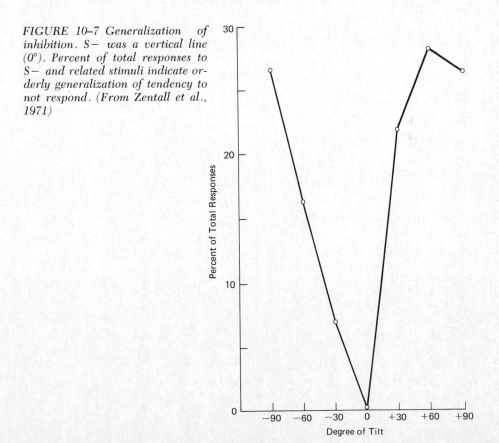

FIGURE 10–7 Generalization of inhibition. S— was a vertical line (0°). Percent of total responses to S— and related stimuli indicate orderly generalization of tendency to not respond. (From Zentall et al., 1971)

posed on it was not reinforced (Zentall, Collins, & Hearst, 1971). After discrimination training a generalization test was conducted with lines of different orientation. It is apparent in Figure 10–7 that virtually no responding took place when the vertical line (0°) was present, but some degree of responding was made in the presence of lines of other orientations. Generally speaking, the more the other lines differed from S−, the greater the degree of responding that took place in their presence. Thus, these data illustrate generalization of inhibition. Inhibition is assumed to be maximal at S− and to decrease as the stimuli become more different from S−. Evidence indicating the generalization of inhibition has been obtained by many others (e.g. Hearst, Besley, & Farthing, 1970; Honig, Boneau, Burstein, & Pennypacker, 1963; Karpicke & Hearst, 1975; Rilling, Caplan, Howard, & Brown 1975; Terrace, 1972).[1]

Thus, it is reasonable to think in terms of gradients of both excitation (tendencies to respond) and inhibition (tendencies to not respond). However, the exact shapes of these gradients and, more importantly, how they interact is not known at this time. It is, of course, just these points, the shape and manner of interaction of the two gradients, that would be crucial for determining the precise adequacy of the Spence model in explaining peak shift (see Hearst, 1969; Mackintosh, 1974, pp. 537–539). All that may be said at the present time is that the model still represents a useful way of thinking about peak shift (Klein & Rilling, 1974), that there is clear evidence of generalization of both excitation and inhibition, that inhibition does seem to be involved in the occurrence of peak shift (Weiss & Dacanay, 1982), but that the degree of precision with which the model can predict peak shift must await further data on inhibition and gradient interactions.

Enhanced Responding in the Postdiscrimination Gradient

The characteristic of the postdiscrimination gradient that we turn to now is the elevation of response rate that is normally found in the postdiscrimination gradient in comparison to the generalization gradient (see Figure 10–5). If Spence's model of discrimination learning is a reasonably adequate account of peak shift, it is readily apparent that it is an inadequate explanation of response enhancement following discrimination training. The Spence model suggests that the peak of responding may be *less* following discrimination training than following nondiscriminative training. This suggestion derives from the assumed summation of excitatory and inhibitory gradients. Following discrimination training, subtraction of the inhibitory tendencies should result in less responding to S+ and related stimuli than comparable responding when no S− has been involved in original training.

---

[1] A gradient showing minimal responding to S− is not sufficient to establish that inhibition is present. Procedures such as the retardation and summation tests described in Chapter 5 would also have to be conducted to obtain evidence for inhibitory control by a stimulus. Such tests have been done and they support the existence of generalized inhibition (see Hearst, 1972; Hearst et al., 1970; Honig & Urcuioli, 1981).

In some situations this prediction has been verified (e.g., Gynther, 1957). However, in most operant experiments that have been conducted, response rate is enhanced following discrimination learning. This enhancement in response rate is now recognized as a form of contrast (see Chapter 7)—a form termed *behavioral contrast*. We will now review some of the data concerning behavioral contrast.

Behavioral Contrast. Behavioral contrast was first recognized by Reynolds (1961a) as an accompaniment of discrimination learning when pigeons were trained on multiple schedules. Recall that in a multiple schedule there are usually two stimuli, each correlated with a particular schedule of reinforcement. These stimuli are presented alternately and the rate at which the subject responds in the presence of each stimulus is measured. The acquisition of a discrimination is indicated when the subject responds at a higher rate in the presence of the stimulus correlated with the highest rate of available reinforcement.

An example of discriminative responding on a multiple schedule was presented in panel A of Figure 10–4 (Halliday & Boakes, 1971). This Figure also illustrates behavioral contrast. In the first stage of this experiment the response disc was either blank or contained an angled line. Responding in the presence of either stimulus was reinforced on a variable interval one-minute (VI-1) schedule of reinforcement. It may be seen in the Figure that the response rates were approximately equivalent to the two stimuli during this stage (labeled VI-1, VI-1). In the second stage of the experiment the reinforcement schedule in effect in the presence of the line was changed to extinction. It is apparent that response rate showed a decline in the presence of the line stimulus (labeled S−). Of particular interest is the response rate during the blank stimulus. Note that this response rate increased even though the reinforcement schedule had not been changed. It is this increase in response rate, compared to preshift baseline, that is termed *behavioral contrast*.

In general, behavioral contrast may be obtained by holding the density of reinforcement constant in one component of a multiple schedule and decreasing the density of reinforcement in the other component. Contrast is then usually measured in terms of an increase in response rate in the *unchanged* component—an increase measured in terms of baseline responding or in terms of control groups that are not shifted in reinforcement schedule (Mackintosh, Little, & Lord, 1972).[2]

---

[2]Strictly speaking, this describes *positive* behavioral contrast. *Negative* behavioral contrast may be obtained by analogous procedures. For example, McSweeney (1982) obtained negative contrast by first training pigeons on a multiple VI 2-minute, VI 2-minute schedule and then shifting one of the schedules to VI-15 seconds. Response rate increased in the presence of the stimulus correlated with this schedule and decreased in the presence of the stimulus correlated with the unchanged VI 2-minute component. This decrease in the unchanged component is negative contrast.

The occurrence of behavioral contrast is important because it is contrary to what is predicted by Spence's theory of discrimination learning. An examination of Spence's model presented in Figure 10–6 shows that the generalization of inhibition from the S− stimulus should subtract from responses to S+. Thus, the rate of responding on the unchanged schedule would be expected to decrease when the alternative schedule is shifted to non-reinforcement. Yet dozens of behavioral contrast studies have shown that the response rate increases where Spence's model predicts a decrease. Thus, Spence's model may provide an adequate account of peak shift, but it clearly does not provide for behavioral contrast. It is behavioral contrast that most likely accounts for the second difference between generalization gradient and the postdiscrimination gradient, that is, the higher rate of response obtained in the postdiscrimination gradient (see Figure 10–5).

Determinants of Behavioral Contrast. Many of the factors that influence the occurrence of behavioral contrast are known. For example, behavioral contrast tends to be greater the greater the difference in reinforcement density between S+ and S− (e.g., Bloomfield, 1967; McSweeney, 1975). This effect is analogous to reward magnitude effects in simple instrumental (nondiscriminative) contrast effects discussed in Chapter 7. One way of stating this relationship is to say that degree of contrast is a function of relative reinforcement rate in the unchanged component; the greater the relative reinforcement (in comparison to that available in alternative schedule) the greater the contrast (see Williams, 1983, p. 347).

A second factor that influences degree of behavioral contrast is the duration of each component of the multiple schedule. Contrast is greater when component duration is short and the two schedules alternate rapidly and often (McSweeney, 1982).[3] This effect of component duration may be related to an enhanced opportunity for the animals to compare the two reinforcement schedules when the components are short.

Another factor that influences degree of contrast is the difficulty of the discrimination. In general, contrast seems to be greater when the discrimination is difficult for the animal (e.g., Bloomfield, 1972; Blough, 1983).[4] For example, in Blough's study contrast was greater when two wavelengths (colors) used as discriminative stimuli were similar than when they were very different. One possible interpretation of the effect of stimulus discriminability might be that similar stimuli enhanced the degree of comparison or "relevance" of one reward schedule for the other.

An aspect of behavioral contrast that has attracted considerable research interest is the role of the decline in response rate to S− in the production of

---

[3]Somewhat different results may be obtained if a response other than pecking on a disc is used with pigeons (McSweeney, 1982).

[4]Mackintosh et al. (1972) reported data that were not consistent with this relationship.

the contrast effect in S+ responding. This research has shown that a decline in response rate is neither a necessary nor a sufficient condition for the occurrence of contrast in S+. One experiment showing that such a decline is not a sufficient condition was done by Halliday and Boakes (1971). In this experiment pigeons were given initial training on a multiple VI 1-minute, VI 1-minute schedule with a blank disc and an angled line as the stimuli. After responding had stabilized, the schedule in effect during presentations of the angled line was shifted from a VI 1-minute to a variable time (VT) 1-minute schedule. On a VT 1-minute schedule, reward is delivered on the average every minute, *without the necessity of a response*. Thus, a VT schedule is like a VI schedule except that the animals do not have to make an instrumental response to get a reward. The results obtained following the shift in schedule are illustrated in Figure 10–8. It is clear that rate of responding in the presence of the line stimulus fell, but there was no corresponding increase in responding during S+, no behavioral contrast. (Compare this Figure with panel A of Figure 10–4.) Thus, a decline in response rate in the presence of one stimulus is not *sufficient* to produce behavioral contrast.

Another study by Halliday and Boakes (1974) shows that a decline in response rate is not a *necessary* condition for the occurrence of behavioral contrast. This experiment also involved a VT schedule, but it was a more complex experiment than the one just described. The general procedure was as follows. Pigeons were first trained to peck at a response disc illuminated by white light. The birds were then separated into two groups. One group was shifted to a multiple VI 1-minute, VT 1-minute schedule with red illumination indicating S+ and green illumination indicating S− (the VT component). As was mentioned in the earlier discussion of a VT schedule, there is a decline in response rate to S− but there is no evidence of contrast. During this stage of the experiment, the second group of pigeons was maintained on a VI 1-minute schedule when the keys were illuminated both red and green.

Comparison of the two groups when responses had stabilized in this stage of the experiment showed that, in the group with the VT component, responses to S− had declined almost to zero and the response rate to S+ was somewhat *lower* than the average response rate of the group maintained on the VI 1-minute schedule for both red and green stimuli. These data are presented for selected birds in the left hand portions of panels A and B in Figure 10–9. Panel A shows the data for one bird maintained on VI 1-minute, VI 1-minute, Panel B for a VI 1-minute, VT 1-minute bird.

In the next and most interesting stage of the experiment both groups were shifted to a *multiple* VI 1-minute extinction schedule with the red illumination as S+. Examination of response rates to S+ showed that behavioral contrast occurred in both groups (note the sudden rise in S+ response rates in the right portions of both Panel A and Panel B).

The occurrence of contrast is not surprising in the animal given standard

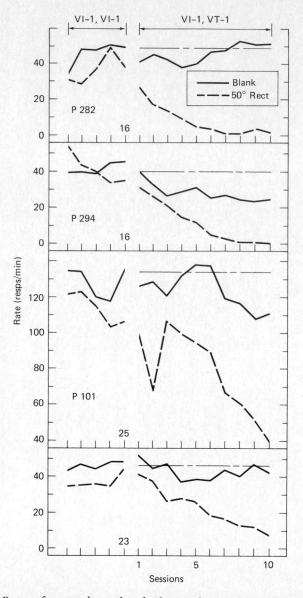

FIGURE 10–8 *Rates of responding when both stimuli were rewarded on a VI 1-minute schedule (left portion) and when the rectangular stimulus was shifted to a VT 1-minute schedule with the blank stimulus left on a VI 1-minute schedule (see text). (From Halliday & Boakes, 1971)*

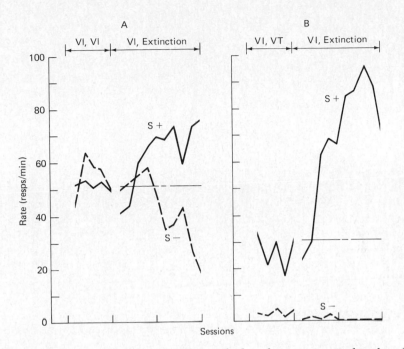

FIGURE 10–9 *Response rates to* S+ *and* S− *of selected pigeons exposed to the sched-*
ules described in the text. Contrast in the S+ *component during the VI/extinction*
phase is apparent in both birds even though a decline in response rate to S− *occurred*
only in the bird shifted from VI 1-minute to extinction. (Modified from Halliday &
Boakes, 1974)

training. However, note that in the animal shifted from the multiple VI, VT
schedule the contrast occurred *without a decline in responding* to S− (Panel
B). Another way of putting this result is that contrast was produced by a
decline in reinforcement frequency without the usually correlated decline in
response rate.

   Thus, these two experiments show that a reduction in response rate is
neither a necessary nor a sufficient condition for the occurrence of behavioral
contrast. The major determinant of contrast seems to be a decline in reinforcement frequency. When reinforcement frequency declines in one component of a multiple schedule, response rate in the alternative component
rises. Evidence other than that described here, that supports this generalization, may be found in Boakes, Halliday, and Mole, 1976; Nevin, 1973; and
Williams, 1983.

   It may be possible to go further than this and suggest that behavioral
contrast is due to the aversiveness of the S− that results from the decline in
reinforcement in its presence (see Amsel, 1971; Bloomfield, 1972; Terrace,
1972). Some evidence in support of this hypothesis comes from a number of

studies: studies showing that degree of behavioral contrast is correlated with degree of aversiveness of the S−, as measured by the subjects' tendencies to escape from S− given the opportunity (Gonzalez & Champlin, 1974); studies showing that adding an aversive electric shock to S− without changing the reinforcement schedule will produce a contrast effect (Farley & Fantino, 1968; cited in Williams, 1983; Terrace, 1968); and studies showing that damage to a part of the brain (the amygdala) which tends to produce a tame animal also reduces contrast (Henke, Allen, & Davison, 1972), whereas damage to a part of the brain (the ventromedial hypothalamus) that produces an emotionally reactive and finicky animal enhances behavioral contrast (Jaffe, 1973). This possibility that emotional responses are involved in behavioral contrast is consistent with our earlier discussion of contrast in Chapter 7.

One final issue regarding behavioral contrast concerns the locus of the comparison that leads to the contrast. In a multiple schedule the S+ and S− stimuli alternate, each signaling its associated schedule of reinforcement. Is the elevated responding that occurs in S+ due to a comparison with the preceding S− period? Many theoretical interpretations of behavioral contrast have assumed that to be the case and, in fact, some data indicate that the transition from S− to S+ may be an important locus of one aspect of contrast (see Rachlin, 1973). However, recent data obtained by Williams and his colleagues indicate quite strongly that it is the *following* S− period that is the major contributor to contrast.

One of the items of evidence comes from a study in which Ben Williams (1981) used a three-component multiple schedule. The first and third components, each signaled by a different stimulus, always had a VI 3-minute schedule of reinforcement associated with them. The reinforcement schedule of the middle component, which was signaled by a third stimulus, was varied. In some stages of the experiment there was a VI 1-minute schedule in effect in the middle component, in other stages there was a VI 6-minute middle component in effect. Of interest was what happened to response rates in the components that followed or preceded the middle component. Ben Williams (1981, 1983) reported that responding in the first component was more affected by changes in the middle component than was responding in the third component. In other words, contrast was primarily influenced by the anticipation of the impending reinforcement schedule rather than by the preceding reinforcement schedule.

Other evidence of the importance of the anticipation of impending rewards was obtained in operant studies by Bacotti (1976); Buck, Rothstein, and Williams (1975); Farley (1980); and Williams (1976). Supporting evidence regarding the role of anticipation of impending rewards was obtained by Flaherty and Checke (1982) in an experiment involving the consumption of sucrose and saccharin solutions.

In summary, behavioral contrast occurs in multiple schedules when animals are switched from equivalent reinforcement schedules in the presence of two stimuli to differential reinforcement schedules in the presence of those same stimuli. The rise in response rate in the unchanged component of the schedule is likely to be responsible for the elevated responding seen in postdiscrimination gradients as compared to generalization gradients. Contrast itself seems to be due to relative differences in reinforcement rate—it is not due to response suppression in the S− component. Contrast is enhanced when component durations are short and when the discrimination is relatively difficult. Contrast may be primarily controlled by the anticipation of the impending schedule of reward.[5]

Steepness of Postdiscrimination Gradient

The third difference (in addition to peak shift and enhanced responding) between generalization and postdiscrimination gradients is that the postdiscrimination gradient is steeper (rises faster) than the generalization gradient. This difference may be seen in Figure 10–5. One obvious fact that may account for this difference in slope is the presence of the S− stimulus in the discrimination group. Since this group responds at a very low level for S−, the postdiscrimination gradient is truncated at the S− side and, thus, the slope is steeper. However, there is also a small but noticeable difference in slope between the two gradients in the side opposite S− (see Figure 10–5). This apparent difference has raised the following questions. Does discrimination training sharpen the generalization gradient *independent of the effects of the S− stimulus on responding during the generalization test?* If so, why does the sharpening occur?

One the earliest studies to raise this question was conducted by Jenkins and Harrison (1960). In this study two groups of pigeons were trained to peck on a response disc for reinforcement. One group had a 1000-hz tone present throughout training. In a generalization test following training, this group showed a flat gradient. That is, the pigeons were about as likely to respond on the disc in the presence of a 300-hz and 3000-hz tones as they were in the presence of the 1000-hz tone that existed during training. These pigeons showed no stimulus control by the tone.

The second group in this experiment was given discrimination training such that they were reinforced in the presence of the tone but not in its absence. A generalization test in this group showed a sharp gradient—stimuli different from the 1000-hz tone were not likely to be responded to. Note that in this study the S− was not a tone of a different frequency from the S+ (the

---

[5]In this brief summary of contrast we have glossed over potentially different types of contrast that may occur in the operant situation. In particular, distinctions may be made between local contrast, which occurs principally at the time of transition from one schedule to another, and steady state contrast, which is a more robust and permanent contrast effect. These, and other distinctions, may be found in several reviews, including Mackintosh (1974); McSweeney, Ettinger, and Norman (1981); McSweeny & Norman (1979); Rashotte (1979); and Williams (1983).

1000-hz tone); the S− was the absence of a tone. Thus, during the generalization test there was no S− presented, there were only values of the tone. This experiment, therefore, indicated an answer to one of the questions posed above, namely, a sharper gradient occurs following discrimination training even if the S− is not present during generalization testing.

Later studies developed more sophisticated experimental procedures for investigating this issue. For example, Switalski, Lyons, and Thomas (1966) used a procedure termed *interdimensional training*. In this procedure the S+ and S− stimuli come from two different stimulus dimensions. This method allows for the determination of a postdiscrimination gradient on the S+ dimension without the presence of any stimuli from the S− dimension.

A description of the details of their experiment may clarify the procedure. One group of pigeons was trained in a discrimination with a green disc as S+ and a vertical white line on an otherwise colorless disc as S−. This is interdimensional training because the two stimuli were derived from two different stimulus dimensions—wavelength (color) and line orientation. Following discrimination training a generalization gradient was obtained using different wavelengths (no line orientations were presented).

A second group of pigeons was also exposed to both a green stimulus and a white vertical line, but, in this case, the pigeons were reinforced equally in the presence of both stimuli. A generalization gradient was also obtained in the wavelength dimension following training with this equal reinforcement group. Comparison of the two gradients showed that the gradient obtained after discrimination training was steeper than the gradient obtained after equal reinforcement. Thus, this study supports the conclusion that postdiscrimination gradients are steeper than generalization gradients even without the presence of the S− stimulus (or dimension) during the generalization test.

Another way of saying this is that the pigeons seemed more sensitive to different wavelengths following discrimination training even though they were never explicitly trained to discriminate different wavelengths. It is as if discrimination training *per se* somehow increased the pigeons' sensitivity to variations in the stimulus dimension, even though they were not trained on that particular dimension.

Another procedure used to investigate this issue is termed *extradimensional training*. An example of this procedure is provided in an experiment by Honig (1969). Honig trained one group of pigeons in a discrimination between green and blue hues. A second group was given equal reinforcement in the presence of both hues. Both groups of pigeons were also trained to peck at three dark vertical lines on a white background. A generalization test was then conducted with lines of different orientations. Honig found that the group given prior discrimination training on hues showed sharper generalization gradients on line orientation than the group given equal reinforcement in the presence of the two colors. Thus again, the results show that prior discrimination training leads to steeper generalization gradients (more stimulus control). In this experiment such a result was found even when neither the S+ nor the S− stimulus was present during generalization testing.

Many other studies have confirmed the finding that either interdimensional or extradimensional discrimination training seems to enhance the degree of stimulus control shown in generalization tests (e.g., Hall & Honig, 1974; Thomas, 1970; Thomas, Freeman, Svinicki, Burr, & Lyons, 1970). Why does this happen? The answer to this question is not certain, but some attempts at the answer have concentrated around the idea that discrimination training somehow facilitates *attention* to the stimulus dimension.

One of the things that an animal may have to learn in a discrimination task is that the difference between red and green, for example, means something—it is correlated with whether reward is obtained or not. Once animals learn to attend to red and green, once they learn that differences between similar stimuli may be important, they may then have a tendency to respond differently to other stimuli varying along a dimension, even if they have not been specifically reinforced for doing so. There is, however, disagreement in the literature as to exactly how these differences in attention may be brought about, or whether such differences are involved at all (cf., Honig & Urcuioli, 1981; Mackintosh, 1974; Rodgers & Thomas, 1982). It seems that the experimental evidence is not complete enough for a definitive answer to the question of why generalization gradients are sharpened by prior discrimination training. The facts, though, are clear: discrimination training narrows the generalization gradient, even if the generalization is on a stimulus dimension different from that used in the prior discrimination training.

Summary

Postdiscrimination gradients differ from generalization gradients in three ways: (a) The peak of responding is usually not at the S+ used in discrimination training but, instead, is shifted to another stimulus in the direction away from the location of S−. (b) Response rate is elevated in the postdiscrimination gradient as compared to the generalization gradient. (c) The postdiscrimination gradient is steeper than the generalization gradient.

The data reviewed indicate that the peak shift may be due to the interaction of excitatory and inhibitory gradients and also possibly may be related to the aversiveness of the S−. The elevated responding obtained after discrimination training was seen to be a type of contrast effect, termed behavioral contrast, which may, in turn, be related to the relative difference in reinforcement level associated with the two discriminative stimuli. Contrast, like peak shift, may be related to the aversiveness of the lower level of reward received in the presence of S−. Regarding gradient steepness, experiments have shown that discrimination training leads to steeper postdiscrimination gradients even if the S−, or neither the S− nor S+, is present during the generalization test following discrimination training.

Sharper gradients indicate that prior discrimination training enhances the tendency of animals to respond differentially to similar stimuli even if they have never been specifically reinforced for differential responding in the presence of those stimuli. This may be related to an increased tendency of animals to attend to stimulus dimensions following discrimination training.

SELECTIVE ATTENTION

. . .without selective interest,
experience is an utter chaos.
William James

In spite of William James' late-nineteenth-century observation and in spite of the importance of the idea of attention in the introspectionists' psychology prominent in America at the turn of the century, the concept of attention did not figure prominently in the earlier history of research on animal discrimination learning. There are at least two reasons for this. First, attention seems to be a subjective, mentalistic concept. It seems to be something that is not verifiable in behavior, something that may only be inferred, never observed. Such concepts were in disfavor throughout much of twentieth-century research in animal learning, particularly after the behaviorists' "revolution" initiated by John Watson (1913). Behavioral psychologists studied only what could be directly seen and measured—only stimuli and responses. Stimuli and responses could be seen and recorded, attention could be neither seen nor recorded.

The second reason was the development of Spence's (1936, 1937) very successful behavioral theory of discrimination learning, which did not employ the concept of attention. We will look first at aspects of Spence's theory of discrimination learning and then examine some data that seemed contrary to Spence's theory—data that seemed to demand the concept of attention for an explanation.

Spence's Theory of Discrimination Learning

As we saw previously, Spence assumed that discrimination learning involved the gradual acquisition of excitatory and inhibitory tendencies to the S+ and S− stimuli, respectively. That is, as a result of differential reinforcement, animals gradually acquire a tendency to respond in the presence of stimuli correlated with reward delivery, and tendencies to withhold responding in the presence of stimuli correlated with the absence of reinforcement.

A key feature of Spence's theory as far as the present discussion is concerned is that he also assumed that *all stimuli* perceived when a reinforcement was presented acquired some excitatory strength, and all stimuli present when a response was not reinforced acquired some inhibitory strength. The stimuli designated as S+ and S− in an experiment eventually come to acquire relatively specific control over behavior because they are the stimuli most reliably present when behavior is reinforced or not reinforced.

The flavor of Spence's theory may be gathered from the following example. Suppose that an animal is allowed to run in a T-maze in which one arm is white, the other is black, and the remainder of the maze is gray. Suppose also that the black arm has been designated as correct (S+) and that therefore there is always a reward at the end of the black arm and never a reward at the end of the white arm. As one further refinement, suppose that the location of the black and white arms on the left or right is randomly varied from trial to trial to ensure that the animal will learn a brightness discrimination, and will not simply learn to turn left or right.

According to Spence's theory, each time the rat encounters the reward in the black arm, black and all other stimuli present gain an added degree of excitatory tendency, and each time the rat enters the white arm and encounters no reward, the white stimulus, and all other stimuli present, gain an added degree of inhibitory tendency. "All other stimuli present" may include such things as odors from the apparatus or from previous rats, visual or auditory cues present in a particular part of the test room or apparatus, stimuli deriving from muscular movements used in running or making a particular turn, etc. Over the long run, the white and black stimuli should gradually gain control over the animals' behavior because they are always correlated with the absence and presence of reward, respectively, whereas the other stimuli may be less predictive of reward.

The point is that Spence's theory explained stimulus control (discrimination learning) without having to assume that the animals "attended" to particular stimuli. Stimulus control developed passively, in a sense, as the result of the automatic strengthening processes of reward (and inhibitory processes of nonreward) delivered in the presence of particular stimuli. This view was not accepted by all experimental psychologists, but the evidence up until about 1950 supported Spence's theory. (See Goodrich, Ross, & Wagner, 1961; Riley, 1968; and Spence, 1951, for reviews of this issue.)

Alternative Theories of Discrimination Learning

Other psychologists argued that discrimination learning is a more active, complex process than that envisioned by Spence. In particular, it was argued that learning about all stimuli present may not proceed at equal rates and, indeed, animals may attend to only some stimuli and ignore others. Learning, according to this view, proceeds only in the case of stimuli attended to (e.g.,

Krechevsky, 1932, 1938; Lashley & Wade, 1946). There are several aspects to more recent theories which emphasize that attention may play a role in discrimination learning. First, it is assumed that stimuli available to an animal in a discrimination problem have different probabilities of being attended to. Thus, learning may proceed at different rates for different stimuli. In that way an animal may form a strong association between one stimulus and the availability of reward, a weak association between another stimulus and the availability of reward, and no association between a third stimulus and the availability of reward. And this may occur *even though the correlation between the stimulus and the reward is the same for all stimuli*. This effect is referred to as *selective attention*, and stimuli for which learning proceeds at different rates are said to differ in *salience* (noticeability).

An example that is somewhat removed from animal discrimination learning but may capture the essence of this idea is the following. Books have a number of stimuli associated with them; they vary in size, color, print, subject matter, etc. If a young child were asked to sort out books in a library, placing together those that seemed to belong together, the child might do the sorting on the basis of size, color, or some such stimulus dimension. An adult, on the other hand, presumably would sort the books according to subject matter. The point is that of all the stimuli associated with a book, some may seem more *relevant* than others for the solution to the problem. Similarly, an animal faced with solving a discrimination problem may find some stimuli more relevant than others and, therefore, learn more about those stimuli.

Another aspect of attentional theories of discrimination learning is that they assume that the salience of a stimulus dimension may change during the course of discrimination learning—the attention-getting properties of a stimulus and their likelihood of entering into associations are not fixed, and its salience may change as a function of the animals' experience with the stimuli in a discrimination task.[6]

A third aspect of attention theories is that they assume that discrimination learning involves two stages or processes. One of these is that animals may learn different response tendencies in the presence of different stimuli (S+ and S−) based on the correlation of these stimuli with the availability of rewards. This aspect of discrimination learning is similar to that envisioned in Spence's model. Attentional theories assume that in addition to learning particular responses in the presence of particular stimuli, animals also attend to the stimulus dimension (e.g., color, brightness, etc.) from which S+ and S− were drawn (e.g., Mackintosh, 1965, 1975; Sutherland & Mackintosh, 1971). For example, if animals are learning a T-maze discrimination task and one arm of the maze is painted black and one white, they learn not only which

[6]Not all attention theories make this assumption (e.g., Mackintosh, 1975).

arm is rewarded and which is nonrewarded, they also learn that there is
something important about brightness of the arms per se as opposed to texture, odor, etc.

Evidence Favoring an Attention Concept

In considering the evidence supporting an attentional concept, we will
examine first the outcomes of two classes of experiments, outcomes which
seemed inexplicable in terms of Spence's theory, but understandable if explained in terms of attention. It should be noted that "attention" was inferred
from the results of these experiments, it was not measured directly. We will
then go on to examine efforts to measure attention in discrimination learning
more directly.

The Overlearning Reversal Experiment

The first class of experiments is concerned with how well animals are
able to reverse a discrimination once it has been learned. In a reversal learning experiment the former S+ is made S−, and vice versa, after the original
discrimination has been learned. The experiments that we will consider were
concerned with the relative ease of reversal learning after different amounts
of training on the original discrimination.

Reid (1953) trained three groups of rats in a T-maze brightness discrimination until they made the correct choice on 18 trials out of a sequence of 20
trials. After this criterion was reached, one group was given training with the
stimulus–reward pairings reversed; the former S+ was now incorrect and the
former S− was now rewarded. One of the remaining two groups was given
an additional 50 trials in the original problem before reversal, and the final
group was given 150 additional trials in the original problem before reversal.
Surprisingly, the result of the experiment was that the latter group, the group
given 150 overlearning trials in the original experiment, learned the reversal
faster than the other two groups.

This finding doesn't seem to follow from Spence's theory. If discrimination learning consists of the gradual strengthening of approach and withdrawal tendencies it would seem that the more training given on the original
discrimination, the more difficult it would be to learn a reversal. Thus, Reid's
data seem to contradict Spence's theory.

In order to explain this finding, Reid adopted a two-stage hypothesis.
He assumed that the acquisition of a task such as a T-maze brightness discrimination actually involves two kinds of learning. At the same time that the
animal is learning to make a response of approaching the correct stimulus and
not approaching the incorrect stimulus, it is also learning to attend to the
stimulus dimension from which the S+ and S− were drawn. For example, if
black and white maze arms are the S+ and S− stimuli, at the same time that

the rat is learning to approach black and not white, it is learning to attend to brightness cues (as opposed to odor, texture, etc.). A second assumption that Reid made in order to explain his data was that this second type of learning, learning to attend to a stimulus dimension, develops more slowly than approach response learning.

This two-stage hypothesis may help explain Reid's data in the following way. The animals that reversed after reaching criterion and after 50 overtraining trials had not yet learned the attentional response to any great degree. Thus, when the correct and incorrect stimuli were reversed, they had to relearn which of the various stimuli in the apparatus (e.g. brightness, odor, location, texture, etc.) to approach and which to avoid. However, in the animals given the 150 overtraining trials, the attentional response had been well learned, so when the S+ and S− were reversed, the animals learned this reversal relatively quickly. They did so because the brightness dimension was still relevant (i.e., the correct and incorrect stimuli were still on the brightness dimension) and, by attending to this stimulus dimension, the animals could quickly learn which aspect to approach (i.e., white).

The finding of faster reversal learning in animals given extra training on the original task led to an explosive growth in the number of experiments conducted to investigate this phenomenon. For some time the results of these experiments were quite confusing; many replicated Reid's findings, but many others did not (see Sperling, 1965a). Eventually, the following conclusion emerged from the mass of experimentation: The overlearning reversal effect (ORE) is likely to be obtained if the discrimination is a relatively difficult one, and if the amount of the reward given for the correct response is large (Mackintosh, 1965, 1969; Sperling, 1965b; Theios & Blosser, 1965).

The importance of the difficulty aspect for attentional theories is the following. It may be assumed that in a simple discrimination there is a high probability that the animal attends to the relevant dimension from the beginning of training, and thus there is little or no learning of an attentional response involved (see Lovejoy, 1966). Under these conditions, overtraining would not be expected to facilitate reversal. In the rat, a spatial discrimination (learning to go left or right in a T-maze) appears to be a relatively easy discrimination, and the ORE is unlikely to occur in a spatial discrimination with rats (Mackintosh, 1965, 1969). However, in a difficult discrimination the animal is likely, at the beginning of the experiment, to be attending to the wrong stimuli. Thus, in a difficult discrimination the learning of the correct attentional response plays a more important role, and it is under these conditions that overtraining is likely to facilitate reversal. For the rat, a brightness discrimination appears to be relatively difficult and it is in a brightness discrimination that the ORE is most likely to occur (Mackintosh, 1965, 1969).

Evidence in regard to this interpretation has been provided by Mackintosh (1965) who found that overtraining facilitated the reversal of a brightness discrimination in rats but not in chicks. It would appear that in birds a brightness discrimination is not difficult since birds may be thought to have a higher probability of attending to visual stimuli than rats. Thus, overtraining a chicken on a brightness discrimination is like overtraining a rat on a spatial discrimination. Further evidence in support of this idea was found in another experiment by Mackintosh (1965) in which it was shown that overtraining would facilitate the reversal of a brightness discrimination in chickens if the discrimination was made difficult enough.

There are other possible explanations for the ORE but at the present time it appears that an explanation involving the concept of attention is most consistent with the data (see Lovejoy, 1966; Mackintosh, 1969). In this regard it is interesting to note the results of experiments that provide an opportunity to "ask" for the stimuli (by making a particular response) any number of times before making a choice between them. In both humans and monkeys, the number of times the subjects choose to produce these stimuli before choosing one increases as problem difficulty increases (D'Amato, Etkin, & Fazzaro, 1968; Premack & Collier, 1966). It is as if more attention to the stimuli is required when the discrimination is complex.

Why a large reward should be necessary to produce the ORE in rats (Mackintosh, 1969) is not clear at the present time. It may be that the large reward is more likely to lead to frustration and thus faster extinction to the formerly correct stimulus (see Chapter 7), or it may be that the large reward is itself involved in directing attention. Mackintosh (1969) seems to favor the latter alternative. In any event, it is apparent why the ORE experiment led to a resurgence of interest in the concept of attention.

Acquired Distinctiveness of Cues

A second line of evidence reviving interest in the concept of attention came from the research of Lawrence (1949, 1950, 1952). Lawrence trained rats in a discrimination task in which they had to learn to approach one stimulus, say a black card, and not another stimulus, say a white card. Both stimuli were present concurrently. During this stage of the experiment other potential stimuli were present in the apparatus. For example, the floors of the choice arms had different textures (rough or smooth) and one arm had small chains hanging from the ceiling whereas the other arm did not. The locations of these stimuli were varied randomly with respect to reward. Thus, they were termed *irrelevant stimuli*—they did not predict the location of reward. The black and white cards, however, were perfectly correlated with the presence and absence of reward. These stimuli were called *relevant stimuli*—they were relevant for finding the reward.

After the animals had learned the black–white discrimination they were trained in a *conditional discrimination* task. In a conditional discrimination, the correct choice response depends upon which stimuli are present. For example, if both left and right choices are covered with a white card, then a left choice is correct (if white cards, go left) whereas if both are covered with a black card then going to the right-hand side would be rewarded (if black, go right). The important aspect of a conditional discrimination is that the animal cannot obtain reward for approaching or avoiding a particular stimulus (black or white); the stimulus serves as a cue for a choice response that is based on something other than direct approach or avoidance of that cue.

Lawrence found that animals trained in the black–white simultaneous discrimination learned the conditional discrimination faster if the black and white cards were used as conditional cues than if different stimuli (irrelevant stimuli from the simultaneous discrimination) were used as conditional cues. For example, if floor texture was used as a conditional cue (if both rough, go right; if both smooth, go left), then learning was not facilitated by having previously learned a simultaneous black–white discrimination.

How are these results related to attention? Lawrence argued that the positive transfer (faster learning) shown between the two tasks could not be accounted for on the basis of excitatory tendencies associated with S+ and inhibitory tendencies associated with S−. A stimulus that served to direct an approach response in the simultaneous task did not serve that function in the conditional task; that is, approaching the black stimulus in the conditional task could not lead to good performance since both choice alternatives were black half of the time and white half of the time.

If commonality of an approach response could not account for the facilitation, what did? Lawrence argued that it was a process of *learning to attend* to the relevant cues that accounted for the transfer. Note that even though the black and white stimulus cards of our example do not direct an approach response in the conditional discrimination, they are still relevant for the solution of the discrimination. Lawrence argued that if the animal learns to attend to the relevant stimulus dimension (e.g., brightness) in the simultaneous discrimination, then the solution of the conditional discrimination should be faster if this same dimension is still relevant. The experiment we have described, as well as others conducted by Lawrence and other investigators, bears out this hypothesis. Lawrence's idea was that the relevant cues acquire distinctiveness in the simultaneous discrimination, and this distinctiveness aids in the solution of the conditional discrimination as long as the same stimulus dimension is relevant for the solution of the conditional problem. By acquired distinctiveness, Lawrence meant that the animals had learned to attend to these cues.

Lawrence (1952) applied this same argument to other experiments in which he showed that learning a difficult discrimination, such as between two shades of gray that are very close in brightness, could be made easier if the animals were first trained on a simpler discrimination, such as that between dark gray and light gray. Lawrence's explanation was that the simpler discrimination taught the animals to attend to the difference in brightness, and it was this difference that predicted the availability or nonavailability of reward.

Thus, the results of these experiments and the ORE experiments seemed best explained if the concept of attention was employed. Animals seemed to learn to attend to a stimulus dimension (e.g., brightness, roughness, color, etc.) as well as learning a particular response during the course of a discrimination learning problem. Many other experiments of this type, and experiments of other types, provided inferential evidence for the usefulness of the concept of attention. (See Riley & Leith, 1976, for a review of these other experiments.)

We turn now to attempts at more direct demonstrations of selective attention.

Demonstrations of Selective Attention

An experiment that seems to demonstrate that animals may selectively attend to one of several available stimuli was conducted by Reynolds (1961b). Reynolds trained pigeons on a multiple VI 3-minute extinction schedule. The S+ and S− during discrimination training were both compound stimuli; a white triangle on a red background was used as S+ and a white circle on a green background was used as S−. After the birds were exhibiting many responses in the presence of S+ and virtually none in the presence of S− (see left half of Figure 10–10), the pigeons were shifted to an extinction schedule in the presence of all stimuli.

In extinction the compound stimuli that had been present during acquisition were separated into their components. That is, sometimes the response key was illuminated red, sometimes green; sometimes just the triangle was presented, and sometimes just the circle. The purpose of this phase of the experiment was, of course, to determine whether the pigeons had selectively attended to any aspect of the compound stimuli present during acquisition. The results of this test are presented in the right half of Figure 10–10. Clearly, pigeon 1 had learned the discrimination primarily on the basis of responding to the white triangle; the red color had no tendency to control its responding. Pigeon 2, however, had learned the discrimination primarily on the basis of attending to color; in this bird the triangle had little control over responding.

This experiment demonstrates that animals may not learn equally about all aspects of the stimuli present in a discrimination situation. They may select some specific aspect of the stimuli present and use that to respond appropriately. It is important to note that in this experiment the animals came into close contact with the compound discriminative stimuli during training— the birds pecked directly on the place where the stimuli were projected. It is also interesting to note that in the Reynolds experiment one of the birds apparently attended to form, whereas the other attended to color.

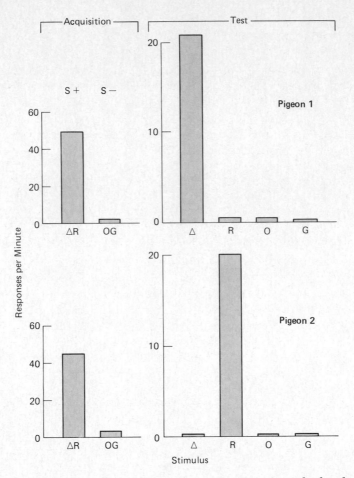

FIGURE 10–10 Responses of two pigeons during training on a multiple schedule with compound stimuli (left panel), and during tests with the compound stimuli broken down into their components (right panel). See text for explanation. (After Reynolds, 1961)

In a conceptually similar experiment, quail were trained in a conditioned food aversion paradigm (see Chapter 4). One group was injected with a toxin after consuming sour water, one group after consuming blue colored water, and a third group after consuming water that was both blue and sour. A test for the formation of a conditioned aversion showed that quail poisoned after exposure to the blue water subsequently avoided blue water and quail poisoned after exposure to sour water subsequently avoided sour water. What of the group exposed to both blue and sour water? In the test for conditioning this group was subdivided so that half were tested with blue water and half with sour water. The results showed that the quail avoided the blue water but not the sour water. Thus, this experiment shows that the quail had selectively associated the color of the water with the toxin, and "ignored" the potential association between the sour water and the toxin. The groups exposed to only single elements (sour or blue) showed that the birds could learn an association to either cue. But, when exposed to both, the birds apparently selectively associated the color with the effects of the toxin (Wilcoxin, Dragoin, & Kral, 1971).

Still another example of this selective attention effect is exemplified by an experiment with fish by Tennant and Bitterman (1975). They trained two groups of carp in a discrimination task. In one group the S+ and S− differed both in color and line orientation; in the second group the S+ and S− differed only in line orientation. After the first group had learned the discrimination, the two aspects of the discriminative stimuli (color and orientation) were presented separately. It was found that the fish learned the discrimination entirely on the basis of the difference in color between the two stimuli. They had apparently learned nothing about the line orientation. The results obtained from the second group showed that the fish could learn a discrimination based on line orientation if that was the only stimulus difference present.

These three experiments (Reynolds, 1961b; Tennant & Bitterman, 1975; Wilcoxin et al., 1971) used *compound stimuli* to assess for the presence of selective attention. This procedure involves the presentation of a conditioning stimulus that is composed of two or more elements. Selective attention is then tested for by decomposing the compound stimulus and presenting the elements alone and measuring responding. The decomposition test is usually conducted in extinction.

Many experiments like this have now been conducted, particularly using Pavlovian conditioning procedures, and the evidence is substantial that animals may learn about only one element, or more about one element than the other (e.g., Baker, 1968; Couvillon & Bitterman, 1982; Mackintosh, 1976). This form of selective attention is often termed *overshadowing* and was first described by Pavlov (1927). These experiments using compound stimuli, and related experiments using more complex procedures (see Riley & Roitblat, 1978) clearly show that animals may learn about only one of multiple stimuli present. Thus, these results are not consistent with Spence's interpretation of discrimination learning but they are consistent with the hypothesis that selective attention may be involved in learning discriminations.

Is Attention Measurable?

Several procedures have been used to measure attention as an ongoing process. For example, a number of experiments have employed an *observing response* technique in which animals must make a specific response in order to have the discriminative stimuli presented to them (e.g., D'Amato, Etkin,

& Fazzaro, 1968; Wyckoff, 1952). As we mentioned earlier, animals make more of these observing responses when discriminations are difficult than when they are easy.

Another procedure measures eye movements directly during the course of discrimination learning. Schrier and Povar (1979, 1982) have measured eye movements in monkeys during the learning of a discrimination between pairs of random dot patterns. They found the amount of eye movement increased initially during the course of discrimination learning, but once the animals learned the discrimination, the number of movements decreased to a level just sufficient for the animal to locate the positive stimulus. Limiting the animals to just one fixation on each stimulus from the start of training seriously impaired a monkey's ability to learn the discrimination. Thus, these experiments indicate that animals actively scan the discriminative stimuli during the course of discrimination learning.

Yet another procedure measures the orienting response (OR) during discrimination learning. Kaye and Pearce (1984) measured the OR to a light CS during the course of several Pavlovian conditioning experiments, including discrimination learning. They found that the OR was maintained at a high level until the discrimination was learned, then it declined, results that are similar to those obtained in the measurement of eye movements. Kaye and Pearce also reported that making a stimulus an unreliable predictor of reinforcement, as when a partial reinforcement schedule was used, served to maintain the OR at high levels.[7]

All of these experiments indicate that animals make overt movements that are indicative of orientation to stimuli during the course of discrimination learning. However, these procedures cannot provide direct information regarding the animals' attentional processes in most experiments using overshadowing experiments. For example, think of the Reynolds' (1961) experiment described earlier. In this case, both cues were superimposed. How could overt behavioral measures indicate which one the animal was attending to?

There is some evidence, from experiments in which the electrical activity of certain brain areas has been measured, that is consistent with the concept of selective attention. For example, the activity evoked by an auditory stimulus in a cat is diminished if an olfactory stimulus is also presented (see Hernandez-Peon, 1961, p. 509). The procedures in these experiments were not discrimination learning tasks, but the data indicate a potential neural basis for selective attention. Eventually, there may be direct measures of neural

---

[7]Kaye and Pearce argue that attention declines as the CS comes to accurately predict a reinforcement. This interpretation is consistent with their OR data, the data of Schrier and Povar, and with the Pearce-Hall model (Chapter 6). It is not consistent with Mackintosh's model of discrimination learning (1965, 1975) nor with current explanations of the ORE and the acquired distinctiveness of cues experiments. Mackintosh (1975) argued that the OR could not be viewed as a measure of selective attention.

activity that can be shown to correlate more closely with selective attention than the behavioral measures taken thus far (see Pritchard, 1981).

Summary and Conclusions Regarding Attention

A large number of experiments using compound stimuli have shown unequivocally that animals may learn more about one stimulus that is available than about others, even though all are equally correlated with reinforcement. In this chapter we presented evidence from overshadowing experiments, in which two or more stimuli are presented from the beginning of training. Another example that could be used to support selective attention was presented in Chapter 6, that is, the blocking experiments. Recall that in blocking, one stimulus is initially paired with a reinforcer and a second stimulus is presented in compound with the first stimulus. The data reviewed showed that very little was learned about the added stimulus element. Thus, both the overshadowing and blocking experiments are consistent with an attentional analysis of discrimination learning.

In this section we have also shown that the results of two experimental classes, the overlearning reversal experiments and the acquired distinctiveness of cues experiments, are consistent with an attentional analysis of discrimination learning and not consistent with Spence's analysis. These experiments suggest a two-stage process of discrimination learning. Animals learn particular responses to particular stimuli as a result of the reinforcement contingencies. And, they also learn to attend to the stimulus dimension that is correlated with reward and nonreward. This attention to the relevant stimulus dimension (the one correlated with reward) is thought to account for the transfer of learning demonstrated in the overlearning reversal experiments and the acquired distinctiveness of cues experiments.

Several behavioral techniques have been used to measure attention during the course of discrimination learning and these procedures (observing responses, eye movements, the orienting response) have shown correlations between the behavior measured and the course of discrimination learning. However, it is questionable whether these techniques have any relevance to selective attention as obtained in experiments using overshadowing procedures.[8]

In general the evidence described above, in addition to the interpretations derived from analysis of the generalization data presented earlier, plus some neurophysiological evidence, favor a role for an active attentional process in discrimination learning.

[8]There is not unanimous agreement that the data presented here absolutely necessitate an attentional explanation (see Bitterman, 1979b; Riley & Leith, 1976), nor is there agreement on the course of attention during discrimination learning (Pearce & Hall, 1980). However, the elaboration of these disagreements is beyond the scope of this text.

What causes selective attention? It could be due to an animal's reinforcement history. This is certainly true in the blocking experiments, and
possibly in some overshadowing experiments. There could also be innate species preferences, as the Wilcoxin et al. and Tennant and Bitterman overshadowing experiments may suggest. One could speculate on the value to the
animal of selective attention, but one could also speculate the other way.
There are not enough data to allow a fruitful pursuit of this question at the
present time.

CHAPTER SUMMARY

In this chapter we have seen that the establishment of a learned response in
the presence of a particular stimulus generalizes to other stimuli not trained.
Typically, responding follows an orderly gradient, decreasing as other stimuli
become less like the trained stimulus on some physical dimension. Data were
presented showing that generalization may be obtained on a temporal dimension as well as on tangible physical dimensions. Included here were data
showing that the shape of the generalization gradient may be influenced by a
number of experimental parameters such as the schedule of reinforcement
used in training.

If one stimulus is consistently paired with reward and another with the
absence of reward, animals will come to show differential responding in the
presence of the two stimuli. Several examples of this discrimination learning
were described.

Prior discrimination training has a substantial effect on the generalization gradient. Typically, generalization testing conducted after discrimination
training yields a gradient (termed a postdiscrimination gradient) that differs
from the usual generalization gradient in three ways. The postdiscrimination
gradient has the peak of responding shifted away from S+, it has a higher
peak rate of responding, and it is steeper. Each of these differences was considered in detail. Peak shift may be related to generalization of inhibition and
the aversiveness of S−. Elevated responding is the result of a contrast effect
related to relativity of reward and possibly to aversiveness associated with the
lower reward value. The sharpened postdiscrimination gradient results from
discrimination training even if the training is conducted with stimuli different
from those used in the generalization test—it may be due to enhanced attention to stimulus dimensions resulting from generalization training.

Overshadowing and blocking experiments demonstrate selective attention. Also, interpretational evidence derived from analysis of the overlearning
reversal experiments and acquired distinctiveness of cues experiments favor
an attentional analysis of discrimination learning. Discrimination learning is
now thought to involve two processes: the learning of particular response
tendencies in the presence of particular stimuli, and the learning of an attentional response to the relevant (reward correlated) stimulus dimension.

11

Instrumental Learning V: Selected Topics

>> **66** *To feed or not to feed, defend the territory, trounce the subordinate, flee the predator, court the lady, build a nest, nurse the young, move, stay put, migrate, hibernate, these are some of the questions continuously facing every animal. . . . These choices govern the continuance, decrease, or increase of an animal's representation in the genetic pool.* **99**

G. H. Collier, *Determinants of Choice,*
1981

CONDITIONED REINFORCEMENT

Most of us are rewarded for our work with money, and most of us value money not for its own sake but for the creature comforts and pleasures that it will bring us in exchange. Money is valuable only because it symbolizes something else.

It has been shown that lower animals may be taught to "work" for symbols that derive their value from their exchangeability. For example, chimpanzees have been taught first that poker chips could be exchanged for food and then that the poker chips could be obtained as rewards in discrimination learning tasks. After the animals had accumulated a number of chips for correct responses they turned them in for food (Cowles, 1937; Wolfe, 1936). Rats too have been trained to accumulate marbles that could later be "traded" for food (e.g., Malagodi, 1967).

The chips and marbles in these experiments are called *conditioned reinforcers.* The term refers to a stimulus that, in and of itself, has no reinforcing value but has come to have such value because the animal has learned of some relationship between the stimulus and a reinforcer. A conditioned reinforcer in instrumental learning is directly analogous to a second order conditioned stimulus in Pavlovian conditioning. Recall that in Chapter 5 it was shown that a CS that had been previously paired with a US could itself act like a US. That is, the CS could be used as the reinforcer for the development of a CR to a new stimulus. Similarly, in instrumental learning a stimulus previously paired with a reinforcer will itself act as a reinforcer. This reinforcing property may be shown by making presentation of the stimulus contingent upon the occurrence of a response. A conditioned reinforcer will enhance the likelihood of a response occurring, much like a natural reinforcer.

This apparent similarity between a second order CS and a conditioned reinforcer naturally raises the question as to whether a conditioned reinforcer for instrumental behavior develops its reinforcing properties through Pavlovian conditioning processes. Is a Pavlovian association between a stimulus and a reward enough to endow that neutral stimulus with the property of reinforcing instrumental behavior? The general conclusion is "yes." A contingent relationship (as in Pavlovian conditioning) between a stimulus and a reinforcer is necessary and perhaps sufficient to establish a stimulus as a conditioned reinforcer for instrumental behavior (e.g., Mackintosh, 1974). Fantino (e.g., 1977) has argued that there may be more to a conditioned reinforcer than this. However, the experimental procedures involved in this argument are somewhat complex and the issue will not be considered in this text.

Measurement of Conditioned Reinforcement

Maze Experiments

One of the classic experiments demonstrating conditioned reinforcement was performed by Saltzman (1949). He first trained rats to run in a straight runway for a food reward. The goal box of the runway was either black or white on different trials. When it was one brightness the rats were rewarded for running, but they found no reward when it was the other brightness. After this training, the rats were tested in a T-maze. One of the goal boxes in the T-maze was the one associated with reward in the runway, the other was the one associated with nonreward in the runway. The rats could not see the goal boxes from the choice point of the maze, thus they had to learn to turn left or right in order to subsequently reach a goal box. The animals eventually learned to go to the goal box previously associated with food. No food was ever presented in the T-maze. Thus, the reinforcement for this learned choice response was simply the attainment of a stimulus that had previously been associated with food.

The Saltzman experiment demonstrated that a conditioned reinforcer would support the learning of a new response (a position discrimination). Other experiments using his and similar techniques for testing conditioned reinforcers have indicated the following generalizations. Conditioned reinforcers are more effective if they are presented intermittently rather than continuously (e.g., D'Amato, Lachman, & Kivey, 1958). A stimulus that had been associated with a large reward is a more effective conditioned reinforcer than a stimulus that had been associated with a small reward (e.g., Butter & Thomas, 1958; D'Amato, 1955). Conditioned reinforcers are reduced in effectiveness if there is a delay between presentation of the conditioned reinforcer and the primary reinforcer (e.g., Stubbs, 1969).

Operant Experiments

Operant schedules have also been used in the analysis of conditioned reinforcers. Some of these schedules will be particularly relevant for the discussion of choice behavior and foraging in the following sections of this chapter. Therefore, the relevant procedures will be described briefly now and covered in more detail in the later sections.

Clock Stimuli. One demonstration of conditioned reinforcement involves the use of *clock stimuli*. A clock stimulus is a stimulus that is correlated with the passage of time on an interval schedule. For example, in one study pigeons were trained on a FI 3-minute schedule. Recall that in a fixed interval schedule the first response after the time interval has elapsed will produce a reinforcer (see Chapter 8). In the study in question there were two response keys on which the pigeons could peck. One of them controlled the delivery of reinforcement on the FI 3-minute schedule. That is, they had to peck on this key in order to obtain the reinforcement. Pecks on the other key resulted in brief presentations of either a white, green, or red light on the key. The white light was presented if the birds responded during the first minute of the three-minute interval, the green light if they responded during the second minute, and the red light during the third minute—hence the term *clock stimuli*.

The results of this experiment showed that the presentations of the red light would maintain responding on the second key. Presentations of the other stimuli would not maintain responding (Kendall, 1972). An interpretation of this result is that the response contingent presentation of the red light acted as a conditioned reinforcer. The white and green lights may have been ineffective in maintaining responding because of their remoteness from the primary reinforcer.

Chained Schedules. In a *chained schedule* there are two or more schedules presented consecutively, each of which is correlated with the presence of a particular stimulus. For example, on a chained variable ratio (VR) variable interval (VI) schedule the animals would first have to complete the ratio requirement (an average of x number of responses) and then they would be reinforced after they had completed the VI requirement (e.g., the first response after an average of y units of time had passed). Only the terminal schedule is reinforced, but each component is signaled by the presentation of a stimulus. Thus, in our example, the key might be illuminated green during the VR component and blue during the VI component.

These two schedules in the chain are usually repeated many times in each daily training session. Eventually, the pattern of responding normally controlled by each type of schedule (see Chapter 8) occurs in the presence of the stimulus correlated with that schedule. In our example, the animals would respond at a very high rate during the VR component, and at a slower rate during the VI component. An interesting aspect of this is that the schedule-appropriate responding occurs during the first link in the chain (the VR component) without any primary reinforcement for this schedule. Thus, the occurrence of the stimulus associated with the second link is thought to act as a conditioned reinforcer for responding on the first link.

Chained schedules may be made quite long, with, for example, five or more links, each correlated with a stimulus. It is not a necessary characteristic of chained schedules that each link be a different schedule. For example, an animal may be required to complete five consecutive FI 5-minute interval schedules prior to reinforcement. Each interval would be correlated with a particular stimulus (notice the similarity in this case to clock stimuli). In chained schedules in which all the links have the same schedule, the rate of responding tends to be lowest in the first link and increases as the terminal link and the time of reinforcement draws closer. Other characteristics of chained schedules and related schedules may be found in reviews by Gollub (1977) and Fantino (1977).[1]

Applications

One of the values of the chained schedule is that it shows that a great deal of behavior can be maintained by a small amount of primary reinforcement delivered at the end of the chain, provided that discriminative stimuli are presented in each link of the chain. This is also a characteristic of conditioned stimuli in general. The deleterious effects of long delays of reward on instrumental behavior were described in Chapter 7. We also described in that chapter how Grice went to some length to remove all sources of stimuli correlated with reward to show just how important is the *immediate* delivery of primary reward if behavior is to be maintained. Conditioned reinforcers are applied to accomplish the opposite task—they are deliberately used to bridge *long* delays between a behavior that is to be reinforced and the delivery of primary reinforcement.

One of the best known examples of this use of conditioned reinforcers is the work of Ayllon and Azrin at Anna State Hospital. The problem that these investigators faced was how to get patients active in the affairs of the ward—how to activate them and keep them busy doing some useful and meaningful task. They wanted to reward the patients somehow if they chipped in and helped, say reward them with a movie if they washed the breakfast dishes. However, it was not feasible to reward each instance of behavior with some primary reinforcement. Such a practice would disrupt ongoing daily events (imagine a two-hour movie after the beds were made, another after breakfast dishes were washed, etc.), and would quickly exhaust the stock of primary reinforcers. What Ayllon and Azrin did was to use con-

---

[1]Other reviews of conditioned reinforcement may be found in Mackintosh (1974), Bolles (1975), and Hendry (1969).

ditioned reinforcers as interim rewards—something that had the promise of a primary reinforcement at some later time. One of the conditioned reinforcers that was used was a token. Different numbers of tokens were given for different behaviors and these tokens were later exchangeable for a primary reinforcement.

An example of the combination of conditioned reinforcement and shaping (see Chapter 7) is seen in the way a patient was brought to work in the hospital laundry. The patient was initially rewarded with 10 tokens for walking on the ward with an attendant, then the same reward was given for walking outside, then for walking to the laundry, then for working in the laundry for five minutes, etc. Eventually, the patient was rewarded with 80 tokens for working in the laundry for six hours without the presence of the attendant (Ayllon & Azrin, 1968).

Another example of conditioned reinforcement occurs in gambling casinos. The slot machine floors in these establishments are something to experience—hundreds or thousands of square feet filled with slot machines and people mechanically feeding coins and pulling handles. The machines are programmed so that small payoffs are fairly frequent and large payoffs are rare. But each time a slot machine pays off, a bell rings and a light mounted on top of the machine flashes. In a room filled with hundreds of people frantically feeding coins into the machines, there is a near constant sound of ringing bells and flashing lights. The feeling that one gets is that winning is frequent—my turn must surely be just beyond the next quarter.

CHOICE BEHAVIOR

In this section we will consider some of the ways in which choice behavior has been studied in animals. Throughout the first fifty years of this century perhaps the predominant apparatus used for the study of choice was the maze.

Maze Learning—Early Studies

Complex Mazes

Much of the early work done with mazes was concerned with the sensory processes used by the rat in learning complex mazes. This early work was reviewed and summarized by Munn (1950). Generally speaking, the rat will use any sense available to it that is useful in finding its way through a maze. Rats solve mazes from which the external environment is visible in terms of visual cues. That is, they learn the relationship between the location of objects outside the maze and the goal area of the maze. Changing this relationship by moving some of the objects, or rotating the maze (see Figure 7–1) has a detrimental effect on maze performance. Rats that cannot use visual cues depend heavily on olfactory cues and, to some extent, on auditory cues to help learn their way through a maze (Honzik, 1936; Munn, 1950).

A number of other characteristics of maze learning were summarized by Munn. Among these are the facts that when there are alternate routes to the goal, rats learn to take the shortest route; that blind alleys which point in the direction of the goal are more difficult for the rat to learn to avoid than blind alleys that point away from the goal; that blind alleys which point in the same direction as the last turn into the goal area are more difficult for the rat to eliminate than blind alleys that point in the opposite direction; and when the momentum of a turn carries the rat to the outside wall of an alley, it tends to follow that wall and make a turn continuous with it.

T-Mazes

From the 1930s through the 1960s extensive work was done using T-mazes. The T-maze may be viewed as a complex maze simplified to the level of a single choice point. Factors that might conceivably influence choice behavior in complex mazes were studied intensively using this simplified apparatus.

Animals that are rewarded for going to one side of a T-maze will soon learn to choose that side. Generally speaking, the larger the reward they receive, the faster they learn the correct choice response (e.g., Hill, Cotton, & Clayton, 1962; Pubols, 1961; Reynolds, 1950). When there are rewards in both arms, the rats will learn to choose the side with the larger reward, but the smaller the difference between the two rewards, the longer it takes them to learn the "correct" choice, and the less often they choose the correct side (e.g., Cakmak & Spear, 1967; Clayton, 1964; Hill & Spear, 1963). Thus, the effects of reward magnitude on choice behavior are what might have been expected from the effects of reward magnitude on behavior in straight runways (see Chapter 7).

Other variables also influence choice in a T-maze in a systematic fashion. For example, rats given partial reward in the correct alternative take longer to learn to choose this alternative than rats given 100 percent reinforcement (e.g., Hill et al., 1962; Wike, Kintsch, & Remple, 1959). Also, rats for whom reward delivery is delayed on the rewarded side of a T-maze take longer to learn than rats for whom the reward is delivered immediately (e.g., Pubols, 1958). A number of experiments have given rats a choice between a small reward delivered immediately and a large reward delivered after some delay. In general, rats choose the side of the immediate reward, but their preference will shift to the delayed reward side if the reward is large enough. Thus, over a range of delays and reward magnitudes, rats will learn to choose either a large, delayed reward or a small, immediate reward, depending on the exact magnitudes of the delay and reward values (e.g., Davenport, 1962; Logan, 1965).

Generally speaking, rats learn spatial discriminations, that is, they go to one side or the other consistently, relatively quickly. This is particularly true when there are visual cues external to the maze which are correlated with the locations of the two arms of the T-maze (e.g., Mackintosh, 1974; Restle, 1957). Rats may also be trained in brightness discriminations in a T-maze. In a brightness discrimination one arm may be white and the other black and the reward is correlated with one brightness, for example, black. In order to ensure that the rats learn this problem on the basis of the brightness difference and not in terms of spatial location, the brightness cues are switched from side to side on a random basis, but the reward always remains with one of the cues (e.g., the black side). For rats a brightness discrimination is more difficult to learn than a spatial discrimination (e.g., Mackintosh, 1965; 1974).

One other aspect of these early T-maze studies is of some interest and importance. When rats are placed in T-mazes with equal rewards in both arms (either no reward in both, or equal amounts of some reward), they show a strong tendency to alternate their choices between the two arms on successive trials (Dember & Fowler, 1958). Thus, if they go to the right side on the first trial they are very likely to go to the left side on the second trial, etc. This alternation is often interpreted in terms of exploratory behavior, and most of the evidence indicates that the alternation is controlled not by the response that the animal last made, but by the place that it last visited. This fact is quite important for an understanding of some aspects of foraging behavior, which will be considered later.

Recent Maze Studies

There has been a recent resurgence of interest in the use of the maze to study choice behavior, a resurgence due in large part to the work of David Olton (Olton, 1978; Olton & Samuelson, 1976). Olton used a radial arm maze, diagrammed in Figure 11–1, to study the choice behavior and memory of rats when they are faced with a large number of choices. Olton's basic procedure was to put food in all eight arms of the maze and place a rat in the center area. The rat was allowed to choose freely among the arms. The question of interest was the number of new arms that the rat would choose before it repeated a choice. In other words, how efficient would the rat be in finding all the available rewards without repeating a choice where it had already consumed the reward? Olton found that the rats did surprisingly well in this task, averaging between seven and eight correct responses out of their first eight choices. Various control experiments showed that this near perfect performance did not depend on the use of stereotyped response patterns as "memory aids" (e.g., always choosing the alley to the right of the last choice),

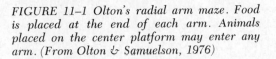

FIGURE 11–1 Olton's radial arm maze. Food is placed at the end of each arm. Animals placed on the center platform may enter any arm. (From Olton & Samuelson, 1976)

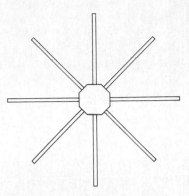

nor did it depend on the use of intramaze cues such as odor trails or other markings. Instead, the choices seemed to be based on the animals' memory of where they had been relative to visual cues lying outside of and around the maze (Olton, 1978; Olton & Collison, 1979). Disturbance of these extra-maze cues disrupted the rat's performance. Consistent with these results is the finding that visual cues, but not auditory or olfactory cues, play a critical role in radial arm maze performance (Zoladek & Roberts, 1978).

Olton did find that the rat's performance suffered the more choices it had to make. Thus, the more choices it had already made, the more likely a rat was to make an error in the eight-choice task. This trend was enhanced when Olton trained rats in a radial arm maze in which there were 17 arms to choose from. In this case, a rat's memory is like some aspects of human memory—it suffers because of interference from prior learning. Olton has found that gerbils do as well as rats in this task, but other investigators have reported that pigeons (Bond, Cook, & Lamb, 1981) and Siamese fighting fish (Roitblat, Tham, & Golub, 1982) do not do as well.

Discussion of interesting hypotheses as to why rats do so well in this task will be deferred until we consider foraging, when an attempt will be made to relate an animal's performance in situations like the radial arm maze to its natural food-seeking habits.

Choice Involving Operant Schedules

Choice behavior has been studied in a number of situations employing operant schedules of reward. Two such situations will be briefly considered—simple concurrent schedules and concurrent chain schedules.

Concurrent Schedules

In a concurrent schedule, two schedules of reinforcement are in effect simultaneously. Each schedule applies to a different manipulandum, and the subject may choose to respond on either manipulandum, and thus on either schedule. An example of this procedure is provided in a study by McSweeney (1975). She used pigeons as subjects in an apparatus in which there were two levers (treadles) mounted on the floor on either side of the area where the reward became available. In addition to these different spatial locations, the two treadles were differentiated by color of the light illuminating them (either blue or white light). The pigeons were free to respond on either treadle and they were reinforced on a variable interval (VI) schedule for responding on either one. This type of schedule is termed a *concurrent VI, VI.*

The pigeons in McSweeney's experiment were exposed to different pairs of VI schedules in effect on the two treadles. Thus, at one time responding on one treadle was reinforced on a VI 30-second schedule and responding on the other treadle was reinforced on a VI 2-minute schedule. At other times the schedule pairs in effect were VI 1-minute and VI 2-minute; VI 2-minute and VI 2-minute; and VI 2-minute and VI 4-minute. The pigeons were allowed extensive experience with each schedule pair before being shifted to another pair.

Of interest in this experiment was how the pigeons would allocate their responses between the two schedules. It could be, for example, that the birds would learn which treadle provided the higher rate of reinforcement and then spend all of their time responding on that treadle. The results obtained by McSweeney are shown in Table 11–1 and Figure 11–2. Data are presented for all four pigeons in her experiment. Table 11–1 shows the average response rate in the presence of each schedule, the average number of reinforcements received in each schedule, the proportion of responses made in each schedule, and the proportion of reinforcements received in each schedule. Plotted in Figure 11–2 are the proportion of responses made and proportion of reinforcements received in the more favorable schedule (the left portion of each pair in Table 11–1).

Several aspects of these results are of interest. First, the animals respond to both available treadles under all schedule conditions—they do not respond only to the most favorable alternative. Second, when the two components produce approximately equal reinforcement opportunities (i.e., the VI 2-minute, VI 2-minute schedule), the animals respond approximately equally to each schedule. Third, when the schedules are unequal the animals respond more often on the schedule that provides the higher frequency of reinforcement availability. For example, VI 30-second responding is at a higher rate than VI 2-minute responding. Fourth, the proportion of responses made to the more favorable schedule approximately equals the proportion of reinforcements received from that schedule. This tendency of the animals' relative response rates in the most favorable component to equal the relative reinforcement rates is apparent in the graph of the proportions presented in Figure 11–2.

TABLE 11–1

Rates of responding (presses per minute) and rates of reinforcement (reinforcers per hour) for four pigeons on four different concurrent VI, VI schedules. Shown also are proportion of total responses made to each component and proportion of total reinforcements received from each component of the concurrent schedules. Note that proportion of responses tends to equal proportion of reinforcements. (From McSweeney, 1975)

Concurrent Schedule Pairs

Bird		VI 30-sec	VI 2-min	VI 1-min	VI 2-min	VI 2-min	VI 4-min	VI 2-min	VI 2-min
8422	responses	17.1	6.8	17.8	9.7	14.7	11.6	12.2	12.5
	reinforce-ments	107.5	30.3	57.8	31.8	30.5	15.4	30.7	31.4
	proportion responses	.72	.28	.65	.35	.56	.44	.49	.51
	proportion reinforce-ments	.78	.22	.64	.36	.66	.34	.49	.51
8772	responses	20.3	6.7	23.0	14.4	23.3	19.9	17.0	18.9
	reinforce-ments	110.8	29.8	58.3	28.7	30.2	13.1	30.6	29.8
	proportion responses	.75	.25	.61	.39	.54	.46	.47	.53
	proportion reinforce-ments	.79	.21	.67	.33	.70	.30	.51	.49
8845	responses	16.8	5.0	14.8	7.7	10.4	8.5	10.1	9.4
	reinforce-ments	110.9	33.9	57.9	28.5	31.6	13.3	31.2	28.7
	proportion responses	.77	.23	.66	.34	.55	.45	.52	.48
	proportion reinforce-ments	.76	.34	.67	.33	.70	.30	.52	.48
8895	responses	24.1	8.8	10.8	9.2	20.0	12.7	11.4	11.2
	reinforce-ments	110.1	30.8	58.3	32.1	30.2	14.0	30.4	31.0
	proportion responses	.73	.27	.54	.46	.61	.39	.50	.50
	proportion reinforce-ments	.78	.22	.64	.36	.68	.32	.50	.50

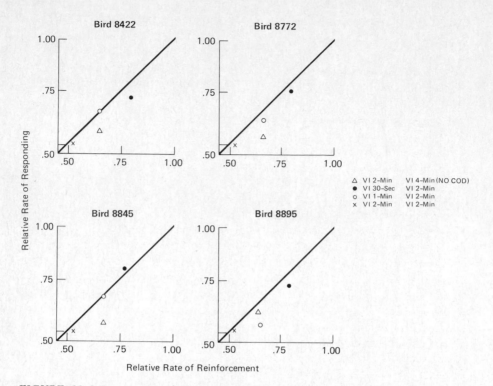

FIGURE 11–2 *Proportion of responses made to schedule that provided the higher rate of reinforcement plotted as a function of the proportion of reinforcements obtained from that schedule. Data were taken from Table 11–1. For example, bird 8422 made an average of 17.1 responses on the VI 30-sec schedule and 6.8 responses on the VI 2-min schedule. In proportions, this bird made 0.72 of its responses on the VI 30-sec treadle. This bird received 0.78 of its reinforcements from responding on that treadle (107.5/[107.5 + 30.3]). In general, proportion of responses tends to approximately equal proportion of reinforcements obtained. (From McSweeney, 1975)*

The relationship of relative response rates to relative reinforcement rates shown in Figure 11–2 may be expressed as a simple equation:

$$\frac{B_1}{B_1 + B_2} = \frac{R_1}{R_1 + R_2}$$

This equation states that the proportion of behavior B emitted to one of two alternatives will equal the proportion of reinforcement R available from that alternative. This equation is termed the *matching law* (Herrnstein, 1970). This matching of responses to reinforcements occurs in concurrent schedules and has been the subject of considerable empirical work and mathematical elaboration (e.g., Baum, 1974; Catania, 1963; Herrnstein, 1970, 1974; Rachlin, Kagel, & Battalio, 1980).

Matching has been found in time allocation as well as in response frequency. For example, pigeons have been placed in a situation in which simply standing on one side or the other of a chamber led to the delivery of reinforcement according to a number of different concurrent VI, VI schedules (as in the McSweeney experiment). In this situation the pigeons allocated their time to the two sides of the chamber in proportion to the reinforcements that they received from each side (Baum & Rachlin, 1969). Similar results were obtained in humans in a study in which they were instructed to search for targets in two locations. The frequency of target occurrence in these locations was programmed according to a concurrent VI, VI schedule. The proportion of time that the subjects spent looking at each location matched the proportion of target sightings that occurred in that location (Baum, 1975).

Many other studies have demonstrated that the matching relationship is obtained with a number of different response measures, with a variety of reinforcers, and across a broad spectrum of animal species (deVilliers, 1977). It should be noted, though, that often special conditions are necessary before the matching relationship is obtained on concurrent schedules. One of these is some mechanism to control an otherwise strong tendency of animals to switch rapidly back and forth between the two choice alternatives. This switching behavior may be reinforced if an animal obtains a reward immediately after switching from one manipulandum to the other. In order to prevent immediate reinforcement, a procedure known as *change over delay* is often employed. In this procedure no reward may be delivered until a delay of several seconds has elapsed after an animal switches from one choice alternative to the other.

Suppose, for example, a pigeon in the McSweeney experiment switched from the treadle rewarded on a VI 2-minute schedule to a treadle rewarded on a VI 30-second schedule, and suppose that during the time the pigeon was responding on the VI 2-minute schedule a reward had become available on the 30-second schedule. Without a change over delay the pigeon would be rewarded for the first response that it made on the 30-second treadle. With a change over delay, however, several seconds will have to elapse after the animal's first response before the available reward will be delivered. Using a change over delay prevents rapid switching and it leads to matching in cases where it would otherwise not occur (deVilliers, 1977).

In summary, animals trained with two choice alternatives on concurrent schedules will learn to choose the alternative that has the higher frequency of reinforcement. Moreover, they will tend to distribute their responses and time in proportion to the reinforcements received from the two alternatives. Perhaps the most important implication of the matching law is that choice behavior in lower organisms performing on concurrent schedules is quite orderly and is capable of being described in mathematical terms. Further evidence on the generality, and limitations, of the matching law may be found in Baum, 1979; deVilliers, 1977; and McSweeney et al., 1983a, 1983b.

Concurrent Chain Schedules

The final procedure employed to study choice that we will be concerned with in this section is the use of *concurrent chain schedules*. In a concurrent chain schedule the animal is faced with two response alternatives. Completion of the response requirement on either alternative, however, does not lead immediately to reinforcement, but instead to another schedule, which is reinforced at its completion. This procedure is diagrammed in Figure 11–3. The Figure shows that the animals are initially exposed to two levers "reinforced" on equal VI schedules. The animals are free to respond on either lever at any time. This first schedule is termed the *initial link* of a concurrent chain schedule. Once the initial link schedule requirement is met on either lever the animal enters the *terminal link* of the schedule.

The entry into the terminal link is accompanied by several changes. First, the opportunity for choice is lost. This is accomplished by rendering inoperative the alternative choice. For example, in a lever-pressing task, the alternative lever may simply be retracted from the apparatus; in a pigeon key-pecking situation the alternative key is darkened and made inoperative. Thus, once the animal chooses one path on the basis of its responses in the initial link, the path not chosen is closed off, at least temporarily. Second, a different schedule is in effect in the terminal link. In the example diagrammed, a FI 10-second schedule is in effect with a reward of three food

FIGURE 11–3 Diagram of concurrent chain procedure. See text for explanation.

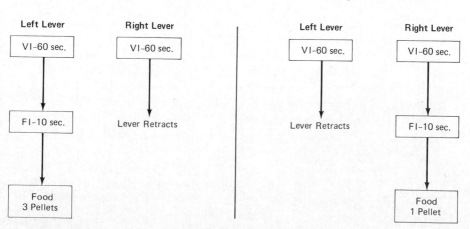

pellets upon completion of the schedule. Third, there is usually some stimulus change correlated with the change to the terminal link. For example, in a pigeon experiment the response key may change from white to green. The stimulus associated with the terminal link is considered to be a conditioned reinforcer because of its predictive relationship with the primary reinforcer that occurs upon completion of the terminal link (see Fantino, 1977; Killeen, 1982). The presentation of this terminal link stimulus may be thought of as the reinforcement for responding on the initial link.

Figure 11–3 also diagrams the events that would take place if the animal chose the other alternative in the initial link of our example. In this case, the terminal link is an identical FI 10-second schedule but the reinforcement magnitude received upon completion of this terminal link is one pellet rather than three pellets. To summarize our example, the animal is faced with two levers, each reinforced on an equal VI schedule by entry into terminal links of equal FI schedules but of differential reinforcement magnitudes. Choice is measured by how much the animal responds to each of the two alternatives in the initial link.[2]

Concurrent chain schedules have been used to ask a number of questions regarding choice behavior. For example, in the experiment from which Figure 11–3 is drawn, Ito and Asaki (1982) were interested in how preference for the large reward alternative would be influenced by the length of the reinforcement delay imposed in the terminal FI schedule. In order to investigate this question, they used different FI terminal links of 5, 10, 20, and 40 seconds. Both terminal links had the same delay, but were reinforced with either one or three food pellets. The initial links available for the animal to choose from were always equal VI 60-second schedules. Thus, the choice that an animal faced at any one time would be as follows: respond on either of two levers, each reinforced on a VI 60-second schedule by entry into either of two terminal links, each reinforced on identical FI schedules (e.g., 10 seconds) but by different amounts of food (one pellet versus three pellets).

The results obtained in this experiment are shown in Figure 11–4. With a constant five-second delay there was a slight preference for the alternative that led to the three pellet reward (bear in mind that the difference between three pellets and one pellet is a very small difference). However, as the length of the terminal link FI schedule increased (as delay of reward increased), the degree of preference for the alternative with the larger reward increased. One interpretation of this result might be that the incentive value

---

[2]A concurrent chain schedule is analogous to the following simpler situation. A rat is faced with two doors, both gray. When the rat goes through one door, the other locks and becomes unavailable as a choice. Once the rat is through the door it has chosen, it must run in a long alley of a particular brightness (conditioned reinforcer). At the end of the alley it finds a reward. The two alleys are of different brightness and contain different reinforcers. The advantage of the concurrent chain procedure is that it provides for a more extended sample of the animal's behavior during the choice phase.

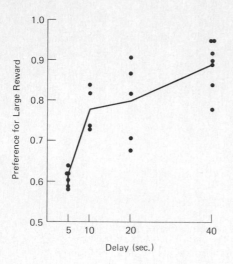

FIGURE 11–4 Percent choice of large reward alternative in concurrent chain procedure as a function of length of the terminal link. As terminal link duration increased, choice of large reward alternative in initial link increased. Filled circles refer to individual animals. (From Ito & Asaki, 1982)

of the small reward decays more rapidly than the incentive value of the large reward over comparable delay intervals; thus, the difference in choice between the two rewarded alternatives becomes exaggerated with long delays. Another way of stating this might be that a long delay is more tolerable when there is a large reward at the end of the delay.

Ito and Asaki also asked another question in their use of the concurrent chain procedure. They asked if points of indifference in choice could be found by increasing the delay associated with the larger of two rewards. In other words, if rats would normally choose the larger of two rewards, could this choice be offset by increasing the delay of the larger reward relative to the delay for the small reward? (Recall that a similar question was investigated in maze tasks by Davenport, 1962, and by Logan, 1965; see Chapter 7.) Ito and Asaki found a number of such equivalences; for example, a 15-second delay for three food pellets was equivalent to a 5-second delay for one food pellet, and that a 5-second delay for three food pellets was equivalent to a 1.7-second delay for one food pellet. In general, they found that the relationship between the delays associated with large and small rewards that would lead to equivalence of choice could be characterized by a power function of the form:

Large reward delay = 7.7(small reward delay)[0.68]

In other words, to find a delay associated with large reward that would just offset the delay correlated with small reward the value of the small reward delay is raised to the 0.68 power and multiplied by 7.7.

Other more detailed investigations of the parameters of reward amount, delay, and schedule that affect choice in concurrent chain schedules may be found in the work of Snyderman (1983), Fantino and Davison (1983), and

Killeen (1982). The work of Snyderman, for example, is an elaboration of the type of experiment conducted by Ito and Asaki. Snyderman found that a more complicated equation than that proposed by Ito and Asaki may be necessary to describe choice behavior or when a wider range of reward amounts and delays are investigated. However, the results of Snyderman's study indicate that satisfactory and general quantitative descriptions of choice behavior in the concurrent chain procedure are possible. The Fantino and Davison study shows that there is a systematic relationship between choice behavior and the relative lengths of the initial and terminal links on concurrent chain schedules. Generally speaking, the longer the initial link (e.g., VI 180-seconds as compared to VI 15-seconds), the less influence the length of the terminal link has on choice behavior.

Our review of choice learning shows clearly that lower animals can learn to make "meaningful" choices in a variety of complex laboratory tasks. Is this choice learning ability related in any way to the animals' survival under natural conditions? In Chapter 1 we discussed how animals were faced with a variety of survival problems, problems such as food procurement, safety from predators, protection from climatic extremes, care of offspring, etc., and we mentioned that natural selection processes may have led to the evolution of both structural specializations and learning abilities as aids in solving these problems.

In the next section we will examine how learning and memory may play a role in one of these problems—food selection. In particular, we will examine some data from the study of foraging by animals in their natural environments, relate some of these data to possible psychological processes described earlier in this text, and then describe some ways in which foraging behavior is studied in the laboratory.

FORAGING

Field Studies

Crows on Mandarte Island, off the west coast of Canada, consume whelks (shellfish with spiral shells). In order to consume these whelks the crows must first find them and then break the shells. The whelks are found after a brief search among the rocks of the intertidal area of the beach (Zach, 1978). Each crow seems to have its own foraging territory. After finding a whelk, the bird flies toward the back of the beach, increases its altitude, and drops the prey. If the shell does not break, the crow will retrieve the whelk and try again, apparently continuing with the same whelk until the shell breaks.

The birds face a number of choices in this behavior. For example, since the whelks vary in size, what size should they select? Where should the whelk be dropped? From what height should it be dropped? If a whelk does not break after x drops should it be abandoned and a new whelk obtained?

Observations and analysis by Zach and Smith (1981) indicated that the larger whelks are more likely to break, in addition to providing more energy when consumed. The crows, it turned out, selected only the largest whelk, even to the point of selecting none when there were only small whelks available. Experimentation indicated that five meters was the optimum height from which to drop a whelk in terms of the likelihood of its breaking, and considering the energy needed to fly to higher altitudes. Observations of the crows showed that 5.2 meters was the average height from which whelks were dropped. Observation also indicated that the crows tended to drop the same whelk repeatedly until it broke, rather than return for a different one. This, Zach and Smith determined, was the optimal strategy because the likelihood of a whelk breaking was the same whether one was dropped repeatedly or a new whelk was dropped. By staying with the same whelk the crows saved the time and energy involved in the search phase of the foraging operation. In addition, the crows dropped the whelks only on rocks, never on grass, bushes, or water, thus increasing the likelihood that the whelks would break when dropped.

All of these decisions made by the crow served to maximize energy gained from consuming the whelk. How were these adaptive behaviors developed? Did individual birds learn by themselves which choices would lead to the most frequent and largest rewards? The laboratory research on choice behavior reviewed in the previous section indicates that such learning would be possible. Did young birds learn from observing older birds? Is learning involved at all? The results of the field study did not provide answers to these questions, but the value of the study in presenting information regarding foraging in a natural situation and in providing questions for further investigation is clear.

For example, one might study the foraging behavior of fledgling crows that have had, or have not had, the opportunity to observe adult crows foraging. One might ask if the selection of the larger whelks is related to discrimination learning processes, as studied in the laboratory. Or, if the persistence of a crow in repeatedly dropping a whelk that doesn't break is related to the partial reinforcement extinction effect (increased persistence).

Other examples of choices made in foraging situations may be derived from field observations of hummingbirds (Gass & Montgomerie, 1981). Hummingbirds must choose what to eat—insects or nectar—a decision that may be dictated in part by internal physiological states associated with breeding condition and by prey availability. If the birds forage for nectar, then there are other decisions to be made. For example, which flower should be chosen? How many flowers in one cluster (inflorescence) should be visited before leaving for another group?

Photograph by Harry L. & Ruth Crockett/National Audobon Collection—Photo Researchers.

Information concerning some of the factors influencing these decisions is available. For example, one type of flower foraged by *Archilochus* hummingbirds remains in bloom for two days but substantial amounts of nectar are usually available on only the first day. The hummingbirds typically do not visit these flowers the second day that they are in bloom. This may be a learned response since, if the nectar supplies were enhanced by the observer, the birds did forage the second day flowers (Gass & Montgomerie, 1981). Thus a discrimination learning process may be controlling the birds' behavior in this situation. Some discriminable cue correlated with the age of the bloom may become associated with a smaller reward magnitude and thus exert only weak control over approach behavior (see Figure 10–4C). Other data show that the likelihood of a hummingbird visiting a patch of flowers is proportional to the number of flowers in the patch (and therefore to the amount of "reward"). Also, the percent of time that hummingbirds spend in a feeding territory is proportional to the quality of the territory in terms of the amount of energy available from the flower sources.

These orderly data are similar to the relationships obtained in laboratory studies of choice behavior described previously and they indicate that reward magnitude and reward frequency variables influence choice in a systematic and quantifiable manner both in the laboratory and in the field.

An important role for memory processes in foraging is indicated by a field study of another nectar-feeding bird, the Amakihi *(Loxops virens)* of Hawaii (Kamil, 1978). Kamil observed that these birds rarely visited flowers in their territory from which they had removed the nectar earlier in the day. The recently depleted flowers were, however, visited by birds intruding on another bird's home territory. The fact that intruder birds visited the depleted flowers might indicate that there were no discriminable stimuli signalling the depleted state of the nectar, and that the avoidance of these flowers by the resident bird was based on the memory that these flowers had already been sampled. One interpretation of the systematic foraging behaviors of the Amakihi is that they remember which flowers they have visited and learn not to make repeat visits to the same flowers until a specified amount of time has passed—time for the nectar supply to be refurbished (Kamil, 1978). This learning could be based on the fact that repeated visits are not rewarded if they are made within too short a time period after the original visit.

There are substantial data from laboratory studies showing how rats, at least, can make accurate time judgments and use the passage of time as a cue. For example, we saw in Chapter 10 how the length of the intertrial interval may be used as a discriminative stimulus signalling the presence or absence of reward (see Figure 10–4B; Mellgren et al., 1983), and that the passage of time has properties much like other stimuli (Figure 10–1; Church & Gibbon, 1982). We have also seen how the passage of time may be used as a cue for avoidance responding (see Sidman avoidance schedules, Chapter 9) and for signaling the availability of reward in operant schedules (see FI and DRL schedules, Chapter 8).

Analysis of foraging in bees has revealed a set of problems similar to that described for the hummingbird, and a similar set of solutions (Waddington & Heinrich, 1981). For example, the amount of time that a bee will spend on any particular flower is directly related to the volume of nectar taken from that flower (reward magnitude effect, see Chapter 7) and the more time a bee spends at one flower on an inflorescence, the more likely it is to visit another flower on that same inflorescence (Pyke, 1978). If a particular flower has a low reward value, the bee is likely to move on to another group of flowers rather than investigate other flowers on the same inflorescence. Thus, the bee's behavior seems to be influenced by the relative amount of nectar (reward) available.

It would also seem that the bees must have some expectancy of the average value of reward to be found in their foraging patches. If the reward available in a particular flower cluster is less than this average, the bee moves on to another group of flowers. This behavior is reminiscent of incentive averaging behavior found in some studies of reward contrast effects (see Chapter 7; Flaherty, Becker, & Osborne, 1983; McHose & Peters, 1975; Peters & McHose, 1974). Indeed, recent analysis of learning in honeybees shows that they exhibit contrast effects as well as many other phenomena of associative learning that occur in vertebrate animals (e.g., Bitterman & Couvillon, 1983; Couvillon & Bitterman, 1980, 1982; Couvillon, Klosterhalfen, & Bitterman, 1983).

Laboratory Studies

Over the past several years many psychologists have become interested in the field work and theories produced by ecologists studying the foraging behavior of animals under natural conditions. This interest has led to several models of foraging behavior in laboratory situations. We will review some of these data and relate the behavior to learning processes covered earlier in this text.

Maze-related Studies of Foraging

The field studies of foraging behavior in nectar-consuming birds and bees indicated that one particular behavioral pattern might be particularly important for the efficient harvesting of energy by these animals. That is, the pattern of going to a different location after food is obtained in one location would seem to be advantageous for these animals. As it happens, some maze learning data obtained in the laboratory indicate that rats may have a similar pattern of responding when seeking food. For example, as mentioned above, some older studies have shown that rats have a strong tendency to alternate choice arms in a T-maze. If they go right on one trial, they are quite likely to go to the left on the next trial (Dember & Fowler, 1958; Zeaman & House, 1951). This alternation behavior occurs under conditions in which both arms are rewarded and under conditions when neither arm is rewarded.

The question arises as to whether this alternation tendency of rats is related to their food gathering behavior. One study examining this question allowed rats freedom to travel in a large area (180 cm by 250 cm) which included three towers with food located at their tops (Olton, Walker, Gage, & Johnson, 1977). Observation of the animals showed that a typical pattern was for the rats to climb one tower, take a few pieces of the food found there, climb down, and consume the food in some favored place in the environment or store it somewhere, usually in corners. They were then likely to repeat this pattern, by climbing a different tower than the one chosen first. In general, the rats tended to alternate their choices among the three towers. In fact, rates of alternation among the food sources were about the same as the alternation rates found in T-maze studies (Olton et al., 1977, p. 322). In experiments in which only one of the towers contained food the pattern of the rats' behavior was to visit all towers initially, and then confine their subsequent food trips to the one tower that held the food.

Thus, the study by Olton and his colleagues shows that when a single food source exists, the rats will learn the location of that source and confine most of their activities to that location, but when multiple food sources exist, the rats will tend to sample from each one before going back to an earlier choice. This latter behavior may be adaptive in the sense that it could allow an animal to exploit all the food sources available to it. This possibility is interesting in the light of Olton's research with the radial arm maze (described previously) which showed that rats have the ability to remember a large number of spatial locations from which they recently obtained food.

If shifting to a different choice did have survival value for rats, then one might hypothesize that rats should find it easier to learn a discrimination based on a "shift" strategy than one based on a "stay" strategy. Will rats perform better in a task that *requires* them to choose a T-maze arm on trial 2 that is different from the arm chosen on trial 1, or will they perform better in a task which *requires* them to choose the same arm on two consecutive trials? An experiment to investigate this question was conducted by Haig, Rawlins, Olton, Mead, & Taylor (1983). In this experiment the rats were forced to go to one of the two arms on trial 1 by blocking the entrance to the alternative arm. On the second trial the animals could freely choose either arm. One set of animals was rewarded on trial 2 only if it chose the arm not taken on trial 1, another set of animals was rewarded on trial 2 only if it chose the same arm as visited on trial 1. The results showed that the rats required to shift after the first choice learned the task more rapidly than the animals required to choose the same arm on two consecutive trials.

These results indicate that the rats' tendency to alternate is a strong one, strong enough to interfere with learning when they are rewarded for not alternating. This study also showed that learning the shift strategy was easier if the available food was depleted on the first trial than if the animal was not allowed to consume all the available food on the first trial.

This brief review of some maze related studies of foraging behavior indicates that there may be a substantial degree of similarity between a rat's performance in a maze and its natural food-seeking behavior. These studies also indicate that the maze may be used to investigate hypotheses concerning the factors that control a rat's natural food-seeking behavior. One question, for example, that has not been resolved concerns the proximal cause for the animals' alternation behavior. While it may be adaptive for the rat to alternate potential food sources, as we have discussed, it is doubtful that each rat alternates for that purpose. There must be some simpler mechanism that has been selected by evolutionary processes to produce that end. Perhaps a consideration of the neural mechanisms controlling maze behavior and alternation behavior will lead to a better understanding of the proximal causes of the rats' habits in visiting potential food sources (e.g., Douglas, 1972; Leaton, 1981; O'Keefe & Nadel, 1978).

Other traditional laboratory techniques have also been applied to foraging related questions. For example, discrimination procedures using pictures of moths under camouflage and noncamouflage conditions have been employed to study "search image" properties in bluejays (Pietrewicz & Kamil, 1981); discriminative autoshaping procedures have been used to study the role of Pavlovian directed behaviors (see Chapter 4) and conditioned reinforcement in the food-seeking behavior of pigeons (Rashotte, O'Connell, & Beidler, 1982); and operant schedules have been used to study the factors controlling "hoarding" in rats (Killeen, Smith, & Hanson, 1981).

Cost-Benefit Analysis

We have seen throughout this text how lower organisms can learn about contingencies beyond their control (Pavlovian CS–US associations) and how they can learn about contingencies between their own behavior and changes in the environment (instrumental associations). Ecologists and ecologically oriented psychologists have recently become interested in a further question: How sensitive are animals to natural environmental contingencies and upon what is this sensitivity based? If behavioral flexibility is to be useful in adapting to one's environment, as we suggested in Chapter 1, then the animal must be sufficiently sensitive to environmental change to respond in an efficient manner. One could suggest that the more efficient an animal is in responding to environmental contingencies the more it is adapted to its environment.

One way of examining such efficiency is in a *cost-benefit* framework: What does each behavior *cost* the animal, in terms of energy expenditure, and how does an animal *benefit* from the behavior, in terms of energy gain? Using a cost-benefit framework, one may ask if an animal is behaving optimally in a foraging situation—optimally in terms of molding its behavior to the best balance that may be obtained between energy expenditure and energy gain. This question may be seen as a restatement of the basic question regarding instrumental learning, the learning of the contingency between responses and consequent changes in the environment.

As a first step in the analysis, foraging behavior itself may be separated into a number of components (Collier, 1983; Collier & Rovee-Collier, 1981). For example, it is reasonable to conceptualize foraging as involving a *search stage* (the animal must seek a food item), an *identification stage* (the animal must be able to recognize a food item when one is encountered), a *procurement stage* (an animal must be able to capitalize on the search and identification processes by actually securing the food item), and a *handling stage* (once obtained, the food item must be consumed).

Each of these stages could be further analyzed in cost-benefit terms. An animal would be most efficient, and perhaps most adapted to its environment, if it could optimize its energy gain in each stage of its foraging behavior. Energy gain would be optimized, for example, if an animal's search pattern were one that maximized the likelihood of encountering a food item (Charnov, 1976). An animal that learns and remembers which locations are most likely to contain food and concentrates its search efforts in such areas would seem to be better adapted than an animal that engages in random or otherwise nonoptimal search patterns. Similarly, an animal may behave optimally in selecting or rejecting a prey item that has been encountered. Should a lion chase a rabbit it has just seen when there may be a zebra a mile across the field? By pursuing a similar line of reasoning, all of the foraging stages could be analyzed in energy cost-benefit terms and related to real life problems that an animal might face.

We will go now to an examination of some laboratory simulations of foraging behavior inspired by cost-benefit analyses. As we proceed through these experiments, the reader may want to consider the learning contingencies potentially involved in each of the examples.

Collier has examined many energy-related factors that might influence an animal's behavior in each of the foraging stages described above (e.g., Collier, 1983). These experiments have been conducted in a standard apparatus shown in Figure 11–5. There is a procurement lever that gains access to food (left side of Figure) and a search lever that activates the procurement lever when the search requirement is completed. Search and procurement costs are manipulated by varying the number of presses that the animal must make on each lever. In these experiments the animals live in the apparatus and they are not food deprived by the experimenter. The animals may initiate food-seeking behavior at any time. In this sense, these experiments come closer to approximating natural conditions than the usual laboratory experiment.

We will begin our examination of these experiments with a fairly straightforward question regarding behavioral flexibility. What is the relationship between meal cost and meal frequency? As meals become more expensive in terms of energy requirements, will animals find a way to reduce the energy expenditure while still consuming enough to remain viable?

It happens that different species of animals have characteristic eating patterns, which include a particular frequency of meal consumption. For example, under laboratory conditions in which meals are available at no "cost," chickens will eat 30 to 40 meals per day, rats 12 to 15, and cats 9 to 10. Collier and his students have shown how meal cost influences these typical meal frequency patterns. Cost in these experiments was manipulated by varying the number of responses required to produce access to a food source. The results of a number of such experiments are summarized in Figure 11–6.

These data show that meal frequency declines in all species as the cost (number of responses required to produce food) of a meal increases (see also Chapter 8). There are, however, some interesting differences among species.

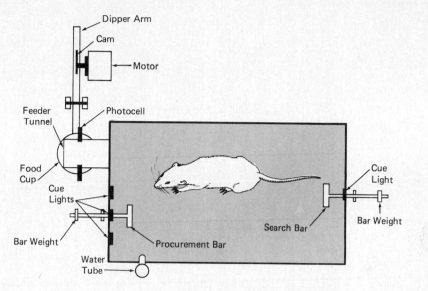

FIGURE 11–5 *Apparatus used by Collier in laboratory simulations of foraging. The animal searches for a food item by completing the operant requirement on the search bar, which is active when the cue light mounted above it is illuminated. When a food item has been encountered as a result of search that fact is signaled by the illumination of a pattern of cue lights at the opposite end of the cage. The particular pattern of lights indicates the cost to the animal of procuring the item that has been encountered. The animal identifies the nature of the prey encountered in terms of its cost and either procures it by completing the prescribed number of presses on the procurement bar or renews searching on the search bar, which may result in the encounter of a less costly food item. When the item has been procured, the door to the feeder tunnel opens and the animal is free to eat a meal of any size (i.e., for as long as it "wishes"). The feeder door closes only after the animal has remained out of the feeder tunnel for ten or more consecutive minutes. Water is continuously available, and weights can be placed on either bar in order to manipulate the energy cost of foraging independent of the time required to complete the bar-press requirements. (From Collier, 1982)*

Adding a requirement of only a single response reduces the meal frequency in chickens from 30 to 40 per day to 15 per day. The cat, however, is not much affected by increased cost until the bar-press requirement goes beyond 20 per meal. It is also interesting to note that wild-caught rats and domestic rats do not differ much in the effects of meal cost on meal frequency.

Collier has shown too that the animals compensate for the reduced meal frequency obtained when the cost increases, by increasing the size of each meal (Collier, 1983; Collier et al., 1972; Kanarek, 1975). This result also seems to occur in the Serengeti lion when meals become "expensive" (Schaller, 1972). Thus, animals apparently get to maximize the energy that

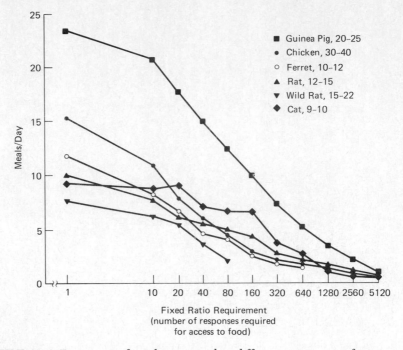

FIGURE 11–6 *Frequency of meals consumed in different species as a function of responses required for feeder access (procurement cost). Characteristic meal frequency when procurement is "free" is listed beside each species. (From Collier & Rovee-Collier, 1981)*

may be gained in the situation—they reduce meal frequency, which saves energy, and they increase meal size, compensating for reduced frequency.

Another series of experiments has examined the relationship between search cost and procurement cost. In one of these experiments the animal was faced with meals that cost either 5 or 100 presses on the procurement lever (left side of Figure 11–5). The two different meal costs were signaled by two lights mounted near the procurement lever. The animal had a choice of accepting the meal by pressing on the procurement lever, or of rejecting the meal and beginning the search over again. Search cost was manipulated by varying the number of responses required on the search lever (right side of Figure 11–5). The data presented in Figure 11–7 show that the animals virtually always accepted the low cost meals (5 presses on procurement lever) when the opportunity was afforded, regardless of the search cost. The high cost meal (100 presses on procurement lever), however, was rejected the great majority of the time when the search cost was low (see five-bar-press search cost in Figure 11–7). As search cost itself became high, then the animals were more likely to take any meal, regardless of the procurement cost.

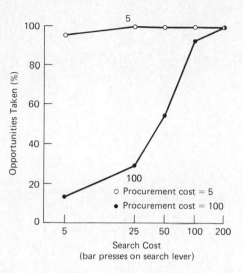

FIGURE 11-7 *Percentage of high cost and low cost meals taken by a rat as a function of search cost. The open circles refer to meals that cost 5 presses on the procurement lever, the filled circles to meals that cost 100 presses on the procurement lever. Number of presses on the search lever necessary to activate the procurement lever was varied from 5 to 200. (From Kaufman, 1979)*

Thus, when search cost was 100 or 200 bar presses, the animals took advantage of any meal opportunity presented to them, whether the procurement cost was five or 100 bar presses. What these results indicate is that when the energy expenditure required to search for a meal is high, then the animal will be likely to accept any meal that is obtainable, regardless of the meal cost, whereas if the energy required for search is minimal, then the animal can afford to be selective in the meals that it takes, rejecting those that are energy expensive.

A related question that Collier and his students have asked is the effect of search cost on meal size. Does the animal's willingness to accept a small or large meal depend on the cost of searching for that meal? In one experiment rats were given access to food for either one minute or five minutes when they completed a search. The differential access times were assumed to simulate differences in prey size (meal size). The procurement cost in this experiment was 50 bar presses. The results showed that the animals would nearly always take the large meal, regardless of search cost. The small meal was often rejected when search cost was low. However, as search cost increased, then the animals were likely to take any meal opportunity offered them, large or small (Kaufman, 1979, presented in Collier & Rovee-Collier, 1981).

These results, showing that animals are selective about small meals when the cost is low, but unselective when the cost is high, clearly parallel the results obtained with procurement cost. In both cases the relative amount of work (bar presses) involved in the search aspect of foraging determines animals' behavior when faced with meals of different costs or different sizes.

The search cost manipulation in Collier's experiments is related to the concept of travel time increases (Krebs, 1978). This follows from a cost-benefit analysis assuming that longer travel time means more energy consumed. The more energy expended in getting to a feeding patch, the more the patch should be utilized (assuming that it will also take a lot of energy to get to another patch).

A way of examining the effects of search cost that is related to travel time is provided in a recent laboratory simulation experiment by Mellgren, Misasi, & Brown (1984). In this experiment, food was located on the tops of towers located at various places in a large laboratory room (see Olton et al., 1977). Two aspects of the towers were varied. First, different towers contained different numbers of food pellets, ranging from 6 to 20 pellets per tower. These food pellets were not readily observable; they were buried in sand pails on the tower tops. Second, the towers differed in height above the ground at different stages of the experiment. Thus, at times all towers were one foot above the floor, sometimes they were all four feet high, and at other times all were seven feet high. Access to the tower tops was gained via a ladder that consisted of nails hammered into the tower post. The animals were given extensive experience in the environment so that they had an opportunity to sample repeatedly from all the towers under all conditions of the experiment.

The data presented in Figure 11–8 show number of pellets consumed from each tower as a function of the number of pellets available on the tower and as a function of the height of the tower. There are several aspects of these data that are interesting. First, it is clear that the more food there was available the more was consumed (linear functions in the Figure). However, it is also interesting to note that not all food was consumed. In fact, the animals tended to leave behind a similar number of pellets in each location. This may be seen by examining Figure 11–8 closely. For example, looking at Subject 1 on the seven-foot tower, a little over three items were consumed, on the average, when six were available, and approximately 18 items were consumed when 20 were available. The LOC value ("left over constant") in the Figure shows the average number of pellets left unconsumed.

The fact that the rats tended to consume the food available on each tower until the amounts *unconsumed* were approximately equivalent on all towers is consistent with a suggestion made by Charnov (1976) that a forager should utilize a patch until the rate of return from that patch equals the average rate of return from the environment. When this state is reached, the forager should give up on the patch. The data obtained by Mellgren et al. (1984) are generally consistent with this notion in that each patch is utilized

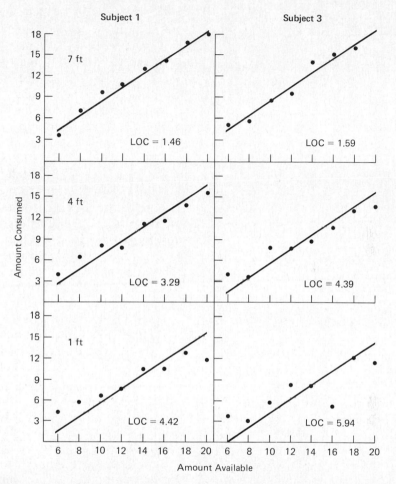

FIGURE 11–8 Food source utilization as a function of quantity available and height of food source above floor (see text). (From Mellgren et al., 1984)

until about the same number of pellets are left over in all patches. Each patch is persistently foraged until it is no better than any other patch.

These data further show that the more difficult it was to reach a patch (travel time increased as tower height increased), the more of the food was utilized from that patch. This can be seen in Figure 11–8 where the left over constant values decrease as tower height increases). This finding is similar to the results obtained by Collier with increased search cost and it is consistent with a cost-benefit analysis of foraging. That is, as energy required for searching/travel time increases, patch utilization should increase (Krebs, 1978). Other data obtained by Mellgren showed that the more difficult it was to reach a tower, the longer the rats stayed there once they had reached it, and the more difficult it was to reach the patches (towers), the fewer towers they visited in a foraging bout. Finally, Mellgren's experiment, like the radial arm maze experiments by Olton (described earlier), showed that the rats had nearly perfect memory for their visits to the eight towers in his experiment. That is, once the rats visited one tower, they were unlikely to return until they had visited all other towers.

This excellent memory for food related items is apparently not unique to rats. Some species of birds hoard thousands of seeds in many hundreds of locations and then, during the winter season, they return to utilize the seed caches. Recent studies of this behavior have indicated that the birds rely heavily on the memory of where they had stored the seeds and the memory of which sites they had already visited (Kamil & Balda, 1983; Shettleworth, 1983). It is interesting to note that the natural selection of an excellent memory in such species might itself be thought of as efficient in cost-benefit terms since a reliance on memory may be energy saving compared to other strategies such as trial and error searching among likely hoarding sites (e.g., near rocks, trees, etc.).

This brief review of laboratory and field studies of foraging should provide an indication of the complementarity of the two modes of investigation. Field studies serve both to generate hypotheses regarding potential learning mechanisms in food procurement behaviors and as a testing ground for principles of learning derived from laboratory studies. The work of Mellgren, Collier, Olton and others described here shows how traditional laboratory learning tasks may be modified to more closely approximate natural food-seeking environments and, thereby, more closely model the problems faced by animals in procuring sustenance. It should be clear also that many of the general principles developed from laboratory work seem to have applications in the field. An animal may learn predictive relationships between environmental stimuli (e.g., physical appearance of a flower) and food availability that would seem to be similar to Pavlovian associations studied in the laboratory. An animal must also learn the relationship between its own behavior and the availability of food (e.g., the crows dropping large whelks on hard surfaces, the rats climbing towers, etc.). Such a relationship would seem to parallel laboratory studies of instrumental learning.

It is also clear that the animals must use memory in these tasks and that their behavior must come under stimulus control to some degree (the crows select only large whelks, birds and bees go to only certain types of flowers, etc.). The extent to which the memory for food items in rats and hoarding birds represents some adaptive specialization for these animals and does not reflect a generalized memory ability awaits further investigation. Similarly, the extent to which stimulus control in foraging behavior is learned, as opposed to innate, awaits further investigation.

This review has also highlighted some similarities between traditional laboratory procedures and "looser," more naturalistic laboratory studies. For example, the food-searching procedures used by Mellgren and Olton were seen to yield behavior from rats that is quite similar to behavior patterns demonstrated in T-maze experiments. Similarly, the foraging simulation employed by Collier has many similarities to the chained schedules used by Fantino and others in the study of choice. There is also a similarity in results. Collier found that increasing search cost by increasing the number of presses required on the search component tended to minimize differences in procurement costs (see Figure 11–7). This result bears a resemblance to demonstrations by Fantino that increasing the length of the initial link on a chained schedule minimizes the differences between terminal links (Fantino, 1977; Fantino & Davison, 1983). It is possible that the effects obtained in both situations have a mediator in common and that this mediator is related to psychological processes controlling decision making by animals in their daily food-gathering rounds.

CHAPTER SUMMARY

Stimuli correlated with the availability of rewards will themselves become capable of reinforcing behavior. The operation of conditioned reinforcers has been demonstrated in maze experiments and in studies using operant techniques such as chained schedules. Generally speaking, stimuli become more potent conditioned reinforcers when their correlation with primary reinforcement is reliable, close in time to the presentation of the primary reinforcer, and when the primary reinforcer itself is substantial. Conditioned stimuli may be used to maintain instrumental behavior over long periods in the absence of primary reinforcement.

Choice behavior has been extensively studied in a variety of experimental situations. Older studies in complex mazes and T-mazes revealed a number of factors that influence an animal's choice behavior. Recent maze studies have shown that rats have an excellent memory for spatial locations which they have previously visited and obtained food from. Choice experiments using concurrent schedules and concurrent chain schedules have shown that the behavior of rats and pigeons is sensitive to small variations in reinforcement magnitude and delay, is very orderly, and may be described by several different mathematical formulations. One of these formulations focuses on the animal's tendency to distribute its behavior between two alternatives in proportion to the reinforcements available from the two alternatives (the matching law).

Animals searching for food in the wild must also make a number of choices. These choices have implications for their survival. Both field and laboratory studies have shown the orderliness of the foraging process and its sensitivity to reward variables. Analysis of both natural foraging behavior and laboratory simulations of foraging in cost-benefit terms has the promise of providing a deep understanding of adaptive behavior, of relating laboratory and field studies of behavior, and of providing a testing ground for learning principles generated from laboratory research.

12

Associative Analysis of Instrumental Learning

❝ *To adapt to its world an organism must learn relations of two sorts: (1) the meaning of stimuli, external or internal, and (2) the consequences of its own response.* **❞**

J. P. Seward, *Conditioning Theory*, 1970

INTRODUCTION

At first glance, the understanding of instrumental learning would seem to be simple. Animals learn responses that provide them with rewards and they learn to not make responses that bring noxious circumstances down upon them. The past five chapters are filled with examples of such behavior. The impression of simplicity is heightened by our own experiences in training pets or watching trained animals perform in circuses, etc. However, a deeper consideration of this behavior has shown that a theoretical analysis is anything but simple. Indeed, nearly ninety years after Thorndike first developed the principles and procedures of instrumental learning, there is still no agreement as to what the animal is actually learning. The various attempts at theoretical understanding that we are about to review will perhaps be more tolerable to the practically oriented student if these efforts are thought of as attempts to peer into the animal mind: to understand the workings of the mind (brain) of a primitive organism, one that does not speak our "language."

The results of these theoretical searches should help us understand the mechanisms by which a lower animal adapts to its world, and perhaps may help us understand our own place in the animal world. In this sense, the theoretical analysis of associative learning is a continuation of the attempt to understand biological evolution. And, to the extent that the principles of associative learning are relevant to human behavior (see Chapter 1), understanding these principles may help us to better understand human cultural evolution (see Mook, 1983; Nevin, 1982).

PROCEDURAL COMPARISON WITH PAVLOVIAN CONDITIONING

One way of thinking about the nature of instrumental learning is to compare it with Pavlovian conditioning. Instrumental learning and Pavlovian conditioning may be distinguished on procedural grounds (see Chapter 7). In essence, the presentation of a reinforcer is stimulus contingent in Pavlovian conditioning, but response contingent in instrumental learning. That is, the presentation of the US in Pavlovian conditioning does not depend on the animal's behavior; it is presented in a certain temporal relationship to the CS by the experimenter independently of the animal's behavior. In an instrumental learning experiment, on the other hand, the animal must engage in some specified behavior before the reinforcement becomes available. The reinforcement is not presented unless the animal performs the "correct" response.

Once this procedural difference is stated, however, it will be recognized that it does not always provide for a clear distinction between Pavlovian and instrumental experiments. This is because many Pavlovian experiments do, in fact, require some degree of behavior on the part of the animal to obtain the US. Even in Pavlov's initial experiments, for example, the dog would have to move its head to the food cup to obtain the US (see Chapter 4 for the discussion of the Zener experiment). The development of directed behaviors once an animal has learned a CS–US association further serves to obscure a procedural distinction. Recall that animals in Pavlovian experiments will approach the CS and/or the US delivery site (see Figure 4–1) and engage in various other behaviors often, but not always, related to the characteristics of the US. The rate at which these behaviors are performed may be partly influenced by response–reinforcer correlations (an instrumental contingency) and partly independent of these correlations (Pavlovian contingency).

Some idea of the degree of control exerted by either contingency may be gained through the use of omission procedures, as described at the beginning of Chapter 7 (see also Boakes, 1977; Jenkins, 1977). For example, the omission procedure shows that autoshaped key pecking in pigeons is very largely under control of Pavlovian stimulus–reinforcer contingencies—it is maintained despite the fact that the occurrence of a response *cancels* a scheduled reinforcement (e.g., D. R. Williams, 1981; Williams & Williams, 1969). Similar effects have been noted in other Pavlovian preparations (e.g., Coleman, 1975; Gormezano & Hiller, 1972). However, even if a behavior may be maintained by Pavlovian stimulus–reinforcer contingencies, that does not mean that it is insensitive to response–reinforcer contingencies. A number of studies have shown that the rate of behavior maintained by stimulus–reinforcer contingencies may be enhanced by the application of instrumental (response–reinforcer) contingencies (e.g., Schwartz & Williams, 1972; and also Figure 7–2).

It is possible to have the US presented internally to the organism, and thus minimize the effect of behavior on the US. Following are some examples. Either food substances or a weak acid solution may be delivered directly to the oral cavity in salivary conditioning or other Pavlovian experiments (e.g., Fitzgerald, 1963; Gormezano, 1971). Electrical stimulation of the brain could be used as the US (see Figure 3–4), or a variety of internal organs could be stimulated in various ways (see Bykov, 1957; Razran, 1961). Drugs may be administered as the US (see Chapter 5, and Eikelboom & Stewart, 1982). Even though these procedures will serve to minimize the effects of the subject's behavior on the US (and thereby minimize the role of instrumental contingencies), it may be impossible to ever completely rule out some modification of the US by "preparatory" responses of one kind or another (see Chapter 6, and the discussion of drug conditioning in Chapter 5).

Thus, the procedural distinction between Pavlovian and instrumental conditioning is useful as a rough way of separating two types of laboratory experiments. But it must be realized that the difference may be one of degree. That is, responses are necessary to obtain the reinforcer in instrumental situations; in Pavlovian experiments there may be a greater or lesser degree of response influence on the US, depending on the nature of the experiment and perhaps on whether the experiment is in the early or later stages of acquisition.[1]

Of more concern in this chapter are possible differences in the nature of the learning that takes place in Pavlovian and instrumental situations. In Chapter 6 we summarized how a stimulus comes to have new effects on behavior after it has been presented in a contingent fashion with a biologically important event. Thus, we saw that a simple stimulus such as a tone may come to cause an animal to blink its eyes, to salivate, to show a change in heart rate, to secrete hormones of stress, etc. Pavlovian procedures seem to endow a stimulus with new "meaning"; Pavlovian procedures change the effects that a stimulus has on an organism.

Instrumental training procedures alter an animal's response probabilities. Thus, a dog may only infrequently lift one paw. Giving the dog a piece of food every time that it does so increases the rate at which this behavior will occur. Similarly, rats will spontaneously press a lever only infrequently, but this rate may be increased by making reinforcement contingent upon this response. Of interest here is the nature of the learning that lies behind these changes in response probabilities. What is causing these changes in behavior?[2]

---

[1]Several theorists have suggested that the natural course of events is for Pavlovian contingencies to merge into instrumental contingencies. For example, once a subject learns of the relationship between a CS and a US, it may engage in behaviors that alter the effect or likelihood of occurrence of the US. Thus, an initial Pavlovian contingency becomes converted to a response-influenced instrumental contingency (e.g., Jones, 1962; Liu, 1964).

[2]Skinner has argued that it is the change in behavior per se that is of interest. What needs to be accomplished is to gain an understanding of the conditions that lead to behavioral change. The theoretical pursuit of internal causes that may be behind these behavioral changes is not necessary nor likely to be fruitful (see Skinner, 1950; Jenkins, 1979).

ASSOCIATIVE STRUCTURE OF INSTRUMENTAL LEARNING

Effectiveness of Response–Reinforcer Contingency

The past five chapters have been filled with examples of the application of a response–reinforcer contingency and its effectiveness in influencing behavior. However, it is worth noting at this point that every instrumental learning situation contains a nested (built-in) Pavlovian contingency (see Spence, 1956, p. 48). This is so because the reinforcement in instrumental learning is delivered in some stimulus context. Thus, in addition to the instrumental response–reinforcer contingency, there is also a Pavlovian stimulus–reinforcer contingency. And, since we have already seen that such a contingency itself will elicit complex behaviors, it must be borne in mind that many of the behaviors that we have seen in the past five chapters may actually be under the complex control of both stimulus–reinforcer and response–reinforcer contingencies. This issue will be considered in more detail later in this chapter. What we will do at this point is simply summarize some evidence which indicates that response–reinforcer contingencies do have an effect in controlling behavior, whatever other effects may be operating because of inherent stimulus–reinforcer contingencies.

Some of the evidence showing the effectiveness of response consequences in influencing behavior is as follows. First are data obtained from the use of the omission procedure as described above and in Chapter 7 (also see Jenkins, 1977). Any decline in behavior that results from the application of an omission schedule indicates that that behavior was being influenced by its consequences, that it was being influenced by a response–reinforcer contingency. Secondly, many of the effects of reinforcement schedules seem to indicate a sensitive relationship between the rate and pattern of behavioral occurrence and the rate and pattern of reinforcement availability (see FR, VR, FI, VI, and DRL schedules in Chapter 8, and negatively correlated reinforcement in Chapter 7). Similarly, rats have been trained to press a lever with a certain force (e.g., Notterman & Mintz, 1965; Samson & Falk, 1974), and hold a lever down for a certain time duration (e.g., Platt & Scott, 1981). Such behavior would seem to indicate a degree of response–outcome sensitivity.

Still more evidence on the importance of a response–reinforcer contingency may be derived from the very effectiveness of shaping by successive approximations in molding behavior (see Chapter 7), and from the improved efficiency that often occurs with experience in an instrumental learning situation. For example, during the initial experience with lever pressing, a rat may sniff, bite, lick, and/or handle the lever with both front paws (see Hull, 1977). But with extended training many rats develop a tendency to press the lever with one paw while keeping their heads close to the site where the food will be delivered (see Figure 7–1e). All of these behaviors imply that rats modify their behavior based on the consequences of that behavior.

There is yet more evidence. Rats may learn a T-maze under conditions in which there are no external cues to guide them. This behavior seems to be based on learning a contingency between making a particular response (e.g., right turn) and the availability of reward (Restle, 1957). Similarly, pigeons can learn to peck a key in total darkness, a situation in which pecking based on sign tracking to predictive stimuli (Pavlovian stimulus–reinforcement contingency) is excluded. Thus, the pecking must have been supported by response-outcome contingencies rather than by stimulus-outcome contingencies (Rudolph & Van Houten, 1977).

Evidence was presented in Chapter 9 that response-contingent termination of a warning signal, or a response produced feedback stimulus will lead to avoidance learning, and that Pavlovian contingencies alone are not sufficient to produce avoidance behavior (see Figure 9–3).

Other support for a role for response learning is the fact that animals may be taught a variety of arbitrary responses that are not related to directed behaviors elicited by Pavlovian CSs. For example, with patience dogs may be taught to roll over to obtain a piece of food, but rolling over is not one of the behaviors typically elicited by a food related CS (see Jenkins et al., 1978; Figure 4–1). Similarly, Jenkins (1977) trained pigeons to obtain food by bobbing their heads at a particular location in the operant chamber defined by the intersection of two photocells. This behavior is not elicited directly as a result of a stimulus–reinforcer contingency. Furthermore, other responses not normally involved in food related behavior, such as scratching and grooming, may, under certain conditions, be brought under the control of response–reinforcer contingencies (e.g., Charlton, 1983; Pearce, Colwill, & Hall, 1978). These, and other considerations, indicate that directed behaviors related to the acquisition of stimulus–reinforcer contingencies are not sufficient to explain all of instrumental behavior. Some degree of response learning takes place. One might also hypothesize that many behaviors occurring in nature, possibly behaviors such as those of the crows dropping whelks on hard surfaces (see Chapter 11) are influenced by response–reinforcer contingencies.

In general, response learning may be considered to be analogous to learned motor skills in humans. In fact, in Thorndike's initial description of instrumental learning, he likened the behavior of his animals to that of humans learning how to play tennis (Thorndike, 1911).

Response–Reinforcer Associations

Given the effectiveness of response–reinforcer contingencies in controlling behavior, a reasonable assumption might be that this effectiveness is based on the learning of an association between the performance of the response and the occurrence of the reinforcement. Such an associative structure for instrumental learning would parallel the stimulus–reinforcer association that is assumed to be learned in Pavlovian conditioning procedures (see Chapter 6). As reasonable as this assumption might appear, however, it has not been the favored theoretical interpretation of instrumental learning throughout most of this century. Instead, the principal interpretation has been that an association is formed between the stimulus complex in which a response occurs and the occurrence of that response. This stimulus–response (S–R) view of conditioning was proposed by Thorndike (1898), and in one form or another has dominated theoretical interpretations of instrumental learning (e.g., Guthrie, 1952; Hull, 1943; Spence, 1956; Watson, 1930).

An interesting aspect of this S–R associationist view was that for most theorists the reinforcement was not part of the association. Reinforcement may be necessary for the association to occur (it "stamped in" the association as Thorndike thought), but the reinforcement itself did not enter into the association. Thus, according to the S–R view, the animal did not perform the instrumental response in order to get the reward, nor did it perform the response because the stimulus situation made it "think of" the correct response. Rather, the particular correct response was performed because it was what was most pleasurable (in Thorndike's words) for the animal to do in that situation.

Thorndike's view of instrumental learning was somewhat reminiscent of William James' view of instinctive behavior.[3] According to James, instinctive behavior is performed without the outcome of that behavior "in mind." That is, there is no purpose or end to the behavior as far as the animal is concerned; the particular behavior is engaged in because that is what feels best. Chickens don't sit on eggs in order to hatch them. They sit on eggs because it feels good to sit on them. For a chicken, an egg is a "never-to-be-too-much-sat-upon object" (James, 1890). Of course, the difference between instinct and instrumental behavior is that the instinctive behavior is unlearned, whereas instrumental behavior is based on an acquired association.

A description of the various nuances in S–R theory, and the relevant evidence, would require almost a history of twentieth-century research in animal learning (see Bolles, 1975; Hergenhahn, 1982). Let is suffice to say that the S–R interpretation is a simple, conservative, parsimonious account of animal learning. It can organize much of the data without assuming that animals think, develop expectancies concerning the reward to be received, or engage in any form of cognitive process whatsoever. All that happens is that a stimulus context comes to control the occurrence of a particular response— the "correct" behavior is automatically drawn out by the stimulus context because of previous reinforcement.

[3]Thorndike took his Master's Degree with James at Harvard before moving on to Columbia for his dissertation work.

There is now, however, substantial dissatisfaction with the S–R account of instrumental behavior (see Mackintosh, 1974, 1983). We will confine our comments here primarily to one aspect of the theory, the presumption that animals do not learn about the conditions of reinforcement. We will see that there is evidence that animals do, in fact, learn about the reinforcement when they learn an instrumental response. These data are, at one and the same time, evidence against S–R theory of the Thorndike variety and evidence in favor of the concept of response–reinforcer associations.

Animals Learn About the Conditions of Reward

Three experimental situations will be described which indicate that animals do learn about the conditions of reward in an instrumental learning task.

Contrast Effects. Recall from Chapter 7 how a shift of reward in a runway situation leads to behavior (positive and negative contrast effects) which indicates that animals are able to compare current reward with reward received in the past. Since contrast effects were considered in some detail in Chapters 7 and 10, this literature will not be considered again here. We will only reiterate that recent reviews have shown that contrast effects, and the comparisons among conditions of reward that underlie these contrast effects, are ubiquitous. They occur in essentially every instrumental learning situation regularly studied in the laboratory (see Flaherty, 1982; Mackintosh, 1974, pp. 213–216; Williams, 1983; and Chapter 7). The widespread occurrence of contrast indicates that learning about the conditions of reward is a fundamentally important aspect of instrumental learning.

Latent Learning and Latent Extinction. Latent learning and latent extinction experiments constitute two situations, other than contrast, which show that changed reward conditions abruptly change instrumental performance.

In latent learning experiments one group of rats was given acquisition training in a maze in the usual fashion, i.e., with a reward in the goal box at the end of each trial. Another group was allowed experience in the maze, but they were not rewarded. After the rewarded group had shown that it had learned the maze by making very few entrances into blind alleys, a reward was introduced for the previously unrewarded group. This group, at the time of reward introduction, had been making considerably more entries into the blind alleys (errors) than the rewarded group. However, within one or two trials after reward was introduced, these animals decreased their error rate to the level of previously rewarded groups. The rapidity of error reduction indicated that these animals must have learned the plan of the maze, in some sense, without reward. When reward was introduced, their instrumental performance improved abruptly (Blodgett, 1929; Tolman, 1948).

The converse effect may be obtained if rats are trained in a maze and then extinguished by simply placing them in the goal box without food. The placement procedure is sufficient to substantially eliminate the running response, even though the response itself is not performed during extinction (e.g., Moltz, 1957).

Both latent learning effects and latent extinction effects are consistent with the possibility that animals normally learn about the conditions of reward during instrumental learning; they do not simply learn S–R associations and perform them without anticipation of the reward.

Discriminative Property of Reinforcers. The final experiment that we will describe in this section is one which shows that the nature of the reinforcement may function as a stimulus in a discrimination learning situation. This discriminative function of the reinforcer is consistent with the hypothesis that the nature of the reinforcer is part of what is learned in instrumental learning.

The experiment involved the formation of a conditional discrimination. Rats were trained in an operant chamber with retractable levers. At the start of a trial both levers were inserted into the chamber. In addition, either a tone or a clicker was sounded. If one stimulus was on (e.g., tone) then one of the levers was correct (e.g., left lever). If the other stimulus was on (clicker) then the other lever was correct. Thus, the rats were faced with the conditional discrimination; if tone, then left; if clicker, then right.[4] The animals learned this discrimination, but the learning was very slow, requiring, for example, 2,000 trials before they were correct on 80 percent of the trials (Trapold & Overmier, 1972).

Of relevance to our considerations in this section was the different rate of learning shown by three groups in the experiment. One group of animals was rewarded with food on all trials, one group was rewarded with sucrose on all trials, and a third group was rewarded with sucrose for one response (e.g., if tone, then left) and with food for the other response (if click, then right). The first two groups did not differ in rate of learning, but both were slower than the third group. The interpretation of these results offered by Trapold and Overmier was that the rats learned to expect the type of reward that they were to receive with each response, and the anticipation of different rewards for different responses helped the animals to discriminate the two responses that had to be learned. (See Peterson, 1984, for other experiments of this type.) For our purposes, this is another experimental situation which is consistent with the idea that animals learn about the conditions of reward.

---

[4]This is very much like the second phase of the Lawrence acquired distinctiveness of cues experiments described in Chapter 10.

Nature of Response–Reinforcer Associations

Given the evidence that animals learn about the conditions of reinforcement in instrumental learning situations, and the assumption that this learning is rooted in the acquisition of associations between the instrumental response and the resultant reinforcement, what further may be said about the nature of these associations? Mackintosh (1983) has developed the argument that these associations may be similar in nature to Pavlovian stimulus–reinforcer associations. We will now examine evidence concerning this topic.

Representational Processes. We saw in Chapter 6 how Pavlovian CS–US associations are assumed to affect representational processes in memory. That is, the presentation of the CS arouses a representation of the US because of the associative link between the two. Some of the evidence in favor of this view of Pavlovian conditioning is that a change in the US by inflation or devaluation procedures (see Chapter 6, p. 128) could change the CR, without the necessity of explicit CS–US pairings. The assumption was that the CS now elicited a representation of the changed US, and this changed representation caused a changed CR.

There is evidence that a similar effect may happen to instrumental behavior. For example, Adams (1982) trained rats to press a lever for sugar pellets. After the animals had earned 100 reinforcements, he allowed a group of animals to eat a sample of pellets without having to press for them. Then he poisoned the animals with a sub-lethal dose of lithium chloride. A second group was also injected with lithium chloride, but without having consumed a "free" bunch of sucrose pellets. Both groups were later tested in the operant chamber in extinction–no sucrose pellets were available. The results showed that the group poisoned after consuming the pellets pressed substantially less than the other group. One interpretation of this result is that these animals had formed an association between bar pressing and the delivery of sucrose pellets so that pressing the lever produced the representation of the sugar, which had been devalued by the formation of a conditioned aversion. Other results consistent with this interpretation have been obtained by Chen and Amsel (1980) and Krieckhaus and Wolf (1968), among others.

Responses as Pavlovian CSs. Other data supporting the concept of response–reinforcer associations may be drawn from studies that measured both instrumental responses and salivation. In the earliest such study, Konorski and Miller (1937) trained dogs to flex one leg for a food reward. They found that the occurrence of the leg flexion response was accompanied by salivation. One interpretation of this result is that the response is functioning like a regular classical CS and eliciting salivation. It elicits salivation because of the formation of an association between the response and the subsequent availability of food. Similarly, Williams (1965) found that responding on a FR schedule was accompanied by salivation, but the salivation did not start until after the animals had made a number of lever press responses. These and other data (e.g., Deaux & Patten, 1964) indicate that the performance of a response can act like a Pavlovian CS in eliciting a CR, a result which supports the hypothesis that animals form response–reinforcer associations. (See Mackintosh & Dickinson, 1979.)

Overshadowing by More Valid Stimuli. Some data indicate that the predictive relationship between the response and the reinforcer is important for the formation of an instrumental association, a parallel to the importance of the predictive relationship between the CS and the US for the formation of a CS–US association (see Chapter 6). An early example of this importance again comes from an experiment by Konorski & Miller (in Konorski, 1967). Dogs were trained to flex their legs for food in the presence of a particular signaling stimulus. In their training method, Konorski and Miller passively flexed a dog's leg and then rewarded it with food. Eventually, the dogs would learn to flex their legs themselves and they were rewarded with food for their efforts. A key to the importance of this experiment was that during training Konorski and Miller sometimes presented the signaling stimulus without flexing the dogs' legs. The dogs were not rewarded under these conditions. They sometimes also flexed the dogs' legs in the absence of the stimulus. The dogs were not rewarded under these circumstances. Thus, only the combination of leg flexion and presence of the signaling stimulus was rewarded.

This procedure is often termed a *discriminated operant,* and the stimulus is termed a *discriminative stimulus* (symbolized often as S^D, see Skinner, 1938). Thus, the total picture of the Konorski and Miller experiment is that passive leg flexion in the presence of S^D led to reinforcement; leg flexion without the S^D present did not produce reinforcement, nor did the presence of the S^D without the leg flexion. Under these circumstances, the animals eventually learned to actively flex their legs in the presence of the S^D.

Konorski and Miller then investigated the effects of omitting the nonreinforced trials in the presence of S^D. In this experiment, the only times the dogs experienced the S^D was when their legs were being flexed—the circumstances in which food was delivered. When this modified procedure was used, the dogs never learned to flex their legs on their own for the food. Why not? An interpretation offered by Mackintosh is as follows (Mackintosh, 1983; Mackintosh & Dickinson, 1979). When the nonreinforced S^D trials are omitted, the S^D becomes a more accurate or valid predictor of the reward than the response. This occurs because a reward is always given in the presence of the S^D (remember that the experimenters passively flexed the dogs' legs), and never in its absence. However, reward sometimes occurs in the presence of leg flexion (when it is made during the S^D period), and sometimes does not occur in the presence of leg flexion (when the flexion response is made in the absence of the S^D). This differential validity of the S^D and the flexion response should lead to the S^D–reinforcement association overshadowing the formation of a leg flexion–reinforcement association. Such reasoning is by analogy with Pavlovian conditioning where a more valid CS–US association overshadows or blocks the formation of an association with a CS which is a less reliable predictor of the US (see the sections on blocking and overshadowing in Chapters 6 and 10, respectively).

This occurrence of overshadowing of a response–reinforcer association by a more valid stimulus–reinforcer association implies that the associative process is the same or similar whether the association is being formed between two stimuli (in Pavlovian conditioning) or between a response and a stimulus (in instrumental learning). Some more recent experiments support this interpretation. For example, Pearce and Hall (1978) have shown that the presentation of a tone correlated with a reinforced lever press when rats are responding on a VI schedule will interfere with the acquisition of the lever press response. Williams (1975, 1978) has demonstrated similar effects in the key-peck response of pigeons. Williams (1978) further demonstrated that a previously established stimulus–reinforcer association will serve to block the acquisition of a response–reinforcer association. Also, Mackintosh and Dickinson (1979) have shown that the acquisition of a response of running in a running wheel can be overshadowed by a stimulus that is a more valid predictor of the reward.

These results are compatible with the hypothesis that response–reinforcer associations are involved in instrumental learning and that the basic associative process is similar to that involved in the formation of stimulus–reinforcer associations (see St. Claire-Smith, 1979).

Effects of Delay. The effects of delay between elements to be associated influence instrumental and Pavlovian associations in a similar fashion. We saw in Chapter 4 how the formation of a CS–US association is critically influenced by the CS–US interval. With a long interval ("long" being somewhat different with different types of USs), CS–US associations apparently are not formed. We found in Chapter 7 that delay of reinforcement in instrumental experiments also has a deleterious effect. There are many different interpretations of the effects of delay of reinforcement in instrumental learning. Of relevance here is that Mackintosh has argued that it is reasonable to consider that delay of reinforcement affects instrumental learning for the same reason that long CS–US intervals affect Pavlovian conditioning. That is, a long delay interferes with the development of an association—a response–reinforcer association in the instrumental learning situation (Mackintosh, 1983).

Contingency Analysis. Another relevant area of research concerns the presentation of the elements of an association in an uncorrelated fashion. In Chapters 5 and 6 we described how random CS, US presentations do not lead to the development of a CR, and furthermore, may lead to difficulties in development of an association when the same CS and US are present in a contingent fashion. Exactly parallel research has not been conducted with instrumental tasks, but the "learned helplessness" experiments described in Chapter 9 are relevant. There we saw that at least part of the deficit in instrumental learning produced by prior experience with an uncontrollable aversive event might be due to an associative deficit—a difficulty in subsequently learning that events are controllable. Thus, there may be a similarity in the effects of uncorrelated CS, US presentations on the later formation of a CS–US association, and the effects of reinforcements that are uncorrelated with responses on the later formation of a response–reinforcer association (see Tomie & Khouri, 1984; Tomie & Loukas, 1984).

Summary and Conclusions. In summary, a number of different pieces of evidence support the interpretation of instrumental learning in terms of the acquisition of response–reinforcer associations, which are associations that are similar in structure to stimulus–reinforcer associations learned in Pavlovian conditioning. This evidence includes: the occurrence of reinforcer representation effects in instrumental learning, evidence that responses can act like CSs in eliciting Pavlovian CRs, evidence showing that a more valid stimulus–reinforcer contingency may overshadow a less valid response–reinforcer contingency, similarities in the effects of delay between the elements of the association in both Pavlovian and instrumental situations, and similarities in the effects of uncorrelated presentations of the elements of the association in both Pavlovian and instrumental situations.

The interpretation of instrumental learning in terms of response–reinforcer associations is appealing not only because of the parallel between Pavlovian and instrumental associative processes that it implies, but, more than that, it hints at the possibility that the neural mechanisms of association may be quite similar or identical in the two procedures. The performance of any response by the somatic musculature is signaled to the central nervous system by a variety of neural feedback mechanisms (see Carlson, 1977) and, indeed, the resting state of muscles is also monitored by complex neural circuits. Thus, a response provides stimulus input to the central nervous system, just as an external stimulus typically used as a CS provides stimulus input to the central nervous system. Thus, at a neural level, all associations may be formed in interacting sensory networks. Pavlovian and instrumental associations may differ only in the origin of the sensory input that is the first element in the association.

Other Associative Structures

The preceding discussion has provided evidence consistent with the interpretation of instrumental learning in terms of response–reinforcer associations. But is that all that is involved in instrumental behavior? Probably not. Earlier in this chapter we indicated that every instrumental learning task includes an inherent set of Pavlovian contingencies. That is, the reward is delivered in some stimulus context, and therefore reward availability is predicted by that context—the same state of affairs that exists in every Pavlovian conditioning experiment. Thus, there is a potential for both response–reinforcer and stimulus–reinforcer associations to influence behavior in instrumental situations. And indeed there is substantial evidence that instrumental behavior is often under such dual influence.

Many experiments have shown that Pavlovian training influences instrumental behavior. For example, the development of an instrumental discrimination in an operant task (multiple schedules, see Chapter 10) may be facilitated if animals are given prior Pavlovian training with the S+ signaling reward and the S− signaling nonreward, or it may be retarded if the signaling relationship in the Pavlovian phase is inconsistent with the stimulus–reward pairings in instrumental training (e.g., Bower & Grusec, 1964; Flaherty & Davenport, 1968; Mellgren & Ost, 1969). Rescorla (1966) has shown that a Pavlovian CS which signals impending shock will increase the rate of instrumental avoidance performance, whereas a Pavlovian CS which signals the absence of shock will reduce the rate of instrumental avoidance performance. Many other experiments in a wide variety of tasks have clearly shown such influence of Pavlovian CSs on instrumental behavior. (For reviews see Davis & Hurwitz, 1977; Dickinson & Dearing, 1979; Dickinson & Pearce, 1977; and Rescorla & Solomon, 1967.)

Other experiments show that behavior established by a stimulus–reinforcer contingency (e.g., autoshaping, see Chapter 4) may be influenced by response–reinforcer contingencies. Conversely, behavior established primarily by response–reinforcer contingencies may be maintained by stimulus–reinforcer contingencies if the response–reinforcer contingency is later withdrawn (e.g., Jenkins, 1977).

There are many explanations for these interacting effects of Pavlovian and instrumental contingencies. A Pavlovian CS could be thought of as providing motivation (because of its reward-signaling function) for the performance of an instrumental task (see Bindra, 1974; Hearst, 1975; Rescorla & Solomon, 1967). Alternatively, the Pavlovian CS could be thought of as eliciting an emotional reaction, which in turn interacts with an emotional reaction "natural" to the particular instrumental situation (see Dickinson & Dearing, 1979; Dickinson & Pearce, 1977). Still another possibility is that the Pavlovian CS could influence instrumental behaviors because of the relationship of directed behaviors elicited by the CS to the behaviors appropriate for the instrumental response (see Karpicke et al., 1977). For example, response–reinforcer and stimulus–reinforcer contingencies should act additively to enhance key-pecking behavior by pigeons since both the instrumental contingency and the directed behavior elicited by the stimulus–reinforcer contingency should have the same effect—lead the pigeon to peck on the key (see Schwartz & Gamzu, 1977). Conversely, if a signal indicating the availability of reward is located away from a lever which must be pressed to obtain that reward, then behaviors directed toward the stimulus, as a result of a stimulus–reinforcer association, could detract from the instrumental behavior controlled by response–reinforcer associations (see Karpicke, 1978; Boakes, 1977).

This discussion of the associative structure of instrumental learning may be summarized, and further discussion aided, by the diagram presented in Figure 12–1. The diagram shows the three elements involved in instrumental behavior: the signaling stimulus (S), the response (R), and the reinforcer (Rnf). The arrows in the diagram indicate possible associative connections. Arrow number 1 indicates the response–reinforcer association assumed to be fundamental to instrumental learning. Arrow number 2 indicates stimulus–reinforcer associations learned during instrumental learning because of the inherent Pavlovian contingency. Arrow number 3 will be discussed later.

Thus far we have presented evidence relevant to the response–reinforcer association and evidence relevant to the influence of a stimulus–reinforcer association on instrumental behavior. We have not shown explicitly, however, that the stimulus–reinforcer association is normally learned during the course of instrumental learning. The experiments discussed above showed that separate training in Pavlovian conditioning would influence instrumental behavior. Next we will describe an experiment which shows that stimulus–reinforcer associations are normally learned during the course of instrumental learning and that these associations occur independently of the particular response involved. The experiment further shows that these associations influence the performance of an instrumental response.

This experiment (Hearst & Peterson, 1973) is fairly complex, but the logic is straightforward. We will outline the experiment and present the logic underlying it. Rats were trained to make a particular response (e.g., lever press) in the presence of a signaling stimulus (e.g., light) in order to obtain reinforcement (milk). After this response was well learned, the rats were then trained on a different response (e.g., chain pull) in the presence of a different signaling stimulus (e.g., tone). What the tone signaled differed in different subgroups of animals. For some it signaled the availability of reinforcement (milk), for others it signaled the absence of reinforcement, and for others it was uncorrelated with the availability of reinforcement. Thus, the situation that existed at the end of this second stage of training was that a light signaled

FIGURE 12–1 Diagram of hypothetical associations that may be formed in an instrumental learning task. See text for explanation.

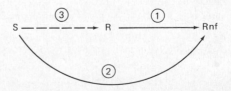

reinforcement for bar pressing; a tone had a different signaling value in different groups—for some it signaled milk, for others the absence of milk, and for others it had no relationship to milk availability. The tone, however, served as a signal for a chain-pulling response, not a lever-pressing response.

The question of interest to Hearst and Peterson was what would happen if the tone and light were both present in a situation in which only the lever-press response was possible. Would the tone have any control over behavior even though it had never been presented when the animals were lever pressing? This question was addressed in the last phase of the experiment by presenting the light alone on some trials, and the light plus tone on other trials. This test was conducted in extinction (no rewards were available) and with only the lever-press response possible.

The results of the experiment were as follows. In the group for whom the tone signaled food availability, the combination of the tone and light led to a 76-percent increase in lever pressing above that occurring when the light alone was presented. In the group for whom the tone signaled the absence of food, the presentation of the tone–light combination led to a 35-percent decline in response rate compared to when the light alone was presented. In the group for whom the tone was uncorrelated with the availability of food, the presentation of the tone–light compound did not reliably change rate of lever pressing. These results support the idea that stimulus–reinforcer associations normally occur during the course of instrumental learning, that these associations are independent of the particular response requirements of the experiment, but that these associations may influence such responding.

Thus the evidence reviewed in this section is consistent with the formation of both Pavlovian stimulus–reinforcement associations and instrumental response–reinforcement associations during the course of instrumental learning. Performance in an instrumental learning task may be considered to be a function of the interaction of these joint associations.

Our diagram of the associative structure included a third possible association, one between the stimulus and the response. Earlier in this chapter we indicated that explanation of instrumental behavior in terms of S–R associations is no longer acceptable and we gave some of the reasons why alternative explanations are more consonant with the data. We might ask, though, whether or not there are any conditions in which S–R associations might be formed and play some part in instrumental performance. In fact, it has been suggested that after extended training in an instrumental task, animals may behave in a manner consonant with some of the original S–R formulations (Mackintosh, 1983). In particular, behavior may become "habitual" in the common use of the term, and be performed without indication that the outcome of the behavior is being taken into account.

One example of this behavior is provided in a study by Adams (1982). We described part of this study earlier (see p. 310). Recall that animals poisoned contingent upon the consumption of sucrose pellets showed a decline in a previously learned lever-press response for those sucrose pellets. These results were taken to support the idea that animals learn response–reinforcer associations, that they learn about the conditions of reinforcement during an instrumental task. The results were obtained after the animals had had 100 training trials in the lever-press task. Adams had two other groups that had 500 training trials in the lever-press task. As in the case with the 100 trial groups, one set of animals was poisoned with lithium chloride after consuming the sucrose pellets used as a reward. The control group was also injected with lithium chloride but did not consume the sucrose pellets before the injection. The data presented in Figure 12–2 show that only the group poisoned after 100 trials dropped below the control group in rate of bar pressing. Poisoning after 500 training trials did not influence instrumental responding.

One interpretation of these results is that associative control may shift from response–reinforcer connections to stimulus–response connections with extended training. When behavior is under the control of stimulus–response associations, animals respond as if their behavior is not immediately influenced by the consequences of that behavior. Instead, responding is controlled by antecedent stimuli, as Thorndike had suggested.

Thus, it is conceivable that three different associative connections may influence instrumental behavior. The relative balance among them, and rate of formation of the associations, may depend on the nature of the instrumen-

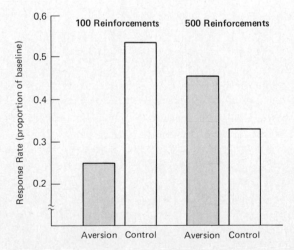

FIGURE 12–2 *Effects of a conditioned food aversion to the reward on rate of bar pressing after different amounts of instrumental training trials. A conditioned aversion formed after one hundred training trials decreased instrumental responding, but a conditioned aversion formed to the reward after five hundred training trials did not reduce response rate. See text for further discussion. (From Adams, 1982)*

tal task and the amount of training administered. For example, some "instrumental" tasks such as key pecking in pigeons and performance in straight runways by rats may be predominantly under the control of stimulus–reinforcer associations and Pavlovian directed responses. Even performance in some complex mazes may be controlled primarily by direct approach responses to stimuli correlated with reward location. They would thus be more under stimulus–reinforcer control than response–reinforcer control (see Bindra, 1974; O'Keefe & Nadel, 1978; Tolman, 1948).

Tasks requiring more of a "skill" component may be more under the control of response–reinforcer associations, or under dual control, as the Hearst and Peterson experiment that we described implies. Also, with extended training, control may pass to a stimulus–reinforcer "subroutine," perhaps requiring less use of representational systems for the production of behavior.

One advantage of such a multiple associative structure is that it may provide for a degree of flexibility in animal behavior in the sense that there may be "back-up" or redundant systems for the associative solution to a problem. In this regard it is interesting to note that rats may use any of a number of sensory systems to solve maze problems (e.g., Munn, 1950; see also Chapter 11), and also that animals in the wild typically have a number of navigational cues that they may use in finding their way around their environment (e.g., Dyer & Gould, 1983).

ALTERNATIVE INTERPRETATIONS OF INSTRUMENTAL BEHAVIOR

We have confined our analysis of instrumental learning to associations between two elements of the three principal aspects of the learning situation: stimulus, response, and reward. Other interpretations are possible. For example, Mackintosh (1983) has suggested that an association may be formed between the stimulus and the response–reinforcement *relationship*. That is, the signaling stimulus is not associated with either response or reinforcement per se, but with the relationship between them. Jenkins (1977) has suggested that it may not be possible to decompose the relationship among the three basic elements into two-element units. Animals may, in fact, learn something about the relationship among all three elements concurrently, in a fashion other than that envisaged by simpler associative theory. Bolles (1972) suggested that animals may, in some sense, "deduce" a three-element relationship from the two-element combinations of stimulus–reinforcer and response–reinforcer associations. This three-element relationship may be something on the order of: "If response X is made in stimulus situation A, then outcome Y will occur."

All of these alternative interpretations seem more complex and "cognitive" than the two-element structures described in this chapter. In fact, such speculations continue a trend toward cognitive interpretations of instrumental and Pavlovian conditioning that was initiated by Tolman (1932) and gathered momentum with the recognized inadequacies of S–R theory. Even the simple associative structure described in this chapter may be recast into cognitive terms. The acquisition of a stimulus–reinforcer association may be characterized as the learning of an expectancy—an expectancy that a particular reward will occur in a given stimulus situation. Similarly, the acquisition of a response–reinforcer association may be characterized as learning an expectancy that a certain response will lead to a certain outcome.

These cognitive interpretations may be treated as current "working hypotheses," perhaps best supported by current data but likely to change if research generated by this theoretical framework proves to be inconsistent with this type of theorizing. The student should be wary of equating "cognitive" with "smart." Although the acquisition of a stimulus–reinforcer association may be conceptualized in cognitive terms, animals may behave quite maladaptively after acquiring such an association. For example, autoshaping may be thought to be based upon a stimulus–reinforcer association, but pigeons in an autoshaping experiment may well lose reinforcers because they peck at the key even when it prevents them from getting reinforced (Jenkins, 1977; Williams & Williams, 1969). Such behavior, although based on a "cognition" may well be thought of as "stupid" (Jenkins, 1977).

The trend toward more cognitive interpretations of instrumental learning and Pavlovian conditioning (see Chapter 6) has helped generate new research in regard to these old questions: Just how smart are animals—can they "think"? Can they solve problems? Can they extrapolate from the present into the future? Can they learn rules and apply them in novel situations? These questions will be considered in the next chapter.

CHAPTER SUMMARY

Instrumental learning and Pavlovian conditioning tasks may be distinguished on procedural grounds. In Pavlovian conditioning the presentation of the US is contingent upon presentation of the CS—there is a stimulus–reinforcer contingency. In instrumental learning the presentation of the reward is contingent upon the occurrence of a particular response on the part of the animal—there is a response–reinforcer contingency. It is probable that these two contingencies rarely operate in isolation in laboratory experiments or in nature. However, the understanding of a simple learning situation has benefited from analysis in these terms. Of concern in this chapter has been the nature of the associations that arise from these contingencies, and their influence on instrumental behavior.

Because of the defining characteristics of a Pavlovian conditioning experiment (a reinforcer is delivered in a stimulus context), every instrumental learning situation also contains a "built-in" Pavlovian contingency.

However, evidence was described which showed that the response–reinforcer contingency that is applied in instrumental learning situations (i.e., the animal must make a specified response in order for the reward to be presented) has effects on behavior that cannot be explained solely in terms of stimulus–reinforcer (Pavlovian) contingencies. This evidence included: the effects of omission training, the differential effects of different reinforcement schedules, the effectiveness of shaping procedures, the occurrence of instrumental learning in situations in which there are no external stimuli available to direct an animal's behavior, and the learning of relationships between arbitrarily selected responses and rewards.

Evidence was then presented relevant to the possibility that the response–reinforcer contingency characteristic of instrumental learning tasks leads to the formation of a response–reinforcer association. A characteristic of response–reinforcer associations is that the animals learn what the consequences of their response will be. Contrast effects, latent learning, latent extinction, and evidence of the discriminative properties of rewards were cited as supporting the hypothesis that animals do learn about the conditions of reward that exist in instrumental tasks. Response–reinforcer associations were further characterized as being similar in nature to stimulus–reinforcer associations. Evidence supporting this contention was drawn from: studies of representational processes in instrumental learning, studies showing that responses may function as CSs, evidence showing overshadowing effects in instrumental learning, effects of delay of reward, and a contingency analysis of instrumental learning.

The possibility that stimulus–reinforcer associations may be formed with extended training was also considered. A characteristic of stimulus–reinforcer associations may be that behavior under the control of such associations is performed regardless of the consequences of that behavior. Behavior under the control of such associations may properly be called *habitual* in the common use of that term.

Finally, brief consideration was given to the possibility that instrumental learning may involve the formation of more complex associations among the three basic elements of the instrumental learning situation: stimulus, response, and reinforcer.

13

Cognitive Processes in Animals

> " . . . *human cognition . . . exists in an organism with a history of adaptive evolution . . . [it] developed in the service of the organism's biological needs, not its intellectual ones.* "
>
> J. L. Lachman & R. Lachman

INTRODUCTION

The term *cognition* means knowledge or perception, and it has been applied to animal learning in a number of different ways. One application is essentially the restatement, in cognitive terms, of the associative structure described in the preceding chapter. Other applications include the description of processes assumed to mediate performance on a variety of tasks more complex than those discussed thus far in this text, topics such as concept and rule learning, making same/different "judgments," and, possibly, language learning. Most of these topics are beyond the scope of this text. In fact, that research seems to be leading to a new field of comparative cognition, a field that continues the story of animal learning from where Pavlovian conditioning and instrumental learning leave off (see Premack, 1983; Roitblat, Bever, & Terrace, 1984). We will present a relatively brief overview of some of these topics. Before launching into this review, however, a few words regarding the appropriateness of cognitive views of animal behavior may be in order.

A variety of forces were most likely involved in the adoption of an S–R approach to understanding animal behavior by the early experimental psychologists. Among these forces was the overenthusiastic acceptance of animal intellectual abilities by the early comparative psychologist Romanes (1883), an acceptance based on anecdotal reports of pet owners rather than on experimental evidence. In this regard, Thorndike wrote the following in his paper on animal intelligence:

> Besides commonly misstating what facts they report, they report only such facts as show the animal at his best. Dogs get lost hundreds of times and no one ever notices it or sends an account of it to a scientific magazine. But let one find his way from Brooklyn to Yonkers and the fact immediately becomes a circulating anecdote. Thousands of cats on thousands of occasions sit helplessly yowling, and no one takes thought of it or writes to his friend, the professor; but let one cat claw at the knob of a door supposedly as a signal to be let out, and straightaway this cat becomes the representative of the cat-mind in all the books. (Thorndike, 1911, p. 24)

Thorndike undertook his research to obtain an objective picture of animal learning abilities, a picture that he chose to describe in noncognitive, S–R terms.

Another factor possibly contributing to the conservative interpretation of animal learning was James' interpretation of instinctive behavior. As we saw in Chapter 12, this interpretation included the notion that instinctive behavior is not goal directed—the animals do not behave in order to accomplish some end in the future. Rather, it is the case that their behavior is determined by the biological and psychological structure that has resulted from the forces of natural selection. Their behavior is determined by the history of their species. Similarly, Thorndike's interpretation of instrumental learning was that the behavior of animals was determined by their past history of reinforcement. They did not engage in instrumental behavior in order to obtain certain ends. They did it because that is what they were reinforced for doing in the past. There was no cognitive component of anticipation or expectation.

The trend toward conservatism that developed in animal psychology at the time was perhaps summarized by the early comparative psychologist Morgan. He suggested that animal behavior should not be explained on the basis of complex or "higher" psychological processes if that behavior may just as well be understood in terms of "lower" psychological processes (Morgan, 1894, 1930). Morgan, in other words, was suggesting that we attribute as little psychological complexity to animals as seems to be necessary to understand their behavior. Morgan's position, sometimes referred to as *Morgan's canon* (meaning rule, standard, or fundamental principle), is related to the earlier admonition of William of Occam (*ca*. 1285–1349) who wrote: "What can be done with fewer [assumptions] is done in vain with more." Occam's principle of parsimony in explanation is sometimes referred to as *Occam's razor*, perhaps derived from the idea of cutting out what is unnecessary.

The reflex model, which had become prominent in physiology, and was adopted by Pavlov (a physiologist), was available as a way of explaining animal learning in psychologically simple terms. And in fact the S–R model of animal learning, adopted by the early experimental psychologists as a parsimonious explanation of animal behavior, adheres to the reflex model. This model, in one form or another, dominated theoretical interpretations of animal learning for the first fifty or sixty years of this century.

The trend away from the S–R interpretation was prompted by several factors, including the failure of the S–R viewpoint to account for experimental results (see Chapter 12 and Flaherty et al., 1977; Mackintosh, 1974, 1983), advances in cognitive interpretations of human behavior, and the widespread use of complex and sophisticated procedures in the study of animal learning. However, a cognitive psychology of animal learning was not the only direction to take. Skinner (1938, 1974, 1977) abandoned S–R psychology without becoming a cognitive psychologist. He has long argued that the study of be-havior per se, and a description of the functional relationships between exter-nal events and the occurrence of behavior, is all that is necessary for the prediction and control of behavior. The attribution of behavior to hypothetical cognitive states somehow lying behind and causing behavior was said to be unnecessary and misleading. Skinner's view, often termed *radical behavior-ism*, is still championed by many psychologists (see Blackman, 1983; Catania, 1983).

However, many others have found varying degree of value in cognitive constructs (e.g., Estes, 1979; Hulse, Fowler, & Honig, 1978; Menzel, 1978; Roitblat, Bever, & Terrace, 1984; Wasserman, 1982). The reasons for this may become clear as we progress through our review.

EXPECTANCY AND ANTICIPATION

The stimulus–reinforcer and response–reinforcer associations discussed in the preceding chapter may be considered as knowledge, knowledge that a rein-forcement will occur in a particular context or follow a particular response. Such bits of knowledge may also be readily characterized as *expectancies*. Thus, a cognitive interpretation of Pavlovian conditioning is that animals learn to *expect* the US when the CS is presented. A cognitive interpretation of instrumental learning is that animals learn to *expect* rewards when certain responses are made, or perhaps when certain responses are made in a partic-ular stimulus context. This was Tolman's view of conditioning (Tolman, 1932, 1948). The evidence favoring such a view is essentially the same as the evi-dence favoring a stimulus–reinforcement interpretation of Pavlovian condi-tioning presented in Chapter 6 and a response-reinforcement interpretation of instrumental learning presented in the preceding chapter. Which language is chosen to describe such learning—associative or cognitive—is, at the pres-ent time, largely a matter of preference.

One area of research that may favor the cognitive language, however, is that of incentive contrast. The idea of expectancy carries more of the flavor of possible disappointment than does the associative language, and disappoint-ment might well be a reasonable way of characterizing negative contrast. For example, in one early study a monkey was regularly given a piece of banana as a reward and then was shifted to a less preferred lettuce reward. Upon first encountering the lettuce the monkey did not touch it. Instead, "She looks under and around her. She picks the cup up and examines it thoroughly inside and out. She has on occasion turned toward observers present in the room and shrieked at them in apparent anger. After several seconds spent searching, she gives a glance toward the other cup, which she has been taught not to look into, and then walks off to a nearby window. The lettuce is left untouched on the floor." (Tinklepaugh, 1928, p. 224).

We saw in Chapter 7 that reward downshifts in rats lead to hormonal stress responses, and that the effects of such downshifts may be alleviated by drugs which reduce anxiety in humans. These various effects of reward downshifts seem compatible with the idea of reward expectancies and disappointment when those expectancies are not met. Casting reward contrast in these terms suggests possible relationships to human behavior in terms of minor disappointments (receiving a B grade when an A is expected), or perhaps even major disappointments such as the loss of a loved one (see Klinger, 1977). Thus, one of the values of a cognitive framework is the suggestion of relationships to human situations and the stimulation of behavioral and physiological research specifically addressing the suggested relationship (Estes, 1979).

Other contrast experiments, too complicated to explain in this text, have suggested that the behavior of rats and pigeons for one reward may be influenced by the learned anticipation of a different reward to be received in the near future. Thus, responding for one reward may be suppressed if the reward to be received soon is more preferred, or enhanced if the reward to be received soon is less preferred (Flaherty & Checke, 1982; Flaherty & Rowan, 1984; B. A. Williams, 1976, 1981, 1983). Other evidence indicating that rats may learn to anticipate future events will be considered when rule learning is discussed.

COGNITIVE MAPS

Tolman's explanation of maze learning in rats was that they formed *cognitive maps* of the maze. That is, they learned the spatial arrangement of the maze units, particularly in regard to visual cues provided by the environment outside of the maze (Tolman, 1948). Their progress through the maze was then guided by the relationship between their location and the location of the goal box, with reference to the external "landmarks." This explanation stood in opposition to the S–R view that maze learning was based on a chain of S–R associations such that each choice point served as a stimulus to which a particular response (right turn or left turn) became associated. This stimulus-response view was contradicted by studies showing that rats could learn mazes if they were driven through them in little carts (e.g., Gleitman, 1955; McNamara, Long, & Wike, 1956), thereby showing that the rats did not have to make responses to learn the maze. These experiments also showed that the rats could not learn the maze by being driven through in carts unless the area outside the maze was clearly visible to the animals and it contained discriminable cues. These results are consistent with the idea that the rats form maps of the maze based on the relationship of locations in the maze to cues in the extramaze environment. This was found also in more recent studies in Olton's radial arm maze (see Chapter 11). We have also had occasion previously to mention that a particular structure in the brain, the hippocampus, may be involved in the use of these extramaze cues as guides (O'Keefe & Nadel, 1978).

Menzel (e.g., 1978) conducted an extensive series of studies with chimpanzees that supports the idea of cognitive mapping of animals. Chimpanzees initially released into a novel, large, outdoor environment travel from one area to another, allocating their time at each location in rough approximation to the prominence of any features located there (e.g., trees, or some object). With time, the chimps will explore virtually the entire environment. Menzel then tested the animals' knowledge of and memory for the environment by altering it in various ways in the chimps' absence. He found that the chimps responded almost immediately to any change. They were most responsive to any new object introduced into the field, less responsive to old objects moved to new locations, and least responsive to the location of a missing object.

Menzel also tested the chimps' memory and knowledge of the environment by hiding food in various places. In this test, one chimp was carried along by the experimenter and shown where the food was hidden (in 18 different locations). After this, the observer chimp was released into the area, along with several other chimps who had not had the opportunity to observe the food being hidden. Over a series of experiments, the observer chimps recovered an average of 12.5 of the hidden items, whereas the other chimps recovered an average of less than one item. This difference indicates that the observer chimps were using their memory of the hiding spots and not some other cue, such as olfaction, which would have been available to all the chimps. Menzel also noted that the observer chimps traveled from location to location generally by taking the shortest path possible, as Tolman had noted that rats would learn to do in a maze. Furthermore, the chimps' patterns of recovering the hidden food were not related in any systematic fashion to the path originally traveled by the experimenter.

Menzel's interpretation was that the observer chimps had remembered the food locations in relation to prominent objects in the environment. This idea was supported by the observation that the observer chimps, during the hiding phase, would seem to scan first the local area where the food was being hidden, and then scan the larger environment, as if first learning local cues that predicted food location, and then learning the location of these cues in relation to prominent objects in the environment.

Thus, these experiments indicate that chimps explore, learn, and remember the locations of objects in their environment. The studies also indicate that chimps can use the locations of these objects as reference points for the locations of hidden food sources. One additional study by Menzel shows the systematic way in which the chimps use these cues as guides. In this study Menzel hid nine piles of preferred food (fruit) and nine piles of unpreferred food (vegetables). In general, the chimps gathered up all the fruit before going to the vegetables.

Menzel's data, as well as the maze data obtained with rats, suggest that cognitive mapping may be a generally used strategy in foraging behavior. The studies by Olton and Mellgren of rats searching for food in a seminatural environment (see Chapter 11) are consistent with this suggestion. Also consistent is the use of landmarks by birds and bees in foraging behavior (e.g., Dyer & Gould, 1983; Shettleworth, 1983). However, whether all behavior that suggests the use of mapping need be explained in cognitive terms must await further research and theoretical advancement. Wasps, which are quite inflexible in many of their behaviors, may be very good at remembering landmarks and using such cues to find a home nest (Tinbergen, 1951). Thus, it is not clear that an ability to form and use spatial maps always indicates cognition.

CONCEPTS AND RULES

Is it possible for lower animals to learn concepts and form rules? Several experimental procedures have been used in the investigation of this question. The results of some of these will now be reviewed.

Learning Set

One of the earliest procedures for demonstrating rule learning in animals was developed by Harry Harlow at the University of Wisconsin. Harlow (1949, 1959) used a variation of discrimination learning in which monkeys were allowed to choose between two objects, one of which was rewarded. The objects were presented side by side on a tray, each covering a well in the tray. The well under one of the objects, the "correct" object, contained food. Thus, if the monkey lifted the correct object it would find a food reward; if it lifted the incorrect object it would see an empty well. The monkeys were allowed only one choice per trial. The experiments were conducted in the apparatus shown in Figure 13–1. This apparatus allowed the experimenter to bait the correct well out of sight of the monkey on each trial. After the well was baited, an opaque screen was removed, the tray was moved forward, and the monkey was allowed to make its choice.

The unusual feature of Harlow's procedure was that the animals were given only limited experience with a particular pair of objects to be discriminated, just six trials in the typical experiment. However, the monkeys were also given many different pairs of objects to discriminate in this fashion, usually several hundred. Thus, a monkey might see a square and a triangle on the first six trials, with, say, the square designated as the correct stimulus. For the next six trials the monkey might have to choose between a baseball and a wooden triangle; for the next six between a spool of thread and a toy

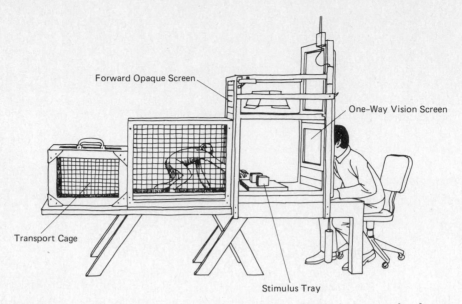

FIGURE 13–1 The Wisconsin General Test Apparatus (WGTA). See text for description. (After Harlow, 1951)

police car, etc. Proceeding in this fashion, the monkeys would eventually be given experience with several hundred different stimulus pairs.

The data from such an experiment may be examined for two trends: the improvement in performance across the six trials with a given pair of stimuli (termed *intraproblem* learning), and the improvement in rate of learning as a function of the number of different stimulus pairs experienced (termed *interproblem* learning). Both of these effects may be seen in Figure 13–2.

The curve labeled 1–8 represents average intraproblem improvement in the first eight discrimination problems presented to the monkeys. Performance on trial 1 should be at chance level (50 percent correct), since the monkeys have no way of determining which of the two stimuli is to be rewarded. Performance improves gradually from trial 1 through trial 6 as the monkeys learn which stimulus is rewarded within each pair presented to them.

The remaining curves in the Figure also show intraproblem improvement across the six trials of each problem, but, in addition, these curves also represent average performance after the monkeys have had experience with more and more different pairs of stimuli. It is evident that the additional experience leads to better performance on the part of the monkeys. This is apparent in the ever improving (approaching 100 percent) correct responses from trial 2 through trial 6. The monkeys apparently learn not only to solve each discrimination, they also learn how to solve this general class of discrim-

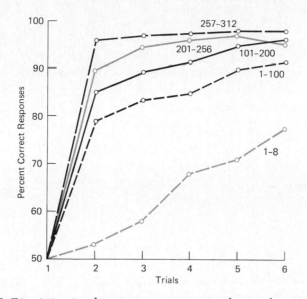

FIGURE 13–2 Discrimination learning curves presented as a function of problem blocks experienced. The lowest curve shows average performance across the six trials with each stimulus pair over the first eight sets of problems (stimulus pairs). The upper curve shows average performance during the last 55 problems. Intervening curves give average performance over intermediate problem sets. Performance improved so that the monkeys were nearly always correct on trial 2 after they had had extensive experience with different problems. (After Harlow, 1949)

ination problem. It is this "learning how to learn" that the term *learning set* refers to—the monkeys develop a "set" to learn.

How do the animals develop this learning set? What is controlling their performance? One possibility is that the monkeys learn a rule or strategy. They learn that the outcome of the first trial of each discrimination problem provides enough information to solve the problem, to be correct on all subsequent trials of that problem. The rule that the animals might learn has been characterized as *win–stay, lose–shift* (i.e., if object chosen on trial 1 is rewarded, stay with it on subsequent trials; if object chosen on trial 1 is not rewarded, shift to other object on subsequent trials). The adoption of such a rule would mean that the monkeys would be 100 percent correct on trial 2 of every problem, regardless of whether they were right or wrong on trial 1.

Is there any evidence that the monkeys do in fact learn such a rule? One study addressing this question trained chimpanzees in an entirely different procedure, but one in which the same win–stay, lose–shift strategy could possibly be utilized. After the chimps had mastered this first task, they were moved to the learning set procedure to see if the proposed strategy transferred to the learning set situation.

The experiment was as follows. The chimpanzees were trained on a long series of successive reversal problems with just two stimuli, one of which was correct (Schusterman, 1962). After the subjects had made the correct choices on 12 consecutive trials, the reward values were reversed. The former S+ was now S−, and training was continued until the animal again made the correct choices on 12 consecutive trails, whereupon the stimuli were reversed again, etc. After extensive training in this task, the chimps were shifted to a learning set situation where they received training with large numbers of different stimuli in the standard learning set procedure.

Schusterman found that it did not require extensive training for the chimps to show the typical learning set behavior—virtually 100 percent correct on trial 2. In fact, the chimps showed such behavior within the first block of 30 problems. This result supports the hypothesis that the same strategy is involved in both successive reversals and learning set. That is, in the successive reversal task, the animal may learn to stay with one stimulus as long as it is rewarded. After the first occurrence of nonreward, the animal will then shift to the other stimulus (which is now rewarded), and so on. But this is the same win–stay, lose–shift strategy that is assumed to be important for learning set formation. The occurrence of positive transfer between the two tasks thus supports the interpretation of learning set behavior in terms of a learned rule—win–stay, lose–shift. A similar interpretation was applied to results from slightly different experimental procedures by Riopelle (1955).

Other experiments have provided further support for the idea that the monkeys have learned a rule. For example, if a win–stay, lose–shift hypothesis is normally involved in the development of learning set, it might be asked if it is possible to train monkeys with procedures that make other hypotheses relevant and then see if a learning set develops on the basis of these other hypotheses. Brown and McDowell (1963) undertook such an experiment. They attempted to capitalize on the tendency of monkeys to shift their responses to the object *not chosen* on the first trial (see the foraging strategy of rats described in Chapter 11). In this experiment the monkeys received only two trials with each pair of stimuli. On the first trial, choice of either stimulus was rewarded. But in order to receive a reward on the second trial the monkeys had to choose the stimulus that was not chosen on the first trial. In other words, the monkeys had to learn to shift responses between trials 1 and 2. Brown and McDowell found that there was a systematic decline in errors as a function of experience in this task so that after 960 problems the percentage of errors on trial 2 had declined from 70 percent early in training to approximately 10 percent. Apparently, the monkeys had adopted a response–shift rule (win–shift, lose–stay). Note that this strategy would be expected to produce negative transfer to a learning set situation.

Other experiments have suggested that monkeys can learn to respond on the basis of abstract "concepts" such as novelty and familiarity, or oddity in color or in form. For example, monkeys can develop a learning set to choose one of three objects that is different from the other two—they will learn to do this on their first experience with a given trio of objects (see Schrier, Harlow, & Stollnitz, 1965, for reviews). Thus, there is substantial evidence that monkeys are able to learn simple rules and respond with a degree of abstraction in learning set situations. Furthermore, there is evidence that this learning is not restricted to monkeys. For example, Kamil has shown that blue jays are able to perform quite well in learning set tasks and, in fact, show many of the same characteristics as rhesus monkeys in their performance (Kamil, Jones, Pietrewicz, & Mauldin, 1977; Kamil & Mauldin, 1975).

Matching to Sample

In the matching-to-sample procedure animals are first shown a single stimulus item as the sample (e.g., a square) and then two items are presented (e.g., a square and a dot), one of which is the same as the sample. The animal's task is to choose the item that matches the sample. Extensive research with pigeons and monkeys has shown that the animals can learn such a task, although it often takes a surprisingly large number of trials (500 to 1000, for example). Once animals demonstrate such learning by being, say, 90 percent correct over a series of choices, what have they learned? Have they learned the concept of "sameness"? The simple fact that animals are able to perform well on this task is not evidence that they have learned a concept—the problem could be solved by some simpler response strategy. For example, the animals could learn to respond to a triangle choice if the sample was a triangle, to a green choice if the sample was green, etc., responding in each case to the *particular stimuli* not in terms of the abstract *concept of sameness* (e.g., D'Amato, Salmon, & Columbo, 1984; Lea, 1984).

A better test of concept acquisition is to present new stimuli to the animal and see if it generalizes the learning from the original set to the new stimuli. Thus, if an animal has learned to choose on the basis of *sameness*, then it shouldn't make much difference that the animal has never seen the particular stimuli before. The specific characteristics of the stimuli are irrelevant to the solution of the problem; all the animal must do is choose on the basis of identity, whatever the stimuli happen to be. Such tests have indicated that monkeys do apparently learn the concept of sameness. They do well when presented new sets of stimuli (e.g., D'Amato et al., 1984), although even in this case the transfer is not perfect. That is, it takes some number of trials for the monkeys to learn with the new set of stimuli, but many fewer than were required with the first set of stimuli. Whether or not pigeons are capable of learning a sameness concept is still open to debate (e.g., D'Amato et al., 1984; D'Amato & Salmon, 1984; Lea, 1984; Zentall, Edwards, Moore, & Hogan, 1981; Zentall & Hogan, 1974).

Even though the monkeys do demonstrate some evidence of concept learning in the visual matching-to-sample procedure, there is also evidence that this concept learning may be relatively specific. For example, D'Amato et al. (1984) found that their monkeys could not learn the matching concept when the match was between flashing and nonflashing stimuli. That is, they treated the image of a square that flashed on and off as being different from a nonflashing square. Similarly, attempts to train monkeys in sameness matching with auditory stimuli have not been very successful, despite giving the animals thousands of training trials (Salmon, 1984; Thompson, 1981). Thus, some degree of sameness concept learning may occur in monkeys, but such learning comes hard (many trials) and may be limited to a narrow range of stimulus conditions.

Natural Concept Learning

A number of experiments have trained pigeons in discrimination experiments using slides made from photographs of natural situations as the discriminative stimuli. Some of these experiments employed a concept training procedure such that all slides containing an instance of some concept (e.g., trees) were S+ stimuli and all slides that were negative instances of this concept (did not contain trees) were S− stimuli. The general procedure in one of these experiments (Herrnstein, Loveland, & Cable, 1976) was to project the slides near a response key and the birds were reinforced for responding in the presence of the S+ on a VI 30-second schedule and not reinforced for responding in the presence of S−. For the tree concept the pigeons were shown 1,840 different pictures, of which half contained trees and half did not. The tree pictures were diverse, including a variety of different kinds of trees with and without leaves. The pigeons learned to respond differentially to the tree and nontree slides by the time they had seen about 700 different instances of trees and nontrees.

Evidence that they were responding on the basis of a concept came from further testing in which they readily responded differentially to tree and nontree slides that they had never seen before. Similar results were obtained in other experiments with the tree concept and using somewhat different procedures (Herrnstein, 1979); with other natural concepts such as water; and with a specific person (1,600 different pictures, half of which contained one specific person, the other half did not contain this person). Recent evidence has also indicated that monkeys may be able to form concepts on the basis of presence or absence of people in slides (D'Amato & Salmon, 1983).

The basis on which the animals identified instances of the concept is not clear at the present time. Sorting on the basis of common elements would seem to be a difficult task, especially in the case of the Herrnstein, Loveland, and Cable study (1976) in which so many instances of the concepts were shown. To quote from the authors: "To recognize a tree, the pigeons did not require that it be green, leafy, vertical, woody, branching, and so on. . . . Moreover, to be recognizable as a nontree, a picture did not have to omit greenness, woodiness, branchiness, verticality, and so on." (Herrnstein et al., 1976, p. 298). Yet, somehow the pigeon apparently learns to sort these various instances (i.e., each slide) into perceptual classes such that a member of the class (tree) is quickly distinguished from a nonmember of the class (nontree). The basis and nature of such learning awaits further research (Lea, 1984).

Serial Pattern Learning

Another instance of rule learning has evolved from a series of studies in which rats were trained in runways with rewards changed in an orderly fashion from trial to trial. These experiments indicate that rats may learn the simple "rule" that reward magnitude is going to change in a specified manner (always decreasing), and extrapolate this rule to new reward sequences. These studies also provide another instance in which the behavior of rats is influenced by the anticipation of events that are going to occur (see section concerning expectancy and anticipation earlier in this chapter).

One example of this research is provided in a series of experiments by Hulse and his colleagues. Rats were trained in a runway with a specific sequence of reward magnitudes, e.g., 14–7–3–1–0 pellets. That is, on the first trial they received 14 pellets in the goal box, 7 pellets on the second trial, etc. This same cycle was then repeated a number of times. Eventually, the rats began to run slowly on the last trial of the sequence—the zero-pellet trial. This result implies that the rats learned to anticipate the reward that would occur on the last trial (remember, in a runway the rats do not encounter the reward until they reach the goal box, and the measure of their behavior is the time that they take).

Does this mean that the rats learned a rule? Hulse has argued that it may be so, because of the following additional data. Rats learn to anticipate the reward on the last trial faster if the structure of the sequence of rewards is simple rather than complex. For example, the learning to anticipate is slower if the sequence is 14–1–3–7–0 pellets than if it is 14–7–3–1–0 (Fountain, Evensen, & Hulse, 1983; Hulse, 1978; Hulse & Dorsky, 1977). This result implies that the rats could be learning a simple rule of "always decreasing" reward magnitude, and that learning such a rule facilitates the anticipation of the last reward in the sequence. A rule for the 14–1–3–7–0 sequence would be more complicated (e.g., decreasing, increasing, decreasing).

Further evidence in support of this rule learning was obtained in other experiments which showed that training on one regularly decreasing sequence facilitated the learning of a different decreasing sequence, and that it was not necessary for the last element in the sequence to be a zero reward in order for such sequential learning to occur (Hulse & Dorsky, 1979; Hulse & O'Leary, 1982).

Additional evidence regarding the anticipation of reward sequences has been provided by Capaldi. In these experiments Capaldi compared the running speeds of rats under two different three-trial reward sequences. For example, in one condition the sequence of rewards received was 10–0–10 pellets, whereas the other sequence was 10–0–0 pellets. The data of interest were the running speeds on the middle trial. The results, presented in Figure 13–3, show that the rats given the 10–0–10 sequence ran faster on the middle trial than the rats given the 10–0–0 sequence. Capaldi's interpretation of these data is that the faster running speeds in the middle trial of the 10–0–10 condition occur because the animals are anticipating the 10 pellet reward on the last trial. This, and other experiments, Capaldi argues, support the idea that animals learn a *serial map* of the events in the series, and are able to anticipate the next event scheduled to occur (Capaldi, Nawrocki, & Verry, 1983; Capaldi & Verry, 1981).

Thus, the Hulse and Capaldi experiments indicate that rats may learn to anticipate an impending reward in a series of different reward magnitudes, and they also indicate that rats learn a "rule" such as "rewards always decrease." The evidence for rule learning comes principally from the facts that orderly sequential structures promote more rapid learning than complex sequential structures (more complex rules?), and that there are savings in learning an ordered sequence once another ordered sequence has already been learned.

MEMORY

Memory is essential for learning. How can an animal show habituation to a stimulus unless it can remember that it had experienced that stimulus before? How can an animal form an association between a CS and a US unless it can remember some aspect of the CS–US sequence? How can an animal learn that a response produces a reward unless it can remember the response it had made when the reward was presented? Despite the importance of memory for learning, the experimental analysis of animal memory has often lagged behind the study of learning itself. The reasons for this are probably many: ambiguous results obtained in the early experiments of this century; inadequate experimental procedures for addressing issues of memory; inadequate theoretical concepts; and the belief of radical behaviorists, including Skinner, that concepts such as memory are not necessary for an understanding of animal behavior.

Recently we have seen a burgeoning interest in animal memory. The new interest has been spurred by new techniques, new concepts, and re-

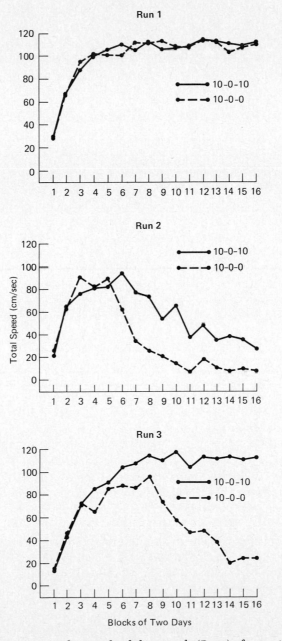

FIGURE 13–3 *Running speed on each of three trials (Runs) of rats given two differ-ent sequences of rewards: 10–0–10 or 10–0–0. Both groups received zero reward on the middle trial, but the group that would receive 10 pellets on trial 3 ran faster in this middle trial than the group that would receive zero pellets on trial 3 (see text). (After Capaldi et al., 1983)*

newed attention to cognitive explanations of animal learning. Along with these is a willingness to apply cognitive concepts used in the study of human memory to the understanding of animal memory. (See Spear, 1978, for a history of memory research in animals; and Roitblat et al., 1984, and Spear & Miller, 1981, for more recent research and theoretical analyses.)

Associative Memory and Memory of Associations

Animal memory is now a major topic of research. In this section we can do no more than present some highlights of this research, concentrating on those issues related to cognitive processing in animals.

One characteristic of current research is the recognition that there are different aspects to memory. For example, it is reasonable to distinguish between the memory necessary to form an association and the memory of an association already formed (Revusky, 1971; Spear, 1978). We have seen at several places in this text that the time between a response and a reward must be relatively brief if an association is to be formed. The degree to which such necessarily short intervals reflect memory functions and other aspects of the associative process, such as a perceived contingency or cause and effect relationship (Mackintosh, 1983), remains to be determined (see Wagner, 1981).

Once an association is formed, it may be retained for a long time period—weeks, months, or years, depending on the conditions of the experiment. The following are some examples. Rats will remember the reward magnitude that they have received in a runway for nearly a month and show a contrast effect if tested with a smaller reward (Gonzalez et al., 1973; Spear, 1967). A spatial discrimination (respond left or right) may be remembered nearly intact after a 44-day retention interval (Gleitman, 1971); conditioned suppression may be remembered virtually intact for 90 days (Gleitman & Holmes, 1967) or possibly even 2½ years (Hoffman et al., 1963).

Other examples could be given, but to do so may invite comparisons among the memories for various tasks. Such comparisons would be inappropriate because the details of original learning and the methods of retention testing are rarely comparable across different experiments. In any case, it is clear that the memory interval necessary for an event to enter into an association is quite short when compared to the memory interval over which an already formed association may be retained.

Active and Inactive Memory

Another distinction made in current research is between active and inactive memories. This distinction is similar to an older distinction between short term and long term memory. In some ways it approaches a distinction that we could make in humans between memories that are in current consciousness and memories of which we are not currently conscious. Active memories are thought to be more labile, more subject to modification, than inactive memories (Wagner, 1981).

One situation in which a memory is likely to be active is just after a learning trial. It has been known for some time that a traumatic experience, such as a blow to the head, electroconvulsive shock, hypoxia (lowered oxygen levels), or hypothermia (lowered body temperature), will interfere with the memory of a recently experienced event more than with one experienced some time in the past (e.g., Duncan, 1949; Riccio et al., 1968; Spear, 1978). These effects are termed *retrograde amnesia* (loss of memory that "works backwards," that is, the traumatic event interferes with a memory that was formed before the traumatic event occurred). Retrograde amnesia gradients have been demonstrated repeatedly in rats. The sooner the traumatic event follows a learning trial, the more likely that the trauma will interfere with the memory of that trial (e.g., Lewis, Miller, & Misanin, 1969; Spear, 1978). One interpretation of this involves the assumption that memories tend to move from an active to an inactive state as a function of time elapsed since the learning experience, and that memories in the inactive state are relatively safe from disruption by traumatic events.

The malleability of memories in the active state has also been shown by studies in which memory has been *improved* by specific treatments administered just after the learning experience. For example, injecting rats with strychnine (a central nervous system stimulant in low doses, a poison in higher doses) within 15 minutes after a discrimination learning trial, enhances the animal's memory of the learning experience. If the strychnine is injected two hours after the trial, it does not have a memory enhancing effect (McGaugh & Dawson, 1971).

Recent research has shown that psychological events as well as physically traumatic events will influence labile memories. For example, the memory of a Pavlovian association can be interfered with by presenting "surprising" events within a short time period following a trial. These events may be the presentation of a CS+ that is not followed by its usual US, or presentation of a CS− that *is* followed by a US (Wagner, Rudy, & Whitlow, 1973). Presenting these surprising events within 3 to 10 seconds following a conditioning trial substantially interferes with learning on that trial, whereas presenting them 5 minutes after a trial has little effect. These data have been interpreted as showing that psychological incongruity can interfere with the processing of active memories, but such incongruity does not interfere with memories that have already entered the inactive state (Wagner, 1981).

Another recent finding is that memories may be "moved" from the inactive to the active state and, once in the active state, they are subject to modification by some of the processes that influence recently acquired memories. For example, an old memory may be reactivated by exposing the animal to some aspect of the original conditioning without giving the animal a complete conditioning trial. Thus, animals briefly exposed to the apparatus, or briefly exposed to a shock outside of the apparatus, will show better performance on an avoidance task after a retention interval than animals not given these "reminder" cues (e.g., Riccio & Ebner, 1981; Spear, 1981). The reminder cues may be thought of as reactivating or retrieving a memory from some long term storage system—they may change a memory from an inactive state to an active state (Lewis, 1979; Spear, 1978). It has been shown that such reactivated memories are subject to retrograde amnesia from hypothermia and that the time period in which reactivated memories are susceptible to retrograde amnesia is much the same as that of newly acquired memories (Mactutus, Riccio, & Ferek, 1979; Riccio & Ebner, 1981).

Reactivated memories are also subject to enhancement by some of the same treatments (e.g., strychnine administration) that enhance newly acquired memories and, as in the case with new memories, the period of susceptibility of the reactivated memory to enhancement is limited to a short time after the reactivation treatment (e.g., Gordon, 1977, 1981; Gordon & Spear, 1973).

Thus, this research indicates that active memories are more malleable than inactive memories, that old memories that are made active may be as malleable as recently acquired active memories, and that employment of retrieval cues is one way of activating inactive memories. This line of research may provide information that will be important in the understanding and modification of human memory and may also provide some clues regarding the nature of consciousness.

Spatial and Temporal Memory

Another aspect of current memory research, one that will be discussed only briefly, is the study of spatial and temporal maps (Honig, 1981, 1984). In considering what evolutionary value memory may have had for animals, three functions are clearly suggested. It would be useful for an animal to remember *what* important events it had experienced, *where* it had experienced them, and *when* it had experienced them.[1]

The memory for associations may be considered to be the *what*, a stimulus that has gained meaning because of its predictive relationship to a US or to a response that will produce a reward. The question of *where* is the study of spatial memory, and we saw examples of this memory in Chapter 11 when the older literature on maze learning was considered, and also the recent work by Olton showing the rats' remarkable spatial memory in the radial arm maze. The work of Menzel described earlier in this chapter points up the spatial memory abilities of chimpanzees and monkeys. And, of course, the

---

[1]Suggested by D'Amato (1984)—personal communication.

work by ethologists on homing behavior provides an even more remarkable example of spatial memory in animals (see Alcock, 1975; Gould, 1982). The analysis of spatial memory in laboratory studies and in foraging behavior is only in its initial stages (see Chapter 11 and O'Keefe & Nadel, 1978; Olton, 1978; Shettleworth & Krebs, 1982).

Honig (1984) has suggested that the concept of a temporal map, something analogous to a spatial map, may be useful in understanding an animal's memory of the temporal order of events—the *when* question. We saw some examples of a rat's ability to estimate time intervals in Chapter 8 (e.g., FI and DRL schedules of reinforcement) and in Chapter 10 (see Figure 10–4B). The study of structured sequences of rewards discussed earlier in this chapter also gives an indication of a rat's ability to learn and to anticipate from the sequential order of events (see Roitblat, Polage, & Scopatz, 1983). In the next topic to be discussed in this memory section we will see how the inability to remember temporal order may be a source of error in some tests of memory.

Working Memory

The term *working memory* has been used to refer to a situation in which an animal must retain some information for a brief period of time to use in the solution of some problem. This memorial function has been studied extensively using the matching-to-sample paradigm (see p. 331). The experiments are conducted as follows. Animals are first trained extensively in the matching procedure. For example, they are initially presented with one stimulus (e.g., red) and then immediately given a choice between that stimulus and another (e.g., green). They are rewarded if their choice matches the sample item. After the animals are performing well in this task, a delay is introduced between the presentation of the sample and the presentation of the choice stimuli. This delay period is thus a retention interval during which the memory of the sample item must be carried. Research using this delayed-matching-to-sample (DMTS) task has provided a number of interesting results.

One finding was that pigeons seem to be able to remember for only seconds, whereas monkeys and dolphins may remember for several minutes (D'Amato, 1973; Herman & Thompson, 1982; Roberts & Grant, 1976). The length of the memory interval over which high levels of performance may be maintained has been shown to be influenced by a number of factors. For example, increasing the duration of sample presentation leads to better performance in pigeons (Roberts & Grant, 1976), but not in monkeys (D'Amato & Worsham, 1972). The monkeys performed well with sample durations of only 0.06 second, and increasing the duration did not facilitate their performance.

Performance on the choice test is also influenced by the lighting conditions during the retention interval. Performance is better in both pigeons and monkeys if they spend the interval in the dark rather than in the light (D'Amato & O'Neill, 1971; Etkin, 1972; Roberts & Grant, 1976). Presenting auditory stimuli during the retention interval does not have any harmful effects on the memory of visual stimuli (Worsham & D'Amato, 1973). One interpretation of these effects is that the memory of the visual samples is interfered with by visual stimuli in the chamber, and turning the lights off during the retention interval removes this interference. This type of interference is termed *retroactive* (backward acting) because it occurs after the memory has been formed. Apparently, auditory stimuli do not retroactively interfere with the memory of visual samples.

What are the animals remembering in the DMTS task? The simplest answer to this question is that they remember the characteristics of the sample stimulus and then, at the choice test, they respond to the choice that matches the memory of the sample. An alternative interpretation is that the animals don't remember the characteristics of the sample per se, but instead they encode an instruction at the time of sample presentation, an instruction of what to do at the time of the choice test. For example, if the sample stimulus is red, the animals remember "respond to red." Memory thought of in these terms is sometimes termed *instructional memory* or *prospective memory* (Adams & Dickinson, 1981; Grant, 1981; Honig, 1984; Macki, 1981).

Support for the instructional interpretation of working memory is derived from experiments with *conditional matching*. In the conditional matching procedure the sample stimulus does not itself appear at the choice test. Instead, the sample symbolizes what stimulus will be correct on the choice test. For example, red as a sample stimulus may indicate that a vertical line stimulus will be the correct choice; a green sample stimulus may indicate that a horizontal line will be correct on the choice test, etc. Conditional matching is more difficult for animals to learn than the identity matching that we described previously. One might also expect that the memory load in a conditional matching experiment would be greater than in an identity matching experiment. That is, animals in a conditional matching task might have to remember something complex, something of the order "green represents horizontal line," whereas animals in an identity task would have to remember only "green."

Forgetting, however, occurs at a comparable rate in the two tasks (D'Amato & Worsham, 1974; Herman & Thompson, 1982; Honig & Thompson, 1984). The fact that rate of forgetting is equivalent in identity matching and conditional matching may mean that the animals' memories are similar. Such would be the case if the instructional interpretation of memory were correct—in both cases animals would remember an instruction of what stimulus to respond to ("respond to green" or "respond to horizontal" in our examples). Other evidence favoring an instructional interpretation of memory may be found in the references cited above.

What is the cause of forgetting in the DMTS task? Several possibilities have been entertained (see Grant, 1981; Macki, 1981; Spear, 1978). One possibility is that animals do not forget that they have seen the stimulus before, but they forget *when* they have last seen that particular stimulus as a sample (D'Amato, 1973). The basis for this temporal discrimination hypothesis is the following. Animals in DMTS tasks experience many hundreds or thousands of trials, usually with a very limited set of stimuli (three to six is not unusual). Thus, the same stimulus is a sample on some trials, and an incorrect choice on other trials. Consider, for example, a series of trials in an experiment in which there are only three stimulus items: a green stimulus, a red stimulus, and a horizontal line. On one trial the green may be the sample and the subject may choose between, say green and line on the choice test. On the next trial the horizontal line may be the sample and the subject would choose between the line and the red stimulus on the test, etc. When the subject sees two stimuli on the choice test (e.g., green and horizontal line), it will have experienced both of them many times as sample and choice stimuli. In order to be correct, it will have to remember which was the sample on the *most recent* presentation of the sample stimulus (or, if the instructional interpretation of memory is correct, it will have to remember when a particular instruction, e.g., "respond to green," was most recently correct).

This temporal discrimination hypothesis of forgetting (D'Amato, 1973) has had some experimental support. For example, it has been shown that the more prior experience a subject has had with the nonmatching stimulus as a sample, the poorer the performance is (Zentall & Hogan, 1977). Interference with memory from prior experience is termed *proactive interference*, and the demonstration of such interference in DMTS is consistent with the temporal discrimination hypothesis—the more prior experience the animal has had with each stimulus, the more difficult it should be to discriminate when it had seen it last. Other evidence in favor of this hypothesis is the fact that animals do better when there is a relatively large set of stimulus items than when there is a small set (Worsham, 1973, 1975). This is consistent with the temporal discrimination hypothesis since the larger the set of stimuli the less likely it is that the noncorrect stimulus on the choice test would have recently been a sample. Also, the fact that performance is better in DMTS with long intertrial intervals (Roberts, 1980) may also be seen as consistent with the temporal discrimination view of forgetting in DMTS. This may be so because long intertrial intervals should serve to temporally isolate successive instances of stimuli as samples, perhaps making it easier for the animal to discriminate that it had not seen the noncorrect choice *recently* as a sample.

Thus, the smaller the stimulus set that an animal experiences, the more prior experience it has had with these stimuli, and the shorter the intertrial interval, the poorer is the animal's performance in a DMTS memory test. All of these factors could be interpreted as making it difficult for an animal to temporally isolate successive instances in which a stimulus last (most recently) appeared as a sample. This failure of a temporal discrimination may be a major contributor to "forgetting" in working memory in the DMTS test. However, it is possible that different mechanisms produce forgetting in monkeys and pigeons (see Grant, 1981; Roberts & Grant, 1976).

Summary

The substantial increase in research on animal memory in recent years has led to hundreds of experiments and many different ways of conceiving memory functions. In this section we have sampled just some of the experimental procedures and conceptual distinctions. We have seen that the memory of an event necessary for the formation of an association involving that event may be distinguished from the memory of an association itself, and that memories of already formed associations may persist over quite long intervals. We have also described research on active and inactive memories, the role of retrieval cues in moving inactive memories into the active state, and various procedures which may be used to modify memories that are in the active state. This research on active and inactive memories may bear some relationship to the concept of consciousness in humans. Memory for spatial and temporal "locations" was also briefly considered, and finally, an analysis of working memory was presented. Research with working memory has indicated that animals may remember instructions of what to do in the future in certain situations rather than exact copies of past events per se. This research has also indicated that poor performance in some tests of working memory may be due to a failure of the animal's temporal map—an inability to discriminate relative recency of events experienced in the past.

INFERENCE

Transitive Inference

Can animals make inferences? If a human is told that A is larger than B and that B is larger than C, the human (at least most of us) will infer that A must also be larger than C. A study with chimpanzees by Gillan (1981) illustrates one attempt to investigate this problem with animals. Gillan trained his chimps in a series of discriminations in which one stimulus always signaled a larger reward than the other stimulus. Thus, the animals learned that stimulus E had more food than D, D had more than C, C had more than B, and B had more than A. After this training, the animals were presented with nonadjacent pairs of stimuli. The results indicated that animals presented with stimuli B and D would tend to choose D, indicating that they had learned a transitive relationship among stimuli.

Other evidence for transitive inference has been obtained with monkeys by McGonigle and Chalmers (1977) and by Salmon and D'Amato (1983). Apparently there are no demonstrations of transitive inference in animals below the level of primates (Salmon & D'Amato, 1983).

Reasoning

Other tests of inference in chimpanzees come close to what is called reasoning in humans. These recent tests resemble the old "insight" problems of the Gestalt psychologists (Köhler, 1926). In these older studies chimpanzees had to combine sticks, pile up boxes, etc., with which they had had previous experience, in order to reach food that was otherwise unreachable. In recent "reasoning" experiments Premack (1983) allowed chimps to watch the experimenter place an apple and a banana in two widely separated containers. Then the chimp was removed from the room for a brief time and, when it returned, it saw the experimenter standing between the two containers eating either an apple or a banana. Subsequently, the chimp was released and allowed to go to either container. Premack found that his chimps performed well on this problem. They went to the presumably untouched container, some immediately, some after a few training trials. Their level of performance was about that of 4 to 5 year old children, and better than 3½ to 4 year old children.

In another problem of this type, the experimenter showed the chimp that he had just one piece of food in his hand. Then, out of sight of the animal he went into a field. When he returned he showed the animal that he was empty-handed. Then the experimenter took the animal into the field, showed it the piece of food in a container, and, with the chimp looking on, removed the food from the container. The chimp was then brought back to the starting point and released. When released, the chimp did not go into the field, but instead sat ". . . grooming itself or gazing into space." (Premack, 1983, p. 131). However, when the same general procedure was repeated—except that the chimp was shown that the experimenter had two pieces of food at the beginning and removed only one piece from the container—when released, the chimp ran right to the container.

Reasoning is often defined as the combining of separate experiences in order to solve a problem. For example, in the experiment just described the chimps saw the two containers stocked with different types of food, then they saw the experimenter eating one of those types. The behavior of the chimps when released indicated that they somehow combined these two pieces of information and "concluded" that only one of the containers still had food. There is a standard test of "reasoning" in rats, as well, one which is based on this definition of combining separate experiences.

The test is the Maier three table reasoning test. One version of the apparatus is shown in Figure 13–4. The basic procedure is to allow rats some

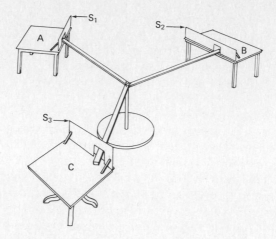

FIGURE 13–4 *The Maier reasoning test. The animal is first allowed to explore the apparatus and then is fed on one of the tables. It is then placed on one of the other tables and must find its way back to the original table. The screens S_1, S_2, and S_3 block any view of food locations (see text). (From Maier, 1932)*

time to freely explore the apparatus, which is usually placed in a room with heterogeneous stimuli. The stimuli in the room allow the animal to locate the several tables in reference to these external cues. After the exploratory experience, the rat is placed on one of the tables and fed. During the feeding experience the view of the other tables is obscured. After these two experiences comes the test for "reasoning." The rat is placed on one of the two tables at which it was *not fed* and allowed to travel down the alleyways and choose one of the other tables. The question is, will it choose the table on which it was previously fed? If so, this is considered reasoning, because the rat will have combined two separate pieces of information: the locations of the tables relative to one another and the room cues, and the table on which it was previously fed.

Many experiments have indicated that rats are able to succeed in this task (Herrmann, Bahr, Bremner, & Ellen, 1982; Maier, 1932; Stahl & Ellen, 1974). Furthermore, it has been shown that the initial exploratory experience is essential; without it the rats cannot solve the problem (Herrmann et al., 1982). Interestingly, this procedure may be adapted to investigate some of the questions considered in regard to foraging in Chapter 11. That is, rats may be taught either a "stay" strategy, going to the table on which they were fed, or a "shift" strategy, going to the table on which they were not fed. The stay strategy is apparently easier in this situation, but rats will eventually learn the shift strategy, particularly if all the food available is consumed during the placement phase of the experiment (Herrmann et al., 1982).

LANGUAGE

The ultimate in cognition involves the acquisition and use of language (and mathematics) for abstract reasoning. The examination of whether animals have a language or are capable of acquiring a language is a matter of much research and debate at the present time, a matter far beyond the scope of a text on conditioning and learning. We mention it here simply to indicate that such research exists and that it is systematically related to the issue of cognition in animals.

One example of the cognitive aspects of "language" training may be seen in Premack's work. Premack language trained his chimps by teaching them to substitute colored pieces of plastic for various grammatical units. These language trained chimps seem to be able to understand cause–effect action sequences. For example, the three-element sequence—apple, knife, cut apple—could represent a causal action sequence: the knife cut the apple. Chimps shown portions of this sequence, e.g., the apple and the cut apple, are able to select the item that will complete the sequence from among a number of other items. In other tests, one chimp, Sarah, was given two items of a three-item sequence, such as paper, blank (no item), then marked paper; or the reverse: marked paper, blank (no item), unmarked paper. Sarah was able to correctly select a pencil as the item needed to complete the first sequence and an eraser as the item needed to complete the second sequence. This indicates that the chimp had learned temporally ordered cause–effect relationships (Premack, 1983).

Chimpanzees trained by Sue Savage-Rumbaugh have been taught to use symbols to request items that they need from among a number of alternative items available. After three years of such training, the chimps spontaneously began naming objects without waiting to be asked to do so by the teacher. Sometimes the chimps would communicate to the teacher. For example, they would select the appropriate symbol for the name of an object, then pick up the object and give it to the teacher, without being so requested—a behavior characteristic of children. At times two chimps would communicate with each other. For example, one chimp would select the symbol for orange and then take a piece of orange and give another chimp a piece of orange. The chimps were never trained specifically to do this (Savage-Rumbaugh, 1984). This behavior is interesting because it indicates that the chimps were using symbols to communicate, not just to manipulate or obtain something that is otherwise unattainable.

Whether the various training procedures used with chimpanzees are actually teaching the chimps a language or not is a matter of extensive debate (Gardner & Gardner, 1975; Premack, 1983; Rumbaugh, 1977; Savage-Rumbaugh, 1984; Savage-Rumbaugh et al., 1980; Terrace et al., 1979). The debate will not be settled or even examined in this text. It is clear, though, that the use of symbols by chimpanzees is substantial, abstract, and possibly creative. The sense of excitement in this research may best be stated by Sue Savage-Rumbaugh:

> The acquisition of functional communicative symbolic skills by chimpanzees is an extraordinary thing for it moves these members of the species beyond their biological heritage in ways that only human beings have ever traveled before. (Savage-Rumbaugh, 1984)

SELF-AWARENESS

There has been interest for some time in the implications of assuming that animals may be aware (Griffin, 1976). In this section we will comment briefly on evidence which may indicate self-awareness in some animals. One way of defining self-awareness is: an animal that is self-aware is "capable of becoming the object of its own attention" (Gallup, 1983). In order to investigate self-awareness, so defined, Gallup undertook a series of experiments in which various animals were exposed to mirrors and tested for self-attention.

Most animals that respond at all to mirror images respond as if the image were another member of the species, directing, for example, social or aggressive behaviors toward the image. Chimpanzees responded this way initially, but after several days of eight hours per day exposure, they began to use the mirror to respond to themselves by making faces, looking inside their mouths, grooming, and assuming various postures, apparently to examine parts of their anatomy not usually visible to them.

As a test of self awareness, Gallup chose chimpanzees that were apparently using the mirror for a self-image and treated them as follows. They were anesthetized, and then had one eyebrow and the top of one ear painted with a red dye. The animals were then allowed to recover in the absence of a mirror. When the mirror was reintroduced, each chimp showed extensive and repeated activity directed toward the marked eyebrow and ear, as seen in the mirror. Some chimps visually examined and smelled their fingers after they had touched the painted area (the dye was odorless and tasteless, to humans anyway). In contrast, when chimps without mirror experience were treated the same way and then introduced to mirrors for the first time, they did not show any special behaviors directed toward the marked areas.

These various data, Gallup suggests, indicate that the mirror-exposed chimps had developed a self-image and, perhaps, self-awareness. Similar experiments indicate that orangutans also develop a self-image, but monkeys and, surprisingly, gorillas, do not. Monkeys are able to use a mirror to recognize individual conspecifics and to manipulate objects they could not otherwise see, but they do not seem to develop a self-image, even after years of exposure to mirrors (Gallup, 1983). It has been reported that pigeons may be trained to respond to a spot painted on them. However, this behavior, which resulted from substantial shaping and operant training, seems to be unrelated to self-image behavior in chimpanzees (Epstein, Lanza, & Skinner, 1981; Gallup, 1983).

One could speculate that the presence of self-awareness, if that is what self-recognition implies, plus the ability to manipulate symbols, as in a language trained chimpanzee, together might lead to further signs of higher cognition in chimpanzees. But such speculations might best be left for future research and another course.

CHAPTER SUMMARY AND CONCLUSIONS

We have presented a brief overview of some of the research procedures, data, and interpretations from the reemerging field of comparative cognition. We say reemerging because, after all, Thorndike began his initial investigations into animal behavior in the 1890s to make discoveries regarding animal intelligence. However, he chose to explain his results in spare, noncognitive terms.

In the first section of this chapter we saw how an associative interpretation of instrumental learning, and Pavlovian conditioning, could be rephrased into cognitive terms. We also recounted some evidence favoring the view that animals develop expectancies, particularly reward expectancies, and evidence that lower animals can remember past events and anticipate the occurrence of future events.

In succeeding sections evidence was presented which supported more complex forms of rule and concept learning in rats, pigeons, and primates. The later sections on inference, reasoning, language, and self-awareness indicated that these more complex cognitive behaviors may be limited to primates, or perhaps only apes and humans, perhaps even only *some* apes and humans. There have been many attempts to develop a comparative psychology of intelligence (e.g., Bitterman, 1975; Maier & Schneirla, 1964; Thorndike, 1911; Warren, 1965). The success of the developing cognitive approach must await the test of time and data. The cognitive view has thus far generated interesting research procedures and experiments that may not have been attempted if a strict behaviorist philosophy guided all research. Bickerton, reiterating a theme of Griffin's (1976), pointed out that:

> . . . if we wield Occam's razor too vigorously, we risk cutting ourselves
> off from the antecedents of our consciousness, our volition, and all
> other things that have made us human. (Bickerton, 1983, p. 142)

Curiously, radical behaviorism (Skinner, 1974) seems to have placed two unnecessary boundaries on psychological investigation. Its restriction against cognitive concepts separates the study of animal learning from its relationship to the evolution of human learning, and its avoidance of physiological aspects of learning and behavior separates the study of learning from biology and the biological evolution of learning ability. Recent physiological research cited earlier in this text, and much other research that we have not had the space to cite, is beginning to remedy these losses. If the biologists who studied genetics had had the same bias toward reductionism that radical behaviorists have, we might still be reading about the descriptive studies of Mendelian genetics rather than participating in the revolution brought about by molecular biology. Perhaps a comparable revolution will occur when animal learning is investigated from the perspectives of brain function and comparative cognition. A hint of the possible applications of such a revolution may be seen in recent studies of transplants of brain sections in rats to ameliorate learning deficits (Labbe et al., 1983) and the study of learning deficits in brain-damaged humans from the perspective of comparative cognition and neural function (e.g., Butters, 1981).

In the next chapter we shall return to an issue raised in Chapter 1, and related to the points we have just made. That is, can the principles of learning discovered in any one animal species be generalized to other animals, or, in fact, is the nature of learning different in each species? We will see that current evidence indicates that neither extreme position seems to be accurate. Rather, there are both general and specific principles of learning.

14

General and Specific Principles of Learning

> **❝** *Human minds may play chess and do calculus, but it was their contribution to eating, mating, and escaping that gave such minds their staying power.* **❞**
>
> J. L. Lachman and R. Lachman, 1981

INTRODUCTION

We have seen examples of learning ranging from habituation to reasoning, from conditioned emotional responses to instrumental skill learning, from approach to avoidance. We have had occasion to discuss experiments conducted with fish, snails, bees, pigeons, hummingbirds, sparrows, blue jays, crows, mice, rats, prairie dogs, cats, dogs, coyotes, monkeys, chimpanzees, and humans. A question of longstanding interest in the investigation of animal learning is the degree to which different species of animals resemble each other in the way they learn. Does habituation in the human follow the same principles as it does in the snail? Do learning principles discovered with the rat tell us anything about human learning or, indeed, anything about learning in the pigeon? Are there, perhaps, a few general principles of learning that apply to all species? Are there some similarities but also some differences? Are any apparent similarities only superficial so that principles of learning will have to be developed independently for each species?

Thorndike, as we stated previously, was interested in this issue when he began his investigations into animal intelligence before the turn of the century. He interpreted his data to mean that there were quantitative differences in learning rate among the various species that he studied, but the basic principles of learning seemed to be the same. Indeed, his law of effect (see Chapter 7) seemed to be equally applicable to all species, including humans (Thorndike, 1911). In the 1930s and 1940s various comprehensive theoretical systems of learning assumed that the same general learning principles applied to all animals, including humans, and that much progress toward the understanding of human learning could be made by studying just one species, the rat (Hull, 1943; Skinner, 1938, 1974; Spence, 1956; Tolman, 1932).

Although there was some evidence of qualitative differences in learning among lower animals (e.g., fish may not show a negative contrast effect when rewards are reduced, something regularly found with mammals—see Chapter 7, and Bitterman, 1975), the general assumption of similarities in learning principles was not seriously challenged until recently.

The challenge arose in the 1960s and 1970s when the results of many experiments seemed to indicate the presence of *biological constraints* on learning. That is, the data indicated that what an animal learns, or is able to learn, may be related to its evolutionary history. A prime source of the evidence on biological constraints was the conditioned taste aversion procedure, which seemed to show that mammals are *predisposed* (by their evolutionary history) to associate taste with illness-producing agents, and that these associations are formed quickly and over delays in which other forms of learning could not occur (see Chapter 4). The presence of such constraints suggested that it may not be possible to generalize principles of learning from one animal species to another, or from one learning paradigm to another (Seligman, 1970). This suggestion of nongeneralizability has been recently extended to the suggestion that general principles of learning are unlikely to be discovered in laboratory research using artificial experimental situations. Rather, learning may be understood only by investigating it in nature, in the context of each animal's natural environment (Johnston, 1981).

We will present some of the data that led to the idea of biological constraints (more accurately, we will re-present the data, since you have seen most of it already in this text), and then examine the implications of these data for general principles of learning. The conclusion that we will arrive at is that the data do, in fact, indicate that knowledge of an animal's biological heritage and knowledge of its behavior in naturalistic situations will contribute greatly to an understanding of its learning abilities. However, the data seem to complement and expand, rather than negate, the learning principles that have been developed over the past century.

In retrospect, it is not surprising that there should be both general and specific laws of learning. It is not surprising because nearly all animals apparently use learning to adapt to their environment, to solve the problems described in Chapter 1 (e.g., finding food, defending the territory, reproducing, caring for offspring, etc.). But the details of the solutions to these problems may differ, sometimes markedly, depending on the environmental niche to which the organism has adapted and on the ability of its genetic endowment to solve the problems without the necessity of learning (see Odling-Smee, 1983; Plotkin, 1983; Plotkin & Odling-Smee, 1979).

PROGRAMMED LEARNING

Imprinting

The term *imprinting* refers to a type of learning that occurs very early in the lives of certain birds and is vitally important for their survival and "identification" as a member of their species (Gould, 1982; Hess, 1959).

These birds seem to be prepared by innate factors to learn social attachment at a specific time in their lives and they learn this attachment by responding with a specific behavior to a moving stimulus—they follow it. We will describe some of the basic facts of imprinting and then show how Pavlovian associative processes may occur at specific stages in this type of specialized learning.

A newly hatched duckling is likely to emit distress vocalizations, but these vocalizations are suppressed if a moving stimulus is presented to it. If the duckling is able to locomote, it will follow the moving stimulus. After some exposure to the stimulus, it develops an attachment in the sense that this stimulus is able to alleviate distress and elicit following and other signs of filial behavior, whereas other stimuli do not have these effects.

An important aspect of imprinting is that there is a critical period during which this learning must take place, usually the first day or two of a duck's life. If an attachment is not formed during this period, all subsequently presented stimuli are likely to elicit distress responses and escape attempts—the duck will have no stimulus to which it is attached. In the wild, this would be a disaster because normally the first moving stimulus that a duck sees is its mother, and through the imprinting process it develops an attachment to its mother. This attachment is essential if the animal is to survive. Thus, the duck seems to be genetically prepared to form an attachment to a stimulus that it is most likely to encounter just after hatching, and to form no attachments to other stimuli that it is likely to encounter after it is a day or two old. Subsequent attachments are not formed because all novel stimuli presented after the critical period has passed tend to elicit distress and escape behavior, whether or not any attachment has already been formed.

Imprinting therefore appears to be different from other forms of learning discussed in this text. However, laboratory studies have demonstrated that there are, in fact, a number of similarities between imprinting and Pavlovian conditioning (Hoffman & Ratner, 1973; Jaynes, 1958a, 1958b; Moltz, 1963). The possibility of similarities between imprinting and other forms of learning was indicated first by the fact that prolonged exposure of a duckling to the imprinting stimulus was necessary before an attachment developed. The requirement of prolonged exposure suggested that gradual learning takes place during the exposure period. Secondly, it was found that a stationary object (e.g., a duck decoy) will not initially elicit filial behavior in ducklings: this happens only after the animal has had some exposure to the same moving object (e.g., Eiserer & Swope, 1980; Hoffman, Eiserer, & Singer, 1972; Hoffman & Ratner, 1973). Also, it was observed that filial behavior generalized to similar stimuli (e.g., Cofoid & Honig, 1961; Jaynes, 1958b) and that filial behavior could be suppressed by punishment (Hoffman, Stratton, & Newby, 1969).

These observations led Hoffman and Ratner (1973) to develop an associative model of imprinting, a model that illustrates the interaction between innate and learned behavior. According to this model, precocial birds (birds that are able to move about freely when newly hatched) are innately disposed to respond filially to moving stimuli. The imprinting stimulus (e.g., a moving duck) thus has the characteristics of a US in that it elicits innate responses (such as following and/or suppression of distress). These responses may be thought of as URs. The imprinting stimulus, like other USs, is assumed to be reinforcing. Therefore, initially neutral stimuli paired with this US should eventually come to elicit filial responses.

This conditioning process is assumed to account for the fact that characteristics of a stationary object (e.g., shape, color, size), stimuli that do not initially elicit filial behavior, eventually come to do so after the animal has had some experience with the moving object. For example, a nonmoving shape of a duck will not suppress stress vocalizations in a newly hatched duckling. However, after the duckling has had some experience following the moving shape of a duck, the stationary shape will suffice to reduce fear. Hoffman and Ratner postulate that the characteristics of the stationary object function as CSs that are paired with the US of the moving object. As a result of this contingent relationship, these characteristics themselves come to elicit filial behavior. The process is one of Pavlovian conditioning. As we have mentioned, this conditioning may then generalize so that stimuli similar to the imprinting stimulus also come to elicit filial behavior. The conditioning and generalization thus may be the basis of conspecific recognition by such birds.

Additional support for this reinforcing model may be drawn from the fact that an imprinting stimulus functions as a reinforcer in other circumstances. For example, ducks will learn an operant response when pecking is made contingent upon the presentation of an imprinted stimulus (e.g., Hoffman et al., 1966). It has also been shown that initially neutral environmental stimuli will come to suppress distress vocalizations if they are paired with an imprinting stimulus (which, thus, is functioning like a US—Hoffman, Ratner, & Eiserer, 1972). In addition, studies derived from the associative model have shown that the "critical period" is not absolute. As we have mentioned, initial observations of the imprinting phenomena had indicated that imprinting must take place within the first day or so of a duck's life. After that, novel objects elicited fear rather than filial behavior, and imprinting could not take place. However, subsequent studies have shown that forcibly exposing older ducklings (5 to 10 days old) to a moving stimulus eventually led to imprinting. This stimulus initially elicited fear (which does not happen in day-old ducks), but eventually, after extended exposure, filial behavior developed.

This experiment shows that older ducklings are not incapable of learning filial behavior. Such learning just normally does not occur because the maturing fear response to novel objects prevents the animal from engaging in approach and following behavior (Gaioni, Hoffman, DePaulo, & Stratton, 1978). If the animal is confined in the presence of the imprinting stimulus the fear eventually is ameliorated (habituates?), and imprinting takes place. It is interesting to note that this would not normally occur in the natural environment since an older duckling would escape from the vicinity of the fear eliciting stimulus and thus there would be no opportunity for filial behavior to develop.

The imprinting research illustrates the interplay between innate behaviors and learning. There is an innately determined reinforcer and critical period defined by the development of fear to novel stimuli. The animal is also innately predisposed to develop an attachment to a stimulus with a certain characteristic (i.e., movement) if it appears during the critical period. However, the learning potential is flexible, so that any moving stimulus that appears during that period may be learned about, and furthermore, other initially neutral characteristics of that object become conditioned as a result of the continuous relationship to the imprinting stimulus.

This "programmed" learning (the animals appear innately programmed to learn a particular response at a particular time) is flexible in the sense that any of a variety of objects will function as an imprinting stimulus if they are present and moving during the critical period. However, the learning is not completely open. If ducklings are exposed to *both* a moving duck and a moving human, they will imprint on the duck (Gould, 1982). This fact shows that there is a certain degree of selectivity in the formation of attachment associations.

Bird Song

The development of singing in some species of birds bears a number of similarities to filial imprinting in precocial birds. For example, the white crowned sparrow apparently needs some form of learning to develop its song. Birds of this species that are hatched and raised in isolation from adult conspecifics do not sing the typical species song. However, if such birds are exposed to the song of their species when they are between 10 and 50 days of age, they will sing the appropriate species song (Konishi, 1965, cited in Alcock, 1975). It is interesting that the birds seem to "learn" the species typical song even though they don't start singing until some four months after they are exposed to the song.

Although this exposure during the critical period is necessary for the development of appropriate adult song, it is not sufficient. If birds are deafened after the exposure period, so that they cannot hear themselves sing when they are adults, they do not develop a fully appropriate song. It is as if the early exposure forms a neural model of the appropriate song, but the birds have to "practice," when they become sexually mature, in order for their singing to match exactly the model (memory?) that they have stored from their early experience. The feedback from the practice seems to shape the output of the vocal apparatus until it matches the model of the species song.

Thus, song learning in white crowned sparrows again demonstrates an interaction between genetic and experiential factors. The birds are innately predisposed to a particular kind of learning that must occur during a genetically determined critical period. Yet, they must practice, and receive feedback from this practice, when they are mature, or they will not sing the correct song of their species (and thus will not be able to attract mates). As in the case of imprinting, there is some degree of selectivity in the song that is learned during the critical period. That is, white crowned sparrows that are exposed to the songs of other birds during the critical period do not learn them; they seem able to learn only the song characteristic of their species (Marler, 1970; Peters, Searcy, & Marler, 1980).

One thing that is not clear from these studies is how the shaping of the song that occurs during the practice period resembles instrumental learning principles. Is there some mechanism by which a "match" between the bird's vocal output and the neural model of the song generates "reinforcement" and the learning is thus supported by this reinforcement? Is this process analogous to the operation of Thorndike's law of effect in more traditional laboratory learning experiments?

Summary of Programmed Learning

Imprinting and song learning by the white crowned sparrow are examples of genetically programmed flexibility.[1] Genetic mechanisms open a brief temporal "window" during which learning may occur. However, the flexibility is limited. Only specific kinds of learning may occur, as if the genetic window was tinted to allow only a certain wavelength of light to come through. Thus, the learning that may occur is constrained in time and it is selective, perhaps more so in the case of sparrow song than in filial imprinting. The learning that does occur, however, may be at least partly similar in process to aspects of Pavlovian and instrumental associative learning traditionally studied in the laboratory.

We turn now to forms of learning more traditional in laboratory research and will examine the possibility that principles discovered in their research may have limited generality.

CONDITIONED TASTE AVERSIONS

A great deal of the interest in the possibility that learning was constrained by an animal's biological heritage followed Garcia's research on conditioned food

---

[1] Different processes control song learning in different species of birds. Doves seem to be entirely inflexible—they have one song and it is innate. On the other hand, parrots, myna birds, and mockingbirds are able to imitate a wide variety of sounds. Sparrows are, in a sense, intermediate.

aversions and the apparent stark differences between such learning and other forms of learning (see Garcia, Hankins, & Rusiniak, 1974). Subsequent research has confirmed the fact that there are some differences between food aversion learning and other forms of learning (see Chapter 4). However, there are also many similarities. In this section we will first briefly discuss some of the similarities—how taste aversion learning shows many of the same effects and phenomena as other forms of learning—and then examine in some detail three aspects of conditioning that initially seemed to be unique to taste aversion learning, but which are now no longer thought to be so.

General Overview

The great amount of research since Garcia's initial discoveries has shown that the learning of food aversions seems to follow many of the same basic principles as other forms of learning in animals. These similarities have been reviewed by Logue (1979), Revusky (1977), and Testa and Ternes (1977). Only brief mention of them will be made here.

Like other forms of conditioning, taste aversions show CS and US intensity effects and CS–US interval functions (see Chapter 4). Conditioned food aversions are also susceptible to blocking (e.g., Rudy, Iwens, & Best, 1977) and other CS–US contingency manipulations (e.g., Monroe & Barker, 1979). Phenomena found in other forms of conditioning, phenomena such as conditioned inhibition, sensory preconditioning, second order conditioning, memory, and extinction, occur also in the food aversion learning paradigm (see Logue, 1979). Thus, although differing in detail (e.g., CS–US interval functions—Chapter 4) conditioned food aversions are clearly related to other forms of conditioning in terms of broad parametric effects and learning phenomena.

We will now examine some specific issues that arose from the conditioned aversion literature suggesting that food aversion learning may be a unique form of learning, one that is not beholden to general principles discovered with other animal learning procedures.

Selective Associations

A general implicit and sometimes explicit assumption of learning research is that it doesn't make much difference what is used as a stimulus in learning studies—any stimulus should be readily associable with any reinforcer. This view was challenged with the publication of the Garcia and Koelling (1966) experiment on conditioned food aversions. This experiment, which was described in Chapter 4, showed that rats seem to be able to associate the taste of saccharin with poisoning, but not with electric shock. Conversely, the rats were able to associate audiovisual cues with electric shock, but not with poisoning. This and similar experiments led to the idea that learned food aversions represented an adaptive specialization in learning, a specialization such that food related stimuli were prepotent in their likelihood of being associated with agents that produce gastrointestinal distress (e.g., Garcia et al. 1968, 1974). The seemingly special character of food aversion learning was enhanced by the fact that associations could be formed so quickly (one trial) and over such long CS–US intervals.

Subsequent research stimulated by the Garcia experiments has indeed shown that there are differences in the readiness with which specific stimuli and reinforcers may be associated (Domjan, 1983; Domjan & Galef, 1983; LoLordo, 1979). Some of the findings obtained in this research will be briefly summarized.

At least in the case of mammals, taste stimuli are more readily associable with toxicosis than shock, and external stimuli are more readily associable with shock than with toxicosis (e.g., Domjan & Wilson, 1972). This seems to be the case even with newborn rats (Gemberling & Domjan, 1982; Gemberling, Domjan, & Amsel, 1980) indicating that differential experience is not at the basis of the differential associability. However, this differential associability is not absolute. Even though taste cues are more readily associated with toxicosis than exteroceptive cues (e.g., Revusky & Parker, 1976), exteroceptive stimuli may be associated with gastrointestinal distress under some circumstances (Best, Best, & Mickley, 1973; Braveman, 1977; Krane, 1980; Revusky & Parker, 1976), particularly if the exteroceptive stimuli are novel (e.g., Krane, 1980; Mitchell, Kirschbaum, & Perry, 1975). The fact that non-taste stimuli may become associated with toxicosis in animals is also consistent with the observation that humans undergoing chemotherapy for cancer may become nauseous at the site of, or mention of anything associated with, their treatment (see Chapters 3 and 6).

It has also been demonstrated that taste stimuli are associable with the aversiveness of shock (Krane & Wagner, 1975). An important condition for the formation of such associations seems to be that the CS should not extend in time past the presentation of the US. Taste is a long lasting stimulus. When a taste is presented as a CS (e.g., consumption of saccharin) and is immediately followed by shock, the taste may linger well after the effects of shock have passed. We saw in Chapter 4 that the extension of a CS past the US presentation period may have a deleterious effect on standard Pavlovian conditioning. Such seems to be the case in taste–shock pairings also. Thus, a taste–shock association is more likely to be formed if the presentation of the shock is delayed for some time after the taste is presented than if the shock is given immediately (Krane & Wagner, 1975).

Selectivity of associations has been found to occur in conditioning situations other than those involving taste stimuli and toxicosis. For example, in both Pavlovian fear conditioning and in avoidance learning situations, a tone is a more effective stimulus than a light when pigeons are used as subjects. Conversely, a light is more effective than a tone when food is employed as a reinforcement (LoLordo, 1979; LoLordo & Furrow, 1976; Shapiro, Jacobs, & LoLordo, 1980). Other studies with rats have shown that noise onset was more effective as a warning signal than as a safety signal in avoidance learning (see Chapter 9). And, consistent with this, noise offset is more effective as a safety signal than as a warning signal. Also, visual stimuli are more effective as safety signals than as warning signals for rats in avoidance learning (Jacobs & LoLordo, 1980).

Thus, the research since Garcia and Koelling (1966) shows that selective associations do occur in taste aversion learning, but that they are not absolute and they are not limited to the taste aversion procedure. This latter finding indicates that selectivity of associations is not a special adaptation for poison avoidance learning but instead may be a general characteristic of conditioning, including imprinting and bird song learning.

The reasons that selectivity occurs in learning are not yet understood. There is some evidence that nonassociative factors such as selective attention or orientation to the stimuli (Gillette, Martin, & Bellingham, 1980), relative novelty of the stimuli (Kalat & Rozin, 1970; Mitchell et al., 1975), and relative similarity of the CS and US (Rescorla & Cunningham, 1979; Rescorla & Furrow, 1977; Testa & Ternes, 1977) may be important. There is also the possibility that the extent to which the CS and US activate the same neural system *before conditioning* may be important (Cohen, 1980; Kandell, 1983; Thompson, 1976) in determining conditionability.

Long Delay Learning

Initial findings showed that conditioned food aversions occurred with long intervals between the consumption of the food and the presentation of the US. These results challenged the typical findings in both Pavlovian conditioning and instrumental learning that there must be only a brief time period between CS and US, or between response and reinforcement, if an association was to be formed (see Chapters 4 and 7). Conditioned food aversion experiments showed that associations could be formed with many minutes or hours between food and toxin (see Figure 4–4).

Recent experiments have shown that some degree of long delay learning may occur under other experimental conditions. For example, visual, olfactory, and tactile stimuli may be associated with toxicosis over long delays (e.g., Braveman, 1977; Domjan & Hanlon, 1982; Galef & Osborne, 1978; Palmerino, Rusiniak, & Garcia, 1980; Revusky & Parker, 1976). Long delay learning has also been shown to occur in T-maze learning (see Lett, 1975, 1977; and the research of D'Amato and colleagues described in Chapter 7).

Why is it that conditioning can occur with long delays? Domjan (1983) has summarized a number of factors that may be important for the demonstration of learning over long CS–US or long response–reinforcer intervals. Among these are: the way in which learning is measured (for example, preference measures taken over time may be more sensitive to the occurrence of learning than a measure of momentary choice—see Chapter 7); the presentation of marking or retrieval cues to enhance memory; and having the stimulus, the response, and the reinforcer centered upon the same object. Whether taste–toxicosis learning over long delays represents something in addition to the operation of these general factors is not known at the present time (see Domjan, 1983; Revusky, 1977).

Potentiation

We saw in Chapters 6 and 10 how blocking or overshadowing may occur when more than one stimulus is used as the CS. In both blocking and overshadowing, the effectiveness of one CS is reduced by the presence of another CS. An effect opposite to this was noted in research on conditioned food aversions. In particular, it was found that learning about nongustatory aspects of a CS may be facilitated by the presence of a taste cue. For example, hawks do not learn an aversion to black mice if they are poisoned with lithium chloride after consuming one. However, they can learn to avoid black mice if the mice are also made bitter-flavored (Brett, Hankins, & Garcia, 1976). The presence of the bitter flavor led to the formation of an aversion to the "color" of the mouse (i.e., they would consume white, but not black mice). Similarly, the presence of a novel taste enhances conditioned aversion formation to an odor cue in rats (Palmerino et al., 1980) and to visual stimuli in rats, pigeons, and quail (Lett, 1980; Galef & Osborne, 1978).[2]

This enhancing effect of flavor on the conditioning of other stimuli is referred to as a *potentiation*. Potentiation is, in a sense, the opposite of overshadowing. Recent research has shown that potentiation effects may also be obtained in conditioning situations other than food aversions. This research was based upon the observation that in conditioned food aversion studies, animals experience nonflavor and flavor cues sequentially as they approach the poisoned substance. Thus, an animal may first encounter odor or visual cues, and subsequently taste cues, as it begins to consume the food. The presentation of multiple stimuli successively as a CS is referred to as *serial compound conditioning* (as opposed to *simultaneous compound conditioning*—the usual case in overshadowing experiments—see Chapter 10).

A conditioning sequence, for example, could consist of the presentation of a tone, then a light, and then the US. The CS in this case consists of the tone and light presented sequentially. Potentiation would be said to take place if this sequence led to conditioning occurring to the tone, but no conditioning occurring to the tone in the absence of the intervening light. The

---

[2] At the present time there is uncertainty over the conditions in which potentiation or overshadowing will occur in the case of quail presented with both color and flavor cues (see Lett, 1980; Wilcoxin et al., 1971).

use of serial compound stimuli has shown that potentiation effects do occur in standard conditioning situations such as nictitating membrane conditioning in rabbits (Kehoe et al., 1979), autoshaping in pigeons (Rescorla, 1982), conditioned suppression in rats (Pearce et al., 1981), and discriminative conditioning in honeybees (Couvillon & Bitterman, 1982).

Thus, initial studies with conditioned food aversions led to the awareness of a phenomenon—potentiation—that was later found to occur in more traditional conditioning paradigms. The apparent key to the occurrence of potentiation, rather than of overshadowing, is the sequential presentation of stimuli as the CS.

Summary

Logue concluded her review of the conditioned aversion literature with the statement: "In virtually all cases the same principles are sufficient for describing taste aversion and traditional learning data" (Logue, 1979). However, she also recognized that there are some differences. For example, the prepotent role of taste stimuli in the formation of conditioned aversions to a toxicant, and the rapidity with which, and long delays over which associations may be formed make the food aversion procedure at least quantitatively different from most other forms of learning.

The important contribution of Garcia's discovery and subsequent research is that it forced learning theorists to rethink the basis of learning principles and to recognize the significance of an animal's biological heritage and the survival problems that it must face in its natural environment. This rethinking has not, thus far, overthrown previous learning principles, but it has led to modifications in such principles (e.g., in terms of selectivity of associations and in terms of the viability of long delay learning). It has led also to an interest in the investigation of learning in naturalistic circumstances (see Chapter 11).

In the next section we will consider another challenge to general laws of learning, namely a challenge to the potency of the law of effect and to principles of instrumental learning.

DIFFERENTIAL REINFORCEABILITY OF RESPONSES

Are all responses equally reinforceable? It has often been an implicit, and sometimes explicit (Skinner, 1938, p. 45 ff.) assumption that this is the case. However, recent research has clearly shown that responses differ in their susceptibility to the law of effect (something that Thorndike [1911] realized).

An extensive study of the differential reinforceability of responses in the golden hamster was made by Shettleworth (1973, 1975, 1978, 1980). She found that the frequency of occurrence of some responses, such as rearing, "scrabbling" (scraping a wall with forepaws while standing), and digging, may be greatly enhanced by making a food reward or brain stimulation reward contingent upon the performance of these responses. However, other responses engaged in by hamsters, such as face washing, scratching, and scent marking, were very resistant to the effects of positive reinforcement. Thus, some responses showed increases when reinforced, others did not. Shettleworth also found that responses are differentially sensitive to the effects of punishment. For example, rearing is hardly suppressed at all when it is punished, face washing is somewhat suppressed, and scrabbling is readily suppressed.

Why is it that responses seem to be differentially reinforceable? Domjan (1983) and Shettleworth (1980) explored a number of possibilities. One suggestion is that a response which is a component of an innate sequence of responses may, in isolation, be resistant to reinforcement. For example, face washing in rats is resistant to the effects of reinforcement. But face washing is part of a sequence that usually begins with paw washing. Interestingly, when face washing is followed by reinforcement, paw washing may show an increase in frequency (Annable & Wearden, 1979). Similarly, scent marking in hamsters is resistant to the effects of reinforcement, but when scent marking is reinforced, the frequency of digging may increase (Shettleworth & Juergensen, 1980). Digging is often a precursor of scent marking in hamsters.

Another suggestion is that some responses are resistant to reinforcement because the animal cannot discriminate that it has made the response— there is little or no feedback to the animal based upon its response. For example, it is difficult to increase frequency of scratching in rats by reinforcement. It has also been shown that rats cannot use self scratching as a discriminative stimulus for the performance of an instrumental response. That is, they cannot learn that reinforcement is available for pressing a particular lever only after they have just scratched themselves. Rats can learn, however, to use rearing responses (standing on their hind legs) as a cue for reinforced lever press responses, and rearing itself, as it turns out, is also susceptible to reinforcement (Morgan & Nicholas, 1979; Shettleworth & Juergensen, 1980).

A third possibility is that Pavlovian directed behaviors may interfere with the performance of the instrumental response thus reducing the effects of instrumental reinforcement. For example, Shettleworth has suggested that face washing in hamsters may be resistant to the effects of reinforcement because face washing is inconsistent with the anticipation of food. That is, once the animals learn to anticipate food (a stimulus–reinforcer association), face washing may be suppressed. The role of stimulus–reinforcer associations in interfering with the performance of instrumental responses will be considered in more detail when we discuss "misbehavior."

Thus, there is little question that some responses are more resistant to instrumental reinforcement than others, and that there may be a number of reasons why such differences exist. One way of categorizing these differences is: *outer directed responses*, which move the animal about in the environment or bring it into contact with environmental stimuli, are relatively readily reinforceable (e.g., rearing, digging, scrabbling, lever pressing, running in a maze, etc.). However, responses that are *self directed* (e.g., face washing, scratching) are less influenced by reinforcement (Shettleworth & Juergensen, 1980).

MISBEHAVIOR

Perhaps the most dramatic failures of a reinforcement contingency to influence responding were noted by Breland and Breland (1961) in the context of preparing animals for commercial demonstrations. For example, the Brelands attempted to train raccoons to "save" tokens by depositing them into a metal box. They were reinforced for doing so. Eventually, however, instead of dropping them into the box, the raccoons began to rub them together and dip them into the container and pull them back out again without letting go. This behavior persisted despite the fact that it prevented the raccoons from obtaining reinforcement. In other instances the Brelands trained a chicken to hit a "baseball" with a bat. If the ball got past the miniature fielders and hit the rear wall, the chicken was reinforced. Unfortunately, the chicken began chasing the ball after it was hit and pecking at it, a behavior that prevented the occurrence of reinforcement. Other problems encountered by the Brelands included: a strong tendency for pigs to "root" coins, instead of placing them in "piggy banks" (which would have led to reward); a tendency for chickens to scratch and peck the floor instead of standing still for a specified time period in order to obtain reward; and porpoises that swallowed stimuli that they were supposed to be manipulating in order to obtain reward.

In all these cases, the presence of a response–reinforcer contingency failed to maintain behavior, as the law of effect would lead one to expect. Why does this failure occur? Is the law of effect limited (perhaps seriously) by some biological predisposition of the animals (as the Brelands argued)?

Current research indicates several factors that may have to be taken into account to understand these instances of *misbehavior*—of the apparent failure of response–reinforcer contingencies to be effective in controlling behavior. One distinct possibility is that behaviors elicited by the formation of Pavlovian stimulus–reinforcer associations (see Chapters 6 and 12) may come to interfere with, and perhaps override, instrumental response–reinforcer associations. In fact, the behaviors we described in the Breland and Breland experiments may well have reminded the reader of autoshaped behaviors discussed in Chapters 4, 6, 7, and 12.

Recall that in autoshaping, birds will approach a stimulus that signals impending reinforcement and engage in behaviors directed toward that stimulus that are often appropriate for the reinforcement. For example, pigeons will peck at a light that signals food, "drink" at a light that signals water, "court" a light that signals a female, etc. (see Chapter 4). In the Brelands' experiments the various objects used (tokens, etc.) functioned as signals predicting the impending occurrence of a reward. The animals in those experiments eventually came to direct species typical behaviors towards those objects that were appropriate for the reward.

The fact that they engaged in these behaviors even if they prevented the occurrence of reward is also consistent with some aspects of the autoshaping literature, which has shown that birds will continue to peck at keys even if such pecking prevents the occurrence of reward (see Chapters 4, 6, 7, and 12). Thus, the misbehavior discovered by the Brelands now seems to be a case of learned stimulus–reinforcer associations overriding response–reinforcer associations (see Chapter 12). Rather than being an example of the failure of learning principles, misbehavior is now seen to be a particularly powerful demonstration of principles of Pavlovian signal directed behaviors discovered in basic laboratory research (see Chapter 4).

There are actually two issues imbedded in the misbehavior phenomenon. First is the source of the misbehavior. The source is now seen to be the Pavlovian conditioning of stimulus–reinforcer associations—the animal's learning about the signaling properties of the stimulus. Second is the nature of the behavior that develops as a result of this learned signaling relationship. Recent research indicates that the characteristics of the behavior are clearly related to the nature of the reward that is predicted. We saw some examples of this: pigeons behave differently to a lighted key depending upon whether the key signals food, water, or a receptive female pigeon. Similarly, it has been shown that the way a rat behaves toward a lever depends on whether the lever signals food, water, or sucrose (Davey & Cleland, 1982; Davey et al., 1981; Hull, 1977). Timberlake has shown that the behavior of rats toward a rolling ball-bearing that predicted a reward differed depending upon whether the reward was food or water (Timberlake, 1983; Timberlake, Wahl, & King, 1982). In general, rats are more manipulative of objects that predict food (i.e., more likely to chew, hold, or carry them) than they are of objects that predict water.

It is also clear that the nature of the predictive stimulus itself influences the characteristics of the stimulus directed behavior. For example, we mentioned previously that the use of a rat as a CS to signal food for other rats eventually leads to social behaviors, not food-related behaviors, being directed at the signal rat (Timberlake & Grant, 1975). It has also been shown that rats will chase, pick up, and chew on a ball-bearing that predicts food (Timberlake, 1983). Many of these behaviors obviously cannot be observed with the usual signaling stimuli (e.g., tone, or stationary light source).

Timberlake suggested that the nature of the behavior that is directed toward a signaling stimulus, once a stimulus–reinforcer association has been learned, is a function of the activation of preorganized neural systems. The systems that are activated, and the behavior that results, depend on the motivational state of the organism (e.g., whether it is food or water deprived), the nature of the reward, the nature of the signaling stimulus, and the nature of the organism. The importance of the nature of the organism is clearly revealed in the original misbehavior studies by the Brelands. After the stimulus–reinforcer association was learned, pigs rooted, raccoons "washed," and roosters pecked the signaling stimulus.

Thus, the outcome of misbehavior research at the present time seems to be that the principles of associative learning are, in fact, probably similar among all species; that the misbehavior occurs because stimulus–reinforcement associations impose their effects into situations in which the experimenter is studying response–reinforcer contingencies; and that the exact nature of the behavior that is elicited by these stimulus–reinforcer associations is a function of a number of motivational factors that influence performance. They are factors such as the nature of the reward, the nature of the signaling stimulus, and the nature of the animal. The evolutionary history of the animal is important possibly because stimulus–reinforcer associations activate ready-made response systems that are related to the animal's natural food directed behavior. A role for such innate response repertoires activated by Pavlovian associations has been suggested by Glickman and Schiff (1967—see Chapter 6) as well as by Timberlake (1983).

SUMMARY AND CONCLUSIONS

The discussions of imprinting, bird song, taste-aversion learning, the reinforceability of responses, and misbehavior show both the generality of learning principles that are based on laboratory research, and some of the limitations of this generality. Exactly how rapidly an animal may form an association, or the conditions that are optimal for the formation of a particular association, or the behavior that results from the formation of an association, all may be influenced to a degree by each animal's biological heritage.

However, in each of the situations discussed in this chapter there is a greater or lesser degree of applicability of the learning principles that have been shown to be effective in the myriad of other experimental situations described throughout this text. Thus, there is clear evidence of generality as well as specificity in the laws of learning. To reiterate a point made earlier, we might have expected that to be the case since the survival problems that all species face are similar in broad outline, but differ in detail depending on the environmental niche.

It seems clear that we need laboratory studies to suggest and test principles of learning. We need field studies to test the generality of these principles and to suggest new ideas for laboratory investigation. We need laboratory studies to develop quantitative principles of learning that may also be tested in the field (see Chapter 11). We need laboratory studies to investigate neural mechanisms of learning, and we need field studies to determine if suggested neural models are applicable for an animal encountering naturalistic problems (e.g., Blanchard & Blanchard, 1972). Finally, we need laboratory studies to investigate *capacities*: the learning that an animal may be capable of but might never have the opportunity or necessity to demonstrate in its natural environment. (What primitive human ever played chess, programmed a computer to play chess, or composed a sonata, or played one?)

How far can current knowledge of animal learning be generalized? We don't know. At various places in this text we have mentioned applications of animal research to practical field problems and to human behavior. For example, we saw that Pavlovian conditioning research with drugs suggests an associative component for drug tolerance, drug addiction, and death from drug overdose. Pavlovian conditioning research has also suggested an associative origin for phobias and a treatment for these "irrational" fears. Research with conditioned food aversions was seen to have potential relevance for people undergoing chemotherapy for cancer.

Recent use of Pavlovian techniques has demonstrated that human infants are able to form Pavlovian associations within a few hours after birth, and these associative processes may well be related to the development of attachment behavior during the feeding process (Blass et al., 1984). The use of instrumental learning techniques with human infants has revealed aspects of infant memory that parallel phenomena discovered in lower animals (Fagan & Rovee-Collier, 1983; Rovee-Collier et al., 1980). Biofeedback, a process related to the role of response–reinforcer contingencies in animal behavior, has been shown to be effective in reducing migraine headache, high blood pressure, and other aspects of stress (cf., Woolfolk & Lehrer, 1984; Yates, 1980). Recent demonstrations that aspects of the immune system are amenable to Pavlovian conditioning have widespread potential application for understanding the role of emotions in physical health and for behavioral medicine in general (Ader, 1982; Jenkins, Chadwick, & Nevin, 1983).

It has been suggested that acquisition of language by humans may have some parallels to the acquisition of species typical songs by birds (Marler, 1970). If this proves to be the case, the study of the neural mechanisms controlling that behavior may help us understand the neural mechanisms in-

volved in human language acquisition and speech (see Geschwind, 1970; Nottebohm, 1980). The study of unpredictable and uncontrollable aversive events
in animals may have relevance to our understanding of the ability of humans
to cope with stress and may provide clues to the mechanisms by which psychological stress may aggravate physical illness (see Chapter 9).

These and other examples discussed in the text suggest many specific
ways in which principles and phenomena discovered in animal research may
be generalized to help in the understanding of human behavior. There is
need for much more research, particularly in terms of the relationship between neural processes and learning. Such research holds the great promise
of the eventual ability to ameliorate learning deficits due to aging and to
various types of mental retardation (*see* Labbe et al., 1983; Gage et al.,
1984).

References

ABBREVIATIONS OF FREQUENTLY CITED JOURNALS

AL&B	*Animal Learning and Behavior*
AJP	*American Journal of Psychology*
JCP	*Journal of Comparative Psychology*
JCPP	*Journal of Comparative and Physiological Psychology*
JEAB	*Journal of the Experimental Analysis of Behavior*
JEP	*Journal of Experimental Psychology*
JEP:ABP	*Journal of Experimental Psychology: Animal Behavior Processes*
JEP:General	*Journal of Experimental Psychology: General*
L&M	*Learning and Motivation*

Abramson, L. Y., Garber, J., & Seligman, M. E. P. Learned helplessness in humans: An attributional analysis. In J. Garber & M. E. P. Seligman (Eds.), *Human helplessness: Theory and applications*. New York: Academic Press, 1980.

Adams, C. Variations in the sensitivity of instrumental responding to reinforcer devaluation. *Quarterly Journal of Experimental Psychology*, 1982, *34B*, 77–98.

Adams, C., & Dickinson, A. Actions and habits: Variations in associative representations during instrumental learning. In N. E. Spear & R. R. Miller (Eds.), *Information processing in animals: Memory mechanisms*. Hillsdale, N.J.: Erlbaum, 1981.

Ader, R. (Ed.). *Psychoneuro-immunology*. New York: Academic Press, 1982.

Alcock, J. *Animal behavior: An evolutionary approach*. Sunderland, Mass: Sinauer, 1975.

Alloy, L. B., & Abramson, L. Y. The cognitive component of human helplessness and depression: A critical analysis. In J. Garber & M. E. P. Seligman (Eds.), *Human helplessness: Theory and applications*. New York: Academic Press, 1980.

Alloy, L. B., & Bersh, P. J. Partial control and learned helplessness in rats: Control over shock intensity prevents interference with subsequent escape. *AL&B*, 1979, *7*, 157–164.

Amsel, A. The role of frustrative non-reward in noncontinuous reward situations. *Psychological Bulletin*, 1958, *55*, 102–119.

Amsel, A. Partial reinforcement effects on vigor and persistence: Advances in frustration theory derived from a variety of within-subjects experiments. In K. W. Spence & J. T. Spence (Eds.), *The psychology of learning and motivation: Advances in research and theory* (Vol. 1). New York: Academic Press, 1967.

Amsel, A. Positive induction, behavioral contrast, and generalization of inhibition in discrimination learning. In H. H. Kendler & J. T. Spence (Eds.), *Essays in neobehaviorism: A memorial volume for Kenneth W. Spence*. New York: Appleton-Century-Crofts, 1971.

Amsel, A., & Roussel, J. Motivational properties of frustration: I. Effect on a running response of the addition of frustration to the motivation complex. *JEP*, 1952, *43*, 363–368.

Amsel, A., & Stanton, M. Ontogeny and phylogeny of paradoxical reward effects. In J. S. Rosenblatt, R. A. Hinde, C. Beer, & M. C. Busnel (Eds.), *Advances in the study of animal behavior*. New York: Academic Press, 1980.

Anderson, B. J., Nash, S. M., Weaver, M. S., & Davis, S. F. Defensive burying: The effects of multiple stimulus presentation and extinction. *The Psychological Record*, 1983, *33*, 185–190.

Andrews, E. A., & Braveman, N. S. The combined effects of dosage level and interstimulus interval on the formation of one-trial poison-based aversions in rats. *AL&B*, 1975, *3*, 287–289.

Anger, D. The role of temporal discriminations in the reinforcement of Sidman avoidance behavior. *JEAB*, 1963, *6*, 477–506.

Anisman, H., deCatanzaro, D., & Remington, G. Escape performance following exposure to inescapable shock: Deficits in motor response maintenance. *JEP:ABP*, 1978, *4*, 197–218.

Anisman, H., Pizzino, A., & Sklar, L. Coping with stress, norepinephrine depletion and escape performance. *Brain Research*, 1980, *191*, 583–588.

Anisman, H., & Sklar, L. Catecholamine depletion in mice upon re-exposure to stress: Mediation of the escape deficits produced by inescapable shock. *JCPP*, 1979, *93*, 610–625.

Annable, A., & Wearden, J. H. Grooming movements as operants in the rat. *JEAB*, 1979, *32*, 297–304.

Annau, Z., & Kamin, L. J. The conditioned emotional response as a function of intensity of the US. *JCPP*, 1961, *54*, 428–432.

Armus, H. L. Effect of magnitude of reinforcement on acquisition and extinction of a running response. *JEP*, 1959, *58*, 61–63.

Ayllon, T., & Azrin, N. *The token economy: A motivation system for therapy and rehabilitation*. New York: Appleton-Century-Crofts, 1968.

Azrin, N. H., & Holz, W. C. Punishment during fixed-interval reinforcement. *JEAB*, 1961, *4*, 343–347.

Azrin, N. H., Holz, W. C., & Hake, D. F. Fixed-ratio punishment. *JEAB*, 1963, *6*, 141–148.

Bacotti, A. V. Home cage feeding time controls responding under multiple schedules. *AL&B*, 1976, *4*, 41–44.

Baker, A. G. Conditioned inhibition arising from a between-sessions negative correlation. *JEP:ABP*, 1977, *3*, 144–155.

Baker, A. G., & Mackintosh, N. J. Excitatory and inhibitory conditioning following uncorrelated presentations of CS and UCS. *AL&B*, 1977, *5*, 315–319.

Baker, A. G., & Mackintosh, N. J. Preexposure to the CS alone, US alone, or CS and US uncorrelated: Latent inhibition, blocking by context or learned irrelevance? *L&M*, 1979, *10*, 278–294.

Baker, A. G., Mercier, P., Gabel, J., & Baker, P. A. Contextual conditioning and the US preexposure effect in conditioned fear. *JEP:ABP*, 1981, *7*, 109–128.

Baker, T. W. Component strength is a compound CS as a function of number of acquisition trials. *JEP*, 1968, *79*, 347–352.

Balaz, M. A., Kasprow, W. J., & Miller, R. R. Blocking with a single compound trial. *Animal Learning & Behavior*, 1982, *10*, 271–276.

Balsam, P. D., & Payne, D. Intertrial interval and unconditioned stimulus durations in autoshaping. *AL&B*, 1979, *7*, 447–482.

Balsam, P. D., & Schwartz, A. L. Rapid contextual conditioning in autoshaping. *JEP:ABP*, 1981, *7*, 382–393.

Banks, R. K. Persistence to continuous punishment and nonreward following training with intermittent punishment and nonreward. *Psychonomic Science*, 1966a, *5*, 105–106.

Banks, R. K. Persistence to continuous punishment following intermittent punishment training. *JEP*, 1966b, *71*, 373–377.

Banks, R. K., & Torney, D. Generalization of persistence: The transfer to approach behavior to differing aversive stimuli. *Canadian Journal of Psychology*, 1969, *23*, 268–273.

Bardo, M. T., Wellman, P. J., & Hughes, R. A. The role of hot plate and general environmental stimuli in morphine analgesic tolerance. *Pharmacology, Biochemistry & Behavior*, 1981, *14*, 757–760.

Barker, L. M. CS duration, amount, and concentration effects in conditioning taste aversions. *L&M*, 1976, *7*, 265–273.

Barnett, S. A. *The rat: A study in behavior*. Chicago: Aldine, 1963.

Barry, H., III. Effects of strength of drive on learning and on extinction. *JEP*, 1958, *55*, 473–481.

Barry, H., III. Effects of drive strength on extinction and spontaneous recovery. *JEP*, 1967, *73*, 419–421.

Baum, M. Extinction of avoidance responding through response prevention (flooding). *Psychological Bulletin*, 1970, *74*, 276–284.

Baum, M., & Poser, E. G. Comparison of flooding procedures in animals and man. *Behavior Research and Therapy*, 1971, *9*, 249–254.

Baum, W. M. On two types of deviation from the matching law. *JEAB*, 1974, *22*, 231–242.

Baum, W. M. Time allocation in human vigilance. *JEAB*, 1975, *23*, 45–53.

Baum, W. M. Matching, undermatching, and overmatching in studies of choice. *JEAB*, 1979, *32*, 269–281.

Baum, W. M., & Rachlin, H. C. Choice as time allocation. *JEAB*, 1969, *12*, 861–874.

Beck, B. B. *Animal tool behavior: The use and manufacture of tools by animals*. New York: Garland STPM Press, 1980.

Becker, D. E., & Shapiro, D. Physiological response to clicks during zen, yoga, and TM meditation. *Psychophysiology*, 1981, *18*, 694–699.

Becker, H. C., & Flaherty, C. F. Influence of ethanol on contrast in consummatory behavior. *Psychopharmacology*, 1982, *77*, 253–258.

Becker, H. C., & Flaherty, C. F. Chlordiazepoxide and ethanol additively reduce gustatory negative contrast. *Psychopharmacology*, 1983, *80*, 35–37.

Becker, H. C., Flaherty, C. F., & Pohorecky, L. Corticosteroid response to consummatory negative contrast. Paper presented at the meetings of the Eastern Psychological Association, Baltimore, 1984.

Beer, B., & Trumble, G. Timing behavior as a function of amount of reinforcement. *Psychonomic Science*, 1965, *2*, 71–72.

Benedict, J. O., & Ayres, J. J. B. Factors affecting conditioning in the truly random control procedure in the rat. *JCPP*, 1972, *78*, 323–330.

Berger, T. W., Clark, G. A., & Thompson, R. F. Learning-dependent neuronal responses recorded from limbic system brain structures during classical conditioning. *Physiological Psychology*, 1980, *8*, 155–167.

Berger, T. W., & Thompson, R. F. Limbic system interrelations: Functional division among hippocampal-septal connections. *Science*, 1977, *197*, 587–589.

Bernstein, I. L. Learned taste aversions in children receiving chemotherapy. *Science*, 1978, *200*, 1302–1303.

Bernstein, I. L., & Sigmundi, R. A. A learned food aversion. *Science*, 1980, *209*, 416–418.

Berry, S. D., & Thompson, R. F. Prediction of learning rate from the hippocampal electroencephalogram. *Science*, 1978, *200*, 1298–1300.

Berry, S. D., & Thompson, R. F. Medial septal lesions retard classical conditioning of the nictitating membrane response in rabbits. *Science*, 1979, *205*, 209–210.

Best, M. R., & Domjan, M. Characteristics of the lithium-mediated proximal US-preexposure effect in flavor-aversion conditioning. *AL&B*, 1979, *7*, 433–440.

Best, P. J., Best, M. R., & Mickley, G. A. Conditioned aversion to distinct environmental stimuli resulting from gastrointestinal distress. *JCPP*, 1973, *85*, 250–257.

Bickerton, D. The last of Clever Hans? *The Behavioral and Brain Sciences*, 1983, *6*, 141–142.

Billman, G. E., & Randall, D. C. Classical aversive conditioning of coronary blood flow in mongrel dogs. *Pavlovian Journal*, 1980, *15*, 93–101.

Billman, G. E., & Randall, D. C. Mechanisms mediating the coronary vascular response to behavioral stress in the dog. *Circulation Research*, 1981, *48*, 214–223.

Bindra, D. A motivational view of learning, performance and behavior modification. *Psychological Review*, 1974, *81*, 199–213.

Bitterman, M. E. The comparative analysis of learning. *Science*, 1975, *188*, 699–709.

Bitterman, M. E. Attention. In M. E. Bitterman, V. M. LoLordo, J. B. Overmier, & M. E. Rashotte (Eds.), *Animal learning: Survey and analysis*. New York: Plenum Press, 1979a.

Bitterman, M. E. Generalization. In M. E. Bitterman, V. M. LoLordo, J. B. Overmier, & M. E. Rashotte (Eds.), *Animal learning: Survey and analysis*. New York: Plenum Press, 1979b.

Bitterman, M. E., & Couvillon, P. A. The overlearning extinction effect and successive negative contrast in honeybees. Paper presented at the meetings of the Psychonomic Society, 1983.

Blackman, D. E. On cognitive theories of animal learning: Extrapolation from humans to animals? In G. C. L. Davey (Ed.), *Animal models of human behavior*. Chichester, Eng.: John Wiley & Sons. 1983.

Blanchard, D. C., & Blanchard, R. J. Innate and conditioned reactions to threat in rats with amygdaloid lesions. *JCPP*, 1972, *81*, 281–290.

Blass, E. M., Granchrow, J. R., & Steiner, J. E. Classical conditioning in newborn humans 2–48 hours of age. *Infant Behavior and Development*, 1984, *7*, 223–235.

Blodgett, H. C. The effect of the introduction of reward upon maze performance of rats. *University of California Publications in Psychology*, 1929, *4*, 113–134.

Bloomfield, T. M. Behavioral contrast and relative reinforcement frequency in two multiple schedules. *JEAB*, 1967, *10*, 151–158.

Bloomfield, T. M. Contrast and inhibition in discrimination learning by the pigeon: Analysis through drug effects. *L&M*, 1972, *3*, 162–178.

Blough, D. S. Steady state data and a quantitative model of operant generalization and discrimination. *JEAB*, 1975, *1*, 3–21.

Blough, P. M. Local contrast in multiple schedules: The effect of stimulus discriminability. *JEAB*, 1983, *39*, 427–435.

Boakes, R. A. Performance on learning to associate a stimulus with a positive reinforcement. In H. Davis & H. M. B. Hurwitz (Eds.), *Operant Pavlovian interactions*. Hillsdale, N.J.: Erlbaum, 1977.

Boakes, R. A., Halliday, M. S., & Mole, J. S. Successive discrimination training with equated reinforcement frequencies: Failure to obtain behavioral contrast. *JEAB*, 1976, *26*, 65–78.

Boakes, R. A., Poli, M., Lockwood, M. J., & Goodall, G. A study of misbehavior: Token reinforcement in the rat. *JEAB*, 1978, *29*, 115–134.

Bolles, R. C. Species-specific defense reactions and avoidance learning. *Psychological Review*, 1970, *71*, 32–48.

Bolles, R. C. Reinforcement, expectancy and learning. *Psychological Review*, 1972, *79*, 394–409.

Bolles, R. C. *Theory of motivation*. New York: Harper & Row, 1975.

Bolles, R. C. The role of stimulus learning in defensive behavior. In S. H. Hulse, H. Fowler, & W. K. Honig (Eds.), *Cognitive processes in animal behavior*. Hillsdale, N.J.: Erlbaum, 1978.

Bolles, R. C., & Collier, A. C. Effect of predictive cues on freezing in rats. *AL&B*, 1976, *4*, 6–8.

Bolles, R. C., & Grossen, N. E. Effects of an informational stimulus on the acquisition of avoidance behavior in rats. *JCPP*, 1969, *68*, 90–99.

Bolles, R. C., Moot, S. A., & Grossen, N. E. The extinction of shuttlebox avoidance. *L&M*, 1971, *2*, 324–333.

Bolles, R. C., & Warren, J. A., Jr. The acquisition of bar-press avoidance as a function of shock intensity. *Psychonomic Science*, 1965, *3*, 297–298.

Bond, A. B., Cook, R. G., & Lamb, M. R. Spatial memory and the performance of rats and pigeons in the radial-arm maze. *AL&B*, 1981, *9*, 575–580.

Born, D. G. Resistance of a free operant to extinction and suppression with punishment as a function of amount of training. *Psychonomic Science*, 1967, *8*, 21–22.

Bouton, M. E., & Bolles, R. C. Conditioned fear assessed by freezing and by the suppression of three different baselines. *AL&B*, 1980, *8*, 429–434.

Bower, G., & Grusec, T. Effect of prior Pavlovian discrimination training upon learning in an operant discrimination. *JEAB*, 1964, *7*, 401–404.

Bower, G., Starr, R., & Lazarovitz, L. Amount of response-produced change in the CS and avoidance learning. *JCPP*, 1965, *59*, 13–17.

Bower, G. H. Partial and correlated reward in escape conditioning. *JEP*, 1960, *59*, 126–130.

Bower, G. H., Fowler, H., & Trapold, M. A. Escape learning as a function of amount of shock reduction. *JEP*, 1959, *58*, 482–484.

Braun, J. J., Lasiter, P. S., & Kiefer, S. W. The gustatory neocortex of the rat. *Physiology Psychology*, 1982, *10*, 13–45.

Braveman, N. S. Visually guided avoidance of poisonous foods in mammals. In L. M. Barker, M. R. Best, & M. Domjan (Eds.), *Learning mechanisms in food selection*. Waco, Tex.: Baylor University Press, 1977.

Breland, K., & Breland, M. The misbehavior of organisms. *American Psychologist*, 1961, *61*, 681–684.

Brett, L. P., Hankins, W. G., & Garcia, J. Prey-lithium aversions. III Buteo hawks. *Behavioral Biology*, 1976, *17*, 87–98.

Brogden, W. J. Sensory preconditioning. *JEP*, 1939, *25*, 323–332.

Brogden, W. J., Lipman, E. A., & Culler, E. The role of incentive in conditioning and extinction. *American Journal of Psychology*, 1938, *51*, 109–117.

Brooks, C. I. Effect of prior nonreward on subsequent incentive growth during brief acquisition. *AL&B*, 1980, *8*, 143–151.

Brown, P. L., & Jenkins, H. M. Autoshaping of the pigeon's key peck. *JEAB*, 1968, *11*, 1–8.

Brown, R. T., & Wagner, A. R. Resistance to punishment and extinction following training with shock or nonreinforcement. *JEP*, 1964, *68*, 503–507.

Brown, W. L., & McDowell, A. A. Response-shift learning in rhesus monkeys. *JCPP*, 1963, *56*, 335–336.

Browne, M. P. The role of primary reinforcement and overt movements in autoshaping in the pigeon. *Animal Learning & Behavior*, 1976, *4*, 287–292.

Brush, F. R. Avoidance learning after fear conditioning and unsignalled shock. *Psychonomic Society*, 1964, *1*, 405–406.

Buck, S. L., Rothstein, B., & Williams, B. A. A re-examination of local contrast in multiple schedules. *JEAB*, 1975, *24*, 291–301.

Burdette, D. R., Brake, S., Chen, F. S., & Amsel, A. Ontogeny of persistence: Immediate extinction effects in preweanling and weanling rats. *AL&B*, 1976, *4*, 131–138.

Burkhardt, P. E., & Ayres, J. J. B. CS and US duration effects in one-trial simultaneous fear conditioning as assessed by conditioned suppression of licking in rats. *AL&B*, 1978, *6*, 225–230.

Burns, R. A. Effects of sequences of sucrose reward magnitudes with short ITIs in rats. *AL&B*, 1976, *4*, 473–479.

Butter, C. M., & Thomas, D. R. Secondary reinforcement as a function of the amount of primary reinforcement. *JEAB*, 1958, *51*, 346–348.

Butters, N. The Wernicke-Korsakoff syndrome: A review of psychological, neuropathological and etiological factors. In M. Galanter (Ed.), *Currents in alcoholism* (Vol. 14), Grune & Stratton, 1981.

Bykov, K. M. *The cerebral cortex and the internal organs*. New York: Chemical Publishing Co., 1957.

Cain, N. W., & Baenninger, R. Effects of prior experience with the US on the formation of learned taste aversions in rats. *AL&B*, 1977, *5*, 359–364.

Cakmak, M., & Spear, N. E. Acquisition of discrimination between rewards. *Psychonomic Science*, 1967, *7*, 97–98.

Camp, D. S., Raymond, G. A., & Church, R. M. Temporal relationship between response and punishment. *JEP*, 1967, *74*, 114–123.

Campbell, B. A. The reinforcement difference linear (RDL) function for shock reduction. *JEP*, 1956, *52*, 258–262.

Campbell, B. A., & Church, P. M. *Punishment and aversive behavior*. New York: Appleton-Century-Crofts, 1969.

Campbell, B. A., & Kraeling, D. Response strength as a function of drive level and amount of drive reduction. *JEP*, 1953, *45*, 97–101.

Campbell, B. A., & Sheffield, F. D. Relation of random activity to food deprivation. *JCPP*, 1953, *46*, 320–322.

Campbell, P. E., Batsche, C. J., & Batsche, G. M. Spaced-trials reward magnitude effects in the rat: Single versus multiple food pellets. *JCPP*, 1972, *81*, 360–364.

Campbell, P. E., Knouse, S. B., & Wrotten, J. Resistance to extinction in the rat following regular and irregular schedules of partial reinforcement. *JCPP*, 1970, *72*, 210–215.

Capaldi, E. D. Resistance to extinction in rats as a function of deprivation level and schedule of reward in acquisition. *JCPP*, 1972, *79*, 90–98.

Capaldi, E. J. Partial reinforcement: A hypothesis of sequential effects. *Psychological Review*, 1966, *73*, 459–479.

Capaldi, E. J. Partial reward either following or preceding consistent reward: A case of reinforcement level. *JEP*, 1974, *102*, 954–962.

Capaldi, E. J. Effects of schedule and delay of reinforcement on acquisition speed. *AL&B*, 1978, *6*, 330–334.

Capaldi, E. J., Nawrocki, T. M., & Verry, D. R. The nature of anticipation: An inter- and intraevent process. *AL&B*, 1983, *11*, 193–198.

Capaldi, E. J., & Verry, D. R. Serial order anticipation learning in rats: Memory for multiple hedonic events and their order. *AL&B*, 1981, *9*, 441–453.

Carlson, N. R. *Physiology of behavior*. Boston: Allyn and Bacon, 1977.

Carlton, P. L. The interacting effects of deprivation and reinforcement schedule. *JEAB*, 1961, *4*, 379–381.

Castellucci, V. F., Carew, T. J., & Kandel, E. R. *Science*, 1978, *202*, 1306–1308.

Castellucci, V. F., & Kandel, E. R. An invertebrate system for the cellular study of habituation and sensitization. In T. J. Tighe & R. N. Leaton (Eds.), *Habituation*. Hillsdale, N.J.: Erlbaum, 1976.

Catania, A. C. Concurrent performances: Reinforcement interaction and response independence. *JEAB*, 1963, *6*, 253–263.

Catania, A. C. Behavior analysis and behavior synthesis in the extrapolation from animal to human behavior. In G. C. L. Davey (Ed.), *Animal models of human behavior*. Chichester, Eng.: John Wiley & Sons, 1983.

Charlton, S. G. Differential conditionability: Reinforcing grooming in golden hamsters. *AL&B*, 1983, *11*, 27–34.

Charnov, E. L. Optimal foraging: The marginal value theorem. *Theoretical Population Biology*, 1976, *9*, 129–136.

Chen, J. S., & Amsel, A. Recall (versus recognition) of taste and immunization against aversive taste anticipation based on illness. *Science*, 1980, *209*, 831–833.

Church, R. M. The internal clock. In Hulse, S. H., Fowler, H., & Honig, W. K. (Eds.), *Cognitive processes in animal behavior*. Hillsdale, N.J.: Erlbaum, 1978.

Church, R. M., & Gibbon, J. Temporal generalization. *JEP:ABP*, 1982, *8*, 165–186.

Church, R. M., Raymond, G. A., & Beauchamp, R. D. Response suppression as a function of intensity and duration of a punishment. *JCPP*, 1967, *63*, 39–44.

Clayton, K. N. T-maze choice learning as a joint function of the reward magnitudes for the alternatives. *JCPP*, 1964, *58*, 333–338.

Cleland, E. A., Williams, M. Y., & DiLollo, V. Magnitude of negative contrast effect in relation to drive level. *Psychonomic Science*, 1969, *15*, 121–122.

Cofoid, D. A., & Honig, W. K. Stimulus generalization of imprinting. *Science*, 1961, *134*, 1692–1694.

Cohen, D. H. The functional neuroanatomy of a conditioned response. In R. F. Thompson, L. H. Hicks, & V. B. Shvyrkov (Eds.), *Neural mechanisms of goal-directed behavior and learning*. New York: Academic Press, 1980.

Cohen, D. H., & Goff, D. M. Conditioned heart-rate change in the pigeon: Analysis and prediction of acquisition patterns. *Physiological Psychology*, 1978, *6*, 127–141.

Coleman, S. R. Consequences of response-contingent change in unconditioned stimulus intensity upon the rabbit *(Oryctolagus cuniculus)* nictitating membrane response. *JCPP*, 1975, *88*, 591–595.

Collerain, I. Frustration odor of rats receiving small numbers of prior rewarded running trials. *JEP:ABP*, 1978, *4*, 120–130.

Collerain, I. J., & Ludvigson, H. W. Hurdle-jump responding in the rat as a function of conspecific odor of reward and nonreward. *AL&B*, 1977, *5*, 177–183.

Collier, G. Consummatory and instrumental responding as functions of deprivation. *JEP*, 1962, *64*, 410–414.

Collier, G. Body weight loss as a measure of motivation in hunger and thirst. *Annals of the New York Academy of Science*, 1969, *157*, 594–609.

Collier, G. H. Determinants of choice. In H. E. Howe, Jr., & D. J. Bernstein (Eds.), *Nebraska Symposium on Motivation*. Lincoln, Nebr.: University of Nebraska Press, 1982.

Collier, G. H. Life in a closed economy: The ecology of learning and motivation. In M. D. Zeiler & P. Harzem (Eds.), *Advances in analysis of behavior*. London: Wiley, 1983.

Collier, G., Hirsch, E., & Hamlin, P. H. The ecological determinants of reinforcement in the rat. *Physiology and Behavior*, 1972, *9*, 705–716.

Collier, G. H., & Rovee-Collier, C. K. A comparative analysis of optimal foraging behavior: Laboratory simulations. In A. C. Kamil & T. D. Sargent (Eds.), *Foraging behavior: Ecological, ethological, and psychological approaches*. New York: Garland STPM Press, 1981.

Collins, J., & D'Amato, M. R. Magnesium pemoline: Effects on avoidance conditioning mediated by anticipatory responses. *Psychonomic Science*, 1968, *12*, 115–116.

Coppock, H. W., & Chambers, R. M. GSR conditioning: An illustration of useless distinctions between "type" of conditioning. *Psychological Reports*, 1959, *6*, 171–177.

Coulter, X., Riccio, D. C., & Page, H. A. Effects of blocking an instrumental avoidance response: Facilitated extinction but persistence of "fear." *JCPP*, 1969, *68*, 377–381.

Couvillon, P. A., & Bitterman, M. E. Some phenomena of associative learning in honeybees. *JCPP*, 1980, *94*, 878–885.

Couvillon, P. A., & Bitterman, M. E. Compound conditioning in honeybees. *JCP*, 1982, *96*, 192–199.

Couvillon, P. A., & Bitterman, M. E. The overlearning-extinction effect and successive negative contrast in honeybees *(Apis mellifera)*. *JCP*, 1984, *98*, 100–109.

Couvillon, P. A., Klosterhalfen, S., & Bitterman, M. E. Analysis of overshadowing in honeybees. *JCP*, 1983, *97*, 154–166.

Cowie, R. J. Optimal foraging in great tits *(Parus major)*. *Nature*, 1977, *268*, 137–139.

Cowles, J. T. Food-tokens as incentives for learning by chimpanzees. *Comparative Psychology Monographs*, 1937, 14.

Craig, W. Appetites and aversions as constituents of instincts. *Biological Bulletin*, 1918, *34*, 91–107.

Crawford, M., & Masterson, F. Components of the flight response can reinforce bar-press avoidance learning. *JEP:ABP*, 1978, *4*, 144–151.

Crespi, L. P. Quantitative variation of incentive and performance in the white rat. *American Journal of Psychology*, 1942, *55*, 467–517.

Crespi, L. P. Amount of reinforcement and level of performance. *Psychological Review*, 1944, *51*, 341–357.

Crowell, C. R., Hinson, R. E., & Siegel, S. The role of conditional drug responses in tolerance to the hypothermic effects of ethanol. *Psychopharmacology*, 1981, *73*, 51–54.

Cunningham, C. L., Fitzgerald, R. D., & Francisco, D. L. Excitatory and inhibitory consequences of explicitly unpaired and truly random conditioning procedures on heart rate in rats. *AL&B*, 1977, *5*, 135–142.

Daly, H. B. Reinforcing properties of escape from frustration aroused in various learning situations. In G. H. Bower (Ed.), *The psychology of learning and motivation* (Vol. 8). New York: Academic Press, 1974.

Daly, H. B., & Daly, J. T. A mathematical model of reward and aversive nonreward: Its application to over 30 appetitive learning situations. *JEP:General*, 1982, *111*, 441–480.

D'Amato, M. R. Secondary reinforcement and magnitude of primary reinforcement. *JCPP*, 1955, *48*, 378–380.

D'Amato, M. R. *Experimental psychology: Methodology, psychophysics and learning*. New York: McGraw-Hill, 1970.

D'Amato, M. R. Delayed matching and short-term memory in monkeys. In G. H. Bower (Ed.), *The psychology of learning and motivation: Advances in research and theory* (Vol. 17). New York: Academic Press, 1973.

D'Amato, M. R., & Worsham, R. W. Retrieval cues and short-term memory in capuchin monkeys. *JCPP*, 1974, *86*, 274–282.

D'Amato, M. R., Buckiewicz, J., & Puopolo, M. Long-delay spatial discrimination learning in monkeys *(Cebus apella)*. *Bulletin of the Psychonomic Society*, 1981, *18*, 85–88.

D'Amato, M. R., & Cox, J. K. Delay of consequences and short-term memory in monkeys. In D. Medin, R. Davis, & W. Roberts (Eds.), *Coding processes in animal memory*. Hillsdale, N.J.: Erlbaum, 1976.

D'Amato, M. R., Etkin, M., & Fazzaro, J. Cue-producing behavior in the capuchin monkey during reversal, extinction, acquisition, and overtraining. *JEAB*, 1968, *11*, 425–433.

D'Amato, M. R., & Fazzaro, J. Discriminated lever-press avoidance learning as a function of type and intensity of shock. *JCPP*, 1966, *61*, 313–315.

D'Amato, M. R., Fazzaro, J., & Etkin, M. Discriminated bar-press avoidance maintenance and extinction in rats as a function of shock intensity. *JCPP*, 1967, *63*, 351–354.

D'Amato, M. R., Fazzaro, J., & Etkin, M. Anticipatory responding and avoidance discrimination as factors in avoidance conditioning. *JEP*, 1968, *77*, 41–47.

D'Amato, M. R., Keller, D., & Biederman, G. Discriminated avoidance learning as a function of parameters of discontinuous shock. *JEP*, 1965, *70*, 543–548.

D'Amato, M. R., Lachman, R., & Kivy, P. Secondary reinforcement as affected by reward schedule and the testing situation. *JCPP*, 1958, *51*, 734–741.

D'Amato, M. R., & O'Neill, W. Effects of delay-interval illumination on matching behavior in the capuchin monkey. *JEAB*, 1971, *15*, 327–333.

D'Amato, M. R., & Safarjan, W. R. Differential effects of delay of reinforcement on acquisition of affective and instrumental responses. *AL&B*, 1981, *9*, 209–215.

D'Amato, M. R., Safarjan, W. R., & Salmon, D. P. Long-delay conditioning and instrumental learning: Some new findings. In N. E. Spear & R. R. Miller (Eds.), *Information processing in animals: Memory mechanisms*. Hillsdale, N.J.: Erlbaum, 1981.

D'Amato, M. R., & Salmon, D. P. Person concept in cebus monkeys. Paper presented at the American Psychological Association meeting, Anaheim, Calif., 1983.

D'Amato, M. R., & Salmon, D. P. Cognitive processes in cebus monkeys. In H. L. Roitblat, T. G. Bever, & H. S. Terrace (Eds.), *Animal Cognition*. Hillsdale, N.J.: Erlbaum, 1984.

D'Amato, M. R., Salmon, D. P., & Colombo, M. Extent and limits of the matching concept in monkeys *(Cebus apella)*. *JEP:ABP*, 1984, in press.

D'Amato, M. R., & Siller, J. Partial reinforcement and response variability. *The Journal of General Psychology*, 1962, *66*, 25–31.

D'Amato, M. R., & Worsham, R. W. Delayed matching in the capuchin monkey with brief sample durations. *L&M*, 1972, *3*, 304–312.

Dantzer, R., Arnone, M., & Mormede, P. Effects of frustration on behavior and plasma corticosteroid levels in pigs. *Physiology & Behavior*, 1980, *24*, 1–4.

Darby, C. L., & Riopelle, A. J. Observational learning in the rhesus monkey. *JCPP*, 1959, *52*, 94–98.

Darwin, C. *The descent of man, and selection in relation to sex*. New York: Appleton, 1871.

Darwin, C. *The origin of species*. New York: New American Library, 1958.

Davenport, D. G., & Olson, R. D. A reinterpretation of extinction in discriminated avoidance. *Psychonomic Science*, 1968, *13*, 5–6.

Davenport, J. W. The interaction of magnitude and delay of reinforcement in spatial discrimination. *JCPP*, 1962, *55*, 267–273.

Davey, G. C. L., & Cleland, G. G. Topography of signal-centered behaviour in the rat: Effects of deprivation state and reinforcer type. *JEAB*, 1982, *38*, 291–314.

Davey, G. C. L., Phillips, S., & Cleland, G. G. The topography of signal-centered behaviour in the rat: The effects of solid and liquid food reinforcers. *Behaviour Analysis Letters*, 1981, *1*, 331–337.

Davis, H., & Hurwitz, H. M. B. (Eds.). *Operant-Pavlovian interactions*. Hillsdale, N.J.: Erlbaum, 1977.

Davis, S. F., Grady, S. M., Klaess, A. M., Petty-Zirnstein, M. K., & Tramill, J. L. Defensive burying of a classically conditioned stimulus. *The Psychological Record*, 1983, *33*, 67–75.

Davis, S. F., Gussetto, J. K., Tramill, J. L., Neideffer, J., & Travis-Neideffer, M. N. The effects of extended insulin dosage on target-directed attack and biting elicited by tailshock. *Bulletin of the Psychonomic Society*, 1978, *12*, 80–82.

Deaux, E. B., & Patten, R. L. Measurement of the anticipatory goal response in instrumental runway conditioning. *Psychonomic Science*, 1964, *1*, 357–358.

DeBold, R. D., Miller, N. E., & Jensen, D. D. Effect of strength of drive determined by a new technique for appetitive classical conditioning of rats. *JCPP*, 1965, *59*, 102–108.

Demarest, J., & Mackinnon, J. R. Effects of chlordiazepoxide and reward magnitude on the acquisition and extinction of a partially reinforced response. *Physiological Psychology*, 1978, *6*, 78–82.

Dember, W. N., & Fowler, H. Spontaneous alternation behavior. *Psychological Bulletin*, 1958, *55*, 412–428.

Denny, M. R. Relaxation theory and experiments. In F. R. Brush (Ed.), *Aversive conditioning and learning*. New York: Academic Press, 1971.

Denny, M. R., Zerbolio, D. J., Jr., & Weisman, R. G. Avoidance learning in heterogeneous and homogeneous shuttle boxes. *JCPP*, 1969, *68*, 370–372.

Deutsch, J. A. *The structural basis of behavior*. Cambridge, Eng.: Cambridge University Press, 1960.

Deutsch, R. Effects of CS amount on conditioned taste aversion at different CS-US intervals. *AL&B*, 1978, *6*, 258–260.

De Villiers, P. A. Choice in concurrent schedules and a quantitative formulation of the law of effect. In W. K. Honig & J. E. R. Staddon (Eds.), *Handbook of operant behavior*. Englewood Cliffs, N.J.: Prentice-Hall, 1977.

Dickinson, A. *Contemporary animal learning theory*. Cambridge, Eng.: Cambridge University Press, 1980.

Dickinson, A., & Dearing, M. F. Appetitive-aversive interactions and inhibitory processes. In A. Dickinson & R. A. Boakes (Eds.), *Mechanisms of learning and motivation: A memorial volume to Jerzy Konorski*. Hillsdale, N.J.: Erlbaum, 1979.

Dickinson, A., Hall, G., & Mackintosh, N. J. Surprise and the attenuation of blocking. *JEP:ABP*, 1976, *2*, 313–322.

Dickinson, A., & Mackintosh, N. J. Reinforcer specificity in the enhancement of conditioning by posttrial events. *JEP:ABP*, 1979, *5*, 162–177.

Dickinson, A., & Pearce, J. M. Inhibitory interactions between appetitive and aversive stimuli. *Psychological Bulletin*, 1977, *84*, 690–711.

Dieter, S. E. Continuity and intensity of shock in one-way avoidance learning in the rat. *AL&B*, 1976, *4*, 303–307.

Domjan, M. Ingestional aversion learning: Unique and general processes. In J. S. Rosenblatt, R. A. Hinde, C. Beer, & M. C. Busnel (Eds.), *Advances in the study of behavior* (Vol. 2). New York: Academic Press, 1980.

Domjan, M. Biological constraints on instrumental and classical conditioning: Implications for general process theory. In G. Bower (Ed.), *The psychology of learning and motivation* (Vol. 17). New York: Academic Press, 1983.

Domjan, M., & Best, M. R. Interference with ingestional aversion learning produced by preexposure to the unconditioned stimulus: Associative and nonassociative aspects. *L&M*, 1980, *11*, 522–537.

Domjan, M., & Galef, B. G., Jr. Biological constraints on instrumental and classical conditioning: Retrospective and prospect. *AL&B*, 1983, *11*, 151–161.

Domjan, M., & Gemberling, G. A. Effects of expected vs. unexpected proximal US preexposure on taste-aversion learning. *AL&B*, 1980, *8*, 204–210.

Domjan, M., & Hanlon, M. J. Poison-avoidance learning to food-related tactile stimuli: Avoidance of texture cues by rats. *AL&B*, 1982, *10*, 293–300.

Domjan, M., & Wilson, N. E. Specificity of cue to consequence in aversion learning in the rat. *Psychonomic Science*, 1972, *26*, 143–145.

Douglass, R. J. Pavlovian conditioning and the brain. In R. A. Boakes & M. S. Halliday (Eds.), *Inhibition and learning*. London: Academic Press, 1972.

Dragoin, W. Conditioning and extinction of taste aversions with variations in intensity of the CS and UCS in two strains of rats. *Psychonomic Science*, 1971, *22*, 303–305.

Drugan, R. C., & Maier, S. F. The nature of the activity deficit produced by inescapable shock. *AL&B*, 1982, *10*, 401–406.

Drugan, R. C., & Maier, S. F. Analgesic and opioid involvement in the shock-elicited activity and escape deficits produced by inescapable shock. *L&M*, 1983, *14*, 30–47.

Duncan, C. P. The retroactive effect of electroshock on learning. *JCPP*, 1949, *42*, 32–44.

Dunham, P. J. Punishment: Method and theory. *Psychological Review*, 1971, *78*, 58–70.

Dunham, P. J. Changes in unpunished responding during response-contingent punishment. *AL&B*, 1978, *6*, 174–180.

Dyck, D. G., Dresel, M., & Suthons, E. Order of partial and consistent reward, reward magnitude shift, and resistance to extinction. *L&M*, 1978, *9*, 219–229.

Dyer, F. C., & Gould, J. L. Honey bee navigation. *American Scientist*, 1983, *71*, 587–597.

Ehrenfreund, D. Effect of drive on successive magnitude shift in rats. *JCPP*, 1971, *76*, 418–423.

Eibl-Eibesfeldt, I. *Ethology: The biology of behavior*. New York: Holt, Rinehart and Winston, 1970.

Eikelboom, R., & Stewart, J. Conditioning of drug-induced physiological responses. *Psychological Review*, 1982, *89*, 507–528.

Eiserer, L. A., & Swope, R. L. Acquisition of behavioral control by static visual features of an imprinting object: Species generality. *AL&B*, 1980, *8*, 481–484.

Elkins, R. L. Attenuation of drug-induced bait shyness to a palatable solution as an increasing function of its availability prior to conditioning. *Behavioral Biology*, 1973, *9*, 221–226.

Ellen, P., & Aitken, W. C., Jr. Absence of temporal discrimination following septal lesions. *Psychonomic Science*, 1971, *22*, 129–131.

Ellen, P., Aitken, W. C., Jr., Sims, T., & Stahl, J. M. Cholinergic blockade, septal lesions, and DRL performance in the rat. *JCPP*, 1975, *5*, 409–420.

Elliott, M. H. The effect of change of reward on the maze performance of rats. *University of California Publications in Psychology*, 1928, *4*, 19–30.

Ellison, G. D. Differential salivary conditioning to traces. *JCPP*, 1964, 57, 373–380.

Epstein, R., Lanza, R. P., & Skinner, B. F. "Self-awareness" in the pigeon. *Science*, 1981, *212*, 695–696.

Estes, W. K. An experimental study of punishment. *Psychology Monographs*, 1944, *57*, No. 3.

Estes, W. K. Stimulus-response theory of drive. In M. R. Jones (Ed.), *Nebraska Symposium on Motivation*. Lincoln: University of Nebraska Press, 1958.

Estes, W. K. The statistical approach to learning theory. In S. Koch (Ed.), *Psychology: A new study of a science* (Vol. 2). New York: McGraw-Hill, 1959.

Estes, W. K. (Ed.). *Handbook of learning and cognitive processes: Vol. 2, Conditioning and behavior theory*. Hillsdale, N.J.: Erlbaum, 1975.

Estes, W. K. Cognitive processes in conditioning. In A. Dickinson & R. A. Boakes (Eds.), *Mechanisms of learning and motivation: A memorial volume to Jerzy Konorski*. Hillsdale, N.J.: Erlbaum, 1979.

Estes, W. K., & Skinner, B. F. Some quantitative properties of anxiety. *JEP*, 1941, *29*, 390–400.

Etkin, M. Light-induced interference in a delayed-matching task with capuchin monkeys. *L&M*, 1972, *3*, 317–324.

Fagen, J. W., & Rovee-Collier, C. K. Memory retrieval: A time-locked process in infancy. *Science*, 1983, *222*, 1349–1351.

Fallon, D. Resistance to extinction following learning with punishment of reinforced and non-reinforced licking. *JEP*, 1968, *76*, 550–557.

Fallon, D. Resistance to extinction following partial punishment of reinforced and/or nonreinforced responses during learning. *JEP*, 1969, *79*, 183–185.

Fanselow, M. S., & Bolles, R. C. Naloxone and shock-elicited freezing in the rat. *JCPP*, 1979, *93*, 736–744.

Fantino, E. Conditioned reinforcement: Choice and information. In W. K. Honig & J. E. R. Staddon (Eds.), *Handbook of operant behavior*. Englewood Cliffs, N.J.: Prentice-Hall, 1977.

Fantino, E., & Davison, M. Choice: Some quantitative relations. *JEAB*, 1983, *40*, 1–13.

Farley, J. Automaintenance, contrast and contingencies: Effects of local vs. overall and prior vs. impending reinforcement context. *L&M*, 1980, *11*, 19–48.

Feierabend, I. K., Feierabend, R. L., & Nesvold, B. A. Social change and political violence: Cross-national patterns. In H. D. Graham & T. R. Gurr (Eds.), *Violence in America: Historical and comparative perspectives*. New York: Signet, 1969.

Fenton, F., Calof, A., & Katzev, R. The effect of controllable and uncontrollable neonatal preshocks on adult escape/avoidance behavior in the guinea pig (*Cavia porcellus*). *AL&B*, 1979, *7*, 372–376.

Ferster, C. B., & Skinner, B. F. *Schedules of reinforcement*. New York: Appleton-Century-Crofts, 1957.

Fitzgerald, R. D. Effects of partial reinforcement with acid on the classically conditioned salivary response in dogs. *JCPP*, 1963, *56*, 1056–1060.

Fitzgerald, R. D., Martin, G. K., & O'Brien, J. H. Influence of vagal activity on classically conditioned heart rate in rats. *JCPP*, 1973, *83*, 485–491.

Fitzgerald, R. D., Vardaris, R. M., & Teyler, T. J. Effects of partial reinforcement followed by continuous reinforcement on classically conditioned heart rate in the dog. *JCPP*, 1966, *62*, 483–486.

Flaherty, C. F. Incentive contrast: A review of behavioral changes following shifts in reward. *AL&B*, 1982, *10*, 409–440.

Flaherty, C. F., Becker, H. C., & Osborne, M. Negative contrast following regularly increasing concentrations of sucrose solutions: Rising expectations or incentive averaging. *Psychological Record*, 1983, *33*, 415–420.

Flaherty, C. F., & Caprio, M. Dissociation between instrumental and consummatory measures of incentive contrast. *American Journal of Psychology*, 1976, *89*, 485–498.

Flaherty, C. F., & Checke, S. Anticipation of incentive gain. *AL&B*, 1982, *10*, 177–182.

Flaherty, C. F., & Davenport, J. W. Noncontingent pretraining in instrumental discrimination between amounts of reinforcement. *JCPP*, 1968, *66*, 707–711.

Flaherty, C. F., & Davenport, J. W. Three-level differential reward magnitude discrimination in rats. *Psychonomic Science*, 1969, *15*, 231–243.

Flaherty, C. F., & Davenport, J. W. Successive brightness discrimination in rats following regular versus random intermittent reinforcement. *JEP*, 1972, *96*, 1–9.

Flaherty, C. F., & Driscoll, C. Amobarbital sodium reduces successive gustatory contrast. *Psychopharmacology*, 1980, *69*, 161–162.

Flaherty, C. F., Hamilton, L. W., Gandelman, R. J., & Spear, N. E. *Learning and memory*. Chicago: Rand-McNally, 1977.

Flaherty, C. F., & Largen, J. Within-subjects positive and negative contrast effects in rats. *JCPP*, 1975, *88*, 653–664.

Flaherty, C. F., & Rowan, G. A. Anticipatory contrast: Within-subjects analysis. AL&B, in press.

Flaherty, C. F., Uzwiak, A. J., Levine, J., Smith, M., Hall, P., & Schuler, R. Apparent hyperglycemic and hypoglycemic conditioned responses with exogenous insulin as the unconditioned stimulus. *AL&B*, 1980, *8*, 382–386.

Fountain, S. B., Evensen, J. C., & Hulse, S. H. Formal structure and pattern length in serial pattern learning by rats. *AL&B*, 1983, *11*, 186–192.

Fowler, H. Suppression and facilitation by response contingent shock. In F. R. Brush (Ed.), *Aversive conditioning & learning*. New York: Academic Press, 1971.

Fowler, H., Fago, G. C., Domber, E. A., & Hochhauser, M. Signaling and affective functions in Pavlovian conditioning. *AL&B*, 1973, *1*, 81–89.

Fowler, H., & Trapold, M. A. Escape performance as a function of delay of reinforcement. *JEP*, 1962, *63*, 464–467.

Franchina, J. J., Kash, J. S., Reeder, J. R., & Sheets, C. T. Effects of exteroceptive feedback and safe-box confinement durations on escape behavior in rats. *AL&B*, 1978, *6*, 423–428.

Frey, P. W. Within- and between-session CS intensity performance effects in rabbit eyelid conditioning. *Psychonomic Science*, 1969, *17*, 1–2.

Frey, P. W., & Butler, C. S. Rabbit eyelid conditioning as a function of unconditioned stimulus duration. *JCPP*, 1973, *85*, 289–294.

Frey, P. W., & Ross, L. E. Classical conditioning of the rabbit eyelid response as a function of interstimulus interval. *JCPP*, 1968, *65*, 246–250.

Frey, P. W., & Ross, L. E. Rabbit eyelid conditioning: Effects of age, interstimulus interval, and intertrial interval. *Developmental Psychobiology*, 1968, *1*, 276–279.

Gage, F. H., Dunnett, S. B., & Kelly, P. A. T. Intrahippocampal septal grafts ameliorate learning impairments in aged rats. *Science*, 1984, *225*, 533–536.

Gage, F. H., Evans, S. H., & Olton, D. S. Multivariate analyses of performance in a DRL paradigm. *AL&B*, 1979, *7*, 323–327.

Gaioni, S. J., Hoffman, H. S., & DePaulo, P. Imprinting in older ducklings: Some tests of a reinforcement model. *AL&B*, 1978, *6*, 19–26.

Galef, B. G., Jr., & Osborne, B. Novel taste facilitation of the association of visual cues with toxicosis in rats. *JCPP*, 1978, *92*, 907–916.

Gallagher, M., Kapp, B. S., McNally, C. L., & Pascoe, J. P. Opiate effects in the amygdala central nucleus on heart rate conditioning in rabbits. *Pharmacology, Biochemistry, & Behavior*, 1981, *14*, 497–505.

Gallup, G. Towards a comparative psychology of mind. In R. L. Mellgren (Ed.), *Animal cognition and behavior*. North Holland, Amsterdam: 1983.

Gamzu, E. The multi-faceted nature of taste-aversion-inducing agents: Is there a single common factor? In L. M. Barker, M. R. Best, & M. Domjan (Eds.), *Learning mechanisms in food selection*. Waco, Tex.: Baylor University Press, 1977.

Gamzu, E. R., & Williams, D. R. Associative factors underlying the pigeon's key pecking in autoshaping procedures. *JEAB*, 1973, *19*, 225–232.

Gantt, W. H. The nervous secretion of saliva: The relation of the unconditioned reflex to the intensity of the unconditioned stimulus. *American Journal of Physiology*, 1938, *123*, 74.

Garber, J., & Seligman, M. E. P. (Eds.). *Human helplessness: Theory and applications*. New York: Academic Press, 1980.

Garcia, J., Ervin, F. R., & Koelling, R. A. Learning with prolonged delay of reinforcement. *Psychonomic Science*, 1966, *5*, 121–122.

Garcia, J., & Hankins, W. G. On the origin of food aversion paradigms. In L. M. Barker, M. R. Best, & M. Domjan (Eds.), *Learning mechanisms in food selection*. Waco, Tex.: Baylor University Press, 1977.

Garcia, J., Hankins, W. G., & Rusiniak, K. W. Behavioral regulation of the milieu interne in man and rat. *Science*, 1974, *185*, 824–831.

Garcia, J., Kimeldorf, D. J., & Koelling, E. L. Conditioned aversion to saccharin resulting from exposure to gamma radiation. *Science*, 1955, *122*, 157–158.

Garcia, J., & Koelling, R. A. Relation of cue to consequence in avoidance learning. *Psychonomic Science*, 1966, *4*, 123–124.

Gardner, B. T., & Gardner, R. A. Evidence for sentence constituents in the early utterances of child and chimpanzee. *JEP:General*, 1975, *104*, 244–267.

Gass, C. L., & Montgomerie, R. D. Hummingbird foraging behavior: Decision-making and energy regulation. In A. C. Kamil & T. D. Sargent (Eds.), *Foraging behavior: Ecological, ethological, and psychological approaches*. New York: Garland STPM Press, 1981.

Gatchel, R. J. Effectiveness of two procedures for reducing dental fear: Group administration and group education and discussion. *Journal of the American Dental Association*, 1980, *101*, 634–637.

Gatchel, R. J., & Baum, A. *An introduction to health psychology*. Reading, Mass.: Addison-Wesley, 1983.

Gemberling, G. A., & Domjan, M. Selective associations in one-day-old rats: Taste-toxicosis and texture-shock aversion learning. *JCPP*, 1982, *96*: 105–113.

Gemberling, G. A., Domjan, M., & Amsel, A. Aversion learning in 5-day-old rats: Taste-toxicosis and texture-shock associations. *JCPP*, 1980, *94*, 734–745.

Gentry, G. D., Weiss, B., & Laties, V. G. The microanalysis of fixed-interval responding. *JEAB*, 1983, *39*, 327–343.

Geschwind, N. The organization of language and the brain. *Science*, 1970, *170*, 940–944.

Gibbon, J. Timing and discrimination of shock density in avoidance. *Psychological Review*, 1972, *79*, 69–92.

Gibbon, J., Baldock, M. D., Locurto, C., Gold, L., & Terrace, H. S. Trial and intertrial durations in autoshaping. *JEP:ABP*, 1977, *3*, 264–284.

Gibbon, J., Farrell, L., Locurto, C. M., Duncan, H. J., & Terrace, H. S. Partial reinforcement in autoshaping with pigeons. *AL&B*, *1980*, *8*, 45–59.

Gibbs, C. M., Cohen, D. H., Broyles, J., & Solina, A. Conditioned modification of avian dorsal geniculate neurons is a function of their response to the unconditioned stimulus. Paper presented at Society for Neuroscience, 1981.

Gibbs, C. M., Latham, S. B., & Gormezano, I. Classical conditioning of the rabbit nictitating membrane response: Effects of reinforcement schedule on response maintenance and resistance to extinction. *AL&B*, 1978, *6*, 209–215.

Gilbertson, D. W. Courtship as a reinforcement for key pecking in the pigeon, *Columba livia*. *Animal Behaviour*, 1975, *23*, 735–744.

Gillan, D. J. Reasoning in the chimpanzee: II. Transitive inference. *JEP:ABP*, 1981, *7*, 150–164.

Gillette, K., & Bellingham, W. P. Loss of within-compound flavour associations: Configural conditioning. *JEAB*, 1982, *1*, 1–17.

Gillette, K., Martin, G. M., & Bellingham, W. P. Differential use of food and water cues in the formation of conditioned aversions by domestic chicks *(gallus gallus)*. *JEP:ABP*, 1980, *6*, 99–111.

Gleitman, H. Place learning without prior performance. *JCPP*, 1955, *48*, 77–79.

Gleitman, H. Forgetting of long-term memories in animals. In W. K. Honig & P. H. R. James (Eds.), *Animal memory*. New York: Academic Press, 1971.

Gleitman, H., & Holmes, P. Retention of incompletely learned CER in rats. *Psychonomic Science*, 1967, *7*, 19–20.

Glickman, S. E., & Schiff, B. B. A biological theory of reinforcement. *Psychological Review*, 1967, *74*, 81–109.

Goldman, L., Coover, G. D., & Levine, S. Bi-directional effects of reinforcement shifts on pituitary adrenal activity. *Physiology & Behavior*, 1973, *10*, 209–214.

Gollub, L. Conditioned reinforcement: Schedule effects. In W. K. Honig & J. E. R. Staddon (Eds.), *Handbook of operant behavior*. Englewood Cliffs, N.J.: Prentice-Hall, 1977.

Gonzalez, R. C., & Champlin, G. Positive behavioral contrast, negative simultaneous contrast, and their relation to frustration in pigeons. *JCPP*, 1974, *87*, 173–187.

Gonzalez, R. C., Fernhoff, D., & David, F. G. Contrast, resistance to extinction, and forgetting in rats. *JCPP*, 1973, *84*, 564–571.

Goodkin, F. Rats learn the relationship between responding and environmental events: An expansion of the learned helplessness hypothesis. *L&M*, 1976, *7*, 382–393.

Goodrich, K. P. Performance in different segments of an instrumental response chain as a function of reinforcement schedule. *JEP*, 1959, *57*, 57–63.

Goodrich, K. P., Ross, L. E., & Wagner, A. R. An examination of selected aspects of the continuity and noncontinuity positions in discrimination learning. *The Psychological Record*, 1961, *11*, 105–117.

Gordon, W. C. Susceptibility of a reactivated memory to the effects of strychnine: A time-dependent phenomenon. *Physiology & Behavior*, 1977, *18*, 95–99.

Gordon, W. C. Mechanisms of cue-induced retention enhancement. In N. E. Spear & R. R. Miller (Eds.), *Information processing in animals: Memory mechanisms*. Hillsdale, N.J.: Erlbaum, 1981.

Gordon, W. C., & Spear, N. E. The effects of strychnine on recently acquired and reactivated passive avoidance memories. *Phystology & Behavior*, 1973, *10*, 1071–1075.

Gormezano, I. Investigations of defense and reward conditioning in the rabbit. In A. H. Black & W. F. Prokasy (Eds.), *Classical conditioning 2: Current theory and research*. New York: Academic Press, 1972.

Gormezano, I., & Coleman, S. R. The law of effect and CR contingent modification of the UCS. *Conditional Reflex*, 1973, *8*, 41–56.

Gormezano, I., & Coleman, S. R. Effects of partial reinforcement on conditioning, conditional probabilities, asymptotic performance, and extinction of the rabbit's nictitating membrane response. *Pavlovian Journal of Biological Science*, 1975, *10*, 13–22.

Gormezano, I., & Hiller, G. W. Omission training of the jaw-movement response of the rabbit to a water US. *Psychonomic Science*, 1972, *29*, 276–278.

Gormezano, I., & Kehoe, E. J. Classical conditioning: Some methodological-conceptual issues. In W. K. Estes (Ed.), *Handbook of learning and cognitive processes: Vol. 2. Conditioning and behavior theory*. Hillsdale, N.J.: Erlbaum, 1975.

Could, J. L. *Ethology: The mechanisms and evolution of behavior*. New York: W. W. Norton, 1982.

Grant, D. S. Short-term memory in the pigeon. In N. E. Spear & R. R. Miller (Eds.), *Information processing in animals: Memory mechanisms*. Hillsdale, N.J.: Erlbaum, 1981.

Gray, J. A. Sodium amobarbital and effects of frustrative nonreward. *JCPP*, 1969, *69*, 55–64.

Gray, J. A. Sodium amobarbital, the hippocampal theta rhythm and the partial reinforcement extinction effect. *Psychological Review*, 1970, *77*, 465–480.

Gray, J. A. Stimulus control of differential reinforcement of low rate responding. *JEAB*, 1976, *25*, 199–207.

Gray, J. A. *The neuropsychology of anxiety: An enquiry into the functions of the septo-hippocampal system*. New York: Oxford University Press, 1982.

Gray, J. A., Davis, N., Feldon, J., Nicholas, P., Rawlins, P., & Owen, S. R. *Animal models of anxiety*. In *Progress in Neuro-psychopharmacology*. London: Pergamon Press, 1981, 143–157.

Gray, T., & Appignanesi, A. A. Compound conditioning: Elimination of the blocking effect. *Learning and Motivation*, 1973, *4*, 374–380.

Green, L., & Rachlin, H. On the directionality of key pecking during signals for appetitive and aversive events. *L&M*, 1977, *8*, 551–568.

Grice, G. R. The relation of secondary reinforcement to delayed reward in visual discrimination learning. *JEP*, 1948, *38*, 1–16.

Grice, G. R., & Hunter, J. J. Stimulus intensity effects depend upon the type of experimental design. *Psychological Review*, 1964, *71*, 247–256.

Griffin, D. R. *The question of animal awareness*. New York: Rockefeller University Press, 1976.

Grossberg, S. Processing of expected and unexpected events during conditioning and attention: A psychophysiological theory. *Psychological Review*, 1982, *89*, 529–572.

Grossen, N. E., & Bolles, R. C. Effects of a classical conditioned "fear signal" and "safety signal" on nondiscriminated avoidance behavior. *Psychonomic Science*, 1968, *11*, 321–322.

Groves, P. M., & Thompson, R. F. Dual-process theory of habituation: Neural mechanisms. In H. V. S. Peeke & M. J. Herz (Eds.), *Habituation: Physiological substrates* (Vol. 2). New York: Academic Press, 1973.

Gustavson, C. R. Comparative and field aspects of learned food aversions. In L. M. Barker, M. R. Best, & M. Domjan (Eds.), *Learning mechanisms in food selection*. Waco, Tex.: Baylor University, 1977.

Guthrie, E. R. *The psychology of learning* (2nd ed.). New York: Harper & Row, 1952.

Gutman, A., Sutterer, J. R., & Brush, F. R. Positive and negative behavioral contrast in the rat. *JEAB*, 1975, *23*, 377–383.

Guttman, N. Equal-reinforcement values for sucrose and glucose solutions as compared with equal sweetness values. *JEP*, 1954, *47*, 358–361.

Guttman, N., & Kalish, H. I. Discriminability and stimulus generalization. *JEP*, 1956, *51*, 79–88.

Gynther, M. D. Differential eyelid conditioning as a function of stimulus similarity and strength of response to the CS. *JEP*, 1957, *53*, 408–416.

Haber, A., & Kalish, H. I. Prediction of discrimination from generalization after variation in schedule of reinforcement. *Science*, 1963, *142*, 412–413.

Haig, K. A., Rawlins, J. N. P., Olton, D. S., Mead, A., & Taylor, B. Food searching strategies of rats: Variables affecting the relative strength of stay and shift strategies. *JEP:ABP*, 1983, *9*, 337–348.

Hall, G., & Honig, W. K. Stimulus control after extradimensional training in pigeons: A comparison of response contingent and noncontingent training procedures. *JCPP*, 1974, *87*, 945–952.

Hall, G., & Pearce, J. M. Restoring the associability of a pre-exposed CS by a surprising event. *Quarterly Journal of Experimental Psychology*, 1982, *34B*, 127–140.

Halliday, M. S., & Boakes, R. A. Behavioral contrast and response independent reinforcement. *JEAB*, 1971, *16*, 429–434.

Halliday, M. S., & Boakes, R. A. Behavioral contrast without response rate reduction. *JEAB*, 1974, *22*, 463–467.

Hamilton, L. W. Active avoidance impairment following septal lesions in rats. *JCPP*, 1969, *69*, 420–431.

Hammond, L. J. A traditional demonstration of the properties of Pavlovian inhibition using differential CER. *Psychonomic Science*, 1967, *9*, 65–66.

Hammond, L. J. Retardation of fear acquisition when the CS has previously been inhibitory. *JCPP*, 1968, *66*, 756–759.

Hannum, R., Rosellini, R., & Seligman, M. E. P. Learned helplessness in the rat: Retention and immunization. *Developmental Psychology*, 1976, *12*, 449–454.

Hanson, H. M. Effects of discrimination training on stimulus generalization. *JEP*, 1959, *58*, 321–334.

Harlow, H. F. The formation of learning sets. *Psychological Review*, 1949, *56*, 51–65.

Harlow, H. F. Primate learning. In C. P. Stone (Ed.), *Comparative psychology*. New York: Prentice-Hall, 1951.

Harlow, H. F. Learning set and error factor theory. In S. Koch (Ed.), *Psychology: A study of a science* (Vol. 2). New York: McGraw-Hill, 1959.

Haroutunian, V., & Riccio, D. C. Acquisition of rotation-induced taste aversion as a function of drinking-treatment delay. *Physiological Psychology*, 1975, *3*, 273–277.

Hearst, E. Excitation, inhibition and discrimination learning. In N. J. Mackintosh & W. K. Honig (Eds.), *Fundamental issues in associative learning*. Halifax, N.S.: Dalhousie University Press, 1969.

Hearst, E. Some persistent problems in the analysis of conditioned inhibition. In R. A. Boakes and M. S. Halliday (Eds.), *Inhibition and learning*. London: Academic Press, 1972.

Hearst, E. The classical-instrumental distinction: Reflexes, voluntary behavior, and categories of associative learning. In W. K. Estes (Ed.), *Handbook of learning and cognitive processes Vol. 2: Conditioning and behavior theory*. Hillsdale, N.J.: Erlbaum, 1975.

Hearst, E. Stimulus relationships and feature selection in learning and behavior. In S. H. Hulse, H. Fowler, & W. K. Honig (Eds.), *Cognitive processes in animal behavior*. Hillsdale, N.J.: Erlbaum, 1978.

Hearst, E. Classical conditioning as the formation of interstimulus associations: Stimulus substitution, parasitic reinforcement, and autoshaping. In A. Dickinson & R. A. Boakes (Eds.), *Mechanisms of learning and motivation: A memorial volume to Jerzy Konorski*. Hillsdale, N.J.: Erlbaum, 1979.

Hearst, E., Besley, S., & Farthing, G. W. Inhibition and the stimulus control of operant behavior. *JEAB*, 1970, *14*, 373–409.

Hearst, E., & Franklin, S. R. Positive and negative relations between a signal and food: Approach-withdrawal behavior to the signal. *JEP:ABP*, 1977, *3*, 37–52.

Hearst, E., & Jenkins, H. M. *Sign tracking: The stimulus-reinforcer relation and directed action*. Austin, Tex.: Monograph of the Psychonomic Society, 1974.

Hearst, E., Koresko, M. B., & Popper, R. Stimulus generalization and the response-reinforcement contingency. *JEAB*, 1964, *7*, 369–380.

Hearst, E., & Peterson, G. B. Transfer of conditioned excitation and inhibition from one operant response to another. *JEP*, 1973, *99*, 360–368.

Hemmes, N. S., Eckerman, D. A., & Rubinsky, H. J. A functional analysis of collateral behavior under differential-reinforcement-of-low-rate schedules. *AL&B*, 1979, *7*, 328–332.

Hemmes, N. S., & Rubinsky, H. J. Conditional acceleration and external disinhibition of operant lever pressing by prereward, neutral, and reinforcing stimuli. *JEAB*, 1982, *38*, 157–168.

Hendry, D. D. (Ed.). *Conditioned reinforcement*. Homewood, Ill.: Dorsey, 1969.

Henke, P. G. Persistence of runway performance after septal lesions in rats. *JCPP*, 1974, *86*, 760–767.

Henke, P. G., Allen, J. D., & Davison, C. Effects of lesions in the amygdala on behavioral contrast. *Physiology & Behavior*, 1972, *8*, 173–176.

Hergenhahn, B. R. *An introduction to theories of learning*. Englewood Cliffs, N.J.: Prentice-Hall, 1982.

Herman, L. M., & Thompson, R. K. R. Symbolic, identity, and probe delayed matching of sounds in the bottlenosed dolphin. *AL&B*, 1982, *10*, 22–34.

Hernandez, L. L., Buchanan, S. L., & Powell, D. A. CS preexposure: Latent inhibition and Pavlovian conditioning of heart rate and eyeblink responses as a function of sex and CS intensity in rabbits. *AL&B*, 1981, *9*, 513–518.

Hernandez-Peon, R. Reticular mechanisms of sensory control. In W. A. Rosenblith (Ed.), *Sensory communication*. Cambridge, Mass.: M.I.T. Press, 1961.

Herrmann, T., Bahr, E., Bremner, B., & Ellen, P. Problem solving in the rat: Stay vs. shift solutions on the three-table task. *AL&B*, 1982, *10*, 39–45.

Herrnstein, R. J. On the law of effect. *JEAB*, 1970, *13*, 243–266.

Herrnstein, R. J. Formal properties of the matching law. *JEAB*, 1974, *21*, 159–164.

Herrnstein, R. J. Acquisition, generalization, and discrimination reversal of a natural concept. *JEP:ABP*, 1979, *5*, 116–129.

Herrnstein, R. J., & Hineline, P. N. Negative reinforcement as shock frequency reduction. *JEAB*, 1966, *9*, 421–430.

Herrnstein, R. J., Loveland, D. H., & Cable, C. Natural concepts in pigeons. *JEP:ABP*, 1976, *2*, 285–302.

Hess, E. H. Imprinting: An effect of early experience. *Science*, 1959, *130*, 133–141.

Heth, C. D. Simultaneous and backward fear conditioning as a function of number of CS-UCS pairings. *JEP:ABP*, 1976, *2*, 117–129.

Heth, C. D., & Rescorla, R. A. Simultaneous and backward fear conditioning in the rat. *JCPP*, 1973, *82*, 434–443.

Hilgard, E. R., & Bower, G. H. *Theories of Learning*. Englewood Cliffs, N.J.: Prentice-Hall, 1975.

Hill, W. F., Cotton, J. W., & Clayton, K. N. Effect of reward magnitude, percentage of reinforcement, and training method on acquisition and reversal in a T-maze. *JEP*, 1962, *64*, 81–86.

Hill, W. F., & Spear, N. E. Resistance to extinction as a joint function of reward magnitude and the spacing of extinction trials. *JEP*, 1962, *64*, 636–639.

Hill, W. F., & Spear, N. E. Choice between magnitudes of reward in a T-maze. *JCPP*, 1963, *56*, 723–726.

Hinson, R. E., & Poulos, C. X. Sensitization to the behavioral effects of cocaine: Modification by Pavlovian conditioning. *Pharmacology, Biochemistry & Behavior*, 1981, *15*, 559–562.

Hinson, R. E. & Siegel, S. Trace conditioning as an inhibitory procedure. *AL&B*, 1980, *8*, 60–66.

Hirsch, E., & Collier, G. The ecological determinants of reinforcement in the guinea pig. *Physiology and Behavior*, 1974, *12*, 239–249.

Hoehler, F. K., & Leonard, D. W. Motivational vs. associative role of the US in classical conditioning of the rabbit's nictitating membrane response. *AL&B*, 1981, *9*, 239–244.

Hoffman, H. S., Eiserer, L. A., & Singer, D. Acquisition of behavioral control by a stationary imprinting stimulus. *Psychonomic Science*, 1972, *26*, 146–148.

Hoffman, H. S., Fleshler, M., & Jensen, P. Stimulus aspects of aversive controls: The retention of conditioned suppression. *JEAB*, 1963, *6*, 575–583.

Hoffman, H. S., & Ratner, A. M. A reinforcement model of imprinting: Implications for socialization in monkeys and men. *Psychological Review*, 1973, *80*, 527–544.

Hoffman, H. S., Ratner, A. M., & Eiserer, L. A. Role of visual imprinting in the emergence of specific filial attachments in ducklings. *JCPP*, 1972, *81*, 399–409.

Hoffman, H. S., Searle, J. L., Toffey, S., & Kozma, F., Jr. Behavioral control by an imprinted stimulus. *JEAB*, 1966, *9*, 177–189.

Hoffman, H. S., Stratton, J. W., & Newby, V. Punishment by response-contingent withdrawal of an imprinting stimulus. *Science*, 1969, 163, 702–704.

Hoffman, J. W., & Fitzgerald, R. D. Bidirectional heart rate response in rats associated with excitatory and inhibitory stimuli. *AL&B*, 1982, 10, 77–82.

Holland, P. C. Conditioned stimulus as a determinant of the form of the Pavlovian conditioned response. *JEP:ABP*, 1977, 3, 77–104.

Holland, P. C. The effects of qualitative and quantitative variation in the US on individual components of Pavlovian appetitive conditioned behavior in rats. *AL&B*, 1979, 7, 424–432.

Holland, P. C. Influence of visual conditioned stimulus characteristics on the form of Pavlovian appetitive conditioned responding in rats. *JEP:ABP*, 1980a, 6, 81–97.

Holland, P. C. CS-US interval as a determinant of the form of Pavlovian appetitive conditioned responses. *JEP:ABP*, 1980b, 6, 155–174.

Holland, P. C. The effects of satiation after first- and second-order appetitive conditioning in rats. *Pavlovian Journal of Biological Science*, 1981a, 16, 18–24.

Holland, P. C. Acquisition of representation-mediated conditioned food aversions. *L&M*, 1981b, 12, 1–18.

Holland, P. C., & Rescorla, R. A. The effects of two ways of devaluing the unconditioned stimulus after first- and second-order appetitive conditioning. *JEP:ABP*, 1975, 1, 355–363.

Holland, P. C., & Straub, J. J. Differential effects of two ways of devaluing the unconditioned stimulus after Pavlovian appetitive conditioning. *JEP:ABP*, 1979, 5, 65–78.

Honig, W. K. Attentional factors governing the slope of the generalization gradient. In R. M. Gilbert and N. S. Sutherland (Eds.), *Animal discrimination learning*. London: Academic Press, 1969.

Honig, W. K. Working memory and the temporal map. In N. E. Spear & R. R. Miller (Eds.), *Information processing in animals: Memory mechanisms*. Hillsdale, N.J.: Erlbaum, 1981.

Honig, W. K. Can animal learning learn anything from animal memory? In H. L. Roitblat, T. C. Bever, & H. S. Terrace (Eds.), *Animal cognition*. Hillsdale, N.J.: Erlbaum, 1984.

Honig, W. K., Boneau, C. A., Burstein, K. R., & Pennypacker, H. S. Positive and negative generalization gradients obtained after equivalent training conditions. *JCPP*, 1963, 56, 111–116.

Honig, W. K., & Thompson, R. K. R. Retrospective and prospective processing in animal working memory. In G. H. Bower (Ed.), *The psychology of learning and motivation* (Vol. 6). New York: Academic Press, 1984.

Honig, W. K., & Urcuioli, P. J. The legacy of Guttman and Kalish (1956): 25 years of research on stimulus generalization. *JEAB*, 1981, 36, 405–445.

Honzik, C. H. The sensory basis of maze learning in rats. *Comparative Psychology Monographs*, 1936, 13, No. 4.

Howard, J. L., Obrist, P. A., Gaebelein, C. J., & Galosy, R. A. Multiple somatic measures and heart rate during classical aversive conditioning in the cat. *JCPP*, 1974, 87, 228–236.

Hull, C. L. *Principles of behavior*. New York: Appleton-Century-Crofts, 1943.

Hull, J. H. Instrumental response topographies of rats. *AL&B*, 1977, 5, 207–212.

Hulse, S. H. Amount and percentage of reinforcement and duration of goal confinement in conditioning and extinction. *JEP*, 1958, 56, 48–57.

Hulse, S. H. Cognitive structure and serial pattern learning by rats. In S. H. Hulse, H. Fowler, & W. K. Honig (Eds.), *Cognitive processes in animal behavior*. Hillsdale, N.J.: Erlbaum, 1978.

Hulse, S. H., & Dorsky, N. P. Structural complexity as a determinant of serial pattern learning. *L&M*, 1977, 8, 488–506.

Hulse, S. H., & Dorsky, N. P. Serial pattern learning by rats: Transfer of a formally defined stimulus relationship and the significance of nonreinforcement. *AL&B*, 1979, 7, 211–220.

Hulse, S. H., Fowler, H., & Honig, W. K. (Eds.). *Cognitive processes in animal behavior*. Hillsdale, N.J.: Erlbaum, 1978.

Hulse, S. H., & O'Leary, D. Serial pattern learning: Teaching an alphabet to rats. *JEP:ABP*, 1982, 8, 260–273.

Humphreys, L. G. Acquisition and extinction of verbal expectations in a situation analogous to conditioning. *JEP*, 1939, 25, 294–301.

Hyson, R. L., Ashcraft, L. J., Drugan, R. C., Gru, J. W., & Maier, S. F. Extent and control of shock affects naltrexone sensitivity of stress-induced analgesia and reactivity to morphine. *Pharmacology, Biochemistry, and Behavior*, 1982, 17, 1019–1025.

Imada, H., Yamazaki, A., & Morishita, M. The effects of signal intensity upon conditioned suppression: Effects upon responding during signals and intersignal intervals. *AL&B*, 1981, *9*, 269–274.

Ison, J. R., & Cook, P. E. Extinction performance as a function of incentive magnitude and number of acquisition trials. *Psychonomic Science*, 1964, *1*, 245–246.

Ison, J. R., & Pennes, E. S. Interaction of amobarbital sodium and reinforcement schedule in determining resistance to extinction of an instrumental running response. *JCPP*, 1969, *68*, 215–219.

Ito, M., & Asaki, K. Choice behavior of rats in a concurrent-chains schedule: Amount and delay of reinforcement. *JEAB*, 1982, *37*, 383–392.

Jackson, R. L., Alexander, J. H., & Maier, S. F. Learned helplessness, inactivity, and associative deficits: Effects of inescapable shock on response choice escape learning. *JEP:ABP*, 1980, *6*, 1–20.

Jackson, R. L., Maier, S. F., & Coon, D. J. Long-term analgesic effects of inescapable shock and learned helplessness. *Science*, 1979, *206*, 91–93.

Jacobs, W. J., & LoLordo, V. M. The sensory basis of avoidance responding in the rat. *L&M*, 1977, *8*, 448–466.

Jacobs, W. J., & LoLordo, V. M. Constraints on Pavlovian aversive conditioning: Implications for avoidance learning in the rat. *L&M*, 1980, *11*, 427–455.

Jaffe, M. L. The effects of lesions in the ventromedial nucleus of the hypothalamus on behavioral contrast in rats. *Physiological Psychology*, 1973, *1*, 191–198.

James, W. *Principles of psychology*. New York: Holt, 1890.

Jaynes, J. Imprinting: The interaction of learned and innate behavior: III. Practice effects in performance, retention, and fear. *JCPP*, 1958a, *51*, 234–237.

Jaynes, J. Imprinting: The interaction of learned and innate behavior: IV. Generalization and emergent discrimination. *JCPP*, 1958b, *51*, 238–242.

Jeffers, V., & Lore, R. Let's play at my house: Effects of the home environment on the social behavior of children. *Child Development*, 1979, *50*, 837–841.

Jenkins, H. M. Sensitivity of different response systems to stimulus-reinforcer and response-reinforcer relations. In H. Davis & H. M. B. Hurwitz (Eds.), *Operant-Pavlovian interactions*. Hillsdale, N.J.: Erlbaum, 1977.

Jenkins, H. M. Animal learning and behavior theory. In E. Hearst (Ed.), *The first century of experimental psychology*. Hillsdale, N.J.: Erlbaum, 1979.

Jenkins, H. M., Barrera, F. J., Ireland, C., & Woodside, B. Signal-centered action patterns of dogs in appetitive classical conditioning. *Learning and Motivation*, 1978, *9*, 272–296.

Jenkins, H. M., & Harrison, R. H. Effect of discrimination training on auditory generalization. *JEP*, 1960, *59*, 246–253.

Jenkins, H. M., & Moore, B. R. The form of the autoshaped response with food or water reinforcers. *JEAB*, 1973, *20*, 163–181.

Jenkins, P. E., Chadwick, R. A., & Nevin, J. A. Classically conditioned enhancement of antibody production. *Bulletin of the Psychonomic Society*, 1983, *21*, 485–487.

Johnson, C. T., Olton, D. S., Gage, F., III, & Jenko, P. S. Hippocampus, hippocampal connections, and DRL. *JCPP*, 1977, *91*, 508–522.

Johnston, T. D. Contrasting approaches to a theory of learning. *The Behavioral and Brain Sciences*, 1981, *4*, 125–173.

Jones, J. E. Contiguity and reinforcement in relation to CS-UCS intervals in classical aversive conditioning. *Psychological Review*, 1962, *69*, 176–186.

Kalat, J. W. Status of "learned safety" or "learned noncorrelation" as a mechanism in taste-aversion learning. In L. M. Barker, M. R. Best, & M. Domjan (Eds.), *Learning mechanisms in food selection*. Waco, Tex.: Baylor University Press, 1977.

Kalat, J. W., & Rozin, P. "Salience": A factor which can override temporal contiguity in taste-aversion learning. *JCPP*, 1970, *71*, 192–197.

Kalat, J. W., & Rozin, P. "Learned safety" as a mechanism in long-delay taste-aversion learning in rats. *JCPP*, 1973, *83*, 198–207.

Kamil, A. C. Systematic foraging by a nectar-feeding bird, the Amakihi *(Loxop virens)*. *JCPP*, 1978, *92*, 388–396.

Kamil, A. C., & Balda, R. P. Spatial memory and food cache recovery by nutcrackers. Paper presented at the Psychonomic Society Meeting, San Diego, 1983.

Kamil, A. C., Jones, T. B., Pietrewicz, A., & Mauldin, J. E. Positive transfer from successive reversal training to learning set in blue jays *(Cyanocitta cristata)*. *JCPP*, 1977, *91*, 79–86.

Kamil, A. C., & Mauldin, J. E. Intraproblem retention during learning-set acquisition in blue jays *(Cyanocitta cristata)*. *AL&B*, 1975, *3*, 125–130.

Kamin, L. J. The gradient of delay of secondary reward in avoidance learning. *JCPP*, 1957, *50*, 457–460.

Kamin, L. J. The delay of punishment gradient. *JCPP*, 1959, *52*, 434–437.

Kamin, L. J. Temporal and intensity characteristics of the conditioned stimulus. In W. F. Prokasy (Ed.), *Classical conditioning: A symposium*. New York: Appleton-Century-Crofts, 1965.

Kamin, L. J. Predictability, surprise, attention, and conditioning. In B. A. Campbell & R. M. Church (Eds.), *Punishment and aversive behavior*. New York: Appleton-Century-Crofts, 1969.

Kamin, L. J., Brimer, C. J., & Black, A. H. Conditioned suppression as a monitor of fear of the CS in the course of avoidance training. *JCPP*, 1963, *56*, 497–501.

Kamin, L. J., & Gaioni, S. J. Compound conditioned emotional response conditioning with differentially salient elements in rats. *JCPP*, 1974, *87*, 591–597.

Kanarek, R. B. The energetics of meal patterns. Unpublished doctoral dissertation, Rutgers University, 1974.

Kanarek, R. B. Availability and caloric density of the diet as determinants of meal patterns in cats. *P&B*, 1975, *15*, 611–618.

Kandel, E. R. Nerve cells and behavior. *Scientific American*, 1970, *223*, 57–70.

Kandel, E. R. Cellular insights into behavior and learning. *The Harvey Lectures, Series 73*. New York: Academic Press, 1979a.

Kandel, E. R. Small systems of neurons. *Scientific American*, 1979b, *241*, 67–76.

Kandel, E. R. Steps toward a molecular grammar for learning: Explorations into the nature of memory. In *Harvard Bicentennial Symposium*, 1983.

Kandel, E. R., & Schwartz, J. H. Molecular biology of learning: Modulation of transmitter release. *Science*, 1982, *218*, 433–443.

Kaplan, P. S. The importance of relative temporal parameters in trace autoshaping: From excitation to inhibition. *JEP:ABP*, 1984, *10*, 113–126.

Kaplan, P. S., & Hearst, E. Bridging temporal gaps between CS and US in autoshaping: Insertion of other stimuli before, during, and after CS. *JEP:ABP*, 1982, *8*, 187–203.

Karpicke, J. Directed approach responses and positive conditioned suppression in the rat. *AL&B*, 1978, *6*, 216–224.

Karpicke, J., Christoph, G., Peterson, G., & Hearst, E. Signal location and positive versus negative conditioned suppression in the rat. *JEP:ABP*, 1977, *3*, 105–118.

Karpicke, J., & Hearst, E. Inhibitory control and errorless discrimination learning. *JEAB*, 1975, *23*, 159–166.

Kaufman, L. W. Foraging strategies: Laboratory simulations. Unpublished doctoral dissertation, Rutgers University, 1979.

Kaye, H., & Pearce, J. M. The strength of the orienting response during Pavlovian conditioning. *JEP:ABP*, 1984, *10*, 90–109.

Keehn, J. D. The effect of a warning signal on unrestricted avoidance behavior. *British Journal of Psychology*, 1959, *50*, 125–135.

Keesey, R. E., & Kling, J. W. Amount of reinforcement and free operant responding. *JEAB*, 1961, *4*, 125–132.

Kehoe, E. J., Feyer, A. M., & Moses, J. L. Second-order conditioning of the rabbit's nictitating membrane response as a function of the CS2-CS1 and CS1-US intervals. *AL&B*, 1981, *9*, 304–315.

Kehoe, E. J., Gibbs, C. M., Garcia, A., & Gormezano, I. Associative transfer and stimulus selection in classical conditioning of the rabbit's nictitating membrane response to serial compound CS. *JEP:ABP*, 1979, *5*, 1–19.

Kehoe, E. J. & Gormezano, I. Effects of trials per session on conditioning of the rabbit's nictitating membrane response. *Bulletin of the Psychonomic Society*, 1974, *2*, 434–436.

Keith-Lucas, T., & Guttman, N. Robust single-trial delayed backward conditioning. *JCPP*, 1975, *88*, 468–476.

Keller, R. J., Ayres, J. J. B., & Mahoney, W. J. Brief versus extended exposure to truly random control procedures. *JEP:ABP*, 1977, *3*, 53–65.

Kendall, S. B. Some effects of response dependent clock stimuli in a fixed interval schedule. *JEAB*, 1972, *17*, 161–168.

Kettlewell, H. B. D. Darwin's missing evidence. *Scientific American*, 1959, *200*, 48–53.

Killeen, P. R. On the temporal control of behavior. *Psychological Review*, 1975, *82*, 89–115.

Killeen, P. R. Incentive theory II: Models for choice. *JEAB*, 1982, *38*, 217–232.

Killeen, P. R., Smith, J. P., & Hanson, S. J. Central place foraging in *Rattus norvegicus*. *Animal Behavior*, 1981, *29*, 64–70.

Kimble, G. A. *Hilgard and Marquis' Conditioning and Learning*. New York: Appleton-Century-Crofts, 1961.

Kimmel, H. D. "Pavlov's Wednesdays": Sensory preconditioning. *American Journal of Psychology*, 1977, *90*, 319–321.

Kimmel, H. D., & Burns, R. A. Adaptational aspects of conditioning. In W. K. Estes (Ed.), *Handbook of learning and cognitive processes: Vol. 2, Conditioning and behavior theory*. Hillsdale, N.J.: Erlbaum, 1975.

King, D. L. *Conditioning: An image approach*. New York: Gardner Press, 1979.

Klein, M., & Rilling, M. Generalization of free operant avoidance behavior in pigeons. *JEAB*, 1974, *21*, 75–88.

Klinger, E. *Meaning and void: Inner experience and the incentives in people's lives*. Minneapolis: University of Minnesota Press, 1977.

Knapp, R. K. Acquisition and extinction of avoidance with similar and different shock and escape situations. *JCPP*, 1965, *60*, 272–273.

Kohler, W. *The mentality of apes*. New York: Harcourt, Brace, 1926.

Konishi, M. The role of auditory feedback in the control of vocalization in the white-crowned sparrow. *Zeitschrift für Tierpsychologie*, 1965, *22*, 770–783.

Konorski, J. *Conditioned reflexes and neuron organization*. New York: Hafner, 1948.

Konorski, J. *Integrative activity of the brain: An interdisciplinary approach*. Chicago: University of Chicago Press, 1967.

Konorski, J., & Miller, S. On two types of conditioned reflex. *Journal of General Psychology*, 1937a, *16*, 264–272.

Konorski, J., & Miller, S. Further remarks on two types of conditioned reflex. *Journal of General Psychology*, 1937b, *17*, 405–407.

Krane, R. V. Toxiphobia conditioning with exteroceptive cues. *AL&B*, 1980, *8*, 513–523.

Krane, R. V., & Wagner, A. R. Taste aversion learning with a delayed shock US: Implications for the "generality of the laws of learning." *JCPP*, 1975, *88*, 882–889.

Krank, M. D., Hinson, R. E., & Siegel, S. Conditioned hyperalgesia is elicited by environmental signals of morphine. *Behavioral and Neural Biology*, 1981, *37*, 148–157.

Krasnegor, N. A. (Ed.). *Behavioral tolerance: Research and treatment implications*. Research Monograph. Washington, D. C.: Department of Health, Education, and Welfare, 1978.

Krebs, J. R. Optimal foraging: Decision rules for predators. In J. R. Krebs & N. B. Davies (Eds.), *Behavioral ecology*. Sunderland, Mass.: Sinauer, 1978.

Krechevsky, I. "Hypotheses" in rats. *Psychological Review*, 1932, *39*, 516–532.

Krechevsky, I. A study of the continuity of the problem-solving process. *Psychological Review*, 1938, *45*, 107–134.

Kremer, E., Specht, T., & Allen, R. Attenuation of blocking with the omission of a delayed US. *AL&B*, 1980, *8*, 609–616.

Krieckhaus, E. E., & Wolf, G. Acquisition of sodium by rats: Interactions of innate mechanisms and latent learning. *JCPP*, 1968, *65*, 197–201.

Labbe, R., Firl, A., Jr., Mufson, E. J., & Stein, D. G. Fetal brain transplants: Reduction of cognitive deficits in rats with frontal cortex lesions. *Science*, 1983, *221*, 470–472.

Lachman, J. L., & Lachman, R. General process theory, ecology, and animal-human continuity: A cognitive perspective. *The Behavioral and Brain Sciences*, 1981, *4*, 149–150.

Lajoie, J., & Bindra, D. Contributions of stimulus-incentive and stimulus-response incentive contingencies to response acquisition and maintenance. *AL&B*, 1978, *6*, 301–307.

Lashley, K. S., & Wade, M. The Pavlovian theory of generalization. *Psychological Review*, 1946, *53*, 72–87.

Laudenslager, M. L., Ryan, S. M., Drugan, R. C., Hyson, R. L., & Maier, S. F. Coping and immunosuppression: Inescapable but not escapable shock suppresses lymphocyte proliferation. *Science*, 1983, *221*, 568–570.

Lawrence, D. H. Acquired distinctiveness of cues: I. Transfer between discriminations on the basis of familiarity with the stimulus. *JEP*, 1949, *39*, 770–784.

Lawrence, D. H. Acquired distinctiveness of cues: II. Selective association in a constant stimulus situation. *JEP*, 1950, *40*, 175–188.

Lawrence, D. H. The transfer of a discrimination along a continuum. *JCPP*, 1952, *45*, 511–516.

Le, A. D., Poulos, C. X., & Cappell, H. Conditioned tolerance to the hypothermic effect of ethyl alcohol. *Science*, 1979, *206*, 1109–1110.

Lea, S. E. A. In what sense do pigeons learn concepts? In H. L. Roitblat, T. G. Bever, & H. S. Terrace (Eds.), *Animal cognition*. Hillsdale, N.J.: Erlbaum, 1984.

Leaf, R. C. Avoidance response evocation as a function of prior discriminative fear conditioning under curare. *JCPP*, 1964, *58*, 446–449.

Leaton, R. N. Habituation of startle response, lick suppression, and exploratory behavior in rats with hippocampal lesions. *JCPP*, 1981, *95*, 813–826.

Leaton, R. N., & Jordon, W. P. Habituation of the EEG arousal response in rats: Short- and long-term effects, frequency specificity, and wake-sleep transfer. *JCPP*, 1978, *92*, 803–814.

Lett, B. T. Long delay learning in the T-maze. *L&M*, 1975, *6*, 80–90.

Lett, B. T. Regarding Robert's reported failure to obtain visual discrimination learning with delayed reward. *L&M*, 1977, *8*, 136–139.

Lett, B. T. Taste potentiates color-sickness associations in pigeons and quail. *AL&B*, 1980, *8*, 193–198.

Levey, A. B., & Martin, I. Shape of the conditioned eyelid response. *Psychological Review*, 1968, *75*, 398–408.

Levine, J. D., Gordon, N. C., & Fields, H. L. The mechanism of placebo analgesia. *Lancet*, 1978, 654–657.

Lewis, D. J. Psychobiology of active and inactive memory. *Psychological Bulletin*, 1979, *86*, 1054–1083.

Lewis, D. J., Miller, R. R., & Misanin, J. R. Selective amnesia in rats reduced by electroconvulsive shock. *JCPP*, 1969, *69*, 136–140.

Lieberman, D. A., McIntosh, D. C., & Thomas, G. V. Learning when reward is delayed: A marking hypothesis. *JEP:ABP*, 1979, *5*, 224–242.

Light, J. S., & Gantt, W. H. Essential part of reflex for establishment of conditioned reflex. Formation of conditioned reflex after exclusion of motor peripheral end. *Journal of Comparative Psychology*, 1936, *21*, 19–36.

Linden, D. R. The effect of intensity of intermittent punishment in acquisition on resistance to extinction of an approach response. *AL&B*, 1974, *2*, 9–12.

Linden, D. R., & Hallgren, S. O. Transfer of approach responding between punishment and frustrative nonreward sustained through continuous reinforcement. *L&M*, 1973, *4*, 207–217.

Liu, I. A theory of classical conditioning. *Psychological Review*, 1964, *71*, 408–411.

Liu, S. S. Differential conditioning and stimulus generalization of the rabbit's nictitating membrane response. *JCPP*, 1971, *77*, 136–142.

Locurto, C. M., Duncan, H., Terrace, H. S., & Gibbon, J. Autoshaping in the rat: Interposing delays between responses and food. *AL&B*, 1980, *8*, 37–44.

Locurto, C. M., Terrace, H. S., & Gibbon, J. Omission training (negative automaintenance) in the rat: Effect of trial offset. *Bulletin of the Psychonomic Society*, 1978, *12*, 11–14.

Locurto, C. M., Tierney, J., & Fitzgerald, S. Omission training and positive conditioned suppression in the rat. *AL&B*, 1981, *9*, 261–268.

Logan, F. A. A note on stimulus intensity dynamism (V). *Psychological Review*, 1954, *61*, 77–80.

Logan, F. A. *Incentive*. New Haven: Yale University Press, 1960.

Logan, F. A. Decision making by rats: Delay versus amount of reward. *Journal of Comparative and Physiological Psychology*, 1965, *59*, 1–12.

Logue, A. W. Taste aversion and the generality of the laws of learning. *Psychological Bulletin*, 1979, *86*, 276–296.

Logue, A. W., Logue, K. R., & Strauss, K. E. The acquisition of taste aversions in humans with eating and drinking disorders. *Behavior Research and Therapy*, 1983, *21*, 275–289.

LoLordo, V. M. Selective associations. In A. Dickinson & R. A. Boakes (Eds.), *Mechanisms of learning & motivation: A memorial volume to Jerzy Konorski*. Hillsdale, N.J.: Erlbaum, 1979.

LoLordo, V. M., & Furrow, D. R. Control by the auditory or the visual element of a compound discriminative stimulus: Effects of feedback. *JEAB*, 1976, *25*, 251–256.

Lore, R., Nikoletseas, M., & Takahashi, L. Colony aggression in laboratory rats: A review and some recommendations. *Aggressive Behavior*, 1984, *10*, 59–71.

Lovejoy, E. Analysis of the overlearning reversal effect. *Psychological Review*, 1966, *73*, 87–103.

Lubow, R. E. Latent inhibition. *Psychological Bulletin*, 1973, *79*, 398–407.

Lucas, G. A., Deich, J. D., & Wasserman, E. A. Trace autoshaping: Acquisition, maintenance and path dependence at long trace intervals. *JEAB*, 1981, *36*, 61–74.

Ludvigson, H. W., McNeese, R. R., & Collerain, I. Long-term reaction of the rat to conspecific (frustration) odor. *AL&B*, 1979, *7*, 251–258.

Lukowiak, K., & Sahley, C. The in vitro classical conditioning of the gill withdrawal reflex of *Aplysia californica*. *Science*, 1981, *212*, 1516–1518.

McAllister, D. E., McAllister, W. R., Brooks, C. I., & Goldman, J. A. Magnitude and shift of reward in instrumental aversive learning in rats. *JCPP*, 1972, *80*, 440–501.

McAllister, D. E., McAllister, W. R., & Dieter, S. E. Reward magnitude and shock variables (continuity and intensity) in shuttlebox-avoidance learning. *AL&B*, 1976, *4*, 204–209.

McAllister, D. E., McAllister, W. R., Hampton, S. R., & Scoles, M. T. Escape-from-fear performance as affected by handling method and an additional CS-shock treatment. *AL&B*, 1980, *8*, 417–423.

McAllister, W. R. Eyelid conditioning as a function of the CS-US interval. *Journal of Experimental Psychology*, 1953, *45*, 417–422.

McAllister, W. R., & McAllister, D. E. Drive and reward in aversive learning. *American Journal of Psychology*, 1967, *80*, 377–383.

McAllister, W. R., & McAllister, D. E. Behavioral measurement of conditioned fear. In F. R. Brush (Ed.), *Aversive conditioning and learning*. New York: Academic Press, 1971.

McAllister, W. R., McAllister, D. E., & Benton, M. M. Measurement of fear of the conditioned stimulus and of situational cues at several stages of two-way avoidance learning. *L&M*, 1983, *14*, 92–106.

McAllister, W. R., McAllister, D. E., Dieter, S. E., & James, J. H. Preexposure to situational cues produces a direct relationship between two-way avoidance learning and shock intensity. *AL&B*, 1979, *7*, 165–173.

McCain, G., Lobb, M., & Newberry, J. Extended training and multiple shifts: Percentage of reward. *Bulletin of the Psychonomic Society*, 1976, *8*, 191–193.

McCain, G., Ward, R., & Lobb, M. Reward magnitude and a comment. *Bulletin of the Psychonomic Society*, 1976, *7*, 90–92.

McGaugh, J. L., & Dawson, R. G. Modification of memory storage processes. In W. K. Honig & P. H. R. James (Eds.), *Animal memory*. New York: Academic Press, 1971.

McGonigle, B. O., & Chalmers, M. Are monkeys logical? *Nature*, 1977, *267*, 694–696.

McHose, J. H. Relative reinforcement effects: S1/S2 and S1/S1 paradigms in instrumental conditioning. *Psychological Review*, 1970, *77*, 135–146.

McHose, J. H., & Peters, D. P. Partial reward, negative contrast effects, and incentive averaging. *AL&B*, 1975, *3*, 239–244.

Macki, W. S. Directed forgetting in animals. In N. E. Spear & R. R. Miller (Eds.), *Information processing in animals: Memory mechanisms*. Hillsdale, N.J.: Erlbaum, 1981.

Mackintosh, N. J. Overtraining, extinction, and reversal in rats and chicks. *JCPP*, 1965a, *59*, 31–36.

Mackintosh, N. J. Selective attention in animal discrimination learning. *Psychological Bulletin*, 1965b, *64*, 124–150.

Mackintosh, N. J. Further analysis of the overtraining reversal effect. *JCPP*, 1969, *67*, 1–18.

Mackintosh, N. J. Distribution of trials and the partial reinforcement effect in the rat. *JCPP*, 1970, *73*, 341–348.

Mackintosh, N. J. *The psychology of animal learning*. London: Academic Press, 1974.

Mackintosh, N. J. A theory of attention: Variations in the associability of stimuli with reinforcement. *Psychological Review*, 1975, *82*, 276–298.

Mackintosh, N. J. Overshadowing and stimulus intensity. *AL&B*, 1976, *4*, 186–192.

Mackintosh, N. J. Cognitive or associative theories of conditioning: Implications of an analysis of blocking. In S. H. Hulse, H. Fowler, & W. K. Honig (Eds.), *Cognitive processes in animal behavior*. Hillsdale, N.J.: Erlbaum, 1978.

Mackintosh, N. J. *Conditioning and associative learning*. Oxford: Oxford University Press, 1983.

Mackintosh, N. J., Bygrave, D. J., & Picton, B. M. B. Locus of the effects of a surprising reinforcer in the attenuation of blocking. *Quarterly Journal of Experimental Psychology*, 1977, *29*, 327–336.

Mackintosh, N. J., & Dickinson, A. Instrumental (Type II) conditioning. In A. Dickinson & R. A. Boakes (Eds.), *Mechanisms of learning and motivation: A memorial volume to Jerzy Konorski*. Hillsdale, N.J.: Erlbaum, 1979.

Mackintosh, N. J., Dickinson, A., & Cotton, M. M. Surprise and blocking: Effects of the number of compound trials. *AL&B*, 1980, *8*, 387–391.

Mackintosh, N. J., Little, L., & Lord, J. Some determinants of behavioral contrast in pigeons and rats. *L&M*, 1972, *3*, 148–161.

Mackintosh, N. J., & Lord, J. Simultaneous and successive contrast with delay of reward. *AL&B*, 1973, *1*, 283–286.

MacLennan, A. J., Drugan, R. C., Hyson, R. L., Maier, S. F., Madden, J., IV, & Barchas, J. D. Dissociation of long-term analgesia and the shuttle box escape deficit caused by inescapable shock. *JCPP*, 1982a, *96*, 904–912.

MacLennan, A. J., Drugan, R. C., Hyson, R. L., Maier, S. F., Madden, J., IV, & Barchas, J. D. Corticosterone: A critical factor in an opioid form of stress-induced analgesia. *Science*, 1982b, *215*, 1530–1532.

McNamara, H. J., Long, J. B., & Wike, E. L. Learning without response under two conditions of external cues. *JCPP*, 1956, *49*, 477–480.

McSweeney, F. K. Matching and contrast on several concurrent treadle-press schedules. *JEAB*, 1975, *23*, 193–198.

McSweeney, F. K. Positive and negative contrast as a function of component duration for key pecking and treadle pressing. *JEAB*, 1982, *37*, 281–293.

McSweeney, F. K., Ettinger, R. H., & Norman, W. D. Three versions of the additive theories of behavioral contrast. *JEAB*, 1981, *36*, 285–297.

McSweeney, F. K., Melville, C. L., Buck, M. A., & Whipple, J. E. Local rates of responding and reinforcement during concurrent schedules. *JEAB*, 1983, *40*, 79–98.

McSweeney, F. K., Melville, C. L., & Whipple, J. E. Herrnstein's equation for the rates of responding during concurrent schedules. *AL&B*, 1983, *11*, 275–289.

McSweeney, F. K., & Norman, W. D. Defining behavioral contrast for multiple schedules. *JEAB*, 1979, *32*, 457–461.

Mactutus, C. F., Riccio, D. C., & Ferek, J. M. Retrograde amnesia for old (reactivated) memory: Some anomalous characteristics. *Science*, 1979, *204*, 1319–1320.

Mahoney, W. J., & Ayres, J. J. B. One-trial simultaneous and backward fear conditioning as reflected in conditioned suppression of licking in rats. *AL&B*, 1976, *4*, 357–362.

Maier, N. R. F. The effect of cerebral destruction on reasoning and learning in rats. *Journal of Comparative Neurology*, 1932, *54*, 45–75.

Maier, N. R. F., & Schneirla, T. C. *Principles of animal psychology*. New York: Dover, 1964.

Maier, S. F., Albin, R. W., & Testa, T. J. Failure to learn to escape in rats previously exposed to inescapable shock depends on nature of escape response. *JCPP*, 1973, *85*, 581–592.

Maier, S. F., Drugan, R. C., & Grau, J. W. Controllability, coping behavior, and stress-induced analgesia in the rat. *Pain*, 1982, *12*, 47–56.

Maier, S. F., & Jackson, R. L. Learned helplessness: All of us were right (and wrong): Inescapable shock has multiple effects. In G. H. Bower (Ed.), *The psychology of learning and motivation*. New York: Academic Press, 1979.

Maier, S. F., & Seligman, M. E. P. Learned helplessness: Theory and evidence. *JEP:General*, 1976, *105*, 3–46.

Maier, S. F., Sherman, J. E., Lewis, J. W., Terman, G. W., & Liebeskind, J. C. The opioid/nonopioid nature of stress-induced analgesia and learned helplessness. *JEP:ABP*, 1983, *9*, 80–90.

Malagodi, E. F. Acquisition of the token-reward habit in the rat. *Psychological Reports*, 1967, *20*, 1335–1342.

Mallott, R. W., & Cumming, W. W. Schedules of interresponse time reinforcement. *Psychological Record*, 1964, *14*, 211–252.

Mallott, R. W., & Cumming, W. W. Schedules of interresponse time reinforcement. In J. A. Nevin (Ed.), *The study of behavior: Learning, motivation, emotion, and instinct*. Glenview, Ill.: Scott, Foresman, 1973.

Manning, A. A., Schneiderman, N., & Lordahl, D. S. Delay versus trace heart-rate classical discrimination conditioning in rabbits as a function of interstimulus interval. *Journal of Experimental Psychology*, 1969, *80*, 225–230.

Mansfield, J. G., & Cunningham, C. L. Conditioning and extinction of tolerance to the hypothermic effect of ethanol in rats. *JCPP*, 1980, *94*, 962–969.

Marler, P. Birdsong and speech development: Could there be parallels? *American Scientist*, 1970, *58*, 669–673.

Marlin, N. A. Contextual associations in trace conditioning. *AL&B*, 1981, *9*, 519–523.

Martin, B. Reward and punishment associated with the same goal response: A factor in the learning of motives. *Psychological Bulletin*, 1963, *60*, 441–451.

Mason, J. W. A review of psychoendocrine research on the pituitary-adrenal cortical system. *Psychosomatic Medicine*, 1968, *30*, 576–607.

Mason, J. W., & Brady, J. V. Plasma 17-hydroxycorticosteroid changes related to reserpine effects on emotional behavior. *Science*, 1956, *124*, 983.

Masterson, F. A., & Crawford, M. The defense motivation system: A theory of avoidance behavior. *The Behavioral and Brain Sciences*, 1982, *5*, 661–696.

Mellgren, R. L. Positive and negative contrast effects using delayed reinforcement. *L&M*, 1972, *3*, 185–193.

Mellgren, R. L., Mays, M. Z., & Haddad, N. F. Discrimination and generalization by rats of temporal stimuli lasting for minutes. *L&M*, 1983, *14*, 75–91.

Mellgren, R. L., Misasi, L., & Brown, S. W. Optimal foraging theory: Prey density and travel requirements in *Rattus norvegicus*. *JCP*, 1984, *98*, 142–153.

Mellgren, R. L., & Ost, J. W. P. Transfer of Pavlovian differential conditioning to an operant discrimination. *JCPP*, 1969, *67*, 390–394.

Mellgren, R. L., Seybert, J. A., & Dyck, D. G. The order of continuous, partial and nonreward trials and resistance to extinction. *L&M*, 1978, *9*, 359–371.

Meltzer, D., & Brahlek, J. A. Quantity of reinforcement and fixed-interval performance. *Psychonomic Science*, 1968, *12*, 207–208.

Menzel, E. W. Cognitive mapping in chimpanzees. In S. H. Hulse, H. Fowler, & W. K. Honig (Eds.), *Cognitive processes in animal behavior*. Hillsdale, N.J.: Erlbaum, 1978.

Meredith, A. L., & Schneiderman, N. Heart rate and nictitating membrane: Classical discrimination conditioning in rabbits under delay versus trace procedures. *Psychonomic Science*, 1967, *9*, 139–140.

Millenson, J. R., Kehoe, E. J., & Gormezano, I. Classical conditioning of the rabbit's nictitating membrane response under fixed and mixed CS-US intervals. *L&M*, 1977, *8*, 351–366.

Miller, N. E. Learning resistance to pain and fear: Effects of overlearning, exposure, and rewarded exposure in context. *JEP*, 1960, *60*, 137–145.

Miller, R. R., & Balaz, R. R. Differences in adaptiveness between classically conditioned responses and instrumentally acquired responses. In N. E. Spear & R. R. Miller (Eds.), *Information processing in animals: Memory mechanisms*. Hillsdale, N.J.: Erlbaum, 1981.

Miller, W. R., Rosellini, R. A., & Seligman, M. E. P. Learned helplessness and depression. In J. D. Mazer & M. E. P. Seligman (Eds.), *Psychopathology: Experimental models*. San Francisco: W. H. Freeman, 1977.

Mineka, S. The role of fear in theories of avoidance learning, flooding, and extinction. *Psychological Bulletin*, 1979, *86*, 985–1010.

Mineka, S., & Gino, A. Some further tests of the brief confinement effect and the SSDR account of flooding. *L&M*, 1979, *10*, 98–115.

Mis, F. W. A midbrain–brain stem circuit for conditioned inhibition of the nictitating membrane response in the rabbit *(Oryctolagua cuniculuc)*. *JCPP*, 1977, *91*, 975–988.

Mis, F. W., Gormezano, I., & Harvey, J. A. Stimulation of abducens nucleus supports classical conditioning of the nictitating membrane response. *Science*, 1979, *206*, 473–476.

Mitchell, D., Kirschbaum, E. H., & Perry, R. L. Effects of neophobia and habituation on the poison-induced avoidance of exteroceptive stimuli in the rat. *JEP:ABP*, 1975, *104*, 47–55.

Modaresi, H. A. Facilitating effects of a safe platform on two-way avoidance learning. *JEP:ABP*, 1978, *4*, 83–94.

Modaresi, H. A., Coe, W. V., & Glendenning, B. J. An efficient one- and two-way avoidance apparatus capable of producing identical one- and two-way avoidance performance. *Behavior Research Methods and Instrumentation*, 1975, *7*, 348–350.

Moltz, H. Latent extinction and the fractional anticipatory response mechanism. *Psychological Review*, 1957, *64*, 229–241.

Moltz, H. Imprinting: An epigenetic approach. *Psychological Review*, 1963, *70*, 123–138.

Monroe, B., & Barker, L. M. A contingency analysis of taste aversion conditioning. *AL&B*, 1979, *7*, 141–143.

Mook, D. G. The state of the art and the fate of the earth. *JEAB*, 1983, *40*, 343–350.

Moore, J. W. Brain processes and conditioning. In A. Dickinson and R. A. Boakes (Eds.), *Mechanisms of learning and motivation: A memorial volume to Jerzy Konorski*. Hillsdale, N.J.: Erlbaum, 1979.

Morgan, C. L. *An introduction to comparative psychology*. London: Walter Scott, 1894.

Morgan, C. L. *The animal mind*. London: Edward Arnold, 1930.

Morgan, M. J., & Nicholas, D. J. Discrimination between reinforced action patterns in the rat. *L&M*, 1979, *10*, 1–22.

Morris, M. D., & Capaldi, E. J. Extinction responding following partial reinforcement: The effects of number of rewarded trials and magnitude of reward. *AL&B*, 1979, *7*, 509–513.

Mowrer, O. H. On the dual nature of learning: A reinterpretation of "conditioning" and "problem-solving." *Harvard Educational Review*, 1947, *17*, 102–148.

Mowrer, O. H., & Jones, H. Habit strength as a function of the pattern of reinforcement. *JEP*, 1945, *35*, 293–311.

Mowrer, O. H., & Lamoreaux, R. R. Fear as an intervening variable in avoidance conditioning. *JCP*, 1946, *39*, 29–50.

Mowrer, O. H., & Lamoreaux, R. R. Conditioning and conditionality (discrimination). *Psychological Review*, 1951, *58*, 196–212.

Moye, T. B., Coon, D. J., Grau, J. W., & Maier, S. F. Therapy and immunization of long-term analgesia in rats. *L&M*, 1981, *12*, 133–148.

Moyer, K. E., & Korn, J. H. Effect of UCS intensity on the acquisition and extinction of an avoidance response. *JEP*, 1964, *67*, 352–359.

Moyer, K. E., & Korn, J. H. Effect of UCS intensity on the acquisition and extinction of a one-way avoidance response. *Psychonomic Science*, 1966, *4*, 121–122.

Muenzinger, K. F., Bernstone, A. H., & Richards, L. Motivation in Learning VIII. Equivalent amounts of electric shock for right and wrong responses in a visual discrimination habit. *JCP*, 1938, *26*, 177–186.

Munn, N. L. *Handbook of psychological research on the rat*. Boston: Houghton Mifflin, 1950.

Myers, A. K. Shock intensity and warning signal effects on several measures of operant avoidance acquisition. *AL&B*, 1977, *5*, 51–56.

Nachman, M., & Ashe, J. H. Learned taste aversions in rats as a function of dosage, concentration, and route of administration of LiCl. *Physiology and Behavior*, 1973, *10*, 73–78.

Nairne, J. S., & Rescorla, R. A. Second-order conditioning with diffuse auditory reinforcers in the pigeon. *L&M*, 1981, *12*, 65–91.

Nation, J. R., Wrather, D. M., & Mellgren, R. L. Contrast effects in escape conditioning of rats. *JCPP*, 1974, *86*, 69–73.

Nevin, J. A. The maintenance of behavior. In J. A. Nevin and G. S. Reynolds (Eds.), *The study of behavior: Learning motivation, emotion, and instinct*. Glenview, Ill.: Scott, Foresman, 1973.

Nevin, J. A. On resisting extinction: A review of Jonathan Schell's *The Fate of the Earth*. *JEAB*, 1982, *38*, 349–353.

Nottebohm, F. Brain pathways for vocal learning in birds: A review of the first 10 years. In J. M. Sprague & A. N. Epstein (Eds.), *Progress in psychology and physiological psychology* (Vol. 9). New York: Academic Press, 1980.

Notterman, J. M., & Mintz, D. E. *Dynamics of response*. New York: Wiley, 1965.

Oakley, D. A., & Russell, I. S. Subcortical nature of Pavlovian differentiation in the rabbit. *Physiology and Behavior*, 1976, *17*, 947–954.

Oakley, D. A., & Russell, I. S. Subcortical storage of Pavlovian conditioning in the rabbit. *Physiology and Behavior*, 1977, *18*, 931–937.

O'Brien, C. P., Testa, T., O'Brien, T. J., Brady, J. P., & Wells, B. Conditioned narcotic withdrawal in humans. *Science*, 1977, *195*, 1000–1002.

O'Connell, J. M., & Rashotte, M. E. Reinforcement magnitude effects in first- and second-order conditioning of directed action. *L&M*, 1982, *13*, 1–25.

Odling-Smee, F. J. Multiple levels in evolution: An approach to the nature-nurture issue via "applied epistemology." In G. C. L. Davey (Ed.), *Animal models of human behavior: Conceptual, evolutionary, and neurobiological perspectives*. Chichester, Eng.: John Wiley, 1983.

O'Keefe, J., & Nadal, L. *The hippocampus as a cognitive map*. Oxford, Eng.: Oxford University Press, 1978.

Olton, D. S. Characteristics of spatial memory. In S. H. Hulse, H. Fowler, & W. K. Honig (Eds.), *Cognitive processes in animal behavior*. Hillsdale, N.J.: Erlbaum, 1978.

Olton, D. S., & Collison, C. Intramaze cues and "odor trails" fail to direct choice behavior in an elevated maze. *AL&B*, 1979, *7*, 221–223.

Olton, D. S., & Samuelson, R. J. Remembrance of places passed: Spatial memory in rats. *JEP:ABP*, 1976, *2*, 97–116.

Olton, D. S., Walker, J. A., Gage, F. H., & Johnson, C. T. Choice behavior of rats searching for food. *L&M*, 1977, *8*, 315–331.

Osborne, S. R. A quantitative analysis of the effects of amount of reinforcement on two response classes. *JEP:ABP*, 1978, *4*, 297–317.

Overmier, J. B., & Seligman, M. E. P. Effects of inescapable shock upon subsequent escape and avoidance learning. *JCPP*, 1967, *63*, 28–33.

Palmer, C. C., Rusiniak, K. W., & Garcia, J. Flavor-illness aversions: The peculiar roles of odor and taste in memory for poison. *Science*, 1980, *208*, 753–755.

Parisi, T., & Matthews, T. J. Pavlovian determinants of the auto-shaped key peck response. *Bulletin of the Psychonomic Society*, 1975, *6*, 527–529.

Pavlick, W. B., & Reynolds, W. F. Effects of deprivation schedule and reward magnitude on acquisition and extinction performance. *JCPP*, 1963, *56*, 452–455.

Pavlov, I. P. *Conditioned reflexes*. Oxford, Eng.: Oxford University Press, (Dover Edition, 1960), 1927.

Pavlov, I. P. The reply of a physiologist to psychologists. *Psychological Review*, 1932, *39*, 91–127.

Pearce, J. M. The relationship between shock magnitude and passive avoidance learning. *AL&B*, 1978, *6*, 341–345.

Pearce, J. M., Colwill, R. M., & Hall, G. Instrumental conditioning of scratching in the laboratory rat. *L&M*, 1978, *9*, 255–271.

Pearce, J. M., & Hall, G. Overshadowing the instrumental conditioning of a lever-press response by a more valid predictor of the reinforcer. *JEP:ABP*, 1978, *4*, 356–367.

Pearce, J. M., & Hall, G. A model for Pavlovian learning: Variations in the effectiveness of conditioned but not unconditioned stimuli. *Psychological Review*, 1980, *87*, 532–552.

Pearce, J. M., Nicholas, D. J., & Dickinson, A. The potentiation effect during serial conditioning. *Quarterly Journal of Experimental Psychology*, 1981, *33b*, 159–179.

Peden, B. F., Browne, M. P., & Hearst, E. Persistent approaches to a signal for food despite food omission for approaching. *JEP:ABP*, 1977, *3*, 377–399.

Peeke, H. V. S., & Veno, A. Stimulus specificity of habituated aggression in three-spined sticklebacks *(Gasterosteus aculeatus)*. *Behavioral Biology*, 1973, *8*, 427–432.

Perkins, C. C., Jr. The relation of secondary reward to gradients of reinforcement. *JEP*, 1947, *37*, 377–392.

Perkins, C. C., Jr. The relation between conditioned stimulus intensity and response strength. *JEP*, 1953, *46*, 225–231.

Perkins, C. C., Jr. An analysis of the concept of reinforcement. *Psychological Review*, 1968, *75*, 155–172.

Peters, D. P., & McHose, J. H. Effects of varied preshift reward magnitude on successive negative contrast effects in rats. *JCPP*, 1974, *86*, 85–95.

Peters, S. S., Searcy, W. A., & Marler, P. Species song discrimination in choice experiments with territorial male swamp and song sparrows. *Animal Behaviour*, 1980, *28*, 393–404.

Peterson, G. B. The differential outcomes procedure: A paradigm for studying how expectancies guide behavior. In H. L. Roitblat, T. C. Bever, & H. S. Terrace (Eds.), *Animal cognition*. Hillsdale, N.J.: Erlbaum, 1984.

Petrinovich, L., & Patterson, T. L. Field studies of habituation: IV. Sensitization as a function of the distribution and novelty of song playback to white-crowned sparrows. *JCPP*, 1981, *95*, 805–812.

Petrinovitch, L., & Patterson, T. L. Field studies of habituation: I. The effect of reproductive condition, number of trials, and different delay intervals on the response of the white-crowned sparrow. *JCPP*, 1979, *93*, 337–350.

Petrinovitch, L., & Patterson, T. L. Field studies of habituation: III. Playback contingent on the response of the white-crowned sparrow. *Animal Behaviour*, 1980, *28*, 742–751.

Petrinovitch, L., & Peeke, H. V. S. Habituation to territorial song in the white-crowned sparrow *(Zonotrichia leucophrys)*. *Behavioral Biology*, 1973, *8*, 743–748.

Pfautz, P. L., Donegan, N. H., & Wagner, A. R. Sensory preconditioning versus protection from habituation. *JEP:ABP*, 1978, *4*, 286–295.

Pietrewicz, A. T., & Kamil, A. C. Search images and the detection of cryptic prey: An operant approach. In A. C. Kamil & T. D. Sargent (Eds.), *Foraging behavior: Ecological, ethological, and psychological approaches*. New York: Garland STPM Press, 1981.

Pinel, J. P. J., & Treit, D. Burying as a defensive response in rats. *JCPP*, 1978, *92*, 708–712.

Platt, J. R., & Scott, G. K. Analysis of the superiority of discrete-trials over free-operant procedures in temporal response differentiation. *JEP:ABP*, 1981, *7*, 269–277.

Plotkin, H. C. The function of learning and cross-species comparisons. In G.C.L. Davey (Ed.), *Animal models of human behavior: Conceptual, evolutionary, and neurobiological perspectives*. Chichester, Eng.: John Wiley, 1983.

Plotkin, H. C. & Oakley, D. A. Backward conditioning in the rabbit *(Oryctolagus cuniculus)*. *JCPP*, 1975, *88*, 586–590.

Plotkin, H. C., & Odling-Smee, F. J. Learning, change, and evolution: An enquiry into the teleonomy of learning. In J. S. Rosenblatt, R. A. Hinde, C. Beer, & M. C. Busnel (Eds.), *Advances in the study of behavior* (Vol. 10). New York: Academic Press, 1979.

Popik, R. S., Stern, S. D., & Frey, P. W. Second-order conditioning: Different outcomes in fear and eyelid conditioning. *AL&B*, 1979, *7*, 355–359.

Porter, J. J., Madison, H. L., & Senkowski, P. C. Runway performance and competing responses as a function of drive level and method of drive measurement. *JEP*, 1968, *78*, 281–284.

Post, R. M., Lockfeld, A., Squillace, K. M., & Contel, N. R. Drug-environment interaction: Context dependency of cocaine-induced behavioral sensitization. *Life Sciences*, 1980, *28*, 755–760.

Poulos, C. X., & Gormezano, I. Effects of partial and continuous reinforcement on acquisition and extinction in classical appetitive conditioning. *Bulletin of the Psychonomic Society*, 1974, *4*, 197–198.

Powell, G. M., Berthier, N. E., & Moore, J. W. Efferent neuronal control of the nictitating membrane response in rabbit *(Oryctolagus cuniculus)*: A reexamination. *Physiology & Behavior*, 1979, *23*, 299–308.

Premack, D. On the abstractness of human concepts: Why it would be difficult to talk to a pigeon. In S. H. Hulse, H. Fowler, & W. K. Honig (Eds.), *Cognitive processes in animal behavior*. Hillsdale, N.J.: Erlbaum, 1978.

Premack, D. The codes of man and beast. *The Behavioral Brain Sciences*, 1983, *6*, 125–167.

Premack, D., & Collier, G. H. Duration of looking and number of brief looks as dependent variables. *Psychonomic Science*, 1966, *4*, 81–82.

Pritchard, W. S. Psychophysiology of p300. *Psychological Bulletin*, 1981, *89*, 506–540.

Prokasy, W. F., Grant, D. A., & Meyers, N. A. Eyelid conditioning as a function of unconditioned stimulus intensity and intertrial interval. *JEP*, 1958, *55*, 242–246.

Pubols, B. H., Jr. Delay of reinforcement, response preservation, and discrimination reversal. *JEP*, 1958, *56*, 32–40.

Pubols, B. H., Jr. The acquisition and reversal of a position habit as a function of incentive magnitude. *JCPP*, 1961, *54*, 94–97.

Pubols, B. J., Jr. Incentive magnitude, learning and performance in animals. *Psychological Bulletin*, 1969, *57*, 89–115.

Pulliam, H. R., & Dunford, C. *Programmed to learn*. New York: Columbia University Press, 1980.

Purtle, R. B. Peak shift: A review. *Psychological Bulletin*, 1973, *80*, 408–421.

Pyke, G. H. Optimal foraging: Movement patterns of bumblebees between inflorescences. *Theoretical Population Biology*, 1978, *13*, 72–98.

Pynchon, T. *Gravity's Rainbow*. New York: Bantam Books, 1973.

Rachlin, H. Contrast and matching. *Psychological Review*, 1973, *80*, 217–234.

Rachlin, H., Kagel, S. H., & Battalio, R. C. Substitutability in time allocation. *Psychological Review*, 1980, *87*, 355–374.

Randich, A., & LoLordo, V. M. Preconditioning exposure to the unconditioned stimulus affects the acquisition of a conditioned emotional response. *Learning and Motivation*, 1979, *10*, 245–275.

Randich, A. & Rescorla, R. A. The effects of separate presentations of the US on conditioned suppression. *AL&B*, 1981, *9*, 55–64.

Rashotte, M. E. Reward training: Extinction. In M. E. Bitterman, V. M. LoLordo, J. B. Overmier, & M. E. Rashotte (Eds.), *Animal learning: Survey and analysis*. New York: Plenum Press, 1979.

Rashotte, M. E. Reward training: Contrast effects. In M. E. Bitterman, V. M. LoLordo, J. B. Overmier, & M. E. Rashotte (Eds.), *Animal learning: Survey and analysis*. New York: Plenum Press, 1979.

Rashotte, M. E. Second-order autoshaping: Contributions to the research and theory of Pavlovian reinforcement by conditioned stimuli. In C. M. Locurto, H. S. Terrace, & J. Gibbon (Eds.), *Autoshaping and conditioning theory*. New York: Academic Press, 1981.

Rashotte, M. E., & Amsel, A. Transfer of slow-response rituals to extinction of a continuously rewarded response. *JCPP*, 1968, *66*, 432–443.

Rashotte, M. E., Griffen, R. W., & Sisk, C. L. Second-order conditioning of the pigeon's keypeck. *AL&B*, 1977, *5*, 25–38.

Rashotte, M. E., Marshall, B. S., & O'Connell, J. M. Signalling functions of the second-order CS: Partial reinforcement during second-order conditioning of the pigeon's keypeck. *AL&B*, 1981, *9*, 253–260.

Rashotte, M. E., O'Connell, J. M., & Beidler, D. L. Associative influence on the foraging behavior of pigeons *(Columba livia)*. *JEP:ABP*, 1982, *8*, 142–153.

Raskin, D. C., Kotses, H., & Bever, J. Autonomic indicators of orienting and defensive reflexes. *JEP*, 1969, *80*, 423–433.

Razran, G. The observable unconscious and the inferable conscious in current Soviet psychophysiology: Interoceptive conditioning, semantic conditioning, and the orienting reflex. *Psychological Review*, 1961, *68*, 81–147.

Reid, L. S. Development of noncontinuity behavior through continuity learning. *JEP*, 1953, *46*, 107–112.

Reiss, S., & Wagner, A. R. CS habituation produces a "latent inhibition effect" but no active "conditioned inhibition." *L&M*, 1972, *3*, 237–245.

Renner, K. E. Influence of deprivation and availability of goal box cues on the temporal gradient of reinforcement. *JCPP*, 1963, *56*, 101–104.

Renner, K. E. Delay of reinforcement: A historical review. *Psychological Bulletin*, 1964, *61*, 341–361.

Rescorla, R. D. Predictability and number of pairings in Pavlovian fear conditioning. *Psychonomic Science*, 1966, *4*, 383–385.

Rescorla, R. A. Pavlovian conditioning and its proper control procedures. *Psychological Review*, 1967a, *74*, 71–80.

Rescorla, R. A. Inhibition of delay in Pavlovian fear conditioning. *JCPP*, 1967b, *64*, 114–120.

Rescorla, R. A. Probability of shock in the presence and absence of CS in fear conditioning. *JCPP*, 1968, *66*, 1–5.

Rescorla, R. A. Pavlovian conditioned inhibition. *Psychological Bulletin*, 1969, *72*, 77–94.

Rescorla, R. A. Summation and retardation tests of latent inhibition. *JCPP*, 1971, *75*, 77–81.

Rescorla, R. A. Effect of US habituation following conditioning. *JCPP*, 1973, *82*, 137–143.

Rescorla, R. A. Effect of inflation of the unconditioned stimulus value following conditioning. *JCPP*, 1974, *86*, 101–106.

Rescorla, R. A. Pavlovian excitatory and inhibitory conditioning. In W. K. Estes (Ed.), *Handbook of learning and cognitive processes: Conditioning and behavior theory* (Vol. 2). Hillsdale, N.J.: Erlbaum, 1975.

Rescorla, R. A. Some implications of a cognitive perspective on Pavlovian conditioning. In S. H. Hulse, H. Fowler, & W. K. Honig (Eds.), *Cognitive processes in animal behavior*. Hillsdale, N.J.: Erlbaum, 1978.

Rescorla, R. A. Conditioned inhibition and extinction. In A. Dickinson & R. A. Boakes (Eds.), *Mechanisms of Learning and Motivation: A Memorial Volume to Jerzy Konorski*. Hillsdale, N.J.: Erlbaum, 1979.

Rescorla, R. A. *Pavlovian second-order conditioning: Studies in associative learning*. Hillsdale, N.J.: Erlbaum, 1980.

Rescorla, R. A. Effect of a stimulus intervening between CS and US in autoshaping. *JEP:ABP*, 1982, *8*, 131–141.

Rescorla, R. A., & Cunningham, C. L. Spatial contiguity facilitates Pavlovian second-order conditioning. *JEP:ABP*, 1979, *5*, 152–161.

Rescorla, R. A., & Furrow, D. R. Stimulus similarity as a determinant of Pavlovian conditioning. *JEP:ABP*, 1977, *3*, 203–215.

Rescorla, R. A., & Holland, P. C. Associations in Pavlovian conditioned inhibition. *L&M*, 1977, *8*, 429–447.

Rescorla, R. A., & Solomon, R. L. Two-process learning theory: Relationships between Pavlovian conditioning and instrumental learning. *Psychological Review*, 1967, *74*, 151–182.

Rescorla, R. A., & Wagner, A. R. A theory of Pavlovian conditioning: Variation in the effectiveness of reinforcement and nonreinforcement. In A. H. Black & W. F. Prokasy (Eds.), *Classical Conditioning II: Current Research and Theory*. New York: Appleton-Century-Crofts, 1972.

Restle, F. Discrimination of cues in mazes: A resolution of the "place-vs-response" question. *Psychological Review*, 1957, *64*, 217–228.

Revusky, S. Aversion to sucrose produced by contingent X-irradiation: Temporal and dosage parameters. *JCPP*, 1968, *65*, 17–22.

Revusky, S. The role of interference in association over a delay. In W. K. Honig & P. H. R. James (Eds.), *Animal memory*. New York: Academic Press, 1971.

Revusky, S. The concurrent interference approach to delay learning. In L. M. Barker, M. R. Best, & M. Domjan (Eds.), *Learning mechanisms in food selection*. Waco, Tex.: Baylor University Press, 1977.

Revusky, S., & Parker, L. A. Aversions to unflavored water and cup-drinking produced by delayed sickness. *JEP:ABP*, 1976, *2*, 342–353.

Reynierse, J. H., & Rizley, R. C. Stimulus and response contingencies in extinction of avoidance by rats. *JCPP*, 1970, *73*, 86–92.

Reynolds, B. Acquisition of a simple spatial discrimination as a function of the amount of reinforcement. *JEP*, 1950, *40*, 152–160.

Reynolds, G. S. An analysis of interactions in a multiple schedule. *JEAB*, 1961a, *4*, 107–117.

Reynolds, G. S. Attention in the pigeon. *JEAB*, 1961b, *4*, 203–208.

Riccio, D. C., & Ebner, D. L. Postacquisition modifications of memory. In N. E. Spear & R. R. Miller (Eds.), *Information processing in animals: Memory mechanisms*. Hillsdale, N.J.: Erlbaum, 1981.

Riccio, D. C., Hodges, L. A., & Randall, P. K. Retrograde amnesia produced by hypothermia in rats. *JCPP*, 1968, *66*, 618–622.

Riccio, D. C., & Silvestri, R. Extinction of avoidance behavior and the problem of residual fear. *Behaviour Research and Therapy*, 1973, *11*, 1–9.

Richter, C. P. Increased salt appetite in adrenalectomized rats. *American Journal of Physiology*, 1936, *115*, 155–161.

Richter, C. P. Experimentally produced behavior reactions to food poisoning in wild and domesticated rats. *Annals of the New York Academy of Sciences*, 1953, *56*, 225–239.

Ridgers, A., & Gray, J. A. Influence of amylobarbitone on operant depression and elation effects in the rat. *Psychopharmacologia*, 1973, *32*, 265–270.

Riley, A. L., & Baril, L. L. Conditioned taste aversions: A bibliography. *AL&B*, 1976, *4*, 15–135.

Riley, A. L., & Clarke, C. M. Conditioned taste aversions: A bibliography. In L. M. Barker, M. R. Best, & M. Domjan (Eds.), *Learning mechanisms in food selection*. Waco, Tex.: Baylor University Press, 1977.

Riley, D. A. *Discrimination learning*. Boston: Allyn and Bacon, 1968.

Riley, D. A., & Leith, C. R. Multidimensional psychophysics and selective attention in animals. *Psychological Bulletin*, 1976, *83*, 138–160.

Riley, D. A., & Roitblat, H. L. Selective attention and related cognitive processes in pigeons. In S. H. Hulse, H. Fowler, & W. K. Honig (Eds.), *Cognitive processes in animal behavior*. Hillsdale, N.J.: Erlbaum, 1978.

Rilling, M., Caplan, H. J., Howard, R. C., & Brown, C. H. Inhibitory stimulus control following errorless discrimination learning. *JEAB*, 1975, *24*, 121–133.

Riopelle, A. J. Learning sets from minimum stimuli. *JEP*, 1955, *49*, 28.

Riopelle, A. J. Observational learning of a position habit by monkeys. *JCPP*, 1960, *53*, 426–428.

Robbins, D. Partial reinforcement: A selective review of the alleyway literature since 1960. *Psychological Bulletin*, 1971, *76*, 415–431.

Roberts, W. A. Distribution of trials and intertrial retention in delayed matching to sample with pigeons. *JEP:ABP*, 1980, *6*, 217–237.

Roberts, W. A., & Grant, D. S. Studies of short-term memory in the pigeon using the delayed matching to sample procedure. In D. L. Medin, W. A. Roberts, & R. T. Davis (Eds.), *Processes in animal memory*. Hillsdale, N.J.: Erlbaum, 1976.

Rodgers, J. P., & Thomas, D. R. Task specificity in nonspecific transfer and in extradimensional stimulus generalization in pigeons. *JEP:ABP*, 1982, *8*, 301–312.

Roitblat, H. L., Bever, T. C., & Terrace, H. S. (Eds.). *Animal cognition*. Hillsdale, N.J.: Erlbaum, 1984.

Roitblat, H. L., Polage, B., & Scopatz, R. A. The representation of items in serial position. *AL&B*, 1983, *11*, 489–498.

Roitblat, H. L., Tham, W., & Golub, L. Performance of *Betta splendins* in radial arm maze. *AL&B*, 1982, *10*, 108–114.

Romanes, G. J. *Animal intelligence*. New York: Appleton, 1883.

Rosellini, R. A. Inescapable shock interferes with the acquisition of an appetitive operant. *AL&B*, 1978, *6*, 155–159.

Rosellini, R. A., & DeCola, J. P. Inescapable shock interferes with the acquisition of a low-activity response in an appetitive context. *AL&B*, 1981, *9*, 487–490.

Rosellini, R. A., DeCola, J. P., & Shapiro, N. R. Cross-motivational effects of inescapable shock are associative in nature. *JEP:ABP*, 1982, *8*, 376–388.

Rovee-Collier, C., & Lipsitt, L. P. Learning, adaptation, and memory in the newborn. In P. Stratton (Ed.), *Psychobiology of the human newborn*. London: Wiley, 1982.

Rovee-Collier, C. K., Sullivan, M. W., Enright, M., Lucas, D., & Fagen, J. W. Reactivation of infant memory. *Science*, 1980, *208*, 1159–1161.

Rozin, P. Specific aversions as a component of specific hungers. *JCPP*, 1967, *64*, 237–242.

Rozin, P. Adaptive food sampling patterns in vitamin deficient rats. *JCPP*, 1969, *69*, 126–132.

Rozin, P. The significance of learning mechanisms in food selection: Some biology, psychology, and sociology of science. In L. M. Barker, M. R. Best, & M. Domjan (Eds.), *Learning mechanisms in food selection*. Waco, Tex.: Baylor University Press, 1977.

Rudolph, R. L., & Van Houten, R. Auditory stimulus control in pigeons: Jenkins and Harrison (1960) revisited. *JEAB*, 1977, *27*, 327–330.

Rudy, J. W., & Cheatle, M. D. A role for conditioned stimulus duration in toxiphobia conditioning. *JEP:ABP*, 1978, *4*, 399–411.

Rudy, J. W., Iwens, J., & Best, P. J. Pairing novel exteroceptive cues and illness reduces illness-induced taste aversions. *JEP:ABP*, 1977, *3*, 14–25.

Rumbaugh, D. M. (Ed.). *Language learning by a chimpanzee: The Lana project*. New York: Academic Press, 1977.

Runquist, W. N., & Spence, K. W. Performance in eyelid conditioning as a function of UCS duration. *JEP*, 1959, *57*, 249–252.

Rzoska, J. Bait shyness, a study in rat behavior. *British Journal of Animal Behavior*, 1953, *1*, 128–135.

Safarjan, W. R., & D'Amato, M. R. One-trial, long-delay, conditioned preference in rats. *The Psychological Record*, 1981, *31*, 413–426.

St. Claire-Smith, R. The overshadowing of instrumental conditioning by a stimulus that predicts reinforcement better than the response. *AL&B*, 1979, *7*, 224–228.

Salafia, W. R., Lambert, R. W., Host, K. C., Chiaia, N. L., & Ramirez, J. J. Rabbit nictitating membrane conditioning: Lower limit of the effective interstimulus interval. *AL&B*, 1980, *8*, 85–91.

Salmon, D. P. An investigation of modality specificity in the cognitive processes of monkeys *(Cebus apella)*. Unpublished dissertation, Rutgers University, 1984.

Salmon, D. P., & D'Amato, M. R. Symmetry and transitivity in monkeys' conditional discriminations. Paper presented at the Eastern Psychological Association Meeting, 1983.

Saltzman, J. J. Maze learning in the absence of primary reinforcement: A study of secondary reinforcement. *JCPP*, 1949, *42*, 161–173.

Samson, H. H., & Falk, J. L. Ethanol and discriminative motor control: Effects on normal and dependent animals. *Pharmacology, Biochemistry, & Behavior*, 1974, *2*, 791–801.

Samuels, O. B., DeCola, J. P., & Rosellini, R. A. Effects of inescapable shock on low-activity escape/avoidance responding in rats. *Bulletin of the Psychonomic Society*, 1981, *17*, 203–205.

Savage-Rumbaugh, E. S. Acquisition of functional symbol usage in apes and children. In H. L. Roitblat, T. C. Bever, & H. S. Terrace (Eds.), *Animal cognition*. Hillsdale, N.J.: Erlbaum, 1984.

Savage-Rumbaugh, E. S., Rumbaugh, D. M., & Boysen, S. Do apes use language? *American Scientist*, 1980, *68*, 49–61.

Schaller, G. B. *The Serengeti lion: A study of predator-prey relations*. Chicago: University of Chicago Press, 1972.

Schmaltz, L. W., & Theios, J. Acquisition and extinction of a classically conditioned response in hippocampectomized rabbits *(Oryctolagus cuniculus)*. *JCPP*, 1972, *79*, 328–333.

Schneider, B. A. A two-state analysis of fixed-interval responding in the pigeon. *JEAB*, 1969, *12*, 677–687.

Schneiderman, N. Interstimulus interval function of the nictitating membrane response of the rabbit under delay versus trace conditioning. *JCPP*, 1966, *62*, 397–402.

Schneiderman, N. Response system divergencies in aversive classical conditioning. In A. H.

Black and W. F. Prokasy (Eds.), *Classical conditioning II: Current research and theory*. New York: Appleton-Century-Crofts, 1972.

Schoenfeld, W. N. *Theory of reinforcement schedules*. New York: Appleton-Century-Crofts, 1970.

Schrier, A. M., Harlow, H. F., & Stollnitz, F. (Eds.). *Behavior of nonhuman primates: Modern research trends*. New York: Academic Press, 1965.

Schrier, A. M., & Povar, M. L. Eye movements of stumptailed monkeys during discrimination learning. VTE revisited. *AL&B*, 1979, *7*, 239–245.

Schrier, A. M., & Povar, M. L. Eye movements of monkeys during discrimination learning: Role of visual scanning. *JEP:ABP*, 1982, *8*, 33–48.

Schusterman, R. J. Transfer effects of successive discrimination-reversal training in chimpanzees. *Science*, 1962, *137*, 422.

Schwartz, B., & Gamzu, E. Pavlovian control of operant behavior. In W. K. Honig & J. E. R. Staddon (Eds.), *Handbook of operant behavior*. Englewood Cliffs, N.J.: Prentice-Hall, 1977.

Schwartz, B., & Williams, D. R. The role of the response-reinforcer contingency in negative automaintenance. *JEAB*, 1972, *17*, 351–357.

Sears, R. J., Baker, J. S., & Frey, P. W. The eye blink as a time-locked response: Implications for serial and second-order conditioning. *JEP:ABP*, 1979, *5*, 46–64.

Seligman, M. E. P. On the generality of the laws of learning. *Psychological Review*, 1970, *77*, 406–418.

Seligman, M. E. P. *Helplessness: On depression, development and death*. San Francisco: W. H. Freeman, 1975.

Seligman, M. E. P., & Beagley, G. Learned helplessness in the rat. *JCPP*, 1975, *88*, 534–541.

Seligman, M. E. P., & Campbell, B. A. The effect of intensity and duration of punishment on extinction of an avoidance response. *JCPP*, 1965, *59*, 295–297.

Seligman, M. E. P., & Hager, J. L. *Biological boundaries of learning*. New York: Appleton-Century-Crofts, 1972.

Seligman, M. E. P., & Johnston, J. C. A cognitive theory of avoidance learning. In F. J. McGuigan & D. B. Lumsden (Eds.), *Contemporary approaches to conditioning and learning*. Washington, D.C.: V. H. Winston & Sons, 1973.

Seligman, M. E. P., Maier, S. F., & Solomon, R. L. Unpredictable and uncontrollable aversive events. In F. R. Brush (Ed.), *Aversive conditioning and learning*. New York: Academic Press, 1971.

Seligman, M. E. P., Rosellini, R. A., & Kozak, M. J. Learned helplessness in the rat: Time course, immunization, and reversibility. *JCPP*, 1975, *88*, 542–547.

Senkowski, P. C. Variables affecting the overtraining extinction effect in discrete-trial lever pressing. *JEP:ABP*, 1978, *4*, 131–143.

Seybert, J. A. Positive and negative contrast effects as a function of shifts in percentage of reward. *Bulletin of the Psychonomic Society*, 1979, *13*, 19–22.

Seybert, J. A., Baer, L. P., Harvey, R. J., Ludwig, K., & Gerard, I. C. Resistance to extinction as a function of percentage of reward: A reinforcement-level interpretation. *AL&B*, 1979, *7*, 233–238.

Seybert, J. A., Mellgren, R. L., & Jobe, J. B. Sequential effects on resistance to extinction at widely spaced trials. *JEP*, 1973, *101*, 151–154.

Seyfarth, R. M., Cheney, D. L., & Marler, P. Monkey responses to three different alarm calls: Evidence of predator classification and semantic communication. *Science*, 1980, *210*, 801–803.

Shanab, M. E., & Biller, J. D. Positive contrast in the runway obtained following a shift in both delay and magnitude of reward. *L&M*, 1972, *3*, 179–184.

Shanab, M. E., & Birnbaum, D. W. Durability of the partial reinforcement and partial delay of reinforcement extinction effects after minimal acquisition training. *AL&B*, 1974, *2*, 81–85.

Shanab, M. E., & Cavallaro, G. Positive contrast obtained in rats following a shift in schedule, delay, and magnitude of reward. *Bulletin of the Psychonomic Society*, 1975, *5*, 109–112.

Shanab, M. E., & Ferrell, H. J. Positive contrast in the Lashley maze under different drive conditions. *Psychonomic Science*, 1970, *20*, 31–32.

Shanab, M. E., Sanders, R., & Premack, D. Positive contrast in the runway obtained with delay of reward. *Science*, 1969, *164*, 724–725.

Shapiro, K. L., Jacobs, W. J., & LoLordo, V. M. Stimulus-reinforcer interactions in Pavlovian conditioning of pigeons: Implications for selective associations. *AL&B*, 1980, *8*, 586–594.

Sheldon, M. H. Contingency theory and the distinction between associative and non-associative effects in classical conditioning. *Quarterly Journal of Experimental Psychology*, 1973, 25, 124–129.

Sherman, A. D., Sacquitne, J. L., & Petty, F. Specificity of the learned helplessness model of depression. *Pharmacology, Biochemistry, and Behavior*, 1982, 16, 449–454.

Sherman, J. E. US inflation with trace and simultaneous fear conditioning. *AL&B*, 1978, 6, 463–468.

Sherman, J. E. The effects of conditioning and novelty on the rat's analgesic and pyretic responses to morphine. *L&M*, 1979, 10, 383–418.

Sherman, J. G. The temporal distribution of responses on fixed-interval schedules. Unpublished doctoral dissertation, Columbia University, 1959.

Shettleworth, S. J. Reinforcement and the organization of behavior in golden hamsters. In R. A. Hinde & J. Stevensen-Hinde (Eds.), *Constraints on learning*. London: Academic Press, 1973.

Shettleworth, S. J. Reinforcement and the organization of behavior in golden hamsters: Hunger, environment, and food reinforcement. *JEP:ABP*, 1975, 1, 56–87.

Shettleworth, S. J. Reinforcement and the organization of behavior in golden hamsters: Punishment of three action patterns. *L&M*, 1978, 9, 99–123.

Shettleworth, S. J. "Constraints on Conditioning" in the writings of Konorski. In A. Dickinson & R. A. Boakes (Eds.), *Mechanisms of learning and motivation*. Hillsdale, N.J.: Erlbaum, 1979.

Shettleworth, S. J. Memory in food hoarding birds. *Scientific American*, 1983, 248, 102–110.

Shettleworth, S. J., & Juergensen, M. R. Reinforcement and the organization of behavior in golden hamsters: Brain stimulation reinforcement for seven action patterns. *JEP:ABP*, 1980, 6, 352–375.

Shettleworth, S. J., & Krebs, J. R. How marsh tits find their hoards: The roles of site preference and spatial memory. *JEP:ABP*, 1982, 8, 342–353.

Shurtleff, D., & Ayres, J. J. B. One-trial backward excitatory fear conditioning in rats: Acquisition, retention, extinction, and spontaneous recovery. *AL&B*, 1981, 9, 65–74.

Sidman, M. Avoidance behavior. In W. K. Honig (Ed.), *Operant behaviour: Areas of research and application*. New York: Appleton-Century-Crofts, 1966.

Siegel, S. Conditioning of insulin induced glycemia. *JCPP*, 1972a, 78, 233–241.

Siegel, S. Latent inhibition and eyelid conditioning. In A. H. Black & W. F. Prokasy (Eds.), *Classical conditioning* II: *Current research and theory*. New York: Appleton-Century-Crofts, 1972b.

Siegel, S. Conditioning insulin effects. *JCPP*, 1975, 89, 189–199.

Siegel, S. Morphine analgesic tolerance: Its situation specificity supports a Pavlovian conditioning model. *Science*, 1976, 193, 323–325.

Siegel, S. Morphine tolerance acquisition as an associative process. *JEP:ABP*, 1977, 3, 1–13.

Siegel, S. A Pavlovian conditioning analysis of morphine tolerance. In N. A. Krasnegor (Ed.), *Behavioral tolerance: Research and treatment implications* (NIDA Research Monograph No. 18). Washington, D.C.: U.S. Government Printing Office, 1978.

Siegel, S., & Domjan, M. Backward conditioning as an inhibitory procedure. *L&M*, 1971, 2, 1–11.

Siegel, S., Hinson, R. E., & Krank, M. D. The role of predrug signals in morphine analgesic tolerance: Support for a Pavlovian conditioning model of tolerance. *JEP:ABP*, 1978, 4, 188–196.

Siegel, S., Hinson, R. E., Krank, M. D., & McCully, J. Heroin "overdose" death: Contribution of drug-associated environmental cues. *Science*, 1982, 216, 436–437.

Siegel, S., Sherman, J. E., & Mitchell, D. Extinction of morphine analgesic tolerance. *L&M*, 1980, 11, 289–301.

Sigmundi, R. A., Bouton, M. E., & Bolles, R. C. Conditioned freezing in the rat as a function of shock intensity and CS modality. *Bulletin of the Psychonomic Society*, 1980, 15, 254–256.

Skinner, B. F. *The behavior of organisms. An experimental analysis*. New York: Appleton-Century-Crofts, 1938.

Skinner, B. F. Are theories of learning necessary? *Psychological Review*, 1950, 57, 193–216.

Skinner, B. F. *Science and human behavior*. New York: Macmillan, 1953.

Skinner, B. F. *About Behaviorism*. New York: Knopf, 1974.

Skinner, B. F. Why I am not a cognitive psychologist. *Behaviorism*, 1977, 5, 1–10.

Sklar, L. S., & Anisman, H. Stress and coping factors in tumor growh. *Science*, 1979, *205*, 513–515.

Small, W. S. Experimental study of the mental processes of the rat, II. *American Journal of Psychology*, 1901, *12*, 206–239.

Smith, J. C., & Roll, D. L. Trace conditioning with X-rays as an aversive stimulus. *Psychonomic Science*, 1967, *9*, 11–12.

Smith, M. C., Coleman, S. R., & Gormezano, I. Classical conditioning of the rabbit's nictitating membrane response. *JCPP*, 1969, *69*, 226–231.

Smith, M. L., & Glass, G. V. Meta-analysis of psychotherapy outcome studies. *American Psychologist*, 1977, *32*, 752–760.

Snyder, H. L. Saccharin concentration and deprivation as determinants of instrumental and consummatory response strengths. *JEP*, 1962, *63*, 610–615.

Snyderman, M. Delay and amount of reward in a concurrent chain. *JEAB*, 1983, *39*, 437–447.

Sokolov, E. N. Higher nervous functions: The orienting reflex. *Annual Review of Physiology*, 1963, *25*, 545–580.

Solomon, P. R. Role of the hippocampus in blocking and conditioned inhibition of the rabbit's nictitating membrane response. *JCPP*, 1977, *91*, 407–417.

Solomon, P. R., Brennan, G., & Moore, J. W. Latent inhibition of the rabbit's nictitating membrane response as a function of CS intensity. *Bulletin of the Psychonomic Society*, 1974, *4*, 445–448.

Solomon, R. L. Punishment. *American Psychologist*, 1964, *19*, 239–253.

Solomon, R. L., & Turner, L. H. Discriminative classical conditioning in dogs paralyzed by curare can later control discriminative avoidance responses in the normal state. *Psychological Review*, 1962, *69*, 202–219.

Solomon, R. L., & Wynn, L. C. Traumatic avoidance learning: The principles of anxiety conservation and partial irreversibility. *Psychological Review*, 1954, *61*, 353–385.

Solomon, R. R., Solomon, S. D., Vander Schaaf, E., & Perry, H. E. Altered activity in the hippocampus is more detrimental to classical conditioning than removing the structure. *Science*, 1983, *220*, 329–330.

Spear, N. E. Retention of reinforcer magnitude. *Psychological Review*, 1967, *74*, 216–234.

Spear, N. E. *The processing of memories: Forgetting and retention*. Hillsdale, N.J.: Erlbaum, 1978.

Spear, N. E. Extending the domain of memory retrieval. In N. E. Spear & R. R. Miller (Eds.), *Information processing in animals: Memory mechanisms*. Hillsdale, N.J.: Erlbaum, 1981.

Spear, N. E., & Miller, R. R. (Eds.). *Information processing in animals: Memory mechanisms*. Hillsdale, N.J.: Erlbaum, 1981.

Spence, K. W. The nature of discrimination learning in animals. *Psychological Review*, 1936, *43*, 427–449.

Spence, K. W. The differential response of animals to stimuli differing within a single dimension. *Psychological Review*, 1937, *44*, 430–444.

Spence, K. W. Theoretical interpretations of learning. In S. S. Stevens (Ed.), *Handbook of experimental psychology*. New York: Wiley, 1951.

Spence, K. W. *Behavior theory and conditioning*. New Haven: Yale University Press, 1956.

Spence, K. W., Haggard, D. F., & Ross, L. E. Intrasubject conditioning as a function of the intensity of the unconditioned stimulus. *Science*, 1958, *128*, 774–775.

Sperling, S. E. Reversal learning and resistance to extinction: A review of the rat literature. *Psychological Bulletin*, 1965a, *63*, 281–297.

Sperling, S. E. Reversal learning and resistance to extinction: A supplementary report. *Psychological Bulletin*, 1965b, *64*, 310–312.

Spetch, M. C., Wilkie, D. M., & Pinel, J. P. J. Backward conditioning: A reevaluation of the empirical evidence. *Psychological Bulletin*, 1981, *89*, 163–175.

Spivey, S. E. Resistance to extinction as a function of number of NR transitions and percentage of reinforcement. *JEP*, 1967, *75*, 43–48.

Stahl, J. M., & Ellen, P. Factors in the reasoning performance of the rat. *JCPP*, 1974, *87*, 598–604.

Stampfl, T. G., & Levis, D. J. Essentials of implosive therapy: A learning-theory-based psychodynamic behavioral therapy. *Journal of Abnormal Psychology*, 1967, *72*, 496–503.

Starr, M. D., & Mineka, S. Determinants of fear over the course of avoidance learning. *L&M*, 1977, *8*, 332–350.

Stellar, J. R., Brooks, F. H., & Mills, L. E. Approach and withdrawal analysis of the effects of hypothalamic stimulation and lesions in rats. *JCPP*, 1979, *93*, 446–466.

Stubbs, A. Contiguity of briefly presented stimuli with food reinforcement. *JEAB*, 1969, *12*, 271–278.

Sutherland, N. S., & Mackintosh, N. J. *Mechanisms of animal discrimination learning*. New York: Academic Press, 1971.

Switalski, R. W., Lyons, J., & Thomas, D. R. Effects of interdimensional training on stimulus generalization. *JEP*, 1966, *72*, 661–666.

Tait, R. W., Kehoe, E. J., & Gormezano, I. Effects of US duration on classical conditioning of the rabbit's nictitating membrane response. *JEP:ABP*, 1983, *9*, 91–101.

Tennant, W. A., & Bitterman, M. E. Blocking and overshadowing in two species of fish. *JEP:ABP*, 1975, *1*, 22–29.

Terrace, H. S. Discrimination learning, the peak shift, and behavioral contrast. *JEAB*, 1968, *11*, 727–741.

Terrace, H. S. Conditioned inhibition in successive discrimination learning. In R. A. Boakes & M. S. Halliday (Eds.), *Inhibition and learning*. London: Academic Press, 1972.

Terrace, H. S., Pettito, L. A., Sanders, R. J., & Bever, T. C. Can an ape create a sentence? *Science*, 1979, *206*, 891–900.

Terris, W., & Barnes, M. Learned resistance to punishment and subsequent responsiveness to the same and novel punishments. *Psychonomic Science*, 1969, *15*, 49–50.

Terris, W., & Wechkin, S. Learning to resist the effects of punishment. *Psychonomic Science*, 1967, *7*, 169–170.

Testa, T. J., & Ternes, J. W. Specificity of conditioning mechanisms in the modification of food preferences. In L. M. Barker, M. R. Best, & M. Domjan (Eds.), *Learning mechanisms in food selection*. Waco, Tex.: Baylor University Press, 1977.

Tevis, L. Behavior of a population of forest-mice when subjected to poison. *Journal of Mammalogy*, 1956, *37*, 358–370.

Theios, J., & Blosser, D. The overlearning reversal effect and magnitude of reward. *JCPP*, 1965, *59*, 252–257.

Thomas, D. R. Stimulus selection, attention, and related matters. In J. H. Reynierse (Ed.), *Current issues in animal learning*. Lincoln: University of Nebraska Press, 1970.

Thomas, D. R., Freeman, F., Svinicki, J. G., Burr, D. E. S., & Lyons, J. Effects of extradimensional training on stimulus generalization. *JEP Monograph*, 1970, *83*, 1–21.

Thomas, D. R., & Switalski, R. W. Comparison of stimulus generalization following variable ratio and variable interval training. *JEP*, 1966, *71*, 236–240.

Thomas, E. Role of postural adjustments in conditioning of dogs with electrical stimulation of the motor cortex as the unconditioned stimulus. *JCPP*, 1971, *76*, 187–198.

Thompson, R. F. The search for the engram. *American Psychologist*, 1976, *31*, 209–227.

Thompson, R. F., Berger, T. W., Berry, S. D., Hoehler, F. K., Kettner, R. E., & Weisz, D. J. Hippocampal substrate of classical conditioning. *Physiological Psychology*, 1980, *8*, 262–279.

Thompson, R. F., & Glanzman, D. L. Neural and behavioral mechanisms of habituation and sensitization. In T. J. Tighe and R. N. Leaton (Eds.), *Habituation*. Hillsdale, N.J.: Erlbaum, 1976.

Thompson, R. F., McCormick, D. A., Lavond, D. G., Clark, G. A., Kettner, R. E., & Mauk, M. D. The engram found? Initial localization of the memory trace for a basic form of associative learning. *Progress in Psychobiology and Physiological Psychology*, 1983, *10*, 167–195.

Thompson, R. F., & Spencer, W. A. Habituation: A model phenomenon for the study of neuronal substrates of behavior. *Psychological Review*, 1966, *73*, 16–43.

Thompson, R. K. R. Nonconceptual auditory matching by a rhesus monkey reflects biological constraints on cognitive processes. Paper presented at the Animal Behavior Society Meeting, 1981.

Thorndike, E. L. Animal intelligence: An experimental study of the associative processes in animals. *Psychological Review Monograph Supplement*, 1898, *2*, 1–109.

Thorndike, E. L. *Animal intelligence: Experimental studies*. New York: Macmillan, 1911.

Thorndike, E. L. Reward and punishment in animal learning. *Comparative Psychology Monographs*, 1932, *8*.

Tiffany, S. T., & Baker, T. B. Morphine tolerance in rats: Congruence with a Pavlovian paradigm. *JCPP*, 1981, *95*, 747–762.

Timberlake, W. Rats' responses to a moving object related to food or water: A behavior-systems analysis. *AL&B*, 1983, *11*, 309–320.

Timberlake, W., & Grant, D. L. Auto-shaping in rats to the presentation of another rat predicting food. *Science*, 1975, *190*, 690–692.

Timberlake, W., Wahl, G., & King, D. Stimulus and response contingencies in the misbehavior of rats. *JEP:ABP*, 1982, *8*, 62–85.

Tinbergen, N. *The study of instinct*. Oxford: Oxford University Press, 1951.

Tinbergen, N. Comparative studies of the behavior of gulls. *Behaviour*, 1959, *15*, 1–70.

Tinklepaugh, O. An experimental study of representative factors in monkeys. *JCP*, 1928, *8*, 197–236.

Todd, G. E., & Cogan, D. C. Selected schedules of reinforcement in the black-tailed prairie dog (*Cynomys ludovicianus*). *AL&B*, 1978, *6*, 429–434.

Tolman, E. C. *Purposive behavior in animals and men*. New York: The Century Co., 1932.

Tolman, E. C. Cognitive maps in rats and men. *Psychological Review*, 1948, *55*, 189–208.

Tomie, A. Interference with autoshaping by prior context conditioning. *JEP:ABP*, 1976, *2*, 323–334.

Tomie, A., Hayden, M., & Biehl, D. Effects of response elimination procedures upon the subsequent reacquisition of autoshaping. *AL&B*, 1980, *8*, 237–244.

Tomie, A., & Khouri, P. The effects of response-reinforcer contingency of time allocation in the open field. *L&M*, 1984, *15*, 1–11.

Tomie, A., & Kruse, J. Retardation tests for inhibition following discriminative autoshaping. *AL&B*, 1980, *8*, 401–408.

Tomie, A., & Loukas, E. Correlations between rat's spatial-location and ICS administration affects rate of acquisition and asymptotic level of time allocation bias in the open-field. *L&M*, 1984, in press.

Tomie, A., Murphy, A. L., & Fath, S. Retardation of autoshaping following unpredictable food: Effects of changing the context between pretraining and testing. *L&M*, 1980, *11*, 117–134.

Tomie, A., Rhor-Stafford, I., & Schwam, K. T. The retarding effect of the TRC response-elimination procedure upon the subsequent reacquisition of autoshaping: Comparison of between- and within-subjects assessment procedures and the evaluation of the role of background contextual stimuli. *AL&B*, 1981, *9*, 230–238.

Trapold, M. A., Carlson, J. G., & Myers, W. A. The effect of noncontingent fixed- and variable-interval reinforcement upon subsequent acquisition of the fixed-interval scallop. *Psychonomic Science*, 1965, *2*, 261–262.

Trapold, M. A., & Fowler, H. Instrumental escape performance as a function of the intensity of noxious stimulation. *JEP*, 1960, *60*, 323–326.

Trapold, M. A., & Overmier, J. B. The second learning process in instrumental learning. In A. H. Black & W. F. Prokasy (Eds.), *Classical conditioning II: Current research and theory*. New York: Appleton-Century-Crofts, 1972.

Traupmann, K. L. Drive, reward, and training parameters and the overlearning-extinction effect (OEE). *L&M*, 1972, *3*, 359–368.

Tyler, D. W., Wortz, E. C., & Bitterman, M. E. The effect of random and alternating partial reinforcement on resistance to extinction in the rat. *American Journal of Psychology*, 1953, *66*, 37–65.

VanDercar, D. H., & Schneiderman, N. Interstimulus interval functions in different response systems during classical discrimination conditioning of rabbits. *Psychonomic Science*, 1967, *9*, 9–10.

Visintainer, M. A., Volpicelli, J. R., & Seligman, M. E. P. Tumor rejection in rats after inescapable or escapable shock. *Science*, 1982, *216*, 437–439.

Waddington, K. D., & Heinrich, B. Patterns of movement and floral choice by foraging bees. In A. C. Kamil & T. D. Sargent, *Foraging behavior: Ecological, ethological, and psychological approaches*. New York: Garland STPM Press, 1981.

Wagner, A. R. Effects of amount and percentage of reinforcement and number of acquisition trials on conditioning and extinction. *JEP*, 1961, *62*, 234–242.

Wagner, A. R. Frustrative non-reward: A variety of punishment? In B. A. Campbell & R. M. Church (Eds.), *Punishment*. New York: Appleton-Century-Crofts, 1969.

Wagner, A. R. Priming in STM: An information-processing mechanism for self-generated or retrieval-generated depression in performance. In T. J. Tighe and R. N. Leaton (Eds.), *Habituation*. Hillsdale, N.J.: Erlbaum, 1976.

Wagner, A. R. SOP: A model of automatic memory processing in animal behavior. In Spear, N. E., & Miller, R. R. (Eds.), *Information processing in animals: Memory mechanisms*. Hillsdale, N.J.: Erlbaum, 1981.

Wagner, A. R., & Rescorla, R. A. Inhibition in Pavlovian conditioning: Application of a theory. In R. A. Boakes & M. S. Halliday (Eds.), *Inhibition and Learning*. London: Academic Press, 1972.

Wagner, A. R., Rudy, J. W., & Whitlow, J. W., Jr. Rehearsal in animal conditioning. *JEP Monograph*, 1973, *97*, 407–426.

Wagner, A. R., Siegel, S., Thomas, E., & Ellison, G. D. Reinforcement history and the extinction of a conditioned salivary response. *JCPP*, 1964, *58*, 354–358.

Wagner, A. R., & Terry, W. S. Backward conditioning to a CS following an expected vs. a surprising UCS. *AL&B*, 1975, *3*, 370–374.

Wagner, A. R., Thomas, E., & Norton, T. Conditioning with electrical stimulation of motor cortex: Evidence of a possible source of motivation. *JCPP*, 1967, *64*, 191–200.

Wahlsten, D. L., & Cole, M. Classical and avoidance training of leg flexion in the dog. In A. H. Black & W. F. Prokasy (Eds.), *Classical conditioning II: Current research and theory*. New York: Appleton-Century-Crofts, 1972.

Wall, J., Wild, J. M., Broyles, J., Gibbs, C. M., & Cohen, D. H. Plasticity of the tectofugal pathway during visual conditioning. Paper presented at Society for Neuroscience, 1980.

Walters, G. C., & Grusec, J. E. *Punishment*. San Francisco: Freeman & Co., 1977.

Wasserman, E. A. Pavlovian conditioning with heat reinforcement produces stimulus-directed pecking in chicks. *Science*, 1973, *181*, 875–877.

Wasserman, E. A. Response evocation in autoshaping: Contributions of cognitive and comparative-evolutionary analysis to an understanding of directed action. In C. M. Locurto, H. S. Terrace, & J. Gibbon (Eds.), *Autoshaping and conditioning theory*. New York: Academic Press, 1981.

Wasserman, E. A. Further remarks on the role of cognition in the comparative analysis of behavior. *JEAB*, 1982, *38*, 211–216.

Wasserman, E. A., Deich, J. D., Hunter, N. B., & Nagamatsu, L. S. Analyzing the random control procedure: Effects of paired and unpaired CSs and USs on autoshaping the chick's key peck with heat reinforcement. *L&M*, 1977, *8*, 467–487.

Wasserman, E. A., Franklin, S. R., & Hearst, E. Pavlovian appetitive contingencies and approach versus withdrawal to conditioned stimuli in pigeons. *JCPP*, 1974, *86*, 616–627.

Watson, J. B. Psychology as the behaviorist views it. *Psychological Review*, 1913, *20*, 158–177.

Watson, J. B. The effect of delayed feeding upon learning. *Psychobiology*, 1917, *1*, 51–60.

Watson, J. B. *Behaviorism*. New York: Norton, 1930.

Watson, J. B., & Raynor, R. Conditioned emotional reactions. *JEP*, 1920, *3*, 1–14.

Weinstock, S. Resistance to extinction of a running response following partial reinforcement under widely spaced trials. *JCPP*, 1954, *47*, 318–323.

Weisman, R. G. On the role of reinforcers in associative learning. In H. Davis & H. M. B. Hurwitz (Eds.), *Operant-Pavlovian interactions*. Hillsdale, N.J.: Erlbaum, 1977.

Weisman, R. G., & Dodd, W. D. The study of association: Methodology and basic phenomena. In A. Dickinson & R. A. Boakes (Eds.), *Mechanisms of learning and motivation: A memorial volume to Jerzy Konorski*. Hillsdale, N.J.: Erlbaum, 1979.

Weiss, J. M., Glazer, H. I., Pohorecky, L. A. Coping behavior and neurochemical changes: An alternative explanation for the original 'learned helplessness' experiments. In G. Serban and A. Kling (Eds.), *Animal models in human psychology*. New York: Plenum Press, 1976.

Weiss, J. M., Glazer, H. I., Pohorecky, L. A., Brick, J., & Miller, N. E. Effects of chronic exposure to stressors on avoidance-escape behavior and on brain norepinephrine. *Psychosomatic Medicine*, 1975, *37*, 522–533.

Weiss, J. M., Goodman, P. A., Losito, B. G., Corrigan, S., Charry, J. M., & Bailey, W. H. Behavioral depression produced by an uncontrollable stressor: Relationship to norepinephrine, dopamine, and serotonin levels in various regions of rat brain. *Brain Research Reviews*, 1981, *3*, 167–205.

Weiss, R. F. Deprivation and reward magnitude effects on speed throughout the goal gradient. *JEP*, 1960, *60*, 384–390.

Weiss, S. J., & Dacanay, R. J. Incentive processes and the peak shift. *JEAB*, 1982, *37*, 441–453.

Weisz, D. J., Solomon, P. R., & Thompson, R. F. The hippocampus appears necessary for trace conditioning. *Bulletin of the Psychonomic Society Abstracts*, 1980, *193*, 244.

Whiting, J. W. M., & Mowrer, O. H. Habit progression and regression: A laboratory study of some factors relevant to human socialization. *Journal of Comparative Psychology*, 1943, *36*, 229–253.

Whittaker, R. H., & Feeny, P. P. Allelochemicals: Chemical interactions between species. *Science*, 1971, *171*, 757–770.

Wike, E. L., Kintsch, W., & Remple, R. Selective learning and habit reversal as a function of partial reinforcement during training and reversal. *Psychological Reports*, 1959, *5*, 665–668.

Wilcoxin, H. C., Dragoin, W. B., & Kral, P. A. Illness-induced aversions in rat and quail: Relative salience of visual and gustatory cues. *Science*, 1971, *7*, 489–493.

Williams, B. A. The blocking of reinforcement control. *JEAB*, 1975, *24*, 215–225.

Williams, B. A. Behavioral contrast as a function of the temporal location of reinforcement. *JEAB*, 1976, *26*, 57–64.

Williams, B. A. Information effects on the response-reinforcer association. *AL&B*, 1978, *6*, 371–379.

Williams, B. A. The following schedule of reinforcement as a fundamental determinant of steady state contrast in multiple schedules. *JEAB*, 1981, *35*, 293–310.

Williams, B. A. Another look at contrast in multiple schedules. *JEAB*, 1983, *39*, 345–384.

Williams, D. R. Classical conditioning and incentive motivation. In W. F. Prokasy (Ed.), *Classical conditioning: A symposium*. New York: Appleton-Century-Crofts, 1965.

Williams, D. R. Biconditional behavior: Conditioning without constraint. In C. M. Locurto, H. S. Terrace, & J. Gibbon (Eds.), *Autoshaping and conditioning theory*. New York: Academic Press, 1981.

Williams, D. R., & Williams, H. Automaintenance in the pigeon: Sustained pecking despite contingent non-reinforcement. *JEAB*, 1969, *12*, 511–520.

Willner, P. J. Effect of chlordiazepoxide on the partial reinforcement extinction effect. *Pharmacology, Biochemistry, & Behavior*, 1977, *7*, 479–482.

Wilson, M. P. Periodic reinforcement interval and number of periodic reinforcements as parameters of response strength. *JCPP*, 1954, *47*, 51–56.

Wilson, M. P., & Keller, F. J. On the selective reinforcement of spaced responses. *JCPP*, 1953, *46*, 190–193.

Wilton, R. N., & Strongman, K. T. Extinction performance as a function of reinforcement magnitude and a number of training trials. *Psychological Reports*, 1967, *20*, 235–238.

Witcher, E. S., & Ayres, J. J. B. Systematic manipulation of CS-US pairings in negative CS-US correlation procedures in rats. *AL&B*, 1980, *8*, 67–74.

Wolfe, J. B. Effectiveness of token rewards for chimpanzees. *Comparative Psychology Monographs*, 1936, *12*.

Wolfe, J. B., & Kaplon, M. D. Effect of amount of reward and consummative activity on learning in chickens. *Journal of Comparative Psychology*, 1941, *31*, 353–361.

Wolpe, J., & Lazarus, A. A. *Behavior therapy techniques*. New York: Pergamon Press, 1966.

Woods, S. C. Conditioned hypoglycemia: Effect of vagotomy and pharmacological blockade. *American Journal of Physiology*, 1972, *223*, 1424–1427.

Woods, S. C., & Kulkosky, P. J. Classically conditioned changes of blood glucose level. *Psychosomatic Medicine*, 1976, *38*, 201–219.

Woods, S. C., Vasselli, J. R., Kaestner, E., Szakmary, G. A., Milburn, P., & Viliello, M. V. Conditioned insulin secretion and meal feeding in rats. *JCPP*, 1977, *91*, 128–133.

Wooldridge, D. E. *The machinery of the brain*. New York: McGraw-Hill, 1963.

Woolfolk, R. L., & Lehrer, P. M. (Eds). *Principles and practice of stress management*. New York: Guilford, 1984.

Worden, F. G. Auditory habituation. In H. V. S. Peeke & M. J. Herz (Eds.), *Habituation. Vol. II: Physiological Substrates*. New York: Academic Press, 1973.

Worsham, R. W. Delayed matching-to-sample as temporal discrimination in monkeys. Unpublished doctoral dissertation, Rutgers University, 1973.

Worsham, R. W. Temporal discrimination factors in the delayed matching-to-sample tasks in monkeys. *AL&B*, 1975, *3*, 93–97.

Worsham, R. W., & D'Amato, M. R. Ambient light, white noise and monkey vocalization as sources of interference in visual short-term memory of monkeys. *JEP*, 1973, *99*, 99–105.

Wyckoff, L. B., Jr. The role of observing responses in discrimination learning. Part 1. *Psychological Review*, 1952, *59*, 431–442.

Wyers, E. J., Peeke, H. V. S., & Herz, M. J. Behavioral habituation in invertebrates. In H. V. S. Peeke & M. J. Herz (Eds.), *Habituation. Vol. I: Behavioral studies*. New York: Academic Press, 1973.

Yates, A. J. *Biofeedback and the modification of behavior*. New York: Plenum, 1980.

Zach, R. Selection and dropping of whelks by northwestern crows. *Behaviour*, 1978, *67*, 134–148.

Zach, R., & Smith, J. N. M. Optimal foraging in wild birds? In A. C. Kamil & T. D. Sargent (Eds.), *Foraging behavior: Ecological, ethological, and psychological approaches*. New York: Garland STPM Press, 1981.

Zahorik, D. M., & Houpt, K. A. The concept of nutritional wisdom: Applicability of laboratory learning models to large herbivores. In L. M. Barker, M. R. Best, & M. Domjan (Eds.), *Learning mechanisms in food selection*. Waco, Tex.: Baylor University Press, 1977.

Zeaman, D., & House, B. J. The growth and decay of reactive inhibition as measured by alternation behavior. *JEP*, 1951, *41*, 117–186.

Zeaman, D., & Wegner, N. Strength of cardiac conditioned responses with varying stimulus duration. *Psychological Review*, 1958, *65*, 238–241.

Zener, K. The significance of behavior accompanying conditioned salivary secretion for theories of the conditioned response. *American Journal of Psychology*, 1937, *50*, 384–403.

Zentall, T., Collins, N., & Hearst, E. Generalization gradients around a formerly positive S−. *Psychonomic Science*, 1971, *22*, 257–259.

Zentall, T., & Hogan, D. Abstract concept learning in the pigeon. *JEP*, 1977, *102*, 393–398.

Zentall, T. R., Edwards, C. A., Moore, B. S., & Hogan, D. E. Identity: The basis for both matching and oddity learning in pigeons. *JEP:ABP*, 1981, *7*, 70–86.

Zentall, T. R., & Hogan, D. E. Short-term proactive inhibition in the pigeon. *L&M*, 1977, *8*, 367–386.

Zoladek, L., & Roberts, W. A. The sensory basis of spatial memory in the rat. *AL&B*, 1978, *6*, 77–81.

Author Index

Subject Index

About the Author

Charles Flaherty is Professor of Psychology and Chairman of the department at Rutgers University. He received his B.A. from Northeastern University and his M.A. and Ph.D. from the University of Wisconsin at Madison. Dr. Flaherty has published numerous research papers and a text on learning and memory.

A Note on the Type

The text of this book is set in CALEDONIA, a Linotype face designed by W. A. Dwiggins. It belongs to the family of printing types called "modern face" by printers—a term used to mark the change in style of type-letters that occurred about 1800. Caledonia borders on the general design of Scotch Modern, but is more freely drawn than that letter.

This book was composed on a Linotron 202 by P&M Typesetting, Inc., Waterbury, Connecticut, printed and bound by R. R. Donnelley & Sons Co., Harrisonburg, Virginia.